1½-2" = best circle on full size

RIVERSIDE HOME ECONOMICS SERIES

Edited by

ALICE F. BLOOD, PH.D.

*Formerly Director of the School of Home Economics
and Professor of Nutrition, Simmons College*

Dress design

DRAPING AND FLAT PATTERN MAKING

MARION S. HILLHOUSE

EVELYN A. MANSFIELD

Michigan State College

HOUGHTON MIFFLIN COMPANY

The Riverside Press Cambridge

COPYRIGHT 1948

BY MARION S. HILLHOUSE AND
EVELYN A. MANSFIELD

ALL RIGHTS RESERVED, INCLUDING THE RIGHT TO
REPRODUCE THIS BOOK OR PARTS THEREOF IN ANY FORM

PRINTED IN THE U.S.A.

To Ethel G. Webb

Whose many years of analytical and inspiring presentation of draping led to the writing of this book.

Contents

1. THE DRESS FORM — Pages 1-15

Part 1. The Dress Form Cover
Part 2. Padding the Dress Form

2. BASIC BLOUSES — Pages 16-59

Part 1. Draping Basic Blouses on the Dress Form
Part 2. The Flat Pattern Method of Designing Blouses on the Master Block Pattern

3. BASIC SKIRTS — Pages 60-111

Part 1. Draping Skirts on the Dress Form
Part 2. The Flat Pattern Method of Designing Skirts on a Master Pattern

4. SLEEVES — Pages 112-192

Part 1. Drafting and Flat Pattern Designing Basic Set-In Sleeves
Part 2. Designing Set-In Sleeves from the Master Pattern One-Piece Sleeve Block
Part 3. Sleeves Cut In One with the Bodice or a Part of the Bodice

5. FITTING — Pages 193-246

Part 1. General Principles of Fitting
Part 2. Preparation of the Master Pattern for Fitting
Part 3. Fitting Problems of the Blouse

Part 4. Fitting Problems of the Skirt

Part 5. Fitting Problems of the Sleeve

Part 6. Completing the Master Pattern after the Fitting

6. COLLARS AND NECKLINES   Pages 247-272

Part 1. Drafting and Flat Pattern Design

Part 2. Draping

7. SOURCES OF INSPIRATION IN DESIGN   Pages 273-318

Suggestion 1. Developing Line Arrangements by Sketching

Suggestion 2. Studying the Fabric

Suggestion 3. Draping for General Effect

Suggestion 4. Draping with Muslin for Details of Design

Suggestion 5. Interpreting Silhouettes as Complete Designs

Suggestion 6. Molding the Fabric to the Form by Seams and by Concealed Darts

Suggestion 7. Developing the Design Theme from Variations of Basic Darts

Suggestion 8. Developing Unusual Skirt Cuts from the Basic Two-, Four-, and Six-Gore Patterns

Suggestion 9. Carrying One Piece of Fabric As Far As Possible without Cutting

Suggestion 10. Deriving Unusual Effects from Asymmetric Cuts

Suggestion 11. Designing from a Detail

Suggestion 12. Introducing Original Details into a Standard Commercial Pattern

INDEX

Preface

The purpose of this book is to explain in detail the principles of draping fabric on the dress form, the principles of flat pattern designing from master pattern blocks, and the dependence of successful flat pattern making on an understanding of draping. We have devoted the entire book to the presentation of these two systems in order to show that a facility in both frees the designer to carry out any original costume with ease and confidence.

Although draping is the oldest method of pattern designing, we have nowhere been able to find a text for our own college classes that shows in detail how to drape flat fabric to fit the curves of the body. Texts that deal adequately with the flat pattern system merely mention draping as a possible method but make no attempt to explain it. We have therefore tried to present draping as adequately and logically as the block system.

From long experience in teaching both systems of pattern making, we have also become convinced that one can work with greater understanding, efficiency, and skill if able to use both. We should therefore not want to present one system without the other. Each has many advantages, and only when one is able to use the system which better suits a particular situation, or even to use a combination of the two, can one derive the utmost satisfaction and pleasure from original costume designing. An understanding of each method helps to explain the other. For example, flat pattern designs developed from drafted patterns will be utterly cold, set, and lifeless unless one has had experience in working with fabric on the form. Such designs may be accurate, but they will lack the finer line placement gained through draping experience. We have, therefore, attempted to show the improvement in design quality that comes when blocking is founded on an understanding of draping.

It is too widely assumed that in order to profit from draping one must have a mysterious feeling for fabric or a gift for line, and that draping at best is a kind of vague hit or miss procedure, too impractical to be generally used. This false assumption is undoubtedly due to the fact that draping has not previously been analyzed and systematized and that procedures easy to follow have not been established. We are not attempting to prove that merely by learning to drape, any one can become a professional designer. Indeed, we wish to make clear our conviction that a successful professional dress designer must be born not only with an innate feeling for line and texture, an interest in and an appreciation of all the arts, but with a keen business sense as well that enables her to design the right clothes at the right time. But we do maintain that any student or homemaker with elementary dressmaking skills at her command can learn to drape deftly and accurately, and that this ability will help her to design original and beautiful costumes. At the very least, she will learn through experience in draping to recognize the qualities of a well designed dress and to tell a good design from a poor one. Draping also teaches one not only to recognize an ill-fitting garment but to correct fitting errors — a learning process that takes years by the trial and error method. The chapter on fitting (Chapter 5) should be of great practical value to all clothing teachers as well as professional dressmakers.

The designs illustrated in this book have been chosen both because of their intrinsically good lines and because they explain a principle of design or pattern making. They are not intended as fashions, and we hope that the students who use this book will not regard them so, but rather as illustrations of principles which no fashion change can influence.

It should be obvious, then, that we have planned the book primarily as a laboratory text for college students and for students of clothing in technical schools of dressmaking and design — students who have already learned elementary dressmaking techniques and are familiar with the rudiments of handling commercial patterns. It should also serve as a practical reference for high school clothing teachers, clothing extension specialists, and teachers of adult evening classes who need help with problems in pattern making as well as with alteration of patterns for both design and fit. This is not a suitable home economics text for high schools, nor is it intended for the homemaker who has never learned to sew. In short, it is primarily intended as a supplement to classroom teaching; yet we believe that the experienced home dressmaker, as well as the professional dressmaker, will find that the detailed directions, and the profuse illustrations and diagrams, will be of value even without benefit of classroom instruction, not only in making and fitting basic patterns, but in designing costumes that are both individual and original.

We wish to express appreciation to M. Rohr, Charles and Esther Kaplan, Harriet Pepin, Mabel Erwin, and Mary Evans for the help derived from their books on pattern making. We wish especially to thank Shirley Hillhouse, the fashion illustrator, for so skillfully converting the rough drawings into finished illustrations. We also wish to give recognition to the students whose draped designs in so many cases served as illustrations for Chapter 7. For the encouragement which so greatly facilitated the writing of this book, we want to express appreciation to Dean Marie Dye of the School of Home Economics at Michigan State College, and to Hazel Strahan, Head of the Department of Textiles, Clothing, and Related Arts.

MARION S. HILLHOUSE
EVELYN A. MANSFIELD

1. The Dress Form

A dress form should so accurately duplicate the size and shape of the person for whom it is made that she can drape clothes on it and be assured that they will fit her with little alteration. Although there are several kinds of forms that can either be bought or made at home, none of them gives the satisfaction of a standard, inexpensive commercial form padded out with cotton to fill a fabric cover which follows the measurements of the individual with absolute precision. The advantages of this type of form are many. If well padded, it is firm yet resilient, and it does not resist pins as do hard unpadded forms. Moreover, the two sides are exactly alike, so that a half garment can be duplicated without the risk of doubling the size of errors. Finally, if the garment is draped carefully, it will fit with only minor alterations.

Another type of form is made by sticking strips of gummed tape on a gauze vest directly on the figure. This type theoretically duplicates not only the individual's measurements but also her posture. Unfortunately this is true in theory only. Actually the model must stand still for so long while the tape is being applied that her figure sags and the form too often becomes a caricature of her real posture. It is thus discouraging both to see and to use. Garments draped on these forms are bound to be inaccurate, and the form, itself — unattractive as it usually is — furnishes no inspiration to the draper. Because this type of form is less satisfactory than the fabric-covered form described above, the following discussion will be limited to the procedure for making and fitting the fabric dress form cover and for padding out a standard commercial form to fit the cover which you have made. The discussion includes the smallest details of procedure in order to ensure a form that will be satisfactory.

THE DRESS FORM COVER

THE PATTERN STYLE

The dress form cover should be a smooth, firm garment fitted to the torso like a knitted bathing suit without wrinkles or looseness. It should follow every curve of the body so that, when it is filled out with padding on the form, it will exactly duplicate every measurement of the figure. Dress forms vary in length but generally extend 12 to 14 inches below the waist. The cover should be 2 or 3 inches longer than this so that it can be pulled down and tacked securely to the wooden brace underneath the form in order to give a tight and smooth surface.

The most satisfactory pattern for the cover is usually known as a *French lining*, a princess-style pattern with center front, side front, center back, and side back vertical panels. The eight vertical seams make it possible for the cover to follow the body curves exactly without the need for a waistline seam. Such patterns are sometimes sold by pattern companies; but since they are not always available, directions are given on pages 9 to 12 for drawing them in sizes 12, 14, 16, 18, and 20. The directions are easy to follow, and the patterns can be drawn in a few minutes with a pencil and a tailor's square. If you are able to buy a regulation French lining pattern, you will simply need to true it up according to your own measurements.

If you cannot buy and do not wish to draw a French

DRESS DESIGN

Fig. 1. Princess style dress pattern, a possible substitute for a regulation French lining pattern.

lining pattern, a regular princess-style dress pattern is a possible substitute (see Figure 1). If you use a pattern of this type, several modifications will be necessary. First, rule the center front line marked on the center front panel and cut off the extension for the lap and lapel. Then alter the dress front slightly for a basic neckline, and cut it off to a 36-inch bodice. Finally, draw the panel lines from the largest hip measurement down absolutely vertically rather than outward on a slant, since a form cover must fit skin-tight all the way to the lower edge.

THE PATTERN SIZE

Because the form cover must be skin tight, buy your pattern one size smaller than the dress size you normally wear, or in the smallest size that will fit the bust. Then, if necessary, add to the seams below the waist to let out the hips. This requires much less alteration than would be necessary to fit out excess above the waistline. Fully half of the college students find their proportions from shoulder to waist somewhat smaller than from waist to hip. By using the smaller pattern size and letting out the seams from waist to hip, you will have to make very little adjustment at the fitting.

For class use, the instructor will find that it saves time to make up in advance muslin French lining samples of all pattern sizes (12, 14, 16, 18, 20). The student can then try them on and select the one which fits her best above the waist.[1]

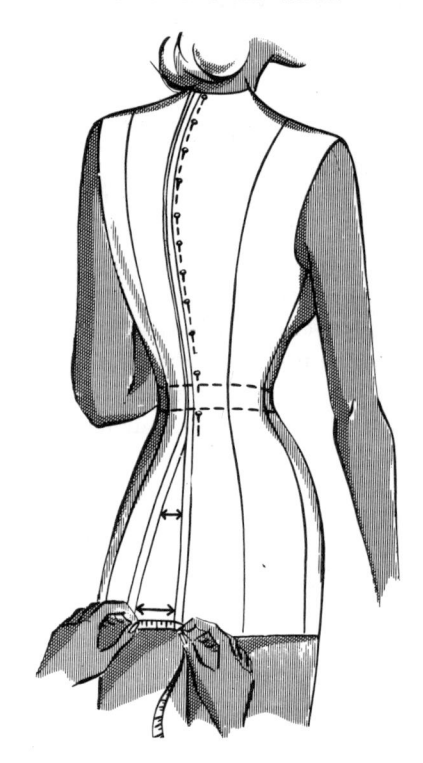

Fig. 2. Checking pattern size by trying on a muslin form cover sample.

---

[1] The sample models should be left open down the center back, and the neckline, armholes, and lower edge should be turned under on the seam lines and stitched twice to prevent stretching. They should be kept in a closed box when not in use to prevent soiling, since they would shrink and be inaccurate after being washed or dry cleaned. For class use the teacher will also find it convenient to cut several sets of each pattern size in tagboard without seam allowances. She should mark the lengthwise grain the full length of the pattern and mark or cut notches, and should put reinforced perforations in the top of each piece and tie together the four parts of each pattern set.

THE DRESS FORM

If some of the body measurements differ from those of the pattern, they can be accurately checked and noted when the muslin is tried on. Figure 2 shows a muslin sample on a model who needs more width from waist to hip on the side and back seams. The vertical seams also need to be indented at a lower point to fit the lower waistline of the figure shown. If one takes carefully detailed notes on such differences, the outline of the pattern can be altered before cutting. This way of checking size and proportion has proved to be quicker and more efficient for a classroom or shop than the method of taking many measurements.

FABRIC FOR THE COVER—QUALITY AND AMOUNT

The principal requirement of the fabric for the cover is firmness without stiffness. Heavy weight muslin or a firm twill, such as khaki, covert, light-weight denim, heavy cotton gabardine, or galatea are all satisfactory. The fabric must be pliable to be closely fitted and easily pinned, but it must also be firm enough to withstand the strain of being pulled over the padded form without stretching, for unless it is pulled very tight, the form will be too soft to retain its shape. Buy two dress form lengths (approximately two yards) of 36-inch material. Press the fabric to smooth out wrinkles, but use no moisture. Then stretch it diagonally to straighten the crossgrain as much as possible.

LAYOUT AND MARKING

1. Fold a two-yard piece of 36-inch fabric crosswise through the center, thus allowing a yard length for the pattern pieces and their duplicates in the under layer.

2. Place the center back line of the pattern 1 inch in from the selvage to allow for a lap. (Since the center back is to be left open, the selvage prevents it from stretching.)

3. Allow ¾ inch for seams on all other pattern edges.

4. Draw around the center back panel with a pencil. Then place the side back, side front, and center front panels as shown in the layout diagram, Figure 3, with the lengthwise grain-marking of the patterns on the lengthwise grain of the fabric.

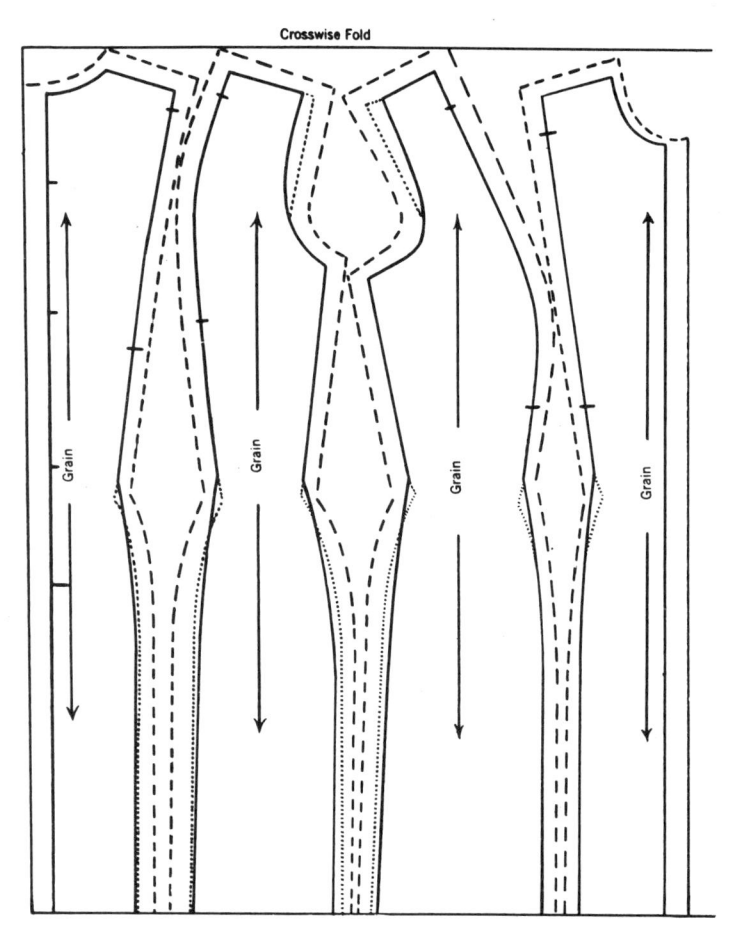

Fig. 3. Dress form cover layout. Dotted lines indicate alterations for lower waistline and let-out on side and back seams from waist to hip.

The dotted lines of Figure 3 show how to alter the seam lines on the fabric to conform to the proportions of the figure in the sketch. The waistline should be ¾ inch lower than the pattern, and there should be a let-out on the side and back seams to provide extra width from the waist to the broadest part of the hips. If the bodice pattern is less than 36 inches in length, rule vertical lines from the largest hip measurement, approximately 8½ to 9 inches below the waist, to the lower edge of the fabric. Unless the pattern has unusually wide shoulders, add ¾ inch to the end of the front and back shoulder seams for possible let-out or for unusually broad shoulders. (The broken lines indicate the cutting lines with ¾ inch seams.)

5. Pencil all notches on the cloth, paying special attention to those on the side front and side back

DRESS DESIGN

seams over the bust and shoulder blades. Mark the center back with four crossmarkings, short horizontal lines which indicate matching points on corresponding seams, to keep the two sides of the back seam balanced when you pin the cover up the back at the fitting.

6. Label each piece — *center front, side front,* and so on — as you cut.

7. Pin the two layers of fabric together to prevent each pattern part and its duplicate from shifting in position and trace all penciled seam lines and crossmarkings, using a tracing wheel on a chalk board or wax carbon paper to transfer them to the under layer.

ASSEMBLING THE PATTERN PARTS

Pin all seams except the center back, and machine-baste them for the first fitting.

Exception. When making a form cover at home without the help of a fitter, leave the center front open rather than the center back.

1. Pin the center front seam first before separating the two layers.

2. Pin the seam, joining the center panels to the side fronts at about one-inch intervals over the bust curve. Beginning at the shoulder, match the notches and distribute the ease evenly on the side front over the curve of the bust.

To join seam lines accurately, direct the pin through the penciled line of the top layer of the fabric and look to see that it comes through the penciled line on the under layer. Pick up with the pin only 1/8 inch of the fabric directly on the seam line. If you pick up more than this, one layer will slip against the other and the seam lines will not match. (See Figure 4.)

3. After pinning side fronts to center fronts and side backs to center backs, machine-baste all seams.

4. Pin and baste the underarm and shoulder seams. For the first fitting, baste the shoulder seam from neck to princess line and from armscye (armhole) to princess line to avoid stitching across the vertical seams.

For basting, adjust the sewing machine to the longest possible stitch and use a hinged presser foot in order to jump the pins without blunting or breaking the needle.

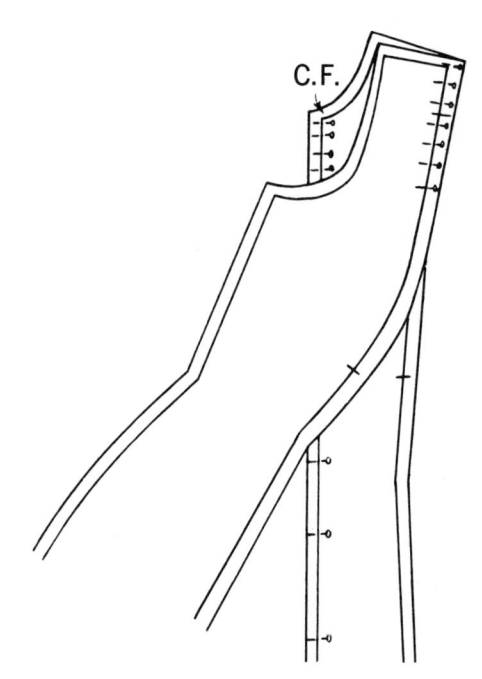

Fig. 4. Method of pinning seams.

5. Press the cover throughout, but without giving any direction to the seams, as creases are a hindrance when making alterations.

FIRST FITTING

Remove your slip to avoid snagging it with pins, but wear a good foundation garment and then put on the form cover wrong side out in order to fit it skin tight. Although this places the right half of the garment on the left half of the body and vice versa, it is wise to ignore small variations in the two sides of the body and to make both sides of a dress form exactly alike, for fitting clothes to minor figure irregularities emphasizes rather than conceals them. Fit only one side and duplicate all alterations on the other side after taking the garment off. Never trim off seam allowances, but use them to match the two sides. If the armscye and neckline are unusually high, the fitter will need to clip the seam allowances at these points before putting the garment on. She should then pin the center back line, being careful to match the neckline and the four crossmarkings, and should pull down the lower edge to settle all lines into place. If the cover fails to settle down at the collar bone and chest, the neckline may need even more clipping.

The fitter should check several important points before making any alterations. The center front and center back lines should be placed on the center of the figure, the garment should be smoothly pulled down, and the shoulder pads should be placed at the armhole end of each shoulder seam. Shoulder pads, of course, are optional; but when broad padded shoulders are in vogue, it is better to fit over them than to pin the pads to the dress form on top of the cover and thus conceal the shoulder and armscye seam lines so helpful when draping.

FRONT OF COVER (see Figure 5)

1. Shoulder seam

(a) *Position.* The seam should be directly on top of the shoulder and should be inconspicuous from either front or back. It should be a straight line from neck to armscye. If it is not, see that the garment is properly adjusted on the figure before altering this line. You may find that if you pull the cover down at the center front, the shoulder seam will fall where it belongs without any alteration.

(b) *Fit.* The shoulder seam should cling closely to the body from armscye to neck. A shoulder pad usually raises the neck end of the seam above the body so that it needs to be hollowed in until it clings to the shoulder.

2. Underarm seam line

The person being fitted should raise her arm enough so that the fitter can pin out any looseness along the underarm seam. With a few pins, pick up the same amount on the opposite underarm seam. This will serve as a check on tightness and will also keep the center lines in position. The final underarm line, however, should be copied from the side first pinned.

3. Armscye

(a) Clip the seam allowance in one or two places along the lower half of the armscye if it is too high to set smoothly.

(b) Pin a dart from the middle of the armscye, directing it toward the bust to fit the hollow below the shoulder ball.

Fig. 5. First fitting of dress form cover — wrong side out.

4. Neckline

Pin out of the center front seam line any excess width across the front at the base of the neck.

5. Princess line

(a) Rip the seam from the point just below the bust to the waistline. (This invariably has to be done.)

(b) Retain the original line of the center front panel, but take in a deeper seam on the side front panel to tighten the form cover under the bust. This increases the curve on the side section.

(c) Follow the same method from waist to hip. Always keep the center panel the same width and take in or let out the seam on the side section.

6. Center front line

Place horizontal darts from the center front seam to the point of the bust to indent the space between the breasts.

DRESS DESIGN

BACK OF COVER

1. Armscye

Clip the armscye seam allowance if it binds when the arm is down. Pin a dart from the center of the armscye to the point of the shoulder blade if there is looseness and wrinkling at the armscye when the arm is down.

2. Princess line

Follow the same procedure as for the front if there is excess above or below the shoulder blades. However, the back princess line from shoulder to waist seldom needs alteration if a small enough pattern has been used.

3. Side seam

The fitter should stand away from the person being fitted and observe the position of the side seam to determine whether or not the line is being pulled either forward or back. It should be as nearly as possible a plumb line from under the arm to the floor, but should divide the figure becomingly, so that the seam itself is inconspicuous from either the back or front view.

MARKING AND DUPLICATING ALTERATIONS

1. Remove the garment.
2. With a pencil, replace all pin markings with short, broken lines and crossmark all seams with pencil.
3. Spread the garment on a table to smooth it out and to true the alteration lines. If the alterations are extensive, rip out all bastings.
4. Duplicate alterations on one panel at a time, carefully matching and pinning together the seam edges of the two layers before placing them on a chalk board or carbon paper to transfer the markings to the one beneath. If the alterations are slight, fold the garment wrong side out on the center front seam and telescope the left half of the garment into the right half. Pin together the raw edges of the two layers along the neckline, armscye, shoulder, and underarm, and then place the unfitted side against the wax carbon paper and trace the alteration lines. Rip the front princess lines below the bust before duplicating that alteration, since more has been taken up on the side front panel than on the center front panel.

PREPARATION FOR THE SECOND FITTING

1. Shorten the machine stitch and restitch all unchanged vertical seams directly on the first stitching. Carefully re-pin and stitch the altered seams, but either hand-baste or pin very closely the exaggerated curve over the bust to keep the line accurate and to distribute properly the ease over the curve. Stitch the shoulder seams in a continuous line from armscye to neck.

2. Press open the center front and underarm seams. Press the side front and side back seams toward the center and press the shoulder seams open.

3. Clip diagonally through all seam allowances at the waistline to within $\frac{1}{8}$ inch of the stitching. Do the same for the front seams of the princess lines below the bust and for the shoulder seams where they curve up to the neckline.

4. Trace the center back lines and crossmarkings to show on the right side of the fabric for accuracy in pinning the garment together for the second fitting.

THE SECOND FITTING

Put the cover on *right side out*. Adjust the shoulder seams correctly and slip in the shoulder pads if they are to be used. Pin the center back, matching the four crossmarkings. Pull firmly on the lower edge of the garment both in back and front to settle all lines down on the body and to smooth out any horizontal wrinkles due to tightness. Ordinarily no further adjustments are necessary if alterations have been made carefully, but do not overlook any possible improvements of fit at this time.

The chief purpose of the second fitting is to mark basic lines on the form cover (see Figures 6 and 7).

1. Neckline

The prominent vertebra at the back of the neck is the center back point of the neckline, and the hollow of the neck establishes its position at the center

THE DRESS FORM

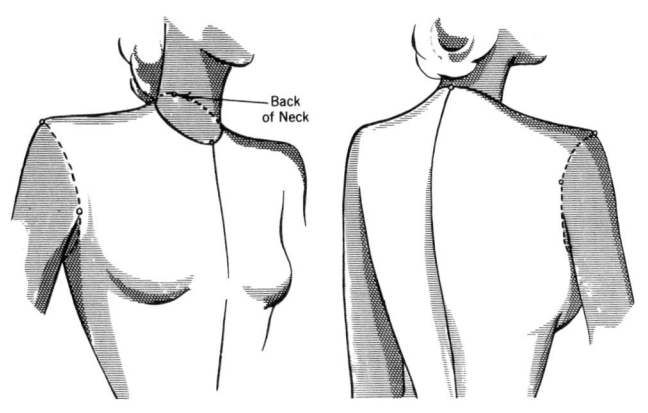

Fig. 6. (*a*) Position of basic neckline; (*b*) Armscye.

front. The line joining these two points should follow the meeting of the neck column with the plane of the shoulder. The center back should be as high as the side or slightly higher, and the center front, of course, is the lowest point. The basic neckline must be high enough to serve as the foundation for a tailored or roll collar. If it is not, the roll line of the collar will buckle away from the neck. If you are in doubt about its accuracy, clip at intervals from the raw edge toward the neckline and turn the raw edge under. Then mark the line from center back to center front with soft lead pencil or pins (see Figures 6*a* and *b*). Check and record the base of neck measurement from center back to front and also the measurement of the neck 1½ inches above the base. Use these two measurements when padding the form.

2. Armscye (Armhole)

Begin to form the line at the shoulder seam. One way to establish the top point of the armscye line is to measure the length of the shoulder seam of your most recent satisfactory dress or suit and use that measurement to determine the shoulder seam length from neck to armscye on your dress form. Another way to establish the top point of the armscye is to lay a long pencil against the outside of the upper arm and extend it to meet a pencil laid along the shoulder seam. The point where these two pencils meet indicates the intersection of the shoulder seam and the armscye. When a broad square-shouldered effect is in fashion, plain sleeves without darts or gathers should meet the shoulder seam line without being pulled inward. From the top point of the armscye curve, mark a line down to the point where the arm and body join — the narrowest point of the curve — keeping the line as straight and nearly parallel to the center front as possible without putting the armscye so far out that it rests on top of the arm rather than at the joining of the arm and the body. From this point continue the curve downward and outward to the underarm seam, the top point of which should be at least one inch below the armpit (see Figures 6 *a* and *b*). Follow the same procedure for establishing the back armscye curve. The person being fitted should bring her arms forward to make sure that there is enough width across the shoulder blades. The under part of the armscye will be a rather narrow oval because of the tightness of the form cover.

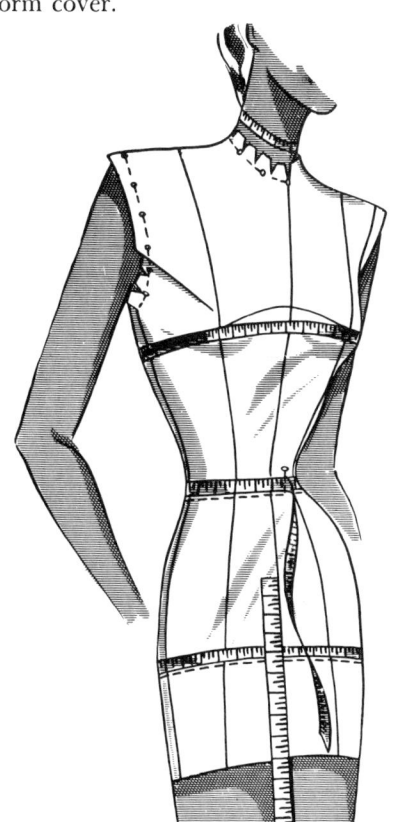

Fig. 7. Second fitting of form cover — marking neckline, armscye, bust line, waistline, hip level and distance from hip level to floor.

3. Waistline

The placement of this line as well as that of the armscye varies with fashion. Place and pin a tape measure around the waist, adjusting it up and down until you find a position that is becoming from back,

DRESS DESIGN

side, and front views. The waistline at the center back should never be lower than the side, and the center front should be as low as or lower than the side. Pencil around the lower edge of the tape from center back to center front. Check and record the waistline measurement (see Figure 7).

4. Hipline

Place and pin a tape around the largest hip measurement. With a yardstick measure from the floor to the tape in order to level and true the line. Mark clearly on the dress form the distance from the hip level line to the floor. This measurement may be used later to indicate whether the dress form is level as well as to show whether it is set at the correct height. Pencil around the lower edge of the tape and record the hip measurement at this level (see Figure 7).

5. Bustline

Place and pin a tape around the largest bust measurement, being sure that the tape is kept level. Pencil lightly around the lower edge of the tape and record the measurement (see Figure 7).

The recorded measurements of neck, bust, waist, and hip are checks on size when you pad the form.

FINISHING THE DRESS FORM COVER

1. Remove the cover and duplicate line markings on the opposite half after folding on the center front line and pinning the raw edges together along the neckline and armscye edges and along the shoulder and underarm seams.

2. Transfer all of the basic lines to the inside of the garment, using a tracing wheel on carbon paper.

3. To make the important basic lines permanent and easy to feel even through heavy fabrics, couch cord or embroidery floss along the penciled lines. To do this, wind the cord or floss on the machine bobbin, but leave the cord out of the bobbin tension. Then if the tension of the top thread is loosened, it will loop down through the fabric over the cord. Stitch all basic lines with the right side of the cloth down against the feed dog so that the cord from the bobbin will lie on the right side of the garment. In addition to the basic neckline, armscye, waist, and hip level lines, shoulder seams and center front can be quickly marked in this way.

4. Machine-stitch with regular thread the center back lines to stay them, as you will have to re-pin the center back line several times during the course of padding the form.

DRAWING THE FRENCH LINING PATTERN

Although it is usually possible to buy a French lining pattern which can be used in making a dress form cover, you may not always be able to secure one readily. If you cannot get a pattern through commercial sources, you can always make one of your own, and it takes but little time and few tools to do so. A large sheet of construction or wrapping paper, a tailor's square, and a well-sharpened pencil are all you need. Moreover, the task requires no special skill, though it does require accuracy in reading and in marking the measurements correctly.

The following pages give you, in tabulated form, all the information you will need for the purpose. This consists of (1) a chart of measurements for the French lining pattern, in sizes 12, 14, 16, 18, and 20; (2) detailed pattern directions; (3) measurements for the four types of panel in each of the five sizes given; and (4) an illustration showing the patterns for the panels and the typical measurements for each (see Figure 8). Before you begin making your own pattern, examine this material carefully.

You should begin by checking the measurements of the five pattern sizes given in the chart against your own measurements. In doing so, select the size which coincides with your own measurements. Be sure to take your hip measure where it is largest, that is, 8 or $9\frac{1}{2}$ inches below the waist, rather than 7 inches below the waist, as is usually done in commercial patterns. Once you have determined the actual measurements you will use, the next step is to substitute these for the average measurements given in Figure 8. Finally, draw the lines of the pattern on the paper. For best results, connect all points which should be joined (see directions below) with ruled pencil lines. Then draw curves freehand wherever they are indicated. The panels can then be cut out and used precisely like those of a commercial pattern.

THE DRESS FORM

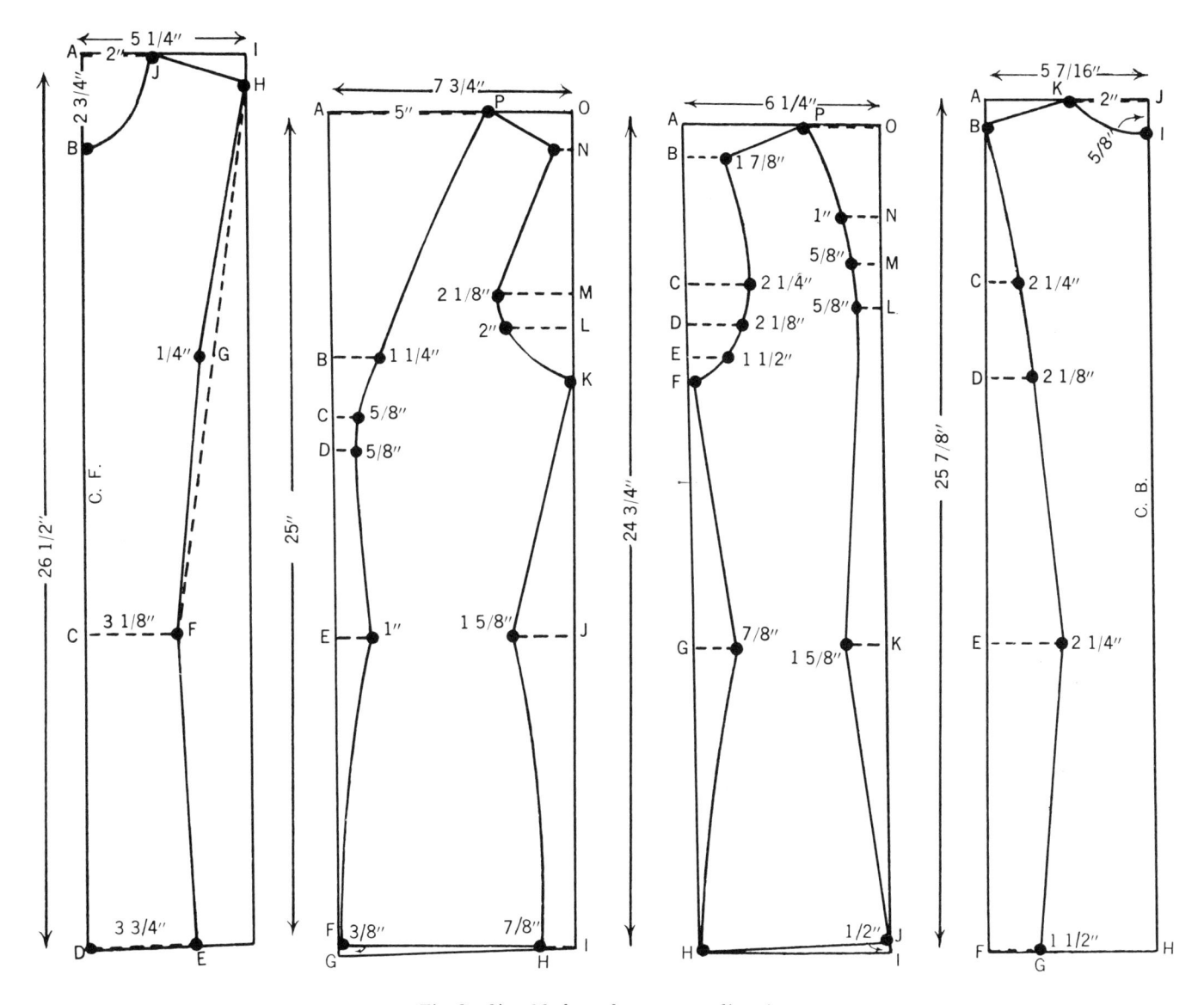

Fig. 8. Size 16 dress form cover directions.

CHART OF MEASUREMENTS
FOR FRENCH LINING PATTERNS

Size	12	14	16	18	20
Bust	34	36	38	40	42
Waist	26½	28	30	32	34
Hip (lower edge of pattern)	36¾	39	41¼	43	45
Length of pattern from base of neck at center front to lower edge	23¼	23½	23¾	24	24¼

PATTERN DIRECTIONS

Lengthwise grain in all pieces is parallel to the long side of the rectangle.

CENTER FRONT PANEL
1. Construct rectangle
2. Measure and dot:
   - A to B
   - A to C
   - D to E
   - A to J
   - I to H

9

DRESS DESIGN

3. Join:

    J to H   H to F
    F to E

   Measure in 1/4 inch from point G (halfway between H and F). Swing inward curve from H to F through point G.

4. Draw neckline B to J beginning with right angle at B and ending with right angle at J.

SIDE FRONT PANEL

1. Construct rectangle
2. Measure and dot:

    A to B   A to C
    A to D

3. Measure up from G to find point F.
4. Square in from line AG the given measurements at B, C, D, E.
5. Measure and dot:

    A to P   O to L
    O to N   O to K
    O to M   O to J

6. Square in from line OI the given measurements at M, L, J, I.
7. Join P to points marked in from B, C, D, with outward curve.
8. Join D to E with inward curve.
9. Join E to F with outward curve.
10. Join F to H and H to I.
11. Join P to N with ruler.
12. Swing inward curve from N to the points squared in from M and L and on to K.
13. Join K to J with slightly inward curve.
14. Join J to I with slightly outward curve over hip.

SIDE BACK PANEL

1. Construct rectangle
2. Measure and dot:

    A to B   A to E
    A to C   A to F
    A to D   A to G

3. Square in from line AH the given measurements at B, C, D, E, F, G.
4. Measure and dot:

    A to P   O to M
    P to O   O to L
    O to N   O to K

5. Square in from line OI the given measurements at N, M, L, K.
6. Measure up from I to J.
7. Join P to point marked in from B. Use ruler.
8. With inward curve join to points marked in from B, C, D, E, F.
9. Join points squared in from F and G and continue to H.
10. Join P to points squared in from N, M, L with outward curve.
11. Join point marked in from L to K with ruler and to J with outward curve.
12. Join J to H, touching line HI at center of panel.

CENTER BACK PANEL

1. Construct rectangle
2. Measure and dot:

    A to B   A to D
    A to C   A to E

3. Square in the given measurements from line AF at C, D, E, F.
4. Measure and dot:

    A to K   K to J
    J to I

5. Join K to B.
6. Join B to points squared in from line AF with inward curve B to E, and outward curve E to G.
7. Draw neckline K to I beginning with right angle at K and ending with right angle at I.

Pattern Measurements for Dress Form Cover

Size 12

Center Front Panel
Rectangle
   Width ...... 5"
   Length .... 25 5/8"
A-B .... 2 1/2"
A-C .... 17 1/4"
C-F .... 2 7/8"
A-D .... 25 5/8"
D-E .... 3 1/4"
A-J .... 1 3/4"
I-H .... 1 3/8"
G—
   one-half of FH   1/4"

Side Front Panel
Rectangle
   Width ...... 6 5/8"
   Length .... 24 1/4"
A-B .... 7 1/2"
B .... 7/8"
A-C .... 9 3/8"
C .... 3/8"

Center Back Panel
Rectangle
   Width ...... 5 1/8"
   Length .... 25 3/8"
A-B .... 1 5/8"
A-C .... 6"
C .... 1"
A-D .... 9"
D .... 1 1/2"
A-E .... 16 5/8"
E .... 2 1/4"
A-F .... 25 3/8"
F .... 1 3/4"
J-K .... 2"
J-I .... 5/8"

Side Back Panel
Rectangle
   Width ...... 5 5/8"
   Length .... 24"
A-B .... 1"
B .... 1 5/8"

THE DRESS FORM

A-D	10 3/8"
D	3/8"
A-E	15 7/8"
E	3/4"
F-G	1/4"
A-P	4 3/8"
O-N	1 1/4"
O-M	5 5/8"
M	1 3/4"
O-L	6 5/8"
L	1 5/8"
O-K	7 7/8"
O-J	15 3/4"
J	1 1/2"
I	5/8"

A-C	5 1/4"
C	2"
A-D	6 1/4"
D	1 3/4"
A-E	6 3/4"
E	1 3/8"
A-F	7 1/2"
F	3/16"
A-G	15 1/2"
G	1"
A-H	24"
P-O	1 15/16"
O-N	3"
N	1 1/16"
O-M	4 5/8"
M	7/8"
O-L	6"
L	3/4"
O-K	15 1/8"
K	1 5/8"
I-J	3/8"

Size 14

Center Front Panel
Rectangle
Width ..... 5 1/8"
Length ..... 26"
A-B ..... 2 5/8"
A-C ..... 17 5/8"
C-F ..... 3"
A-D ..... 26"
D-E ..... 3 1/2"
A-J ..... 1 7/8"
I-H ..... 1 3/8"
G—halfway between F-H ..... 1/4"

Side Front Panel
Rectangle
Width ..... 7 1/16"
Length ..... 24 1/2"
A-B ..... 7 1/2"
B ..... 7/8"
A-C ..... 9 3/8"
C ..... 3/8"
A-D ..... 10 3/8"
D ..... 3/8"
A-E ..... 16 3/8"
E ..... 7/8"
F-G ..... 3/8"

Center Back Panel
Rectangle
Width ..... 5 3/16"
Length ..... 25 5/8"
A-B ..... 1 3/8"
A-C ..... 6"
C ..... 7/8"
A-D ..... 9"
D ..... 1 3/8"
A-E ..... 16 7/8"
E ..... 2 1/8"
A-F ..... 25 5/8"
F ..... 1 3/8"
J-K ..... 2"
J-I ..... 5/8"

Side Back Panel
Rectangle
Width ..... 5 7/8"
Length ..... 24 3/8"
A-B ..... 1 1/16"
B ..... 1 1/2"
A-C ..... 5 1/4"
C ..... 2"
A-D ..... 6 1/4"
D ..... 1 3/4"
A-E ..... 6 3/4"

A-P	4 9/16"
O-N	1 1/4"
O-M	5 5/8"
M	2"
O-L	6 5/8"
L	1 7/8"
O-K	8"
O-J	16"
J	1 1/2"
I	3/4"

Size 16

Center Front Panel
Rectangle
Width ..... 5 1/4"
Length ..... 26 1/2"
A-B ..... 2 3/4"
A-C ..... 18"
C-F ..... 3 1/8"
A-D ..... 26 1/2"
D-E ..... 3 3/4"
A-J ..... 2"
I-H ..... 1 3/8"
G—halfway point between F and H ..... 3/8"

Side Front Panel
Rectangle
Width ..... 7 3/4"
Length ..... 25"
A-B ..... 7 1/2"
B ..... 1 1/4"
A-C ..... 9 3/8"
C ..... 5/8"
A-D ..... 10 3/8"
D ..... 5/8"
A-E ..... 16 5/8"
E ..... 1"
F-G ..... 3/8"
A-P ..... 5"
O-N ..... 1 1/2"
O-M ..... 5 3/4"
M ..... 2 1/8"

E	1 3/8"
A-F	7 5/8"
F	0
A-G	15 3/4"
G	3/4"
A-H	24 3/8"
P-O	1 7/8"
O-N	3"
N	7/8"
O-M	4 5/8"
M	3/4"
O-L	6"
L	3/4"
O-K	15 1/2"
K	1 3/4"
I-J	1/2"

Center Back Panel
Rectangle
Width ..... 5 7/16"
Length ..... 25 7/8"
A-B ..... 1 1/2"
A-C ..... 6"
C ..... 1"
A-D ..... 9"
D ..... 1 1/2"
A-E ..... 17 1/8"
E ..... 2 1/4"
A-F ..... 25 7/8"
F ..... 1 1/2"
J-K ..... 2"
J-I ..... 5/8"

Side Back Panel
Rectangle
Width ..... 6 1/4"
Length ..... 24 3/4"
A-B ..... 1 3/16"
B ..... 1 7/8"
A-C ..... 5 1/4"
C ..... 2 1/4"
A-D ..... 6 1/4"
D ..... 2 1/8"
A-E ..... 7 1/4"
E ..... 1 1/2"
A-F ..... 8"
A-G ..... 16"
G ..... 7/8"
A-H ..... 24 3/4"

11

DRESS DESIGN

O-L	6¾"
L	2"
O-K	8⅜"
O-J	16¼"
J	1⅝"
I	⅞"

P-O	1⅞"
O-N	3"
N	1"
O-M	4⅝"
M	⅝"
O-L	6"
L	⅝"
O-K	15¾"
K	1⅝"
I-J	½"

Size 18

Center Front Panel

Rectangle
- Width ...... 5⅜"
- Length ..... 27"

A-B	2⅞"
A-C	18"
C-F	3⅜"
A-D	27"
D-E	4"
A-J	2"
I-H	1¼"

G—Point Halfway between F and H ..... ⅜"

Side Front Panel

Rectangle
- Width ...... 8¼"
- Length ..... 25³⁄₁₆"

A-B	7½"
B	1⅜"
A-C	9⅜"
C	¾"
A-D	10⅜"
D	¾"
A-E	16⅝"
E	1¼"
F-G	½"
A-P	5⅝"
ON	1⅝"
O-M	5¾"
M	2⅛"
O-L	6¾"
L	2"
O-K	8⅝"
O-J	16¼"
J	1¾"
I	1¼"

Center Back Panel

Rectangle
- Width ...... 5½"
- Length ..... 26³⁄₁₆"

A-B	1½"
A-C	6"
C	¹⁵⁄₁₆"
A-D	9"
D	1⅜"
A-E	17¼"
E	2⅛"
A-F	26³⁄₁₆"
F	1⅜"
J-K	2³⁄₁₆"
J-I	⅝"

Side Back Panel

Rectangle
- Width ...... 6⁹⁄₁₆"
- Length ..... 24¾"

A-B	⅞"
B	2½"
A-C	5¼"
C	2¾"
A-D	6¼"
D	2⅝"
A-E	7¼"
E	2"
A-F	8⅛"
F	⅜"
A-G	16"
G	1"
A-H	24¾"
P-O	1⁵⁄₁₆"
O-N	3"
N	½"
O-M	4⅝"
M	¼"

Size 20

Center Front Panel

Rectangle
- Width ...... 5⅝"
- Length ..... 27⅜"

A-B	3"
A-C	18"
C-F	3⅝"
A-D	27⅜"
D-E	4¼"
A-J	2"
I-H	1⅛"

G—Halfway point between F and H ..... ⅜"

Side Front Panel

Rectangle
- Width ...... 8"
- Length ..... 25½"

A-B	8"
B	½"
A-C	9½"
C	¼"
A-D	11¼"
D	¼"
A-E	16¾"
E	1⅛"
F-G	⅜"
A-P	4⅝"
O-N	1⅝"
N	¾"
O-M	5¾"
M	2¼"
O-L	6¾"
L	2⅛"
O-K	8⅞"
O-J	16½"
J	1½"
I	½"

Center Back Panel

Rectangle
- Width ...... 5¾"
- Length ..... 26⅜"

A-B	1⅝"
A-C	6"
C	1¹⁄₁₆"
A-D	9"
D	1½"
A-E	17⅜"
E	2¼"
A-F	26⅜"
F	1½"
J-K	2⅜"
J-I	⅝"

Side Back Panel

Rectangle
- Width ...... 6⅝"
- Length ..... 25³⁄₁₆"

A-B	1"
B	2⅛"
A-C	5¼"
C	2¾"
A-D	6¼"
D	2⅜"
A-E	7¼"
E	1¾"
A-F	8¼"
F	0
A-G	16"
G	¾"
A-H	25³⁄₁₆"
P-O	1⅝"
O-N	3"
N	¾"
O-M	4⅝"
M	½"
O-L	6½"
L	⅝"
O-K	16"
K	1⅝"
I-J	½"

THE DRESS FORM

PADDING THE DRESS FORM

SELECTION OF THE DRESS FORM

Buy any make of form you prefer, as long as it has a heavy iron base to prevent it from tipping over easily. An inexpensive form will serve you as well as a high priced one if it is well padded.

If you can try the completed cover on two or three unpadded forms in your own size range, you can select the right size most accurately. There should be space for enough padding under the cover to give a resilient foundation to pin into. The most important measurement to check is the size of the form *at the level where the waistline of the cover will come.* The waistline of the form may be exactly the right size, but if the waistline marked on the cover falls far below that point, the form will not serve your purpose. If you are exceptionally long-waisted, select a form which is as small around the upper hip as your own waistline measurement.

An individual who wears a size 12 dress pattern should usually choose a size 30 form; one who wears a size 14, a 32 form; and a size 16, a 34. If your waistline is under 24 inches, use a size 28 form.

PADDING MATERIALS

Cotton batting is by far the most satisfactory padding. Soft tissue paper can also be used, but is much slower and more awkward to handle. Or, it is possible to use the two together, first filling out with batting and then covering with tissue. Even newspapers are sometimes used for first layers where a great deal of padding is required. Paper is often unsatisfactory, however, because it has to be pinned onto the form, and unless the pins are well pushed into the form, the heads tend to punch through the finished covering. Cotton batting, on the other hand, clings to the form with little or no pinning if placed directly against the cotton jersey — the usual surface of a standard commercial form.

If the shoulders of the form are narrower than those of the cover, cut half circles of tagboard or other flexible cardboard and tack or pin them to the dress form to widen the shoulders as much as necessary before beginning to pad (see **Figure 9**).

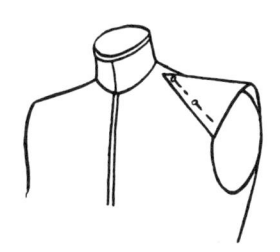

Fig. 9. Cardboard pinned to the shoulder of the form to widen it.

PADDING

First try the finished cover on the form, pinning it together at several points along the center back opening. Adjust the shoulder seams so that the cover tips neither to the back nor to the front, and so that the waistline and hipline are level. Then determine how much padding to add to the front and back to keep the side seams centered in position.

Check the places needing the most padding as well as those which need the least. Do this by reaching under the cover and chalking any lines or points on the form at places which need special consideration. Also chalk the position of the basic neckline of the cover to serve as a guide for measuring down to the bust, waist, and hip level and down to the shoulder blades in the back. Then remove the cover.

Carefully unroll the cotton batting in preparation for the actual padding. Throughout the entire process use it *in thin sheets,* never in clumps, handling it lightly to avoid matting it. Begin to pad by covering the entire form with a thin layer, letting each sheet extend as far as it will, then smoothing the edges into those of the adjoining sheet. By blending one layer into another, you can pad the entire form without using any pins. Even those places which need large amounts of padding can be built up without pins if the material is applied one layer at a time and if each layer is pressed carefully into the one underneath.

Do not add any more than a first thin layer of cotton for a radius of two or three inches around the base of the neck. For usually if you pull the cover down firmly in the final adjustment, you need little padding around the neckline. Too much on the top of the shoulder near the neck raises the entire covering too high.

DRESS DESIGN

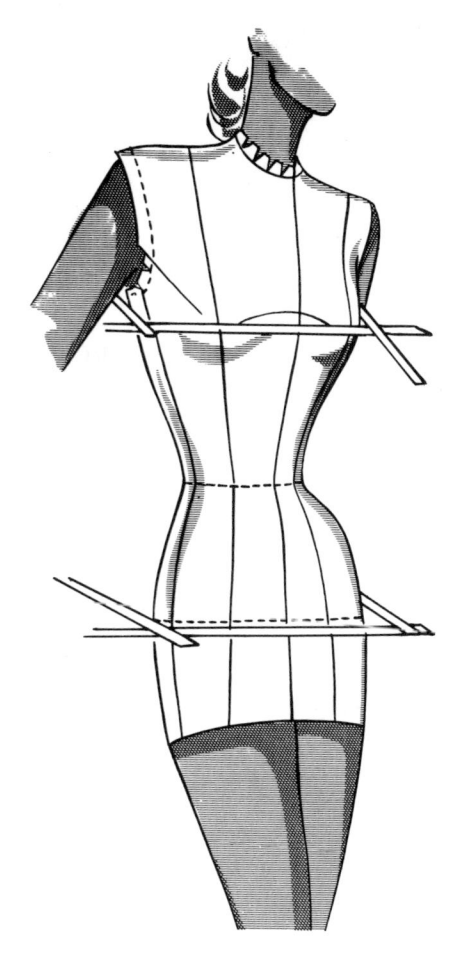

Fig. 10. Measuring bust and hip widths and thickness from front to back.

As you pad, check the recorded measurements of bust, waist, and hip, and those from neck to waist, bust, and hip. Note the curve of the body from waist to hip at the side and back, comparing the padding on the form to the contour of the figure. If you are padding your own dress form, stand in front of a full-length mirror with the form beside you, raised to your own height, and cross two tailor's squares at the hip level to measure the hip width from side to side as shown in Figure 10. Also cross tailor's squares from back to front to determine the thickness of the body and compare this measurement with that of the form. The same method should be used to check the width of bust and shoulders from side to side and their thickness from front to back. Even though the hip measurements of two different figures may be the same, the effect of the two can differ greatly if one is wide from side to side and the other thick from front to back. The form must round out exactly like the figure, or garments draped on it will hang most disappointingly when tried on.

Padding always puffs up much larger than a person's actual size before the covering compresses it. If the batting seems very bulky and difficult to manage, bind bias strips of muslin around the waist and hips and diagonally from the shoulder to the waist to hold it down. Check the various circumferences by pulling the tapeline tightly over the padding, and when the measurements check with your own, try the covering on the form. Do this carefully to avoid shifting the cotton. Place the shoulder seams correctly and see that the neckline is well up in the back and as much higher than the side of the neck as it appeared to be when you tried it on yourself. Pin the cover together every two or three inches down the center back. Then examine the form for flaws. Ordinarily there will be many places which are still too soft and which need more padding. If so, remove the cover and make the final corrections. Before putting the cover on for the last time, give it a thorough pressing, but still without moisture.

The importance of placing the covering on the form correctly cannot be overemphasized. To avoid having it tip to the back, pull the fabric down firmly along the lower edge at the center front. Before pinning the center back, also examine the shoulder seam, the neckline, the waist, and the hipline for correctness of position. Begin to pin at the neck and work down, matching the four crossmarkings on the center back line. Try to avoid pulling the garment downward in back as you pin. Pin the first time with the seam allowance toward the outside. After making a final check for errors, start re-pinning at the neckline, removing one or two pins at a time and lapping the right side over the left. Pin every half inch and bury all but the very head of each pin in the padding. Either leave the form pinned or slipstitch it together.

Pull the lower edge of the cover down firmly to smooth out all horizontal wrinkles and tack it securely to the wooden brace underneath the base of the form. If you expect to use the form for a long time without unpadding it, it will be worth your while to cover the armhole opening and add a shaped collar to the neck.

THE DRESS FORM

THE ARMHOLE COVER

1. Place a piece of paper against the armhole opening and trace its shape, crossmarking it at the shoulder and underarm seams.

2. True the pattern, cut it out, and lay it on the fabric so that the lengthwise grain runs between the two crossmarks, that is, from the shoulder seam to the underarm seam.

3. Pencil around the pattern on the fabric and pencil the crossmarks.

4. Cut it with a 3/8 inch seam.

5. Turn the seam under and place the oval against the armhole, matching the crossmarkings. Then pin the turned edge to the armscye line on the form cover and finish by slipstitching.

COLLAR

The base of the neck is, of course, determined by the neckline marked on the cover. The measurement of the neck 1½ inches above the base (recorded at the fitting) will be at least 1 inch and sometimes 1½ inches less than the base measurement. Pin the tape measure in a circle equal to the circumference of the upper neck and drop it over the neck of the form in order to determine how much to pad the neck. Ordinarily the neck of a dress form is too erect at the back. If your head tilts forward, it may be difficult to give the neck of the form the same slant. Place all of the padding on the sides and front of the upper neck, building it up until it duplicates your own neck as nearly as possible.

To draft the collar pattern, follow the directions below and see Figure 11.

1. Draw a rectangle the length of the basic neckline from center back to center front and 3 inches high.

2. On the center front line measure up ½ inch from the lower line of the rectangle.

3. On the center back line measure down ½ inch from the upper line of the rectangle.

4. For the base of the collar follow the lower line

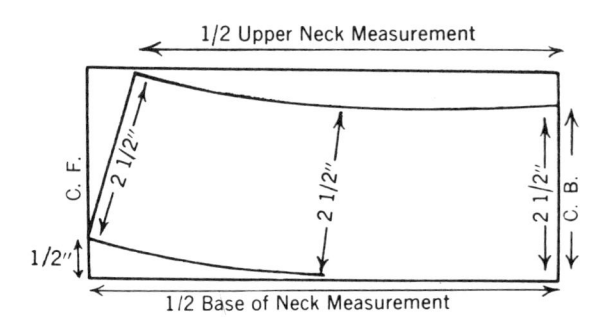

Fig. 11. Dress form collar draft.

one-half its length and then swing up in an outward curve to meet the point ½ inch up on the center front line (see Figure 11).

5. Measure up at right angles from this base line 2½ inches at center front, center back, and at a point halfway between. Beginning at the center back, draw a line for the upper edge of the collar through these three points. Mark off along this line one-half the circumference of the upper neck measurement. Join this point to the end of the lower line for the center front of the collar.

6. Cut out the pattern.

7. Place it on the fabric with the center back on the lengthwise thread and allow a 3/8 inch seam on all edges.

8. Pin the two collar pieces together along the center back and try it on before pinning it to the dress form. The collar should fit closely at the upper edge as well as at the base of the neck, where it will sew to the basic neckline of the cover. The center front and back seams may need to be sloped more to fit your neck exactly.

9. Turn under the lower edge and pin it to the form cover just above the cord couched on the neckline. Then slipstitch the collar to the cover at the base of the neck and to the form at the center front and back seams. Turn the upper edge over the padding and slipstitch it to the form.

The dress form is now finished and should exactly duplicate your measurements and your body contours so that it will serve as a perfect model for all garments which you will design by draping.

2. Basic Blouses

PART I

DRAPING BASIC BLOUSES ON THE DRESS FORM

The Fundamental Dart

The systems of draping and flat pattern design are both founded on a clear understanding of the purpose of the fundamental dart. When you first began to sew, if you ignored the little v-shaped wedges marked on your commercial pattern, you probably wondered why the dress did not fit. Those wedges, or *darts*, take up the excess in the outer edge of the pattern, converting a flat piece of fabric to a rounded or conical shape that conforms to the contour of the figure. Darts always radiate outward from the highest point of the bust in front (Figure 1) and from the shoulders and the shoulder blades in the back. A dart placed anywhere around the outside edge of the blouse-front pattern will always point toward the bust (see Figure 2).

The necessity of shaping a pattern to fit the body curves is the foundation of most of the best dress designs and certainly of the most functional ones. In the following pages, directions will be given for placing the basic dart on the shoulder, under the arm, and under the bust. This will be followed by a discussion of possible variations in design produced by handling the dart or the fullness from the dart in a less conventional way. It is therefore of first importance to understand the function of the dart before even starting to drape, and to consider its possibilities for inspiration in design while draping the first basic blouse patterns. If the beginning draper will carry out each of the following practice problems, she will not only gain a thorough understanding of draping principles, but will also be able to apply them to the more difficult designs included in Chapter 7.

Fig. 1. Darts radiating from the bust.

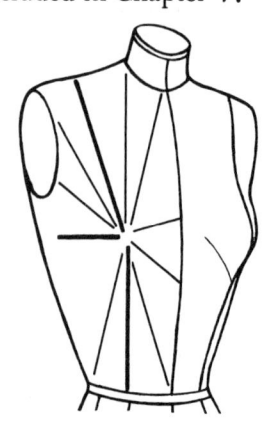

Fig. 2. Possible dart positions (heavy lines show standard positions).

BASIC BLOUSES

For all practice draping use light-weight unbleached muslin or a similar inexpensive material that is easy to handle. Unless otherwise stated, the directions given are for draping a half pattern.

Problem 1

DRAPING THE BLOUSE WITH SHOULDER AND WAISTLINE DARTS

The first problem is to drape a basic waist with shoulder and waistline darts. This is the dart combination that makes the best fitting basic or foundation pattern from which to develop designs through the flat pattern blocking method. A foundation pattern is commonly called a master pattern. See page **44** for a complete explanation of the master block pattern. The following directions for draping the basic waist with shoulder and waistline darts explain not only how to place and pin the fabric, but also how to check results and judge patterns after they are draped in order to predict their accuracy of fit before trying them on.

WAIST FRONT

Estimating The Fabric and Marking The Center Front Line
(see Figure 3)

1. Measure the dress form vertically from the highest point on the shoulder (intersection of the neck and shoulder seam lines) over the fullest curve of the bust to the waistline. Add 3 inches for seam allowances (1 inch for the shoulder and 2 inches for the waistline). The total lengthwise measurement will be approximately 21 inches.

2. Measure the dress form horizontally from the center front across the fullest curve of the bust to the underarm seam and add 3 inches (1 inch for ease and 2 inches for a large let-out seam under the arm). For a size 16 pattern this will total about $12\frac{1}{2}$ inches.

3. Measure in from the selvage of the fabric the width needed and mark the center front with a pencil line on the exact straight lengthwise grain. Figuring the approximate amount of material needed instead of using the exact center of a 36 inch width helps you to acquire the habit of saving fabric. Obviously this can become valuable practice whether the fabric you are working with is expensive or cheap (see Figure 4).

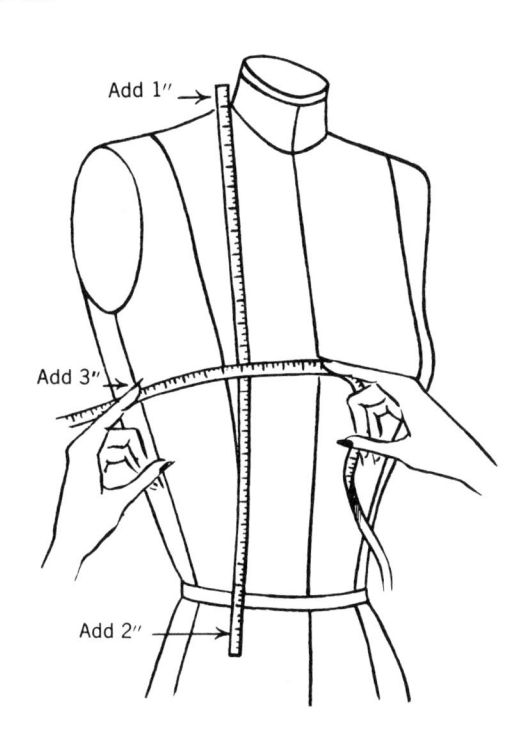

Fig. 3. Method of measuring for blouse.

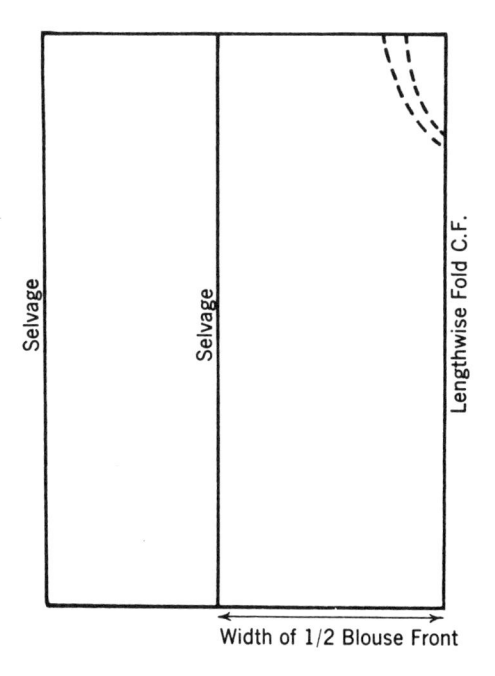

Fig. 4. Location of center front.

DRESS DESIGN

Note. Always use the lengthwise grain of the cloth vertically in garments and always drape with only a single thickness of fabric.

4. Tear off the needed length of muslin, a block approximately 21 inches long by 25 inches wide.

Shaping the Neckline

For a size 16, the front neckline without seam allowances is a curve about 3 inches deep at the center front and 2½ inches wide measured horizontally from the center front to the neck end of the shoulder seam (see Figure 5).

1. Draw on the muslin the neck oval, 4 inches deep at the center front and 2½ inches wide, measured horizontally from the center front to the neck end of the shoulder seam. The 4 inch depth includes a 1 inch shoulder seam.

2. Draw a second line along which to cut. This should be ½ inch above the first line at the center front in order to allow a ½ inch seam. To allow for a slight stretching of the fabric away from the center front as you drape, mark the cutting line closer to the center line as it nears the shoulder seam. The cut neckline should be about 1½ inches wide at the shoulder seam by 3½ inches deep at the center front.

3. Cut out the neckline on the upper pencil line.

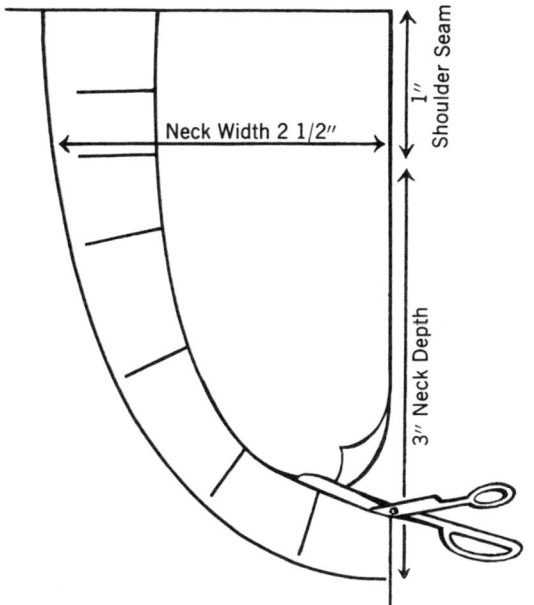

Fig. 5. Shaping the neck.

Placing the Fabric on the Form (see Figure 6)

1. Place the fabric along the center front matching the penciled center front line of the muslin and the center front of the form and pin it at the following points:

(a) The base of the neck. The penciled neckline on the muslin should be at the exact base of the neck on the form.

(b) Chest.

(c) Waistline. Ease the cloth above this last pin to allow length for slight blousing and for action.

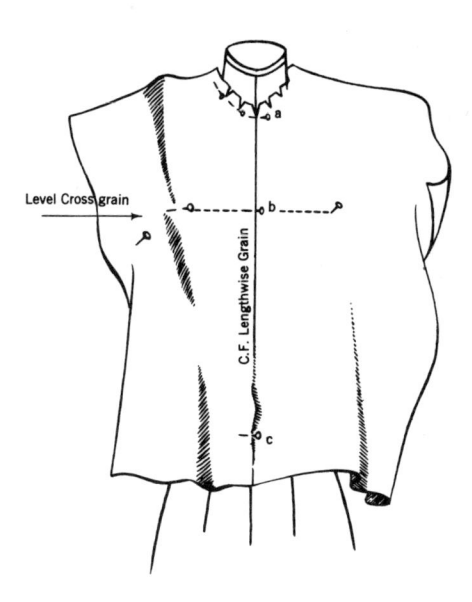

Fig. 6. Pinning the fabric to the form.

2. Start draping at the neckline. Smooth the fabric slightly away from the center front and up toward the shoulder seam, forcing the muslin to cling closely to the side of the neck. Pin the cloth to the form as you proceed and clip the neckline seam so that it fits more smoothly.

Caution. Overstretching causes an ugly diagonal wrinkle and looseness at the chest. Too little stretching causes looseness at the center front neckline and chest (see Figures 7 and 8).

3. Smooth the fabric across the chest and pin it to the form to support it so that the filling threads are perpendicular to the center front as far as the point of the bust.

18

BASIC BLOUSES

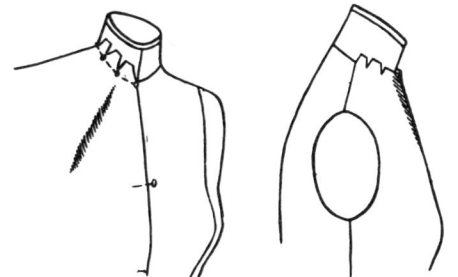

Fig. 7. Neckline over-stretched causes diagonal wrinkle to the bust.
Fig. 8. Neckline loose at center front.

4. Place another pin at the underarm to support the filling threads horizontally all across the bust. Ease the fabric forward to provide looseness at the point of the bust.

Note. (a) Acquire the habit of pinning the fabric to the form as little as necessary. Do this to gain speed and to let the fabric hang as it would when being worn.

(b) It is a general rule to pin at right angles to the edge except when forming a line. When this is being done, place pins head to point on the line.

Forming the Shoulder Dart (see Figure 9)

1. Take up the excess at the shoulder in a dart laid smoothly with its under edge folded inward toward the center front. Pin this dart to the form lightly with one or two pins at and near the shoulder end. Place it tentatively at first so that you can experiment with both its size and its position.

2. Pin the remaining excess under the bust into a tentative waistline dart. Judge the size of each dart, and if desirable, shift the fabric to divide the excess more suitably between the two. The size of the bust will, of course, determine the size of the darts, and the position of the bust, high or low, may make it necessary to shift the excess from one dart to the other in order to keep the crosswise grain at the bust line parallel to the floor.

3. Pin the shoulder dart accurately but leave the waistline dart pinned in the approximate size.

(a) Decide on the best position for the shoulder dart. The normal line is from the center of the shoulder to the point of the bust and slants slightly toward the center front from the top to the bottom (see Figure 11). Figure 10 shows a dart that has been carelessly placed.

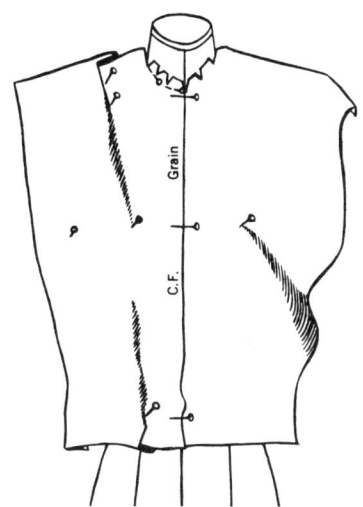

Fig. 9. Shoulder and waistline darts placed tentatively.

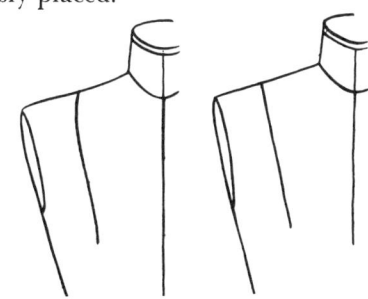

Figs. 10 and 11. Incorrect and correct shoulder dart placement. Note that in Fig. 10, the dart line wavers and curls toward the neck, whereas Fig. 11 shows the normal shoulder dart position.

Note. Since the direction of the dart changes somewhat with fashion, you should not consider the above statement a hard and fast rule. Your feeling for contour will help you place this line to emphasize the fashion silhouette desired. In the 1920's the line ran practically parallel to the center front (see Figure 13). Throughout the 1940's it was fashionable to emphasize broad shoulders and a slender waistline by starting the dart slightly farther out from the neck at the shoulder and pointing somewhat more sharply inward toward the center front (see Figure 12). But in spite of fashion, the direction varies so little that the dart always points toward the center of the bust.

DRESS DESIGN

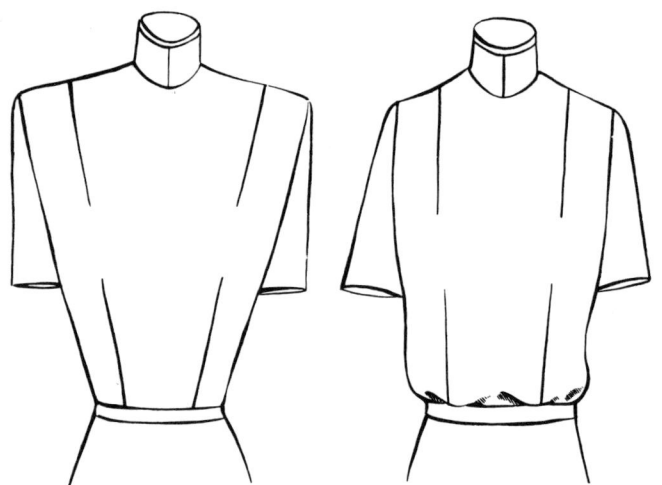

Figs. 12 and 13. Influence of fashion silhouette on dart placement.

(b) Fold the excess under toward the center front and pin the dart perpendicular to the edge. Slip the fingers under the cloth to prevent pinning into the form (see Figure 14).

Caution. Never pin a dart wrong side out. It may be quicker, but it is impossible to form a good line by this method.

Rule for Establishing All Vertical Darts: Determine the position and line direction of the dart first. Fold on this line, sliding the excess toward the center under the folded edge. Pin frequently, placing pins perpendicular to the folded edge.

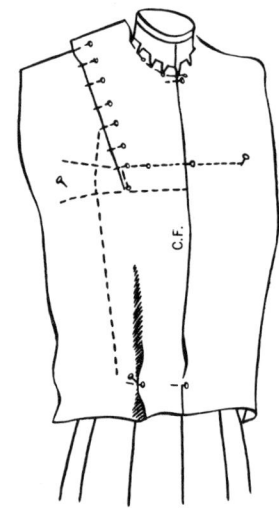

Fig. 14. Shoulder dart accurately pinned (dotted lines indicate the effect of the dart on the grain).

(c) Slip the fingers under the fabric near the point of the dart in order to stop it at the place desired. This should be before it reaches the point of the bust. Doing this introduces some ease across the chest. Avoid fitting so tightly across the chest that the blouse caves in between the shoulder seam and the bust.

Placing the Shoulder Seam (see Figures 15, 16, 17)

The standard position of the shoulder seam (Figure 15) is from the cord at the base of the ear along the top of the shoulder out to a point 1/4 inch back of the bone at the tip of the shoulder. The line slants slightly toward the back. It should appear to be directly on top of the shoulder and should not be visible from either the direct front or back when viewed at the shoulder level. Follow the line already established on the form if it appears to be a good one.

The following variations from the normal are due to faulty posture or to a very large bust: (*a*) For round shoulders and forward head (see Figure 16), move the outer point of the shoulder line back slightly to minimize the defect; (*b*) For a large bust (see Figure 17), move the outer point of the shoulder line slightly forward to reduce the apparent bust size.

1. Standing at the side of the form, fold the fabric along the shoulder line, turning the excess forward over the right side (see Figure 18). Keep the cloth taut along the shoulder line so that it bridges over the hollow in front of the shoulder.

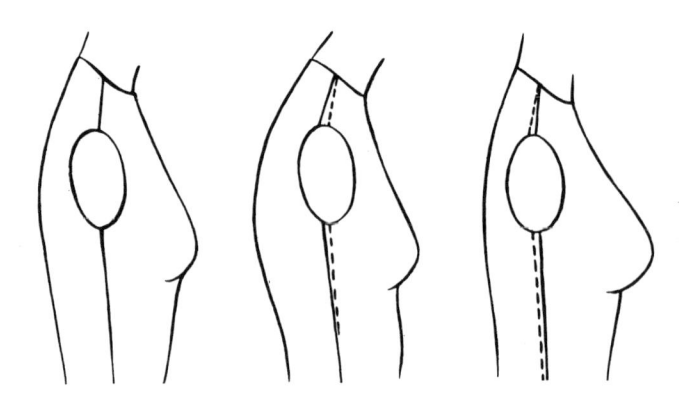

Figs. 15, 16, and 17. Shoulder seam position for three different figures. Fig. 15. Normal position of shoulder seam. Fig. 16. For round shoulders, move seam back at outer end. Fig. 17. For large bust, move seam forward at outer end.

BASIC BLOUSES

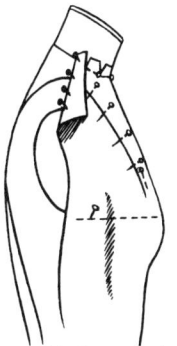

Fig. 18. Shoulder seam folded toward right side.

2. Crease the fold-line with the thumbnail and pin it to the form, being careful not to stretch the bias fold.

3. Cut away the excess, allowing 1 inch for the seam.

4. Turn the seam allowance under to the wrong side (see Figure 19) and pin the turned fold perpendicular to the edge. Pin to the form only at the ends of the seam, as all pins must later be removed to slip the back shoulder seam forward under the front.

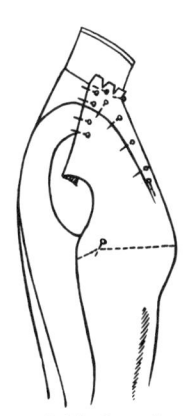

Fig. 19. Shoulder seam folded under and pinned.

Forming the Armscye Curve (see Figure 20)

Three points serve as guides in forming a good armscye curve. (The terms *armscye* and *armhole* are synonymous.)

1. The tip of the shoulder, which should be the starting point. The line normally starts at the junction of the plane of the shoulder and the plane of the arm (see Chapter 1). If shoulders broader than normal are in fashion, move this point out the desired width. Although shoulder widths vary, few shoulder seams should measure less than 5 inches. It is wise, however, to measure the shoulder length of your own favorite dress or suit and gauge the width accordingly.

2. The narrowest point of the chest. From the tip of the shoulder, the armscye line curves slightly inward toward the center front until it reaches the deepest point of the curve at the chest. To find this point, measure down 3 inches from the pit of the neck on the center front line and square out to the armscye. The inward curve is so slight that the line appears to be almost straight when on the figure. If you adjust this curve so that it is practically parallel to the shoulder dart line, the two lines will harmonize.

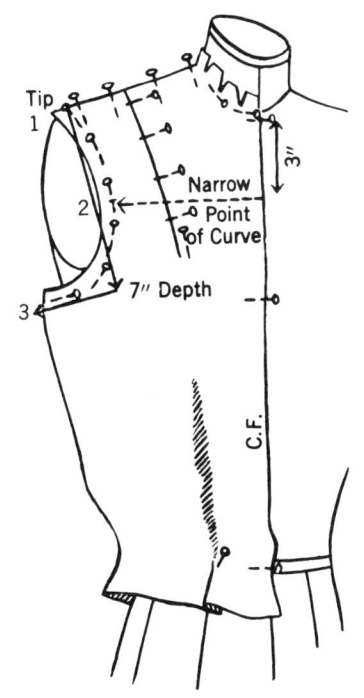

Fig. 20. Armscye curve.

Caution. Do not stretch the fabric across the chest when establishing the armscye line.

3. Depth of the underarm curve. From the pin at the narrowest point of the chest, curve the line outward in a smooth arc toward the underarm. Determine the depth of the underarm by measuring down in a straight vertical line from the tip of the shoulder a distance of 7 to 7½ inches. Then square out from this point to the underarm seam line.

DRESS DESIGN

4. Armscye curve. Cut, allowing a ½ to ⅝ inch seam for the lower half of the armscye, and a ¾ inch seam for the upper half. Extra width on the upper half of the armscye allows for a possible increase in the size of the shoulder dart or added length on the shoulder seam. A narrow seam allowance under the arm is necessary to prevent the armhole from binding when the arm is down.

Placing the Waistline Dart

Before finally pinning the waistline dart, examine the blouse around the armscye, especially toward the underarm. If the fabric tends to gap at the side front of the armscye (see Figure 21) deepen the waistline dart.

1. Push the muslin with the flat of the hand downward and forward toward the center front to fit the armscye smoothly but not tightly (see Figure 22). Pin the muslin to the form at the waistline on the side seam.

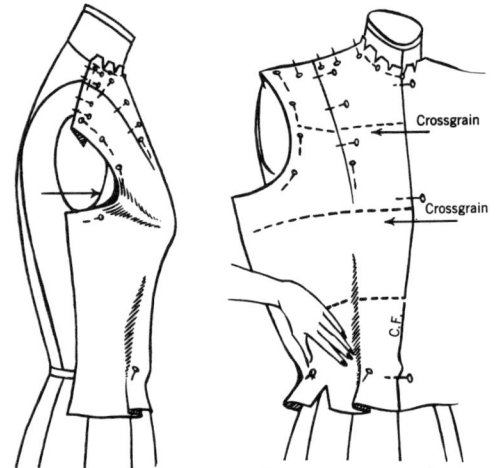

Fig. 21. The armscye may gap if the grain is raised too high at the underarm.
Fig. 22. The fault shown in Fig. 21 may be corrected by lowering the grain and pushing the excess into the waistline dart.

2. Clip the extension below the waistline to make the waistline fit closely.

3. Smooth any excess ease along the waistline toward the tentatively pinned dart.

4. Determine the dart direction and placement. It should slant toward the center as it approaches the waistline and should curve ever so little in order to enter the waistline at a right angle (see Figure 23).

Form the waistline dart carefully, since you will use it later as basic paneling for blocking original designs. It will also determine the spacing of the skirt panel, since the two must coincide. If the dart line is allowed to run parallel to the center front from the bust to the waistline, it thickens the waist and makes the figure appear stocky. If the figure is slender, the dart usually starts at a point about 2¾ inches from the center front and slants away from the center front about ½ inch at its top end. If the figure is very heavy, the panel may be as wide as 3½ inches at the waistline.

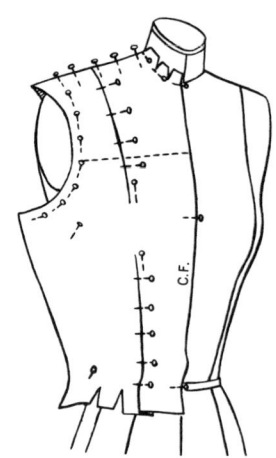

Fig. 23. Waistline dart accurately pinned.

5. Push the excess fabric under the dart line toward the front and pin it perpendicular to the edge.

Placing the Underarm Seam (see Figure 24)

1. The line of the underarm seam should fall at the center of the figure from the underarm to the waist. Place it so that it is inconspicuous from either the back or the front view. On the average figure, it slants slightly forward, because the center of the body at the armpit is usually slightly farther back than it is at the waistline. This is even true of a standard dress form underarm line. If your posture is poor and you carry your shoulders either very far back or very far forward, make any necessary adjustment in the total underarm line along the underarm seam line of the blouse. The arm will hang over this section and will conceal effectively any correction due to faulty posture.

22

BASIC BLOUSES

Before draping, mark the best location on the form with two pins, one at the top under the arm and the other at the center position on the waistline.

2. Stand directly at the side of the form and fold the fabric along the line thus established. Turn the excess forward over the right side. Leave no horizontal ease at the waistline but slant the line outward to allow ¾ to 1 inch of ease over the bust at the top of the underarm seam. This excess forms a small vertical fold in front of the armscye when the arm is down and supplies ease for chest expansion and for body action.

3. Crease the fabric without stretching it and pin it perpendicular to the edge, but not into the dress form.

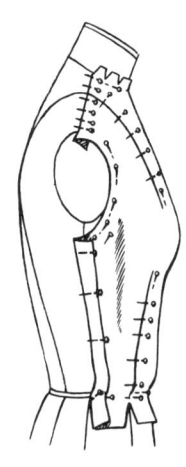

Fig. 24. Underarm seam.

4. Cut, allowing a 1½ to 2 inch seam. The wide seam allowance provides for correcting errors and for let-out when fitting.

5. Turn the seam allowance under to the wrong side on the creased line and re-pin it.

6. Before finally pinning the fabric to the waistline of the form, push the material upward above the waistline from the dart to the side seam. The slight blousing lengthens the underarm seam enough to permit raising the arm easily (see Figure 24).

Note. To acquire speed and deftness in draping technique, do not attach the fabric to the form when pinning darts, the armscye line, or the underarm seam line except at the lower end.

Leave the front of the blouse on the form and proceed with the back.

WAIST BACK

Estimating the Fabric (see Figure 25)

Estimate the amount of cloth needed for the back of the waist as you did for the front. If you expect to fit the blouse, however, cut the back in two separate pieces, allowing for a ½ inch lap at the center.

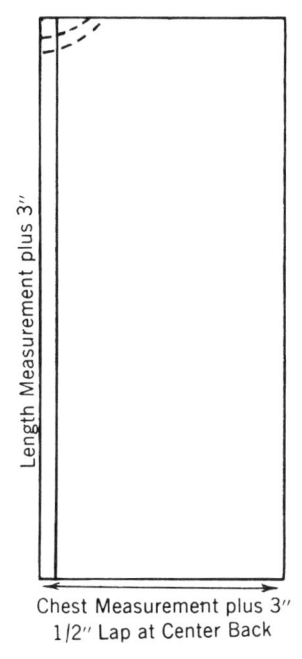

Fig. 25. Fabric estimate for half of the blouse back.

Shaping the Neckline (see Figure 26)

For a size 16, the back neckline without a seam allowance is ½ inch deep at the center and 2½ inches wide at the shoulder seam.

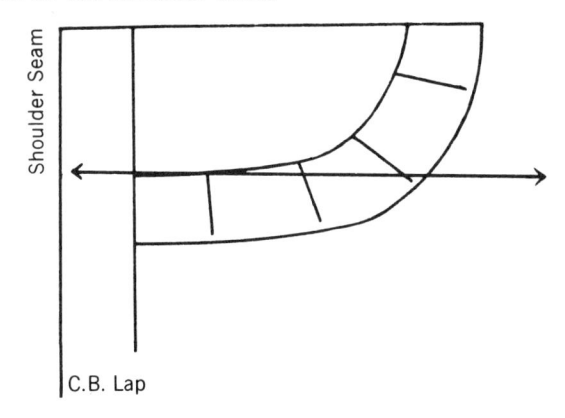

Fig. 26. Back neckline shape.

23

DRESS DESIGN

1. Draw the neck curve. This should be 1½ inches deep at the center back and 3 inches wide at the shoulder. These measurements include 1 inch of depth for the shoulder seam and ½ inch of width for a lap allowance at the center back.

2. Draw the cutting line ½ inch above the actual neckline marked in step 1. The cut curve will be 1 inch deep at the center back and 2½ inches across at the shoulders. There is now a ½ inch seam allowance around the neck, a 1 inch shoulder seam, and a ½ inch center back lap.

Placing the Fabric on the Form (see Figure 27)

1. Fold under and crease the ½ inch center back lap allowance.

2. Pin the fabric along the center back at: (a) the base of the neck, (b) the shoulder blades, and (c) the waistline. The fabric should be eased above the pin at the waistline for blousing.

3. Clip the fabric to the basic neckline. Smooth it slightly away from the center back and up toward the shoulder seam, forcing the fabric to cling closely to the side of the neck. As you do so, keep the filling threads perpendicular to the center back, and pin the cloth to the form as you proceed.

4. Pin the fabric to the form at the underarm seam just below the armscye to support the crossgrain level.

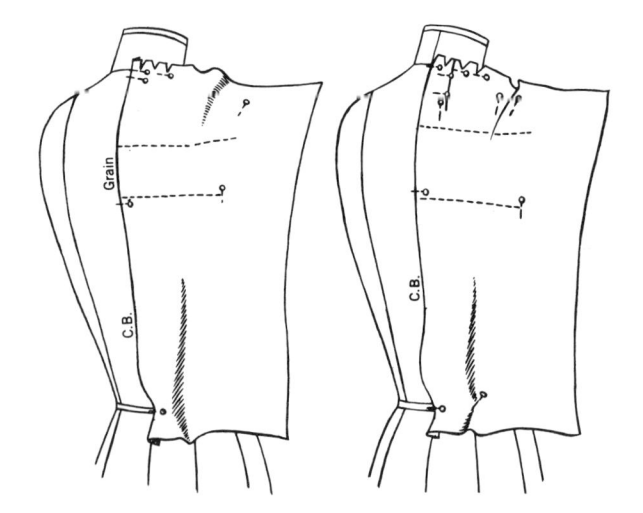

Fig. 27. Fabric placement (crossgrain rises slightly at armscye).
Fig. 28. Neck dart plus ¼"–⅜" of shoulder ease.

Placing the Shoulder Dart

1. *Location.* Just as the purpose of the darts in the front of the blouse is to take care of the contour of the bust, the purpose of those at the back is to shape the fabric over the curve of the shoulder blades and at the top of the shoulder. There are three conventional ways of doing this:

(a) By allowing ¼ to ⅜ inch ease along the back shoulder seam (see Figure 27).

(b) By placing a small dart at the back of the neckline (see Figure 28).

(c) By placing a small dart at the center of the shoulder seam (see Figure 29).

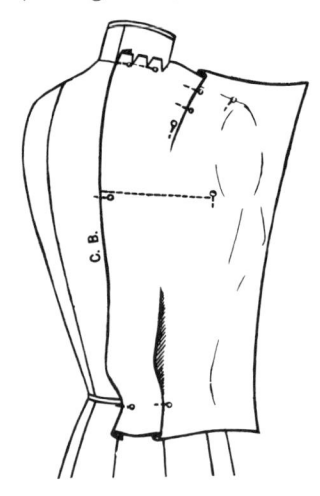

Fig. 29. Shoulder dart pinned and waistline dart tentatively placed.

The ease of ¼ to ⅜ inch along the back shoulder seam is always used. If the shoulders are somewhat round, either method (*b*) or (*c*) is usually used in addition for extra shaping. A figure with flat, erect shoulders, however, may need only the ease along the back shoulder of the pattern.

2. *Shoulder ease.* The amount of shoulder ease possible depends on the flexibility and shrinking quality of the fabric. To keep the filling threads level, lift and swing the fabric from the end of the shoulder up and in toward the center. This forms excess along the shoulder which should be pinned into a temporary dart, later to be eased across the shoulder when the back is joined to the front. By keeping the filling threads horizontal around the underarm, you avoid

24

BASIC BLOUSES

the gapping which sometimes occurs at the lower curve of the back armscye.

3. If you also use method (b) place a dart at the back of the neckline (see Figure 28), and place it when pinning the neckline to the form. The woman having a more mature figure with a prominent bone at the top of the spine, or the girl who carries her head forward, will find this the better dart position. Place it from 1½ to 2 inches from the center back of the neckline. It should not be longer than 2½ to 3 inches and should be almost parallel to the center back, slanting outward not more than ¼ inch at its lower end. Fold the dart under toward the center back and pin it perpendicular to the edge.

4. If in addition to shoulder ease you use method (c) instead of (b), that is, a dart at the shoulder seam (see Figure 29), this may be placed in line with the front dart, since both should start at about the middle of the shoulder (see Figure 30). The dart line should appear to be almost parallel to the center back, but by actual measurement it should slope toward the center back slightly at its lower end. Keep the filling threads horizontal at the lower armscye and swing the excess above this up and inward to form the dart at the shoulder line. Fold the fabric under toward the center back and pin it perpendicular to the edge.

Note. Before establishing the shoulder seam line, check the ease over the shoulder blades. If the fabric clings to the form too closely, lower the filling threads a little from the outer end of the shoulder seam line.

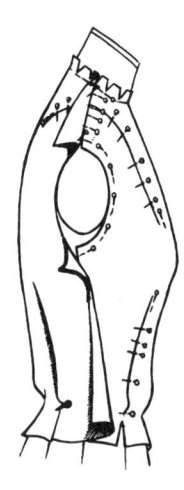

Fig. 30. Shoulder seam turned back ready to be cut.

5. Place the waistline dart tentatively 2½ to 3 inches from the center back at the waistline (see Figure 29). This is the main dart in the back of the blouse. Push the excess material under the dart line and point it toward the center of the shoulder or toward the shoulder dart if there is one. If the waistline dart tends to point too far outward toward the tip of the shoulder, this indicates that the crosswise grain has been raised too high at the outer tip of the shoulder. To correct this, lower the grain at the end of the shoulder until the waistline dart points toward the center of the shoulder, or until it is about ½ inch farther from the center back line at the point than at the lower end.

Placing the Shoulder Seam Line (see Figure 30)

1. Smooth the fabric along the neckline and shoulder, then fold the excess back over the right side, with the edge of the fold flush against the edge of the front shoulder seam.

2. Crease and cut, allowing a 1 inch seam.

3. Unpin and turn the back seam allowance forward, lapping the front edge of the shoulder seam over it.

4. Keep the fabric taut along the front shoulder line so that the blouse when tried on will bridge over the hollow in front of the shoulder seam.

5. Stand directly at the side of the form while pinning this seam. Pin first the neck end, then the outer point. Then, leaving the ease along the back shoulder seam pinned in, finish pinning the shoulder seam, placing the pins perpendicular to the edge.

Note. The shoulder seam should appear to be a true straight line. Overhandling of the bias while pinning may make it curve. This effect should be avoided.

Forming the Armscye Curve (see Figure 31)

Two points of the back armscye curve have already been determined by the blouse front — the shoulder point and the armscye depth. Only one point is unknown, the point of the curve where the back is narrowest.

1. Start the line at the shoulder tip and form a smooth continuation of the front armscye curve. Placing the pins head to point, curve the line slightly

DRESS DESIGN

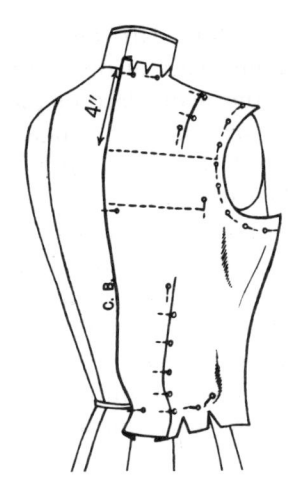

Fig. 31. Armscye curve — upper dotted line indicates the narrowest point of the curve, 4 inches below center back of neck.

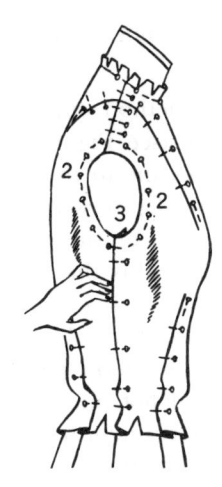

Fig. 32. Finished blouse — hand pressed against form to test looseness around bust. Vertical folds form on each side of underarm.

inward toward the center back line as it goes down toward the shoulder blades.

2. Find the narrowest point of the back by measuring down on the center back line 4 inches (or one-fourth the length of the blouse at the center back) and square out at this level across to the armscye. Continue the curve from this point outward to the underarm, where it meets the lower end of the front armscye curve.

Notice the appearance of the armscye oval from the side view shown in Figure 32. To allow the arm to swing forward, the curve established between points (2) and (3) is somewhat higher than the curve on the front armscye between the same two points.

3. Cut, allowing a 1/2 to 5/8 inch seam on the lower half of the armscye and increase the allowance to 3/4 inch for the upper half.

Placing the Waistline Dart (see Figure 31)

1. Smooth the fabric downward from the armscye area toward the side seam and tentatively pin it at the waistline (see Figure 29). Take up any excess along the waistline between the center back and the side seam by increasing the size of the waistline dart.

2. Pin the waistline dart, placing it accurately to form good panel spacing. It should taper in toward the center back at the waistline and should slant outward about 1/2 inch at the top end. It should be stopped before it reaches the shoulder blades or the blouse will fit too closely at the point of the dart.

3. Check to see that the armscye clings closely to the form. Any gapping along the side of the armscye indicates that a larger dart is needed either at the waistline or at the shoulder.

4. Clip the extension below the waistline in order to fit the waistline closely.

Placing the Underarm Seam (see Figure 32)

1. Fold the excess fabric on the blouse back over toward the right side. Leave no ease at the waistline but slant the line out at the top to allow 3/4 to 1 inch of ease. This makes a slight vertical fold behind the armscye when the arm is down.

2. Crease the fabric lightly and pin it perpendicular to the edge, but do not catch the pins into the form.

3. Cut, allowing a 1 1/2 to 2 inch seam.

4. Before finally anchoring the fabric to the waistline at the side seam, push the material upward above the waistline to blouse it slightly.

5. Remove the pins, lap the front over the back, and re-pin the seam perpendicular to the edge.

Note. To avoid pinning into the form, slip your hand inside the blouse when pinning the underarm seam.

BASIC BLOUSES

THE BLOUSE ON THE FORM

The two basic sections of the blouse, the front and the back, are now essentially complete, but certain adjustments must still be made before the blouse is removed from the form and a master pattern is made from it.

Ease Around the Bust (see Figure 32)

Press your fingertips against the draped blouse on the underarm seam to determine whether or not there is enough ease around the blouse at the bust level. A beginner tends to fit too closely. When you press your fingers against the form, two vertical folds should form, one in front and one in back, in line with the narrowest point of the armscye. Lack of ease around the bust makes the fabric draw and form diagonal folds from the bust to the underarm.

Placing the Waistline (see Figure 32)

1. Place a line of pins along the waistline following the line marked on the form cover. Check to see that there is adequate length for blousing above the waistline.

2. Trim the seam allowance below the waistline to 2 inches. (See The Dress Form Cover, Chapter 1, page 7, for the standard waistline placement.)

Forming the Neckline Curve (see Figure 32)

Place a smooth continuous line of pins along the neckline following the line established on the dress form cover. (See The Dress Form Cover, Chapter 1, page 6, for the basic neckline placement.)

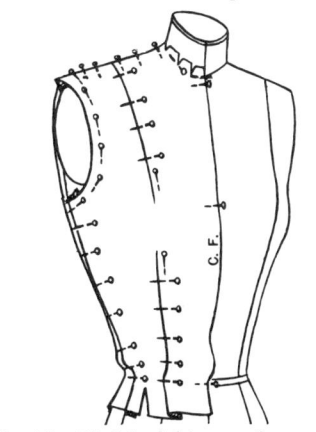

Fig. 33. Finished blouse, front view.

The Final Checking

Before removing the blouse from the form, study Figures 32 and 33. Then stand away from the form and view your draping to check the following points:

1. The general effect of the entire blouse from all angles.

2. The direction of all darts. These should slant in toward the center from the shoulder to the waistline.

3. The straightness of the lines of shoulder and underarm seams.

4. Ease through the bust. (This should be about 1½ inches from the center front to the center back.)

5. Ease in length above the waistline to allow for blousing and reaching.

6. The shape of the armscye oval from the side view.

7. Finally, you should compare your blouse with the illustrations.

MAKING A MASTER PATTERN FROM THE DRAPED BLOUSE

The next steps in the procedure are to remove the blouse from the form to true it, and to transfer it to the opposite half.

Removing the Blouse from the Form (see Figure 34)

1. Take out the pins at the center front and center back, and wherever they have caught into the form. Leave the shoulder and underarm seams, darts, neckline, armscye, and waistline pinned.

2. Mark all important lines. Use a soft pencil when working with practice material and colored thread lines or dressmaker's chalk when using dress fabric. Before trueing the pattern, mark with a broken line and not too heavily the following lines:

(a) Both edges of all seams, with crossmarks to match corresponding edges. Crossmarks, sometimes also called balance points, are equivalent to notches on commercial patterns. There should be a crossmarking at either end of ease and at either side of a dart.

27

DRESS DESIGN

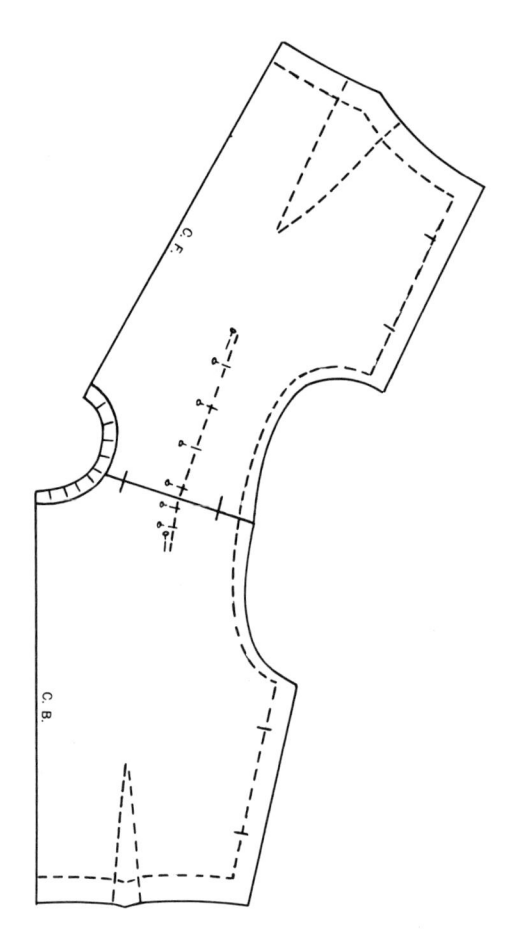

Fig. 34. Blouse pattern after removal from the form — seams marked and crossmarked.

(b) Both edges of darts.

(c) The arm curve, neck curve, and waistline.

Trueing the Pattern (see Figure 35)

Even though patterns are carefully draped, all lines that should be straight must be ruled with a ruler, and all curved lines must be either drawn with the aid of a curve or smoothed up freehand.

1. Remove all pins from the pencil-marked pattern.

2. Smooth the pattern out flat on the table.

3. Pressing a ruler down firmly against the cloth on the table, rule each of the following lines to straighten them:

(a) The underarm seam.

(b) The outer section of the shoulder seam, from the dart to the shoulder tip. The inner section of the shoulder seam, when heavy padding is used, is a slight inward curve dipping about $\frac{1}{4}$ inch near the base of the neck. Smooth the curve in this section freehand.

(c) Dart edges: Shoulder dart — both edges.
Waistline dart — both edges.

4. When ruling darts and seam lines, check to be sure that there are right angles at the intersections of the following lines:

(a) Neckline and shoulder seam.

(b) Shoulder dart and shoulder seam.

(c) Shoulder seam and armscye. (If the shoulder seam slants back more than the normal amount, the angle of the intersection will be slightly less than 90 degrees on the front and slightly more on the back.)

(d) Armscye and underarm seam.

(e) Underarm and waistline.

(f) Waistline and each edge of the waistline dart.

(g) Waistline and center front.

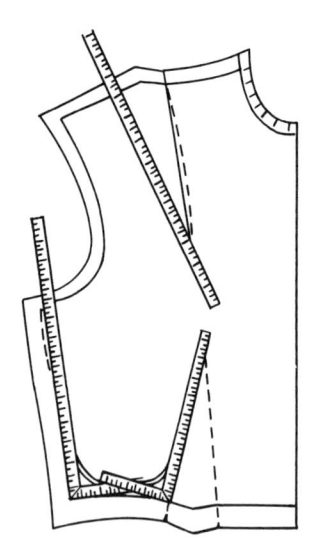

Fig. 35. Method of trueing pattern.

5. True up the following curves either freehand or with a curved ruler:

(a) The neckline. This should enter the shoulder seam and the center front at a right angle. The curve should be close to the neck at the side.

28

BASIC BLOUSES

(b) The armscye. In the front, this has its narrowest point 3 inches down below the base of the neck measured on the center front. In the back, the narrowest point is 4 inches below the neckline measured on the center back. The line curves toward the center front or back from the shoulder tip to the level of the chest, and curves away from the center from the chest to the underarm.

(c) The waistline of the pattern is a smooth curve between the right angles at the intersection of seams and darts.

6. Mark lines to indicate the seam allowance on all pattern edges except the center front and center back, as follows:

(a) Neck curve — ½ inch, clipped.

(b) Shoulder — 1 inch, clipped near the neck end.

(c) Armscye — ¾ inch top half; ½ inch lower half.

(d) Underarm — 2 inches.

(e) Waistline — 2 inches, clipped.

Transferring the Pattern to the Opposite Half

1. Smooth the pattern out with a warm dry iron. Press carefully in the direction of the grain to avoid stretching.

2. Fold the pattern along the center front line and smooth the fabric flat on a table to be sure that the filling threads run perpendicular to the lengthwise threads. Pin the two layers together.

3. Transfer all markings to the opposite half of the pattern with a tracing wheel used on either chalk board or colored carbon paper. Trace against a ruler wherever the lines should be straight. Press down hard on the ruler to keep the cloth from slipping.

4. Open up the muslin pattern and trace all the lines through to the right side in order to mark the right as well as the wrong side. This is for convenience when fitting and is done only on muslin proof — a muslin pattern that is to be basted and tried on to show that it fits.

Note. This procedure of trueing should be followed with all master patterns. Laying the pattern flat on the table and trueing it teaches you to observe pattern shapes in detail. The procedure for preparing a master pattern for a fitting can be found in Chapter 5.

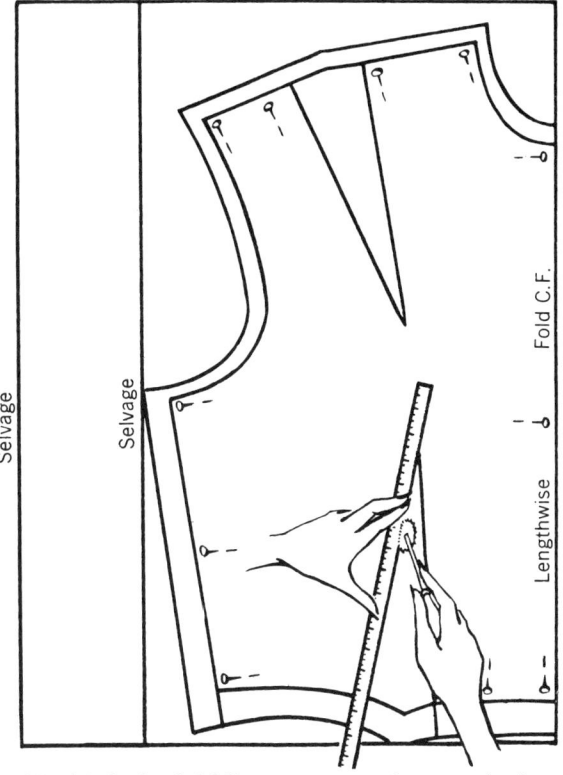

Fig. 36. Method of folding on center front and of transferring markings to opposite half of pattern by a tracing wheel used on carbon paper.

Problem 2

DRAPING THE BLOUSE WITH A HORIZONTAL UNDERARM DART

The procedure for draping a blouse with a horizontal underarm dart is in many respects a repetition of Problem 1. It is therefore advisable to review thoroughly the directions for Problem 1 before starting Problem 2.

An underarm dart may be substituted for a shoulder dart, but is most suitable for the loosely fitting blouse shown in Figure 41 or for a supplementary fitting dart, because if as much excess is fitted out at the underarm as at the shoulder, the underarm dart runs all the way to the point of the bust (see Figure 37). Figure 38 shows graphically why this is true. The distance from the underarm to the point of the bust is much shorter than from the shoulder seam to the point of the bust. The dart must therefore be smaller and shorter to taper out well. The longer dart is, of course, possible

DRESS DESIGN

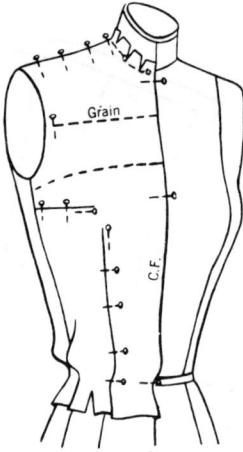

Fig. 37. Underarm dart allowed to run to point of bust, possible only for a master block pattern.

in a master blouse pattern, but is most unbecoming in a blouse that is to be worn. Only when it is used for a loosely fitted blouse is it possible to make the dart enough smaller and shorter so that it will disappear at the front of the armscye line and be concealed by the arm. The remainder of the excess can be put into a waistline dart or can be worked into ease along the waistline. The underarm dart can be successfully used as a concealed fitting dart but never as an ornamental one. Figure 41 shows the finished blouse with the underarm dart shortened and concealed by the sleeve.

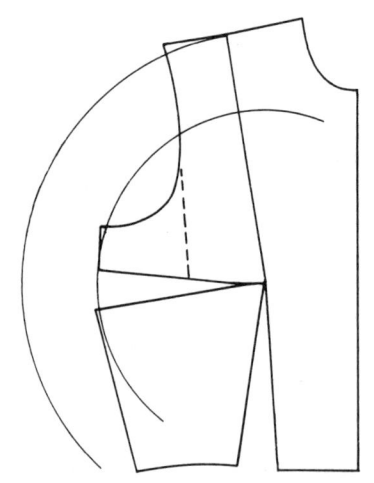

Fig. 38. Compass lines show comparative distances of shoulder and underarm darts from bust point. Underarm dart, if large, cannot be shortened without being divided into two or more smaller darts.

WAIST FRONT

Forming the Neckline Curve

Follow the directions given in Problem 1 for draping the blouse with shoulder and waistline darts.

Placing the Fabric on the Form

1. Pin as in Problem 1 — at base of neck, chest, and waistline.

2. Pin at the chest near the armscye. The filling threads should be level across the chest.

3. Pin around the neck as in Problem 1.

Placing the Shoulder Seam Line

1. Stand directly at the side of the dress form and fold the excess fabric above the shoulder forward to form the shoulder seam line.

2. Pin and crease lightly to avoid stretching the bias fold.

3. Cut, leaving a 1 inch seam allowance, and fold this under.

4. Re-pin, fastening the fabric securely to the form at each end of the shoulder seam.

Forming the Armscye Curve

Proceed as in Problem 1.

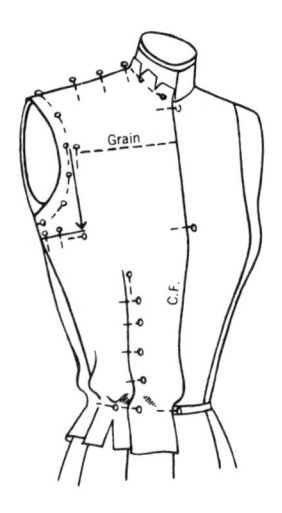

Fig. 39. Underarm dart shortened to disappear at front of armscye.

30

BASIC BLOUSES

Placing the Underarm Dart (see Figures 37 and 39)

All the excess is now at the waistline edge of the pattern. Problem 1 demonstrated that it is impossible to take up the entire basic dart in one place and still taper it out smoothly. It is even more obvious that an underarm dart cannot take up all the excess and that it must be divided between the underarm and a supplementary dart or gathers along the waistline (see Figures 37 and 39).

Notice that the filling threads drop downward toward the underarm seam below the pin at the chest on the armscye and above the underarm dart (Figure 37).

1. Fold in a dart about 1 inch below the armscye and direct it toward the point of the bust.

2. Turn the fold upward and pin it tentatively to see whether or not it is small enough to taper to a point in line with the front of the armscye (see Figure 39).

3. Take up the remaining excess in a waistline dart as in Problem 1. This will be larger than the waistline dart in Problem 1 unless part of the fullness is distributed along the waistline into gathers.

4. Pin the underarm dart perpendicular to the edge. If it is impossible to taper it out in line with the armscye front, divide it into two or three smaller darts that will taper out more smoothly (see Figure 40).

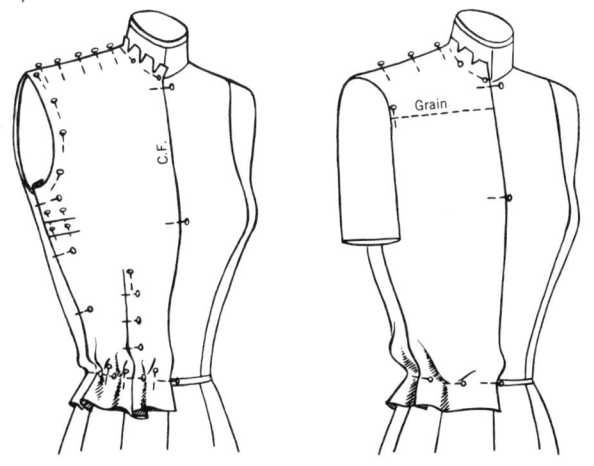

Fig. 40. Underarm darts divided and shortened, part of excess put into waistline gathers.
Fig. 41. Underarm dart concealed by sleeve. Waistline excess put into blousing.

Placing the Waistline Dart

1. Decide on the location as in Problem 1.

2. Pin accurately, but save some of the excess for gathers along the waistline. Distribute the gathers evenly by picking up tiny pin tucks (see Figure 40).

Placing the Underarm Seam

1. Smooth the fabric downward and forward under the arm and pin it at the side on the waistline.

2. Turn the fabric forward over the right side and proceed as in Problem 1.

WAIST BACK

With this waist front use the back pattern draped in Problem 1, but since the front has ease for blousing along the waistline, distribute part of the back waistline dart into gathers along the waistline to unify the back and front designs. Figure 41 shows all of the excess on the waistline put into gathers.

For the method of dividing one dart into two or more parallel darts, see Figures 42 and 43.

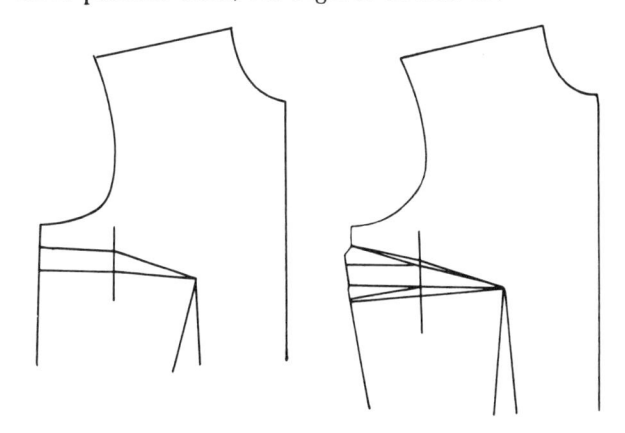

Fig. 42. Procedure for dividing a dart into two or more parallel darts: Step 1.
Fig. 43. Procedure for dividing a dart into two or more parallel darts: Step 2.

Problem 3

DRAPING A FRENCH DART BODICE

The French dart (see Figure 44) is formed by the meeting of the vertical shoulder and waistline darts. The pattern is therefore in two parts, a center panel and a side section. It is used for tight evening bodices

DRESS DESIGN

Fig. 44. Variation of French dart bodice.

and is also preferred by some designers as a foundation pattern. When fitted with ease, it also makes a basic pattern for tailored garments and is a fertile source of original design development (see Chapter 7, Suggestion 7).

BLOUSE FRONT CENTER PANEL (ONE-HALF PATTERN)

Proceed as in Problem 1.

Shaping the Neckline

Hollow out as for the basic waist in Problem 1.

Placing the Fabric on the Form

1. Place the selvage at the center front with the base of the neck in the fabric (marked ½ inch below the cut neck line) at the base of the neck as marked on the form.

2. Pin the fabric at: (a) the neckline, (b) the chest, and (c) the waistline, easing it a little above the last pin.

3. Place a fourth pin at the chest to anchor the fabric to the form and to support the filling threads so that they are level.

4. Clip the seam above the basic neckline. Smooth the fabric around the neck exactly as in Problem 1.

5. In order to support the filling threads, pin the fabric to the form at the shoulder near the neckline.

Forming the French Dart Line (Figure 45)

Place the French dart line where it is most becoming to the individual figure. The standard position is from the center of the shoulder across the point of the bust to the waistline. The line should slant in toward the center all the way from the shoulder to the waist. At the waistline end, it may be somewhat closer to the center front than is the waistline dart of the basic blouse.

Note. If the line does not slant in enough, it seems rather to tilt out, and thus to thicken the waistline. If the bust is large, the French dart line will be more slenderizing if it begins out beyond the center of the shoulder seam in order to broaden the shoulders and reduce the apparent bust size. Figure 46 shows poor panel spacing. The line curves in toward the neck at the top and is too far from the center at the bust.

1. Fold under a half-inch tuck to establish a satisfactory French dart line (see Figure 45).

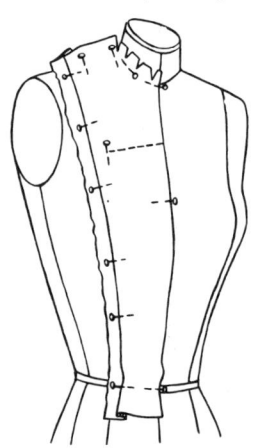

Fig. 45. Formation of French dart line by folding a tuck.

2. Place pins through the two upper layers of the muslin only and at right angles to the edge of the tuck.

3. Turn the edge of the tuck back toward the center front in order to cut off the seam allowance beyond the folded edge. Allow ⅝ to ¾ inch for the seam.

4. Clip the seam over the bust. The pins hold the tuck in position and at the same time turn under the seam allowance to the wrong side.

Note. To enter the shoulder at a right angle, the top of the French dart line curves slightly outward. If it did not, it would appear to curl in toward the

32

BASIC BLOUSES

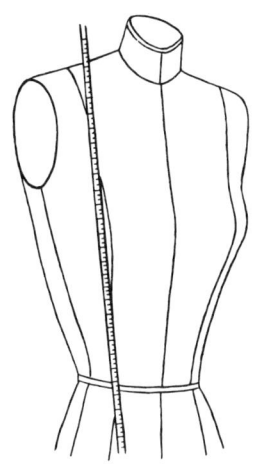

Fig. 46. Tapeline showing poor line formation.

neck as it goes over the shoulder, as in **Figure 46**. The normal French dart line also enters the waistline at a right angle and curves slightly away from center front in order to do so.

SIDE FRONT SECTION

Placing the Fabric on the Form (see Figure 47)

1. Place the fabric on the form with the lengthwise grain running up through the center of the side front section so that it is perpendicular to the waistline as far up as the bust. Pencil the grain line on practice material. Hold the fabric in this position with the left hand and smooth it forward with the right hand to make sure that you have allowed enough material to meet the front panel and to provide a seam allowance as well. There also should be at least a 1 inch seam allowance above the shoulder.

2. Pin the vertical center grain line to the form at the bust level and again at the waistline as shown in Figure 47.

Placing the French Dart Line (see Figure 47)

1. Smooth the fabric forward and upward against the edge of the center front section.

2. Smooth the lengthwise grain above the bust line toward the side front seam enough to force the material to cling around the armscye. The more you direct the lengthwise grain above the bustline inward toward the center front panel, the more ease there will be between bust and shoulder. If you overdo this, however, you will tighten the blouse too much in front of the armscye.

3. Pin the fabric to the form near the shoulder.

4. Fold the fabric back on itself along the French dart line with the edge of the side section just touching the edge of the center front panel. Pin it perpendicular to the edge.

5. Cut, leaving a 1 inch seam to allow for any adjustment which may be necessary when you pin the center front panel to the side section.

Note. There should be more length on the side front section than on the center panel over the bust curve. The narrower the center front panel is, the more vertical ease there should be over the bust on the side front section. A small amount of horizontal ease should also be allowed over the bust curve.

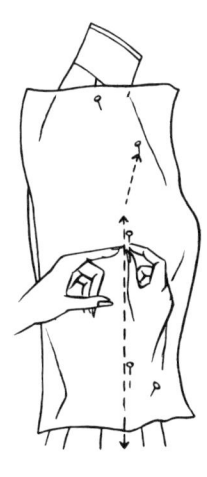

Fig. 47. Side front section — grain perpendicular to waistline up to armscye and then forced forward at chest.

6. Crease the turned line lightly with the thumbnail, unpin, and slip the seam allowance on the side section forward under the center front panel. Then re-pin to join the two sections. Starting at the top, pin down toward the bust; then from the waistline, pin up to the bust. This forces the ease over the bust curve (see Figure 48).

7. Clip the excess below the waistline to fit the bodice very closely around the waist.

33

DRESS DESIGN

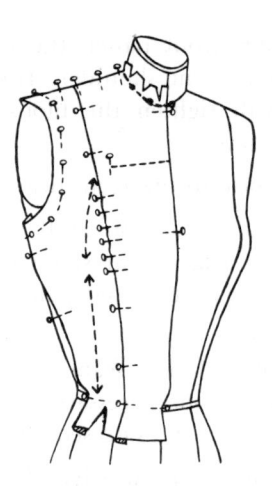

Fig. 48. Joining of center and side front: (1) Dotted lines show grain position; (2) Pins close together show position of ease.

Placing the Shoulder Seam

1. Follow the directions for establishing the shoulder seam in Problem 1.

2. Check the armscye to see that the fabric clings closely enough to the form and yet does not draw too tightly. If there is still looseness around the armscye, push it forward under the side front line.

Forming the Armscye Curve (see Figure 48)

Follow the directions given in Problem 1. The French bodice should cling to the figure somewhat more closely than the basic blouse in Problem 1.

Placing the Underarm Seam Line

Follow the directions given in Problem 1, except that this bodice should fit somewhat more closely around the bust.

Placing the Waistline

1. Clip the fabric below the waistline at the center of the side front section so that it fits tightly along the waistline. A French dart bodice should have no ease whatever along the waistline. Between this clipped point and the underarm seam, ease the fabric upward above the waistline to allow extra length below the armscye for raising the arm (see Figure 48).

2. Mark the fabric with a line of pins following the waistline indicated on the form.

CENTER BACK PANEL

The procedure for draping the back of the French dart bodice is very similar to that for the front. The following directions are therefore condensed to avoid repetition.

Estimating the Fabric. See the estimate for Problem 1.

Shaping the Neckline. See the back of the basic blouse.

Placing the Fabric on the Form. See the center front panel.

Forming the French Dart Line

1. The French dart line in the back of the blouse is a continuation of the side front line. It should enter the shoulder perpendicular to it, should curve slightly inward over the shoulder blades, and should enter the waistline at a right angle. Figure 49 shows a good position for the back French dart line.

2. Study the slope of the line to find the most becoming position over the shoulder blades. If you exaggerate the inward curve, you will emphasize round shoulders, as Figure 50 shows. Keep the shoulder area broad, but slope the panel in at the waistline to slenderize it (see Figure 49).

3. Follow the directions for pinning and cutting the front French dart line.

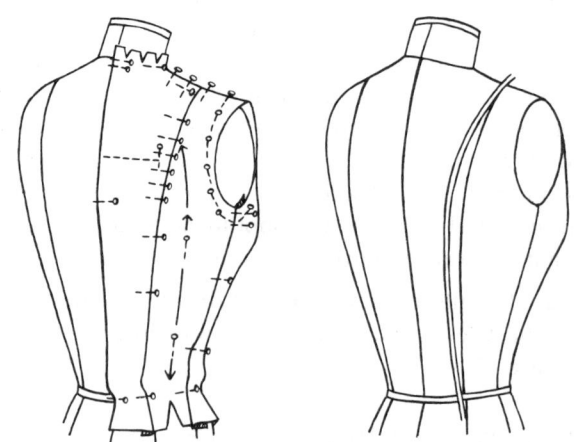

Fig. 49. Joining of center and side back: (1) Well placed French dart line at back (compare with Fig. 50); (2) Arrows show grain position; (3) Pins close together show position of ease.

Fig. 50. Poor French dart line. An exaggerated curve emphasizes round shoulders and narrows the back across the shoulder blades.

34

BASIC BLOUSES

SIDE BACK SECTION

Placing the Fabric on the Form. See direction for the side front.

Forming the French Dart Seam Line (see Figure 49)

1. Smooth the fabric toward the center back and up against the edge of the center back panel.

2. Force the lengthwise grain above the shoulder blades inward enough to keep the fabric smooth around the armscye. Round shoulders need this more than flat ones, but if the forcing is overdone, the roundness will be exaggerated. Rather than overfit round shoulders, use shoulder pads to take up the excess.

3. Pin the side back section to the form near the shoulder.

4. Fold the fabric back on itself along the French dart seam line and follow the directions for pinning, creasing, cutting, and repinning the front French dart line and for clipping the extension below the waistline.

Placing the Shoulder Seam Line

Follow the directions for establishing the shoulder seam given in Problem 1.

Forming the Armscye Curve

Follow the directions for establishing the armscye given in Problem 1.

Placing the Underarm Seam Line

1. Follow the directions given in Problem 1.

2. Check the contour of the blouse around the bust, shoulder blade, and armscye while forming this line. Lap the side front over the back. Sometimes raising or lowering the crosswise grain of the front or back along the side seam line improves the lines of the blouse.

Placing the Waistline

Before marking the waistline, raise the side back slightly to allow enough length below the armscye so that the arm can be raised easily.

Observe the entire bodice to see that the garment fits closely at the neckline, the shoulder seam line, and the waistline. Although the French dart bodice fits more closely than either of the two blouses earlier discussed, there should still be 2 to 3 inches of ease around the entire bust for action and breathing and to avoid horizontal wrinkles around the bust when the blouse is worn. It is better to err on the side of too much rather than too little ease around the bust.

Crossmark the French dart lines in front and back to distribute the ease over the bust and shoulder blades.

Marking and Trueing the Pattern (see Figure 51)

1. Remove the pattern from the form.

2. Pencil all seam lines.

3. Crossmark (*a*) the shoulder seam, (*b*) the French dart line above and below the ease, (*c*) the underarm seam.

4. True the pattern, ruling all straight lines and smoothing all curves freehand.

Figure 51 shows the shape of the French dart bodice pattern when it is flat. Notice the ease over the bust in the side front section.

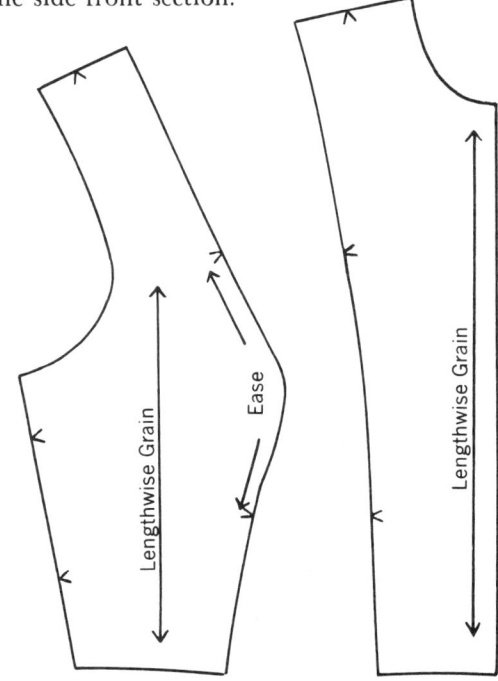

Fig. 51. French dart bodice pattern.

DRESS DESIGN

Note. It is better not to use the French dart style for a striped fabric, as the stripes will seem to curve around the bust. However, if there is no way to avoid using it, remedy the situation by bringing the stripes together in a V or chevron at the French dart line, or possibly by using the stripes horizontally in one section and vertically in the other.

Problem 4
DRAPING A HIP LENGTH FRENCH DART JACKET

This is a popular standard pattern for jackets and suits and offers many possibilities for variation in design (see Chapter 7).

CENTER PANEL — FRONT OR BACK

Estimating the Fabric Length

Measure the length of the blouse from the highest point of the shoulder over the bust in front and the shoulder blades in the back to the waist and add to this measurement the length of the jacket below the waist.

Draping from Shoulder to Waistline

Follow all the directions for draping the center panels of the waist length French dart bodice given in Problem 3, except those for establishing the waistline.

Draping from Waistline to Lower Edge (see Figure 52)

1. Cut off the center panel, working downward to a point 1 inch above the waistline. At this point clip diagonally through the seam allowance to within 1/8 inch of the intersection of the French dart line and the waistline. The reason for doing this is that diagonal clipping is not so likely to tear as one cut on the grain. It also lets the grain drop down for a flare in the peplum section.

2. Let the fabric drop from the clipped point and establish the French dart line from the waist to the hip. The line should slant outward slightly (away from the center front) from the waist to the hip (see Figure 52).

SIDE PANEL — FRONT OR BACK

Draping from Shoulder to Waistline

Follow all the directions for the waist length French dart blouse from shoulder to waistline except those for establishing the waistline.

Draping from Waistline to Lower Edge (see Figure 53)

1. Clip through the seam allowance on both the underarm and the French dart seams from a point 1 inch above the waistline downward diagonally to within 1/8 inch of the waistline.

2. Let the fabric drop from the clipped points for extra width below the waist to fit the hips smoothly or to produce a flare.

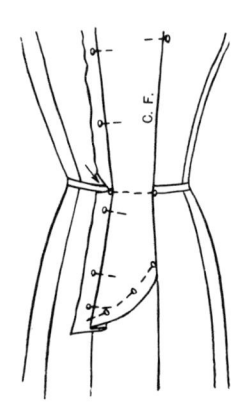

Fig. 52. Center front section. Seam clipped from 1 inch above waistline to the waistline.

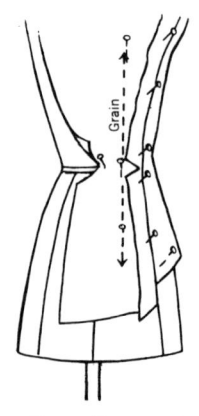

Fig. 53. Side front section. Seams at waistline clipped at both sides, front and side.

36

BASIC BLOUSES

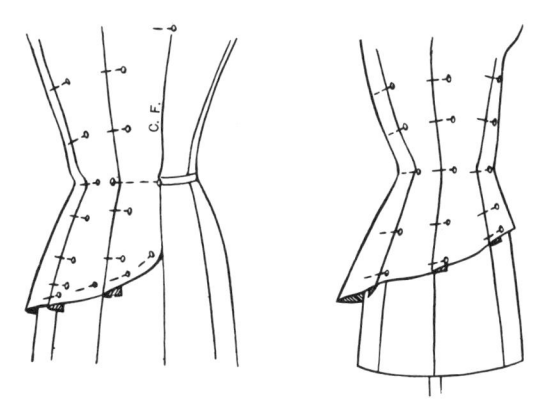

Fig. 54. Completed hip length bodice, front view.
Fig. 55. Completed hip length bodice, side view (flare introduced at the back).

Check to see that the waistline is on the crosswise grain and does not rise at either the underarm or the French dart seam lines, and that the lengthwise grain at the center of the section crosses the waistline at a right angle.

3. Pin the seams from waist to hip, lapping the center section over the side, and the side front over the side back on the underarm seam.

Figures 54 and 55 show the front and side views of the completed French dart hip length jacket.

Note. The line from the waistline to the hip is always an outward slanting line. It is possible either to fit the figure smoothly at the hipline or to introduce some flare on the peplum section by slanting the line out more than enough to fit the hips (see Figure 55). A seam at the center back of the French dart jacket adds still another line either for fitting more smoothly below the waist or for introducing a flare.

To acquire an experimental attitude and to develop a feeling for draping even while working with standard designs, try out the minor variations in design suggested above. However, always follow exactly the fundamental rules of *grain position*.

Problem 5

DRAPING BLOUSES WITH COWL NECKLINES — HIGH, MEDIUM, AND LOW VARIATIONS

The cowl is inherited from classic Greek drapery, but the term itself is derived from the drapery of a monk's hood. The cowl neckline is created by picking up two opposite corners of a piece of fabric and allowing the center to drop downward. Cowls exemplify draping in its most literal sense. Since the beauty of cowls depends on the texture of the material in which they are interpreted as well as the relationship between the fold-lines and the figure curves, the most graceful cowls are usually those which are draped on the form directly in the dress material.

A cowl neckline can absorb all, part, or none of the excess usually taken up in a dart, depending on the depth of the cowl. It absorbs the entire excess and therefore shapes the fabric to the figure only when it falls at least as low as the bustline.

Although most exactly balanced designs can be draped on one-half the form only, a cowl must be draped on both sides to balance the pull on the folds. After draping the cowl in this way, however, use one side only as a pattern so that the two sides will be exactly alike.

A High Neckline Cowl

This absorbs none of the excess and therefore requires the usual amount of darting.

1. Fold the fabric on a true bias and place the bias at the center front of the form (see Figure 56). Pencil this fold line on muslin or thread mark it on an actual garment.

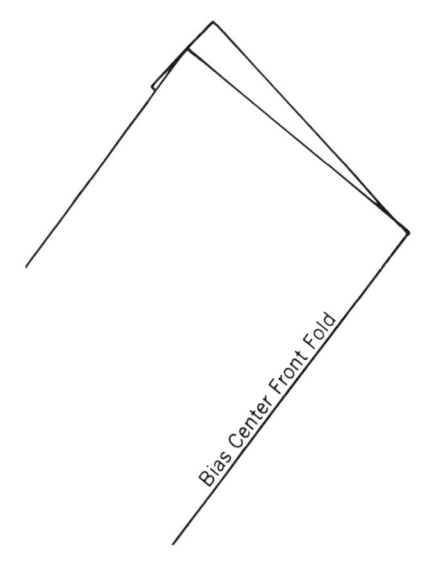

Fig. 56. Fabric folded for **cowl neckline**.

DRESS DESIGN

2. Turn under 1½ to 2 inches along the top for a hem. The hem will also be a true bias.

3. Measure from shoulder seam to shoulder seam horizontally across the front of the dress form neck above the basic neckline (see Figure 57).

4. Measure the fabric from the center front bias fold one-half the amount measured in step 3, and mark both right and left sides with pencil or pins. Pin these marked points to the form on each side of the neck at the shoulder seam line. The center front line of the fabric should coincide with the center front of the form.

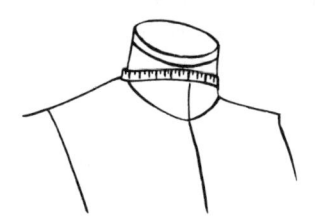

Fig. 57. Measurement for a high cowl neckline.

5. Pull the drapery down at the center front. Since the center front line of the fabric is bias, it is possible to adjust it into small folds instead of one large one (see Figure 58). Weights placed at the lower edge of the top fold help to retain the folds as draped.

Note. To spread the folds more horizontally, stretch the fabric along the shoulder seam from the neckline end toward the armscye in the following order: stretch, stab a pin through the shoulder line at a point 1 inch from the neck, and clip from the raw edge to the pin in order to give direction to the second fold (see Figure 59). Repeat for more folds if desired.

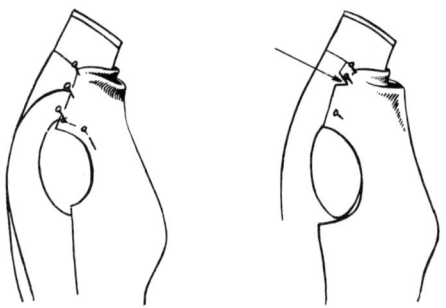

Fig. 58. High cowl. Folds fall from neck end of shoulder seam.
Fig. 59. High cowl. Folds distributed by clipping shoulder seam and stretching away from neck.

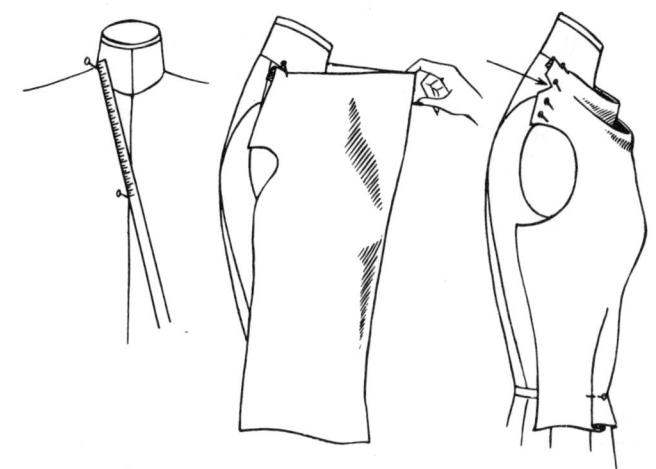

Fig. 60. Measurement for cowl neckline ending above the bust.
Fig. 61. Fabric pinned at sides of neck, true bias fold at center front.
Fig. 62. Shoulder clipped to distribute folds more horizontally.

A Cowl Ending Above the Bust Line

This absorbs some of the excess usually taken up into darts, the amount depending on the depth of the neckline. The center front line of the fabric stands away from the bust line of the form about 1 inch, though the amount increases with the depth of the neckline.

Follow all the steps for draping the high-neckline cowl except number 3, which gives the measurement. For this substitute the following direction: Measure on the dress form the distance from the shoulder seam at the neckline to the desired neckline depth at the center front (see Figure 60). Figures 61 and 62 show the procedure for pinning and clipping to establish the desired folds.

A Deep Cowl from the Neckline

This absorbs most of the necessary pattern shaping and therefore requires little darting.

1. Follow steps 1 and 2 given in the procedure for draping the high neckline cowl.

2. With the fabric 3 inches above the highest point of the shoulder seam, pin the center front line marked on the fabric to the center front of the form at: (*a*) the waistline, and (*b*) a point five inches above the waistline.

BASIC BLOUSES

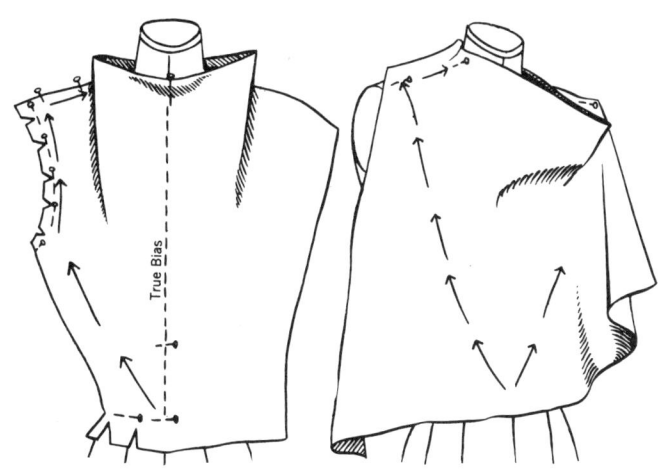

Fig. 63. Deep cowl, folds fall from neckline. Step 3 — Method of pinning to form. For steps 4 and 5, drape in the direction of the arrows.

Fig. 64. Step 6—Deep cowl draped from the neckline.

3. To fit the fabric to the form, begin at the center front of the waistline and smooth the fabric upward and outward to the armscye at the side seam, following the direction of the arrows in Figure 63. Do not tighten the fabric around the bust. Leave ease.

4. Smooth the fabric from the armscye up to the shoulder point, again following the direction of the arrows in Figure 63. Pin the cloth to the form at the end of the shoulder.

5. Smooth the fabric from the end of the shoulder seam inward toward the neckline and pin it to the form. You have now transferred the basic dart to the neckline (see Figure 64).

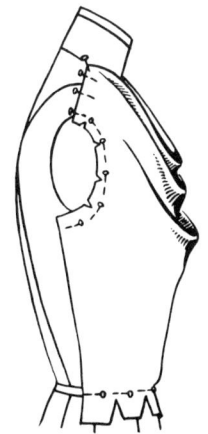

Fig. 65. Deep cowl draped from the shoulder. Step 7 — Folds fall from the intersection of neck and shoulder.

6. Pull the excess fabric in toward the center front and drop it into two or three folds falling vertically from the intersection of the neckline and the shoulder seam (see Figure 65).

Note. This neckline will probably be at least 5 inches below the base of the neck at the center front. For a higher neckline, follow the same procedure, but pivot the fabric less decidedly toward the center front. This leaves some ease below the bust line which must be taken up into a supplementary dart below the bust. Because the center front is on the bias, run the added dart from the lower end of the side seam up toward the bust. It will then more nearly follow the grain and will press better when stitched than if it were on the bias. Figure 66 shows the dart from the waistline.

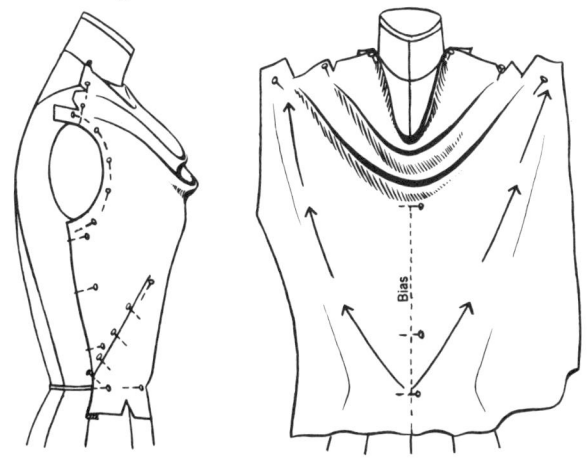

Fig. 66. Cowl draped from shoulder and with part of excess placed in a waistline dart.

Fig. 67. Deep cowl draped from the shoulder.

A Deep Cowl from the Shoulder (see Figure 67)

As in the cowl last discussed, this design transfers the entire dart into the center front at the neckline.

1. Follow steps 1 to 4 for a deep cowl from the neckline.

2. Smooth the fabric from the armscye up to the outer end of the shoulder seam. Pin at this point and clip from the raw edge to the pin as indicated in Figure 67.

3. Drop the grain from this pin in order to form a fold that runs toward the center front at the bust level. Adjust the fabric in the same way on the opposite shoulder.

DRESS DESIGN

4. Pin the fabric to the line of the shoulder seam at a point halfway between the neckline and the armscye, and clip from the raw edge to this pin.

5. Drop the grain toward the center front again from the center of the shoulder seam to make a second fold. Adjust the opposite side in the same way.

6. Pin to the shoulder line at the neck for the third and top fold, as shown in Figure 67. Figure 66 shows the completed effect from the side view when a small dart has been retained at the waistline.

Note. The amount which the grain is dropped toward the center front from the outer end of the shoulder and the halfway point on the shoulder determines both the depth of each fold and the depth of the neckline.

A Deep Cowl from the Armhole

Follow the same procedure, but start tilting the grain toward the center front from a point halfway up the armscye. This directs a fold from the armscye toward the center front.

Cowl Yokes (see Figure 68)

Cowl yokes are often set into blouses to get deep cowl folds and yet to retain a high neckline and avoid heavy folds over the bust line. They are also used when the bias would be unsatisfactory in the lower half of the bodice either because of a conspicuous fabric weave or because the bias draws too tightly around the bust if the fabric is very soft and clinging.

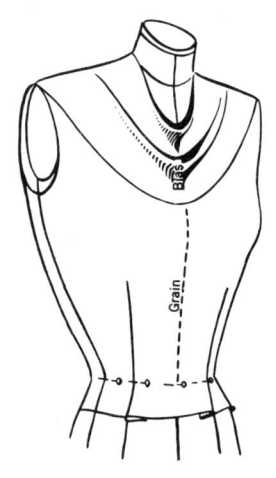

Fig. 68. Cowl yoke.

LAP DIRECTIONS FOR BUTTONS AND BUTTONHOLES AND BUTTONS AND LOOPS

Although the correct method for making buttons and buttonholes, and buttons and loops is not, strictly speaking, a draping problem, it seems desirable to give directions for these procedures at this point since so many of the blouses that you will make involve the techniques required.

Buttons and Buttonholes (see Figure 69)

1. Mark a vertical center front line on both the right and left halves of the pattern. Buttons are attached to the exact center line of the left half of the garment. Buttonholes are placed on the right half of the garment; they begin $\frac{1}{16}$ to $\frac{1}{8}$ inch to the left of the center line marking and extend back to the right side of the center. Since the button slides to the very end of the buttonhole, the latter should extend by only the thickness of the button shank beyond the center front line in order to keep the garment balanced on left and right sides of the center.

2. Decide on the width of the overlap, that is, the amount of fabric on the buttonhole side from the center line to the edge of the closing. Since one-half the width of the button will extend to the left of the center, the overlap should equal the radius of the button plus at least $\frac{1}{4}$ inch for a margin beyond the button edge. Thus, a 1 inch button requires at least a $\frac{3}{4}$ inch overlap. Rule a line to mark the edge of the overlap.

3. Decide on the width of the underlap, that is, the amount of fabric on the button side extending beyond the center line.

(a) If the fabric is transparent, extend the underlap the same amount beyond the center line as the overlap, so that there will be exact symmetry on both sides of the center front.

(b) If the fabric is opaque and the buttonholes are long, make the underlap wide enough so that it extends at least as far as the opening of the buttonhole.

Finish the edges of the overlap and underlap with fitted facings or with wide extensions cut in one with the fronts. If extensions are used, cut the pattern for them by folding under along the lap line and cutting the top edge of the under extension so that it follows the neckline shape (see Figure 69*a*).

BASIC BLOUSES

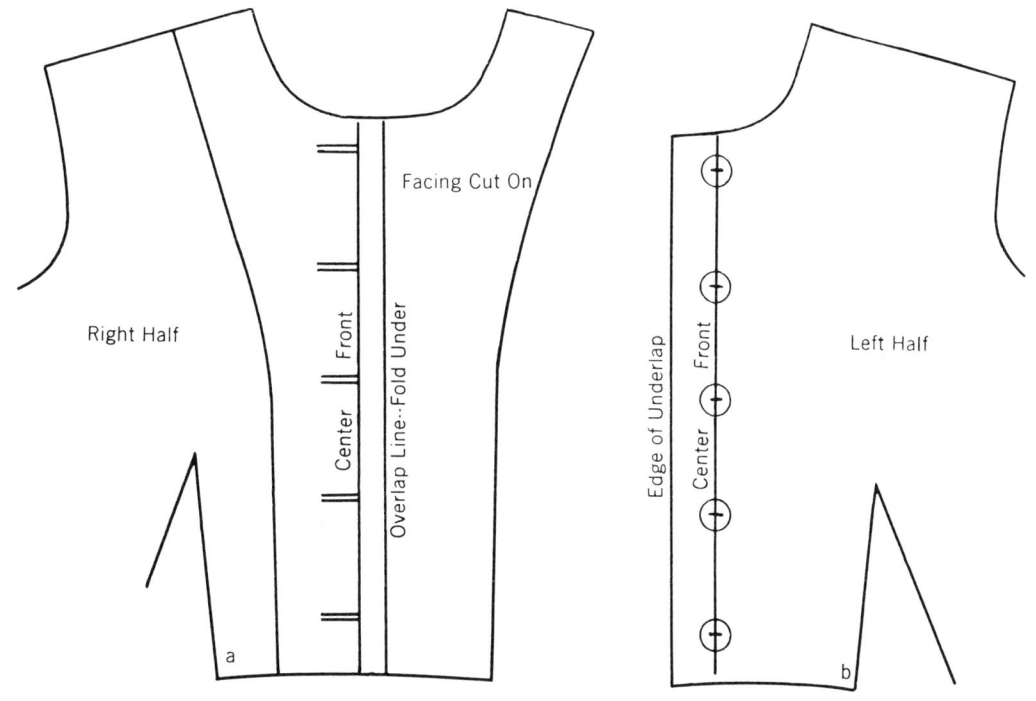

Fig. 69. Lap for buttons and buttonholes. Either cut facing on as in (*a*) or cut facing as a separate piece.

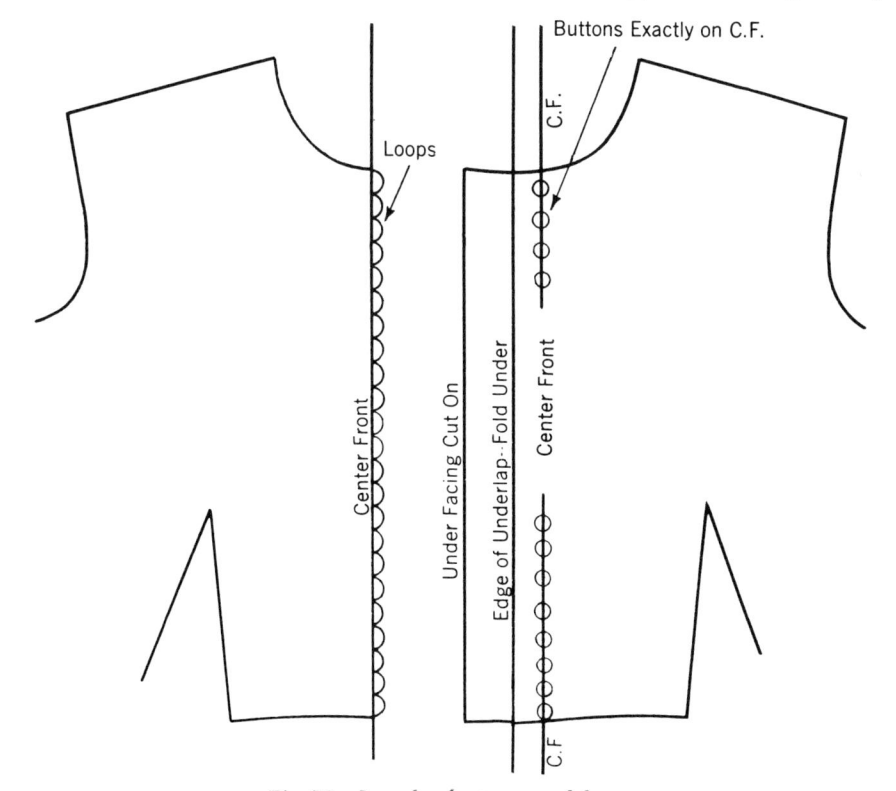

Fig. 70. Lap for buttons and loops.

DRESS DESIGN

Buttons and Loops (see Figure 70)

1. Mark a vertical center front line on both the right and left halves of the pattern.

2. Place the loops exactly on the center front line of the right half and finish the center front line with a fitted facing.

3. Allow an underlap on the left half (the button side) of at least ½ inch if the loops are closely spaced and if they are extended from the center line not more than ¼ inch. Increase the width of the underlap if the loops are extended more than this from the center line on the right side.

4. Face the underlap with a separately cut fitted facing or with an extension folded back from its edge to stay the buttons which are placed on the exact center line.

Problem 6

DRAPING A BLOUSE WITH A YOKE

Instead of running darts to the outer edges of the blouse in order to shape it, it is possible to distribute part or all of the excess along the edge of a yoke. A yoke in a blouse is a small section of pattern around the neck or across the shoulders used to support the lower section of the blouse, which is usually gathered along the yoke edge.

WAIST FRONT — YOKE SECTION

Draping the Upper Part of the Yoke

Use a small scrap of fabric to drape the yoke and follow the standard directions for establishing the neckline, for placing the fabric on the form, and for forming the shoulder and armscye lines of the basic blouse in Problem 1, but omitting the shoulder dart line. Allow extra width at the center front for a button lap if the design requires one.

Designing the Lower Edge of the Yoke

Before designing the lower edge there are three points to consider in the spacing of a yoke (see Figures 71, 72, 73).

1. Scale the yoke to the proportions of the figure. A small yoke looks best on a small figure and a proportionately larger one on a larger figure.

2. Whatever the size of the yoke on which you decide, place the line above the middle of the blouse to avoid dividing it horizontally into two equal parts. A half and half division is not only poor in design, but also cuts unbecomingly across the fullest curve of the bust. A division above the center is usually better than one below because it is less heavy in appearance.

3. To produce the effect of a straight yoke, curve the line slightly upward from the center front to the armscye. This avoids a droopy effect. A line cut on

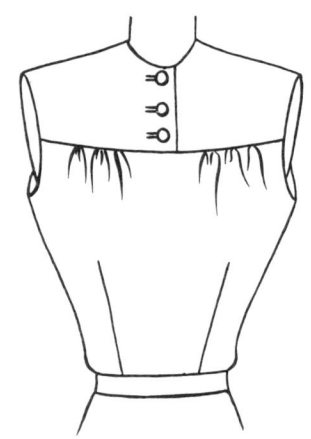

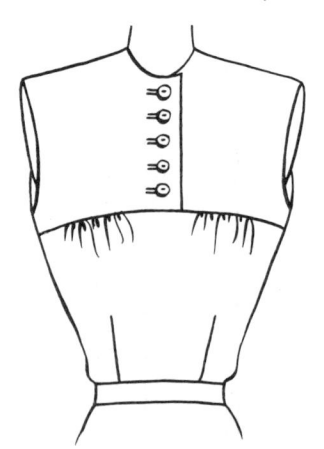

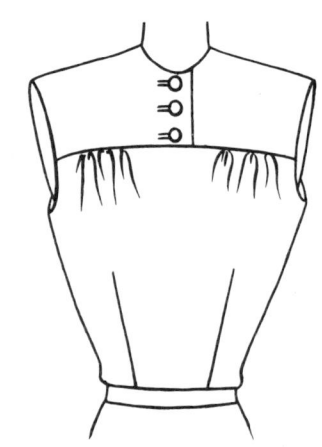

Fig. 71. Good yoke spacing: (a) Pleasing proportion of yoke to lower section; (b) Yoke curves upward toward the sides.
Fig. 72. Poor yoke spacing: (a) Line divides the blouse into equal parts horizontally; (b) Line droops downward toward the sides.
Fig. 73. Good spacing but poor line. Line droops downward toward the sides.

BASIC BLOUSES

the straight crosswise grain always seems to curve downward as it nears the side of the figure, an optical illusion due to the curves of the figure. This principle applies to the establishment of all design lines that should appear to be horizontal.

Mark with pins the lower edge of the yoke and cut, leaving a 5/8 inch seam allowance. Then turn the seam allowance under, pinning it perpendicular to the edge.

WAIST FRONT — LOWER SECTION (see Figure 74)

Placing the Fabric on the Form

1. Pin the straight lengthwise grain or selvage to the center front of the form at the top of the section. Allow a 3/4 inch seam above the lower edge of the yoke.

2. Pin at the chest on the center front.

3. Pin at the waistline on the center front, easing the fabric upward above this pin for blousing.

4. Smooth the fabric across the bust line and pin at the bust so that the crossgrain is level.

5. Pin the fabric to the form at the underarm to support the crossgrain so that it is either level or very nearly so under the arm. Ease the fabric forward to provide at least 3/4 inch of ease. For full gathers along the yoke edge a larger amount may be desirable.

Distributing the Excess

There will be excess fabric both above and below the bust as the fabric is now pinned. Decide whether to force all of it upward to the yoke edge or to divide it between tucks or gathers along the yoke edge and a dart or ease along the waistline. It is probably wiser to keep the grain nearly level across the bust, for if it rises very much it is liable to wrinkle diagonally from the yoke edge toward the underarm.

1. Pinch up tiny tucks along the top of the lower section, starting to work in the fullness over the bust and continuing to within 1½ inches of the armscye. Do not distribute fullness across the entire line, but center it over the bust. Convert the tucks to gathers later when joining the seam. Work in as much fullness as is becoming, releasing the underarm pin if necessary to ease the fabric farther forward horizontally.

2. Take up the remaining excess into a tentative waistline dart or distribute it into pin tucks along the

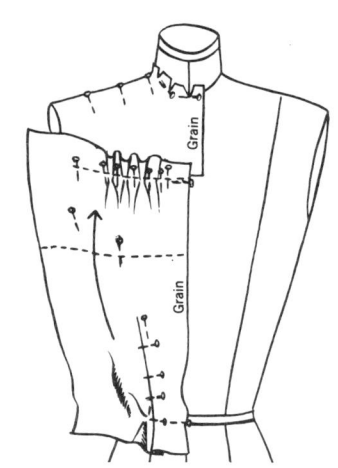

Fig. 74. Procedure for draping blouse section below the yoke.

waistline directly below the gathers in the yoke. Push the fabric upward slightly to provide greater length for blousing.

Joining the Yoke and Lower Section

Lap the yoke edge over the lower section and pin it perpendicular to the edge.

Forming the Lower Section of the Armscye Line

Continue the pin line from the yoke down to the underarm seam, following the directions given in Problem 1 for establishing the armscye line.

Placing the Underarm Seam

Handle according to the directions given for Problem 1.

Forming the Waistline

Trim the waistline seam, leaving a 2 inch extension. It is unnecessary to clip the extension below the waistline if the blouse is gathered at the waistline. If a waistline dart is used the blouse will fit the waistline closely and the extension below it must be clipped as explained in Problem 1, page 22.

WAIST BACK — YOKE SECTION

Draping the Upper Lines of the Yoke

Proceeding as in Problem 1, page 24:

1. Mark the center back.

2. Cut out the neckline.

43

DRESS DESIGN

3. Pin to the form.

4. Form the shoulder line as in Problem 1, except that it is unnecessary to have a dart at the back of the neck or at the shoulder. The ease along the back edge of the shoulder is, of course, necessary.

5. Establish the upper armscye line.

Designing the Lower Edge of the Yoke

The back yoke should be approximately the same depth as the front so that it appears to continue the front line. The effect is better, however, if the back is slightly shallower than the front. The line of the yoke should curve upward very slightly as it goes across the shoulder blades toward the armscye.

Mark the yoke line with pins from the center back to the armscye and trim, leaving a ¾ inch seam allowance. Turn this under and pin it perpendicular to the edge.

WAIST BACK — LOWER SECTION

Proceed as for the front, though there will be less excess to take up into gathers or in a waistline dart. If the blouse is designed for active sports wear, push in extra fullness, more than the amount needed for shaping, but not so much that the figure appears round shouldered. Whenever the design is to have gathers at the edge of a yoke, it is consistent to have gathers at the waistline edge as well. Always push the fabric up above the waistline for extra blousing length whenever there are gathers.

Form the lower armscye line and the underarm line of the back in the same way as for the lower section of the front. Lap the front over the back at the underarm seam.

Note. When using gathers as a form of fullness, use them throughout an entire design wherever fullness appears. Never mix gathers and pleats, or gathers and tucks, in one design, as these various forms of fullness are too unlike. Tucks and pleats, however, have the necessary similarity of line to harmonize with each other. If you do not want gathers at the waistline, use a dart and press it so that it will be practically invisible.

SUMMARY: PRINCIPLES OF DRAPING BASIC BLOUSES

1. It is always necessary to take up excess at the outer edge of a pattern into darts, folds, or gathers in order to make flat fabric conform to body curves.

2. All darts, starting from whatever points around the outer edge of a pattern, point toward the bust in front and toward the curve of the shoulders and shoulder blades in the back.

3. Always place the fabric on the form with the straight lengthwise grain at the center unless the design demands true bias as shown in cowl drapery.

4. Always drape with enough ease around the bust so that the fabric falls free at the front and back of the armscye and forms a small vertical fold.

5. Vertical design lines should usually slant toward the center as they run from the shoulder down to the waistline in order to harmonize with the silhouette of the figure.

6. Horizontal design lines should cut across the figure above or below the bust but never directly at its highest point, and should curve slightly upward as they approach the underarm in order to appear level.

PART II

THE FLAT PATTERN METHOD OF DESIGNING BLOUSES ON THE MASTER BLOCK PATTERN

Before attempting to compare the two systems of pattern making — draping and flat pattern designing — it is essential to understand thoroughly the meaning of the terms *master block pattern* and *flat pattern blocking*. The master block pattern is a foundation pattern made by either draping on the individual dress

BASIC BLOUSES

form or drafting from body measurements. It always lacks the details of an individual design and is never intended to serve as a pattern for a garment to be worn, but rather is to be used as a pattern from which to derive other designs for garments to be worn. The draped muslin pattern must be fitted, or if the pattern has been drafted from measurements, it must be cut in muslin and then fitted, in order to prove its accuracy. This muslin is called "proof." After the muslin has been fitted and corrected, the pattern is cut in tagboard, a kind of cardboard. It is then ready to be used as a master block pattern. The draped blouse shown in Part I, Problem 1, Blouse with Shoulder and Waistline Darts (page 27), is suitable to use as a master block pattern and directions for fitting it are given in Chapter 5.

In contrast, the flat pattern blocking method of developing designs consists in drawing the desired design on a duplicate copy of the master pattern, after which the pattern is cut apart on the new design lines. The whole purpose of this procedure is to change the design without changing either the size or fit of the original master pattern. This method of pattern making will be explained in detail in the following pages.

Even a little experience in draping on the dress form shows clearly that functional design is founded on the adaptation of flat fabric to the curves of the body. After draping even one standard waist, it becomes obvious that to make this adaptation successfully, one must take up all excess along the outer edges of the fabric into darts. It is advantageous to learn this fundamental fact through practice in draping before attempting to understand the flat pattern blocking method of shifting a dart from one position to another in order to change the design of a pattern without changing its size or fit.

After some experience in designing blouses on a master block, you will also be aware of the fact that the two systems — draping and blocking — supplement one another, and that an understanding of one helps to clarify the other. Since most designs are developed by using one system or the other, or more often a combination of the two, it is essential to learn to use both with facility and independence in order to design original costumes. That is why in this book the draping of basic blouses is followed by the principles and techniques of designing them by the flat pattern blocking method.

PROCEDURE

To save time and to simplify the process of learning the system of blocking on a foundation master pattern, it is suggested that you practice the first blocking problems on the quarter-size patterns supplied for that purpose (see Figures 75 and 76). You can trace these patterns and make duplicate copies very quickly. The quarter-size blouse patterns are exactly like the draped master pattern explained in Problem 1 on pages 17-29, except that for convenience in blocking, the entire excess taken up by a dart is in one place — at the waistline. Pattern blocks may have the dart at the waistline, the shoulder, the underarm, or the center front. The waistline dart has been chosen for the present purpose because that is a very convenient location for the master dart.

In all flat pattern designing the master pattern should be used without seam allowances and with the darts cut out. The designs in this book developed from the master pattern, whether they are blouses, skirts, sleeves, or entire dresses, are also shown without seam allowances. When a pattern is laid on the cloth from which it is to be cut, it is very much easier to trace the outline and mark the darts accurately if seam allowances are out of the way. When dress fabric or muslin proof is cut, seam allowances must always be marked on the fabric and darts must never be cut out.

After practicing with the quarter-size pattern, you will want to cut your own full-size draped and fitted master pattern in tagboard and to proceed in exactly the same way as with the smaller one. Directions for doing this are given at the end of this chapter (see pages 58-59).

Before you begin the actual blocking, it will be necessary for you to have the following supplies:

1. Quarter-size master blouse front and back patterns traced from this book.

2. A generous supply of duplicate copies of this pattern in heavy brown paper.

3. A supply of mounting paper.

4. Scotch tape.

DRESS DESIGN

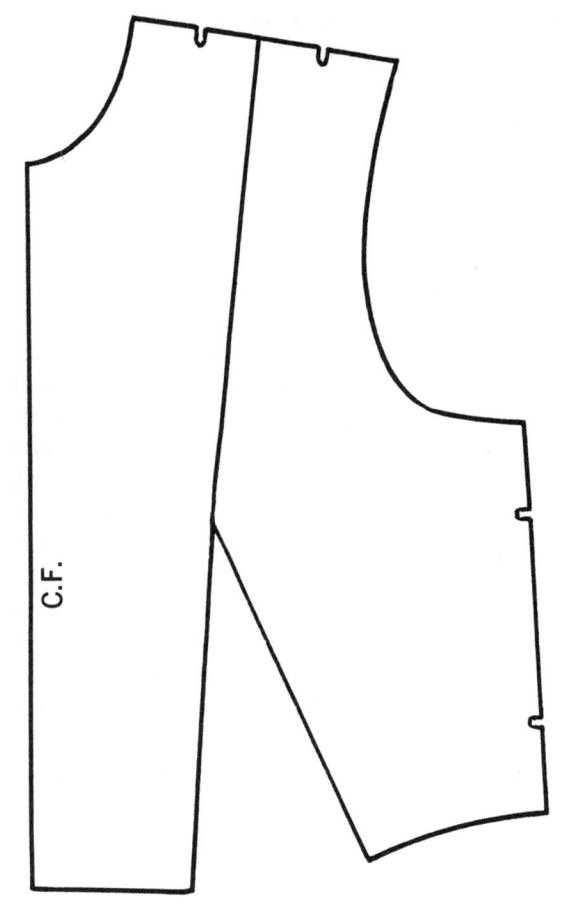

Fig. 75. Master pattern blouse front with shoulder dart transferred to waistline.

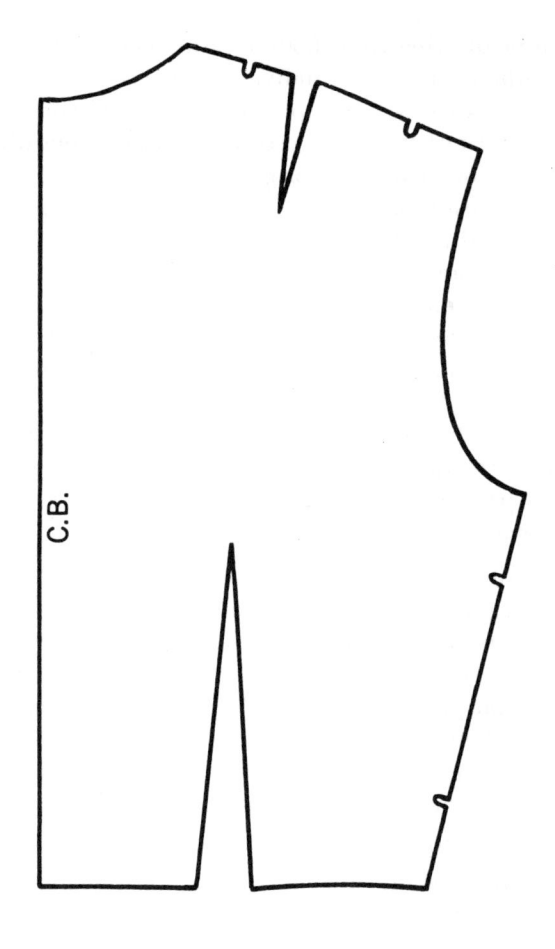

Fig. 76. Master pattern blouse back.

5. Pins.
6. Shears.
7. A sharp pencil.
8. Rulers, a triangle and curves if possible.
9. A large flat work table.

Problem 1

TRANSFERRING THE WAISTLINE DART TO THE SHOULDER (see Figure 77)

1. Draw a straight ruled line from the point of the master dart to the shoulder position. Re-read the discussion of shoulder dart location in Part I, Draping Basic Blouses on the Dress Form (page 19).

2. Cut on the pencil line, close the basic waistline dart, and transfer it to the new position on the shoulder. Although the position of the dart and the shape of the pattern have both been changed by this operation, the size and fit have not been altered in any way.

3. Redraw the new dart, curving it so that it enters the shoulder at a right angle (see Figure 78). True up all vertical darts, following the side of the dart next to the center of the garment.

As it is originally drawn, the dart will be so large that it will run all the way to the point of the bust. This is not only unattractive but causes the blouse to fit too closely. On the other hand, a single dart in a blouse front is too large to be shortened without bulging awkwardly at its tip. Problem 2, illustrated by Figure 79, shows the dart divided, a design which gives a much better distribution of fullness in a blouse that is to be worn.

46

BASIC BLOUSES

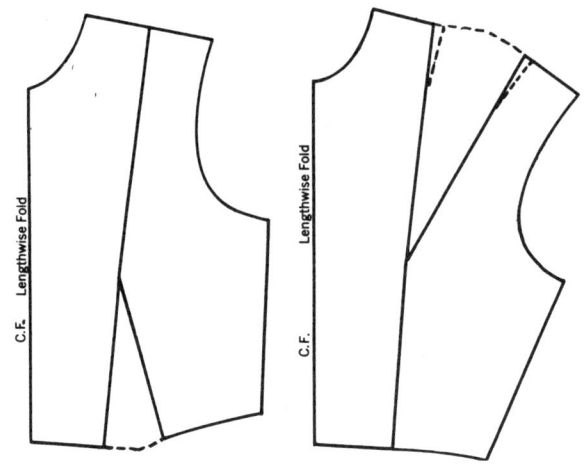

Fig. 77. Step 1 — Transfer waistline dart to shoulder.
Fig. 78. Step 2 — Curve dart to enter shoulder at a right angle.

Problem 2

DIVIDING THE MASTER DART BETWEEN WAISTLINE AND SHOULDER (see Figure 79)

The preceding problem showed that a blouse fits better if the excess is divided between two darts radiating from the bust outward to two different edges of the pattern, since two smaller darts taper out more smoothly when shortened than a single large one.

1. Draw the pencil line and slash exactly as in the preceding problem.

2. Pivot the pattern at the point of the old dart to retain part of the dart at the waistline and shift part of it to the shoulder.

3. Redraw both darts to shorten them, following the inside edge — that is, the edge toward the center line of the garment.

Never change the size of darts at the outside edge of the pattern when trueing them up.

Problem 3

DIVIDING THE MASTER DART BETWEEN WAISTLINE AND UNDERARM (see Figure 80)

The underarm dart is usually placed as high up under the arm as possible without interfering with the armscye seam. This is done because it is not at all decorative and is used only as a supplementary fitting dart in conjunction with the waistline dart and occasionally with a small shoulder dart as well. The underarm dart should always be invisible. (For further discussion, see Part I, Problem 2, Draping the Blouse with a Horizontal Underarm Dart, pages 29-31.)

1. Draw a line from the point of the waistline dart to the location of the projected new dart under the arm. This should be 1 to 1½ inches below the armscye seam.

2. Partly close the old basic dart, pivoting it at its point to divide it between the two positions.

3. Redraw both darts to shorten them.

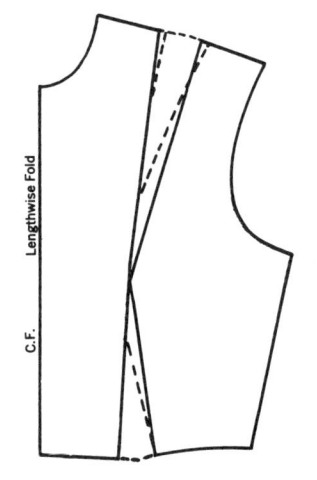

Fig. 79. Master dart divided between shoulder and waistline. Dotted line shows method of trueing vertical darts.

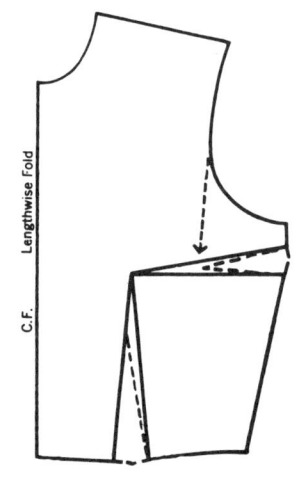

Fig. 80. Master dart divided between waistline and underarm. Dotted lines show method of shortening darts.

DRESS DESIGN

(a) The waistline dart should follow the edge of the pattern toward the center front.

(b) The underarm dart should taper to the center, ending in line with the front of the armscye so that it will be hidden by the front of the sleeve (see **Figure 80**).

Although the shoulder, waistline, and underarm are the three standard positions for darts, the only limit to the possible location of a dart is the design itself. The use of the fundamental dart as a source of the design motif is a basically functional concept in dress designing. Thus a dart pointing to the neck may be the source of any number of ideas, such as gathers under a yoke, a bow tie, a draped neckline with a clip, a cowl, and so on. The transfer of a dart to the center front supplies excess to put into gathers, tucks, or spaced knots along the center front. (See Chapter **7**, Suggestion 7, for further discussion of the use of the basic dart as a starting point in working out new designs.)

Problem 4

DIVIDING THE MASTER DART BETWEEN NECKLINE AND UNDERARM SEAM (see Figure 81)

1. Draw a line from the point of the basic dart to the new position, the neck at the center front.

2. Slash the new line and close the old dart; or

3. Divide the dart, placing part of it at the underarm seam near the waistline. This placement generally harmonizes with folds radiating from the neck to the bust.

Fig. 82. Dart transferred to neck to form a bow tie.

4. Add fabric for a tie if the design calls for one (see Figure 82).

5. To add more ease around the bust than the basic dart provides, spread the pattern apart at the top of the basic dart (see Figure 83).

A good foundation pattern fits very closely, with nearly all of the excess taken up in the basic dart. This makes a very satisfactory block pattern from which to cut designs because it includes no superfluous fullness. It usually fits too closely, however, to be worn, and more ease should be allowed around the bust. Figure 83 shows a blouse pattern with the entire

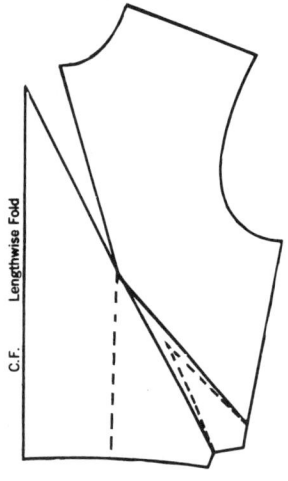

Fig. 81. Master dart divided between the center front neckline and the underarm near the waistline.

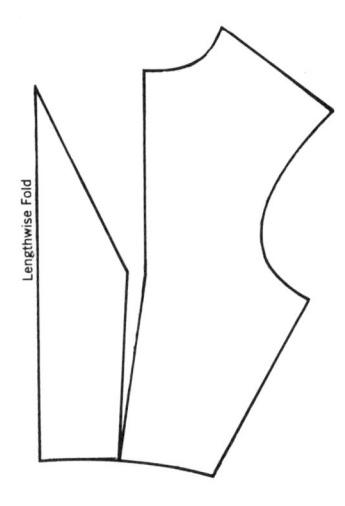

Fig. 83. Method of adding extra width around the bust.

48

BASIC BLOUSES

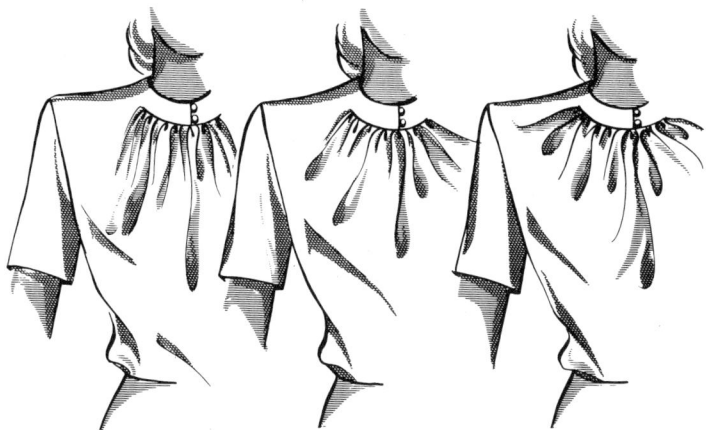

Figs. 84, 85, and 86. Fullness generally follows the direction of slashes.

dart transferred to the neck and with the point of the dart pivoted outward for extra ease around the bust, but with the waistline the same size. Notice that the waistline curve increases as the dart point is pivoted outward.

(a) Figure 87 shows a pattern slashed so that all the folds will tend to fall vertically from the neck to the waistline. The fullness radiates very little because the slashes are nearly vertical. Spreading the slashes intensifies the curve of the waistline, and fullness therefore tends to spring from that curve.

(b) Figure 88 has slashes to the underarm seam. The fullness in this case tends to spring from the underarm, and the lines radiate outward more than in Figure 87. This design will be somewhat less slenderizing.

(c) Figure 89 shows slashes distributed both to the underarm and to the armscye. The fullness lines radiate outward still more and thus emphasize the bust more emphatically.

If you compare these three illustrations carefully, you will be able to draw the conclusion that folds and gathers tend to run in the direction in which you slash. Be cautious, however, in assuming that this will always happen, because there is one other factor that

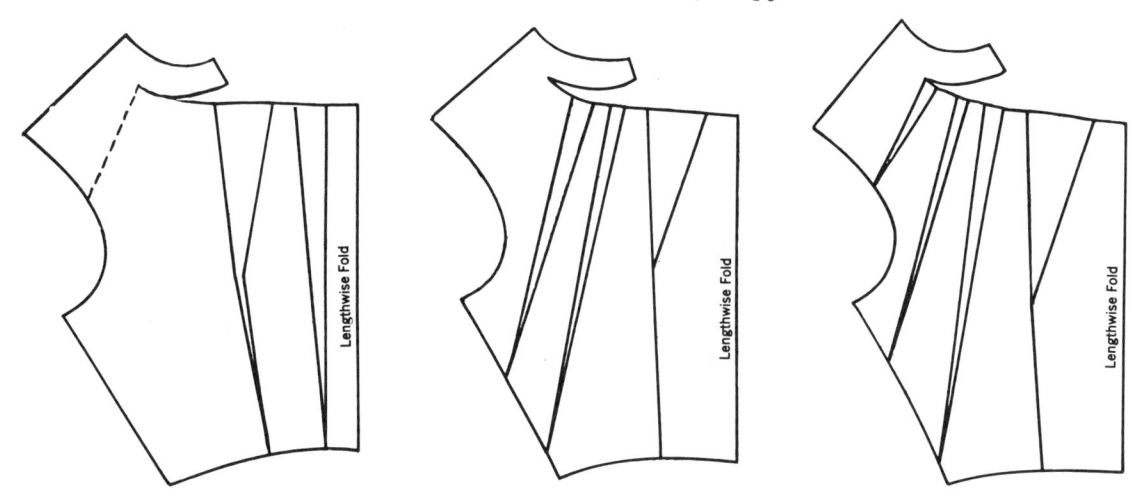

Figs. 87, 88, and 89. Gathers or folds tend to run in the direction of slashes. In Fig. 87, the fullness tends to fall vertically from vertical slashes. In Fig. 88, the fullness tends to radiate toward the underarm. And in Fig. 89, the fullness tends to radiate toward the underarm and the armscye.

6. The factors that control the direction of folds or gathers are (1) the direction of the slashes, and (2) the contour of the figure. Note that the three finished blouses in Figures 84, 85, and 86 have the same partial-yoke design but that the lines of fullness fall differently in each. In Figure 84 the lines of fullness are nearly vertical; in Figure 85 they radiate outward somewhat more; and in Figure 86 they radiate out still more.

determines the direction of fullness lines — the contour of the individual figure. Always take into account the effect of the curves of the body on the final pattern. It is safe to say that body contour is the greatest single factor in determining the direction that fullness lines will take. This, of course, is why flat blocking cannot produce the same sureness of effect in design as does draping on the individual form.

DRESS DESIGN

Upward Curving Simulated or Partial Yokes

A simulated or partial yoke has the appearance of a real yoke cut as a separate pattern segment, but is actually cut in one piece with the main body of the blouse. Figures 84, 85, and 86 illustrate simulated yokes. When you slash and spread a pattern vertically to introduce fullness along the edge of a simulated yoke that curves upward at its outer end, you will discover that the pattern pieces in the lower section overlap the yoke. This shortens the pattern so that it draws at the outer corner of the yoke. To correct this, slash once from the outer corner of the yoke line either to the underarm seam or to the armscye. When it is spread out, this one slash swings the yoke section up out of the way of the vertically slashed lower section and lengthens the blouse enough at the outer end of the yoke line to fit without drawing. This difficulty arises only when you slash vertically, as in Figure 87, and when the yoke is both simulated and curves upward. (See Chapter 7, Figures 31-33, for a similar example applied to simulated yokes in skirts.)

Interpreting the Center Front Dart at the Neckline as a Cowl

1. Reread the directions for draping cowls, pages 37-40

2. On a copy of the master pattern, draw a line from the point of the basic dart to the center front neckline. Cut this line and pivot the pattern at the point of the dart to transfer the basic dart to the neckline at the center front.

3. Square out from a continuation of the center front line to the neckline end of the shoulder seam. An L square makes this operation easy. Measure the length of the top edge of the square from the neck end of the shoulder seam to the center front, and then measure the same amount on the form from the neck end of the shoulder seam down to the center front. This measurement gives you the depth of the cowl neckline. From the side of the neck to a point just above the bust, the fabric will fall into shallow folds formed out of the excess from the master dart (see Figure 90).

4. To increase the depth of the folds and the depth of the neckline, it is possible to proceed in two ways.

(a) Measure down from the side of the neck on the form the desired neckline depth. Placing an L square on the center front line, pivot the front pattern section outward from the waistline until the center front forms a right angle with the cowl neck at the point of the desired neck depth (see Figure 91).

Pivoting the pattern outward in this way increases the intensity of the waistline curve and forces some of the cowl drapery to spring from the point on the waistline where the pattern was pivoted.

If you prefer a cowl that hangs heavily at the center front, follow Method (b).

(b) Pivot the L square (not the pattern) out from the center front at the waistline so that the upper edge touches the neck end of the shoulder seam at the desired depth measurement of the cowl neck. Draw the new center front line and the cowl neckline.

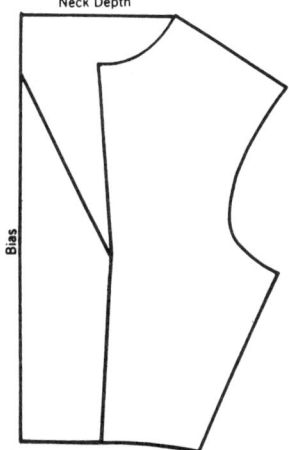

Fig. 90. Cowl interpretation of the master dart transferred to the center front neckline.

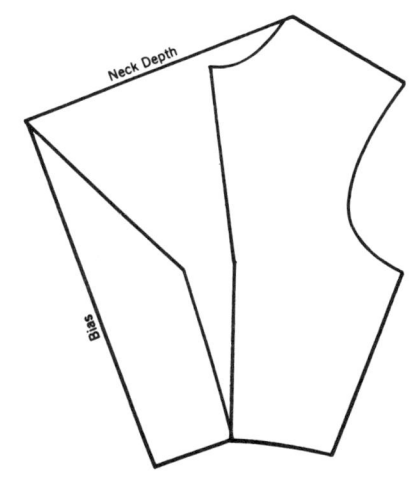

Fig. 91. Deep cowl made by pivoting outward the center front pattern segment.

BASIC BLOUSES

The deeper the neckline, the heavier the drapery and the more mature and dignified the design appears to be. The deep cowl is, therefore, more suitable for an older woman than for a young girl. Since it also decidedly thickens the figure over the bust, it is most becoming to a tall slender woman. For a short girl, the very shallow cowl is generally a better choice. To block a shallow cowl (see Figure 92) retain part of the master dart at the waistline. It is probable that all of these designs need a little extra width at the bust, the amount depending, of course, on the tightness of the original master pattern.

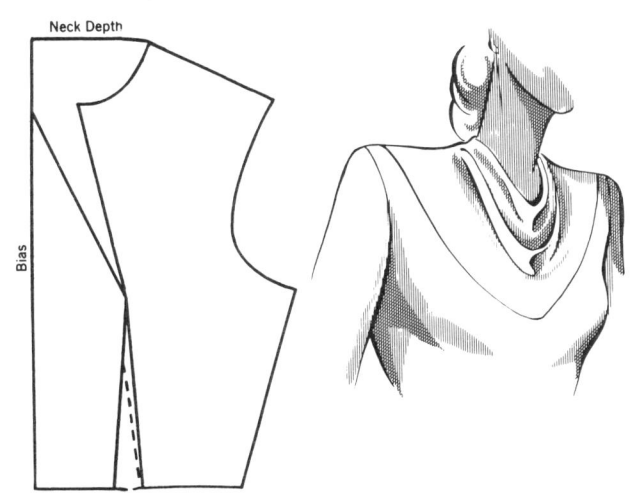

Fig. 92. Very shallow cowl with part of the master dart retained at the waistline.

Fig. 93. Cowl drapery in a yoke.

5. Place the center front of the pattern on the true bias of the fabric. This automatically places the cowl neck edge of the pattern on the bias.

Figure 93 shows cowl drapery in a yoke. This cut has deep folds and yet fits more loosely around the bust because the center front of the lower section is on the straight grain whereas the yoke section is cut with the center front on a true bias. Fabrics used for cowl draping should have grain which is very inconspicuous. Figures 94 and 95 show the procedure for blocking a cowl yoke. Figure 96 shows two steps in making a cowl yoke with fitted folds falling from points along the shoulder and with a seam at the center front of the yoke. Figure 97 shows the finished effect of this cowl yoke.

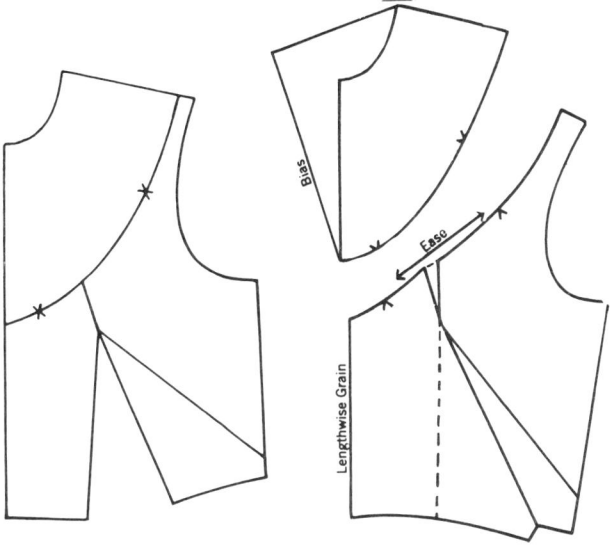

Figs. 94 and 95. Procedure for blocking the cowl yoke: (1) Draw the yoke line and a line from the dart to the edge of the yoke; (2) Cut off the yoke and add cowl drapery; (3) Spread the lower section for ease at the yoke edge and insert a dart to the underarm near the waistline.

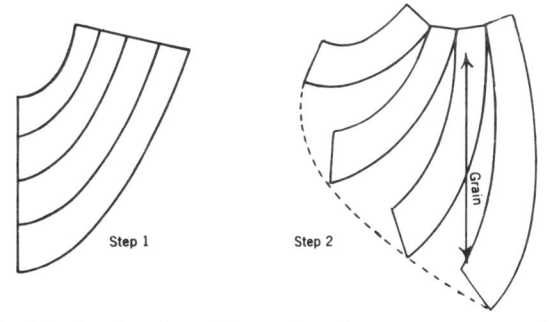

Fig. 96. Cowl yoke with a shaped seam at center front: Step 1 — Mark as shown. Step 2 — Slash and spread the pattern.

Fig. 97. Cowl yoke with a seam at center front.

51

DRESS DESIGN

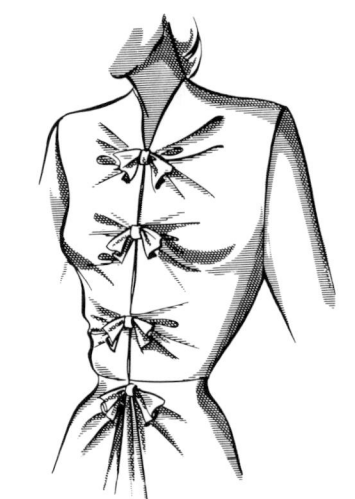

Fig. 98. Spaced bow ties at the center front.

Problem 5

TRANSFERRING THE MASTER DART TO THE CENTER FRONT

This dart position should be used for designs that involve gathers along the center front line, spaced bow knots at the center front, or any design with dart interest at the center front. Figure 98 shows a blouse with spaced knots.

1. Draw a horizontal line from the point of the basic waistline dart to the center front.

2. Slash the line and transfer the original dart to the center front position. The basic dart alone does not provide enough fullness at the center front for gathers, because the distance from the point of the basic dart to the center front is very short (see Figure 99).

3. To increase the fullness at the center front (see Figure 100):

(a) Slash from the point of the basic dart to the underarm seam and spread the pattern.

(b) Slash again at points where knots are to be placed from the center front to the underarm seam, and spread the pattern.

Note. Always slash perpendicular to the gathered edge, if possible.

4. Place the grain indicator perpendicular to the waistline at the center of the section. Figure 100 shows the placing of the grain.

Notice that, as a result of the slashing, the underarm seam is curved and the armscye curve is intensified. The center front is also an intense curve and therefore the grain must be placed at the center of the pattern perpendicular to the waistline.

5. To add width over the bust (see Figure 101), slash vertically from the point of the basic dart up to the shoulder. Spread the slash over the bust but keep it closed at both ends. Thus the waistline and shoulder line remain unchanged in length, but the curve of each increases. Do not forget to trace the exact curve in the final pattern.

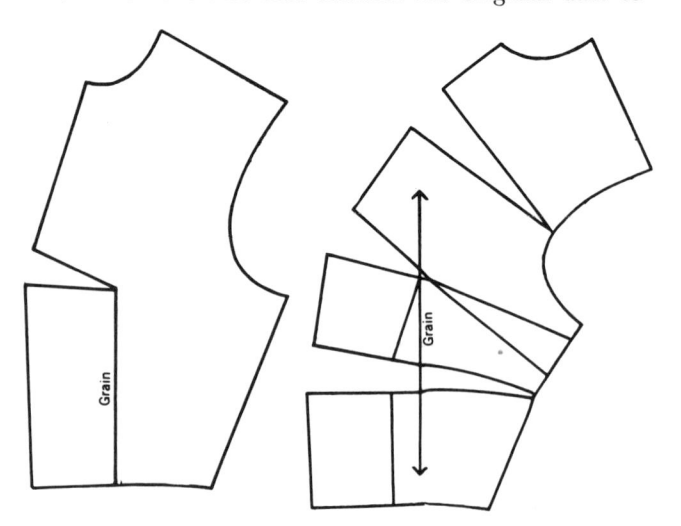

Fig. 99. Transfer of the master dart to the center front.
Fig. 100. Pattern slashed to interpret design in Fig. 98.

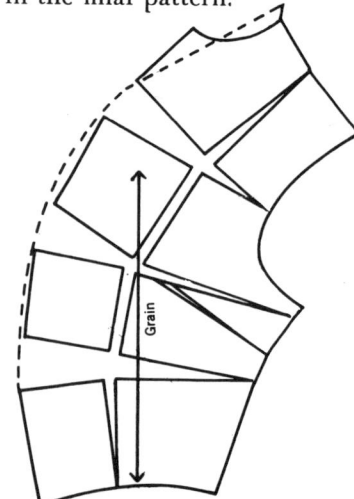

Fig. 101. A vertical slash spread for width around the bust (top and bottom ends are not spread).

BASIC BLOUSES

Note. If you wish to convert the same pattern into one for a design with gathers distributed evenly along the entire center front line, measure the original length of the center front of the master pattern and then spread the horizontal slashes enough so that the center front length after it is spread will equal one and one-half to two times the original measurement. It is a general rule that gathers require one and one-half to two times the length of the space that is to be gathered, the amount depending on the desired fullness and also on the texture and thickness of the fabric which is used.

Problem 6

CONVERTING THE MASTER DART TO A FRENCH DART SEAM LINE

French Dart Line Position

To determine the French dart line, see the instructions for draping the French dart (pages 31-36). First rule a line from the point of the waistline dart to the shoulder position (see Figure 102). Then, using the ruled line as a guide, redraw the line by hand, putting in enough curve so that it enters the shoulder at a right angle, curves slightly toward the center over the bust, and enters the waistline at a right angle. The line may coincide with the basic waistline dart (see

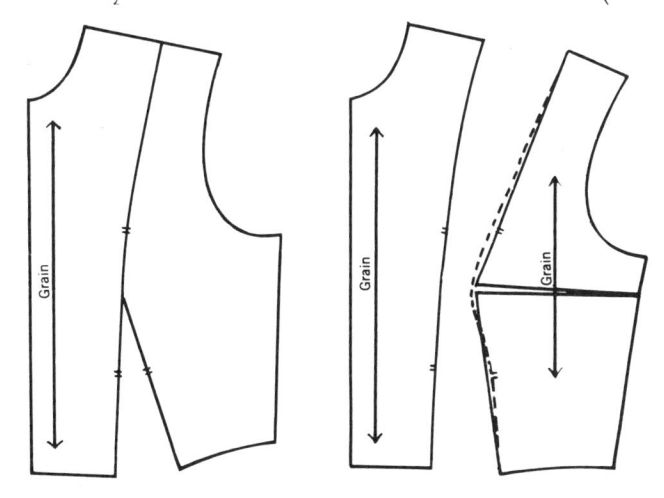

Fig. 102. French dart line drawn as a continuation of the master dart (line curves slightly).

Fig. 103. French dart pattern with ease introduced over the bust on the side front section (dotted line shows final side front line).

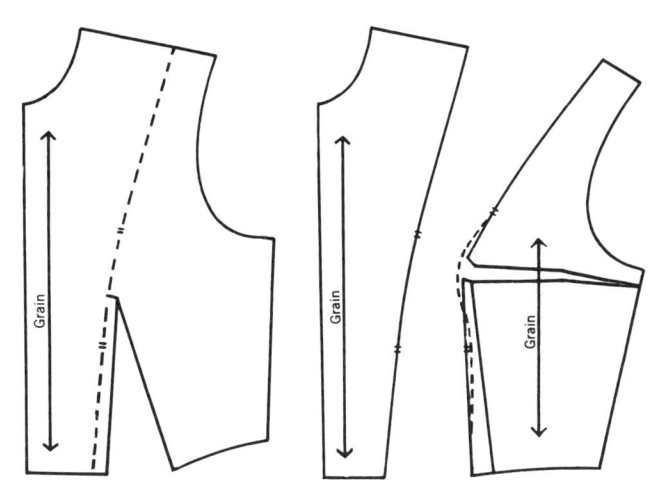

Fig. 104. French dart line drawn closer to center front than the master dart.

Fig. 105. French dart pattern cut on line drawn in Fig. 104: (1) Length increased for ease over bust; (2) Dotted line indicates a more pronounced curve over bust.

Figure 102), although in some cases the spacing may be improved if the front panel is narrowed at the waistline (see Figure 104). Place the master pattern against the form or hold it up against yourself in order to sketch in a becoming line.

1. Pencil the French dart line and crossmark it above and below the bust.

2. Cut the pattern apart along this line.

3. Add ease both lengthwise and crosswise, because the side front section of a French dart blouse always fits better if the ease is increased over the bust.

(a) For extra length, slash from the point of the master dart to the underarm and spread the pattern slightly at the bust (see Figure 103). Spreading over the bust has the same effect as forcing the grain inward above the bust when draping the French dart.

(b) To provide extra width and to smooth up the side front line, redraw it, rounding the sharp point at the bust into a smooth curve (see Figure 103).

4. Mark the straight grain in the side front section perpendicular to the waistline at the center.

For a variation in the position of the French dart line, see Figure 104. Because a French dart bodice fits tightly and is frequently used to provide contrast with a bouffant skirt, the French dart line is sometimes widened at the shoulder and narrowed at the waist,

DRESS DESIGN

as in Figure 104, where the line is closer to the center front. Both the length and the width of the side front section can be increased by cutting the sliver of pattern between the old and the new dart positions from the center front panel and attaching it to the side front section (see Figure 105). This provides some of the ease which is required over the bust. The more the center front panel is narrowed, however, the more ease the side front panel needs to provide a smooth fit over the bust curve.

Problem 7

TRANSFERRING THE MASTER DART TO A YOKE EDGE (see Figure 106)

A yoke is simply a combination of horizontal and vertical darts. It acts as a support for ease or even for visible fullness over the bust as well as to introduce a line along which to shape the pattern. A dress with a yoke simply overlaid on a flat pattern, with no transfer of the dart to its edge, is a serious mistake; not only because the dart positions are unrelated to the line of the yoke, but also because no ease is introduced along the edge joining the yoke to the body section. The design is therefore stiff, tight, and totally unrelated to the body contour. Figure 107 illustrates this error. Figure 108, on the other hand, shows the transfer of part of the waistline dart to the yoke edge in

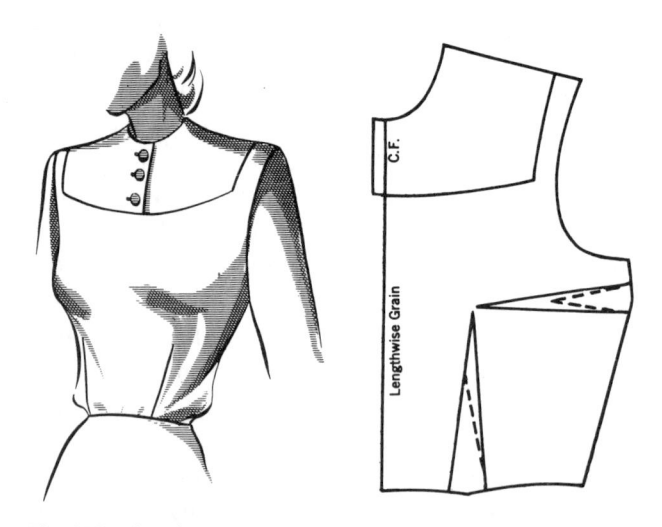

Fig. 106. A yoke.
Fig. 107. Incorrect. Dart should be transferred to yoke edge.

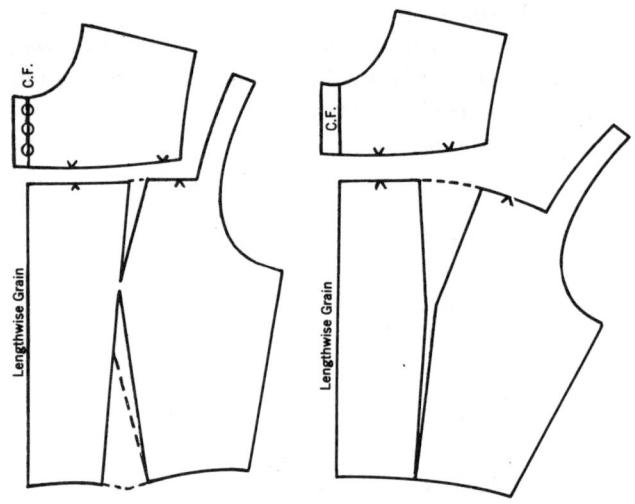

Fig. 108. Correct. Part of dart transferred to yoke edge.
Fig. 109. Master dart entirely transferred to yoke edge and pattern pivoted outward for extra fullness.

order to introduce a little ease. Notice also the shaping along both the lower and side edges of the yoke. This shows that the dart was really transferred from the waistline to the yoke edge. Figure 109 shows the same design except that gathers at the yoke edge have been obtained by transferring the entire waistline dart to the yoke edge and by spreading the pattern at the bust to let in even more fullness.

1. Draw the yoke line on the master pattern while holding the pattern up against the form in order to relate the yoke spacing to the figure. Do not draw the line with a ruler, but curve it slightly upward along its lower edge as it approaches the armscye. (See yoke spacing in Draping a Blouse with a Yoke, pages 42-44.)

2. Crossmark and cut the yoke line.

3. Draw a line from the point of the basic dart to the yoke edge and slash it.

4. Pivot the pattern outward at the point of the basic dart to shift part of the waistline dart to the yoke. Figure 109 shows the pattern pivoted and all of the dart transferred to the edge of the yoke. Retaining some of the waistline dart is optional. Tuck, gather, or ease the excess along the upper edge of the lower section into the yoke.

For a more complicated and unusual yoke design, see Chapter 7, Figures 58 and 59.

BASIC BLOUSES

Problem 8

TRANSFERRING THE MASTER DART TO AN ASYMMETRIC DESIGN WITH BALANCED FULLNESS (see Figures 110 and 111)

An asymmetrically balanced blouse pattern, that is, one that is balanced off center, may be either very easy or very complicated to cut. If, for example, the blouse is exactly the same on the right and left sides, but has a side front or surplice opening, the pattern for the right side will be duplicated for the left even though the opening is off center. On the other hand, if for example the design has gathers or drapery radiating from one shoulder and the other shoulder is smooth, the right and left sides of the pattern will be shaped entirely differently and the pattern will be much more complicated to cut. This latter type of asymmetric design will be discussed in Chapter 7, Suggestion 10. The method discussed here applies to an asymmetrically balanced blouse with all the pattern edges alike on the right and left sides but with the opening off center. It is blocked exactly like a symmetrically balanced one except that it is necessary to draw the design on an entire front of the master block pattern rather than on a pattern for only half the front.

1. Make a paper copy of the entire front of the master pattern with the center front clearly marked. On this pattern, sketch in the design of the overlapped side, the right side only (see Figure 110). The left side should duplicate the right as the under extension on the left usually equals the overlap on the right.

2. Transfer most of the basic waistline dart to the edge of the shoulder yoke (see Figure 111). In addition, spread the pattern slightly for extra ease over the bust. To increase the gathers still more, pivot the pattern outward to spread the full edge.

3. Place the straight grain at the center front. Draw around the final pattern.

Problem 9

DESIGNING BLOUSE BACKS ON THE MASTER BLOUSE BACK PATTERN

The principles of blocking designs on the back of the master pattern are essentially the same as for the front. There are, however, a few points typical of blouse backs only. Because the curves of the figure at the back are divided between the top of the shoulder and the shoulder blades, the foundation master pattern has two darts — a very small one either at the back of the neck or at the shoulder seam, and a second larger one from the waistline up to the shoulder blades. See draping procedure for the Waist Back, Problem 1, pages 23-27.

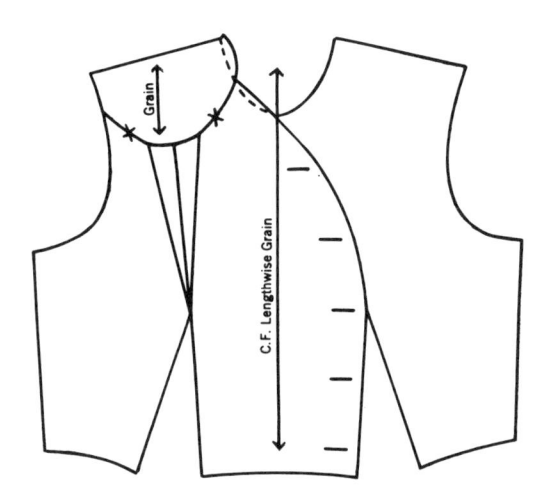

Fig. 110. Complete master pattern front with lines drawn for asymmetric design.

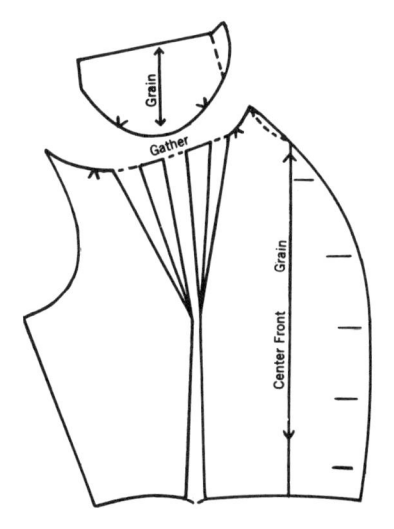

Fig. 111. Right or overlapped side of pattern with slashes spread for gathers at yoke edge.

DRESS DESIGN

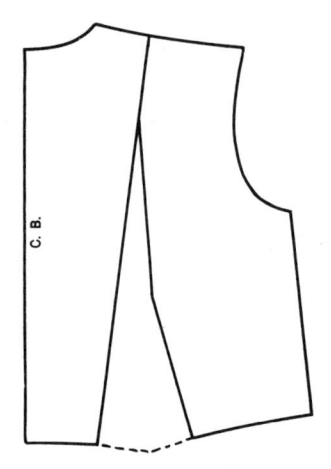

Fig. 112. Transfer of the shoulder dart to the waistline. The great size of the dart increases the width across the shoulder blades.

It is possible to transfer all of the dart from the shoulder to the waistline. It is seldom desirable to do so, however, because this throws a great deal of fullness over the shoulder blades and a tremendous amount at the waistline, and this is usually difficult to control, as Figure 112 shows. It is, however, possible to transfer the basic shoulder or neck dart to a yoke edge, or to change the dart at the back of the neck to a shoulder dart if this change improves the design. Figures 113 and 114 show the procedure for this transfer. It is also possible to divide the waistline dart into two or more smaller darts or to distribute the fullness in gathers along the waistline. Generally, you should take your cue for the design of the back of blouse from the front, and let the back carry out the motifs expressed in the front. Very complicated blouse backs, especially those involving gathers, too often tend to round the shoulders and distort the figure from the profile view. It is generally wiser to keep the backs of blouses comparatively simple and flat for the sake of the complete silhouette.

Transferring the Blouse Back Darts to a Yoke Edge

1. Draw the yoke line and cut the pattern apart. (See the discussion of yoke spacing on pages 42-44.)

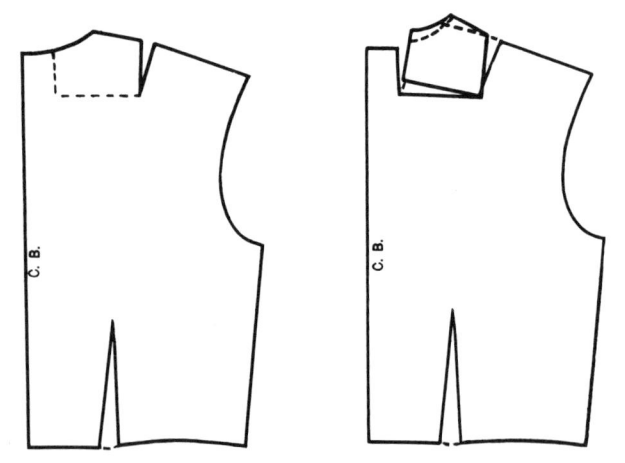

Fig. 113. Master blouse back with lines drawn for the transfer of the shoulder dart to the neck.

Fig. 114. Shoulder dart transferred to neck (dotted line shows necessary dart length and shoulder height corrections).

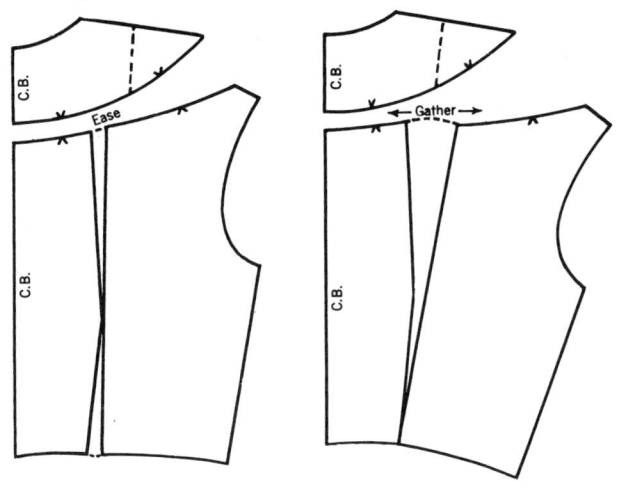

Fig. 115. Closing of shoulder dart and transfer of part of waistline dart to yoke edge.

Fig. 116. Pattern pivoted outward at point of waistline dart to introduce fullness at yoke edge.

2. Close the shoulder dart. The lower edge of the yoke is now slightly longer than the upper edge of the body section and should be the reverse. To get some ease along the upper edge of the body section, transfer a small part of the waistline dart up to it, as shown in Figure 115. For actual gathers, completely close the waistline dart. For still fuller gathers, pivot the waistline dart at its point, as shown in Figure 116.

If the yoke section is deep, more of the shoulder dart should be transferred to its lower edge. But when all of the shoulder dart is transferred to the lower edge of a deep yoke, it fits too loosely. It is better to leave some of the dart at the shoulder where it can be worked in as ease along the shoulder seam. However, the portion of the dart at the lower edge of the

BASIC BLOUSES

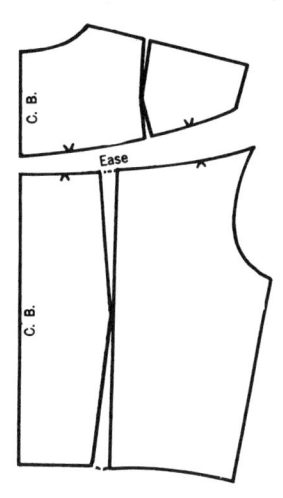

Fig. 117. Deep yoke — part of shoulder dart retained and part transferred to lower edge of yoke.

yoke supplies ease for arm movement. Figure 117 shows this. To avoid tightness over the shoulder blades, there should always be slightly more length on the top edge of the body section than on the lower edge of the yoke section. A deep yoke is not well adapted for use in sports garments, for it obviously restricts action more than a shallow yoke with fullness below it.

Problem 10

DESIGNING A HIP-LENGTH JACKET PATTERN FROM THE MASTER BLOUSE COMBINED WITH THE TWO-GORE SKIRT

It is possible to convert the basic pattern for a blouse to a hip-length jacket (Figures 118 a and b) without a waistline seam by combining the basic blouse pattern with the top of the two-gore basic skirt. (For the two-gore skirt pattern, see pages 65 71.)

1. Trace the outlines of the basic waist pattern on construction paper.

2. Place the waistline of the two-gore skirt against the waistline of the basic blouse pattern. The darts of the waist and skirt are draped to coincide but are not equal in size. First draw around the center section of the skirt and then move the skirt pattern so that the side section fits against the side section of the blouse.

3. Draw the line for the lower edge of the jacket parallel to the waistline and about 7 to 9 inches below it. Notice that there is a slight curve along the waistline of both the master blouse and skirt patterns. Leave this curve as it is, because no overblouse or jacket without a waistline seam should be fitted as snugly around the waistline as a blouse with a separate peplum attached at the waistline.

Note. If the dart in the back of the blouse is smaller than that at the back of the skirt, equalize them by slashing to the shoulder dart and transferring part of the shoulder dart to the waistline.

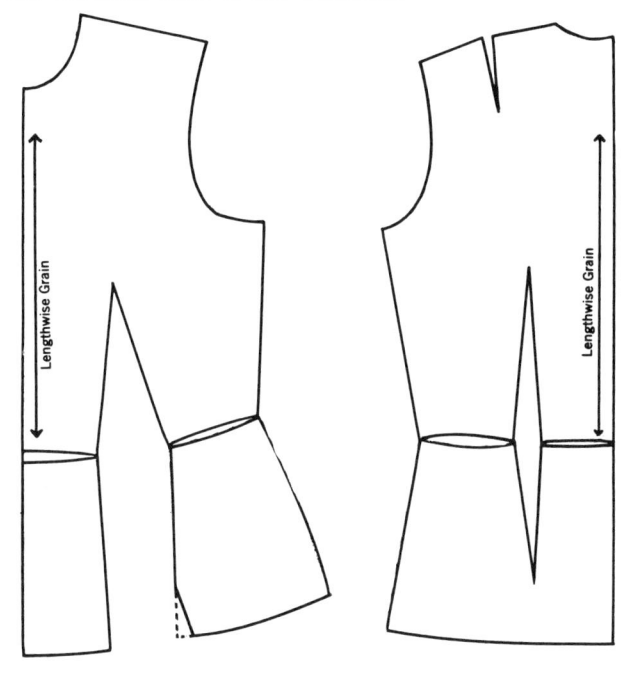

Fig. 118. (a) Front of master pattern hip-length jacket; (b) Back of master pattern hip-length jacket.

French Dart Hip-Length Jacket

Use this pattern for long torso lines that fit very snugly (see Figures 119 a and b).

1. Place the lengthwise grain at the center of the side front and side back sections so that it runs across the waistline perpendicular to it.

2. Slash the side front section of the blouse horizontally from the bust to the underarm seam to add ease over the bust. (See directions for blocking the French dart waist, pages 53 54.)

57

DRESS DESIGN

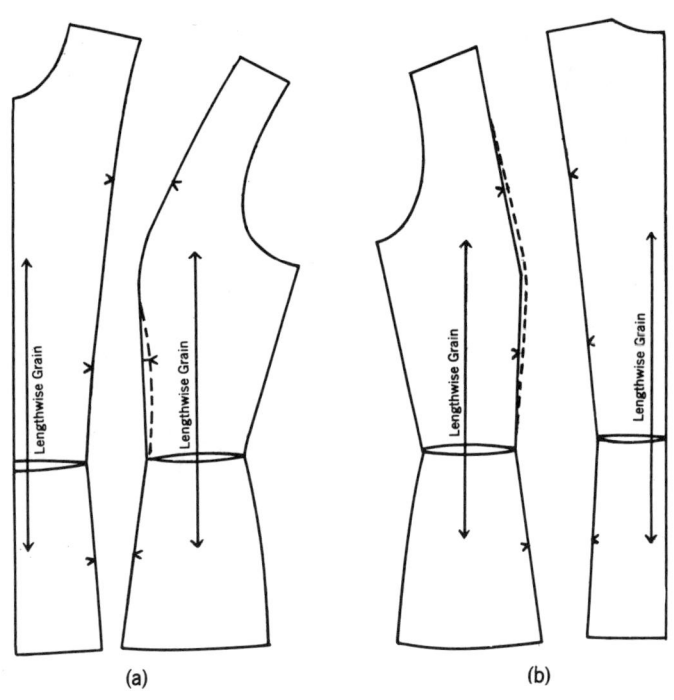

Fig. 119. (a) Front of French dart hip-length jacket; (b) Back of French dart hip-length jacket.

3. Intensify the curve over the bust to define the bust line more sharply.

French Dart Hip-Length Jacket as a Princess Line Dress Pattern

To adapt this bodice to a dress pattern, continue the slope from waist to hip and rule the seam lines for the desired skirt length. The lines are ruler-straight, and slant from the hip to the lower edge.

Blouse Extended Below Waistline Eliminating Part of Waistline Seam

Attach part of the two-gore skirt to part of the basic blouse for dresses which have only a partial waistline seam. Examples of this combination are discussed in Chapter 7.

CUTTING A TAGBOARD MASTER PATTERN FROM THE BLOUSE

After experimenting with the quarter-size pattern, cut your own master tagboard pattern from the draped and fitted muslin waist with shoulder and waistline darts. This is the blouse discussed in Problem 1, pages 17-29. This should be done as follows:

1. Press with a warm iron both the front and back of the fitted and corrected master blouse patterns with darts at the shoulder and waistline. Cut the pattern vertically on the center front and the center back, and use just half a pattern. Be careful that you press with the lengthwise grain in order to guard against stretching the muslin pattern. Press without moisture.

2. Pin the pattern securely to construction paper.

3. Trace around the pattern with a tracing wheel. Hold the wheel tightly against a ruler wherever the line should be straight. Trace curves freehand or with the aid of a curved ruler.

4. Remove the muslin from the paper, and pencil all traced lines on the paper pattern to make them clearer and more exact.

5. Cut out the paper pattern carefully. Cut out darts, cut away all seam allowances, and cut out crossmarkings with little U-shaped cuts which a pencil can be slipped into.

6. Transfer the shoulder dart to the waistline.

It was essential to drape the master blouse with darts at both shoulder and waistline because a blouse fits better when so draped. After the pattern has been fitted, however, it should be prepared for use as a master block by having all of the dart transferred to one place, preferably the waistline. Do this to simplify the blocking procedures, even though the dart will certainly look too wide at its lower end in relation to its length.

(a) Draw a line from the point of the shoulder dart to the point of the bust.

(b) Cut through this line and pivot the pattern to close the shoulder dart and to transfer it entirely to the waistline.

(c) Redraw the waistline dart with a ruler, carrying it up to the highest point of the bust. Follow the inside line of the dart (the edge nearer to the center line) when trueing it.

(d) Cut out the dart.

7. Place the brown paper pattern on tagboard, and pencil around the entire paper pattern, letting the

58

BASIC BLOUSES

pencil run into the crossmarkings and along both edges of the large master dart.

8. Cut out the tagboard pattern without seam allowances.

9. Cut the back blouse pattern in tagboard exactly as it was draped.

Your master pattern should be very similar to the quarter size master pattern shown in Figures 75 and 76.

SUMMARY: PRINCIPLES OF DESIGNING BLOUSES ON A MASTER BLOCK PATTERN

1. The system of designing on a master block pattern is founded on an understanding of the transfer of the dart to the location of the design detail, thereby making the dart both ornamental and functional.

2. The shift in the position of the dart changes the pattern design without changing its size or fit. All change takes place within the edges of the pattern.

3. Two factors control the direction of lines of fullness:

(a) The direction of the slashes usually indicates the direction of the lines of fullness, but

(b) The body contour is the chief determining factor and will often upset all flat-paper calculations.

4. Slashes should be made perpendicular if possible to an edge that is to be gathered.

5. Although it is easiest for blocking purposes to concentrate all excess in one large master waist-front dart running to the point of the bust, the dart in a blouse to be worn is usually divided into two or more smaller darts pointing toward the bust from two or more different edges of the pattern, because the smaller darts taper out more smoothly.

3. Basic Skirts

PART I

DRAPING SKIRTS ON THE DRESS FORM

Draping skirts differs fundamentally from draping blouses in several respects. A blouse fits the figure on all of its edges and there is just enough ease to allow bending and reaching, whereas a skirt may fit the figure from waistline to hips, but from there down to the hem, it swings free of the body. The lines from hip to hem must therefore be established without the contour lines of a dress form to follow and to pin against. To be beautiful, a skirt must have enough freedom below the hipline to swing easily with the motion of the figure, and to do this it must widen as it lengthens. Both gored and circular skirts increase in width at the lower edge, and if cut with enough flare to swing freely, are both comfortable to wear and graceful in motion if the flare is placed within the silhouette so that it slenderizes the hips and thighs. Draped skirts, on the other hand, have fullness drawn up to the waistline, thus narrowing the lower edge, and they tend to restrict motion — sometimes so much that they must be slashed at the hem to allow the wearer to move at all. It is possible, however, to produce a peg-top effect, yet to introduce enough fullness at the lower edge to let the wearer move unhampered. Because it is so important that a skirt be graceful in motion, it should always be finally judged when the wearer moves as well as when she stands still.

The skirts presented in the following pages are classified as *straight, gored, circular,* and *draped,* in the order listed. So that you may become familiar with each type and explore its possibilities, you should practice draping and blocking the examples shown.

STRAIGHT SKIRTS

Straight skirts have seams on the straight lengthwise thread, and hem and hipline on the straight crosswise thread. They include the all-around gathered (the dirndl, or peasant skirt), the all-around pleated, and the wrap-around skirt.

Most children try to make a straight skirt at some time or other, usually on their first attempt at sewing for a doll. A child's natural procedure is to sew the seams, put in a hem on the grain, and gather the excess fabric at the top to fit the waistline. This perfectly simple, natural procedure proves to be good with one exception. The seams and hem should be on the straight grain, it is true, but the waistline should not. The length from the waist to the hip level (a line approximately eight or nine inches below the waist and parallel to the floor) is normally somewhat shorter in the front than in the back. On a figure with a very flat abdomen but with a prominent back hip curve, this difference in length is very pronounced; whereas on a person with a prominent abdomen and flat hips, quite the opposite is true. For illustrations of the effect of posture on skirt length from waist to hip, see Chapter 5, Figures 2 *c, d, e,* and *f.*

Problem 1

DRAPING THE STRAIGHT GATHERED SKIRT

This skirt has become a spring perennial and is extremely popular, especially with the teen-age girl.

BASIC SKIRTS

Fig. 1 · (a) and (b). Influence of texture on silhouette.

Known as a dirndl, it is made in striped, plaid, and flowered fabrics of both stiff and soft, shiny and dull textures, and is worn alike by the fat and the lean, the tall and the short. Because it is so easy to make without a pattern, it is attempted by both the skilled and the unskilled seamstress, though not always with success, for like all designs, the dirndl must be planned in relation to the silhouette it produces. This depends upon the height and slenderness of the wearer and particularly upon her hip and waistline proportions, the texture of the fabric, and the size and line direction of the fabric pattern. A soft clinging material in a dull texture and color without pattern may be fairly successful even on a moderately plump girl — but not a glazed chintz with a large flower pattern. The dirndl is generally at its best on the over-tall, over-slim girl, for it rounds out her sharp hip bones and appears graceful when gathered in to her tiny waistline. Figures 1 a and b show the influence of texture on the silhouette.

Estimating the Fabric

1. The average straight gathered skirt requires two widths of 36 inch fabric, minus a straight lengthwise band taken off next to the selvage for a belt.

DRESS DESIGN

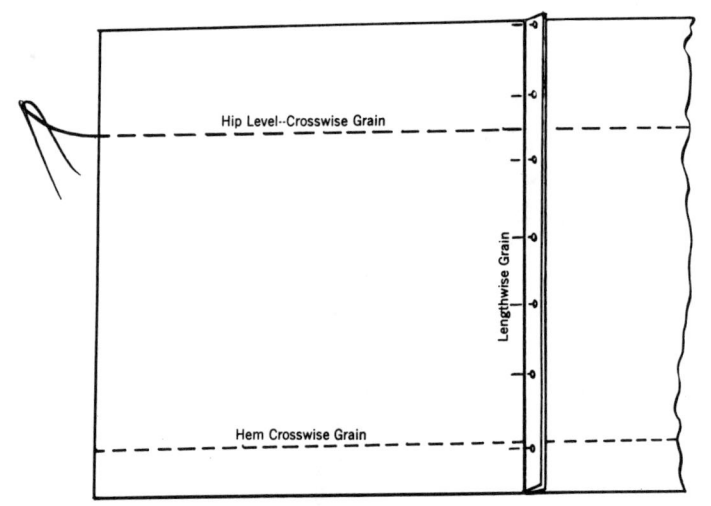

Fig. 2. Straight skirt showing seams joined, hem turned, and gathering thread at the hip level.

2. To determine the length of cloth required, measure from the waistline the desired length and allow a hem on each piece.

Cutting a Waistband

Cut off a straight lengthwise strip along the selvage twice the width desired.

Finishing Seams and Hems

1. Pin and stitch the seams and press them open. If there are two seams, plan to have one on each side, in line with the side seams of the blouse.

2. Turn the hem on a straight crosswise thread.

Adjusting the Skirt from Hip to Waistline

1. Using a double thread, mark a line with long basting stitches 8 or 9 inches from the top and parallel to it (see Figure 2).

2. Draw the thread up to fit the hipline and adjust the skirt on the form, pinning the gathered line to the hip level marked on the form (see Figure 3). (For an explanation of hip level, see page 8.)

3. Place a tape around the waistline, smoothing the fullness up under it to get the correct waistline.

4. Mark the waistline from the center front to the center back with pins. Remove the skirt from the form, smooth up the line, and transfer the markings to the opposite half.

Fig. 3. Straight skirt gathered 8 or 9 inches below the top and pinned to the form at the hip level.

5. Machine-gather the waistline, using several parallel rows.

6. Draw all the gathering threads up at the same time to make all of the rows equally tight.

7. Attach the skirt to a waistband. If the band is very narrow, use a straight lengthwise strip with no shaping. However, if it is more than 1¼ inches wide, it will fit better if shaped slightly.

Problem 2

DRAPING THE STRAIGHT ALL-AROUND PLEATED SKIRT

This skirt can be estimated and made with little adjustment on the form. It is at its best in firm wool that stays pleated, and when well made is justly popular, for it hangs with trim neatness and is even becoming to a girl with fairly large hips.

Note. Since it is a laborious process to pleat an entire skirt by hand, stitch all of the seams except one, finish the hem, and have the skirt pleated by a professional pleater. Pressed pleats actually help to slenderize hips if the pleats are well scaled to the size of the figure. A pleated skirt is not a good choice, however, for a girl with a small waistline and a large hipline, as Figure 4 shows. For this type of figure, it is better to mount a pleated lower section onto a fitted yoke.

BASIC SKIRTS

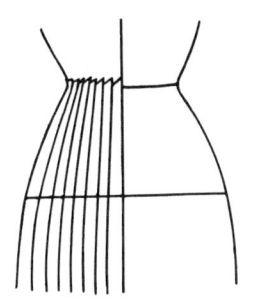

Fig. 4. Difficulty of adjusting a straight pleated skirt to a figure with a small waistline and large hips.

Estimating the Fabric

1. If the skirt is to have deep pleats, the width of the material required will be three times the largest hip measurement, since each pleat takes three times its own depth (see Figure 5). Thus for a 37 inch hip measurement, the entire skirt width should be three yards and three inches plus the seam allowances and plus any necessary allowance for shrinkage.

2. Measure the length as for a straight gathered skirt.

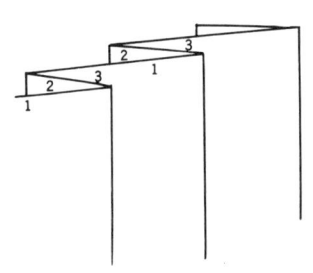

Fig. 5. The width requirement of deep pleats is three times the depth of the pleats.

Finishing Seams and Hem

1. Pin and stitch all except one of the lengthwise seams.

2. Turn the hem on the straight crosswise thread, finish and press it.

3. Have the skirt pleated. Indicate the kind and size of pleats desired.

4. After it has been pleated, rip back the hem on each side of the open seam and join the last seam.

5. Turn the hem over the seam, finish, and press it.

Fig. 6. Pleated skirt is adjusted at hip level and each pleat is tapered from the hip to the waistline.

Fig. 7. Poorly made skirt. All excess at waistline is fitted out at side seams (compare with Fig. 6).

Adjusting the Skirt from the Hip to the Waistline (see Figure 6)

1. Run a basting 7 to 9 inches from the top and parallel to it. Pin this line to the form parallel to the floor.

2. Taper each pleat slightly so that it enters the waistline perpendicular to it. It is far easier to adjust pleats on a form than to do it mathematically. If there is an 8 inch difference between hips and waistline distribute it among all of the pleats equally. Sometimes in a cheaply made skirt the excess at the waistline is fitted out at the side seams with the unfortunate effect shown in Figure 7.

Conceal the seams at the under-creases of the pleats.

3. Baste and edge-stitch the pleats from waistline to hips.

4. Mark the waistline, following the waistline marked on the dress form. The waistline should not be on the crossgrain but should curve downward at the center front for a normal figure.

5. Mount the skirt on a waistband cut on the lengthwise grain.

63

DRESS DESIGN

Fig. 8. Straight wrap-around skirt.

Problem 3

DRAPING THE STRAIGHT WRAP-AROUND SKIRT
(see Figure 8)

When there is a vogue for the very narrow, stem-like skirt, the wrap-around often comes into fashion. It is a skirt cut in one piece which is wrapped closely around the hips as its name suggests. This style gives a narrower front and back silhouette than the two-gore skirt, which flares almost entirely at the sides. For this reason it is often used for a suit skirt, particularly when the jacket opens at the side front in line with the wrapped edge of the skirt. The skirt may, of course, be wrapped to open at the side back instead of at the side front. It is also a favorite cut for bordered materials, since the border follows and accents the wrapped line. Figure 12 shows the pattern shape.

Adjusting the Fabric on the Form (see Figure 9)

Drape the whole skirt on the form. As the final step in the procedure, make the adjustment from hip to waist, as for all straight skirts.

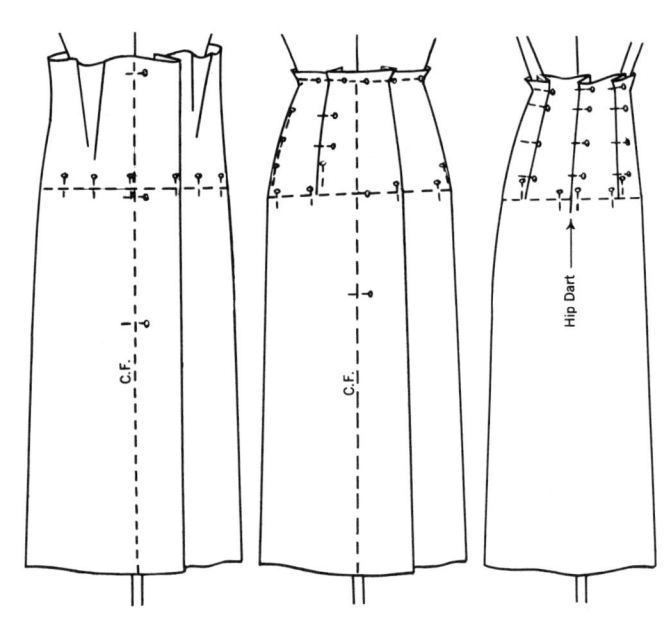

Fig. 9. Procedure for draping a straight wrap-around skirt with the hem on the crossgrain and the hip level parallel to the hem.
Fig. 10. Adjustment of straight wrap-around skirt from hip to waistline (excess taken up into darts).
Fig. 11. Wrap-around showing darts at side, side front, and side back.

1. Decide on the amount of overlap at the left of center front, mark the center front the desired distance back from the overlapped edge, and pin the center front securely at the hip level. Keeping the crosswise grain parallel to the floor, continue to pin around to the center back at the hip level (see Figure 9).

Adjusting the Skirt from Hip to Waist (see Figure 10)

1. Fit out the excess with darts from hip to waist. It is usual to place darts at the side of the figure in line with the underarm seam of the blouse, at the side back in the normal panel position, and at the side front to balance the line of the opening. Slant off the line of the overlapped edge slightly from the waistline to the hem so that it harmonizes with the hip silhouette. If a bordered or striped material is used, it is better to keep the edge straight on the grain all the way from waist to hem. The less difference there is between the size of the hipline and the waistline of the form which is being used, the fewer and smaller the darts will be, and the less slant there will be on the overlapped edge.

BASIC SKIRTS

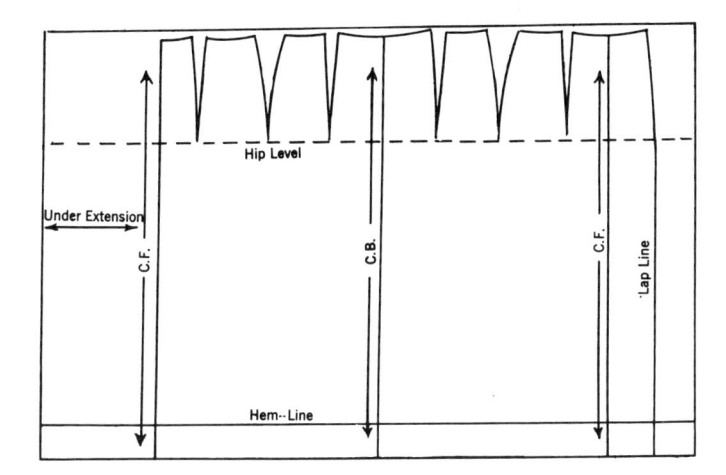

Fig. 12. The wrap-around skirt pattern.

2. Mark the waistline with pins from center front to center back. Figure 11 shows the side view.

3. Remove the skirt from the form and transfer all lines to the opposite half with a tracing wheel used on carbon paper or on a chalk board.

4. Mount the top on a band.

Figure 12 shows the pattern for the wrap-around skirt.

GORED SKIRTS

Draping a gored skirt differs fundamentally from draping a straight skirt, and since the gored skirt is by far the most important type, this difference should be thoroughly understood. In all straight skirts the seams, hip level, and hem run parallel to the grain, and are either gathered, pleated, or darted to fit the waistline. All gored skirts, on the other hand, are composed of wedge-shaped pieces (called *gores*) which are always wider at the hem than at the hip, and wider at the hip than at the waistline. A gored skirt fits the waistline and hipline smoothly and flares outward toward the hem line so that the seams never run on the same lengthwise thread for their entire length, and the hem line and hip level are never on the same crosswise threads. Because a gored skirt is composed of wedges that fit the waistline and hip line, it can be adjusted to flare at any desired point and can be made to take on almost any silhouette. It is justly the most popular of all skirts because it is so adaptable not only to all fashion silhouettes but also to all figure proportions.

Problem 4

DRAPING THE TWO-GORE SKIRT

This skirt is composed of two gores. One makes the entire front and one the entire back of the skirt. It serves as a foundation from which to design other skirts through the flat-pattern blocking method, and together with the basic waist makes a master pattern from which to design the complete body of any desired costume. It is not, however, a good skirt to wear, since most of the flare is certain to swing toward the side seams, and since the back of the skirt tends to cup under the hips because of the lack of any goring at the center or side of the back. For this reason it is an especially unfortunate choice for the heavy, broad-hipped figure (see "General Principles of Fitting", Chapter 5, pages 193-196. Another reason for confining its use to the master pattern is that if a two-gore skirt fits smoothly when the wearer is standing, it often seems uncomfortably tight when she is sitting. Although it is also sometimes used as a suit skirt, it is not particularly well adapted to this purpose. It serves very well, however, as a master block pattern. Before draping the two-gore skirt look at the diagram of the pattern shown in Figure 22 to see the shape of the gores that you are going to drape.

FRONT OF SKIRT

Estimating the Fabric (see Figure 13)

1. Measure from the waistline the desired skirt length and add 5 inches (3 inches for a hem allowance plus 2 inches for curving down the waistline from the side seam to the center front).

2. Estimate the probable width at the lower edge and allow for a wide seam plus a little extra to experiment with as you drape. Plan to make the circumference of the skirt at the lower edge somewhat less than one and one-half times the hip measurement. For instance, if the hips measure 36 inches, the hem sweep should be about 50 inches.

3. To find the center front, measure horizontally from the selvage one-half the estimated width of the skirt front at the hemline (see Figure 14). Mark the center front line clearly. Use a pencil if you are working with practice material and thread markings if you are draping the actual dress fabric. The center front line should be on the straight lengthwise grain.

DRESS DESIGN

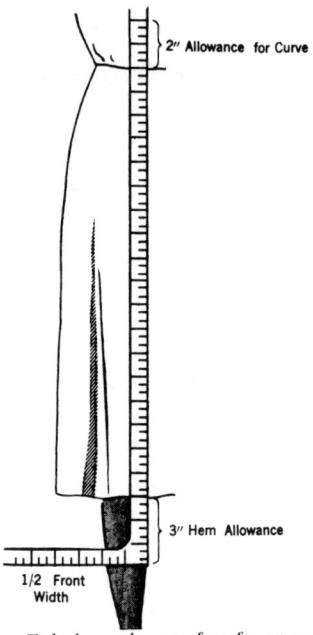

Fig. 13. Fabric estimate for front gore.

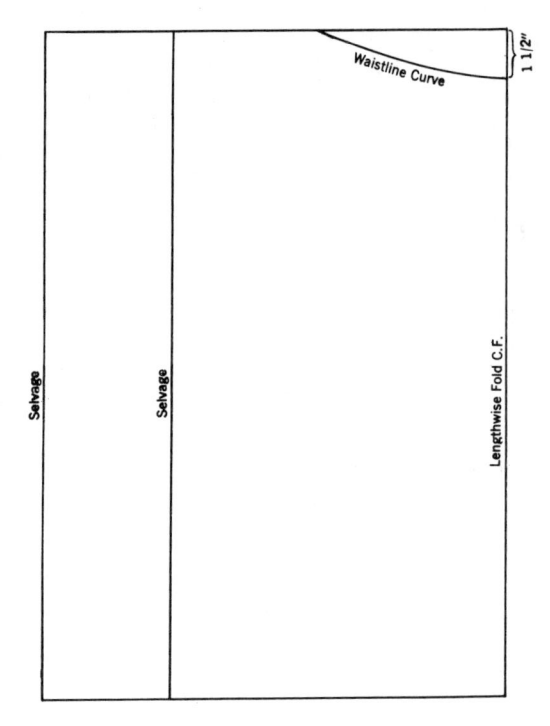

Fig. 14. (1) Center fold position; (2) Shape of waistline.

Shaping the Waistline (see Figure 14)

Place the shears perpendicular to the center front 1½ inches below the top and cut a freehand curve that tapers up to the side seam position. The length of the curve equals the waistline measurement of the form from the center front to the side seam.

Adjusting the Fabric on the Form

1. Pin the center front line marked on the fabric to the center front of the form, with the top edge of the cloth about ⅝ inch above the waistline.

2. Pin the center front at the hip level. Check to see that the center front hangs in a plumb line.

Establishing the Side Seam Position (see Figures 15 a and b)

Study the dress form from the side view. Ideally, the side seam should fall through the center of the waist and the center of the hip in a plumb line to the floor. It should be directly on the side, so that it is not noticeable from either the straight front or the direct back view. It should appear to fall perpendicular to the floor from hip to hem line, and perpendicular to the waist from waistline to hip.

If the figure has a sway back which throws the waistline forward and the hips back, some adjustment is

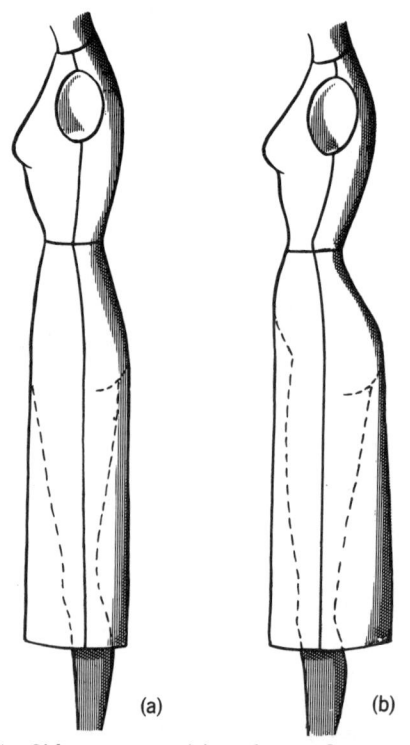

Fig. 15. (a) Side seam position for a figure with good posture; (b) Side seam adjustment for a sway-backed figure.

BASIC SKIRTS

necessary or the side seam will tend to swing toward the back. To adjust the skirt for this posture, tilt the side seam slightly forward from the center of the hip to the center of the waistline where it meets the underarm seam of the blouse (see Figure 15 b). If, on the other hand, the hips are prominent in back, and the front of the figure is very flat, place the side seam slightly farther back to reduce the apparent hip size. If the hips are flat in back and the abdomen is relatively large, move the side seam line slightly forward. In general, however, place the line at about the center of the hip, but always where it is most becoming to the individual figure being fitted.

Adjusting the Grain at the Hip Level (see Figure 16)

The character or "fall" of two-gore skirts is controlled by the amount the crosswise grain is lowered along the hip level toward the side seams. The more you lower the grain at the hip level, the more the gore flares at the hem; and conversely, the less you lower it the less it flares. The flare falls from the points at which you lower the grain.

1. Smooth the fabric from the center front toward the side seam along the hip level line marked on the form. Check the lengthwise grain to make sure that it stays perpendicular to the floor at the center front of the skirt. Supporting the crosswise grain level for about 3 inches from the center front, pin the cloth to the form at this point. This should be done because lowering the grain directly at the center front throws an awkward flare at the center of the figure.

2. Experiment with lowering the grain from the pin established in step 1 to the side seam. Notice that if the grain drops enough to fit the form smoothly at both waist and hip, an undesirable flare falls near the side seam. This flare can be reduced by lowering the grain just enough to produce an easy straight-hanging line from the hip to the lower edge at the side seam. Do not worry about the excess from hip to waist at this stage.

3. In order to retain the silhouette as draped, pin the fabric to the form along the hip level line, beginning 3 inches from the center front and ending at the side seam. If the hip measurement of the dress form exactly corresponds to your own, ease slightly between the pins until the skirt has approximately

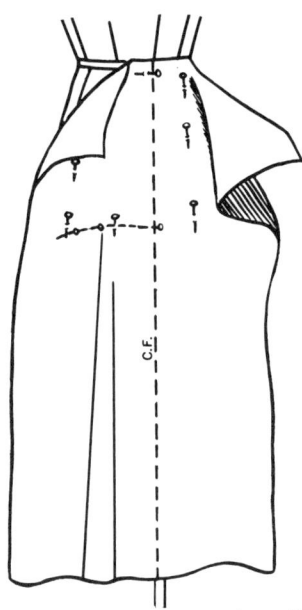

Fig. 16. Two-gore skirt, showing grain adjustment at the hip level.

½ inch of ease from the center front to the side seam. This should be done because the total hip measurement of the skirt around the hips should be at least 2 inches larger than that of the body. The hip expansion when one is sitting determines the exact amount of ease needed.

Adjusting the Side Seam (see Figure 17)

1. Fold the fabric back over itself so that it drops in a line perpendicular to the floor from the hip level to the lower edge. This fold will be the side seam line.

2. Place a pin in the fold at the lower edge. Holding the fold taut, crease it carefully without stretching, and pin the fold perpendicular to the edge.

3. Judge the width of the front gore from the center front to the side seam at the lower edge of the gore. Since this distance is approximately one-fourth the circumference of the entire skirt, it should probably be about 12 to 13 inches for a 35 inch hip measurement.

4. Cut the side seam with a generous seam allowance (1½ to 2 inches) for possible changes at the fitting. Wide seams are especially necessary if it is the first time you have used your dress form in draping a skirt of this type.

DRESS DESIGN

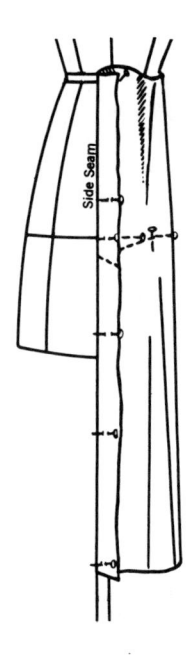

Fig. 17. Side seam adjustment, side view.

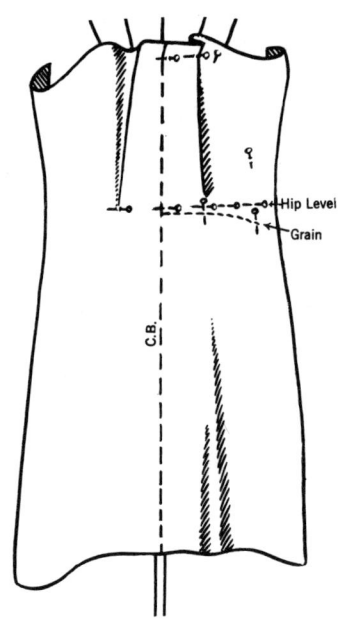

Fig. 18. Back gore showing grain adjustment at the hip level.

5. Turn the seam allowance to the wrong side and re-pin it. Leave the skirt unfinished from hip to waistline.

Note. The procedure for draping all gored skirts is the same in the following details: (1) The line from hip level to hem should be adjusted, and that from hip to waist should be left unfinished until the entire character of the skirt is established at all seams. (2) The side seam from hip level to lower edge should be a straight line slanting outward.

BACK OF SKIRT

Estimating the Fabric. See directions for the front gore.

Shaping the Waistline. See directions for the front gore.

Adjusting the Fabric on the Form. See directions for the front gore.

Adjusting the Grain at the Hip Level (see Figure 18)

Before draping the back of the skirt from hip to hem, it is necessary to understand the relationship of the vertical hip dart to the proportions of the figure and to the skirt silhouette. Because of the outward curve of the hips at the back, the excess at the top edge of the skirt pattern has to be taken up into darts. The more the grain is dropped at the side of the hip to increase the fullness at the lower edge, the smaller these darts will be. Conversely, the narrower the skirt is at the lower edge, the larger the darts will be. The size of the dart also increases with an increase in the difference between waistline and hipline sizes.

1. Smooth the fabric toward the side seam across the hips, keeping the crosswise grain level at the hipline from the center back for a distance of $3\frac{1}{2}$ to 4 inches, the approximate end of the hip dart, and pin the fabric to the form at this point.

2. Lower the crosswise grain toward the side seam enough for a slender skirt that neither cups under the hips nor flares out at the side — in short, for a satisfactory silhouette for a foundation master skirt.

3. Pin the fabric to the form at the hip level in one or two places from the point of the dart to the side seam (see Figure 18) to retain the established silhouette. Remember that any lowering or raising of the crosswise grain at the hip entirely changes the fall of the skirt.

4. Fold the excess above the hip into a dart running from waist to hip and pin it temporarily.

BASIC SKIRTS

Adjusting the Side Seam from Hip to Hem (see Figure 19)

1. Fold the fabric over on itself from the hip level to the lower edge. This line, when it falls free, should be perpendicular to the floor and should flare enough to meet the front edge easily.

2. Crease the fold slightly without stretching it. Then pin it from the hem to the hip, holding it taut as you do so.

3. Trim off the excess, allowing a seam of 1½ to 2 inches.

4. Pencil a clear crossmarking on the side seam at the hip level. This is the balance point of the side seam and controls the hang of the skirt.

5. Unpin the back edge of the seam and slip the seam allowance forward under the front edge. Re-pin the seam from hip to hem, matching the balance points exactly.

6. Check the seam to see that it is perpendicular to the floor from the hip to the lower edge.

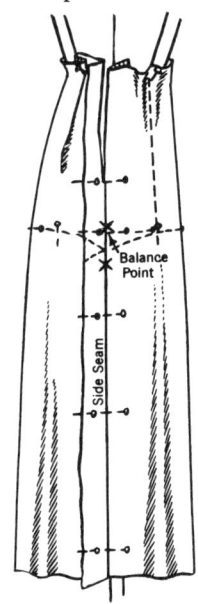

Fig. 19. Side seam from hip to hem.

Position of the Hip Dart in the Skirt Back (see Figure 20)

Notice that the waist dart in the back of the blouse slants inward toward the waistline, conforming to the contour of body. The dart in the back of the skirt also slants inward, and meets the waistline at the point

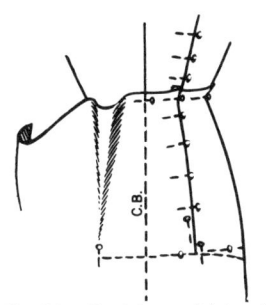

Fig. 20. Position of hip dart.

where the waist dart meets it. The dart in the skirt should carefully conform to the contour of the hip. The greater the difference in size between waistline and hipline, the greater this outward slant should be. Too much outward slant increases the apparent width of the hips. On the other hand, if the dart is parallel or nearly parallel to the center back, the waistline appears heavy and blocky. Learn to place the dart where it will be most becoming to the figure, and always make it appear to continue the vertical dart at the back of the blouse.

1. Fold the dart line, pushing the excess at the waistline under toward the center back (see Figure 20).

2. Pin the dart carefully. The pins should be perpendicular to the edge, and the dart should be long enough to take up all excess smoothly. That is, it should be 6 to 7½ inches long.

Placing the Side Front Waistline Dart (see Figure 21)

There must be ease or darting to shape the fabric over the hip bones just in front of the side seam. Figures with hips which are small in comparison to the waistline need only a very small side front dart and may need none at all. Normally, however, a two-gore skirt front without a dart has too much ease along the side seam from waist to hip. Although ease can be worked in reasonably well, a skirt which is to serve as a master pattern is more satisfactory if the excess is taken up into a dart. Some master pattern skirt fronts place the dart near the side seam so that it points toward the front hip bone, especially if the hip bone is sharp and exaggerated. For the normal figure, however, the dart in the skirt should be placed in line with that in the blouse front in order to form good panel spacing for the master block pattern.

DRESS DESIGN

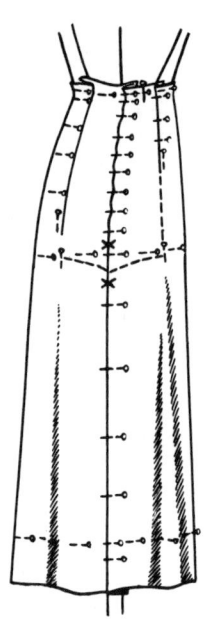

Fig. 21. Side front dart and side seam from hip to waist.

1. Smooth the lengthwise grain upward from the hips so that it is perpendicular to the waistline at a point halfway between the front dart and the side seam. Pin the fabric to the form at this point.

2. Work the excess between the pin and the center front into the dart, and the excess between the pin and the side seam into the shaping of the side seam.

3. Lay a dart which coincides with the blouse dart and which slopes slightly outward from the waist to the hip. Push the excess under toward the center front, and pin it perpendicular to the edge. This dart is much smaller than the one at the back and is therefore shorter. It is usually not more than 4 to 5 inches in length.

Forming the Side Seam Line from Hip to Waist (see Figure 21)

This line should be a smooth continuation of the line from the hip to the lower edge, but usually curves slightly forward in order to enter the waistline at a right angle.

1. Turn under the front seam allowance from waist to hip and pin it perpendicular to the edge but not into the form. Be careful not to stretch the slight curve.

2. Smooth the back gore from the dart to the side seam and slip the back seam allowance forward under the front.

3. Pin the front over the back at very close intervals over the hip curve, easing the front to the back slightly between the pins.

4. Study the entire seam. The forward curve from hip to waist should be so slight as to be almost imperceptible.

Marking the Waistline

Mark the waistline with pins from the center front to the center back, following the waistline of the form. If the waistline seems to be slightly loose, take it in later when easing the skirt to a belt. A little ease is usually retained along the waistline above the hip bone at the side front.

Marking the Hem Line

1. Check to see that the form is level and that it is adjusted to exactly the correct height.

2. Mark with pins, measuring with a tailor's square from the floor, or for speed, measuring from one pin to the next at not more than 3 inch intervals.

Checking the Skirt

Before removing the skirt from the form, check it for the following points:

1. The center front and center back lines should hang perpendicular to the floor.

2. The side seam line should divide the figure becomingly at the waistline and hipline.

3. The side seam should fall perpendicular to the floor from hip to lower edge.

4. The side seam should enter the waistline perpendicular to it.

5. Crossmarkings or hip balance points on the side seams should match exactly.

6. The back dart should be becomingly placed and in line with the blouse dart.

7. The side seam of the front gore should be slightly eased to the side seam of the back gore from hip to waist over the hip bone.

BASIC SKIRTS

8. The waistline and the hem line should be clearly marked with pins.

9. The skirt should hang straight and free from hip to hem without any trace of cupping in back or front, and without any sudden awkward flaring at the side.

PREPARING THE MASTER PATTERN FROM THE DRAPED TWO-GORE SKIRT

Marking the Pattern

1. Remove the skirt from the form, taking out only those few pins which are attached to the form.

2. Mark and crossmark the seams.

(a) Mark practice material with pencil and all other fabric with colored thread lines or sharpened chalk before removing the pins that hold the seams together.

(b) Mark the edge of each seam and each balance point with clear lines, and crossmark once below and twice above the balance point at the hip level.

(c) Mark the waistline and hem line.

(d) Remove all pins.

Trueing the Pattern (see Figure 22)

1. Smooth both sections of the skirt out flat on the table.

2. Draw a smooth curve at the waistline, starting perpendicular to the center front and center back and ending perpendicular to the side seams.

3. Smooth up the curves from the waistline to the hipline.

4. Rule the side seam lines from the balance point to the hem. Press the ruler down against the fabric as you do so, to prevent slipping.

Rule. Gore edges in all gored skirts must be straight, outward-slanting lines from the point on the hip at which the skirt breaks away from the body to the hem line. Always mark these edges with a ruler.

5. True up all dart lines with a ruler. The back dart as pinned is usually a slight outward curve that emphasizes the hollow of the back. Replace this curve with ruler lines.

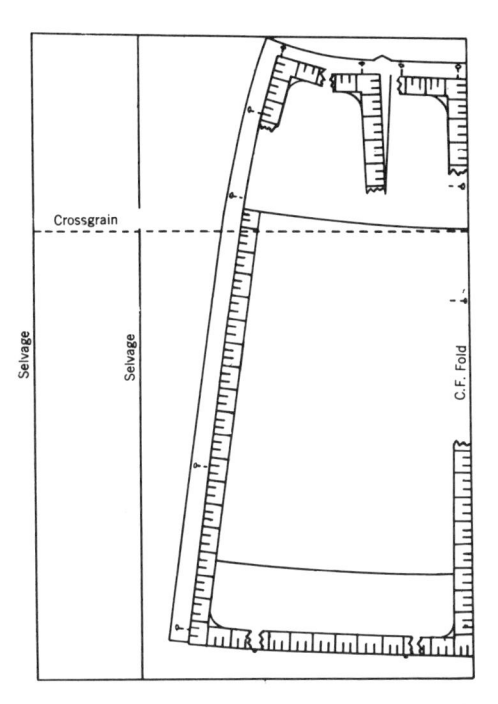

Fig. 22. Trueing the two-gore master skirt.

Note. When stitching the dart, curve the line slightly inward toward the fold to taper the point and to bridge over the hollow of the back.

6. True the hem line by squaring out with the L-square from the center front and from the side seam until the two lines intersect. On each of these lines, find the halfway mark between the intersection and the starting point at center front and side seam. Join the two halfway points with the ruler. Then redraw the line by hand, curving it smoothly (see Figure 22).

Transferring the Markings to the Opposite Half of Front and Back Gores

1. Fold both the front and back gores of the skirt on the center lines. The crosswise grain must be kept perpendicular to the lengthwise grain in both layers since it is liable to slip out of position in the under layer.

2. Pin the two layers together.

3. Trace around the trued up pattern with a tracing wheel on carbon paper or chalk board to transfer all seam lines and crossmarks to the under layer.

4. Cut with seam and hem allowances.

DRESS DESIGN

Problem 5

DRAPING THE SIX-GORE SKIRT

The six-gore skirt, consisting of three front and three back panels, has long found favor among women of all ages and sizes. With minor silhouette changes it has been adapted to many periods of fashion in the past, and is likely to be popular in the future because of its general becomingness. If the panels are skillfully placed for the individual figure, the skirt has a distinctly slenderizing effect. The vertical seam lines themselves seem to decrease the width of the hips by placing nearly all of the flare over the knees, thus producing a slender side silhouette. It is a graceful skirt, not only when the wearer stands still, but also when she moves.

Before draping the six-gore skirt, consider the following points on panel spacing and study Figures 23, 24, and 25.

(1) Always avoid equal spacing (see Figure 23). The central panel is usually wider than the two side ones unless the figure is very slight or the design requires a narrow central panel.

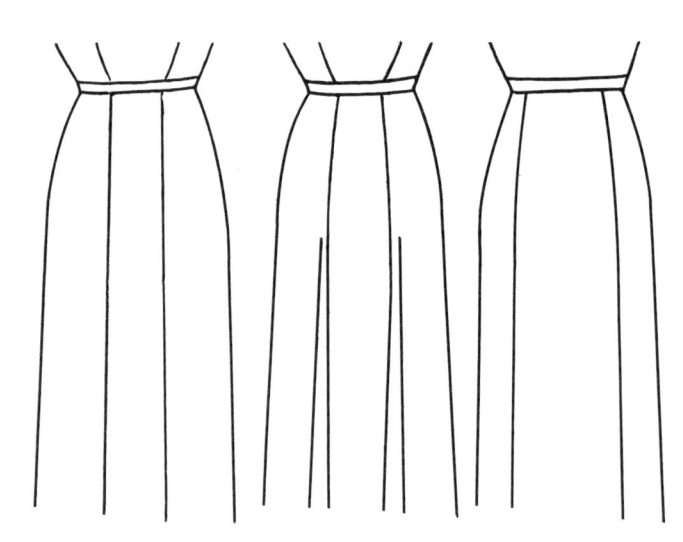

Fig. 23. Poor panel spacing: (1) Panel divides skirt into three equal spaces; (2) Central panel is parallel to center front.
Fig. 24. Good panel spacing: (1) Panel divides skirt becomingly; (2) Panel tapers at waistline.
Fig. 25. Central panel is too wide and does not taper into waistline.

(2) Always taper the panels at the waist (see Figure 24) so that they are in harmony with the contour of the figure as well as consistent with the silhouette of the skirt.

Constantly study trends in design and think of draping as a means of interpreting fashion silhouettes. Do not place seam lines mathematically, but try to relate them to the silhouette. Your designs will then have grace and individuality and will not be set or stereotyped. This is never more true than in draping skirts, since each one is certain to show the individuality of the draper.

Estimating the Fabric

Because the top and bottom edges both curve, allow extra length to shape them when figuring the length of fabric required. Measure from waistline to hem line and add the hem width plus an allowance of 3 inches for the curves at the top and bottom.

Draping the Center Front Panel (see Figure 26)

1. For a half muslin pattern, start with the selvage at the center front; for an entire skirt to wear, estimate the approximate width of the center panel at the hem line (the widest part of the panel) and add a generous seam allowance on each side. Here the directions are given for a half muslin pattern only so that they may be kept as simple as possible.

2. Pin the selvage at the center front of the form at both waist and hip, allowing about 1 inch above the waistline.

3. Smooth the fabric across the waistline and hip line. Pin it to the form at the waistline 2½ to 3 inches from the center front in order to hold the muslin in position while you drape the skirt.

4. Decide how far below the waistline the flare should begin. The point where the skirt begins to swing away from the body is called the *break*.

Note. The placing of the break is an important factor in establishing the final silhouette of the skirt. Although often at the hip level, it may be placed above or below that line at the point where the seam begins to slope outward more sharply.

5. Mark the panel width at the break point and also at the hem line.

72

BASIC SKIRTS

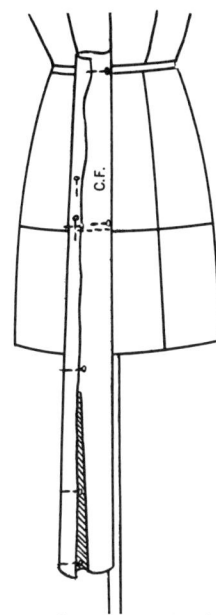

Fig. 26. Center front panel, six-gore skirt.

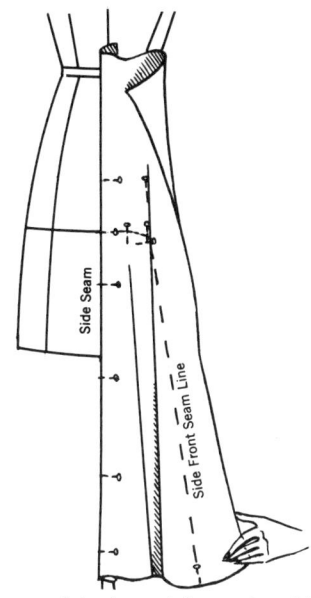

Fig. 27. Side front panel is draped from the side seam forward to meet the center front panel.

6. Crease a line between these two points, holding the fabric taut without stretching it.

7. Cut with a generous seam allowance (1½ inches) from the lower edge to the waistline. The panel narrows from the hip level to the waistline. Adjust the panel spacing at the waistline later.

8. Either take the panel off the form to true it up from hip to lower edge or turn the seam allowance under on the crease and pin it perpendicular to the edge while it is still on the form.

Draping the Side Front Panel (see Figure 27)

It would be possible to pin the straight lengthwise grain to the form at the center of this panel and to drape outward in both directions, but it is easier, and it saves fabric, to start at the side seam and work forward to the side front.

1. Establish the side seam line before placing the fabric on the form. To do this, fold under the seam allowance, putting in the desired flare from hip to hem. For a narrow silhouette, do not slope out the side seam more than 1½ inches at the hem line. For a slender figure and for a very narrow, stem-like skirt silhouette, an increase of ¾ inch from hip to hem may be enough. To save fabric, use the slanting edge just cut from the center front panel and reverse it. Pencil the straight grain, if it is not easy to see, so that the exact amount of outward slant can be checked.

2. Crease and pin the fold.

3. Place it at the side seam position so that it falls perpendicular to the floor. Pin it firmly to the form in two places — at the hip and again above it (see Figure 27).

4. Smooth the fabric forward at the hip level and pin it to support the crosswise grain in a practically level position for about 3 inches from the side seam. From this point let the grain drop toward the side front to introduce the flare. Continue to pin and drop the grain slightly to the side front seam.

Note. If the grain drops at once from the side seam it throws the flare toward the side. By supporting the grain level for at least 3 inches, the flare tends to fall at the side front rather than at the side seam.

5. Fold the fabric back on itself, slanting it forward enough so that the panel hangs perpendicular to the floor and so that it introduces the right amount of flare at the side front seam line.

6. Mark the width of the panel at the lower edge of the skirt with a pin and crease the line carefully between the break point and the pin at the lower edge.

7. Cut, leaving a 1½ inch seam allowance.

DRESS DESIGN

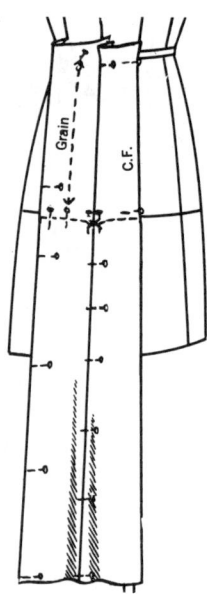

Fig. 28. Joining of center front and side front panels.

8. Crossmark clearly at the break point.

9. Turn the side front seam allowance forward and lap the center section over it. Join the two (see Figure 28), pinning perpendicular to the edge from the break point down to the hem line.

Note. Both the side seam and the side front seam should fall perpendicular to the floor from hip to hem. If either does not, lower or raise the crosswise grain at the hip until the seam is a plumb line, and then re-mark the seams.

Leave the skirt unfinished from hip to waist and proceed to drape the back.

Draping a Center Back Panel with a Low-Placed Flare
(see Figure 29)

Ordinarily, draping the back of the six-gore skirt is largely a repetition of draping the front. But in order to introduce a new problem here, we give the procedure for adding a low-placed rippling flare at the side back. The two kinds of flares may not be used in the same skirt, but there is no reason as far as design is concerned why a skirt should not have a slight flare at the front and a decided ripple at the back.

1. Pin the center line, which should follow the straight lengthwise grain, to the center back of the form at both waist and hip.

2. Smooth the fabric across the hip and pin it to the form with two pins, one to indicate the panel width at the hip, and a second to indicate the break point. Do not place the break point so low that it divides the skirt in half. The proportion will be better if the flare starts well above the center (see Figure 29).

3. Measure at the lower edge the width of the center back panel and mark it with a pin. Allow enough width for a pronounced ripple.

4. Cut the center panel down from the waistline to the point where the flare is to start. This should be done with a seam allowance of 1½ inches.

5. Clip the seam allowance at the break point to within a few threads of the seam line in order to let the panel fall perpendicular to the floor even though the flare is pronounced. The panel should be wide enough at the lower edge to ripple, but not so wide that the flare is heavy and clumsy.

6. Turn the fabric back over itself to get a straight slanting line from the point of break to the lower edge, then crease and pin the fold perpendicular to the edge (see Figure 29).

7. Cut with a wide seam allowance (1¼ to 1½ inches) to allow for let-out.

8. Fold under the seam allowance and re-pin it carefully without stretching the bias line. Figure 30 shows the panel when it falls free.

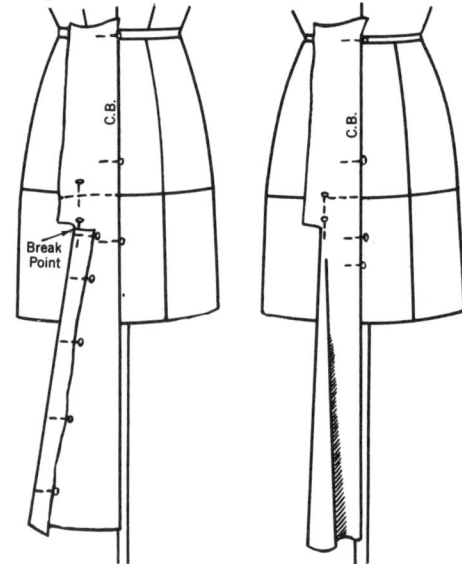

Fig. 29. Center back panel flaring low.
Fig. 30. Panel falling perpendicular to the floor after the seam is clipped.

74

BASIC SKIRTS

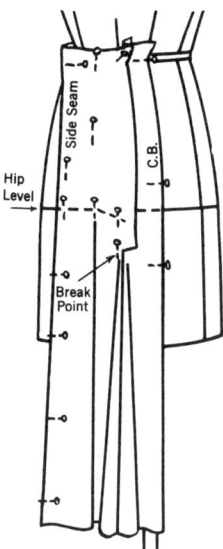

Fig. 31. Side back panel is draped from the side seam toward the side back and pinned to the center back panel from hip to hem.

Draping the Side Back Panel (see Figure 31)

1. Start the side back gore the same way as the side front one. For a slender side silhouette, slant out the side seam about 1½ inches from hip to lower edge. Fold and pin the side seam line to the form in two places, at the hip and again above it. The line should fall against the side seam edge of the skirt front.

2. Smooth the fabric across the form toward the center back. Support the grain nearly level for about 3 inches, then drop the grain toward the center back panel to introduce flare at the lower edge.

3. Pin the side section against the center back panel at the point of break. The point of break on the side back and center back panels must exactly coincide.

4. Trim the seam from the waistline to the point of break, leaving an allowance of 1½ inches. At the break, clip the seam allowance as you clipped the center panel.

5. Let the grain drop from this point for a ripple equal to that of the center panel.

6. Place a pin at the lower edge to indicate the panel width. The seam usually hangs better if it flares equally on both edges. However, if you place more flare on the center panel, a one-sided ripple swings out over the seam away from the center back. An equalized flare, on the other hand, balances the ripple on each side of the seam or falls into a deep unpressed fold or pleat.

7. Fold the fabric back on itself and pin it between the point of break and the lower edge.

8. Cut with a 1¼ to 1½ inch seam allowance.

9. Pin the seam from the break point to the hem, this time with pins running in the direction of the seam so that the ripple falls as if it were stitched. Stretch the seam slightly to make it hang perpendicular to the floor.

Note. Since a bias line tends to bow out in the center when it is stretched, straighten this line with a long ruler when trueing up the pattern after removing it from the form.

Caution. When you drape the side section of a gored skirt, it is easy to become confused and cut *in* on the grain at the lower edge of the side section. Since every gore edge must always be an *outward* slanting line, check this carefully before cutting the edge of the side gore.

Adjusting the Skirt from Hip to Waistline (see Figures 32 and 33)

Although the skirt is still unfinished from hip to waistline, its character has by this stage been completely established.

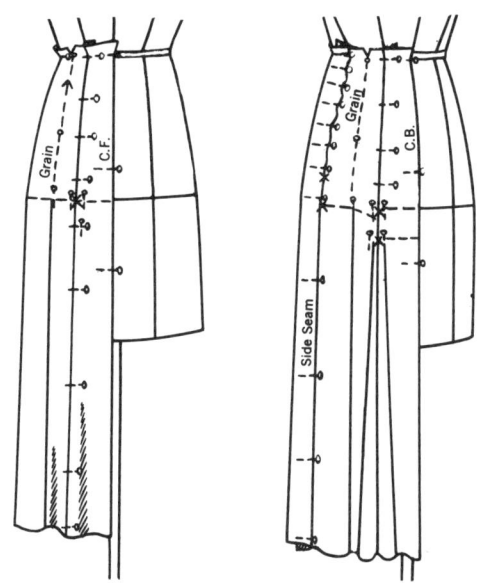

Fig. 32. Six-gore skirt front completed.
Fig. 33. Six-gore skirt back completed.

75

DRESS DESIGN

1. Decide on the width of both center front and center back panels at the waistline. They should taper in toward the waistline to meet the panel-spacing of the blouse. The line should be a straight slanting line, not a curved one, as that would emphasize the abdomen. The slant may continue the one from hip to hem or it may be smaller, but it should not be greater.

2. Fold under the seam allowance from hip to waist.

3. Trim the seam above the waistline to ⅝ inch.

A wider seam would make it impossible to fit the curved waistline closely.

4. Smooth the lengthwise grain in both the side front and side back panels up toward the waistline so that it is perpendicular to it at the center of each gore. Clip the waistline seam above these points and pin the fabric to the form at the waistline.

5. From the center of each side gore, work the excess fabric toward the center front and back, and lap the center panels over the side ones, pinning at right angles to the edge.

6. From the center of each side gore, push the excess toward the side seam and pin to the form at the waistline. Do not stretch the waistline seam, but do not leave any ease.

7. Lap the front edge of the hip seam over the back, easing the front slightly as you attach it to the back, and pin it at close intervals. (See directions for pinning the hip seam of the two-gore skirt, page 70.)

8. Mark both the waistline and the hem line with pins.

DRAPING THE SIX-GORE SKIRT WITH A PLEAT IN THE GORE

The pleated skirt explained on pages 62-63 was a straight skirt and was pleated all around. A side pleat in a gored skirt, however, hangs awkwardly if laid on the grain, and the center panel if absolutely parallel to the center front appears narrower at the lower edge than at the hips. This is because the silhouette line of the skirt flares outward all the way from hip to hem, whereas the center panel line remains the same width as shown in Figure 34a. The optical illusion is even more apparent on a figure with heavy hips and

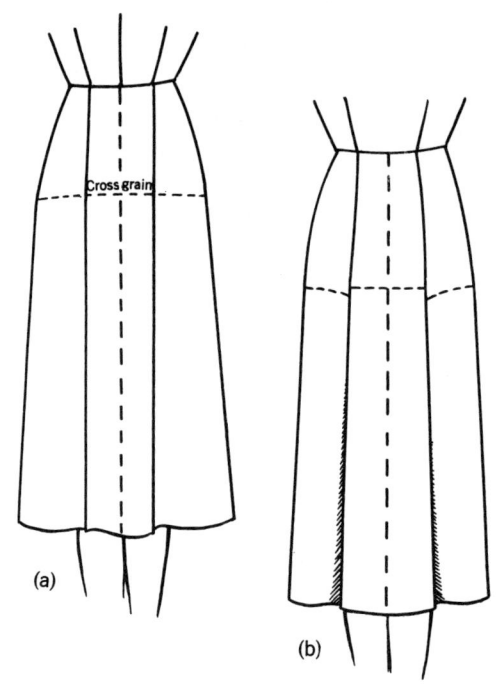

Fig. 34. (a) Poor. Side pleats laid on the grain form a panel which appears narrower at the hem; (b) Better. Side pleats gored out slightly harmonize with the contour and also increase the hem width.

thighs and a relatively small waistline, since the eye always unconsciously compares the shape of a skirt panel with the silhouette of the figure. Another reason for goring the pleat line slightly outward (see Figure 34b) is to widen the lower edge so that the pleat will not spread apart and will hold a press better. Pleats popping open at the lower edge contribute nothing to neatness and slenderness. But since it is impossible to press pleats that are very far off the grain, there must be a seam at the undercrease of the pleat, and wherever there is a group of two or more pleats, there must be a seam at the undercrease of each one. Otherwise each pleat folded into the cloth takes on more bias than the one before and neither presses nor hangs well.

The fiber and weave of fabric for a pleated skirt must also be considered. The fabric should not only take and hold creases but should stand many pressings. A firm wool is obviously the best choice unless it is too bulky or heavy. Pleats in heavy tweed, for example, stand out awkwardly, and the seams at the undercreases are thick and clumsy.

BASIC SKIRTS

Draping the Center Panel with a Side Pleat in the Side Front Seam (see Figure 35)

1. Follow the same procedure as for the center front panel of a regulation six-gore skirt, but add to its width the depth of the pleat plus a seam allowance.

2. Pin the panel to the form at the waist and hip on the center front.

3. Measure the width of the panel at the hip and also at the hem. It should not increase more than ¾ to 1 inch at the lower edge, which is just enough to make the panel appear to be straight. The amount of increase varies slightly with the silhouette of the individual figure.

4. Mark with pins the panel width at hip and hem.

5. Decide on the top point of the pleat.

6. Decide on the depth (width) of the pleat.

7. Remove the panel from the form and rule the line marking its edge, then, parallel to it, the line marking the depth of the pleat.

8. Cut with a seam allowance, fold on the panel line, and pin.

9. Replace the panel on the form and pin it along the center front line at waistline and hip, and again at the side front at the hip to support the crosswise grain.

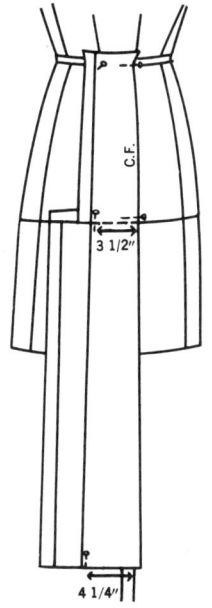

Fig. 35. Center front panel with a side pleat in the side front seam.

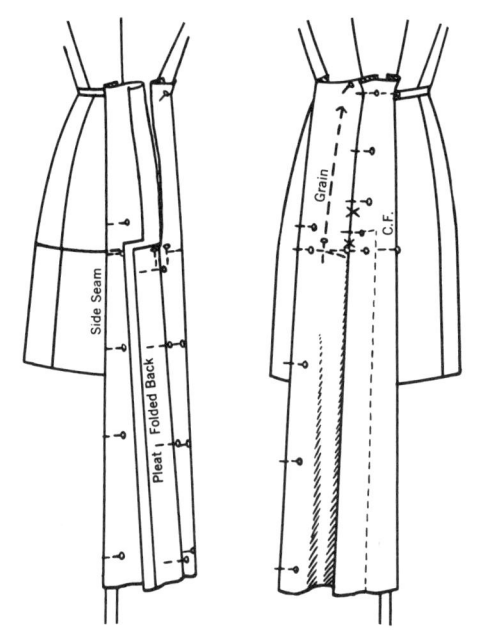

Fig. 36. Side front panel showing allowance for pleat.
Fig. 37. Side front joined to center front panel and pleat pinned at undercrease (shown by dotted line).

Draping the Side Panel with a Side Pleat in the Side Front Seam (see Figure 36)

1. Follow the same procedure as for the side front panel of a regulation six-gore skirt, but add the depth of the pleat plus a seam allowance to the side front edge.

2. Establish the side seam position and pin it to the form, and pin it to the form again at a point about three inches in from the side seam. Then lower the crosswise grain slightly toward the front to introduce just enough width on the side section so that the pleat will stay closed. A sudden dropping of grain would produce a ripple which would be inconsistent with the sharply pressed pleat edge next to it. Anchor the side section to the form along the hip level up to the point where it meets the center panel edge.

3. Mark the width of the panel at the lower edge.

4. Fold the fabric back on itself between the hip and the hem, and pin the fold.

5. Mark the top of the pleat in line with the marking on the center panel, and measure back from the fold the depth of the pleat plus the seam allowance.

6. Trim, leaving a 1¼ inch seam allowance.

DRESS DESIGN

7. Crossmark the break point carefully. Unpin the seam from hip to hem, and lap the front over the side front, pinning the pleat edge of the center panel to the side section (see Figure 37). Later, when trueing up the side front panel, rule the line on which the pleat crease falls and crossmark it between hip and hem. Always match the pleat crease with this line before pinning the seam at the back of the pleat.

8. Finish the top from hip to waist exactly as for the top of a standard gored skirt.

Note. The fabric is more nearly bias on the side front panel at the pleat line than on the center front pleat crease, as Figure 37 shows. This is the principal advantage of a side pleat over an inverted or box pleat in a side gore. The side pleat allows plenty of room over the thighs at the side front, and yet the pressed edge is nearly straight and therefore holds a crease. Figure 38, on the other hand, shows an inverted box pleat which must be pressed on both edges. Hence the grain at the side front edge must also be nearly straight. Try both kinds and you will see that this is true.

When stitching is objectionable across the top of a pleat (for example, in a soft crepe), carry the pleat up to the waistline so that it can be supported at the belt line. It can then be stitched down as far as you wish on the wrong side in order to avoid top stitching.

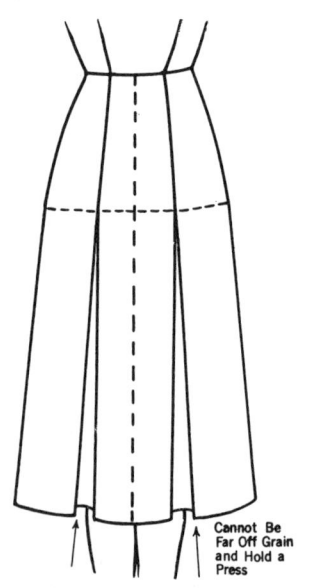

Fig. 38. An inverted box pleat in a side front gore. Pleats are apt to spread apart.

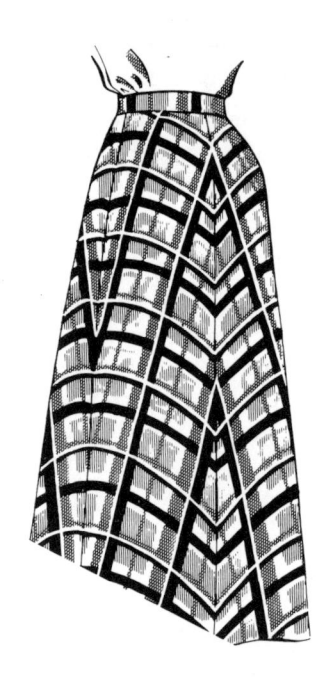

Fig. 39. The lines of a plaid curve in a four-gore skirt.

Problem 6

DRAPING THE FOUR-GORE SKIRT

The four-gore skirt with center front and back seams can be adapted to either tailored or soft styles depending on the amount of flare introduced. Since it has only one seam in front and one in back, the possibility of introducing flare by slanting the seams outward is very limited, and any pronounced ripple must come primarily from lowering the crosswise grain toward the seams. This produces a softer, more circular type of skirt than one that is gored out at the seams. If any appreciable amount of flare is to be introduced, the center front and back seams have to be so much on the bias that the design is not suitable for fabrics that are loosely woven or stretchy, since such fabrics need more seams to "stay" them. The pattern of the fabric must also be considered in choosing this type of skirt. The diagonal lines of a twill, for example, appear mismatched at the bias center front and back seams, and stripes and plaids take on curving diagonal lines such as shown in Figure 39. But for a firm, soft fabric without pronounced pattern, the four-gore skirt is a good choice of cut, especially when the design of the dress focuses interest at the center of the figure.

78

BASIC SKIRTS

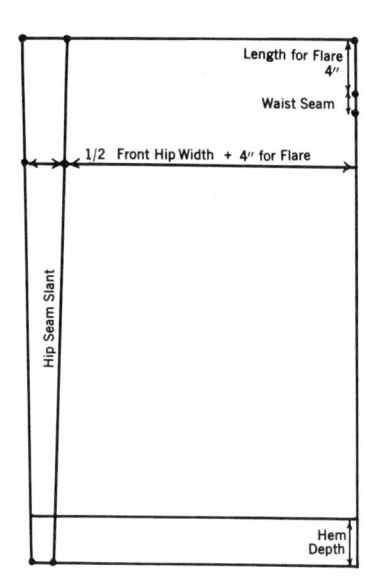

Fig. 40. Fabric estimate for four-gore skirt.

Estimating the Fabric (see Figure 40)

1. To determine the length of the panels, measure from the waistline to the hem line and add a hem allowance and a waistline seam plus approximately 4 inches for lowering the grain to produce flare at the lower edge.

2. Measure around the hips from the center front or back to the side seam and add at least 5 inches for flare at the lower edge. As the flare increases, the extra length for lowering the grain must also be increased.

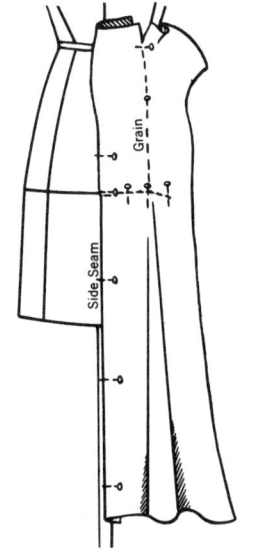

Fig. 41. Four-gore — adjustment on the form.

Adjusting the Fabric on the Form (see Figure 41)

1. Establish the side seam line before placing the fabric on the form. Fold the seam allowance under, sloping out 1 inch from hip to hem for a narrow silhouette. On a selvage, fold the fabric back 1 inch at the lower edge and 2 inches at the hipline, and pin the fold perpendicular to the edge.

2. Place the creased fold against the form at the side of the hip so that it falls perpendicular to the floor from hip to hem.

3. Pin the fold to the form once at the hip level and again 2 or 3 inches above the hip level, so that the seam will not shift. Except for a generous hem, the excess length should all be above the waistline.

Adjusting the Flare at the Center Front (see Figures 41 and 42)

1. Smooth the crosswise grain along the hip level line from the side seam toward the center front. Decide at what point you wish the first flare to fall. This will usually be over the knee and about 5 inches in from the side seam toward the front. Pin the fabric to the form at this point on the hip line. Above this pin, smooth the lengthwise grain upward so that it is perpendicular to the waistline. Then pin the fabric to the form at the waistline. If the lengthwise grain is not anchored perpendicular to the waistline at this point, the flare will swing out toward the side seam.

2. To drop the grain from this point toward the center front, slash through the excess fabric above the waistline down to within $1/2$ inch of the waistline seam (see Figure 41).

3. Drop the grain at the hip level for the center front flare and pin to the form along this line to the center front (see Figure 42).

4. Smooth the fabric up to the waist and pin along the waistline toward the center front, stretching the fabric slightly.

5. Trim the waistline seam to $1/2$ inch.

Note. A very slight drop in grain produces a practically straight skirt, whereas a decided drop creates a circular, flared effect. However, there is a limit to the amount that you can lower the grain and still fit the figure closely from hip to waist. The greater the flare, the higher up it must begin. A skirt which flares

DRESS DESIGN

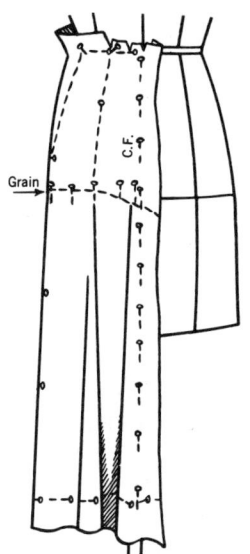

Fig. 42. Four-gore — arrangement of the flares.

directly from the waistline should more properly be classified as a circular skirt. See directions for draping the circular skirt, page 85.

It is also true that the more the skirt flares the more curved the waistline becomes, which makes it necessary to clip and stretch the waistline to fit the figure closely above the hips.

Study the skirt contour for both amount and placement of flare. Guard against placing the flares far out toward the side of the figure, leaving a flat area at the center, for the flares would then have the same broadening effect as a wide panel. Yet if you place all of the flare at the center front seam, the flare swings out awkwardly from the body. Try to place flares so that the silhouette is good from all angles.

Marking the Center Front Line (see Figure 42)

1. Mark with pins a line perpendicular to the floor from waistline to hem.

2. Trim the seam with a 1½ inch allowance.

Marking the Hemline

1. Adjust the form to the correct height.

2. Mark the hem line with pins.

3. Cut, allowing a generous hem (4 inches, at least). If the flares are too exaggerated, raise the grain to remove some of the fullness. This reduces the hem sweep but shortens the skirt.

Checking the Side Seam from Hip to Hem

Keeping the skirt anchored at the hip level on the side seam line, check to see that the side seam falls perpendicular to the floor from the hip down.

Draping the Skirt Back

Follow the same procedure as for the front. More flare falls from the hips at the back because of the hip curve, even though the skirt still fits smoothly from hips to waist.

Adjusting the Side Seam from Hip to Waistline

1. Smooth the fabric from the center of the gore toward the side seam line. Pin the waistline to the form at the side seam and trim the excess above it to ¾ inch. Allow a more generous side seam near the waistline for let out, since a prominent hip bone at the side front, or a decided side curve on the hip, throws the flare to the side. To offset this it is necessary to lower the grain at the waistline near the side seam and to ease the excess into the seam from the hip to the waist.

2. Fold the fabric back upon itself and trim the seam to leave an allowance of about 1¼ inches.

3. Crease the folded seam line, turn the fabric under to the wrong side on the crease, and lap the front over the back, pinning it perpendicular to the edge.

Caution. Crossmark clearly the hip level balance points.

Marking and Trueing the Pattern (see Figure 43)

1. On the side seam, crossmark the back and front, at the hip level and twice above it, in order to distribute ease along the front edge. Rule the side seam from the widest point of the hip curve to the hem.

2. The waistline should be marked clearly and accurately. Since the curve of this line controls the position of the ripples, any variation in it will affect the hang of the skirt. Support the waistline on a snug waistband to preserve the curve exactly before fitting the skirt.

3. Since the center front and center back seam lines are on a sharp bias, stretch them slightly. This, although necessary, bows out the bias line even though

BASIC SKIRTS

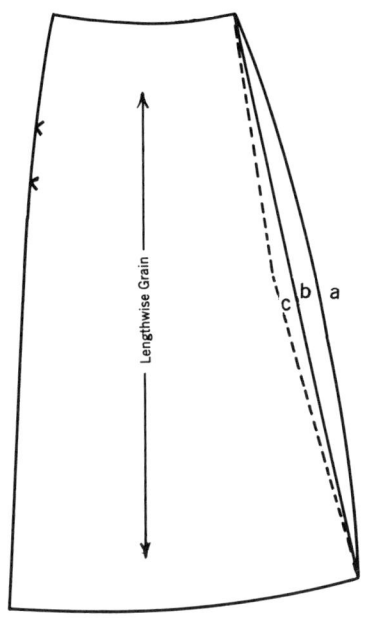

Fig. 43. Line *a* shows how the center front seam bends outward when stretched. Line *b* shows the center front trued with a ruler. Line *c* shows the center front line after tension is relaxed.

it originally appeared to be straight. To correct this bowed effect, follow the directions below (see Figure 43):

(a) Lay the pattern flat on the table with the crosswise threads at right angles to the lengthwise threads.

(b) Stretch both center front and center back biases.

(c) Lay a yardstick on each of these lines and chalk new straight lines.

SUMMARY: PRINCIPLES OF DRAPING ALL GORED SKIRTS

After you have draped a two-, four-, and six-gore skirt and have introduced pleats as well as flares into the gores, the draping of eight, ten, or even more gores presents few new problems. The principles and procedures are always very much the same with one exception. As the gores increase in number and consequently become narrower, the flares must be introduced more by slanting out the edges of the gores than by lowering the grain within the gores.

Keeping in mind this one variable, it is possible to summarize the principles of draping all gored skirts. The factors determining the character (the position and amount of flare) of all gored skirts are:

1. The amount and the side of the gore toward which the crosswise grain is dropped at the hip line within the gore.

2. The amount that the seam edges are slanted out from the point of the break to the lower edge and the high or low placement of the break point.

3. The size and location of body curves, that is, the contour of the figure itself.

Shape of Gore Edges

1. All gored skirts have ruler-straight outward slanting lines at all seam edges from the point of the break down, and the seams fall perpendicular to the floor if the fabric is soft and clinging. The seams enter the hem line perpendicular to it.

2. The lines of the skirt from the point of the break to the waistline are all straight lines slanting inward at all edges except the side seam, which is curved. All seams enter the waistline perpendicular to it.

3. The waistline and hem line are curves meeting the sides of the panels at right angles.

Position of the Lengthwise Grain

1. Drape center gores for two-, six-, and ten-gore skirts with the straight lengthwise grain at the center of the gore.

2. Drape all gores which have evenly balanced flares with the lengthwise grain at the center.

3. Drape side gores and those with more flare at one edge than the other by establishing the less flared edge first between the hip and the hem line. The minimum flare should be ¾ to 1½ inches.

CIRCULAR SKIRTS

The hem sweep of a circular skirt is determined for the most part by the intensity of the arc or curve of the waistline of the skirt in relation to the waistline

81

DRESS DESIGN

curve of the body, whereas the fullness in a typical gored skirt is determined by the sloping out of each gore on the seams as well as the lowering of the grain within the gore. The gored skirt generally flares from the hip level or lower, but the full circular skirt starts to flare from the waistline or immediately below it.

Circular skirts are of four general kinds, according to the amount of sweep at the hem line. These may be called:

(1) the normal,
(2) the less-than-normal,
(3) the greater-than-normal,
(4) the maximum.

1. *The Normal Circular Skirt* (see Figures 44 *a* and *b*) fits the waist and hip lines smoothly. The hem sweep is determined by the difference between the waistline and hipline measurements of the individual figure. That is, the greater the difference between the waist and hip sizes of the individual, the greater the hem sweep will be (see Figure 44 *a*). A skirt for a figure with a normal waistline but with very slender hips (see Figure 44 *b*) will have practically no flare in the front and only a little in the back. The most marked difference between waist and hip size is usually in the back, but on a few figures there is a decided curve on the side of the hip. If you observe a number of different figures and note carefully the differences between them in waist and hip measurements, it is easy to understand why normal circular skirts vary so much in the amount of hem sweep and in the location of the flare.

2. *The Less-Than-Normal Circular Skirt* (see Figure 45) fits the hips smoothly but has less flare at the hem than would ordinarily result from the difference between waist and hip measurements. The hem sweep is controlled either to fit the limitations of a narrow fabric or to get a particular silhouette. An example of this is a skirt designed with a very flat, plain front in order to contrast with a bustle back. Such contrast is essential to relieve the flatness of the contour. This skirt seldom has a side seam. Instead, the fabric is usually carried beyond the side toward the back to the limit of its width. Darts must be used at the waistline to dispose of the excess above the hips, and often a peplum or girdle drapery is used to conceal the darts.

3. *The Greater-Than-Normal Circular Skirt* (see Figure 46) is the typical one. It fits only at the waistline and flares from well above the hips. The lower edge may have any sweep desired. The relation of the waistline size to the sweep of the hem will determine the fullness over the hips. This cut is usually limited to evening dresses, hostess gowns, and skating and ballet skirts, and is at its best on a slim-waisted figure. It may, however, be used to camouflage broad hips if the waistline is small and the fabric is stiff enough to give the illusion that the extension around the hips is due to folds in the fabric rather than to hip size. The greater-than-normal circular skirt can be interpreted in both stiff and soft fabrics, and its silhouette is the direct result of the character of the fabric chosen.

4. *The Maximum Circular Skirt* is a complete circle with a hole cut in the center to fit the waistline. It flares straight out to the hem without fitting the body at all below the level of the waist. Although this cut is called "maximum," it is possible to increase the sweep still further. If the complete circle has a hole

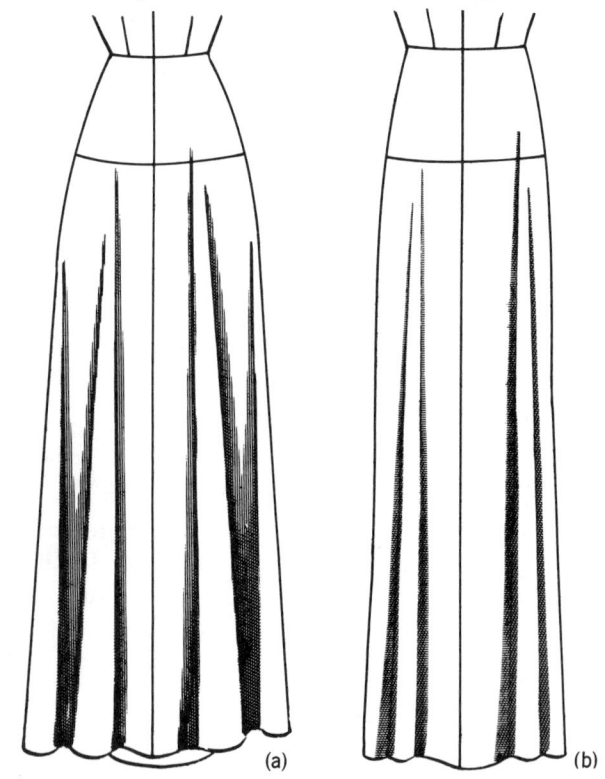

Fig. 44. (*a*) Normal circular skirt. The waistline of the figure is small in relation to the hips; (*b*) Normal circular skirt. The waistline of the figure is large in relation to the hips.

BASIC SKIRTS

Fig. 45. Less-than-normal circular skirt, showing excess darted out of waistline.

Fig. 46. Greater-than-normal circular skirt that fits only at the waistline.

cut in the center to fit not the entire waistline but just the waistline front, and this circle is slashed from the center to the outer edge and seamed to a' circle that fits the back, there will be twice as much fullness. Nets, marquisettes, and chiffons, unless buoyed up by unusual fullness, hang limp and appear to be skimpy. The fold upon fold of these exaggerated circular cuts also deepens the color of transparent fabrics. The fluffy bouffant effect at the upper edge of the skirt can even be increased by cutting the hole at the center of the circle larger than the waistline of the figure in order to gather it. Flares that come so close together and start at the waistline are becoming to petite, small-waisted figures only, and their exaggerated extension must be contrasted by slender, closely fitted bodices that define a tiny waistline. Without this contrast the whole effect is bulky and clumsy.

Now that we have seen something of the general types of circular skirts, and the principles on which they are designed, let us examine the procedures for draping them.

Problem 7
DRAPING THE NORMAL CIRCULAR SKIRT
(see Figures 47 and 48)

This, you will remember, is the skirt in which the sweep of the hem is controlled largely by the difference between the waist and hip measurements and by the contour of the body. The following directions are for draping a half-pattern in muslin. The estimate of material required will depend largely on the desired length of the skirt.

Adjusting the Fabric on the Form (see Figure 47)

1. Place the selvage of the muslin at the center front of the form with the top at least $2\frac{1}{2}$ inches above the waistline. Use the excess above the waist to drop the crosswise grain toward the side seam and to allow for a $\frac{1}{2}$ inch waistline seam.

Note. Since this is a half-pattern, the center front should be placed on a lengthwise fold when you cut the pattern from actual dress fabric.

2. Pin the cloth to the form on the center front at the waist and hip with the selvage falling in a plumb line to the floor. Clip the selvage if it draws or curls.

Adjusting the Crossgrain

Drop the crosswise grain from the center front toward the side seam enough to fit the waistline snugly and the hips with slight ease.

1. Pin the fabric at the waistline about 2 inches from the center front, keeping the crosswise grain level.

2. Clip through the excess above the waist to the pin.

3. Drop the grain from the pin outward just enough to fit the waist closely and the hips with slight ease.

Place a second pin at the waist level two inches farther toward the side and in the same manner continue to pin, clip, and drop the grain to the side seam. Stretch the fabric slightly to make it fit more tightly at the waistline and to throw more flare at the lower edge.

DRESS DESIGN

Marking the Waistline

Mark the waistline with pins from the center front around to the center back.

Marking the Hemline

Mark this line with pins. To mark a floor length hem, adjust the form to the correct height, place it on a table, and mark against a corner of the table.

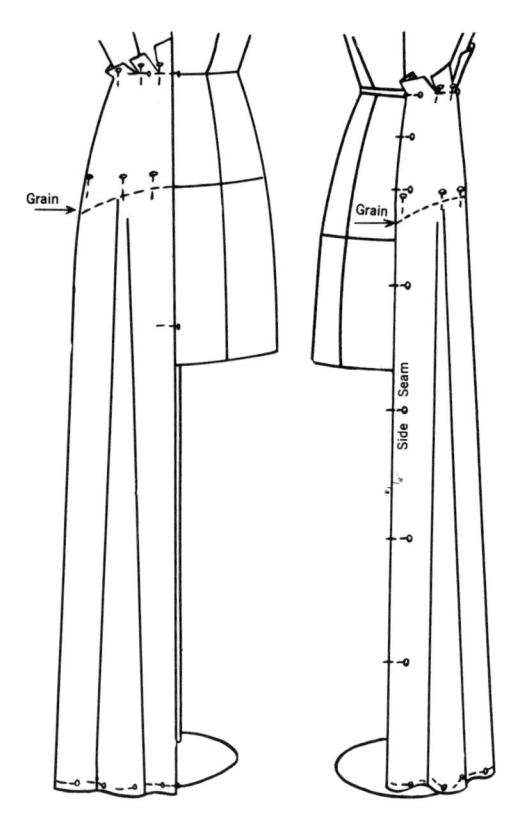

Fig. 47. Draping procedure for the normal circular skirt.

Fig. 48. Side seam adjustment for the normal circular skirt.

Adjusting the Side Seam Line (see Figure 48)

1. Turn the fabric back on itself and pin a line perpendicular to the floor from the waist to the hem. In the normal circular skirt, continue this outward curve from the hip to the hem line with a straight ruled line slanting outward.

2. Cut with a 1¼ inch seam allowance.

3. Crease the edge, remove the pins, turn the seam to the wrong side, and re-pin it perpendicular to the edge. If the fabric is wide, the seam can be placed at the side back and concealed under a flare or fold if doing so improves the design.

Draping the Skirt Back

1. Drape the back like the front.

2. Pin the front and back together, lapping the front over the back.

Problem 8

DRAPING THE LESS-THAN-NORMAL CIRCULAR SKIRT (see Figures 49 and 50)

This type of skirt is controlled by the size of the hips and by a specified hem width.

Adjusting the Fabric on the Form (see Figure 49)

1. Place the selvage on the center front or center back line of the form with the top edge less than 2 inches above the waistline.

2. Pin the cloth to the center front or center back of the form at the waist and hip, with the selvage falling perpendicular to the floor. As in Problem 7, this is a half-pattern.

Adjusting the Crossgrain

1. Determine the width at the hem line according to the silhouette effect desired and mark the hem width with a pin. Drape from hip to hem line first, since these are the two determining circumferences.

2. Smooth the fabric over from the center front or the center back to the side seam along the hip level, allowing the crosswise grain to drop just enough for the desired hem sweep. (Marked by a pin in step 1.)

Note. A variation of this method is given at the end of the directions for this problem.

3. Anchor the fabric to the form at the hipline so that the side seam falls perpendicular to the floor from hip to lower edge.

4. To fit the waistline, take up the excess above the hipline into darts placed to meet the dart lines of the blouse at the waistline.

BASIC SKIRTS

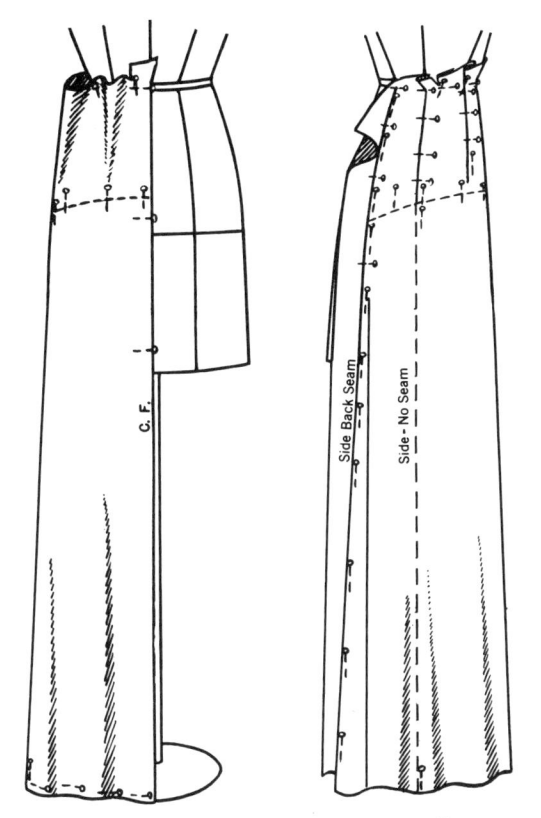

Fig. 49. Less-than-normal circular skirt — adjustment on the form.

Fig. 50. Less-than-normal circular variation. A seam is placed at the side back and a dart substituted for the hip seam.

Marking the Waistline and Hemline

Mark with pins while the fabric is on the form.

Note. Variation beginning with step 2 under "Adjusting the Crossgrain." Because this skirt is very narrow, the side seam may be omitted and the front panel may be carried around to the side back as far as the width of the fabric will allow. This places the seam at the side back and substitutes a long curved dart for the seam at the side of the hip (see Figure 50).

Problem 9

DRAPING THE GREATER-THAN-NORMAL CIRCULAR SKIRT (see Figures 51, 52, and 53)

The character of this skirt is formed by the waistline and hemline arcs.

Adjusting the Fabric on the Form (see Figure 51)

1. Place the selvage of the muslin on the center front line of the form, with the top of the fabric extending 5 to 7 inches above the waistline, depending on the amount of flare to be introduced. When actually cutting the skirt from dress goods, place the center front of the pattern on a lengthwise fold.

2. Pin the muslin to the center front of the form at the waist and hip, and check to see that it hangs perpendicular to the floor.

Method of Draping Flares

1. Pin the fabric to the waistline at a point 2 inches away from the center front, keeping the crosswise grain level.

2. Clip the excess above the waistline down to the pin.

3. Drop the grain enough to produce a flare of the desired depth.

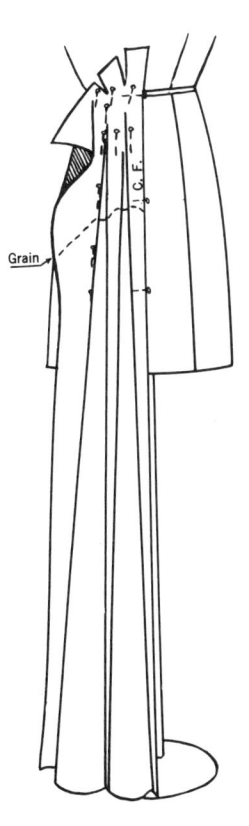

Fig. 51. Full circular skirt — adjustment on the form.

85

DRESS DESIGN

Note. By holding the bulk of the fabric up in the left hand and lifting or lowering the grain to allow the right hand to shape the flare in the lower edge of the skirt, you can set each flare carefully and control its size. In such fabrics as heavy faille, costume velvet, and moiré taffeta, flares several inches deep are effective because they round out in clean-cut lines, whereas flares in silk crepe or jersey of the same depth fall into soft limp folds. This indicates that the grain should be lowered more to form the flares in a stiff fabric than in a soft one. Notice also that as the depth of each flare is increased, the space between flares can also be increased.

4. Place the next pin at the waistline to support the grain for the flare just determined and to place the next flare. Stretch the fabric along the waistline to keep the skirt smooth immediately below it, and continue to pin, clip, and lower the grain to the side seam.

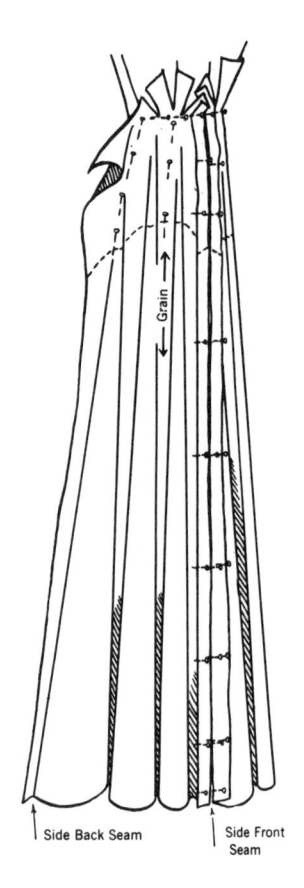

Fig. 52. Full circular with seams at side front and side back.

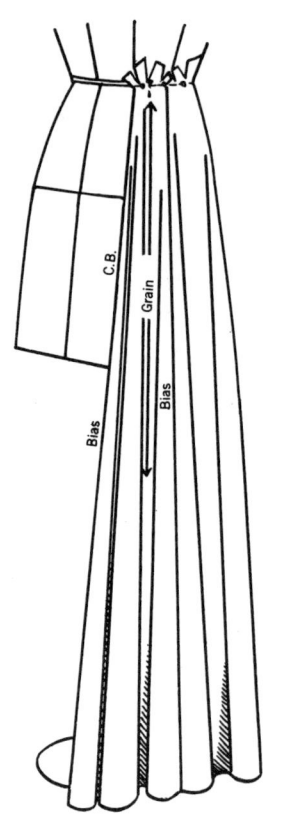

Fig. 53. Full circular back view. Note the position of the grain.

Note. If the flares are at all deep and the skirt is floor length, the fabric will be too narrow at the lower edge to reach the side seam without piecing. This is undesirable in any fabric that shows the piecing, so that it is advisable when using such materials to place seams at the side front and back as well as directly on the side. See Figures 52 and 53.

5. Mark the side seam as for a normal circular skirt.

Standards for Draping Circular Skirts

In draping circular skirts, the following three points should always be kept in mind:

1. Becoming placement of flares. If placed out too far on the sides, they broaden and shorten the body.

2. Correct size of flares for the texture of the fabric and the height of the wearer.

3. Consistency in depth of all flares.

BASIC SKIRTS

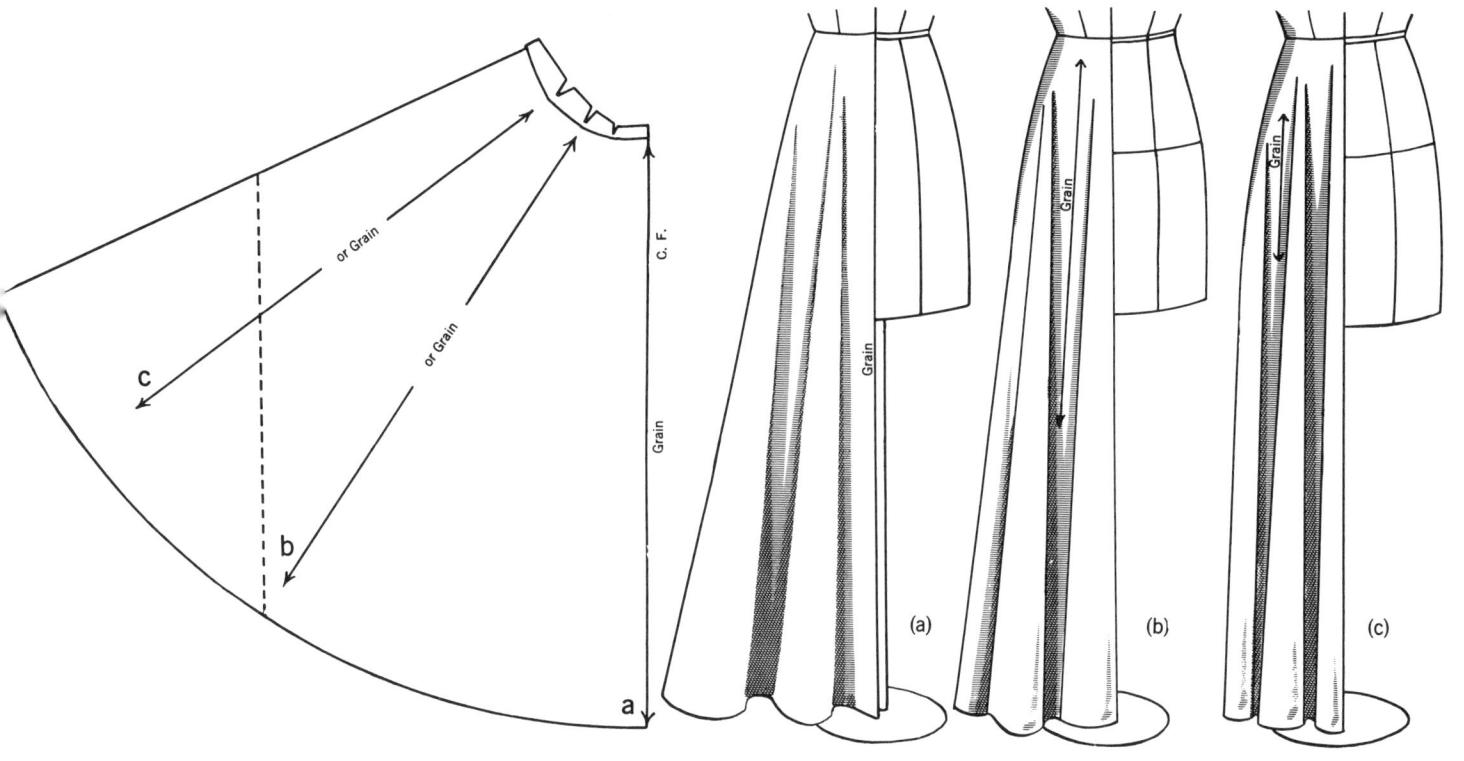

Fig. 54. Three possible grain positions in a full circular skirt: (1) Line *a* shows the grain position in Skirt 55 (*a*); (2) Line *b* shows the grain position in Skirt 55 (*b*); (3) Line *c* shows the grain position in Skirt 55 (*c*). (The dotted line shows the position of piecing for narrow fabric, if the center front is placed on the grain.)

Fig. 55. Three silhouettes produced by the three grain positions diagramed in Fig. 54.

Placing the Grain on a Circular Skirt Pattern

There are three possible ways in which the grain may be placed in a full circular skirt. The one you choose should depend on the width of the dress fabric you are using and the silhouette you desire.

1. If the fabric is wide enough to accommodate the entire skirt front, place the center front of the circular skirt pattern on the lengthwise fold. In some fabrics, inconspicuous piecing can be made at the lower edge along the side seam by joining along a lengthwise thread on both the main panel and the piecing. Always piece in the direction of the wale of a piqué or the floats of a satin weave.

2. When you use a separate width for each half of the skirt front, place the lengthwise grain-marking at the center of the pattern section perpendicular to the waistline so that the center front seam will be on the bias or partially on the bias.

3. Follow the procedure given in step 2, but place the lengthwise grain perpendicular to the waistline at a point about 3 inches in from the side seam at the hip level, so that the grain is nearly straight at the side of the body and practically on a true bias at the center front. Figure 55 *a*, *b*, and *c* show three variations in silhouette brought about by the three different ways of placing the grain.

PEPLUMS

Peplums should be draped in much the same manner as circular skirts. One that fits the figure at both waistline and hipline should be treated exactly like the top section of the normal circular skirt, and one that ripples should be draped like the upper part of a greater-than-normal circular skirt.

DRESS DESIGN

Problem 10
DRAPING A PEPLUM WITH A CENTER BACK FLARE

A peplum may ripple all the way around, only at the front, or only at the back. Generally the silhouette is more becoming if it fits the figure smoothly at the front and concentrates the flare from the side back to the center back.

The following procedure is given for draping those peplums which vary somewhat from the standard.

PEPLUM FRONT

Placing the Fabric on the Form (see Figure 56)

1. Place the fabric on the form with the straight grain at the center front, allowing 2½ inches above the waistline for dropping the grain and for hollowing out the waistline.

2. Pin the fabric at the center front at waistline and hipline.

Adjusting the Crossgrain

1. Smooth the cloth downward toward the side seam, clipping from the top edge to the waistline. Drop the grain enough to allow the lower edge to stand slightly away from the figure.

2. Pin the waistline at the side seam.

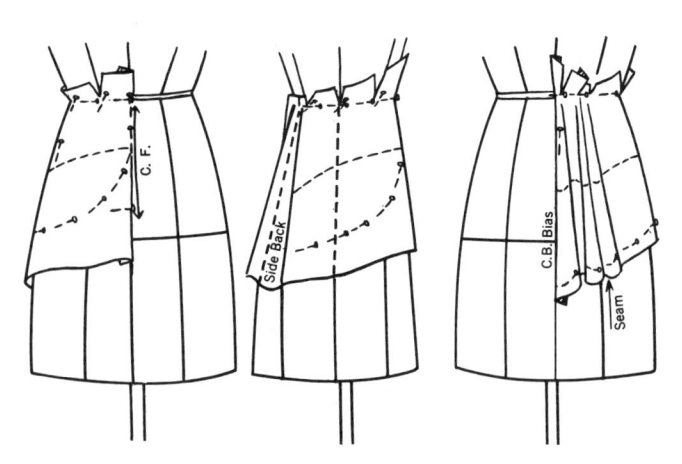

Fig. 56. Peplums — placement of the fabric.
Fig. 57. Fabric carried around to the side back.
Fig. 58. Center back panel, bias at center back.

Side Seam to Center Back

The object is to get a rippling flare at the center back and to place the seam lines wherever they harmonize with the design lines of the entire costume.

Procedure A. Place a seam on the side over the hips.

Procedure B. Omit the side seam and carry the fabric around to the side back (see Figure 57). Figure 58 shows the center back panel with the bias placed at the center back of the form.

Procedure C. Carry the fabric all the way to the center back. To do this, smooth the fabric along the waistline and pin, clip, and drop the crosswise grain around to the center back. Multiple ripples place the center back seam on a bias beyond the crossgrain, and therefore the waistline will be a deep arc.

PEPLUM BACK WITH A SIDE SEAM (see Figure 59)

Placing the Fabric on the Form

1. Place the fabric on the form with the straight grain perpendicular to the waistline at the side back rather than at the center back of the dress form. Leave at least 3½ inches above the waistline at that point.

2. Pin the straight grain to the form at the waistline and hipline, and clip the excess above the waistline down to the pin.

3. Work outward from the pin toward the center back, clipping and dropping the grain until there is enough flare at the center back.

Marking the Center Back Line

Mark with pins and cut with a seam allowance.

Adjusting the Side Seam Line

1. Smooth the fabric from the pin at the center of the back section forward toward the side seam. It may improve the effect to drop the grain slightly toward the side seam.

2. Form the side seam line and trim it with a 1¼ inch seam allowance.

3. Pin the seam, lapping the front over the back. Force any looseness out of the waistline and even stretch it slightly.

88

BASIC SKIRTS

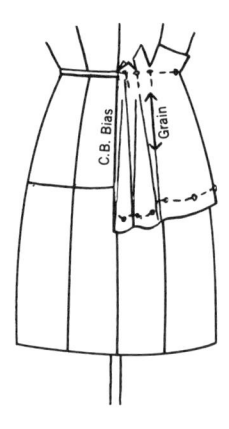

Fig. 59. Back peplum draped from side back toward hip seam and toward center back.

Marking the Lower Edge

Mark the lower edge with a line of pins parallel to the waistline in order to produce a level effect if the peplum is short. Pin the edge on a level with the floor if the peplum is longer than hip level and is actually a tunic. The flare of a short peplum with definite fullness at the back will be more emphatic if the lower edge curves downward from center front to center back. You should always, however, form the lower edge line in harmony with the other lines which determine the design of the costume.

Marking the Waistline

Mark the waistline from center front to center back with pins.

PEPLUMS FORMED BY EXTENDING THE BLOUSE BELOW THE WAISTLINE (see Figure 55, Chapter 2, page 37, Draping a Hip-Length French Dart Jacket)

SUMMARY: PRINCIPLES OF DRAPING CIRCULARS

It is possible to formulate three general rules for controlling the position of the flare:

1. Flares result from dropping the grain at any given point. This changes the waistline curve.

2. Flares result from placing the bias wherever the greatest amount of flare should fall.

3. Flares will always tend to fall from the outward curves of the body — the back of the hips, the side of the hips, and the hip bone at the side front.

DRAPING "DRAPED" SKIRTS

Up to this point we have used the term "draping" to mean modeling or shaping fabric on the dress form. Literally the word "draped," applied to skirts, means raising the grain up to one or more points of suspension, thereby reducing the width of the skirt at the lower edge in contrast to skirts either equal in size at the top and bottom (straight skirts) or larger at the bottom than at the top (gored and circular skirts). A "draped" skirt clings to the figure sometimes as far down as the thighs or even the ankles, is actually "draped" or pulled in against the legs, and has fullness drawn up into gathers or folds at the top. The draped skirt at its worst was pulled in so excessively around the ankles that it was called in ridicule a "hobble skirt" — an awkward and ungainly cut that had to be slashed to the knees at the center front to allow the wearer to move at all. But draped skirts can be lovely. Their beauty depends largely on the skill of the draper in handling soft pliable fabrics so that they form deep folds that define the figure without restricting motion. Peg-top skirts, cowl skirt folds, and funnel hip pockets all belong in the category of "draped" skirts, and can be handled so that they are wide enough at the front lower edge to allow movement with ease and freedom. When worn by a person who is slender and well proportioned below the waist, the draped silhouette defines the slender waistline and hips, and its folds emphasize the play of light on a lustrous silk or rayon.

Although individual directions for draped skirts would, of course, differ somewhat with each change in design, the example given is a conservative and wearable version that explains the principles underlying the manipulation of all draped skirts. Before draping the skirt in muslin, experiment directly with the fabric to be used to see what lines it takes and to get the "feel" of the cloth without cutting into it. (See Chapter 7, suggestion 3.)

DRESS DESIGN

Problem 11
PROCEDURE FOR DRAPING A "DRAPED" SKIRT
(see Figures 60 and 61)

Estimating the Fabric

Measure from the waistline to the hem line and add a generous hem allowance (4 inches) plus extra length for drawing folds up from the bottom and down from the top. This should be at least 2 inches at the top and 2 at the bottom, or a total of 4 extra inches of length for the drapery. Increase this allowance for a more exaggerated draped effect.

Placing the Fabric on the Form (see Figure 60)

1. Starting at the side seam, place the fabric up against the form at the hip level and pin it at least 5 inches in from the selvage, allowing at least 2 inches above the waistline. The 5 inch extension at the side provides for slanting out the seam at the lower edge. The more you draw the fabric up from the bottom, the more biased the side seam eventually becomes.

2. Smooth the fabric forward along the hip level line, supporting the crosswise grain level for about 4 inches. Pin the cloth to the form at this point.

3. *Smooth the fabric upward above this pin and anchor it to the form at the waistline* (see arrow, Figure 61).

Folds from the Waistline toward the Side Seam (see Figure 60)

1. Draw these folds forward and downward from the excess beside the hipline and above the waistline. Do not shift the grain along the hip level.

2. Clip through the excess beyond the side seam at the outer end of the lowest fold, stretch the fabric to make the fold cling to the figure, and pin it to the form at the side seam.

3. Clip through the excess beyond the side seam at the outer end of the second fold above the lowest one, stretch the fabric again to make it cling, and pin it to the form at the end of the second slash.

Both these folds point toward the hip level or above it. If they were directed toward the side seam much below the hip level — as low as the thighs, for instance — they would be very difficult to manage. They would

Fig. 60. The draped skirt — folds from the waistline to the side seam.
Fig. 61. The draped skirt — folds from the pin supporting grain at the waistline to the center front.

either draw too tightly against the legs or they would not be drawn tightly enough to keep the side seam from wavering. To get the effect of low side drapery, it is sometimes necessary to attach it as a separate piece to avoid just this difficulty. It is one thing to drape beautiful folds on a piece of statuary and quite another to drape a skirt that is graceful in motion.

Forming the Waistline from the Folds to the Side Seam

1. Smooth the fabric along the waistline to the side seam, clipping the excess above the waistline.

2. Pin the cloth to the form at the side seam on the waistline.

Laying the Folds from the Side Front to the Center Front (see Figure 61)

1. Lay a fold at the side front which runs from the waistline toward the lower edge at or near the side seam. To get this fold, lift the crosswise grain from the bottom so that the fold radiates outward. It will disappear a little below the hips.

2. Draping toward the center front, lay a second fold at the waistline directed toward the lower edge,

90

raising the grain so that the fold disappears just before it reaches the hem. The crosswise grain has been raised noticeably to make these folds radiate. The second fold should go lower than the first.

3. Lay a third fold at the waistline still closer to the center front, this time keeping the grain level. This one falls *through* the lower edge because the grain was not raised.

4. Lay another fold near the center front either keeping the grain level or dropping it slightly toward the center front if a very deep fold running through the lower edge improves the design.

If the grain is not dropped at the center front, this line can be placed on a lengthwise fold of the fabric. This procedure works very well in rayon crepe because of its heavy "fall." However, if the grain is dropped a little toward the center front, the center front seam will slant outward, producing a wider hem sweep and a more graceful fall of fabric, especially if the texture is not a very clinging one.

Marking the Center Front Seam Line (see Figure 61)

1. Mark with pins from waistline to hem.
2. Trim to a 1½ inch seam allowance.

Forming the Side Seam Line (see Figure 60)

1. Fold the excess fabric beyond the seam forward from the lowest clipped point to the hem to form a plumb line.

2. Pin it perpendicular to the edge and trim it to leave a 1½ inch seam allowance.

3. Form the line from the hips up to the waistline by marking it with pins stabbed into the form. Stretch the fabric slightly toward the side to make the folds cling. Pencil this line and trim the seam to 1 inch. This seam line will be a decided inward curve (see Figure 62).

Marking the Waistline

Pin a line following the waistline of the form, clipping the excess above the waistline. Then smooth the fabric toward the side seam beside the folds to eliminate any ease along the waistline. (The grain tips forward sharply toward the center front in this space beside the side seam.)

Marking the Hem Line

Mark the hem line with an L-square and pins while the skirt is on the form.

The Back of the Skirt

The back of the skirt should be as flat and closely fitted as possible to offset the thickening effect of drapery at the front. The back of a narrow six-gore skirt is a good choice, as it fits closely without cupping under the hips.

The greatest disadvantage of a draped skirt is the above-mentioned tendency to thicken the figure over the abdomen from the profile view. To counteract this effect, it is possible to attach the draped folds to a yoke, or to stitch the folds down over the curve of the abdomen. Some such device usually improves the appearance of the skirt unless the figure is unusually flat and slender across the abdomen. For variations of the draped skirt see Chapter 7, suggestion 8.

Marking and Trueing the Pattern (see Figure 62)

1. Remove the pattern from the form and mark all seam lines, the waistline, and the hem line with a pencil.

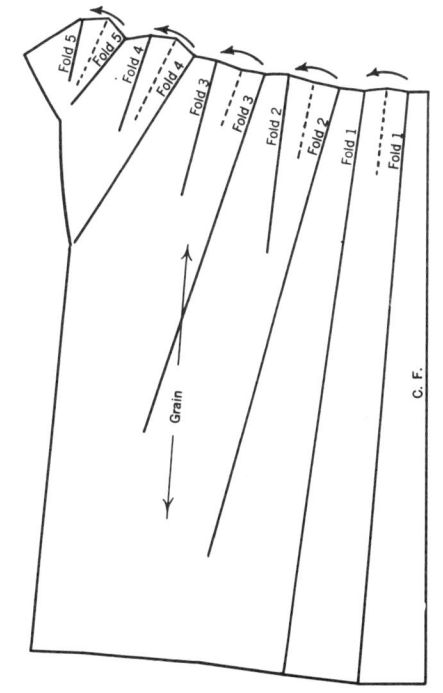

Fig. 62. Draped skirt pattern with folds and edges trued up.

DRESS DESIGN

2. Mark both edges of each draped fold carefully with a pencil.

3. Crossmark the folds.

4. Remove the pins and lay the pattern flat.

The shape of this pattern may be a surprise. The skirt is slightly narrower at its lower edge than at the top. The side seam from hip to waistline reverses the natural shape and curves inward. The waistline curves upward from the side seam to the first fold, then curves downward, and then slightly upward at the center front into a center front seam on the bias. The hem line curves upward slightly at the side front. When trueing up edges, retain the curves and angles *exactly* as they were draped. *Do not smooth them over.*

5. True up and space evenly all drapery folds.

PART II
THE FLAT PATTERN METHOD OF DESIGNING SKIRTS ON A MASTER PATTERN

With one fundamental difference, the general principles of designing waist patterns from a master block apply to the designing of skirts from a foundation pattern. The difference is that the skirt hangs free of the body from the hip to the lower edge and is therefore shaped to fit the figure only from hips to waistline. Therefore you should always draw the hip level on the pattern block to indicate the extent of this fitted area. Notice too that the curve from hip to waist on the side seam is a significant part of the skirt shaping. You draped it to duplicate your side hip curve exactly. Hence any change in the degree of this curve made by taking in or letting out the side seam at the waistline will alter the hang of your skirt. Increasing the hip curve lengthens the seam and allows it to sag; letting out or straightening the hip seam shortens it and allows it to flare sidewise.

All of the four main kinds of skirts and their variations can be blocked from the two-gore master pattern, but since it is so easy to make patterns for straight skirts either on paper or cloth from figure measurements, and since that has already been explained in Part I of this chapter, the examples of blocking here given will be confined to gored, circular, and draped skirts.

THE TWO-GORE MASTER PATTERN FRONT BLOCK

The standard two-gore master pattern may or may not have been draped with a small vertical waistline dart in the front gore, but it makes a much better master block pattern if it has one. The dart takes up the ease between hip and waist at the side seam edge of the pattern and makes it possible to fit the skirt with little side flare below the hips. Then, too, indefinite ease along a pattern edge is undesirable in a master block pattern. Results are more certain when all of the excess is taken up into a definite dart. Although the skirt-front dart falls naturally above the hip bone well around toward the side seam, for convenience in blocking, place it to form panel spacing which coincides with the spacing of the basic waistline dart of the blouse.

Introducing a Waistline Dart at the Front of the Master Pattern (see Figures 63 and 64)

If you have draped your master pattern without a dart at the waistline it is possible to introduce one to take up the ease at the side of the pattern between hips and waistline by following the directions below:

1. Compare the measurements from the balance point at the hip to the waistline on both the back and the front of the skirt to determine the amount of ease on the skirt front. In other words, find out exactly how much longer the front edge is than the back from hip to waist.

2. Draw a horizontal line on the skirt pattern front parallel to the waistline and about 5 inches below it.

3. Draw a vertical line from a point on the waist-

BASIC SKIRTS

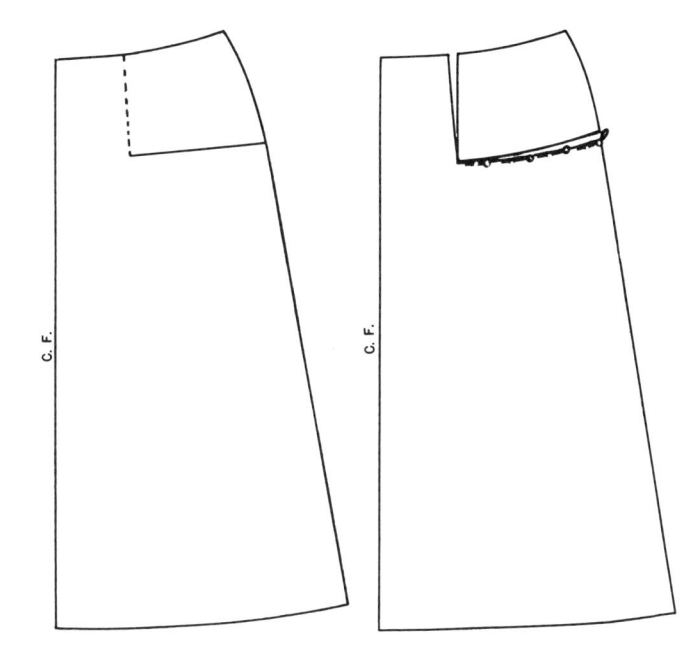

Fig. 63. Introduction of a dart into a master pattern draped without one. Step 1 — Draw the dart line and the line from the point of the dart to the side seam.

Fig. 64. Step 2 — Pin the hip ease into a tuck and open the waistline dart.

line which matches the spacing of the blouse dart to meet the horizontal line. Slant it slightly outward (½ inch from waist to hip). Slash this vertical line.

4. Fold in a dart on the horizontal line, taking up the ease on the side seam of the skirt and taper the fold to end at the vertical slash. The vertical slash then opens automatically, thus transferring the ease from the side seam to the new vertical waistline dart.

5. If you wish to reduce the width at the hem, slash the vertical dart line on through the lower edge of the skirt and overlap the slashed pieces a little at the hem line. Let the pattern pieces touch at the point of the waistline dart and spread apart a little more at the waistline, thus increasing the size of the waistline dart. However, the waistline dart should be kept small. (See pages 69-70.)

6. Smooth the pattern at the point on the side seam where the dart was pinned in. It is now ready to use as a master block pattern.

For convenience and speed in practicing the first basic problems, trace the quarter-size two-gore skirt pattern placed in the book for that purpose (see Figures 65 and 66) and delay using the full size master pattern until you understand the principles of blocking skirts. The supplies required for blocking skirt patterns are the same as those listed for blocking blouses (page 45). Cut many duplicates of the two-gore skirt front and back patterns in heavy brown paper in preparation for this practice.

Problem 1

DESIGNING FOUR-GORE SKIRTS ON THE TWO-GORE MASTER PATTERN

There are many possible variations in the silhouette of the four-gore skirt. It may have more or less flare at the hem line, depending on the fashion and the style of the skirt. The flare may also start at a high or low break point, and may be either concentrated or evenly distributed, as you discovered when you draped four-gore skirts.

Narrow Skirt Front with Waistline Dart Retained
(see Figure 67)

This narrow four-gore style with the small waistline dart retained is excellent for the skirt of a tailored suit made of a firm fabric. What little flare there is should be distributed between the center front and the side seam, but slightly more flare should be thrown toward the center front (see Figure 68). The only change in the master pattern that needs to be made is to shift the grain position from the center front (grain position on a master pattern) to a new position that will throw the skirt flare more toward the center than toward the side. To do this, proceed according to the following directions *which apply to establishing the grain in all gored skirts that flare more on one side of the gore than on the other side.*

1. Mark a point at the center of the gore at the hip level and measure from that point to the side which is to flare less. (This is almost invariably the side seam.)

2. At the lower edge of the same side, measure in the same distance and add to it the amount of flare desired — at least ¾ to 1½ inches — and place a second point.

93

DRESS DESIGN

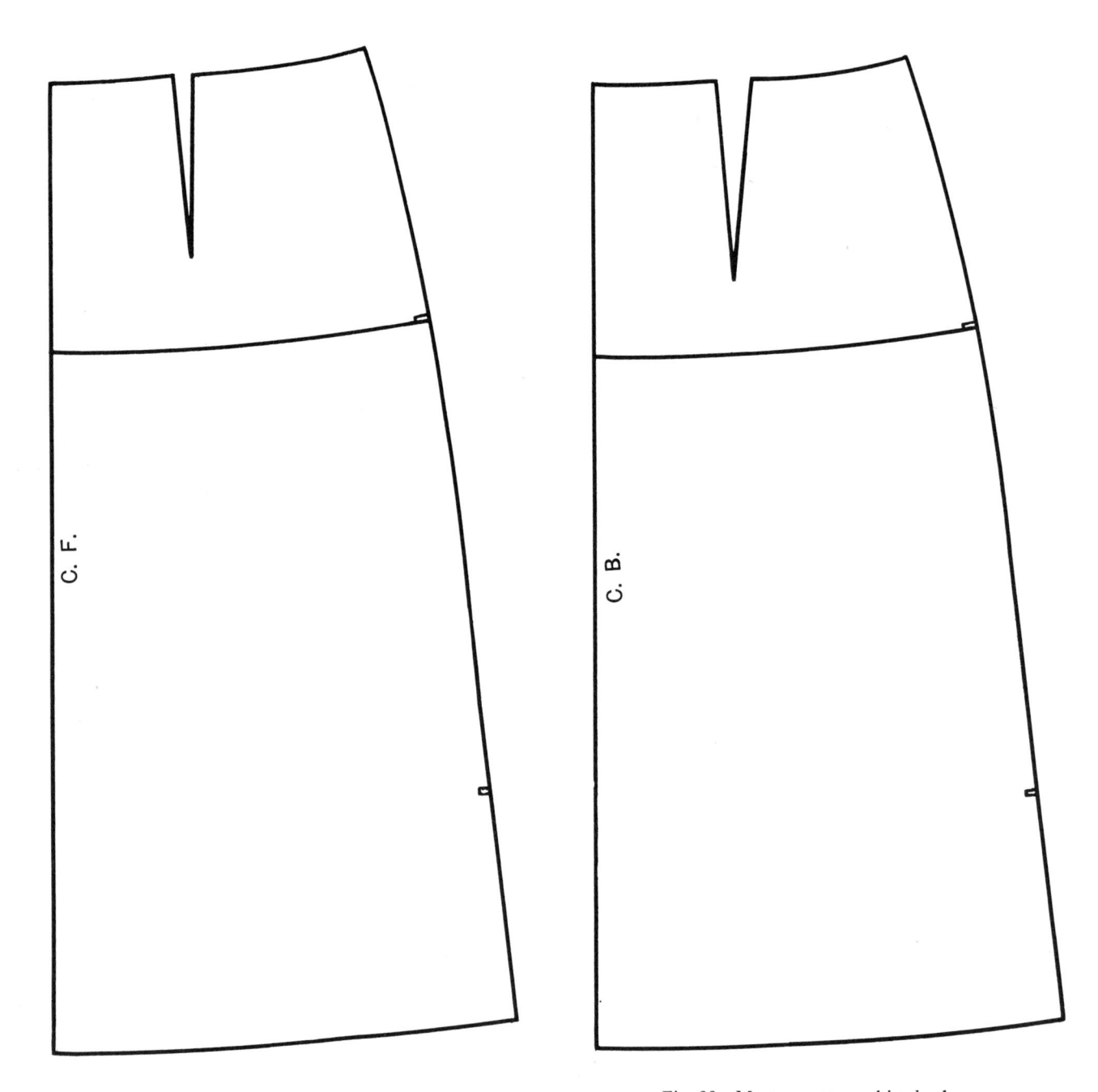

Fig. 65. Master pattern skirt front.

Fig. 66. Master pattern skirt back.

BASIC SKIRTS

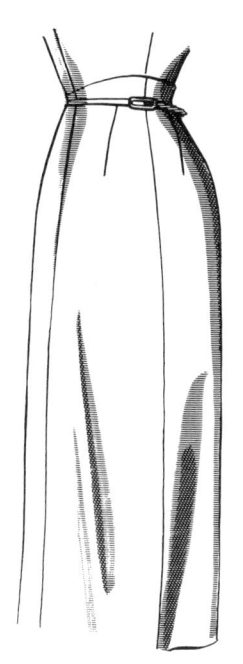

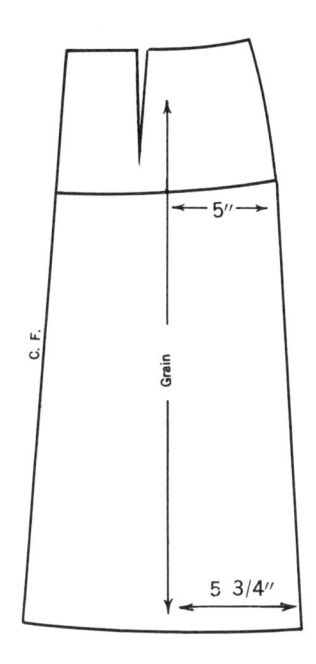

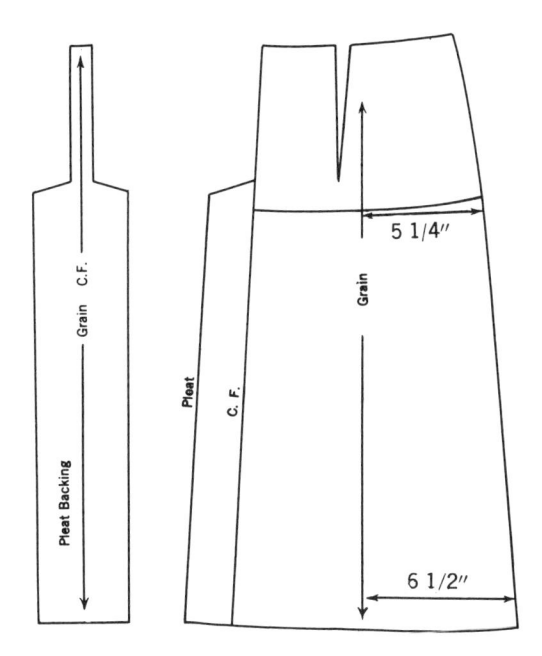

Fig. 67. Very narrow four-gore skirt.
Fig. 68. Very narrow four-gore skirt — master pattern with grain shifted to introduce flare at center front.
Fig. 69. Very narrow four-gore with inverted box pleat at center front.

3. Connect the two points to establish the line along which the grain will run and continue the line through to the waistline.

The advantage of this skirt over the two-gore skirt with no center front seam has already been explained (see Draping the Four-Gore Skirt, page 78). To retain a very narrow silhouette and yet provide enough width for walking, you can add an inverted box pleat at the center front seam (see Figure 69).

Slightly Wider Four-Gore Skirt Front (Dart Transferred)
(see Figures 70 and 71)

1. Draw a ruled pencil line from the point of the dart to the lower edge and slash the line (see Figure 70).

2. Close the dart at the waistline and transfer it to the lower edge. This skirt will still fit closely (see Figure 71).

3. Follow the procedure given on page 93 for placing the grain in a gore that flares more on one side than on the other.

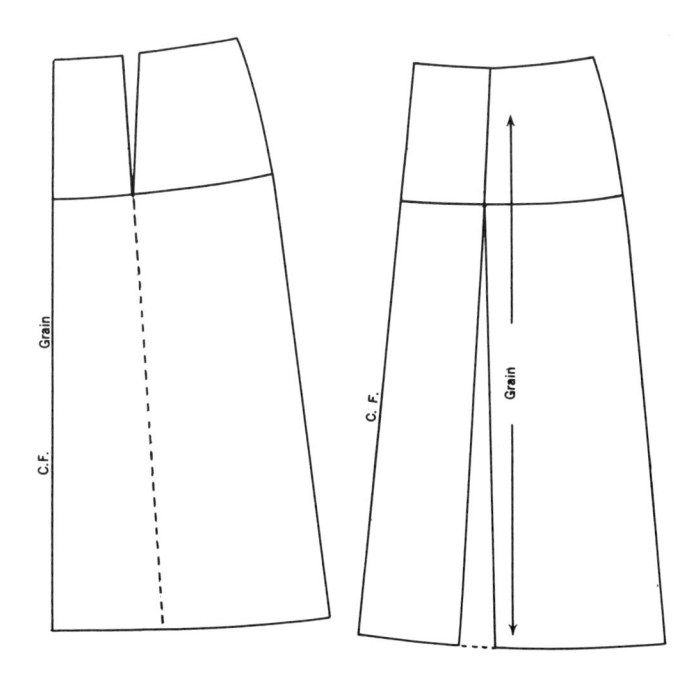

Fig. 70. Line drawn from end of dart to lower edge.
Fig. 71. Dart closed and transferred to lower edge.

95

DRESS DESIGN

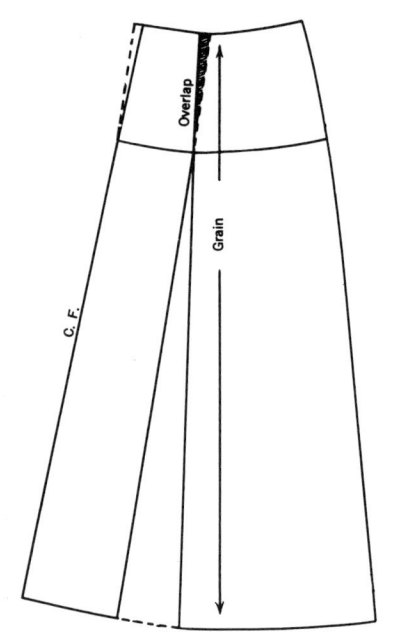

Fig. 72. Four-gore wider at lower edge. Pattern overlaps slightly at waistline, touches at break-line, and spreads at lower edge.

Four-Gore Skirt Front with Greater Sweep (see Figure 72)

All gored skirts should fit exactly at the waistline and as far below as desired.

1. At the level at which the flare is to start breaking away from the figure, draw a line parallel to the waistline. For this skirt place the break-line high, about 5 inches below the waistline, since the fullness is to start above the hip level.

2. Slash from the end of the dart through the hem line and pivot the pieces at the break-line so that they overlap at the waistline, touch at the break-line, and spread at the lower edge (see Figure 72). Notice that the waistline is now a more intense arc, and that a ripple will probably fall at the point where the pieces overlap, since this is the sharpest point of the arc. If the hip bone at the side front is very prominent, however, the ripple may tend to fall from that bulge too far around at the side. As already explained, the body curves are even more important than the pattern shapes in determining the fall of the fabric. This is the unknown quantity in flat pattern designing.

3. Overlapping the pieces has decreased the waistline size. Correct this by placing the basic pattern against the new waistline and adding the necessary width at the center front. This should be not more than ½ inch. True the center front line from waist to hip. Over-tighten the waistline slightly to allow for stretching.

4. Mark the direction of the grain from waist to hem according to the method given on page 93 for a skirt that flares more on one side than on the other.

Four-Gore Skirt Front with High Break-Line, Wide Sweep at Hem Line, and Flare at the Side (see Figure 73)

1. Raise the break-line so that it is not more than 2 or 2½ inches below the waistline and parallel to it (see Figure 74).

2. Slash from the end of the dart through the hem and proceed as for the previous skirt. Let the pieces just touch at the high break-line and spread apart below it. This spreads the lower end of the dart.

3. Because this skirt is to flare at the side as well as at the center front, place the lengthwise grain perpendicular to the waistline at the center of the gore, dividing the flare about equally between the seams at the center front and the side. Notice that the skirt flares almost from the waistline and that the waistline arc is more intense than in the design previously described. Because it is so sharply curved and will stretch, the waistline should be shortened slightly.

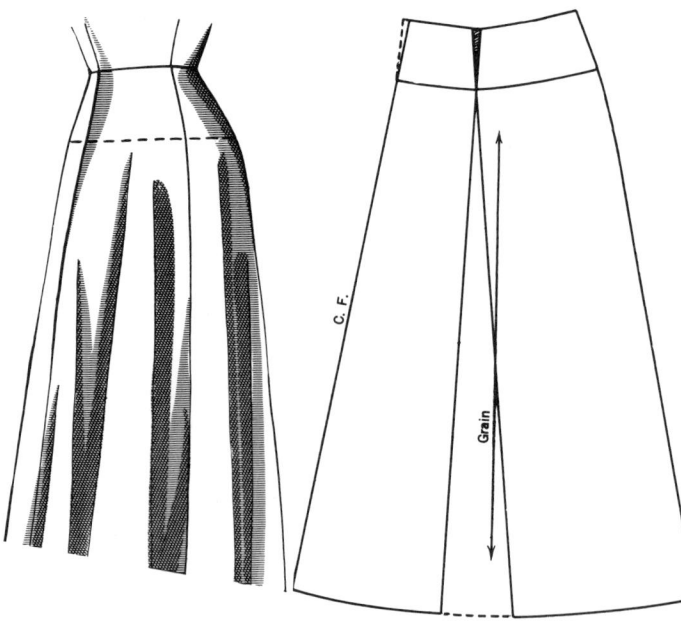

Fig. 73. Four-gore with wide hem sweep and side flare.
Fig. 74. Wide four-gore flare starts at a high break-line and is divided evenly between center front and side seam.

96

BASIC SKIRTS

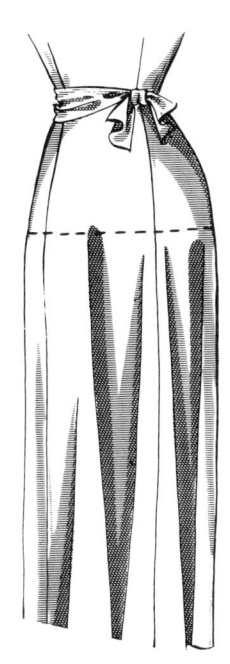

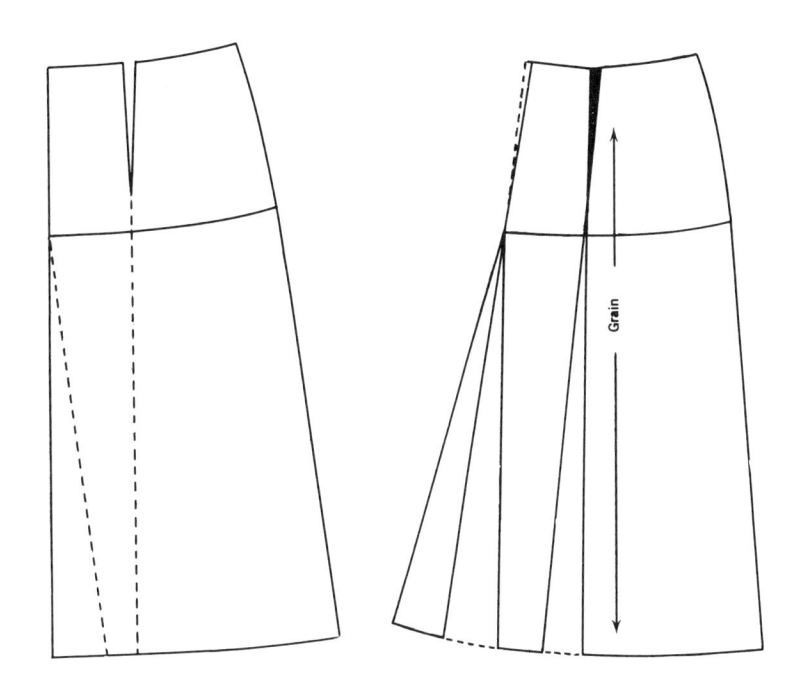

Fig. 75. Four-gore flare — begins low.
Fig. 76. Step 1 — Slash lines for low placed flare as indicated by dotted lines.
Fig. 77. Step 2 — Spread slashes and overlap pattern at waistline.

Four-Gore Skirt Front with a Low Placed Flare (see Figure 75)

This skirt should fit very low around the hips, but the flare should ripple out noticeably around the hem line at the center front and side front, producing a very slenderizing effect.

1. Mark the break-line from 7 to 9 inches below the waistline.

2. Slash from the point of the dart through the lower edge, and pivot the pieces so that they will spread slightly at the break-line, overlap at the waistline, and spread at the lower edge. Figure 76 shows step 1.

3. Slash again, this time nearer the center front, from the lower edge up to the break point. Swing this segment out in order to provide flare along the center front seam. This produces a ripple at the center front and another at the side front, and yet the skirt fits snugly from hips to waist (see Figure 77).

4. Correct the waistline size by adding to the center front the amount subtracted when the dart was overlapped. Rule a new center front line from the corrected point at the waist to the point of break.

5. Mark the position of the grain according to the procedure given on page 93 for a gore that flares more on one side than on the other. This insures a slim side silhouette and throws practically all of the flare at or near the center front.

Problem 2

DESIGNING SIX-GORE SKIRTS ON THE TWO-GORE MASTER PATTERN

The following examples of six-gore skirt blocking show how to develop both tailored and rippling silhouettes. They also clarify the draping of the six-gore skirt (see Figures 23, 24, and 25 for silhouette effects and panel spacing).

97

DRESS DESIGN

Narrow Six-Gore Skirt Front
Center Panel (see Figure 78)

1. Place a line to indicate the level of the break points, 7 to 9 inches below the waistline. This level is variable and depends on the current fashion silhouette, the particular lines of the dress, and the becomingness of the design to the individual.

2. Since the dart was originally placed to form good panel spacing, draw a line that follows its inner edge and continues to the lower edge of the skirt. The center section is now complete except for the straight grain marking. Place the center front on a lengthwise fold of the fabric.

Side Front Section (see Figure 79)

1. Place a ruler along the dart edge at the top of the side front section and continue the line to the lower edge. Slanting the line out in this way adds flare to the side front section and eliminates the bulge on the side front edge at the point of the dart. Both seam edges of the gores that are to be attached should slant outward about equally. The flare does not necessarily have to be equalized, but it is easier to handle if it is.

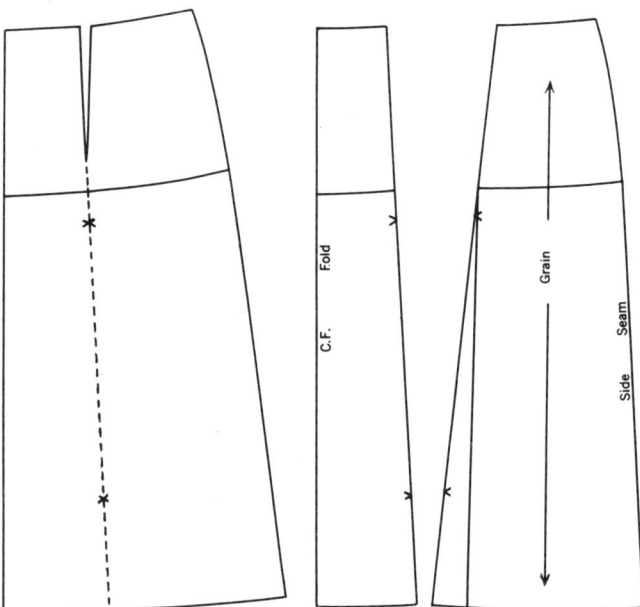

Fig. 78. Narrow six-gore. Step 1 — Draw slash lines on master pattern.

Fig. 79. Step 2 — Slash patterns, add flare at side front, and mark the grain in both sections.

2. Mark the grain so that there is an outward slant of at least 1 to 1½ inches on the side seam from hip to hem.

Note. These directions assume that the master pattern for the skirt front has a *small* waistline dart. (See method for the narrow six-gore skirt back, pages 101-103.)

Six-Gore Skirt Front with a Ripple at Side Front and a Low Break Point (see Figures 80 and 81)

It has already been explained that the ripple in a gored skirt is produced (1) by dropping the grain toward the center of the figure or toward both side and center, and (2) through increasing the outward slant at the seam line. Too much of either is not advisable, because exaggerated lowering of grain produces a circular skirt rippling from the waistline, and too much flare at any one seam produces heavy bunchiness at the seam. A little of each makes a much more graceful four- or six-gore skirt with more flattering distribution of ease.

Center Panel (see Figure 80)

1. Draw in the line to indicate the height of the break, placing it 8 or 9 inches below the waist for a closely fitted hipline.

2. Draw a ruled line from the point of the waistline dart to the lower edge parallel to the center front, and cut the pattern apart on this line. Slope the line out from the break point to the hem the desired amount. Clip the seam allowance at the break point.

3. Mark the grain at the center front to be placed on a fold.

Side Front Section (see Figure 81)

1. On the side front section draw a line from waistline to hem at about the center of the section or wherever a flare is desired, and slash it.

2. Pivot the pieces so that they touch at the breakline, overlap at the waistline, and spread for a small ripple at the hem. Then draw around the pieces in this position. This slashing and spreading produces an extra ripple which corresponds to the one created by dropping the grain from a point about 3 to 4 inches in from the side seam when you draped.

98

BASIC SKIRTS

Rule. Slash and pivot the pattern at a given point when blocking to produce a result comparable to dropping the grain from a given point when draping.

3. Along the side front edge of the side gore, draw a line from the break to the lower edge that slants outward at about the same degree as the side edge of the center gore. This introduces flare at the seam. Clip the seam allowance at the break point.

4. Correct the waistline size by adding to the side front edge of the gore enough to restore the original waistline measurement.

5. Mark the lengthwise grain with a minimum amount of flare at the side seam, thus throwing most of the flare toward the side front.

Gored Skirt with Side Front Lap (see Figure 82)

A gored skirt with a side front lap may be used when the opening at the side harmonizes with the design of the costume, or when you want a side-lapped skirt wider at the lower edge than the straight wraparound. The procedure is exactly the same as for the gored skirts already discussed, except that the entire front of the master pattern must be used and the center front line must be clearly marked (see Figures 83 and 84).

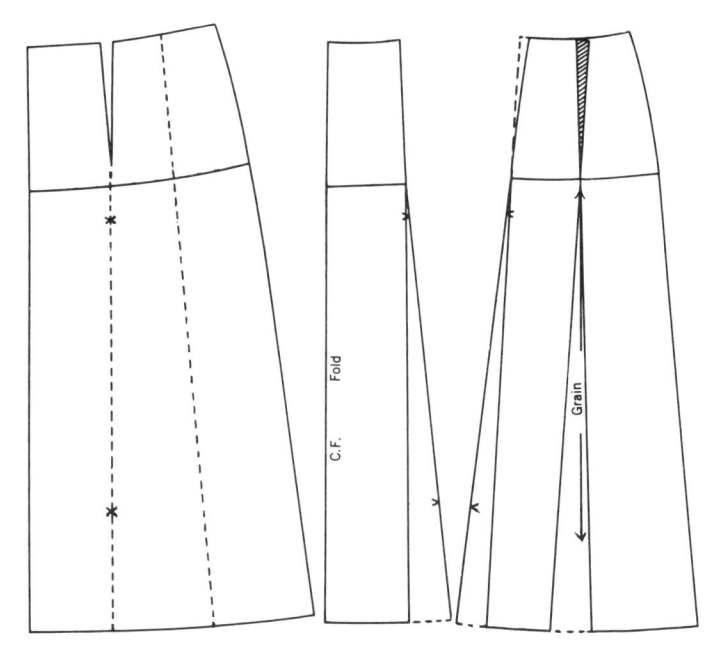

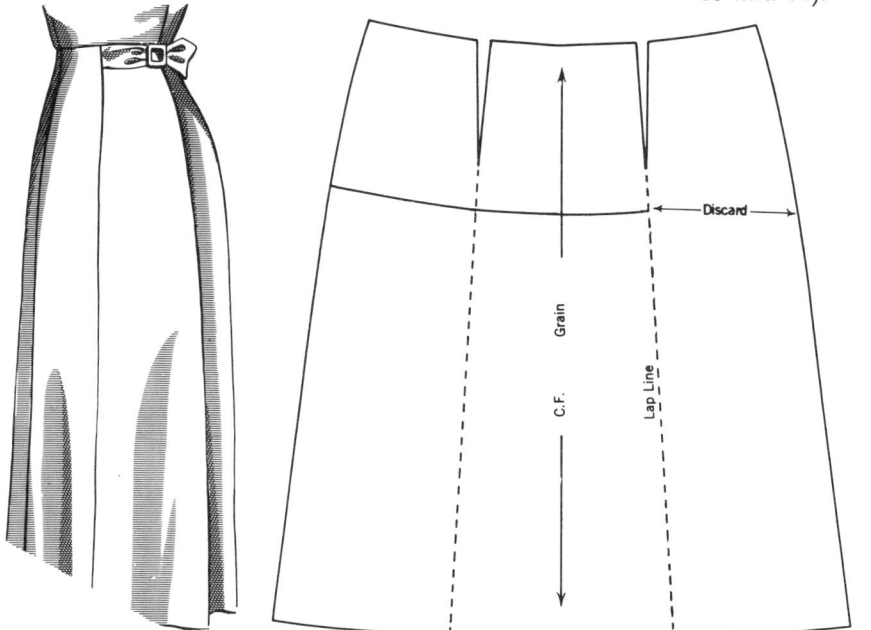

Fig. 80. Rippling six-gore. Step 1 — Draw slash lines on master pattern for two ripples starting from a low breakline.

Fig. 81. Step 2 — Spread pattern to add flare at the side front seam and also within the side gore.

Fig. 82. Six-gore skirt lapped at side front.

Fig. 83. Six-gore skirt with side front lap. Step 1 — Mark lap line to balance center panel.

Fig. 84. Lap allowance and placket should be added at left side front.

DRESS DESIGN

Problem 3

DESIGNING MULTI-GORE SKIRTS ON THE TWO-GORE MASTER PATTERN

Skirts with more than six gores derive the flare almost entirely by slanting the gore edges outward. The sections are too narrow to get much effect by lowering the crossgrain toward the seam. Block the seven- and eight-gore skirts, however, exactly like the rippling six-gore skirt, but add flare at the center front and center back seams and shift the grain position so that it runs through the middle of each center section (see Figure 85).

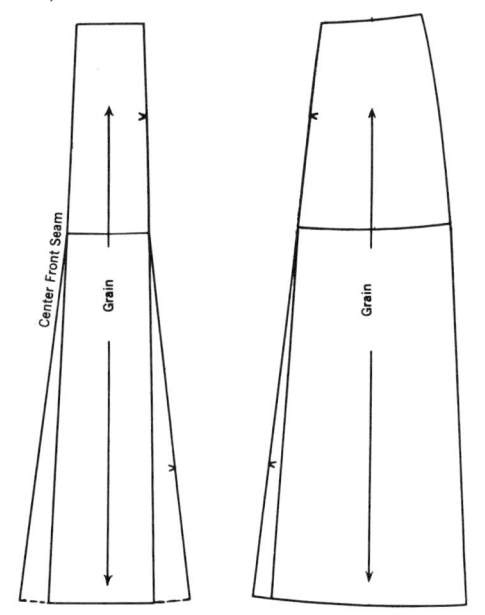

Fig. 85. Eight-gore — Flare added to center front of six-gore and grain placed at middle of center panel.

The Ten-Gore Skirt (see Figures 86, 87, and 88)

As it is usually monotonous to divide the hip width into ten equal spaces, space the center panel somewhat wider than the two side front panels, or so that the three form a group in the center of the skirt. The side panels should be somewhat wider than the side front sections, because panel lines placed too close to the side seams are judged against the hip curves and always appear to be too straight to harmonize with the contour of the figure.

1. Draw in a low break-line, about 9 inches below the waistline.

2. Determine the width of each gore at the break-line and again at the waistline. Slope the lines outward slightly from waist to break-line and continue to rule them to the lower edge (see Figure 87).

3. Slash the pattern apart along the gore lines and also slash from the point of the waistline dart (the dart is in the side front gore) to the lower edge in order to close the dart. There is now a slight flare along the center panel, and there is also flare on each edge of the side front panel due to the closing of the dart. When the dart is closed the pattern automatically opens from the point of the dart to the hem. This increases the hip width slightly at the break-line.

4. Slant the edges of the gores outward from the break-line to the lower edge (see Figure 88).

5. Mark the grain position on each section as follows:

(a) On the center front section, the center front line should come on a fold.

(b) On the side front sections, the lengthwise grain should be perpendicular to the waistline at the center of the panel, with equal flare on each edge.

(c) On the side panels there should be 1 to 1½ inches of slope from hip to hem, thus throwing most of the flare at the front edge.

In this skirt almost all of the flare comes from slanting out the edges of the gores. Notice also that the flares are equal on all edges except the side seam. It is also possible to obtain a different kind of ripple by adding a large flare on one edge of each seam, keeping the other edge fairly straight. This makes a one-sided ripple that falls over the seam. If gores have more flare on one edge of a seam than on the other, always place the edge with more flare on the side nearer the center so that the ripples curl outward rather than toward the center.

GORED SKIRT PATTERNS FOR FABRICS WITH GEOMETRIC DESIGNS

When a six- or eight-gore skirt is to be made in a stripe, a check, or a plaid, two points must be considered. First, introduce the flare by sloping out the seams rather than by lowering the cross-wise grain.

BASIC SKIRTS

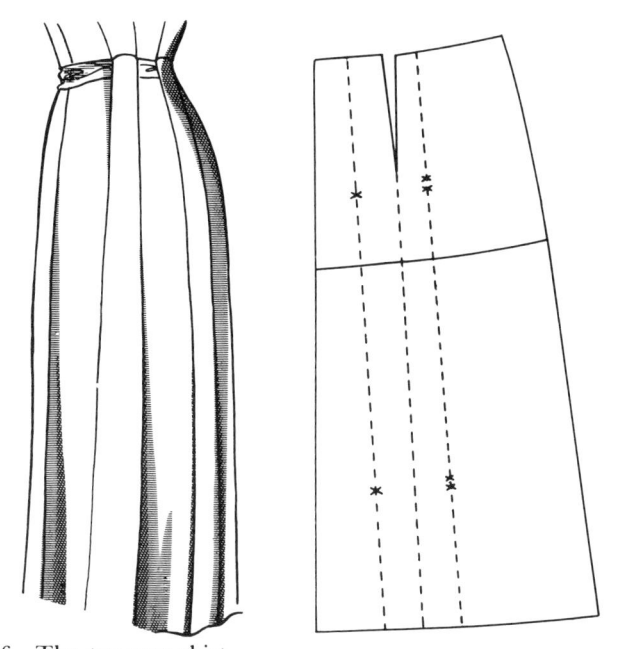

Fig. 86. The ten-gore skirt.
Fig. 87. Step 1 — Draw slash lines on master pattern.

This should be done so that the horizontal lines of the fabric pattern appear parallel to the floor rather than tipped down, thus avoiding confusion in the direction of lines. Second, in order to match the stripes on adjoining seam lines, equalize the angle of slope on each seam edge.

Problem 4

DESIGNING THE BACKS OF GORED SKIRTS ON THE TWO-GORE MASTER PATTERN

Follow the same procedures for blocking the backs of skirts as for the fronts, but introduce more ease at the back, as a skirt is ugly when it fits too closely or cups in under the hips.

Narrow Six-Gore Skirt Back

The directions for cutting a pattern for the back of this skirt are given in detail because the larger back dart makes the procedure different from that for the skirt front.

Center Panel (see Figure 89)

1. Draw in the level desired for the break points.

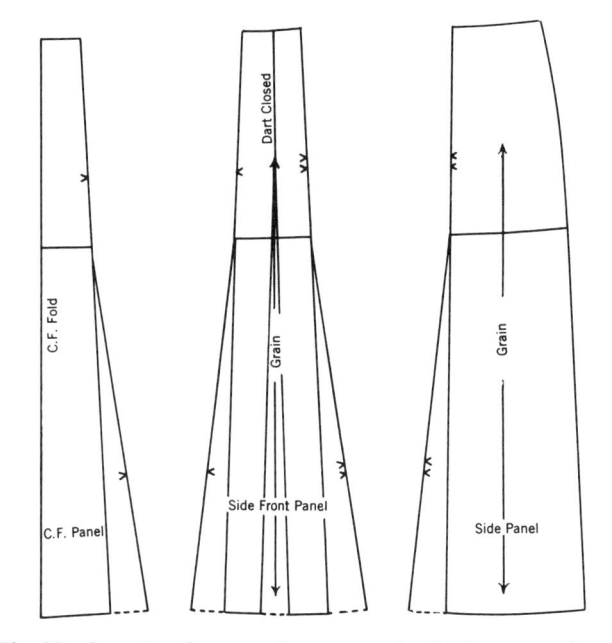

Fig. 88. Step 2 — Cut panels apart and add flares at edges.

This should be 7 to 9 inches below the waistline for a narrow skirt.

2. The panel spacing at the hip and waistline usually follows that on the master pattern and coincides with the spacing on the blouse.

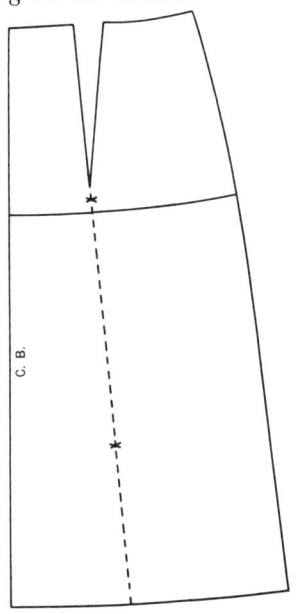

Fig. 89. Narrow six-gore skirt back. Step 1 — Draw slash line for center back panel.

DRESS DESIGN

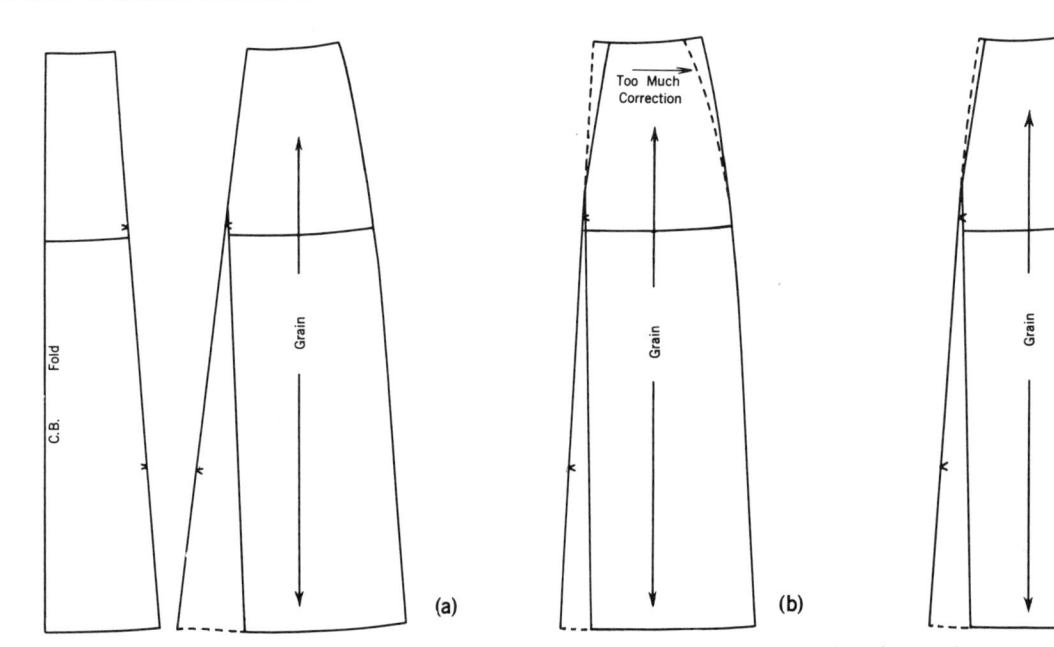

Fig. 90. Step 2 (a) – Incorrect. Bulge at point of dart has been completely taken out, but flare is too wide at lower edge; (b) Incorrect. Lower edge width is correct, but waistline size correction is too large; (c) Better method. Bulge at dart point has not been completely taken out but waistline correction is reasonably small.

3. Draw a line following the inner edge of the dart (edge next to center) and continue it to the hem line.

4. Crossmark and cut the pattern apart on this line. The center section of the pattern is now complete. Mark the grain with the center back line on a lengthwise fold of the cloth.

Side Back Section (see Figures 90 a, b, and c)

There will be a decided bulge at the end of the dart on the side back section compared to the very small one on the front. This bulge varies in prominence with the size of the dart. A figure with a small waistline and large hips requires an unusually large dart and will therefore have a pattern with a very prominent bulge at the end of the dart.

If the dart is small, it is possible to follow the side of it and continue the line down to the hem in the same way as on the front. But if the dart is large, too much flare falls at the side back edge (see Figure 90a). If it does, place a ruler at the peak of the bulge, tilt it until the flare equals that on the center panel, and then continue the line at the same angle up to the waist (see Figure 90b). This reduces the size of the original dart, thereby making the waistline too large. A small amount of the excess (¼ to ⅜ inch) can be subtracted from the waistline along the side seam, but if too much correction is necessary this method will not prove satisfactory. Look at Figure 90c which shows a compromise correction. The waistline shows less correction and a little of the bulge at the point of the dart still remains. This proves to be the best solution of the problem of adapting the back of a very narrow six-gore skirt to a person who requires a large dart at the back of her master pattern.

To summarize the three procedures:

(a) The dotted line exactly follows the dart edge; in other words, it transfers the entire dart to the lower edge, producing too much flare on the side section (see Figure 90a).

(b) The line with the right amount of flare, if continued straight up to the waistline, eliminates the bulge at the peak of the dart, but enlarges the waistline so much that it cannot be corrected at the side seam (see Figure 90b).

(c) The compromise correction at the top leaves a little bulge in the side line which reduces the amount of waistline correction so that it can easily be subtracted from the side seam (see Figure 90c).

Note. When stitching the side seam and the side

BASIC SKIRTS

back seam shown in Figure 90c, avoid stretching them along the curve from hip to waist. Ease the curve to keep it from sagging and cupping under the hips.

This whole problem arises only when an attempt is made to adapt a narrow six-gore skirt, or one which flares out from a very closely fitted hipline, to a figure with a small waistline and prominent back hips. A somewhat wider hem sweep and higher break-line is more becoming to a figure with these particular waist and hip proportions.

Problem 5

DESIGNING A GORED SKIRT WITH A YOKE ON THE TWO-GORE MASTER PATTERN

The Yoke Line (see Figure 91)

1. Draw in the desired yoke line on the two-gore master block pattern and crossmark it. Space the skirt yoke in relation to other lines of the dress. As with blouse yokes, the lower edge should never be a perfectly straight cross line perpendicular to the center front, for if it is, it appears to curve downward as it approaches the side seams. Moreover, skirt yokes should be scaled to the size of the figure and should be shallow for short women and deeper for tall ones. It is always preferable to design this line with the pattern held up vertically on the form in order to see the best proportion rather than to figure it out mechanically.

2. Cut the pattern along the yoke line and close the original dart, thereby transferring it to the lower edge of the yoke (see Figure 91).

The Lower Skirt Section (see Figures 92 a, b and c)

1. To add a circular ripple to the edge joining the yoke (see Figure 93):

   (a) Slash and spread the lower section at the lower edge. The upper and lower skirt sections will fit exactly at the joining, and the skirt will flare at the hem.

   (b) Place the grain so that most of the bias is at the center front with a slope at the side seams of 1 to 1½ inches from hip to hem.

2. To add gathers or folds to the edge joining a yoke (see Figure 94), slash in the same way, but spread the pieces at both top and bottom. They may be spread equally, or they may be spread more at one edge than at the other, depending on the desired effect. Figure 95 shows how the folds may be spread more at the top than at the bottom to produce a modified peg-top with the center folds running through the hem and the side front folds stopping before they reach the hem.

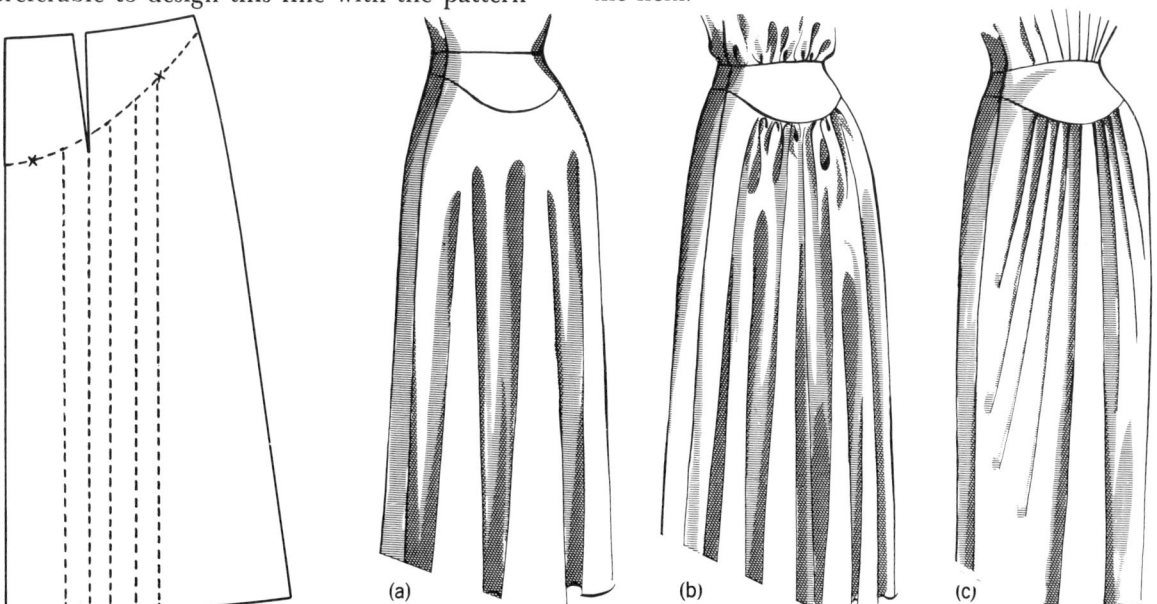

Fig. 91. Gored skirt with a yoke and fullness in the lower section: Step 1.

Fig. 92. The lower skirt section is spread in (a) for circular ripples, in (b) for gathers, and in (c) for draped folds.

DRESS DESIGN

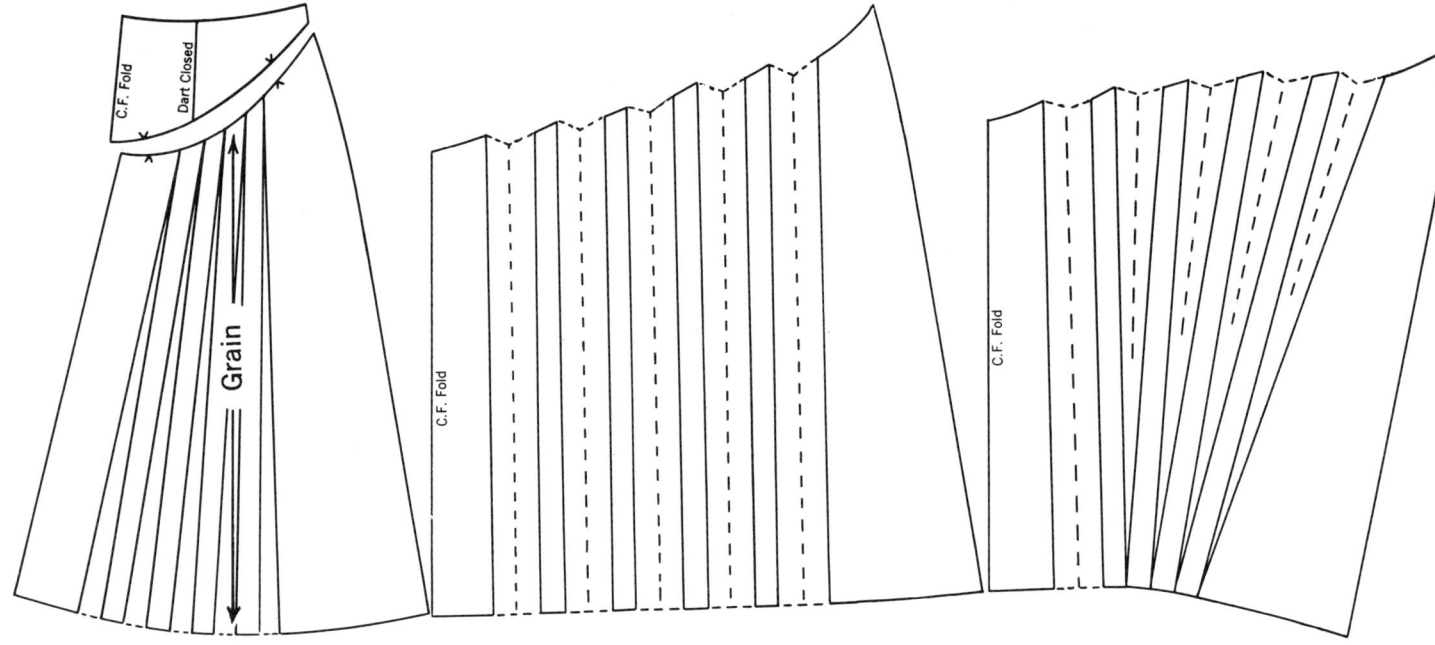

Fig. 93. Dart closed and slashes in lower section spread for circular ripples.

Fig. 94. Lower section spread equally at top and bottom for straight folds or gathers.

Fig. 95. Lower section spread at top for draped folds.

Problem 6

DESIGNING FOUR-GORE SKIRT WITH SEAMS AT SIDE FRONT AND SIDE BACK ON THE TWO-GORE MASTER PATTERN

Seams are commonly found at the exact sides of the figure, because the figure curves most on the side and requires the most fitting over the hips. Sometimes, however, the other design lines of the costume demand that the seams be placed at the side front and side back instead of at the side of the hip. When the straight grain instead of an outward gored line is placed at the side, the skirt is liable to draw tightly against the thighs and legs and to define every little bulge and hollow. Thus if the side seam is omitted, a deep curved dart over the hip must be substituted for it in order to fit the skirt from hip to waist, and on the left side, to serve as a placket. The following directions will explain how to cut the pattern.

Procedure, Using a Copy of the Two-Gore Master Pattern (see Figure 96)

1. Place the side edge of the skirt front against the side edge of the skirt back from the lowest point of the hip curve to the lower edge, and attach the two with Scotch tape. If there is too much flare along the side seam of the master pattern, overlap the front and back patterns slightly at the hemline, but decrease the overlap until it disappears at the hip level. This is done to make the side silhouette of the new skirt hang straight and perpendicular to the floor.

2. Draw a line for the break parallel to and the desired depth below the waistline.

3. Follow the panel spacing established by the basic darts at the side front and side back, and continue to rule the lines down to the lower edge.

4. Slash these lines to form the center panels. Add flare from the break line to the hem on both the side front and side back panels.

5. Mark the center front and center back panel lines to be placed on lengthwise folds (see Figures 97 *a* and *c*), or gore out the seam at the center back for extra flare, as illustrated in Figure 97 *b*.

6. Place the straight lengthwise grain indicator at the side seam position, that is, the line on which the front and back patterns are joined (see Figure 96).

BASIC SKIRTS

7. When you draw around the completed pattern, trace the dart at the side from hip to waist, retaining the curve exactly. It will necessarily be a very large long dart on most figures.

Always slope the front and back edges of the side gore outward enough so that they will meet the center front and back panels easily. Be sure to allow for some flare as well.

Summary: Principles of Designing Gored Skirts on a Two-Gore Master Pattern

Flares may be introduced into a gored skirt by any one of three methods:

1. Transferring the waistline dart to the lower edge.

2. Slashing the pattern vertically so that the two portions overlap at the waistline, touch at the breakline, and spread apart at the hem line.

(Methods 1 and 2 introduce flare within the pattern edges where there is no seam. Flares tend to fall where the pattern is slashed, but are always influenced by body contour.)

3. Slanting the seam line outward from the breakline to the lower edge.

(Flares cannot be introduced but can be greatly intensified by placing the bias where the flares should fall.)

The student should refer to the summary of principles common to the draping of all gored skirts, page 81, for shaping edges of gores and placing the grain of the cloth. The same rules apply whether the pattern is draped or blocked.

Problem 7

DESIGNING CIRCULAR SKIRTS ON THE TWO-GORE MASTER PATTERN

Since the proportions of the figure are the greatest determining factor in producing attractive circular flares, it seems reasonable that the most graceful circular skirts will always be developed by draping rather than by flat pattern blocking. However, after some experience in draping circular skirts and in observing their effectiveness on particular figures, it is possible to estimate with considerable certainty the probable success of any particular circular cut when you use the flat pattern blocking method.

The principle of cutting any circular skirt from the two-gore master pattern is founded on (1) the transfer

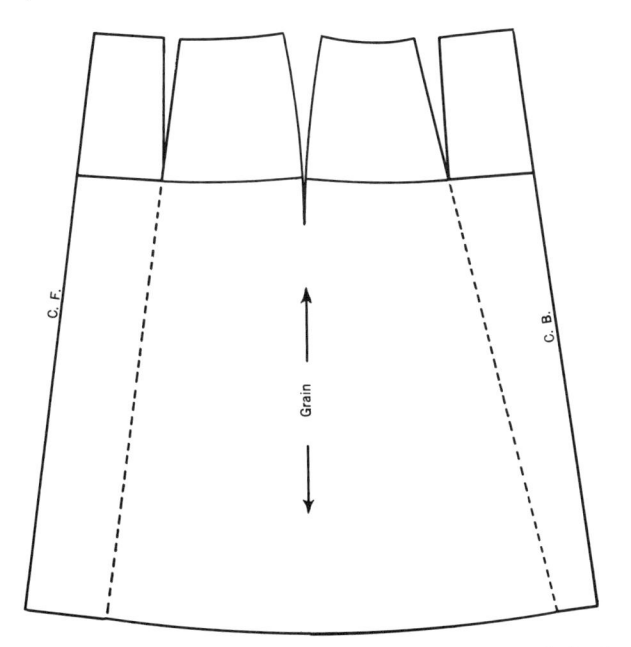

Fig. 96. Gored skirt with seams at side front and back (dotted lines show seam position).

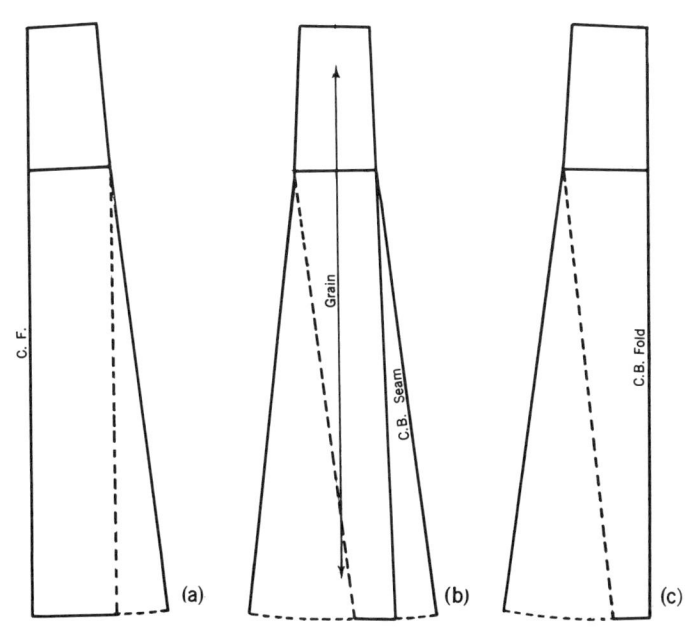

Fig. 97. (a) Pattern of center front; (b) Center back panel with seams on both edges; (c) Center back panel placed on a fold.

DRESS DESIGN

of the dart from the waistline to the lower edge, and (2) slashing from the lower edge to the waistline and spreading to increase circularity. Study the illustration of circular cuts shown under Draping Circular Skirts, pages 81-87.

The Normal Circular Skirt (see Figure 98)

1. Slash the two-gore master pattern from the lower edge to the point of the dart.

2. Close the dart at the waistline and spread the pattern at the hem.

3. Follow the side seam of the master pattern from waist to hip; but to get the line from hip to lower edge, place a ruler on the side seam so that it connects the waist and hip points, and rule from the hip through to the lower edge.

4. If a center front seam is desired, place the grain at the center of the pattern (halfway between the side seam and the center front) perpendicular to the waistline. If you do not want a center seam, place the center front on a fold. (See Placing the Grain on a Circular Skirt Pattern, page 87.)

5. For an evening skirt, continue the ruled seamlines to floor length.

Without any other change, this creates the pattern for a normal circular skirt — one that fits the waistline and the hipline with the flare determined by the difference between the waistline and hipline sizes on the individual master pattern. It is here that the circular and the gored types show their similarity. The normal circular skirt is like the four-gore skirt, except that in the latter, the hem sweep is controlled, whereas the characteristic flare of the normal circular skirt is simply the result of the difference between the two arcs of waistline and hipline.

The Less-than-Normal Circular Skirt, Closely Fitted at the Front but with a Decided Flare at the Back (see Figures 99 a and b)

1. Place together the front and back hip seams of the two-gore master skirt pattern and draw a line for a seam at the side back, as far toward the back as the width of the fabric allows, or at least close enough to the center back to form good panel spacing. Retain the darts at the side front and at the side, and even enlarge them by slashing from the dart points through the lower edge and overlapping the skirt at the lower edge if necessary in order to cut the pattern in one piece from 39 inch fabric.

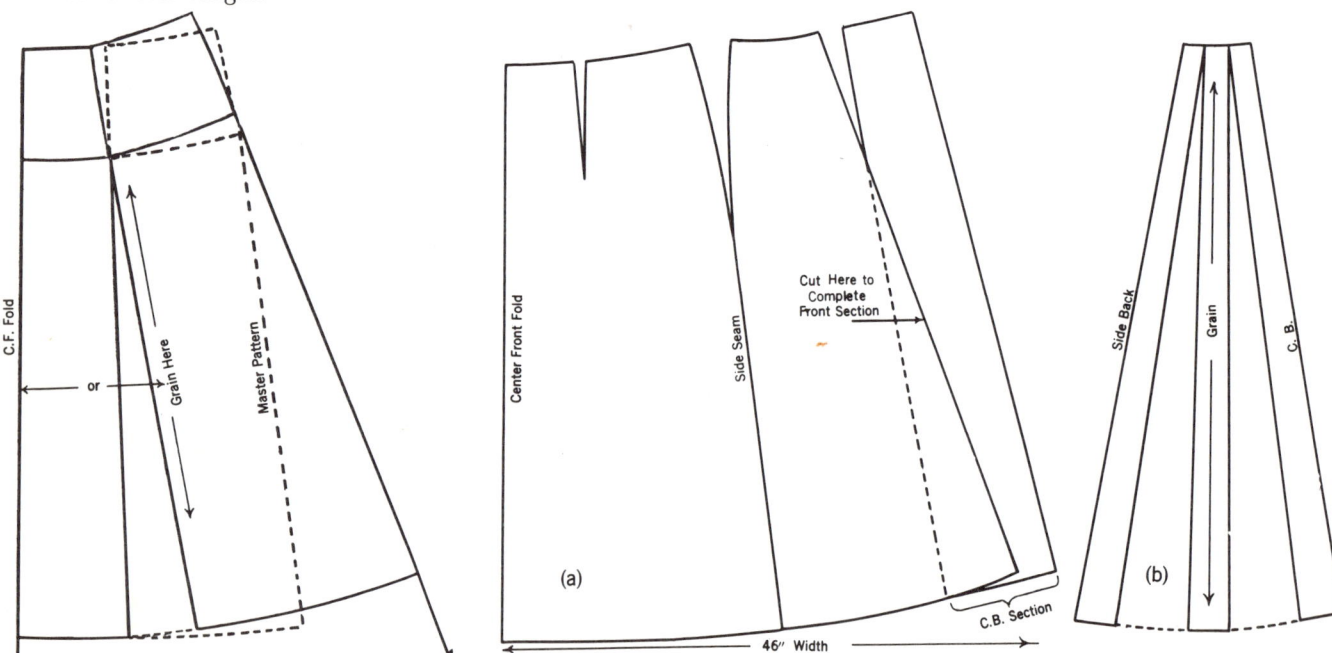

Fig. 98. Normal circular skirt from two-gore.

Fig. 99. Less-than-normal circular skirt with flare added at center back: (*a*) Slash lines drawn; (*b*) Center back section spread for flare.

BASIC SKIRTS

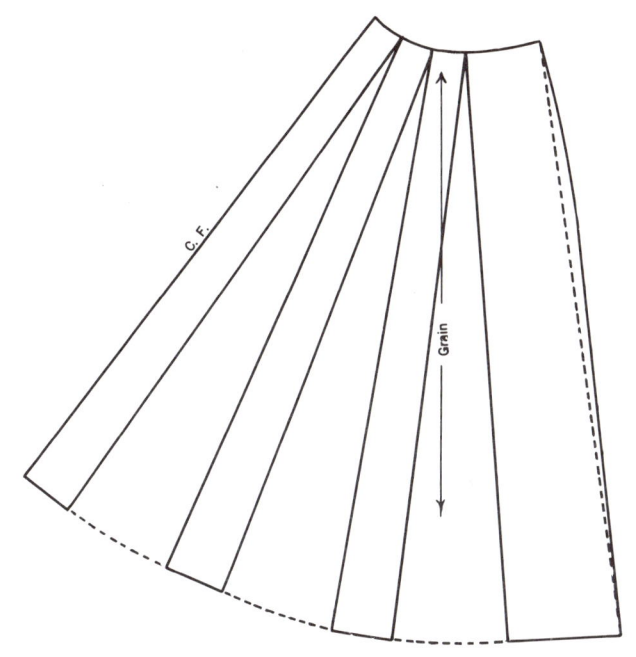

Fig. 100. Greater-than-normal circular skirt (dotted line shows the hip seam with hip curve removed).

2. Add to the center back panel enough to equal the space marked on the diagram by the dotted line.

3. Slash and spread the center back section of the master pattern to form a circular wedge which introduces an emphatic back flare to give contrast to the flatness of the front (see Figure 99 b). A peplum or skirt drapery can be used to conceal the front dart as well as to relieve the plainness of the front. The silhouette is usually more effective, too, if there is a bias seam at the center back to emphasize further the contrast between the flat front and the pronounced back flare.

The Greater-than-Normal Skirt (see Figure 100)

1. Slash from the lower edge to the point of the waistline dart. Close the dart and spread the lower edge.

2. Draw additional lines from the waistline to the lower edge wherever you wish to introduce flares.

3. Slash these lines to the waistline and pivot the pattern outward from the waistline arc. The more the pattern spreads at the hem the more intense the waistline arc becomes, and yet the two arcs (waistline and hem line) will always remain parallel. If you make few slashes and spread the pattern a great deal in one place, the fullness will break into a few large flares. If you make many slashes and spread a small amount at each one, the flares will break into ripples around the entire skirt.

4. Place the straight grain where the least amount of flare should fall. (See Placing the Grain on a Circular Skirt Pattern, page 87.)

5. True up the side seam (see dotted line, Figure 100), cutting off the curve from hip to waistline. The side seam of a greater-than-normal circular skirt does not need to curve since the skirt does not fit the figure over the hip.

Note. Do not ignore or smooth over the abrupt changes in line direction along the waistline arc, as the flares fall from those points.

Figure 101 shows a circular skirt with a maximum flare, in which one-fourth of a skirt pattern equals one-fourth of a circle.

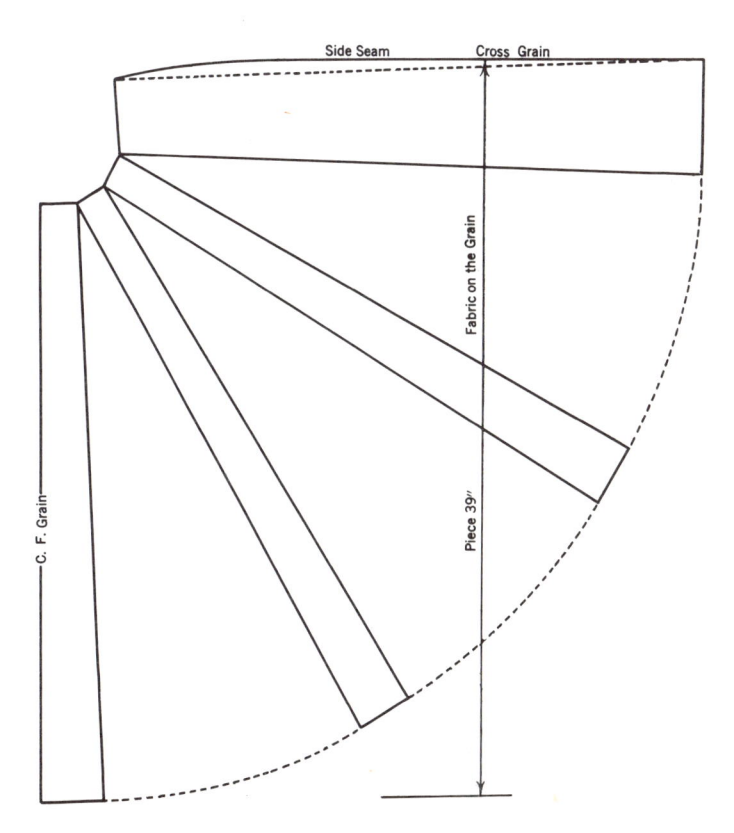

Fig. 101. Maximum circular skirt. One fourth skirt pattern equals one fourth circle.

DRESS DESIGN

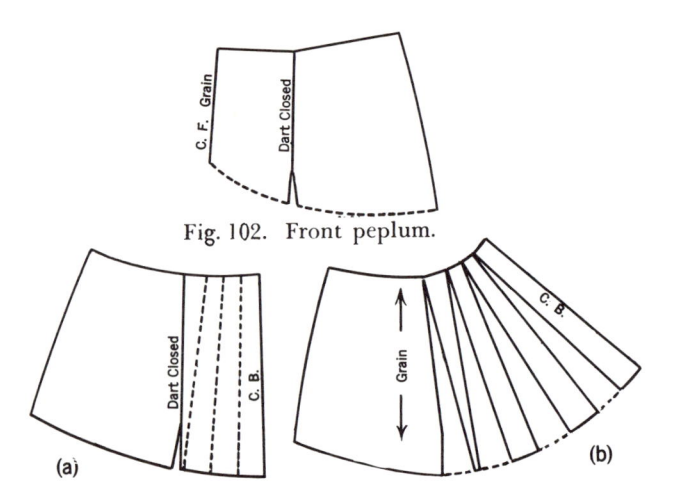

Fig. 102. Front peplum.

Fig. 103. Back peplum: (a) Step 1 — Draw flare lines; (b) Step 2 — Spread slashes for flare and mark grain.

Peplums

Block peplums in the same way as you would block circular skirts, but mark the lower edge of the peplum on the master pattern and cut the pattern off on that line. Figures 102 and 103 a and b show the procedure.

Problem 8

DESIGNING "DRAPED" SKIRTS ON THE TWO-GORE MASTER PATTERN

(See the discussion of the characteristics of this classification, in Part I of this chapter, Draping, pages 90 - 92.)

Placing the Folds (see Figure 104)

1. On the master pattern waistline, space the number of folds desired.

2. Draw radiating lines downward from the points on the waistline. From those which are near the center front draw lines to the lower edge, and from those nearer the side, direct the lines toward the side seam at and above the hip level. Remember that slashes directed too low on the side seam where the skirt should fall free will cause the side seam to waver.

3. Slash along all of the fold-lines, and spread the slashes according to the effect desired (see Figure 105). A skirt is always more graceful if there is enough fullness at the lower edge so that one can move unhampered and sit without having the skirt balloon up into one's lap. To achieve this effect, spread the slash nearest the center front along its entire length. It may even be spread more at the bottom than at the top if desired. Spread the next slash (or slashes) at the top but not at the lower edge. These folds are directed toward the hem but do not run through it. Since the point of the dart intersects this slash line, pivot the dart to close it and increase the spread of the slash line at the waist. Spread the slash toward the side seam at the top edge only. Spread all the shashes equally at the waistline, so that all the folds will be of the same depth.

Center Front

Either mark the center front to be placed on a lengthwise fold, or place the straight grain perpendicular to the waistline over the hip in front of the side drapery. This places the side seam almost on the straight grain and places some flare at the center front. The side seam sometimes even cuts in on the grain at the lower edge if the peg-top effect is very pronounced.

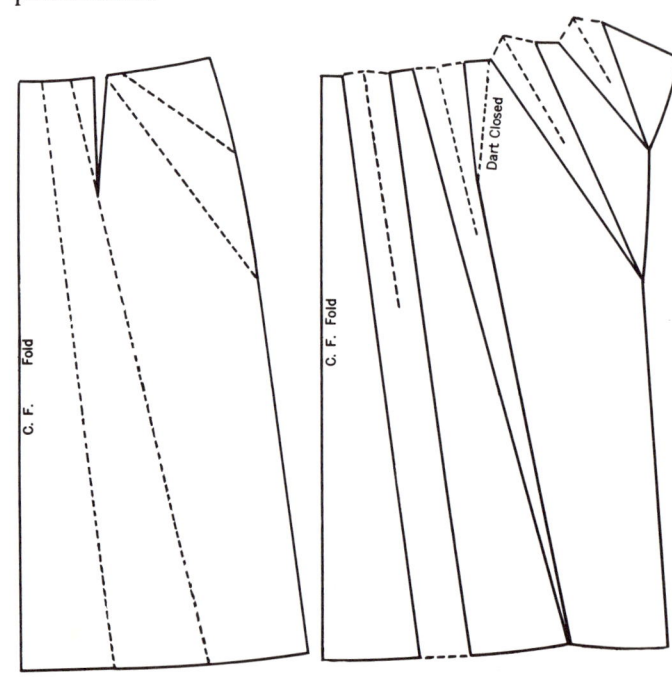

Fig. 104. Draped skirt. Step 1 — Draw slash lines on master pattern.

Fig. 105. Step 2 — Close dart and spread slashes equally at waistline.

108

BASIC SKIRTS

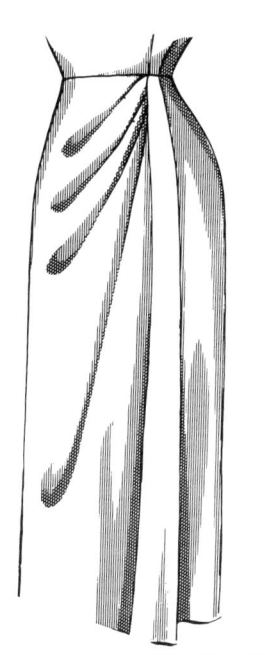

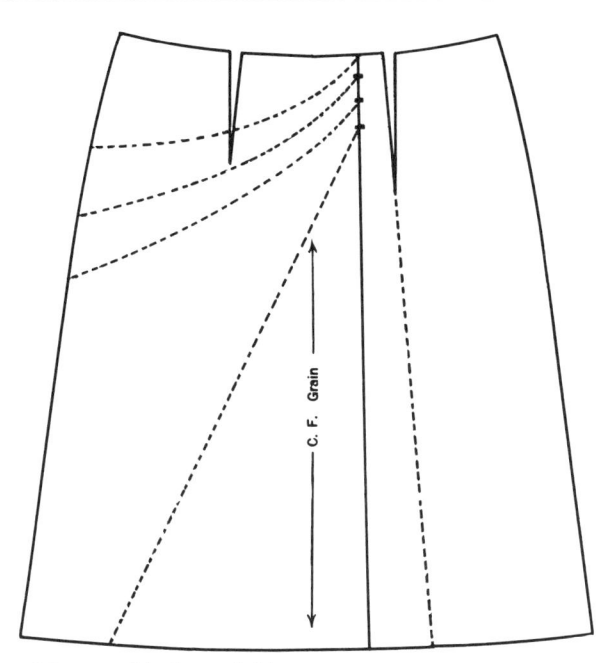

Fig. 106. Skirt draped into a side front fold.
Fig. 107. Skirt draped into a side front vertical fold.
Step 1 — Draw drapery lines and side front opening.

Caution. Do not fail to follow exactly the inward curve along the hipline. To straighten the curve would merely add bulk and destroy the draped effect.

This blocked pattern for a draped skirt is almost an exact duplicate of the draped example, but when draping on the form, the effect at each step is perfectly clear. Flat pattern designing, on the other hand, requires more ability to visualize an idea and is likely to be done with more feeling for contour when it follows experience in draping.

Draped Skirt with a Side Front Opening

An interesting interpretation of the "draped" skirt is one with folds caught into a side front opening (see Figure 106). When the folds are carried from the right side across the center front to an opening on the left, there is more space for them than when they end at the center front. Asymmetric balance is often more graceful and less set than formal symmetry but must be carried throughout the entire costume. Thus, if there is definite emphasis on the side front of the skirt, the asymmetrical motif should be repeated in another part of the garment so that the total design will have unity.

Side Front Line

1. Attach the right and left master pattern skirt fronts at the center front.

2. Draw in the line of the side opening on the left side front. This line should slant outward slightly from the waistline to the hem line and should probably continue in the same direction from the inner edge of the waistline dart.

3. Draw a second vertical line to the hem nearer the center front in order to form the vertical panel shown in Figure 106.

Fold Lines (see Figure 107)

1. Draw lines where the draped folds are to radiate from the fold at the edge of the vertical panel at the left side front, to the right hip seam, fanning out the lines from points very close together at the left side to points farther apart along the right hipline. Do not draw any fold-lines much below the hip level, 9 inches below the waist.

2. Draw another fold-line to the lower edge near the side seam but not running through the lower edge.

3. Slash along these lines, to the side seam, to the

109

DRESS DESIGN

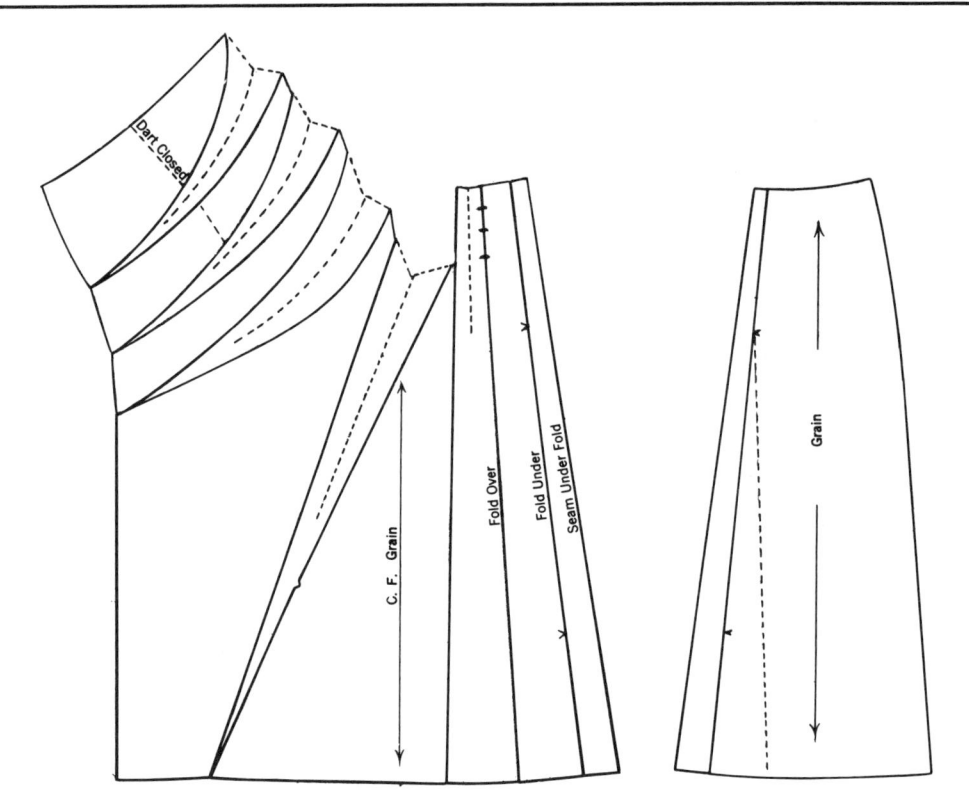

Fig. 108 (a). Skirt draped into side front vertical fold. Step 2 — Spread slashes for folds.

Fig. 108 (b). Left side front section.

lower edge, and all the way through the vertical fold-line that runs through the hem line.

4. Close the waistline dart when you spread the top slash.

5. Spread the slashes directed toward the hip and the hem at the left side front only, but spread the lengthwise slash through the hem at both top and bottom edges, fanning out the lower edge slightly more than the upper one to make the vertical fold deeper.

Center Front

Place the straight lengthwise grain marking at the center front of the pattern from the hem line up to the lowest diagonal slash line.

Left Side Front

Because all of the folds are on the right side front, the pattern shapes for the right and left sides are very different.

1. Use the left side front which was cut away from the entire skirt front (see Figure 107). The dotted line shows where it was cut.

2. Rule down to the lower edge following the side of the dart. This takes out the bulge at the dart point. Then add the same depth of vertical fold to the pattern edge as that added to the side front on the right side (see Figure 108 b).

3. Place the grain with a minimum flare at the side seam.

DESIGNING A "DRAPED" PEPLUM ON A TWO-GORE MASTER PATTERN

Follow the same procedure as for designing a "draped" skirt on a master pattern.

1. Mark on the master pattern the lower edge of the peplum and cut the pattern off along this line.

2. Close the dart. If the end of the dart falls above

the lower edge of the peplum, slash from the lower edge up through the end of the dart, and overlap slightly near the end of the dart to keep the lower edge of the peplum touching. The bias folds of the peplum will stretch enough to make up for the amount overlapped.

3. Slash from the waistline near the center front or from the edge of the center front panel of the peplum to the side seam. Spread at the center front to create the diagonal folds. Add an extension at the center front if you wish to tie the ends of the folds into a knot.

Note. For an all-around draped peplum cut a length of fabric on the true bias and adjust it into folds around the dress form or on the individual figure.

SUMMARY: PRINCIPLES OF DESIGNING GORED SKIRTS ON A TWO-GORE MASTER PATTERN

The character (depth and position of flares) of circular skirts is determined by the following factors,

1. The number, placement, and spread of slashes at the hem edge of the skirt.

(*a*) Many slashes spread equally equalize the flares.

(*b*) Flares occur where slashes are made and fall from the points at which the waistline arc changes direction.

(*c*) One wide spread at the hem produces one deep flare and a correspondingly sudden change in the direction of the waistline arc.

2. The location and size of the outward curves of the individual figure being fitted. Careful observation of these curves enables the designer to predict the probable position of the flares.

3. Grain position. Place the straight grain where least flare is desired and the bias where most flare is wanted. The position of the crosswise grain must be carefully studied in circular skirts. The crosswise grain is bound to hang vertically in some part of the skirt, and the flares will fall most stiffly and awkwardly at this position.

The character or silhouette of a draped skirt is determined by the direction and amount the slashes are spread at the waistline edge of the skirt.

1. Slashes directed entirely toward the side seam of a skirt and spread only at the waistline produce a silhouette that is very narrow at the hem and extremely peg-topped.

2. At least one slash cut through the hem edge near the center and spread apart at the lower edge produces width at the hem that usually improves the silhouette and makes the skirt more graceful and comfortable to wear than the extremely narrow peg-top.

3. Slashes for radiating folds from the waistline can be successfully directed to the side seam at and above the largest hip measurement, but when they are directed toward the side seam below the hips they merely cause the side seam to waver.

4. Sleeves

METHOD OF DESIGN: DRAFTING

The principle of shaping a flat piece of fabric to the contour of the body by darting or easing applies as well to the sleeve pattern as to the blouse or skirt. The arm has two main points of articulation — the elbow and the shoulder ball. At each of these points, darts or ease must provide shaping for the sleeve. The arm must be free to move forward and upward, and even when relaxed, to bend slightly at the elbow. Only when rigid does the arm form one straight axis from shoulder to wrist. Therefore, a dart must be provided for the elbow on the back edge of a long fitted sleeve. And since the shoulder ball rounds outward at the top of the arm, ease must be supplied across the top of the cap of all set-in sleeves to shape them over this curve. The trunk of the body moves comparatively little, whereas the arm performs a great number of movements of a great many kinds. The adaptability which the sleeve must have to accommodate the arm in these positions makes it the most complicated of all pattern shapes and requires absolute accuracy of line.

A method must be chosen to develop a basic master sleeve pattern that fits smoothly and yet gives freedom. One method commonly used but not generally satisfactory is to pad a tightly fitted two-piece muslin sleeve to duplicate the arm at ease, and then to drape sleeves on this form. But draping is not accurate enough for the demands of the sleeve, and results vary widely with each individual draper. Another common method, and also a generally unsatisfactory one, is to cut a heavy cardboard replica of a flat, folded two-piece long sleeve, and to drape over this flat board. The success achieved by this method also varies with the draper, and even the same person finds that her results will differ from sleeve to sleeve.

Drafting, the method of developing a pattern from body measurements, is really the one reliable way, even for a beginner, to make a master sleeve pattern that proves to fit exactly each part of the arm in all positions. Since the master sleeve involves no problems of design and no choice in the placing of darts and curves, but rather hinges on the problem of meticulous accuracy of shape, the drafting method is obviously most suitable. From the drafted master sleeve, all of the more unusual cuts can be speedily derived through blocking. Sleeves so designed will fit with the same precision as the original drafted master sleeve. The draping of sleeves can best be relegated to minor alterations in design and fit.

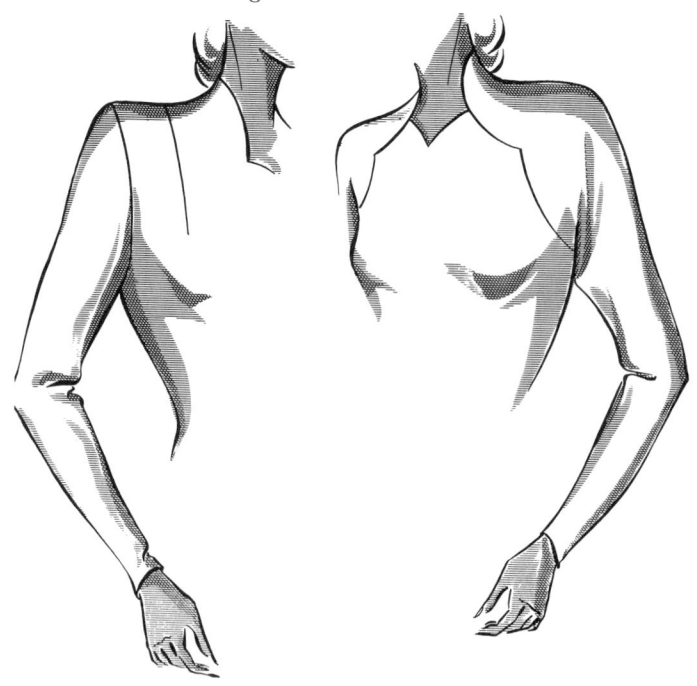

Fig. 1. The set-in sleeve.
Fig. 2. The sleeve cut in one with the bodice.

SLEEVES

CLASSIFICATION OF SLEEVES

Set-in Sleeves (see Figure 1)

Any sleeve that joins the body of the blouse with a seam at the point where the plane of the shoulder joins the plane of the arm is a set-in sleeve.

1. *The one-piece set-in sleeve* is the master pattern for which draft directions will be given. From this drafted pattern, sleeve designs can be derived by using the flat pattern blocking method.

2. *The two-piece set-in sleeve,* because it is made in two sections, fits even more exactly than the one-piece. It is used for tailored garments, suits and coats, and can also be used as a master pattern from which to design variations of two-piece sleeves by blocking.

Sleeves Cut in One with the Bodice or Some Part of the Bodice (see Figure 2)

1. *Raglan-type sleeves* are cut in one with the bodice for the overarm section, but retain the underarm curve which all set-in sleeves have.

2. *Kimono-type sleeves* are cut in one with the bodice through both the overarm and underarm sections, retaining none of the original underarm curve. They therefore give a soft, loose, draped line around the armhole area.

PART I

DRAFTING AND FLAT PATTERN DESIGNING BASIC SET-IN SLEEVES

Problem 1[1]

DRAFT OF ONE-PIECE, LONG, FITTED MASTER SLEEVE

Arm Measurements (see Figures 3 a and b)

Before drafting the sleeve, take accurate arm measurements. Working in pairs, measure each other and take all measurements over the bare arm. For measurements 1, 2, 3, and 4, let the arm hang relaxed and close to the side.

1. *Overarm.* Measure from the tip of the shoulder (the point where arm and shoulder hinge together) over the elbow straight down to a point just below the wrist bone. Since the elbow dart will give additional length for the bend of the arm, measure with the arm almost straight.

2. *Underarm.* Measure from the armpit down the inside line of the arm to the center of the palm at the wrist. To hold the end of the tape in the correct position, pin or sew the tapeline around a pencil and place it under the arm close to the armpit, remembering to subtract the length of the tape around the pencil from the underarm measurement.

3. *Girth or bicep muscle.* Measure around the arm near the armpit with the tape loose enough so that it does not indent the flesh. Then add two inches to this measurement for ease.

Note. If the upper arm is thin compared to the elbow size, more than 2 inches of ease may be required to maintain the correct relationship between the girth and elbow circumferences. The sleeve girth should not be less than 12½ inches. If the upper arm is unusually large, add only 1 to 1½ inches of ease, since a fleshy arm has less muscle and expands less when flexed. (See Chapter 5, Fitting Problems of the Sleeve, page 237 for unusual arm proportions.)

4. *Cap height.* (The cap of the sleeve is the portion above the girth line.) Measure from the girth line to the tip of the shoulder. Increase this measurement ½ to 1 inch for shoulder pads or for a sleeve that is to be set into an armhole slightly deeper than average.

---

[1] For the general methods used in the following sleeve draft, the authors wish to make grateful acknowledgment to M. Rohr, author of *Pattern Drafting and Grading.*

DRESS DESIGN

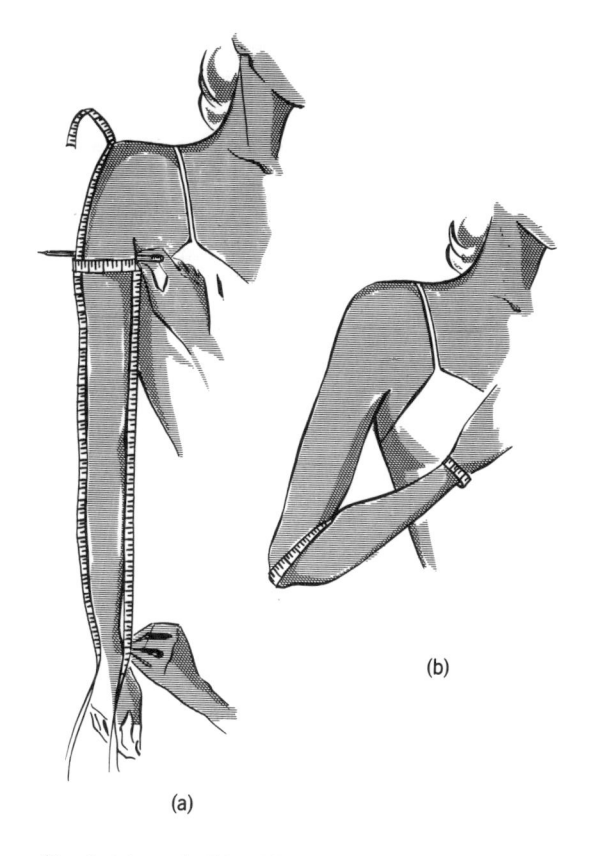

Fig. 3 (a) and (b). Measurements for sleeve draft.

Note. Use this measurement only to check the accuracy of the comparative overarm and underarm measurements. The cap height of the draft is really determined by the difference between the two. Taking the overarm measurement with the arm bent too much increases the difference between it and the underarm length and gives a false cap height. The cap height measurement may indicate that the overarm and underarm measurements should be taken again to correct the error.

The cap height for a dress with a normal armhole and thin shoulder pads varies from 5⅜ to 6¼ inches. Although there is a great deal of individual variation, cap heights generally increase ¼ inch between sizes 12 and 14, 14 and 16, and so on.

5. *Elbow.* Measure around the elbow point with the arm bent sharply. This measurement normally equals the exact girth size, but since no ease is added to it, the elbow will be two inches less than the girth in the sleeve draft.

Note. Try to maintain this two-inch difference between girth and elbow in the draft, because any variation from this throws the cap width out of proportion. A large girth with a small elbow widens the cap too much, and a small girth with a large elbow narrows the cap too much.

6. *Wrist.* Measure around the wrist joint and add one inch to a close measurement for comfortable ease.

Take the measurements for a coat sleeve pattern over a dress sleeve, allowing ½ to 1 inch of extra ease through the girth, elbow, and wrist. Also add extra height to the cap to allow for shoulder pads in the dress and to provide a deeper armscye. The underarm measurement for a coat sleeve should not be taken as high under the armpit as for the dress sleeve. Thus there will be a greater difference between underarm and overarm lengths.

Master Sleeve Draft, Size 16

The following draft is for a basic sleeve with an elbow dart in a standard size 16. To understand the procedure for sleeve drafting and to avoid errors, practice drafting the standard size 16 before drafting a pattern from your own measurements.

The list of supplies required is as follows:

1. Smooth unwrinkled construction or wrapping paper, approximately 27 inches long and 18 inches wide,
2. A tailor's L square,
3. A well sharpened pencil (a fuzzy line is too inaccurate for satisfactory drafting),
4. An eraser.

For accuracy, point the pencil in against the ruler edge in drawing ruled lines.

The measurements for sample size 16 sleeve are as follows:

1. Overarm   23   inches
2. Underarm   17¾   inches
3. Girth   13   inches (11 plus 2 inches of ease)
4. Elbow   11   inches
5. Wrist   7   inches

114

SLEEVES

PROCEDURE FOR DRAFTING (see Figures 4-8)

Vertical Measurements

1. Draw a line 23 inches long down the center of the paper, ending at least 2 inches above the lower edge.

2. Square out in both directions from the center line at the top point *A* and the bottom point *B*.

3. Measure up from point *B* the underarm length, 17¾ inches, and mark point *C*.

4. Measure down on the center line ¾ inch below *C* and mark *D*. Square out at point *D* for the girth line.

5. Mark *E*, the halfway point of the underarm length (one-half the length from *C* to *B*). Measure up 1 inch from *E* and mark *F*. Square out at *F* for the elbow line.

Horizontal Measurements

1. Measure from *F* one-fourth of the elbow measurement, or 2¾ inches, on each side of the center line.

2. Measure from *D* one-fourth of the girth measurement, or 3¼ inches, on each side of the center line.

3. Join with straight lines the points marked on elbow and girth in steps 1 and 2. Continue these lines to both top and bottom horizontals. (Check for equal distances on each side of the center line at *A* and *B*.)

The Sleeve Cap

1. Divide the vertical sides of the cap into halves, but locate a dot ¾ inch above each halfway point. Mark *I* and *J* on these dots.

2. Divide each half of the top line squared out from *A* into halves and mark points *G* and *H*.

3. Divide the lower line on the front of the cap into halves and mark *K*. *It is customary to draft a sleeve with the front edge to the left and the back edge to the right.*

4. Mark point *L* on the lower line of the back of the cap 1 inch from the center line.

5. Connect these points with ruled lines as shown in Figure 4 to provide guide lines for drawing the curves of the sleeve cap.

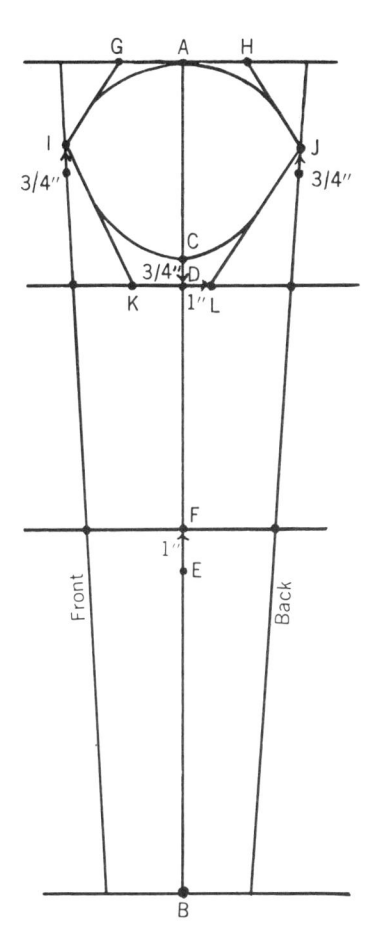

Fig. 4. Locate the sleeve measurements.

Cap Curves

1. On the upper half of the front, follow the guide line up from *I* for slightly over half the distance to *G* before curving toward the center line at *A*.

2. On the upper half of the back, draw a curve from *A* that touches the guide line *HJ* ⅛ inch below its halfway point. On the upper half, the back curve is slightly flatter than the front.

3. For the lower half of the cap, follow the guide lines *IK* and *JL* down one-half their length before curving in toward the underarm at point *C*.

The Open Sleeve

The sleeve is now essentially complete but is in a folded position with the underarm seam at the center line.

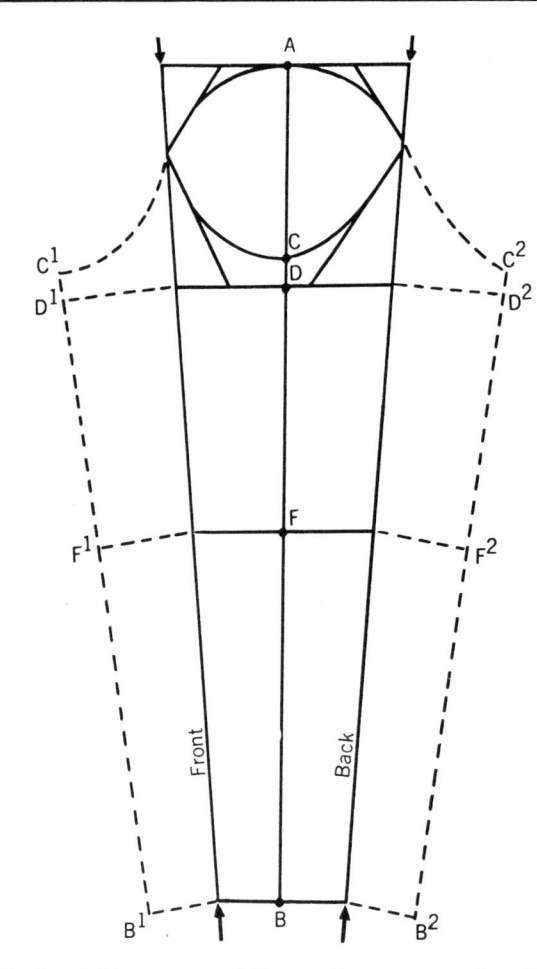

Fig. 5. Fold on arrowed lines and trace to produce lines indicated by dotted lines.

1. Fold the paper under and crease it exactly on the front lengthwise line. With a tracing wheel, follow the lines of the lower half of the sleeve cap, the center line, the girth, the elbow, and the wrist lines. Then open the paper again and you have the outside lines of the sleeve front. The center line becomes the underarm seam line on the newly traced pattern.

2. Repeat direction 1 for the back.

Wrist Width Correction and Provision for Bending the Elbow

1. Measure the sleeve at the wrist and subtract from it the correct wrist size. The lower edge of the sample sleeve measures $8\frac{1}{2}$ inches. The wrist measures 7 inches, so the difference shows $1\frac{1}{2}$ inches of excess. Divide the excess into halves and subtract one-half from the back and one-half from the front seam line at the wrist.

2. From these newly established points on the wrist, draw lines to the outer edge of the elbow line.

3. Overtrace this new lower section from elbow to wrist on another piece of paper placed underneath the draft.

4. Cut out the traced lower sleeve section and place it on top of the original sleeve, pivoting it so that the back elbow point F^2 of the traced section falls $1\frac{1}{2}$ inches below the elbow point F^2 on the sleeve. The space between the two points is the elbow dart.

5. Draw around the pivoted section to get a new bias back line from elbow to wrist and a new front line from elbow to wrist which may end slightly in front of the original wrist point.

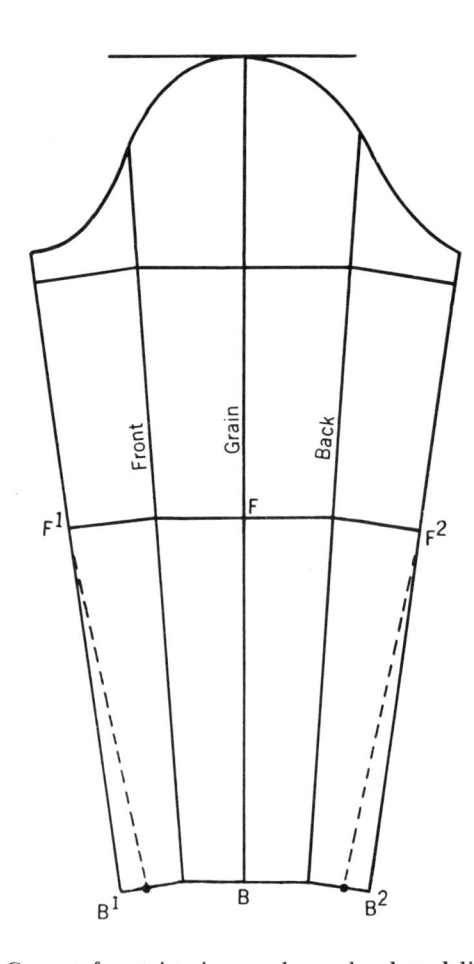

Fig. 6. Correct for wrist size, as shown by dotted lines.

SLEEVES

Balance Points on Seams (Matching Marks or Notches)

1. On the front line, measure up 2½ inches from the elbow and down 2½ inches from the elbow to mark the balance points.

2. To obtain corresponding markings on the back seam line, measure down on the front seam from the underarm to the top balance point and up from the bottom to the lower balance point and mark both points at the same distances down from the underarm and up from the wrist on the back seam. This places the extra length at the elbow on the back seam line between the two notches if the dart is to be put in as ease. Elbow ease should never go above or below these two points.

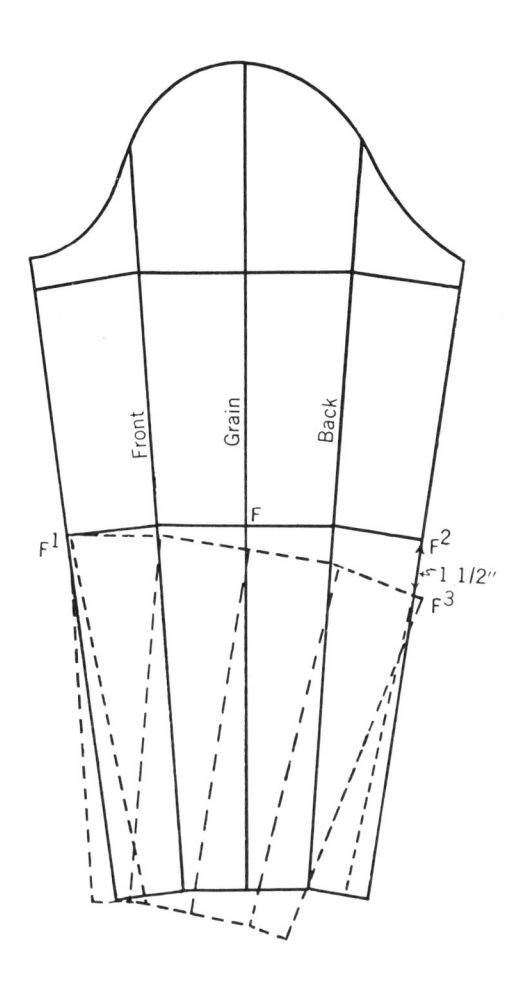

Fig. 7. Making the elbow dart.

The Elbow Dart

1. Begin the point of the dart one-third of the sleeve width in from the back seam line and halfway between the original elbow line on the sleeve draft and the elbow line on the traced section. This is the correct dart length for pattern blocking, though the sewed dart should not be more than one-fourth the sleeve width at the elbow.

2. Draw a line from the point of the dart to the original elbow line on the back seam at F^2.

3. Measure the length of the upper dart edge and mark off the same length for the lower edge. Rule a line from the wrist to this point in order to clear away whatever excess there may be on the back edge from wrist to elbow.

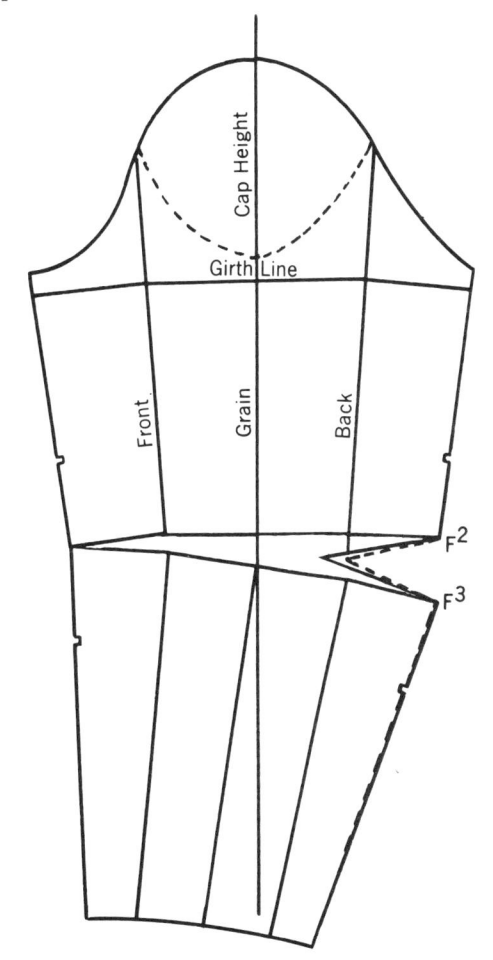

Fig. 8. The one-piece master sleeve draft.

DRESS DESIGN

THE DRAFT FOR THE INDIVIDUAL MASTER PATTERN SLEEVE

Follow the standard size 16 draft directions exactly, but substitute individual arm measurements. The standard measurements for locating guide lines for the cap and the placement of the girth and elbow lines remain constant for all sizes.

Record your own measurements below:

1. Overarm
2. Underarm
3. Girth (plus 2 inches)
4. Elbow
5. Wrist

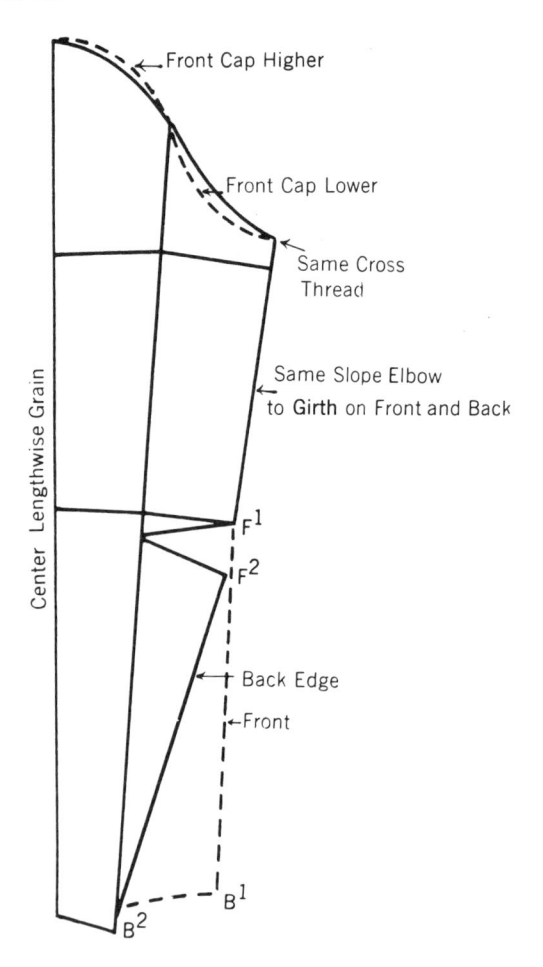

Fig. 9. Sleeve folded on center line (elbow and wristline coincide when the dart is closed).

ANALYSIS OF MASTER ONE-PIECE SLEEVE

In order to check the accuracy of the drafted master pattern sleeve which you have just finished, and better to understand the principles underlying the making of the sleeve patterns, make the following study.

Sleeve Folded on Center along Lengthwise Grain Line (see Figure 9)

1. The girth corner of the front of the sleeve cap should fall directly on the girth corner of the back. The same crosswise thread should run from corner to corner.

2. The slope should be identical on both front and back seam lines from girth to elbow.

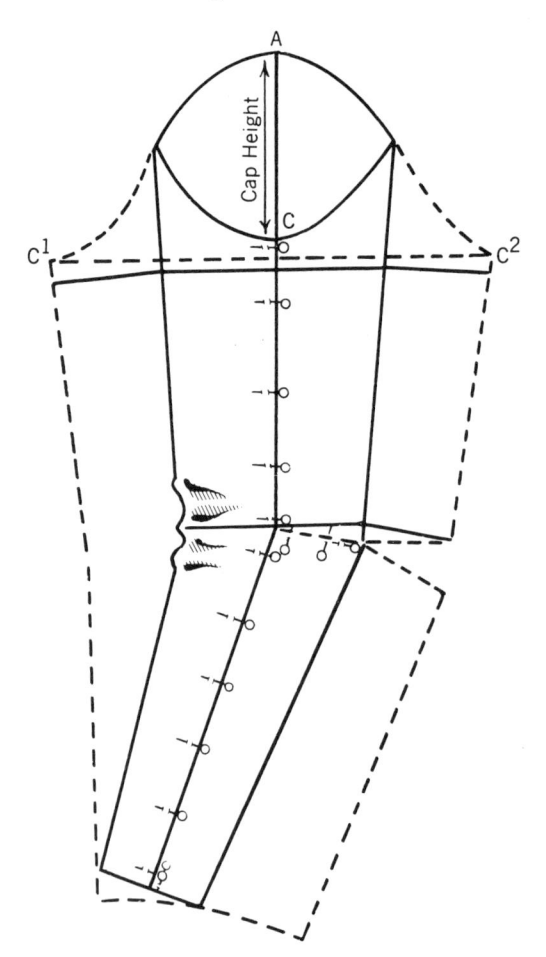

Fig. 10. Sleeve folded with front and back edges meeting on center line (dotted line indicates sleeve opened flat).

SLEEVES

3. The curve on the front of the cap should rise slightly (1/8 to 1/4 inch) above that of the back at the top of the sleeve. The front of the cap dips slightly (1/4 inch) below the back curve at the underarm.

Note. These comparisons of front and back conform to the needs of the average arm. From the shoulder seam forward, the arm has a rounder and higher curve than from the shoulder seam back. The back underarm curve should be hollowed out less than the front one, so that it will be possible to swing the arm forward comfortably without ripping the back of the sleeve from the garment. A deeper curve is needed on the front underarm so that the armscye seam will not bind when the arm swings forward.

Sleeve Folded so that Front and Back Seam Lines Meet on Center Line (see Figure 10)

This will enable you to determine the actual height of the cap, the distance from A to C. It is incorrect to estimate the height of the cap by measuring from A to a straight girth line drawn across the opened sleeve from C^1 to C^2.

Sleeve Opened Flat (see Figure 10)

When the sleeve was drafted, the lower half of the pattern was pivoted forward to give the necessary spread at the back for the elbow dart. This usually causes the front seam line from elbow to wrist to slope forward slightly more than it does from girth to elbow. It would be wrong to draw this as a straight line from girth to wrist, because the front slope from girth to elbow would then no longer be the same as the back slope, and the sleeve would tend to twist when back and front seam edges were joined.

Problem 2

THE LONG FITTED SLEEVE PATTERN MODIFIED FOR BLOCKING SLEEVES LOOSE AT THE LOWER EDGE (see Figures 11-13)

If the original sleeve draft with the basic lines marked on it is not available, you can easily modify the long sleeve with an elbow dart and a fitted wrist to make a workable block for the designing of patterns unfitted from elbow to wrist, such as bishop,

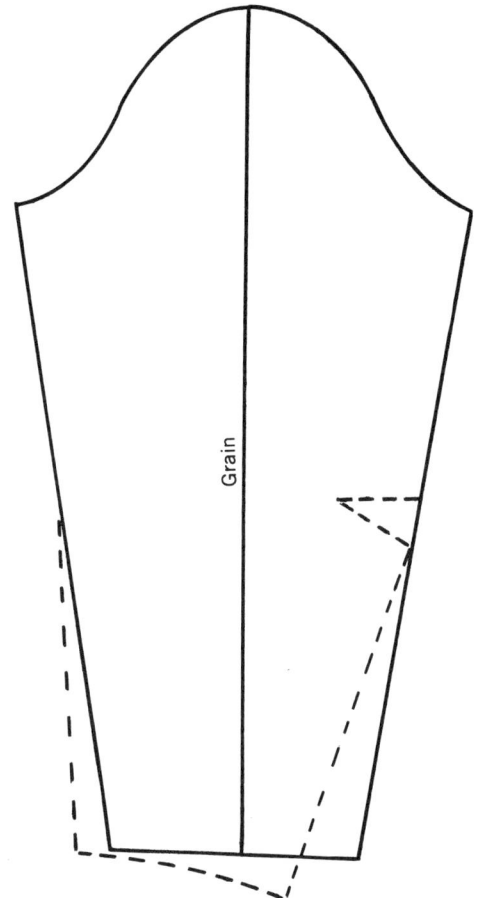

Fig. 11. Front and back underarm seams straightened so that slope from girth to elbow is continued from elbow to wrist.

bell, and straight-hanging sleeves. You will find this a convenient procedure for changing a long fitted sleeve in a commercial dress pattern, or in reversing your cut-out master sleeve pattern to its original drafted form before it was altered to fit from elbow to wrist.

1. To establish the lengthwise center line, fold the sleeve so that the front and back seam lines coincide from girth to elbow, crease the fold along the center line from the top of the sleeve to the wrist, and rule it.

2. Trace the sleeve and the center line on a second sheet of paper.

3. To establish straight back and front underarm seam lines, place a ruler on the original seam line from girth to elbow and with a pencil, continue this line to the wrist (see Figure 11).

119

4. Measure the front underarm seam line from girth to wrist, and mark off the same measurement on the back underarm seam line. At the wrist, rule a line from front to back edges to serve as a temporary cutting line.

5. Cut out the sleeve.

6. Fold the pattern so that the underarm seam lines drawn in step 3 meet along the ruled center line (see Figure 12).

(*a*) Crease along the sides of the pattern, and pencil the fold lines to show the quarter divisions. Folding the sleeve in this way indicates the top and the underside of the sleeve when it is worn.

(*b*) Trace the lower armscye curve.

(*c*) Rule a line across the bottom of the sleeve perpendicular to the center line to get the correct slope for the lower edge.

7. Open the sleeve and use it for blocking (see Figure 13).

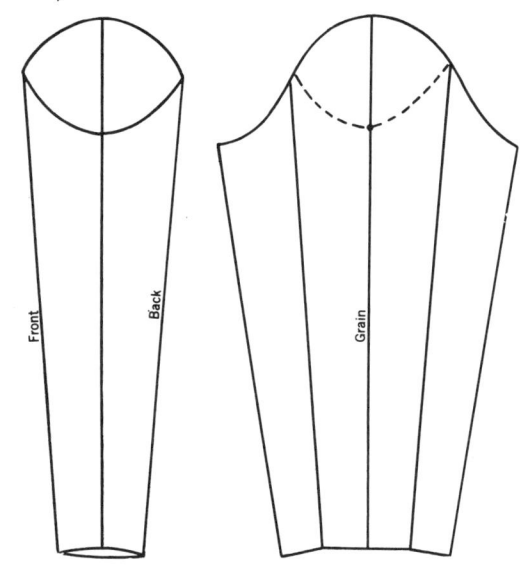

Fig. 12. Sleeve folded to center, in order to determine sleeve quarter division lines, cap base, and correct lower edge.
Fig. 13. Sleeve ready for slashing and spreading.

Problem 3

THE BISHOP SLEEVE FROM MASTER PATTERN
(see Figure 14)

The bishop sleeve derives its name from its clerical source. It is a long sleeve that blouses down over a narrow band at the wrist with the fullest and longest part of the blousing falling away from the body around the little finger side of the hand (see Figure 15).

Either of two methods may be used to produce the bishop sleeve from the master pattern. (*A*) One is to use the master pattern sloper, the draft of the central section of the sleeve with the underarm seam lines folded in to the center line. (*B*) The other is to use the draft for the master pattern opened flat before wrist size is corrected or the elbow dart put in.

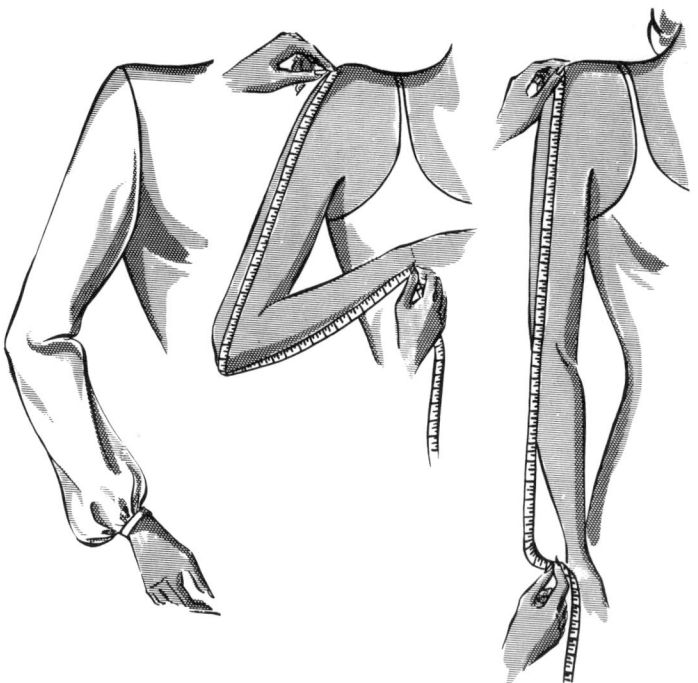

Fig. 14. Bishop sleeve.
Fig. 15. Back of arm measurement for bishop sleeve.

Method A: From Master Pattern Sloper[1] (see Figures 16 and 17)

1. Draw around the sleeve sloper, marking in the lower armscye curve and the center line.

2. Determine the depth of the cuff and mark off this amount on the center line. The cuff is 2 inches deep on the sleeve illustrated.

---

[1] For the general methods used in the sleeve draft that follows, the authors wish to make grateful acknowledgment to M. Rohr, author of *Pattern Drafting and Grading*.

SLEEVES

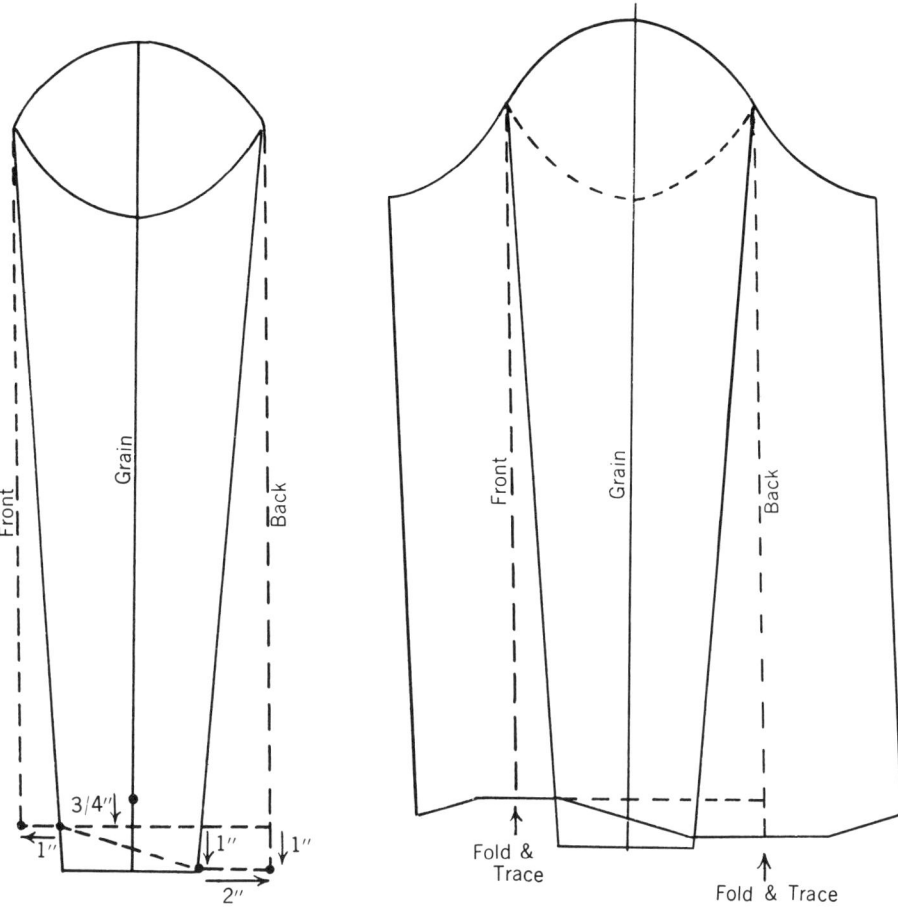

Fig. 16. Bishop sleeve from master pattern sloper. Lines are drawn for increase in width of wrist.

Fig. 17. Pattern is folded under on the dotted lines of Fig. 16, and the sides and lower edge traced.

3. Measure down 3/4 inch from the point marked in step 2. This added length is needed on any sleeve gathered into a tight band to allow for reaching and blousing. Square out in both directions from the center line to establish the construction line of the lower edge of the sleeve (see Figure 16).

4. Increase the sleeve width by measuring forward on the wrist line one-half the amount desired on the front half of the sleeve. Figure 16 shows the wrist line extended 1 inch at the front edge of the sloper. Increase twice this amount at the back. The diagram shows 2 inches. Always maintain this proportion.

5. Join the points marked on the wristline to the top points of the front and back edges of the sloper at the armscye.

6. Lengthen the back of the sleeve 1 inch by dropping down that amount on the back edge of the sloper and also on the newly drawn back line. The additional back length provides for the difference between the measurement over the back of the arm when held straight and when bent at the elbow (see Figure 15). Add more than 1 inch for exaggerated blousing.

7. Rule a line joining the lengthened back line of the sloper to the front line of the sloper at the wrist construction line. The lower edge of the sleeve will be perpendicular to the center line between the original lines of the sloper and the newly drawn lines at the back and front.

8. Fold the pattern under on the new front line and trace the front lower armscye, the center line, and the shaped wrist line to complete the front half of the sleeve (see Figure 17).

9. Repeat the same procedure for the back.

DRESS DESIGN

Method B: From Opened Master Pattern (see Figure 18)

1. Measure up on the center line from the lower edge the cuff width minus ¾ inch allowed for blousing. From this point square out a line across the center section of the sleeve.

2. Slash the vertical lines at the side front and side back of the sleeve (the quarter division lines).

3. Rule a vertical line on a separate sheet of paper and pin the center lengthwise grain line of the pattern to this line at the top and the bottom.

4. Spread the front slash 1½ to 2 inches at the lower edge and the back slash twice that amount. Pin the side sections down to the paper.

5. Extend the length 1 inch on both edges of the back slash to allow for bending the elbow.

6. Rule a wrist line joining the lengthened inner edge of the back slash to the inner edge of the front slash.

7. Measure the length of the center line from point B, marked for the base of the cap, to the bottom line of the sleeve at point F ruled in step 6.

8. Measure off this amount on both the front and back underarm seam lines to determine the points of the sleeve lower edge.

9. Join the points established in step 8 to the outer front and back slash lines and continue as a level line across the space between the outer and inner edges of both back and front slashes to complete the sleeve bottom line.

Problem 4

THE BISHOP SLEEVE WITH EXAGGERATED WIDTH AND LENGTH FOR BLOUSING
(see Figures 19 and 20)

A Long Sleeve

In a sleeve which is very full all across the outside of the arm, the entire spread should not be at the side front and side back edges of the central section. In addition, vertical slashes should be made through the center section and a small amount of flare should be introduced at each slash. However, even with the fullness so distributed, the slash at the side back should be spread more than the others, because the silhouette is more effective if the flare and blousing are most pronounced on the outside of the arm toward the back. As the width of the sleeve increases, the length must also increase in order to produce blousing at the lower edge.

The width of a sleeve can be successfully increased through spreading at the side front and side back slashes up to the point where the width at the lower edge equals that at the girth. If you widen the lower edge much more than this, it is usually more satisfactory to introduce some of the width on the top of the arm by slashes at the center of the sleeve, so that the sleeve will retain a column shape rather than a flattened two dimensional shape flaring entirely at the side front and side back of the arm.

A Three-Quarter-Length Sleeve

This sleeve length is suitable for the mature figure, since it does not have the childish silhouette of a short

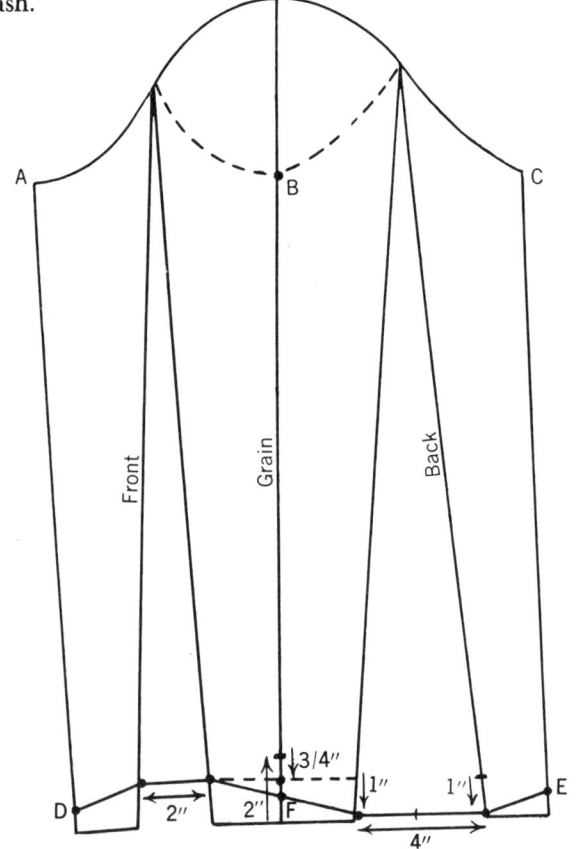

Fig. 18. Bishop sleeve from opened master pattern (shown in Fig. 13). AD and CE should equal center line BF.

SLEEVES

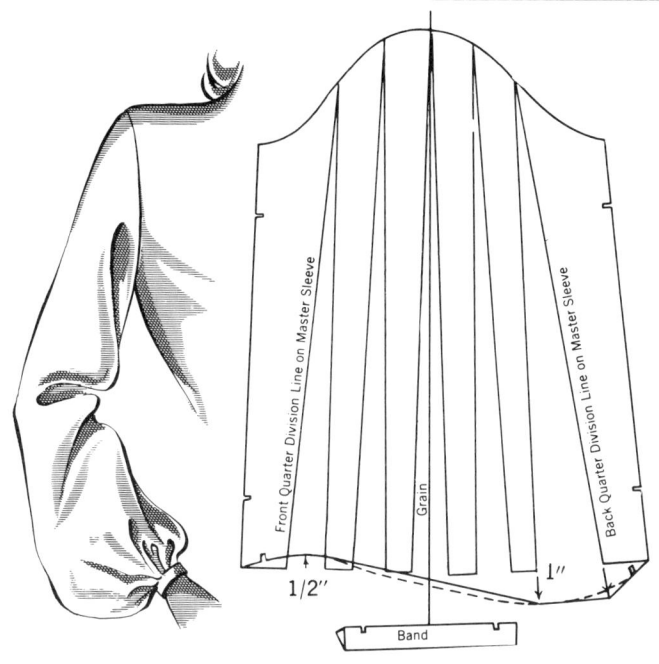

Figs. 19 and 20. Exaggerated bishop sleeve. Fig. 20 shows the fullness distributed evenly all across the top of the sleeve and extra blouse added on the back.

puff sleeve. However, blousing that falls at the outside of the arm below the elbow is at the level of the hips and therefore broadens them.

1. Proceed as for the long full-length sleeve.
2. Measure up from the wrist for the desired sleeve length.
3. Cut off the bishop sleeve already designed on lines exactly parallel to the lower edge.

Problem 5

THE BELL SLEEVE

The bell sleeve, a variation of the bishop sleeve, flares out like a bell, wider at the lower edge than at the girth. It is exactly like the bishop sleeve except for the lower edge which hangs free. Sleeves that hang in a straight tubular column from shoulder to wrist are also often loosely classified as bell sleeves, even though they may be the same size at girth and wrist or even slightly narrower at the wrist.

1. Check the drafted bishop sleeve for correct wrist width. To increase the flare still further, slash and spread at the side front and side back where fullness has already been introduced. (See Problem 4 concerning the extent to which a sleeve can satisfactorily be widened at side front and side back.) To reduce the flare, slash and lap out along these same lines from the bottom of the sleeve to the armscye.

2. Check the lower edge of the pattern to see that the sleeve will be parallel to the floor when the arm hangs at the side of the body. Since the bell sleeve hangs free, remove the allowance for blousing added to the lower edge of the bishop sleeve, but retain the one inch of added length at the side back of the sleeve necessary to go over the bend of the elbow. You may even increase this length as you increase the bell flare.

3. The finish for the lower edge depends on the amount of shaping necessary. If the bottom of the sleeve has to be shaped to hang gracefully, finish the lower edge with a deep shaped facing. Trace the pattern for the facing from the lower section of the sleeve, matching the grain exactly. However, if the sleeve is a column shape, or is only very slightly flared, a deep hem hangs more softly. For the hem pattern, fold the paper pattern under at the hemline and trace the side seams to the top of the hem.

THE CORRECT METHOD FOR INCREASING OR DECREASING SLEEVE WIDTH

The correct method for increasing or decreasing sleeve width (see Figures 21 *a, b,* and *c*) is to slash the sleeve where the alteration is to be made and either spread to widen the sleeve or lap to narrow it.

The first sleeve (Figure 21a) has the usual shape of a master sleeve pattern before being adjusted to wrist size. The seam lines slope inward from girth to wrist. Dotted lines indicate the height of the cap and show the position of the underarm half of the sleeve when it is folded in to the center. This diagram illustrates that if the front and back seam lines slope inward from the girth to the wrist, the girth points at the front and back when brought together will meet *above* a straight horizontal line drawn between them when the pattern is laid flat. It also follows that the bottom edge of this sleeve must curve upward at the center and down at the seam lines in order to appear straight when the seam is joined. The dotted underarm seam lines and the overlapping on the quarter division

123

DRESS DESIGN

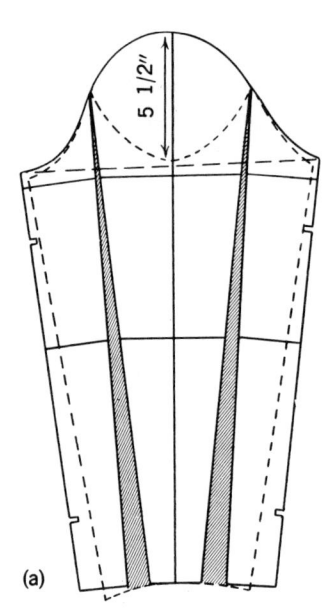

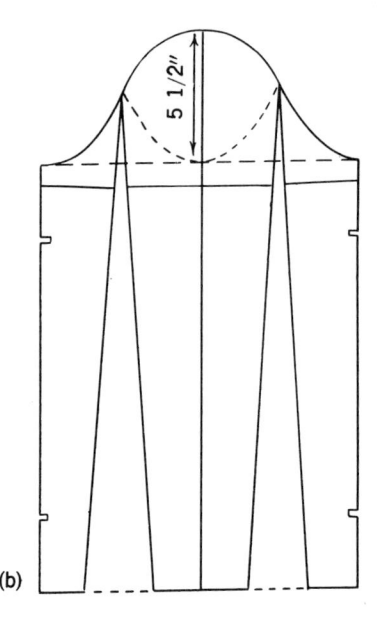

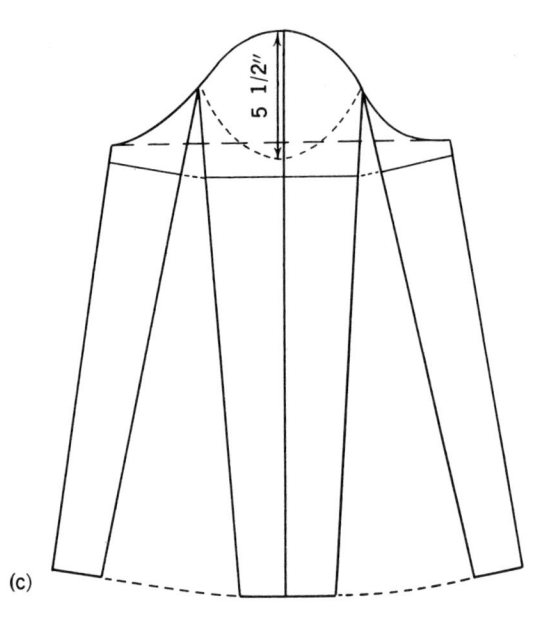

Fig. 21. Correct method of increasing or decreasing width of sleeve at lower edge: (1) Cap same height in each case; (2) Lower edge automatically corrected; (3) Flare falls at sides of arm rather than at underarm seam. (*a*) Slashing and overlapping at quarter division lines; (*b*) Slashing and spreading at quarter division lines; (*c*) Slashing and spreading at quarter division lines.

lines show the correct method for decreasing the sleeve width. The cap height of the sleeve which has been narrowed in this way remains the same as in the original master sleeve.

The second sleeve (Figure 21*b*), made correctly by slashing and spreading the master pattern, shows seam lines at right angles to the girth line. They therefore fold in to the center on a straight horizontal drawn from the front to the back. The bottom edge is also a straight line when the sleeve is open.

The third sleeve (Figure 21 *c*), also made correctly by slashing and spreading the master pattern, slopes outward along the seam lines from girth to wrist. The front and back seam lines when folded in to the center, meet below a straight horizontal line drawn between the front and back girth points when the pattern is laid flat. The bottom edge also curves downward at the center in order to appear straight when the front and back seam lines are joined.

Since the front and back girth corners in Figure 21*a* have dropped with the lapping, and since those in Figures 21*b* and 21*c* have risen with the spreading of the slashes in the sleeves, they will fold in to meet at the original points, and the cap will remain the same correct height in all three. The width added to the sleeve hangs exactly where the pattern was slashed and spread, that is, below the points at the front and back of the armscye where the slash has increased the intensity of the armscye curve.

In contrast, note what has happened to the armscye curves in Figures 22*a, b,* and *c*. These illustrations show why increasing or decreasing sleeve width by simply redrawing the underarm seam line is incorrect. If you compare each of these sleeves with the corresponding one in the correct group, you will notice that the wrong method causes the following errors:

1. The armscye line is not automatically changed to correspond to the new slope of the seam lines in order to retain the original cap height. Inward sloping of the seam lines shortens the cap height (Figure 22*a*) and outward sloping increases it (Figures 22*b* and *c*). (See Fitting Problems of the Sleeve, Chapter 5, pages 232-4.)

SLEEVES

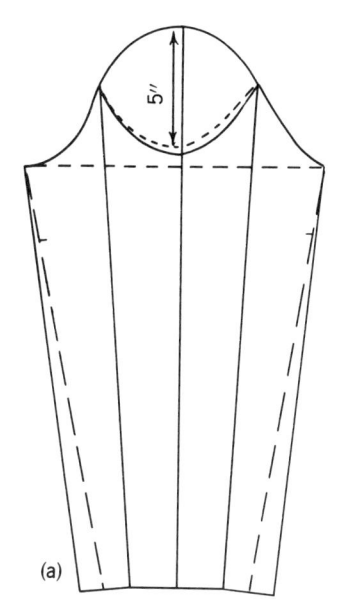

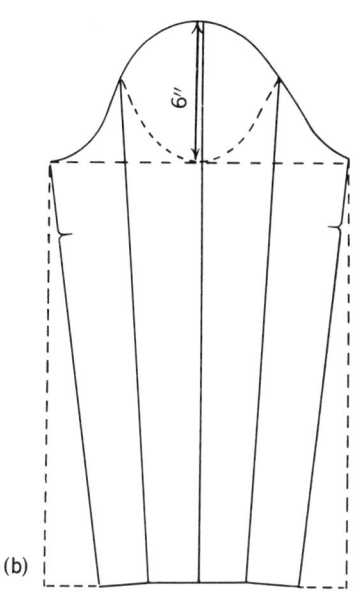

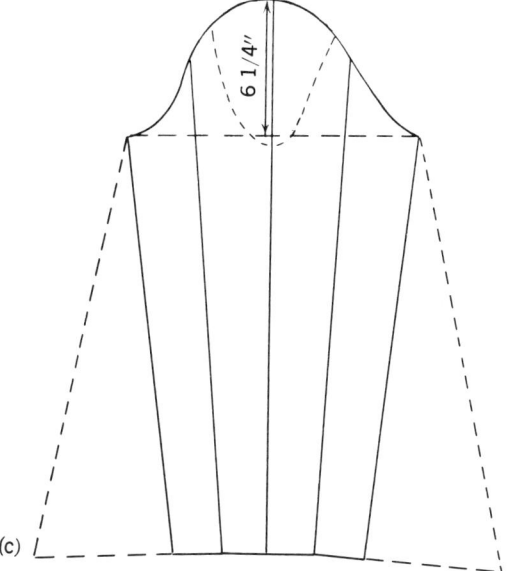

Fig. 22. Incorrect method of increasing or decreasing sleeve width at lower edge: (a) Narrowing sleeve at edges decreases cap height; (b) widening sleeve at edges increases cap height; (c) Widening sleeve at edges not only increases cap height, but throws all flare at underarm.

2. The correction for the lower edge of the sleeve is not indicated, and thus the sleeve will hang unevenly when on the arm.

3. The width added to the sleeve hangs underneath the arm at the seam line, and the sleeve continues to hang in a narrow column at the sides and top of the arm.

Note. This comparison of right and wrong methods in changing sleeve size further emphasizes the dangers of altering *on pattern edges. Most changes should be made within the pattern.*

Problem 6

THE MASTER SLEEVE MODIFIED FOR CAP HEIGHT

The Lower-than-Normal Cap Height (see Figures 23a, b, and c)

Very short sleeves and those for sports or working garments require a cap which is shorter than normal in order to provide freer arm movement. The master pattern sleeve block can be modified to decrease the height of the cap without changing the measurement of the armscye line. When such a change is made, the height of the cap decreases as the width of the cap and of the girth increases, but the armscye length remains constant.

Procedure.

1. Trace the master sleeve pattern, including the center line and the quarter division lines (see points B and D on the armscye).

2. Draw lines from the center top of the sleeve cap to the front and back girth points, lines AC and CE (see Figure 23a).

3. Slash from A and E to the cap edge at the center top, C.

4. Slash on the quarter divisions from line AC up to point B and from line CE up to point D on the side of the armscye.

5. Spread along the slashes A to C and E to C to lengthen the underarm seam lines about 1½ inches. (This may vary with the amount that you wish the cap to be shortened.) The more the underarm seam is lengthened and the cap thus shortened, the more the bottom edge of the sleeve extends away from the arm.

125

DRESS DESIGN

6. Spread about 1/8 inch at the short slashes out to B and D in order to lower slightly the curve on the side of the armscye.

7. Draw a new underarm seam line. To retain the original width at the lower edge, draw sloping lines from points A and E to G and F. To widen the lower edge, rule lines from the girth at A and E parallel to the original underarm seam line. Figure 23c shows that the sleeve with more sloping underarm seam edges will have a shorter cap than the sleeve with less sloping edges and a wider lower edge.

8. Trace off the new sleeve pattern.

Note. The length of the armscye line has not been altered. The loss in cap height has been transferred to increased girth. This pattern is suited to the very short sleeve pictured in Figure 24a. Figure 24b shows a sleeve with a shortened cap, but with the flare which usually swings away from the top of the arm taken out by lapping on the center line. (Figure 25 shows this procedure.) Figure 24c illustrates how underarm tucks also reduce the flare at the center top. The man-tailored shirtwaist (see Figure 26), has a short cap so that the arm can be raised comfortably without pulling the blouse and skirt apart. Dresses for active sports, smocks, and nurses' uniforms are other examples of garments using the shorter cap. It is sometimes used in very bouffant puffed sleeves because of its tendency to flare more than the normal sleeve with a deeper cap.

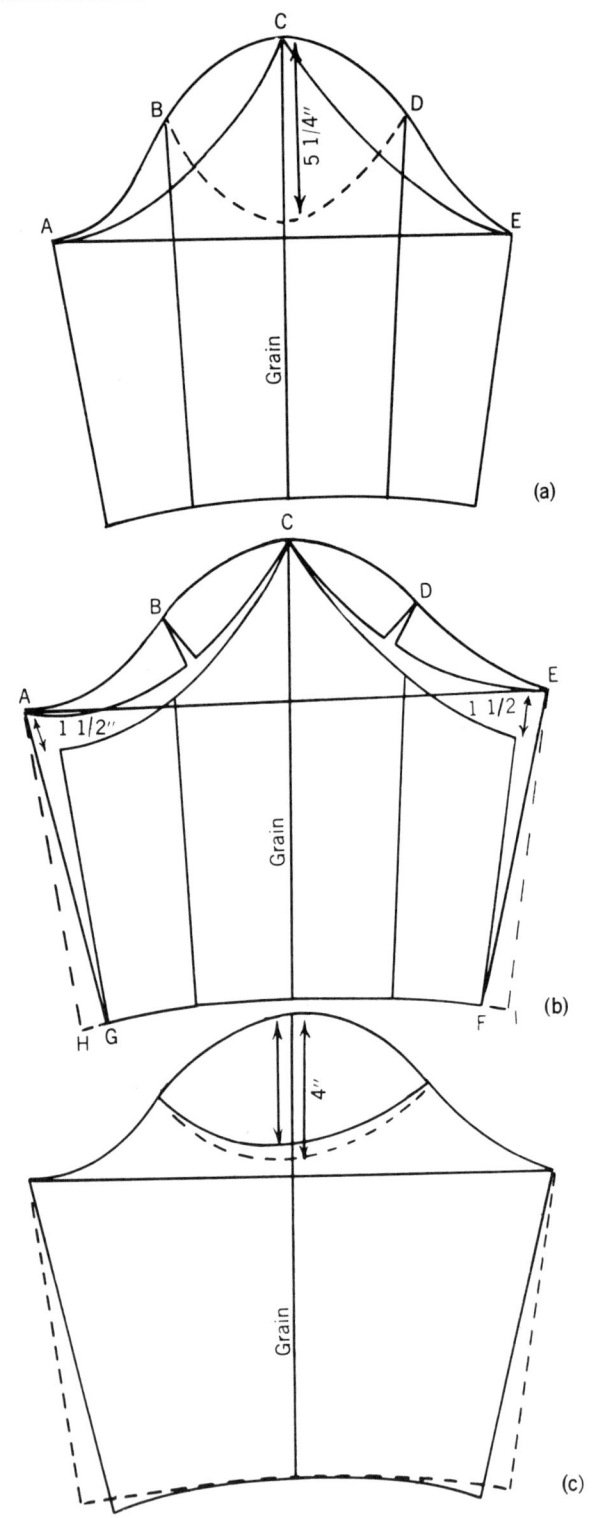

Fig. 23 (*a*), (*b*), and (*c*). Decreasing the normal cap height on the master sleeve.

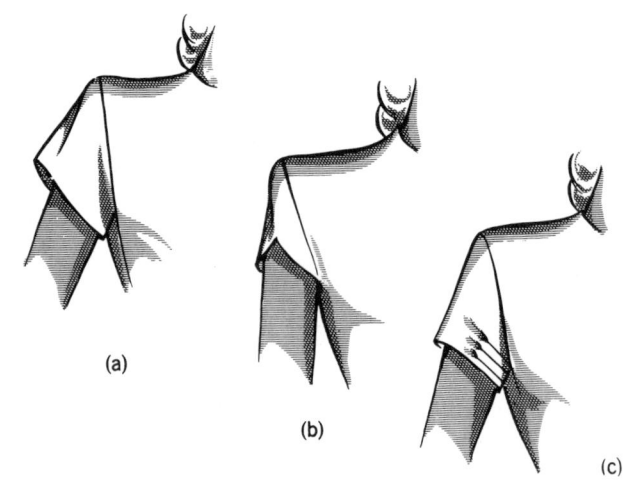

Fig. 24 (*a*), (*b*), and (*c*). Sleeves with less-than-normal cap height.

126

SLEEVES

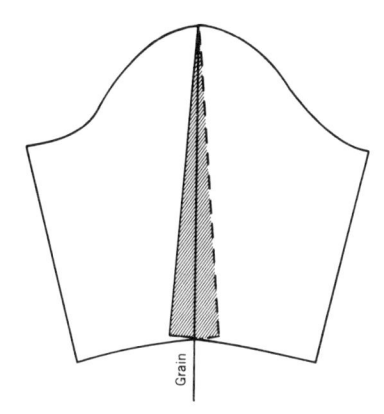

Fig. 25. Pattern for Fig. 24 (b). Top of arm flare lapped out on center line of sleeve.

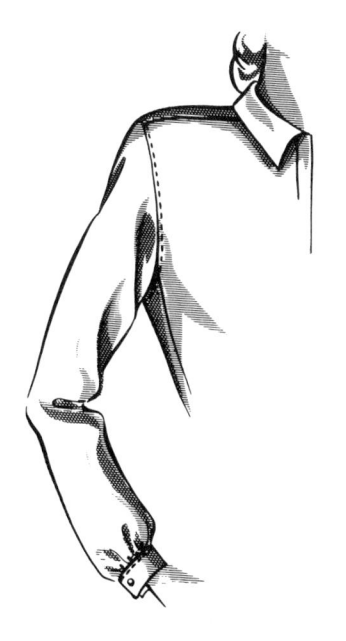

Fig. 26. Shirtwaist sleeve. Less-than-normal cap height allows free arm movement.

The Higher-than-Normal Cap Height (see Figures 27a and b)

The normal cap height of a foundation sleeve may be too short for shoulder padding, and obviously, the thicker the padding the higher the cap needs to be. Check the height of the master sleeve cap accurately by folding the underarm seam lines to the center before measuring from the base of the cap at the center up to the top (see Page 119.)

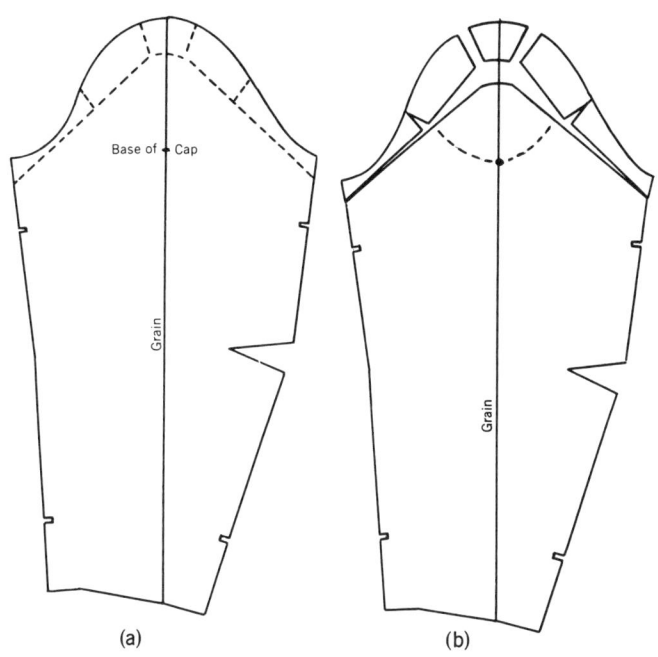

Fig. 27. Extension of cap height for shoulder pads: (a) Slash lines drawn; (b) Slash lines spread and cap pushed up.

Procedure.

1. Place a pencil mark at the exact base of the cap on the center line of the master sleeve pattern.

2. Draw a wedge-shaped piece at the exact center top of the sleeve cap (see Figure 27a).

3. Draw lines from a point on the side seams just below the base of the cap up to the lower corners of this wedge (dotted lines in Figure 27a).

4. Slash along the lines drawn in step 3 to the side seam and push up the wedge to get the necessary height.

5. To raise the height of the cap without distorting the underarm curve of the armscye line, make additional slashes at the back and front to the armscye line just below the midpoint between the top center of the armscye and the base of the cap. You can then raise the top half of the cap without appreciably lifting the underarm curve (see Figure 27b).

6. For gathers held right at the top of the sleeve, use the same method, but push the wedge up still higher. This increases the height of the cap and the width also to some extent, but adds very little width at the girth line.

DRESS DESIGN

Problem 7
THE MASTER SLEEVE MODIFIED FOR A DEEPER-THAN-NORMAL ARMSCYE (see Figures 28 and 29 a and b)

From time to time fashion emphasizes designs having armscyes deeper than normal, and at such times this sleeve variation is adapted to all types of costumes. It is especially desirable for coats and suits in order to allow for easy fitting over dresses and blouses.

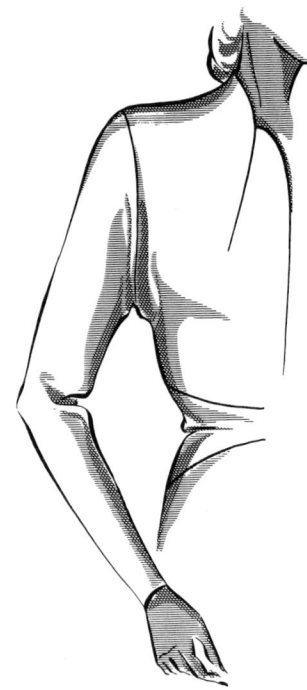

Fig. 28. Sleeve with deeper-than-normal armscye.

The main problem in designing and fitting a set-in sleeve with a deep armhole is to provide the necessary freedom for raising the arm, especially in a garment fitted snugly at the waistline. If the cap of the sleeve is lengthened to correspond to the additional depth of the armhole, the top of the sleeve will form a vise that holds the arm down at the side. Any attempt to raise the arm causes the garment to pull up at the waistline, because the lower armhole has shortened the underarm seam of the blouse. *Lengthening the underarm seam of the sleeve* an amount equal to that lost on the side seam of the blouse overcomes these difficulties.

1. Measure down the new armhole depth on the front and back edges of the underarm seam of the blouse.

2. Redraw the underarm curve for front and back (see dotted line in Figure 29a).

3. Trace the sleeve master pattern and draw a horizontal line extending through the front and back corners of the girth line.

4. Extend the sleeve girth line at front and back an amount equal to the increase in the length of the blouse armhole. With a flexible ruler, measure the armscye of the blouse front from A to B, and subtract from this the measurement from A to C. Repeat for the back.

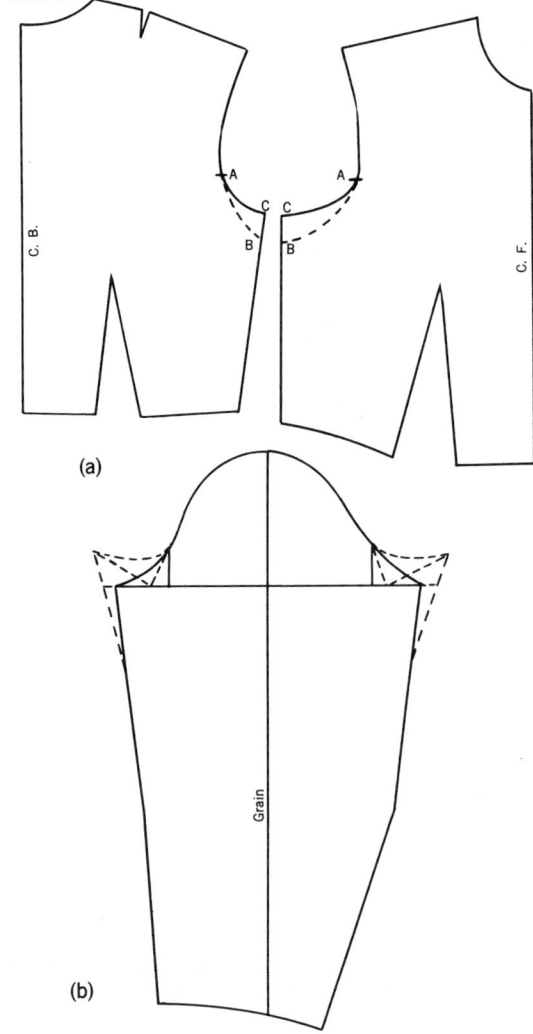

Fig. 29. (a) Blouse armhole deepened; (b) Sleeve armscye and underarm seam lengthened to fit deeper armhole of blouse.

128

SLEEVES

5. Measure in from the original front and back corners of the sleeve girth a minimum of 2 inches. At these points erect perpendiculars and extend them to the armscye.

6. Cut out the sleeve, slash in from the front and back girth corners to the perpendiculars and up to the armscye. Pivot up the wedge-shaped pieces to lengthen the underarm seam as much as the blouse armhole has been lowered.

7. Retrace the sleeve. Draw a new underarm line, curving it from the raised girth corner inward and downward to meet the old sleeve seam at a point 2 or 3 inches below the position of the original girth corner.

Problem 8

MODIFICATION OF SLEEVE LENGTH
Master Sleeve Pattern Cut Off Above the Elbow
(see Figure 30)

1. On a sleeve pattern outline, trace the line at the base of the cap and the center lengthwise grain line from the master pattern.

2. Fold the seam lines in to the center lengthwise grain line.

3. Measure down the desired sleeve length from the base of the cap on the center line, and square out from this point. This is the lower edge of the sleeve. When the pattern is opened out, this line will slant downward toward the underarm seam lines at the ends, and will be parallel to the girth line in the center section.

Note. This method for trueing the lower line by folding the underarm seams in to the center cannot be used for a sleeve which has been derived by slashing and spreading the center section, since the fullness of the under and upper sections of the sleeve are not the same. However, if the lower edge of the sleeve block is correct, the slashed and spread parts will automatically indicate the correct lower line of the new sleeve.

4. To add a hem to the sleeve, measure 2 inches down from the lower edge to provide the hem depth before cutting off the pattern. Fold the hem up and trace the side edges against the side of the sleeve line in order to duplicate the exact side edges of the sleeve. A sleeve can be successfully hemmed only when it is practically straight at the lower edge.

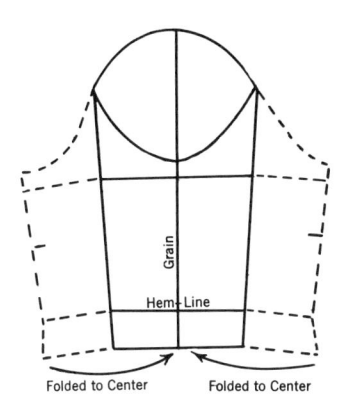

Fig. 30. Method of cutting off a sleeve above the elbow.

Sleeve Cut Off at Three-Quarter Length (see Figure 31)

1. Measure the desired distance up from the wrist on each seam, at the center, the side front, and the side back. Connect these points with a pencil line to form the lower edge of the sleeve.

2. Cut along this line which should be parallel to the wrist line.

Note. This edge is always too curved to have a hem and should therefore be finished with seam ribbon or a shaped facing.

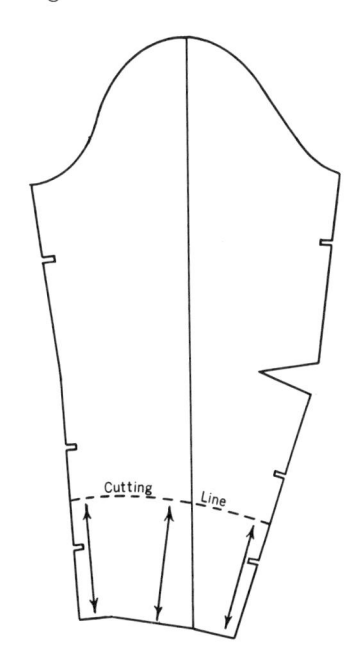

Fig. 31. Method of cutting off a long sleeve to the three quarter length.

DRESS DESIGN

Problem 9

THE CUTTING OF CUFFS
(see Figures 32 a, b, c, and d)

Narrow Cuff Band

A narrow cuff band of 1 to 1½ inches is a straight lengthwise piece folded at the lower edge. (See Figures 32a and 33.)

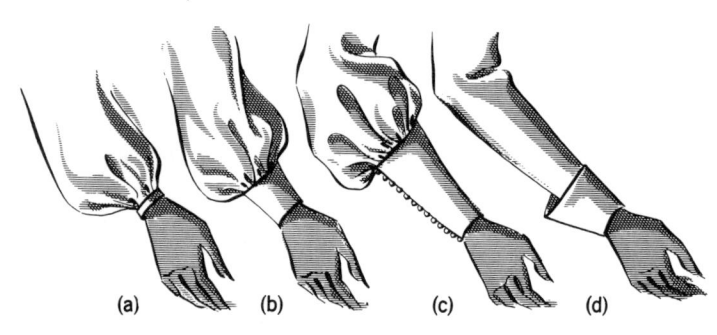

Fig. 32 (a), (b), (c), and (d). Cuff variations.

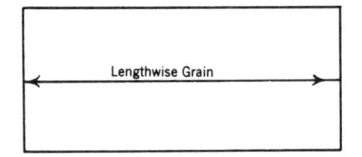

Fig. 33. Narrow cuff band.

Cuff Wider Than Two Inches (see Figures 32b and c)

Take the pattern from the lower part of the one-piece master sleeve (see Figure 34a). For a tightly fitted cuff, use the master pattern with a vertical dart (see page 135 for the pattern). Cut the top of the cuff on a curve parallel to the wrist edge of the master pattern and mark the grain running in the same direction as in the sleeve, that is, along the center line. When you use a buttoned closing, place it at the vertical dart line. If the cuff is to be free at the upper edge, cut the pattern apart along the vertical dart line and join the two sections on the underarm seam line so that the cuff itself can be cut in one piece and retain the grain line marked from the sleeve (see Figure 34b). Allow for a lap on the placket line. A cuff sewed to the sleeve along its upper edge retains the underarm seam (see Figure 32c).

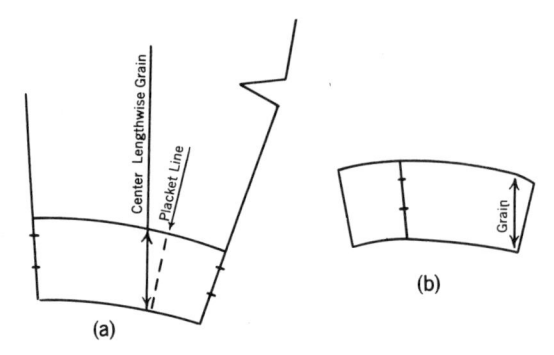

Fig. 34. (a) Wider cuff pattern cut from lower edge of sleeve; (b) Cuff cut in one piece, with a buttoned closing and a free upper edge.

Flared Cuff (see Figure 32d)

Use the cuff pattern made according to the directions in B for the shaped cuff, draw slash lines from the upper edge to the wrist for the flares, slash and spread (see Figure 35). Cut the new curved pattern, and mark the straight lengthwise grain to coincide with the center lengthwise grain of the sleeve.

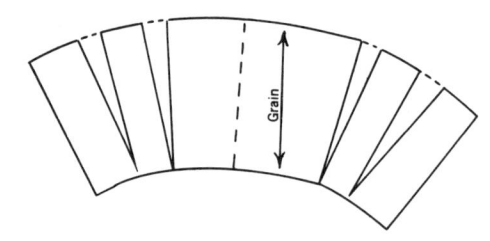

Fig. 35. Flared cuff.

Problem 10

TWO-PIECE SLEEVE DRAFT FROM MASTER ONE-PIECE COAT SLEEVE (see Figures 36-42)

Draft and cut out a pattern for a one-piece sleeve, using the measurements for a coat or a jacket and allowing no elbow dart. A difference of 1¾ inches between girth and elbow will be more satisfactory than the two-inch difference usually used for a dress sleeve (see Figure 37).

Division Lines

Figure 38 should be followed carefully in performing steps 1 through 6.

SLEEVES

1. Draw line *BRO* to divide the front quarter of the sleeve, *ACNP,* in half.

2. On the girth line, measure ⅝ inch toward the back edge from the back quarter division line, *EK,* and mark *X*.

3. On the elbow line, measure ¼ inch from the back quarter line and mark *V*.

4. Rule a line connecting *X* and *V* and extend it through the armscye at *F*.

5. From the wrist measurement of this one-piece sleeve draft, subtract the desired wrist measurement for the new two-piece sleeve, and measure one-half of the difference on each side of the back quarter line *EK* at the wrist, marking *L* and *J*.

6. Draw the lines *VL* and *VJ.*

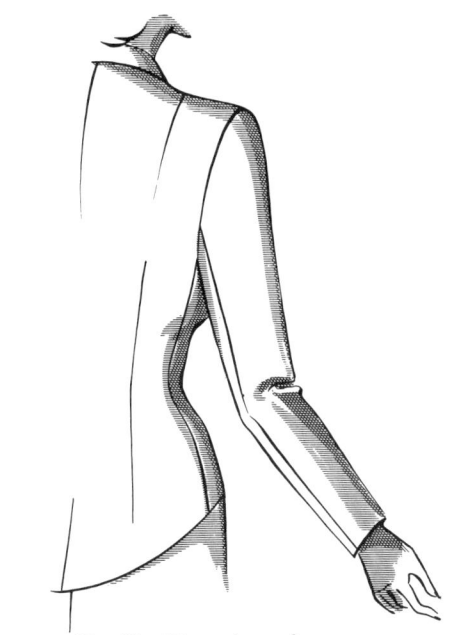

Fig. 36. Two-piece sleeve.

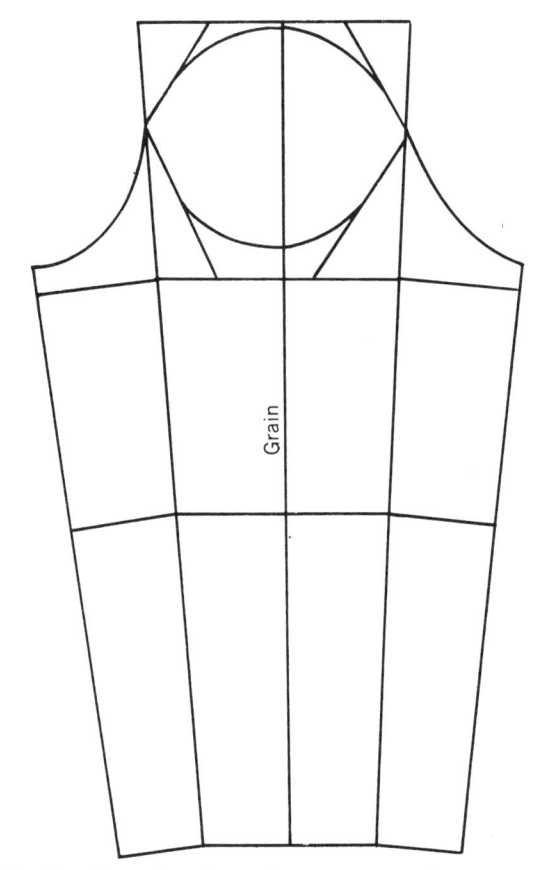

Fig. 37. One-piece sleeve from coat or suit measurement.

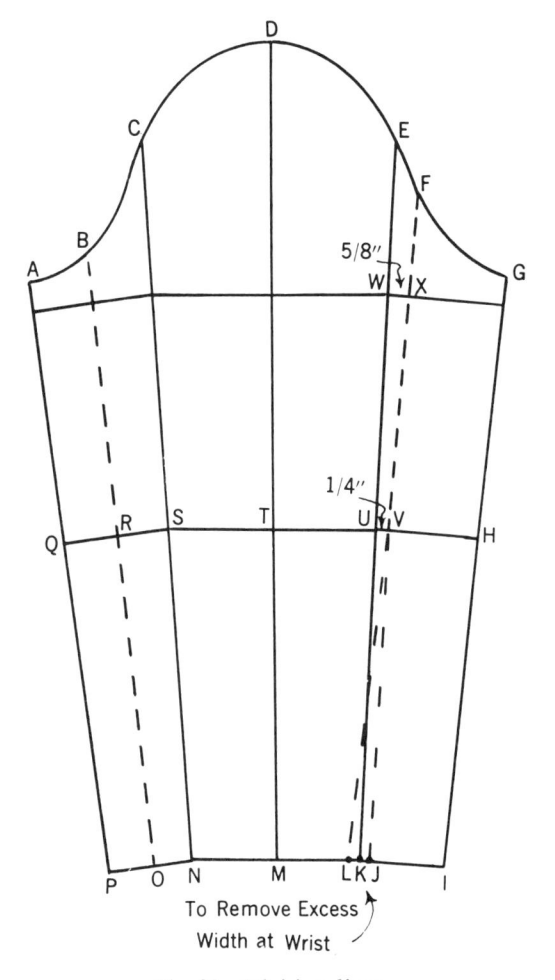

Fig. 38. Division lines.

131

DRESS DESIGN

Separating the Pattern on Vertical and Horizontal Lines

1. Cut on lines *BRO, FXVL,* and *VJ* (see Figure 39).

2. Cut through the elbow line *VUTSR* to the new front edge at *R* (see Figure 40).

3. Slash the front quarter line *CS* from the elbow to the edge of the cap at *C.*

4. Slash the back quarter line *UE* from the elbow up to the cap at *E.*

Upper Section of Sleeve (see Figure 41)

1. Now, on a second sheet of paper, draw a straight line the length of the sleeve plus 4 or 5 inches. Mark it *DY,* and on this line place the center lengthwise grain of the upper section.

2. Draw a second line parallel to this and to the left of it the distance between the center line and the front corner *B* of the girth line.

3. Pin the center line of the sleeve pattern from *D* to *T* to the line *DY.* Place the front girth corner *B* of the pattern against the parallel line.

4. The front edge of the sleeve in the crook of the elbow should be 5/8 inch or more from the parallel line depending on the amount of shaping desired in the sleeve (Figure 41 shows 7/8 inch.) Overlap the two sections along the front quarter line *CS* to indent line *BR* the desired distance from the vertical line.

5. Pivot the back quarter line, *EU,* out at the elbow to add the amount subtracted in the front at point *S.*

6. Pivot the lower section down to add at least 1 1/4 inches of length at the elbow point. Along the back edge of the upper section, make the distance between *V* and *V¹* 1/2 inch longer than the distance between these points on the back edge of the underarm section. This will provide extra ease over the elbow.

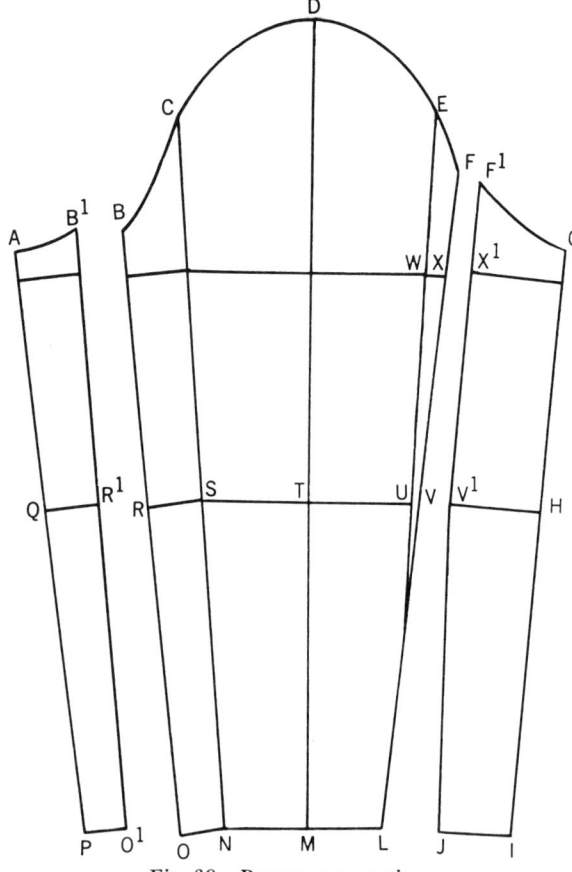

Fig. 39. Pattern separation.

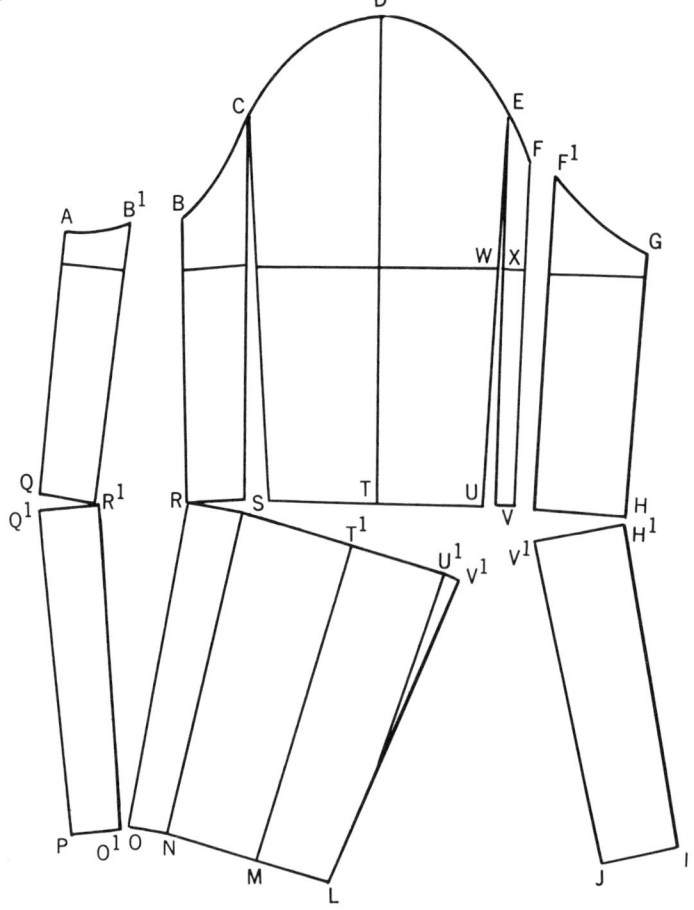

Fig. 40. Separation on vertical and horizontal lines.

SLEEVES

7. Pencil around the pattern and mark the pattern for the lengthwise grain to follow the line *DY* on the under paper.

Under Section of Sleeve

1. On a second sheet of paper, rule a straight line the length of the under section plus 2 or 3 inches. Label this line *AZ*.

2. Rule a second line parallel to it and to the right the distance from *A* to *B* along the girth line.

3. Place section AB^1O^1P so that *A* rests on the line *AZ* and B^1 on the parallel line.

4. At the elbow point R^1, indent the front section from the parallel line at least ½ inch. The indentation in the crook of the elbow on the under section is just slightly less than that on the top section.

5. Place the narrow back section, F^1GIJ, up against the front section AB^1O^1P.

6. Pivot the two sections forward below the elbow line to open the elbow point at V^1 about ¾ inch, ½ inch less than the opening on the top section.

7. Draw around the pattern and trace the lengthwise grain from the line *AZ* on the under paper. (See Figure 42 for the final pattern.)

8. Mark notches on the back line *FL* of upper section at points 1¼ inches above *V* and 1¼ inches below V^1. Measure from *F* to upper notch, and mark off an equal number of inches from F^1 on under section for the matching notch. Measure from *L* to the lower notch and mark off an equal distance from *J* on under section for the matching notch. The ½ inch excess on the upper section will be eased to the lower section between these two notches.

9. Round off the sharp corners and straight lines with slight curves.

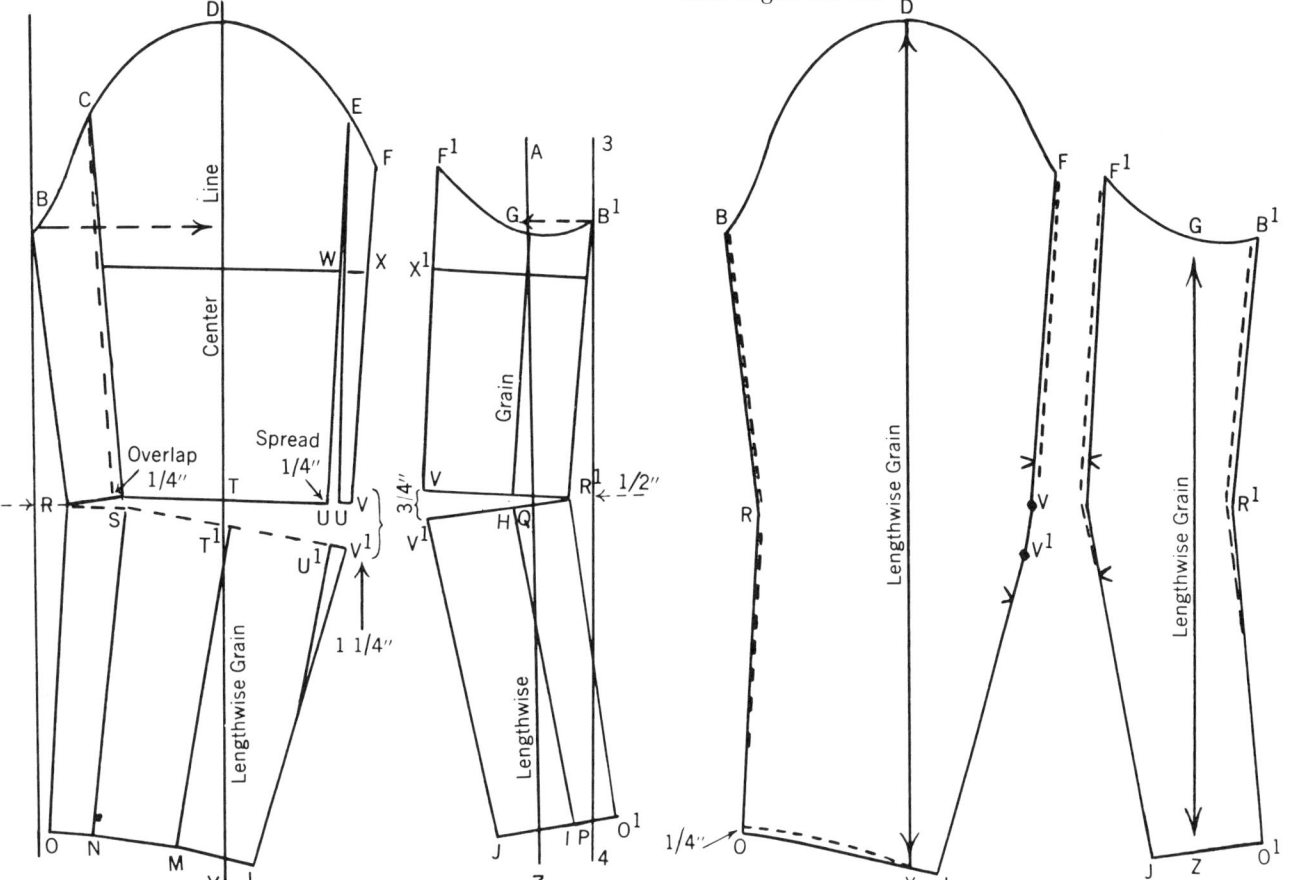

Fig. 41. Top section and underarm section of sleeve.

Fig. 42. Completed pattern for two-piece sleeve.

DRESS DESIGN

PART II

DESIGNING SET-IN SLEEVES FROM THE MASTER PATTERN ONE-PIECE SLEEVE BLOCK

The procedure for developing designs from the one-piece master sleeve pattern is similar in principle to that used in designing from the master blouse and skirt. In all sleeve patterns, the ease (at least 1½ inches) at the top of the master pattern should be retained for fitting over the curve at the top of the arm, but the elbow dart can be shifted at will to produce changes in the design.

For convenience and speed in practicing sleeve design, trace the quarter-size pattern from Page 136 and proceed as for blocking blouses and skirts.

Problem 1

TRANSFER OF THE HORIZONTAL ELBOW DART TO A VERTICAL ONE (see Figure 43)

The elbow dart is often transferred in this manner in designs with the principal interest between the elbow and the wrist. This may take the form of a line of ornamental buttons at the little finger line, gathers blousing into a simulated cuff, or even a moderately loose sleeve with the dart material hanging free. The vertical dart is longer than a horizontal one and can be used for a sleeve that should fit very closely from elbow to wrist, or to fit an arm unusually large below the elbow but with a small wrist.

Procedure (see Figures 44 and 45)

1. Draw a line from a point marking the back third of the elbow width to a point marking the back third of the wrist width (see Figure 44). The position on the arm is approximately from elbow to little finger.

2. Slash along the new line and close the old dart.

3. Redraw the dart to stop it before it reaches the elbow (see Figure 45), but not much below this point because the dart is so large. Taper it off equally on both edges by placing a point directly below the end of the slash and ruling lines to that point.

Note. Part of the horizontal dart of the master sleeve pattern can be transferred to the wrist width for a casual sleeve with wrist circumference large enough to slip over the hand without a placket. Follow the directions for the transfer of the horizontal to the vertical dart, but instead of completely closing the horizontal dart, close it just enough to spread the sleeve at the wrist for the additional width desired.

Problem 2

THREE-QUARTER-LENGTH SLEEVE WITH GATHERS RADIATING FROM ONE OR TWO VERTICAL SLASHES

Gathers Radiating from One Vertical Slash Line

The same procedure applies also to a full-length sleeve, but the design seems to be particularly suited to the three-quarter length (see Figure 46a).

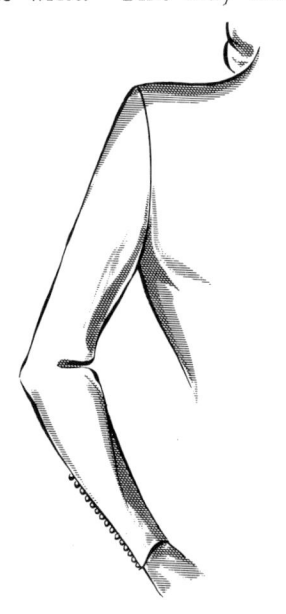

Fig. 43. Vertical placket dart.

SLEEVES

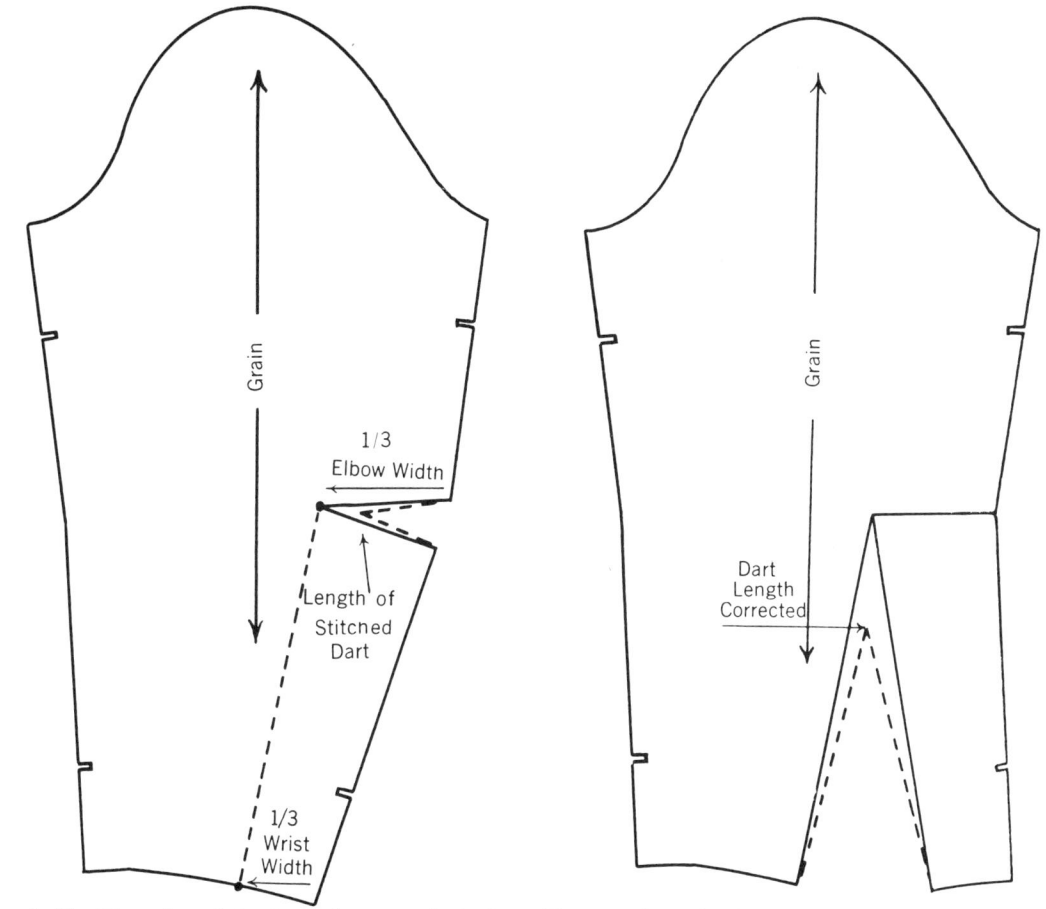

Figs. 44 and 45. Transfer of horizontal to vertical dart. To transfer a horizontal dart to a vertical dart like that shown in Fig. 43, lines are drawn for transferring the dart (Fig. 44) and the vertical dart is spread and the horizontal dart closed (Fig. 45).

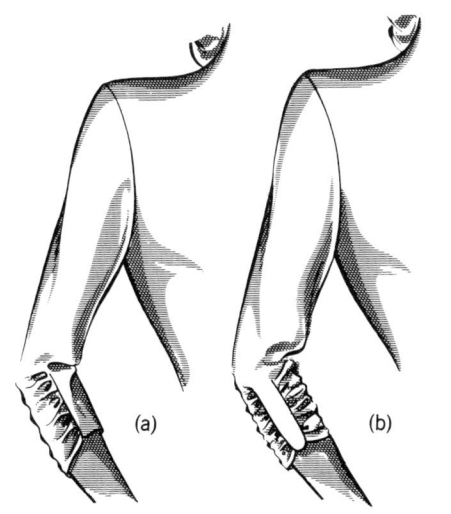

Fig. 46 (a) and (b). Sleeves with gathers radiating from one or two vertical slashes.

1. Cut off the full-length master sleeve pattern at the three-quarter length. Remember always to cut parallel to the lower edge.

2. Decide on the position of the vertical line from which the fullness is to radiate. It would never do to place it at the back of the sleeve, as this would throw the fullness under the arm. Place it at the center or even in front of the center, and draw it perpendicular to the lower edge of the sleeve. Do not continue it much above the elbow (see Figure 47a).

3. Draw lines from this vertical slash line to the back edge of the sleeve and slash to the back seam edge.

4. Close the horizontal elbow dart and thus automatically transfer it forward to the vertical slash line. (See Figure 47b).

135

DRESS DESIGN

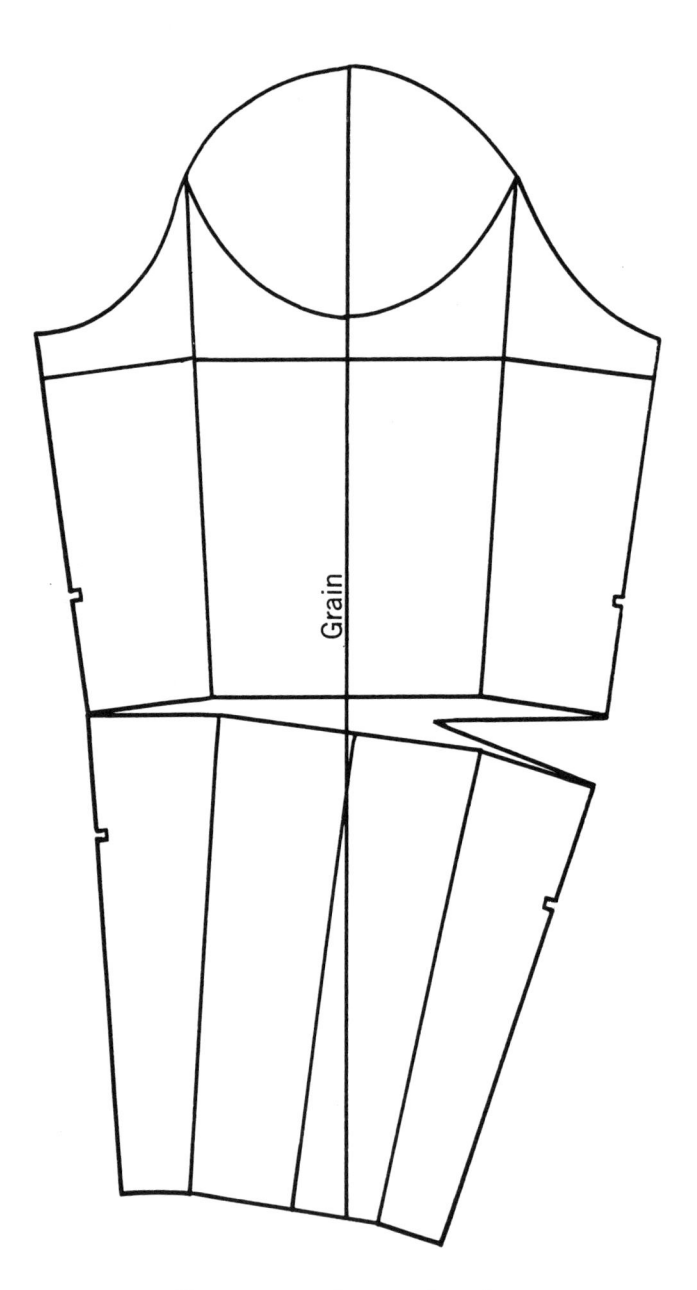

Master pattern for one-piece sleeve.

SLEEVES

Fig. 47 (a). Slash lines are drawn (as indicated by the arrow perpendicular to the lower edge of the sleeve) (b). Shows the slashes spread on the edge to be gathered.

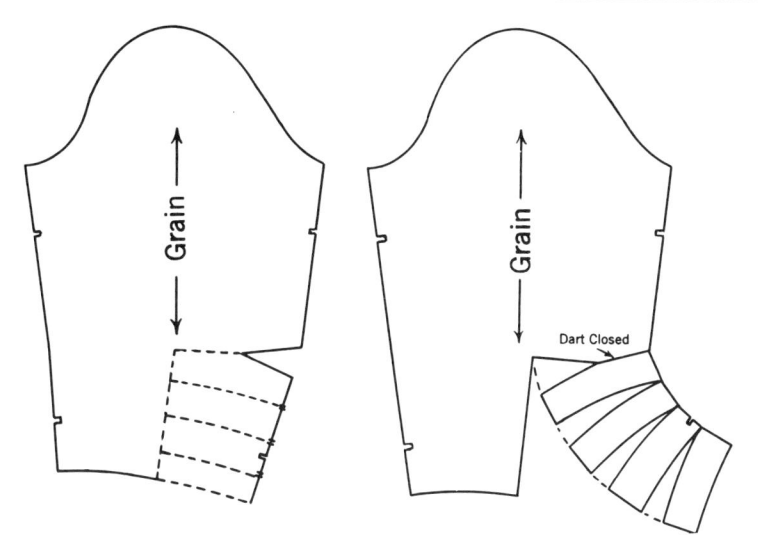

5. Spread the slashes, pivoting from the back edge for gathers but leaving the length of the underarm seam line unchanged. For gathers moderately full, allow one and one-half times the length of the vertical cut; for full gathers, at least twice the length.

Gathers Radiating from Each Side of a Double Vertical Slash Line

The same principle employed for a sleeve with gathers radiating from one vertical slash line may also be applied to a sleeve with fullness radiating in both directions from two vertical cuts that form the edges of a band or panel (see Figure 46b).

1. On the three-quarter-length sleeve pattern, draw two parallel lines perpendicular to the lower edge and running up to but not much above the elbow. Place these lines not more than 1 to 1½ inches apart, one at about the center of the sleeve and one in front of center (see Figure 48).

2. Draw lines perpendicular to the vertical slashes running out in both directions to the underarm seam lines.

3. Slash to each underarm seam line.

4. Close the underarm dart.

5. Spread equally at the edges to be gathered, adding enough length to equal at least one and one-half times the vertical slash length.

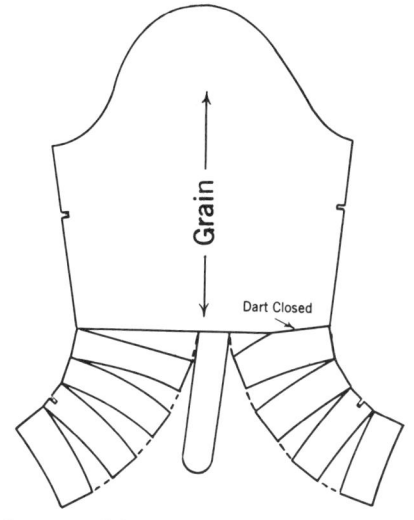

Fig. 48. Slashes spread for gathers on each side of a vertical band.

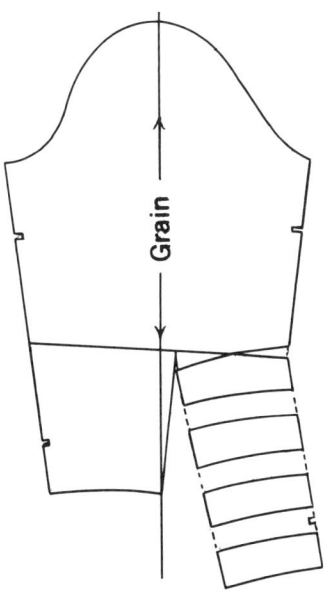

Fig. 49. Both edges spread equally for gathers. Gathers lie parallel and effect is heavier.

Since the underarm seams have not been increased in length, both the seam edges and the gathered edges have become decided arcs.

Another possible design using this principle is achieved by slashing through the underarm seam lines and spreading the pattern at both ends of the slashes for gathers running across the underarm seam. The effect, however, is heavier and more "clothy," because the fullness lines lie parallel and tend to look flat and crushed (see Figure 49).

137

# DRESS DESIGN

Problem 3

SLEEVE WITH SIMULATED CUFF
(see Figures 50, 51a and b)

This sleeve illustrates another way to introduce detail at the lower edge. It is similar in silhouette to the bishop sleeve, but has the cuff and sleeve cut all in one piece (see Figure 50).

1. On the master pattern sleeve, draw in the design line of the cuff. That is, measure up from the lower edge the depth of the cuff and draw a line parallel to the lower edge, but extend it only through the center of the sleeve, not out to the underarm seam lines. Start the line approximately 1 inch from the back edge and end it approximately 2 inches from the front edge (see Figure 51a).

2. Transfer the elbow dart to a vertical dart on the little finger line. (See directions for the transfer of the horizontal to the vertical dart, Page 135).

3. Slash across the design line of the cuff to the marked points. The line on which the cuff has opened will be the correct position for the placket opening, the little finger line. Add a lap if buttons and buttonholes are to be used.

4. Slash vertically at the side back and side front from the ends of the design line of the cuff to the top of the sleeve. Draw these slash lines equidistant from the center line to keep the sleeve balanced.

5. Spread the pattern equally to add fullness at the lower ends of the two slashes. These slashes, plus the spread derived from the transfer of the elbow dart to the lower edge, will supply enough fullness (one and one-half to two times the length of the slash for the cuff). The sleeve will be fullest toward the back because two of the three points spread are back of the center of the cuff (see Figure 51b).

6. Redraw the line to be gathered, curving it downward for enough extra length toward the back to allow the arm to bend sharply.

Figure 52 shows the same idea adapted to a three-quarter-length sleeve with curved line detail on the simulated cuff.

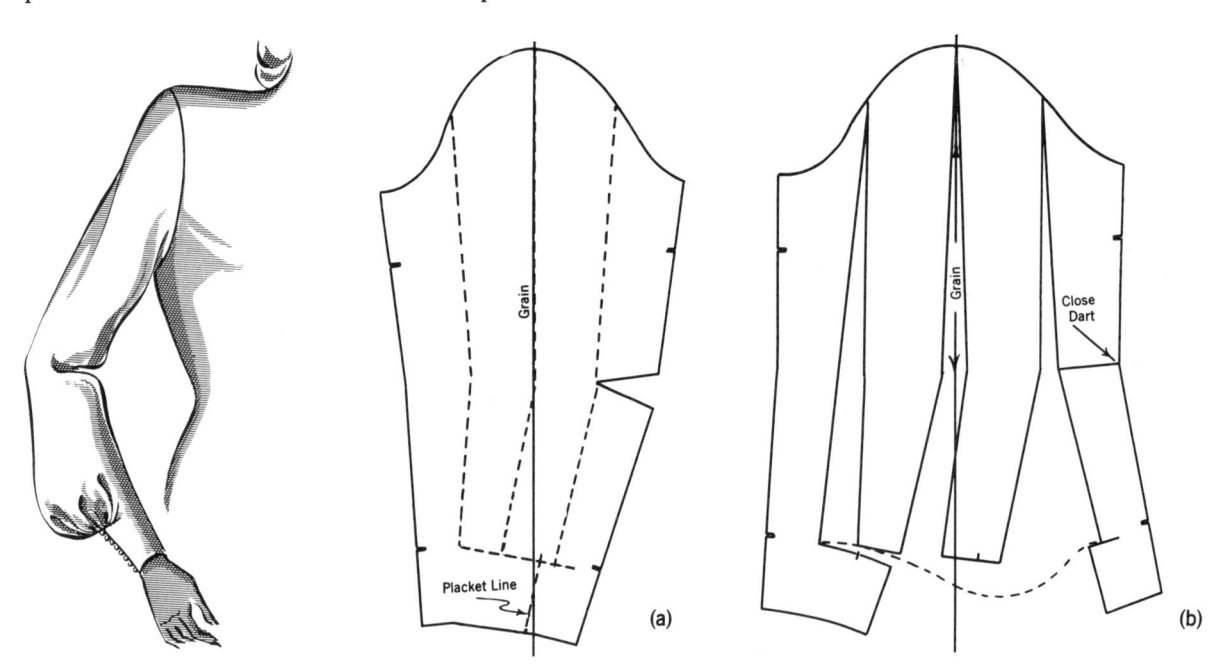

Figs. 50, 51 (a) and (b). Sleeve with bloused fullness above a simulated cuff. Fig. 50 shows bloused fullness above a simulated cuff. In Fig. 51 (a), slash lines are drawn; and in Fig. 51 (b), the slashes are spread for blousing and the full section is lengthened (see dotted line).

SLEEVES

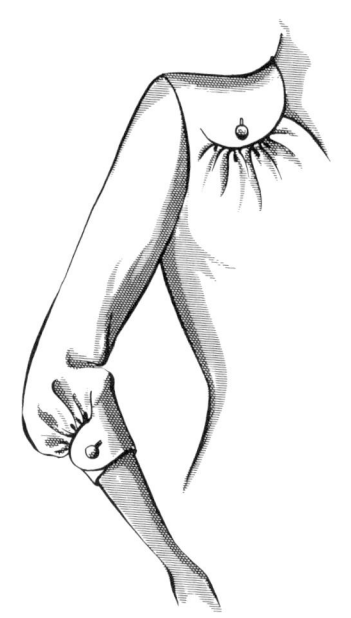

Fig. 52. Simulated cuff on three-quarter-length sleeve.

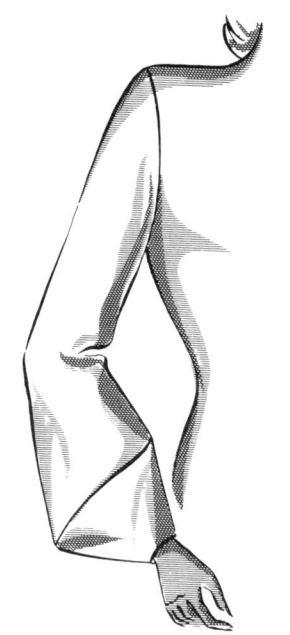

Fig. 53. Lantern sleeve.

Problem 4

SLEEVE WITH WIDTH BELOW THE ELBOW AND A FITTED WRIST — LANTERN SLEEVE
(see Figures 53, 54a and b)

The following directions explain how to design a lantern sleeve with one horizontal seam below the elbow. It is easy to overdo intricate seaming. The sleeve is a very small part of the entire garment, and the smoother and less cut up it is, the better the general effect will be. Silhouette is far more important than detail, and the design will be less fussy and usually better if made with few seams rather than many.

1. On the one-piece master sleeve pattern draw a line parallel to the lower edge. This line divides the sleeve into upper and lower sections. It should be about 5½ inches up from the wrist or any other distance that produces good proportion.

2. Crossmark the line.

3. Rule lines from the top of the cap and parallel to the center line down to the division line established in step 1. Make the lines equidistant from the center.

4. Continue the same lines drawn in step 3 through the lower section so that they are perpendicular to the wrist edge.

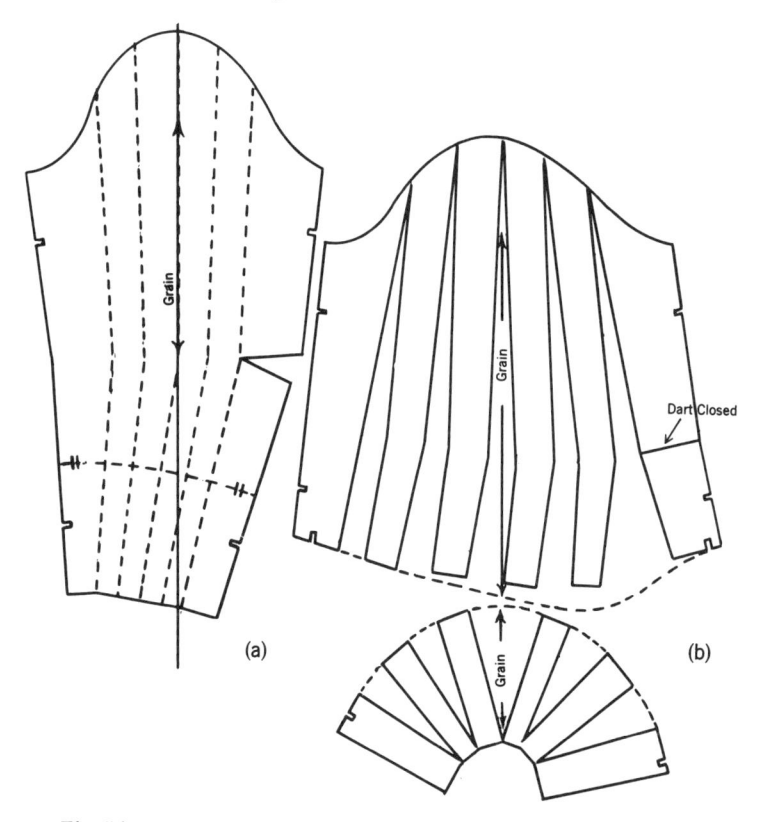

Fig. 54. (*a*) Slash lines drawn (dotted line). (*b*) Slashes spread. The matching edges of both sections must be the same length.

DRESS DESIGN

5. Cut the upper and lower sections apart.

6. Close the elbow dart and transfer it to a vertical slash line at the point of the dart.

7. Slash the vertical lines of the upper section and spread them at the lower end enough to produce the desired width at the lower edge (see Figure 54b).

8. Measure the arm from the shoulder tip over the sharply bent elbow to the wrist (see Figure 15). Since the total sleeve length over the back of the arm must equal this measurement, at least 1½ inches must be added to the upper section. Drop the bottom line of the upper section to lengthen it at the vertical dart position at the side back, and then curve the line up toward the back seam so that it enters the seam at a right angle. The dotted line in Figure 54b indicates the shape this line should take.

9. Slash the vertical lines in the lower section and spread at the upper edge until it exactly equals the lower curved edge of the upper section. The lower section now has a sharply curved wrist line, and its upper edge is a far more rounded curve than the lower edge of the upper section.

Problem 5

SLEEVE WITH PARALLEL DARTS AT THE TOP OF THE CAP (see Figure 55a)

Use the basic master pattern for a fitted sleeve with an elbow dart, but for a bell, bishop, or other sleeve wide at the lower edge, change the basic sleeve into the desired style before slashing and spreading it for a darted cap.

Sleeve with Three Parallel Darts (see Figures 55 b, c, d, and e).

1. Trace and cut out the master sleeve pattern. Include lines marking the center lengthwise grain, the girth, and vertical quarter division lines.

2. According to the placing given in Figure 55b, mark the dart positions: E, center of cap; D, 2½ inches forward from E along the armscye curve; F, 2½ inches behind E. (This series of measurements is variable.)

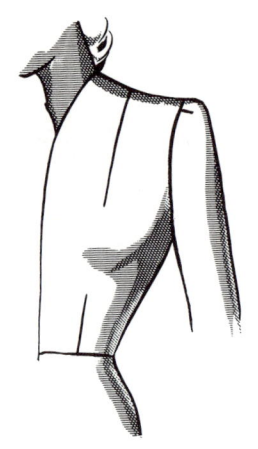

Fig. 55 (a). Sleeve with three parallel darts at the top.

3. Rule from D, E, and F to point Q on the girth line.

4. Measure 1 inch down from point C (the halfway point between A and E) and mark B. Repeat the measurement from G to H.

5. Draw lines from B to Q and H to Q.

6. Slash from E to Q; from Q to P; from Q to R.

7. Slash from Q to B; from Q to H.

8. Slash from D and F to point Q.

Note. The direction *slash to* means cut to a certain point but not through that point.

9. Rule a vertical line on a second sheet of paper and place the center lengthwise grain line of the sleeve pattern along this line.

10. Decide on the new cap height before spreading the slashes.

Note. Cap heights vary with fashion and depend on the prevailing silhouette and the length of the shoulder seam of the blouse. Figure 55c shows the cap height of the foundation sleeve increased 1¾ inches. Since the original height of the cap was 5¼ inches, it is now 7 inches high.

11. Spread vertically between Q and JO 1 inch, and between JO and KN ¾ inch. Notice that the slashes from J to B and O to H make it possible to increase the height without overincreasing the width of the lower part of the cap. The outer dotted line indicates the cap shape without the slash from B to J, and the inner dotted line shows the original armscye.

140

SLEEVES

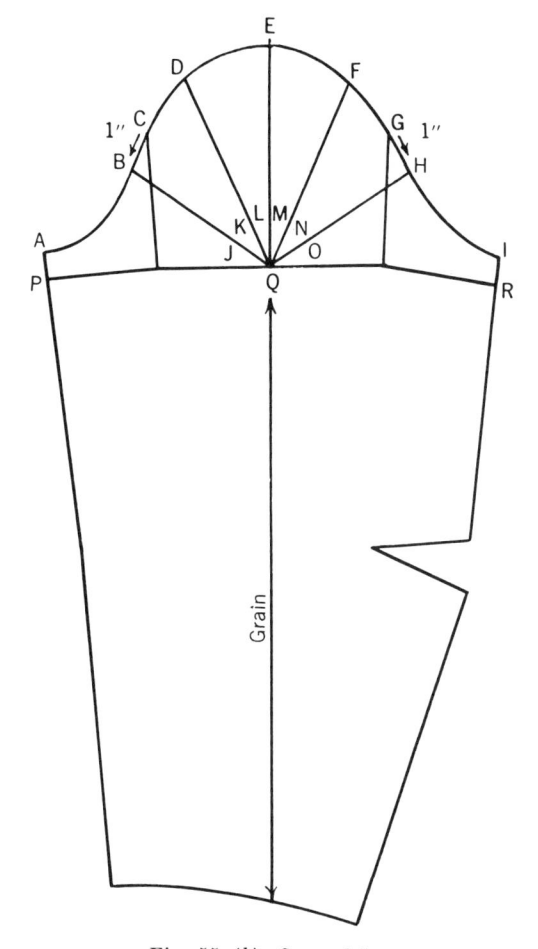

Fig. 55. (b) Steps 1-5.

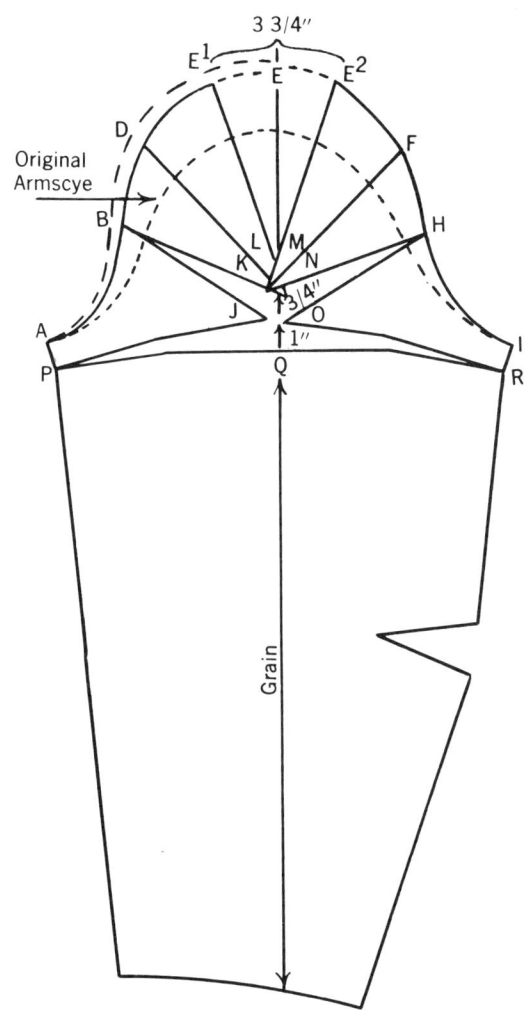

Fig. 55. (c) Steps 6-12.

12. Determine the width of the darts. Push section *DEL* against section *BDK* to estimate the distance from E^1 to E, the amount added to the length of the armscye line. Repeat on the opposite half for the distance from E^2 to E. Figure 55c shows a total spread of 3¾ inches from E^1 to E^2. Since darted sleeves do not require easing over the top of the cap, add to the 3¾ inches excess the amount of ease allowed in the master pattern sleeve (the difference in measurement between the sleeve armscye and the dress armscye). The foundation sleeve in Figure 55b had 1¼ inches of ease. This added to the spread of 3¾ inches on the sleeve provides 5 inches to be divided among the three darts. Thus each will be 1⅝ inches wide.

13. Draw the center dart *SUT* 1⅛ inches long (see Figure 55d).

14. Measure from the center dart 2½ inches to establish *VW* parallel to *SU*.

15. Measure 1⅛ inches on line *VW* and mark point *W*.

16. Measure along the armscye line and mark the dart width from *V* to *X*.

17. Join *X* and *W*. Then mark the correct dart length 1⅛ inches on this line by measuring from *W* and ending at X^1. Note that making darts parallel narrows the sleeve cap.

19. Follow the same method in placing the third dart.

20. Dip the armscye line slightly between the darts to make the corners right angles as shown from *S* to *V* and *T* to *Y* in Figure 55e.

21. To shape the **cap edge** correctly, fold the darts in before cutting along the armscye.

141

DRESS DESIGN

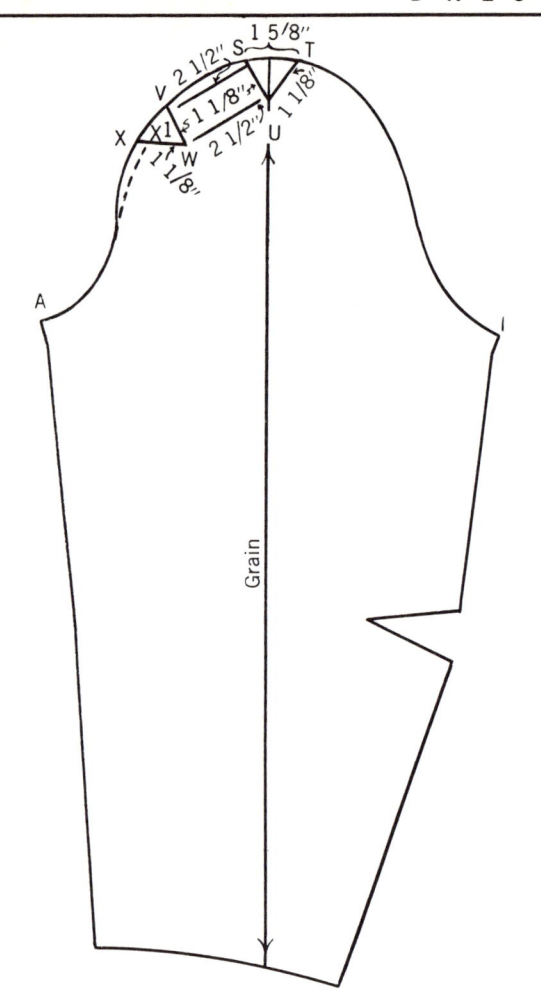

Fig. 55. (d) Steps 13-19.

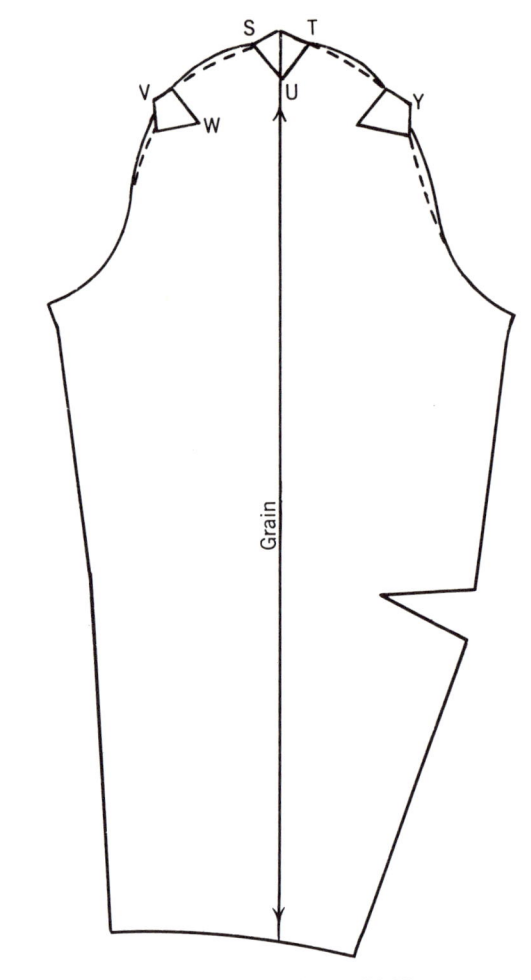

Fig. 55. (e) Steps 20-21.

Sleeve with Five Parallel Darts (see Figures 56 a, b, and c)

1. Trace and cut out the one-piece master sleeve pattern. Include lines marking the center lengthwise grain line at *F*, the girth, *TUV*, and vertical quarter divisions at *C* and *I* (see Figure 56a).

2. Mark the position of the darts: *F* at the center of the cap; *E* 1½ inches forward from *F*; *D* 1½ inches from *E*; *G* 1½ inches back from *F*; *H* 1½ inches from *G*.

3. Rule from *D*, *E*, *F*, *G*, and *H* to *U* on the girth line.

4. Measure 1 inch down from point *C* and mark *B*. Repeat this measurement from *I* to find *J*.

5. Draw lines from *B* and *J* to *U*.

6. Draw a line *WXY* parallel to the girth line *TUV* and at least 1 inch below it. Slash from *F* through *U* to *X*. Slash on the girth line from *U* to *T* and from *U* to *V*; from *X* to *W* and from *X* to *Y*.

7. Slash from *U* to *B*; from *U* to *J*.

8. Slash from points *D*, *E*, *G*, and *H* to point *U*. For ease in handling and spreading the sections, avoid cutting through point *U* in order to keep the triangular pieces together at their tip point *U*.

9. Spread along the horizontal slash lines to lengthen the center line of the sleeve ½ inch above *X*, ½ inch above *U*, and ¾ inch above points marked *L* and *S*.

10. Follow the same procedure in placing the darts as in the sleeve with three darts. The cap height should not be over 7 inches for this sleeve and may be even less. Determine the amount of excess to divide among the darts. The darts shown in Figure 56c are 1 inch long.

142

SLEEVES

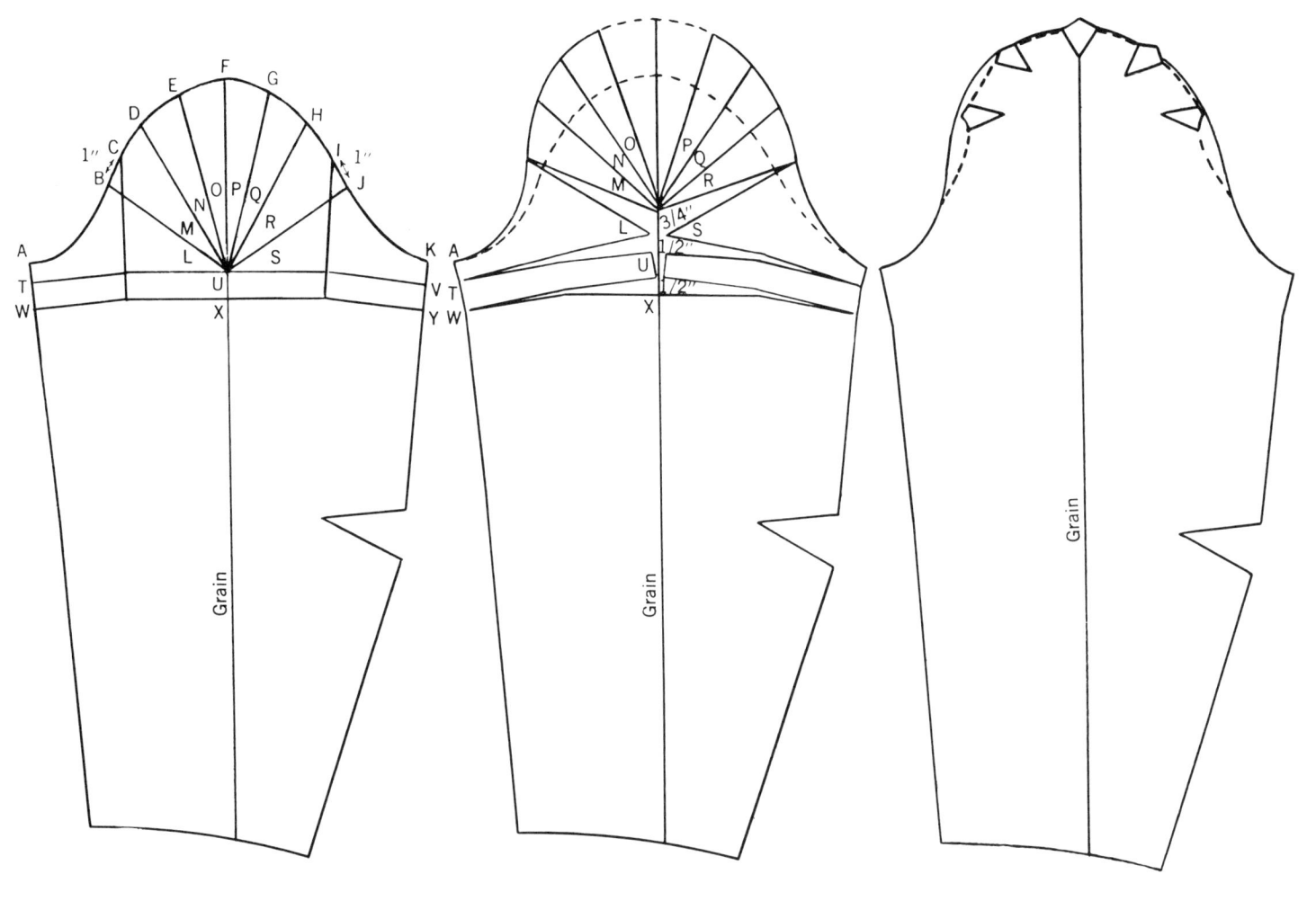

Fig. 56 (a). Sleeve with five parallel darts at the top.   Fig. 56 (b).   Fig. 56 (c).

Problem 6

SLEEVE WITH A SEAM ACROSS THE TOP OF THE CAP PARALLEL TO THE ARMSCYE
(see Figure 57)

An interpretation of the square-shouldered silhouette somewhat out of the ordinary is the sleeve with a seam line curved over the top and parallel to the armscye. This is the squarest of all shoulder lines and introduces an interesting variation of the square-shouldered theme whenever such a silhouette is in vogue (see Figures 58a and b).

1. Mark a line around the center of the top of the basic sleeve parallel to the curve of the top edge and about 1¼ inches below it. Extend this line about 3 to 4 inches to the front and to the back of the center of the sleeve.

2. Draw lines, spaced about 1½ inches apart, from the top edge to the inner curve and perpendicular to it.

3. Cut around the inner curve, then slash out on each line marked in point 2, up to but not through the outside edge except at the center top. Cut the center slash clear through the top edge.

143

DRESS DESIGN

4. Spread these slashes along the inside edge until the cap edge runs up to form a straight vertical band (see Figure 58b).

5. Since it has had 1¼ inches cut from the top, the cap now is too short, and must be increased 1¼ inches at the top center to meet the band-like section over the top of the sleeve cap without drawing down (see Figure 58b).

6. The central curve is also narrow and pointed unless some width is added to the cap at the lower end of the inner curve marked in step 1. To do this, rule lines from the lower ends of the curve down to a point on the underarm seam below the armscye. Slash and spread to increase cap width (see Figure 58b).

Problem 7

SHORT PUFF SLEEVE

There are three kinds of puff sleeves, and each can be developed from the same slash lines. The puff may be all at the shoulder and may fit closely at the lower edge, it may be full at both the top and bottom edges, or it may fit smoothly at the top and puff at the lower edge. Figures 59a, b, and c show the three sleeves developed from the same pattern but with the slashes spread in three different ways to obtain the three effects. Place the gathers in the finished sleeve

Fig. 57. Sleeve with a dart parallel to the armscye (very square-shouldered effect).

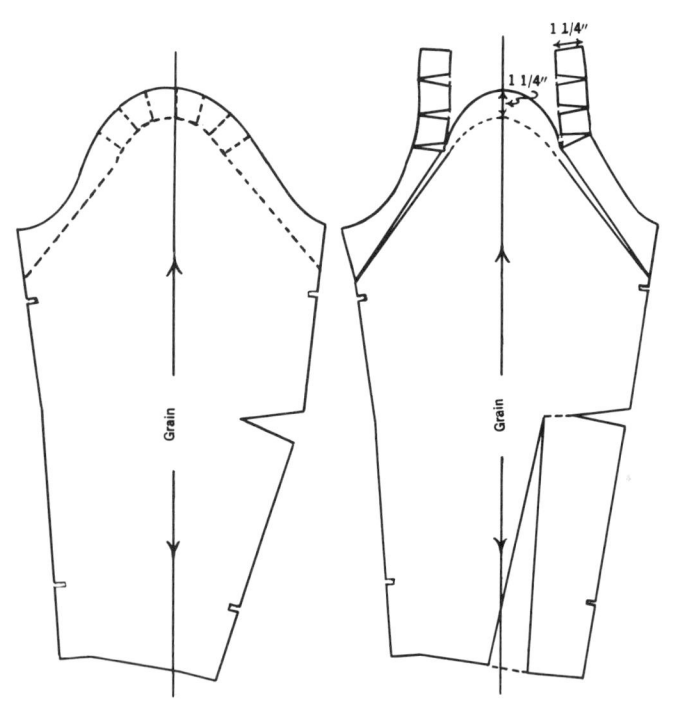

Fig. 58. (a) Slash lines drawn; (b) Slashes spread and cap center increased in height and width. Part of the elbow dart is transferred to the wrist width.

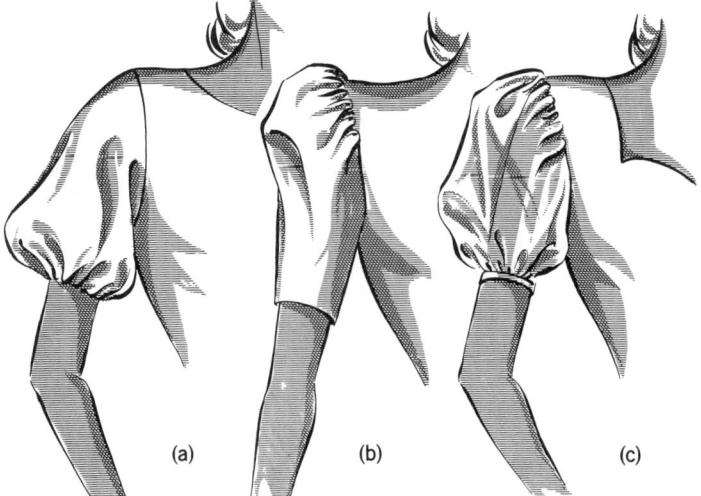

Fig. 59. Short puff sleeves: (a) Fullness on bottom edge; (b) Fullness on top edge; (c) Fullness on both top and bottom edges.

144

SLEEVES

where the slashes come, that is, through the central section of the basic pattern. They should not spread over the top of the cap for more than 3 inches on each side of the shoulder seam. Never allow gathers to continue to the underarm. Notice also the dotted lines at the top of the cap that indicate an increase in length. As a sleeve increases in width for fullness, it must also increase in length or height correspondingly to provide blousing or puffing, as a full gathered sleeve without height enough for puffing at the top will draw down flat against the arm.

An extremely abbreviated puff sleeve is expressive of youth, and is suitable for a child or a slender girl. Short puff sleeves, in general, have exuberant youthful lines.

Figures 60a, b, c, and d should be studied carefully in connection with the following directions.

1. Cut off the master pattern sleeve the desired length. (See method for cutting off a short sleeve, page 129.)

2. Draw lines through the central section of the master sleeve pattern from the top to the lower edge.

3. Spread the slashes in any of the three ways previously explained, depending on the effect desired. Spread all slashes equally to keep the sleeve balanced on each side of the center.

4. Draw around the edge of the pattern exactly, but increase the length or the height directly below or above the points where the slashes are spread in proportion to the increase in width. Increase the height more for more upward puffing, and determine the amount by the silhouette desired and the texture of the fabric used.

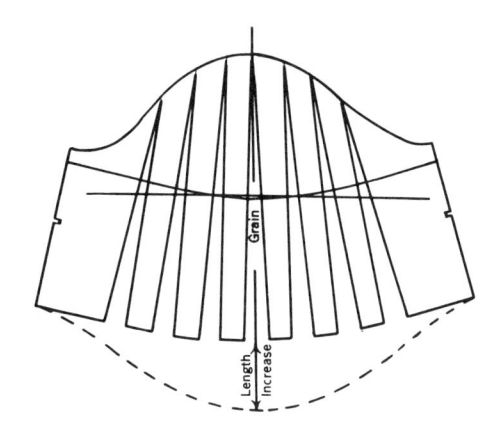

Fig. 60 (b). Spread slashes for puff at lower edge (increase length in proportion to width).

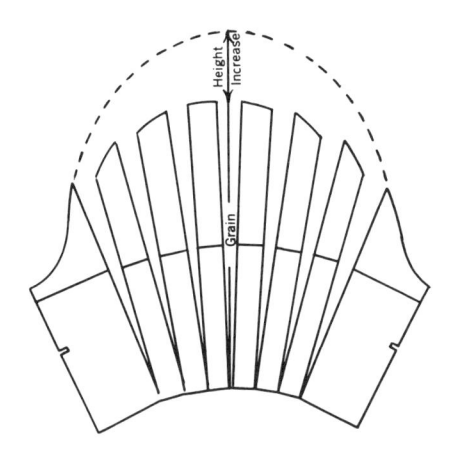

Fig. 60 (c). Spread slashes for puff at top edge (increase height in proportion to width).

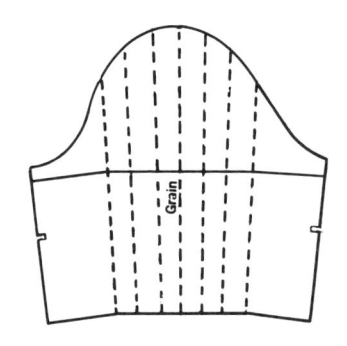

Fig. 60 (a). Short puff sleeve pattern: Draw slash lines.

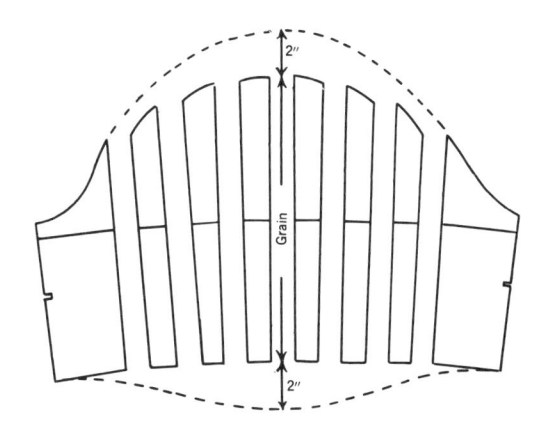

Fig. 60 (d). Spread slashes evenly for puff at both upper and lower edges.

DRESS DESIGN

Fig. 61. Leg o'mutton sleeve.

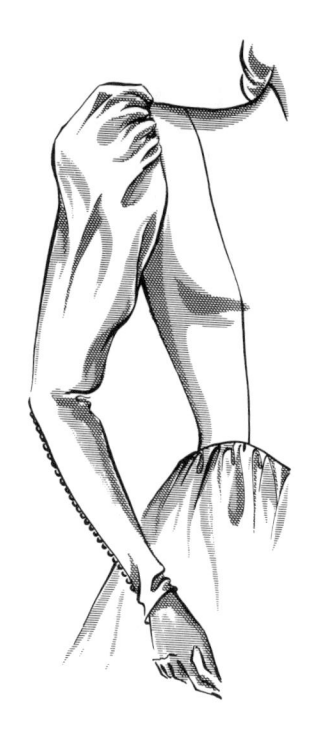

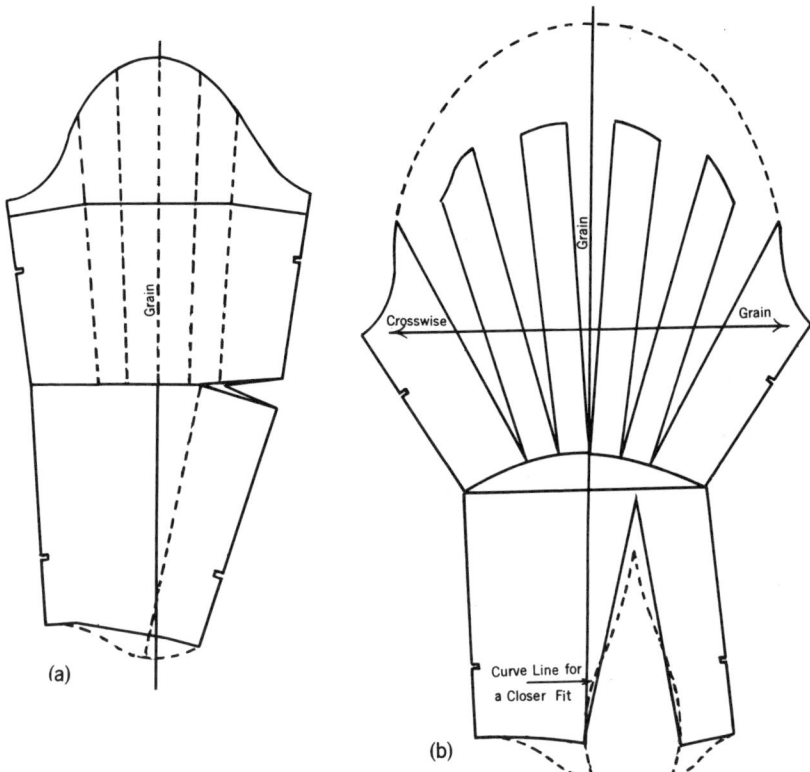

Fig. 62 (*a*). Draw slash lines.

Fig. 62 (*b*). Spread slashes, add height, and shape wrist dart to curve down over hand.

Problem 8

LEG O' MUTTON SLEEVE (see Figures 61, 62a and b)

This is a long fitted sleeve with an extreme puff extending both upward and outward at the shoulder. It is a type of sleeve which comes into fashion from time to time, usually to accent a very tight bodice and a bouffant skirt. Often it is effective to combine the exaggerated puff over the top of the arm with a vertical elbow dart, which provides both a lap for a line of buttons and the opportunity to shape the line down over the hand (see Figure 61).

1. Transfer the horizontal elbow dart to the standard vertical position (see page 135). Plan to button the line nearly to the elbow, and shape it so that it exactly follows the curve of the arm.

2. Slash horizontally from the point of the elbow dart straight across the sleeve (see Figure 62*b*).

3. Draw vertical slash lines at the side front and back and also at the center running from the elbow slash to the top of the sleeve. Spread them at the top, being sure to balance the fullness evenly on each side of the center. *Do not lengthen the underarm seam lines.*

4. Draw a new line over the top, extending it upward at the center for puffing the cap. The extent should be at least one-fourth the original height of the cap.

Notice that the seam lines now slant outward sharply above the elbow, supplying extreme outward extension to the top of the sleeve. *Follow this side seam line exactly as it is.* Do not smooth over the change in the direction of the seam lines at the elbow or the sleeve will not fit the elbow.

5. To extend the sleeve downward over the hand below the normal wrist line, add a curved extension below this line as indicated by the dotted line in Figure 62*a*, and curve the sides of the wrist dart as shown in Figure 62*b*. Notice that the extension flares out at its lower point to fit over the hand.

SLEEVES

Problem 9

SHORT SLEEVE LAPPED ACROSS THE TOP OF THE ARM WITH THE UNDERARM SEAM ELIMINATED
(see Figures 63, 64a and 64b)

The pattern for this very short sleeve lapped across the top of the arm can be made without an underarm seam. The sleeve can be lapped either toward the front or toward the back and can be lapped as much as you wish but probably not more than 3 inches each side of the center of the sleeve.

1. Mark on the basic one-piece sleeve pattern the curve for the desired lower edge and continue it from the center at the lower edge up to the top curve of the sleeve cap as far past the center line as you wish the overlap to be. Then duplicate the overlapped portion of the line on the other side of the center line. This will be the under extension.

2. Cut the pattern along the lower edge of the sleeve.

3. Rule a straight vertical line on a second piece of paper.

4. Place the back edge of the underarm seam against this line and trace the back half of the sleeve plus the under extension drawn in step 1.

5. Place the sleeve with the front edge of the underarm seam against the traced back section and trace the front half of the sleeve plus the overlapped part drawn in step 1.

6. If you wish to tighten the sleeve at the lower edge, slash the basic pattern at the side front and side back, overlapping the lower edge (see Figure 21a, page 124).

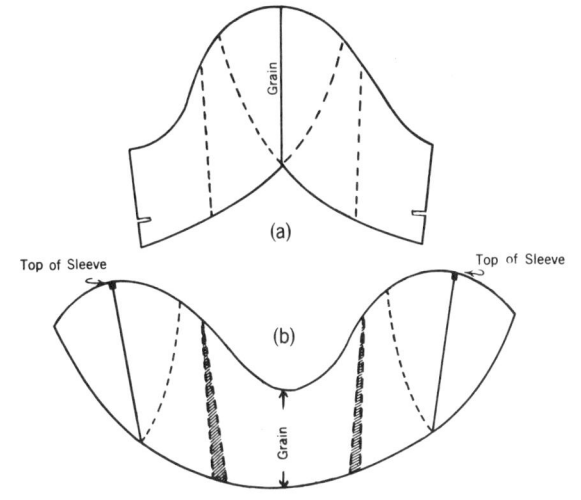

Fig. 64 (a). Step 1 — Draw slash lines. (b). Step 2 — Cut sleeve apart, join underarm seam, and take out a little width by overlapping slashes at side front and back.

Problem 10

LONG SLEEVE WITH COWL FOLDS AT THE SHOULDER (see Figures 65, 66a and b)

This sleeve has dignity and should be made of soft clinging fabric such as transparent velvet or rayon crepe. It is appropriate for very dressy afternoon wear or for a long formal dinner gown.

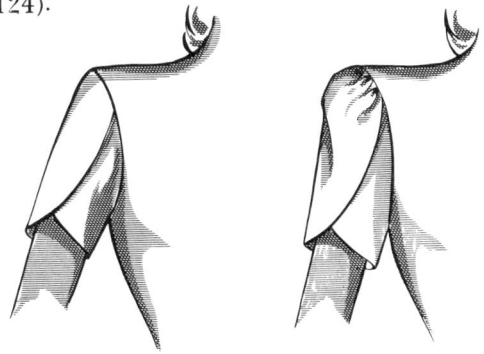

Fig. 63. Lapped sleeve with underarm seam closed.

Fig. 65. Long sleeve with cowl folds.

DRESS DESIGN

The principle of blocking this sleeve is exactly the same as for blocking the cowl folds at the neck of a blouse. Excess added at the center falls down on the outside of the arm into cowl drapery (see Figure 65).

1. Draw the center lengthwise grain line on a duplicate of the master pattern and rule the cowl fold lines from the top of the armscye curve to the center (see Figure 66a).

2. Draw a line across the sleeve from the point of the elbow dart to the opposite side.

3. Slash along these lines (see Figure 66b) and pivot the pattern outward, separating the two sides of the upper sleeve section. Spread the top of the sleeve twice the depth of the fold that hangs from the tip of the shoulder. The fold can have a hem allowance added to the top edge and can fall open to show the arm.

4. Draw a straight line lengthwise through the center of the sleeve and place this line on the true bias.

After practicing these typical cuts you will see possibilities for applying the same principles of designing on a master pattern to any other set-in sleeves that you may choose to try.

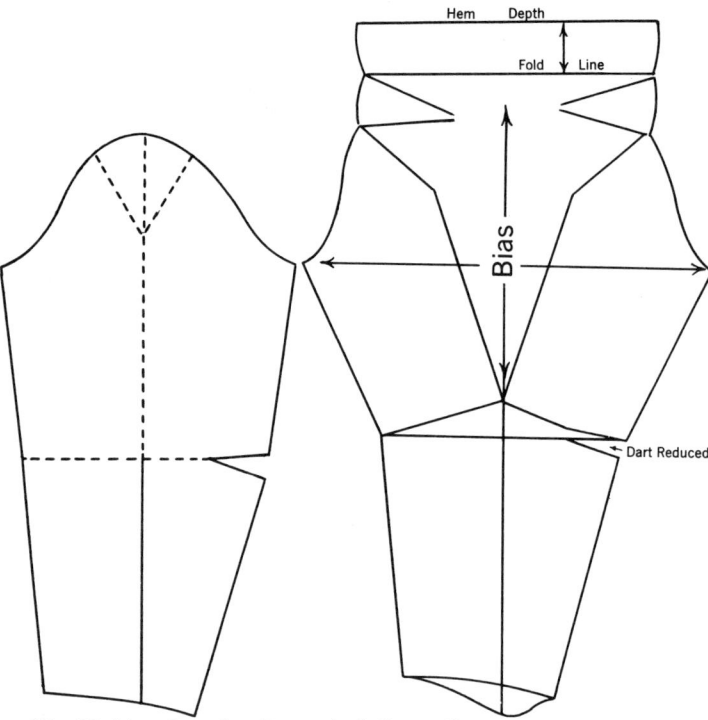

Fig. 66 (a). Step 1 — Draw slash lines. (b). Step 2 — Spread slashes for cowl drapery. A hem is added at the top, and the lower edge is curved down over the hand.

PART III

SLEEVES CUT IN ONE WITH THE BODICE OR A PART OF THE BODICE

Sleeves cut as a part of the bodice are frequently classified as a form of the kimono cut, but there is a distinction between the raglan type, which retains the identity of the lower armscye of the sleeve, and the true kimono type, which loses the original curve of the lower armscye.

RAGLAN TYPE

This includes (1) the raglan, (2) the epaulet (or strap) sleeve, (3) the sleeve cut in one with a yoke, and (4) the sleeve set on to the drop shoulder line.

Problem 1

THE RAGLAN SLEEVE (see Figure 67)

The raglan sleeve is fundamentally different from the true kimono type in that it retains its original lower armscye line, whereas kimono and dolman sleeves completely lose the lower armscye curve in the blending of the sleeve with the bodice. Because the raglan does retain the lower armscye curve, it fits the underarm more exactly and with fewer underarm folds than the kimono type. If the depth of the armscye is normal, the raglan falls in the same manner as

SLEEVES

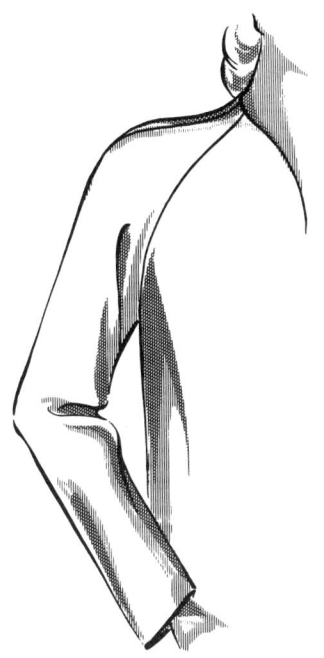

Fig. 67. Raglan sleeve.

any set-in sleeve. However, the deepening of the armhole beyond the normal requires not only the lengthening of the underarm seam of the sleeve, but also the widening of the girth, so that the arm can be raised comfortably. This added length and width at the underarm produce some wrinkling when the arm hangs at the side of the body. Only in loose hanging coats which are free to rise with the movements of the arm is it possible to use a raglan sleeve with a low armscye and long sleeve cap rather than a lengthened underarm sleeve seam. Since the raglan sleeve curves out from the underarm to form the upper shoulder area of the blouse, the armscye is often deepened for a more graceful transitional line between blouse and sleeve. The raglan with both the normal and the deeper-than-normal armscye will be explained in the directions which follow.

Because the raglan is really a modification of the regular set-in sleeve, let us analyze the basic difference between the two. The normal set-in sleeve has 1½ to 2 inches of ease distributed over the upper half of the cap. But when the upper section of the sleeve is cut in one with the blouse, there is no overarm seam along which to distribute the ease. The raglan therefore employs a shoulder line dart as a means of holding in a part of this ease.

Procedure for Designing a Raglan Sleeve (see Figure 68a, b)

1. Trace around the master sleeve pattern and mark the lengthwise center and quarter divisions at top and bottom. Remove the master pattern block and rule the vertical lines.

Note. Figure 68a shows the master sleeve block for designing sleeves loose at the lower edge. The regular master pattern with the elbow dart should be used for fitted sleeves.

2. Transfer the dart from the back shoulder line, but leave ¼ inch of ease on the shoulder seam.

3. Determine and mark the points where the raglan line swings into the normal armscye line on the front and back blocks.

4. Measure on the blouse front armscye the distance from the underarm seam to the point marked in step 3. Measure this same distance on the sleeve armscye from the underarm seam and mark a point. If the raglan line swings into the normal sleeve armscye line above the halfway point between the top of the sleeve and the underarm seam, add ¼ inch before marking the point on the sleeve armscye and work this in when joining the sleeve to the bodice.

5. Repeat for the back.

6. Place the front blouse block against the front of the sleeve, matching the points on the armscye. Repeat for the back.

7. Match the armscye curve of the bodice front to the front of the sleeve cap as far as the curves will blend without overlapping. If the shoulder corner of the blouse is ¼ inch above the sleeve cap, the raglan will have about the same cap height as the master sleeve. Tilt this corner in or out from the sleeve cap according to the cap height on your original master sleeve and according to the increase you wish on the cap height of the new sleeve.

8. Repeat for the back, adjusting it to match the front in distance of shoulder corner from sleeve cap.

9. Draw the shoulder dart lines. Rule from the neck end of the shoulder seam to a point ½ inch below the top of the sleeve.

DRESS DESIGN

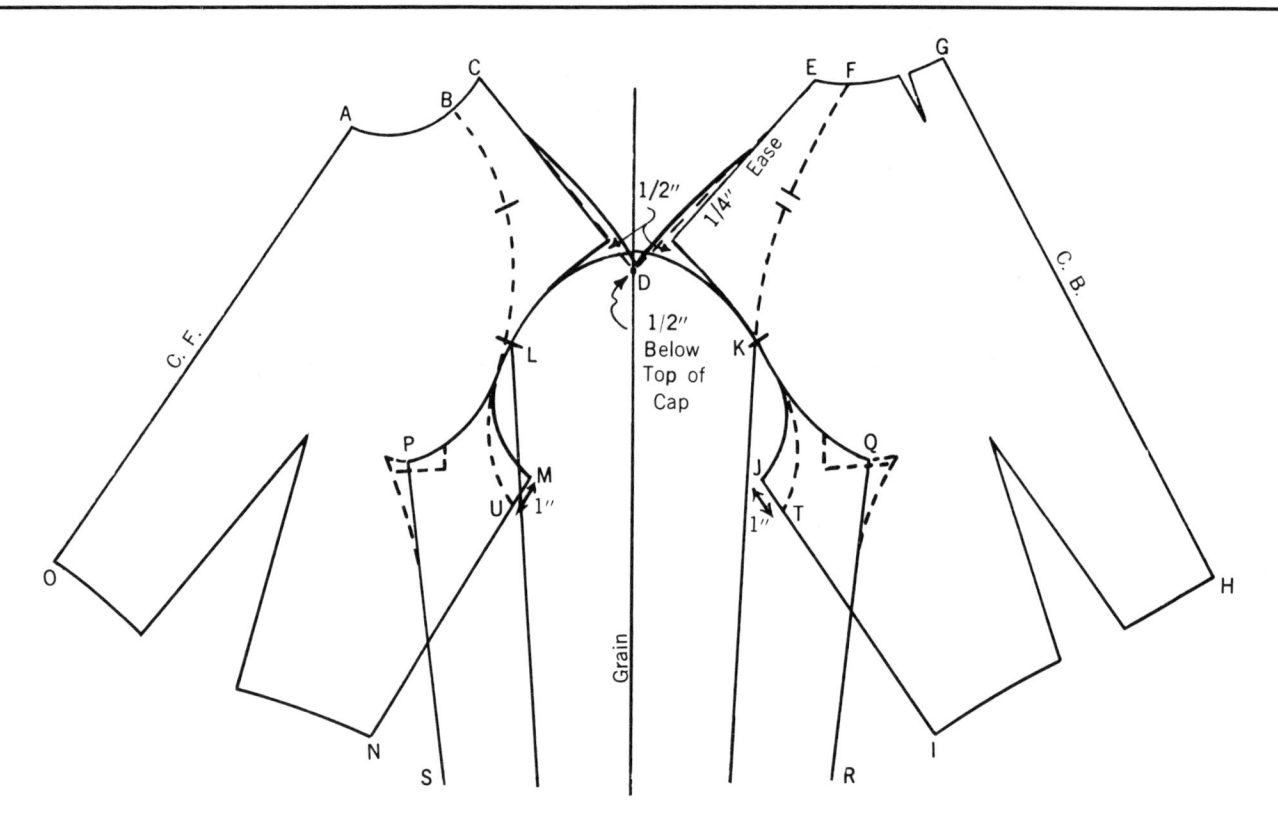

Fig. 68 (a). Raglan sleeve draft. Dotted lines at sleeve girth and lower part of bodice armscye indicate changes if deeper armhole is desired (see Figs. 29 (a) and (b) for sleeve with deepened armscye).

Note. This dart removes a small wedge from the top center of the sleeve cap to eliminate some of the excess on the sleeve ordinarily eased into the upper half of the blouse armhole. The length and width of the dart increase as the shoulder corners of the front and back blocks are pivoted farther away from the sleeve cap. This is the chief variable in the drafting of the raglan sleeve, and you may need to experiment before producing a sleeve in which the dart has the correct length and width. As the dart increases in length and width, the sleeve extends farther out and broadens the shoulders.

10. Modify the straight dart lines drawn in step 9 to taper the dart and to curve the sleeve down over the top of the arm. Begin near the center of the front and back lines and curve into the point as shown in Figure 68a.

11. Draw the raglan line. This may vary, but if the sleeve is to fit like a set-in sleeve, it should cross from the bodice into the sleeve at a point not much lower than halfway down the armscye. The raglan line is usually a compound curve (see Figure 68a). Place crossmarkings.

12. Place a new sheet of paper under the draft and trace off the sleeve, the area marked by the letters *PLBCDEFKQRSP*. Place a second sheet under the draft and trace off the front and back of the bodice, the areas *ABLMNOA* and *GHIJKFG* respectively (see Figure 68b). Include crossmarkings on all tracings. If ¼ inch of excess was left on the front and back armscye of the sleeve, ease it into the bodice at or above the halfway point of the blouse armscye.

13. Slash the sleeve pattern from the lower edge up to points *L* and *K* and spread as much as desired at the lower edge of the sleeve. This step should be omitted in drafting a fitted sleeve.

150

SLEEVES

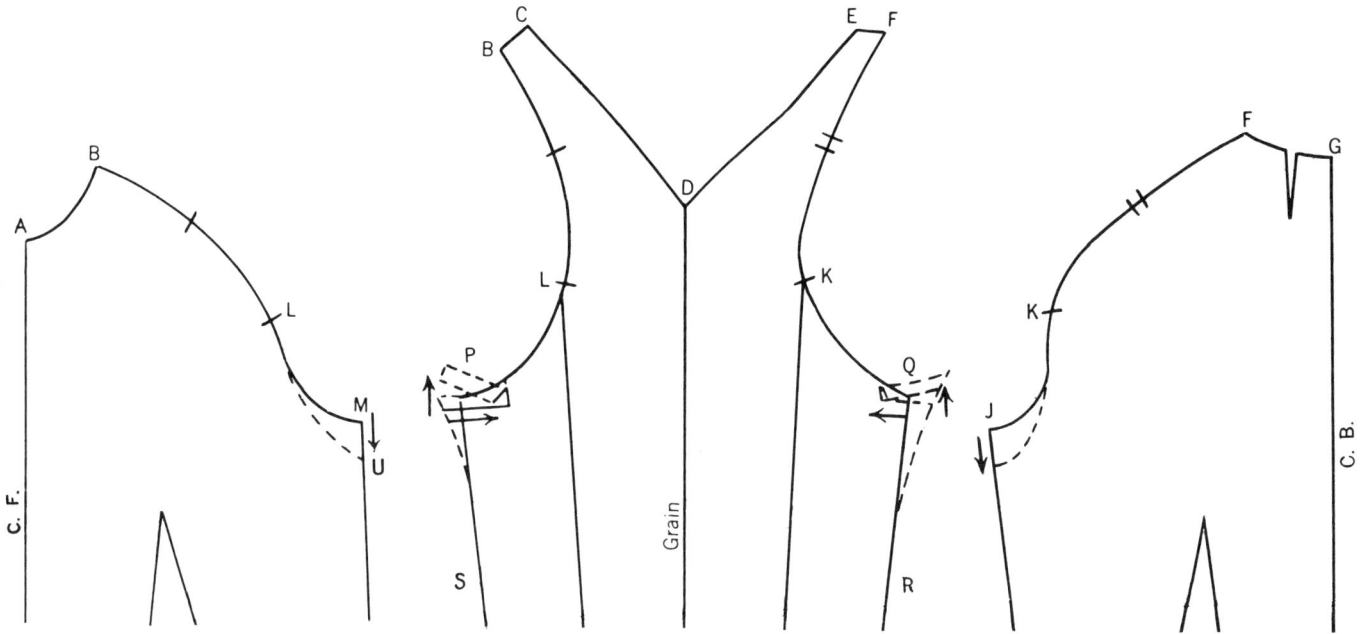

Fig. 68 (b). Raglan draft traced and cut apart (dotted lines indicate variation for deep armscye).

Variation A

To Lower the Armscye

Perform the first ten steps in the standard procedure for the raglan sleeve outlined just above. Then follow the directions below.

1. Drop the armhole 1 inch on the underarm seam of the front and back of the bodice and redraw a smooth curve into this lowered point (see Figure 68b).

2. Increase the sleeve girth by ruling a line through the front and back girth points and extending it until the increase in the sleeve armscye equals that in the armhole of the bodice. You can determine the increase in the length of the bodice armhole by measuring the lower curve of the original blouse armscye from L to M and subtracting it from the new length LU.

3. Rule a horizontal line in from the new front and back girth points of the sleeve 1¼ inches plus the amount added in step 2. If a softer underarm drape is desired, the 1¼ inch measurement can be increased. Erect a perpendicular from the end of this line to the armscye line (see Figure 68a).

4. Connect the new girth end points to the original underarm seam by an inward curving line as indicated by the dotted line in Figure 68a.

5. After tracing the sleeve pattern from the draft, slash the lines drawn in step 3 and raise the wedges to lengthen the underarm seam ¾ to 1 inch. The underarm seam should be lengthened as much as the armhole in the bodice is lowered (see Figure 68b).

Variation B

To transfer part of the shoulder dart to ease along the raglan line of the sleeve where it curves into the normal armscye line, begin with the finished raglan sleeve draft and perform the following steps:

1. Slash from the point on the front of the sleeve where the raglan line swings into the normal armscye, point L, (see Figure 68b) to the end of the dart D. Repeat at the back of the sleeve.

2. Spread the front and back edges of the sleeve to introduce ¼ to ½ inch of ease which will partially close the shoulder line dart. The amount of ease that is possible to work into the curve of the sleeve depends on the shrinking quality of the fabric. This variation transfers some of the cap width away from the top center of the arm to the side of the arm and improves the contour of the sleeve.

DRESS DESIGN

Variation C

To transfer part of the shoulder dart to fullness along the raglan line of the sleeve above the point where it curves into the normal armscye line (see Figures 69a, b, and c):

1. Repeat step 1 in Variation B or make several slashes spaced for distributing gathers or darts.

2. Spread at the front and back edges of the sleeve (or only along the front edge if you prefer a smooth back line) to partially close the shoulder dart.

3. Take up the excess into gathering along a corded seam line or as decorative darts.

Variation D

To transfer part of the shoulder dart to fullness at the center of a bishop sleeve:

1. Slash from the center of the lower edge of the sleeve to the end of the shoulder dart.

2. Spread the sleeve at the center line and partially close the shoulder dart line.

3. Lengthen the sleeve below the center of the bottom line in proportion to the increase in width.

Note. The transfer of the shoulder dart to the center of the sleeve is suitable only for sleeves gathered at the lower edge, since the flare would swing out awkwardly from the top of the arm in a sleeve loose at the lower edge. It may be necessary to slash and spread the sleeve on the vertical lines which divide the sleeve into fourths in order to balance the additional width at the center of the sleeve.

Variation E

To transfer part of the shoulder dart to width at the top center line of the sleeve in order to create a barrel silhouette (see Figure 70a):

Slash as in Variation D and see Figures 70b and c, which show two methods of removing width at the lower part of the sleeve: the one by a shaped seam line on the top of the arm which serves as a long dart from the top of the wrist to a point well above the elbow; and the other by a horizontal slash above the elbow which when overlapped reduces the width at the wrist by shortening the length of the top of the sleeve in relation to the length of the underarm seam.

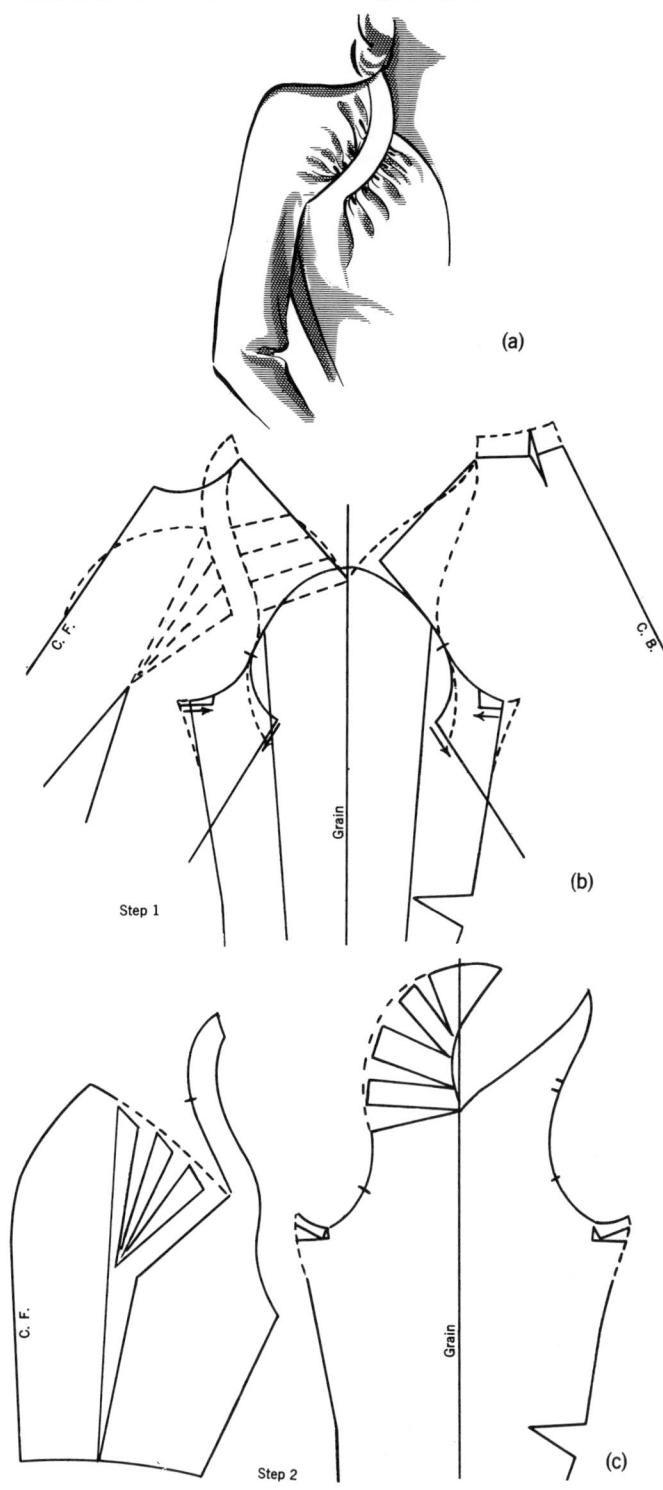

Fig 69. (a) Raglan sleeve with part of shoulder dart transferred into fullness along the front raglan line; (b) Step 1; (c) Step 2.

SLEEVES

(a)

(b)

(c)

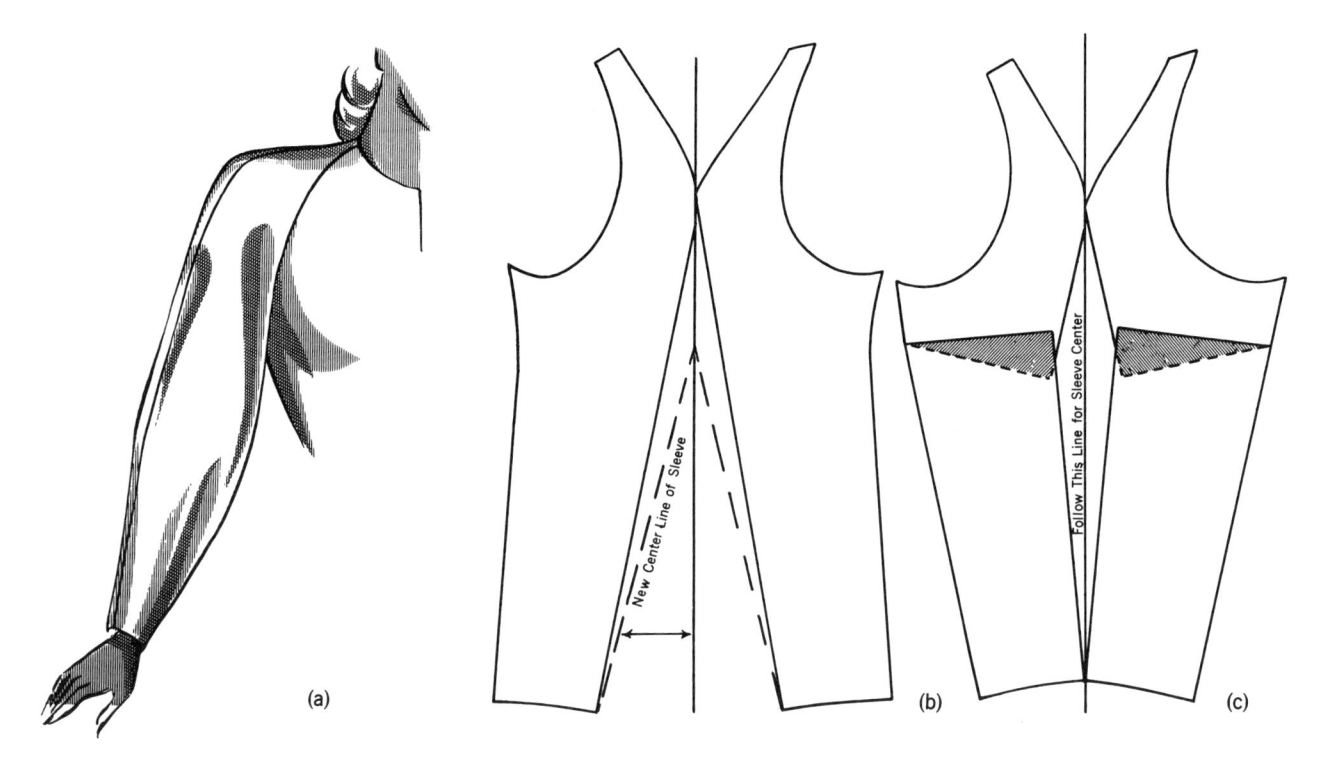

Fig. 70 (*a*). Raglan sleeve with barrel silhouette having part of shoulder dart transferred to center line.

Fig. 70 (*b*). Width removed from lower part of sleeve by center dotted lines.

Fig. 70 (*c*). Width removed from lower part of sleeve by overlapping on horizontal line near girth.

Problem 2

THE EPAULET OR SHOULDER STRAP SLEEVE
(see Figures 71a and b)

The epaulet varies little from the normal set-in sleeve except that it is cut in one with a narrow strip from the top of the shoulder. The regular shoulder seam is omitted, but seams at the front and back of the strap are substituted for it. Decorative detail on the epaulet focuses interest on it, especially if the strap is continued into a high neckline or a collar. Also, the edge of the strap can serve as a yoke line to hold gathers or folds in the bodice front. Its horizontal emphasis tends to broaden the shoulder line and to increase the height by holding interest at a point high on the figure.

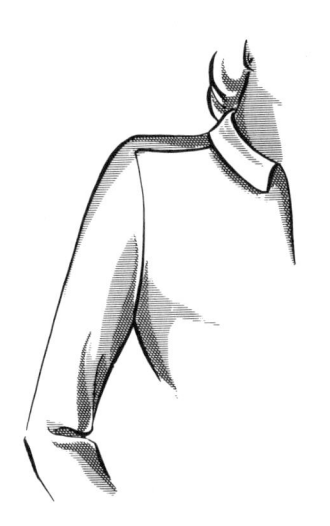

Fig. 71 (*a*). Epaulet sleeve.

153

DRESS DESIGN

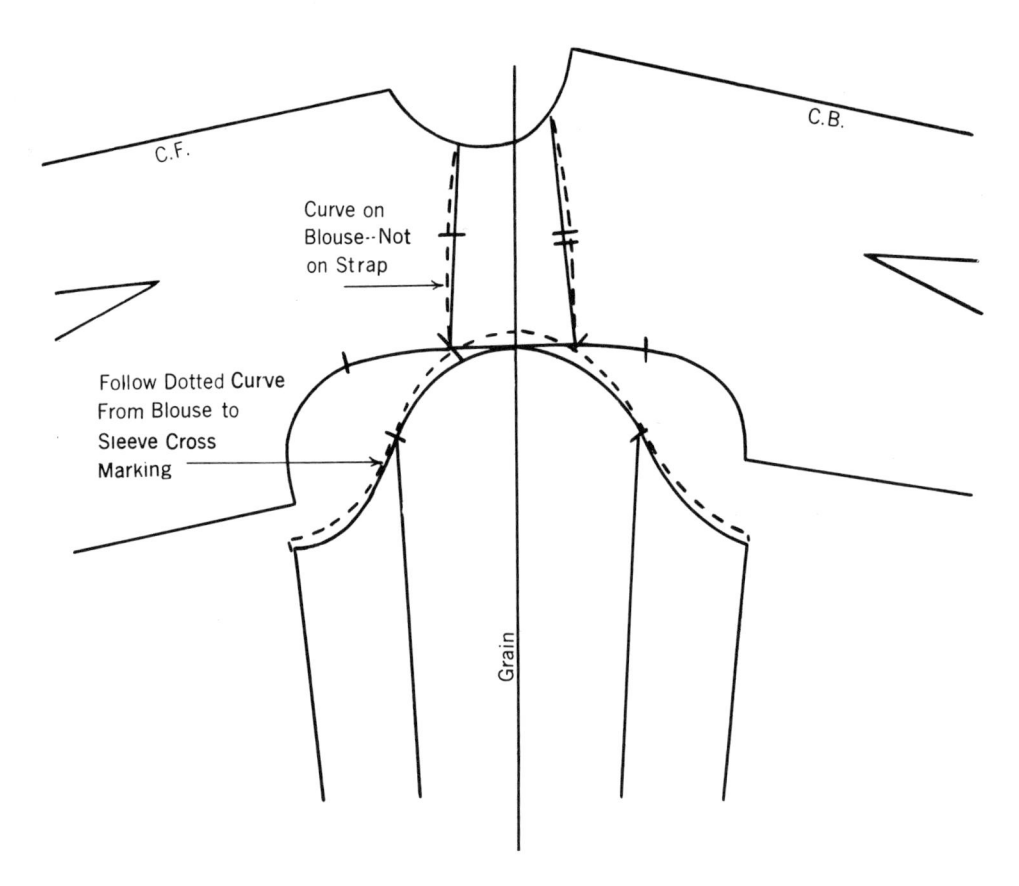

Fig. 71 (b). Draft for epaulet sleeve.

1. Trace the front and the back bodice blocks with shoulder seam lines meeting. Fold out the ease in the back shoulder seam line.

2. Rule a straight line to extend the shoulder seam from the armscye the length of the sleeve.

3. Place the center lengthwise grain line of the sleeve on the line drawn in step 2 with the front half of the sleeve facing the bodice front. The highest point of the center of the sleeve should touch the armscye end of the shoulder seam. Overlapping them reduces the cap height and should be done only for sport sleeves. (The dotted armscye line shows a sleeve cap that touches at the front and back strap lines and overlaps at the center, thereby reducing the original height of the sleeve cap.)

4. Draw the strap design on the back and front of the bodice. At the armscye it should not extend more than 1½ inches either in front or in back of the shoulder seam, since there is no opportunity to ease the sleeve armscye into the armhole of the dress across the strap area. Draw a smooth curved line extending the upper part of the cap to meet the strap line on the back and front of the bodice. Do not rule straight lines to the edge of the sleeve cap. *The extension must be on the sleeve.*

5. Mark front and back notches on both the sleeve and dress armscye lines, on the strap, and on the front and back of the bodice.

6. On the front and back of the bodice, curve the seam lines adjoining the strap ⅛ inch outward from the strap at a point halfway between the neck and the armscye in order to allow more ease below the strap line. Do not change the line on the strap itself.

7. Place the draft over another sheet of paper and trace off the sleeve and the connecting strap. Trace the front and back of the bodice separately.

SLEEVES

Epaulet Variation with Darts Extending into the Sleeve from the Ends of the Strap (see Figures 72a, b, and c)

When very broad shoulders are in vogue, extend the strap into the head of the sleeve by means of darts at the strap edges (see Figure 72a).

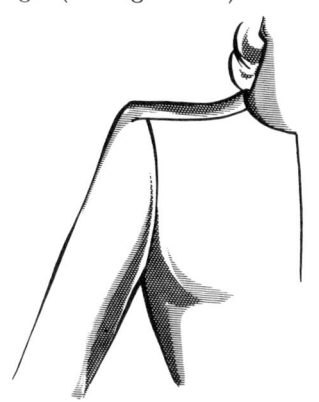

Fig. 72 (a). Epaulet sleeve with darts extending into sleeve from ends of the strap.

1. Trace off the strap sleeve previously described.
2. Draw in the following slash lines:

(a) Center lengthwise line.

(b) Girth line at right angles to center line.

(c) Extension of strap lines at front, N, and back, O, to the girth line.

(d) Lines from the extended strap to the front and back underarm seam lines at points M and L, 3 inches below the girth.

(e) Lines from the girth to points B and D on the front and back armscye halfway between the edge of the strap and the girth (see Figure 72b for placement of the slash lines).

3. Slash along lines HN and IO; slash NM and OL to the underarm seam; slash NB and OD to the armscye; slash NO.

4. Without spreading the slashes, pin the slashed pattern to a new piece of paper, placing the center lengthwise grain line on a vertical line drawn on the under paper.

5. Raise the strap section from the base of the sleeve at the girth, NO, the amount the strap is to be extended beyond the armscye line, in other words, the length of the dart (usually 1¼ to 1¾ inches).

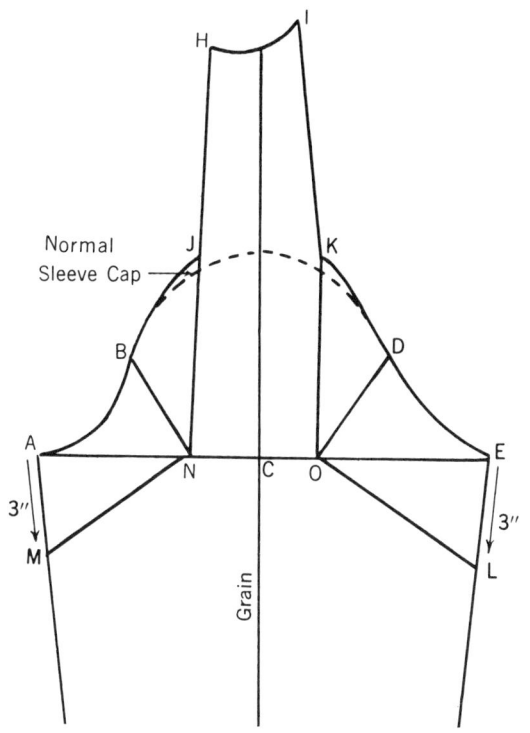

Fig. 72 (b). Slash lines drawn on epaulet sleeve.

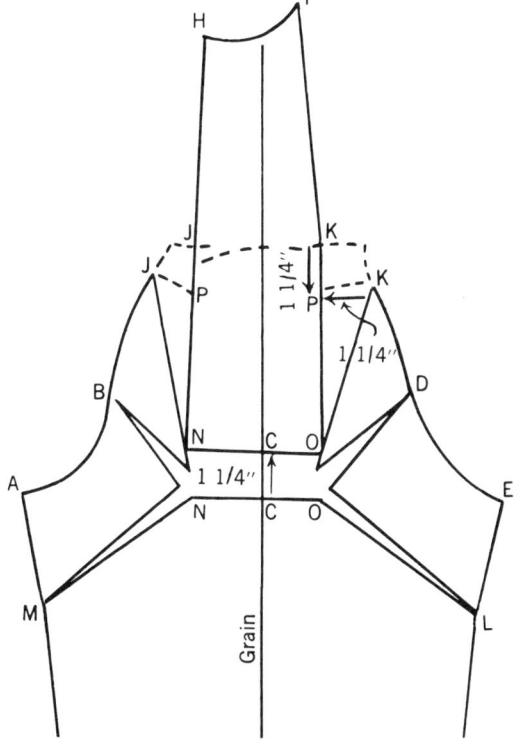

Fig. 72 (c). Slash lines spread and darts drawn.

155

DRESS DESIGN

6. Compare the armhole measurement of the dress from the strap to the underarm seam at back and front with the sleeve armscye measurements. The sleeve cap appears smoother if there is no more than ½ inch of ease on the back and ½ inch on the front. Place the remaining excess in the dart width.

7. Spread the pattern for the increased height and width of the cap as shown in Figure 72c. Rule the darts, following the strap edge for the inner dart edge. Measure the inner edge of the dart from J to P and make the outer edge the same length.

Note. The slashes B to N in the front and D to O in the back provide a higher cap without overlifting the lower curve of the armscye (see Figure 72c).

Problem 3

YOKE AND SLEEVE CUT IN ONE (see Figures 73a and b)

Many interesting designs can be developed by cutting the sleeve in one with the yoke, thus making the yoke a more important space division. Eliminating the top half of the armscye seam gives continuity to the space without sacrificing the advantages of the neatness of a set-in sleeve at the lower armscye.

The lower half of the armscye controls the freedom with which the arm can be moved, and therefore the yoke line should not enter the armhole below the center of the armscye.

Fig. 73 (a). Yoke and sleeve cut in one.

1. Draw the yoke line on the master pattern blouse.

2. Measure the front bodice armhole from the underarm seam to the yoke.

3. Measure the same amount on the sleeve armscye and mark this point.

4. Repeat both measurements for the back.

5. Trace the sleeve on paper, leaving room for the addition of the yoke to the upper cap at both front and back.

6. Place the front and back yoke against the sleeve at the points marked in steps 3 and 4. However, if the yoke line is above the halfway point on the sleeve armscye, leave some ease on the sleeve. The sleeve armscye from underarm to yoke can be ¼ inch longer than the dress armhole.

7. Place the armhole edge of the yoke so that it follows the curve of the upper half of the sleeve cap but with the shoulder seam corner of the yoke (the point where the armscye line and the shoulder seam come together) rising ¼ inch above the sleeve cap. It then has about the same cap height as the master sleeve. To shorten the cap, let the shoulder corner of the yoke dip down into the sleeve. Do this for active sports dresses which need arm freedom. To increase the height of the cap, let the shoulder corners of the yoke rise above the curve of the sleeve cap ½ inch. Do this if the master sleeve does not have enough cap height to go over shoulder padding, or in designing coats and jackets which need extra shoulder room to slip over dresses and blouses with puffed or padded sleeves.

8. Draw the shoulder line dart as for the raglan sleeve.

9. Trace the new sleeve and yoke pattern on a second sheet of paper.

10. Trace the blouse front and back and crossmark the yoke and the lower sections of the bodice.

Note. See variations of the raglan draft (pages 151-152) if, after trying out a muslin proof, you find that the shoulder dart holds too much of the sleeve cap width at the top center of the arm. See Variation A under the Raglan Sleeve (page 151) for instructions on lowering the armscye.

SLEEVES

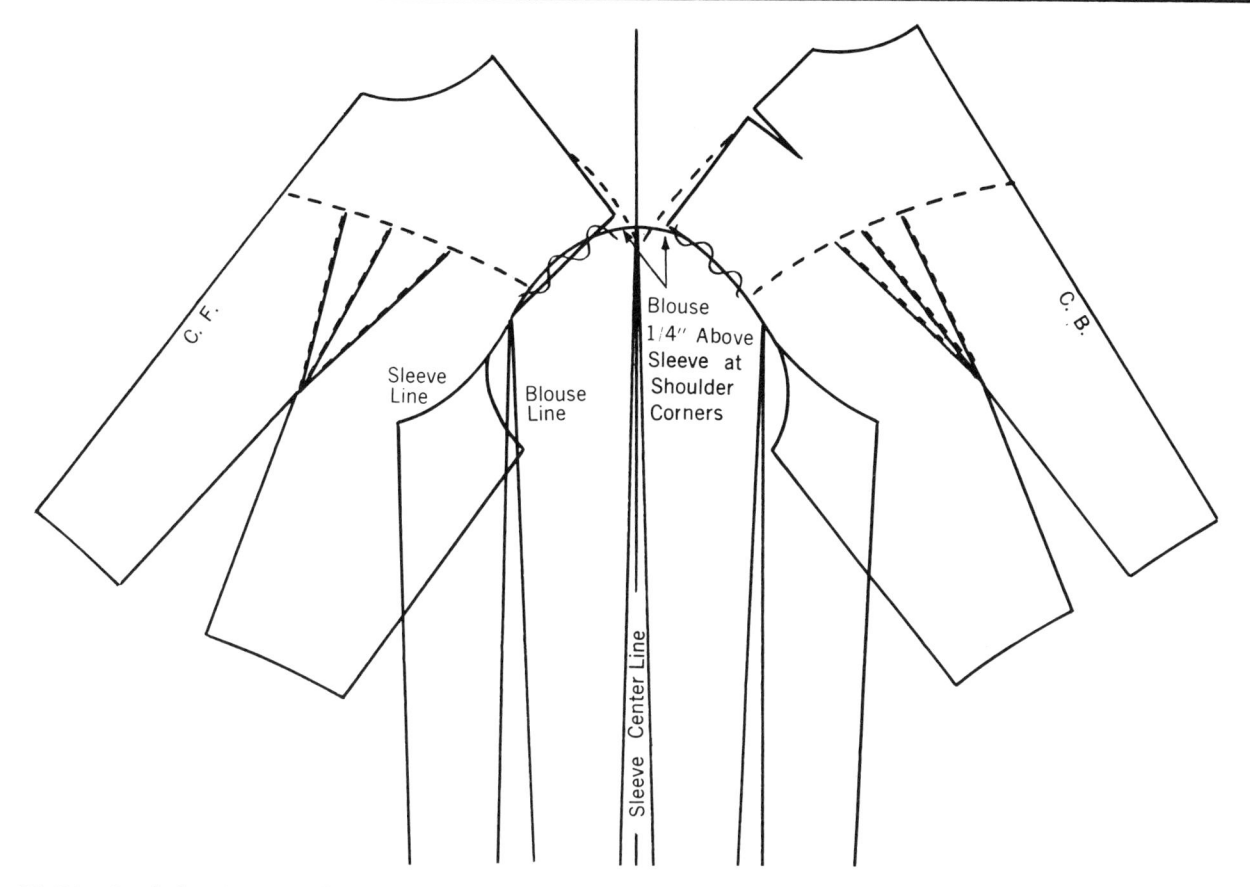

Fig. 73 (b). Draft for sleeve cut in one with yoke. (Sleeve block has been spread on center and quarter verticals for a loose straight-hanging sleeve.)

11. Plan grain placement carefully. The lengthwise grain through the center of the sleeve places the center front and center back of the yoke on the bias or semibias. Straight grain at the center front of the yoke places the center line of the sleeve on the bias and the center back on the crosswise grain or on the semibias depending on the angle of the shoulder line dart. A seam at the center line of the sleeve provides more possibilities for the placement of the grain, but the grain must be matched at the center line of the sleeve on the front and back halves if such a seam is used.

Problem 4

SLEEVE WITH DROP SHOULDER (see Figures 74a, b, and c)

The drop shoulder provides another way of carrying the design lines of the dress into the sleeve, some-

Fig. 74 (a). Sleeve with a drop shoulder.

DRESS DESIGN

times as an extension of a yoke or a French dart line, and sometimes as an extension of the blouse into a simulated yoke. This cut is frequently used to emphasize a graceful shoulder line in evening dresses or hostess gowns with an extremely full gathered or cartridge-pleated sleeve mounted on it, the tubular folds on the sleeve contrasting with the close fitting shoulder line.

1. Trace around the master sleeve pattern on a sheet of paper large enough for the front and back of the blouse as well as the sleeve.

2. Measure the blouse front armscye from the underarm seam to the point chosen for the lower edge of the drop shoulder line (see Figure 74b). Measure the same amount on the sleeve. If the drop shoulder line is above the halfway point, add $\frac{1}{4}$ to $\frac{1}{2}$ inch to the measurement of the sleeve to ease in when setting it into the armhole. Crossmark the sleeve and blouse front.

3. Repeat for the back.

4. Place the armscye edges of the front and back of the blouse against those of the sleeve, matching the marks on the sleeve to points marked for the dropped shoulder line on the bodice.

5. Match the curve of the blouse front armhole to the curve of the sleeve cap, so that the shoulder corner of the bodice extends above the sleeve cap no more than $\frac{1}{8}$ to $\frac{1}{4}$ inch, but without overlapping the sides of the upper sleeve cap.

Note. It must be taken into account that the amount which the corner of the bodice shoulder extends above the sleeve cap depends on several conditions. Direction 5 is for a master sleeve with correct height, ready to use without alteration. For more cap height to go over thicker shoulder pads, the shoulder corner of the bodice may extend $\frac{1}{2}$ inch above the sleeve cap. If the dropped cap is to fit the shoulders closely without padding, overlap the sleeve somewhat.

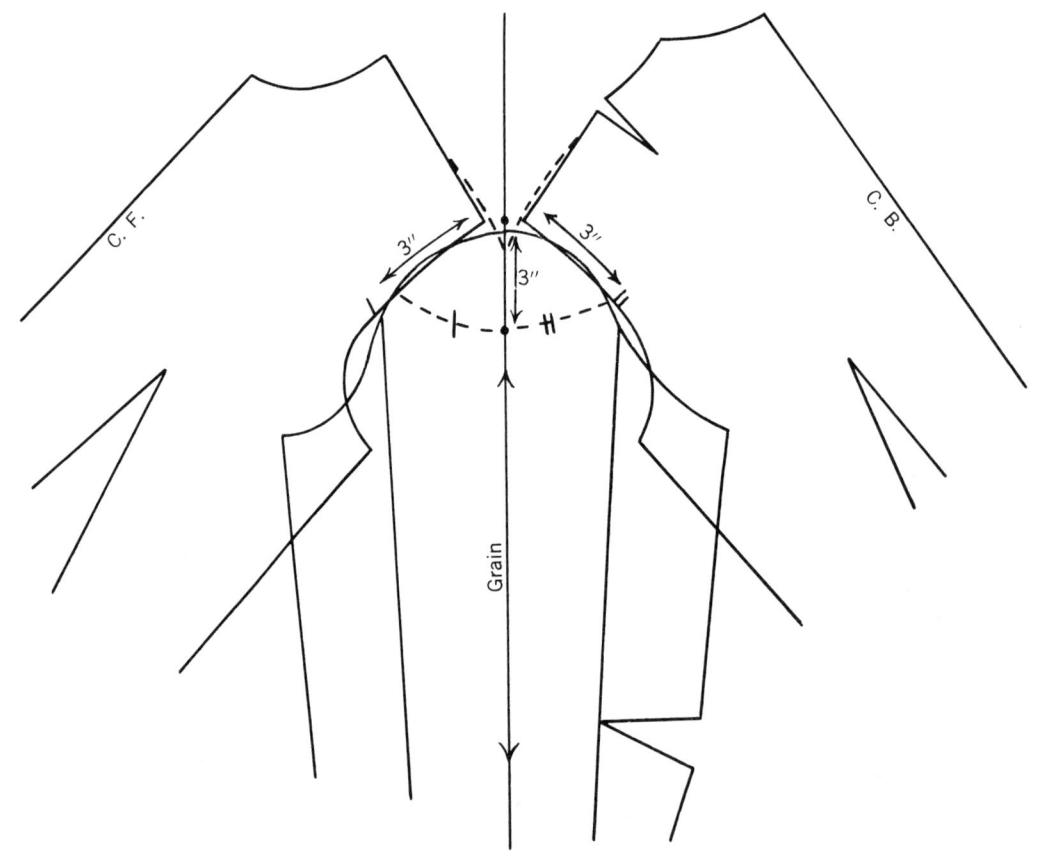

Fig. 74 (b). Draft lines drawn.

Fig. 74 (c). Completed pattern.

6. Pivot the armscye of the back bodice into position against the sleeve, keeping the same relationship between shoulder of bodice and sleeve cap as on the front.

7. Measure the bodice armscye from the shoulder seam to the drop shoulder line. Mark this same distance on the center line of the sleeve, measuring from a point on the center line even with the back and front shoulder corners (see Figure 74b). Draw a smooth curve from this point on the center line of the sleeve to the front and back armscyes to establish the lower line of the drop shoulder. This line may dip downward at the center, but the directions given produce a level line.

8. Establish a shoulder dart line as for the raglan sleeve, but continue it through the drop shoulder as a seam.

9. Crossmark the front and back halves of the drop shoulder line and the point of the shoulder line dart.

10. Trace the sleeve on another sheet of paper.

11. Trace the bodice front and back, including the drop shoulder section. Crossmark.

12. Cut the back and front apart on the center line of the sleeve.

Note. If the drop shoulder section is to fit smoothly, slash and spread the sleeve after making the draft if you wish fullness in the lower sleeve section. However, if the fullness is to hang from the top of the arm, use the spread sleeve from which to draft, so that there will be ripples in the cap area as well as in the lower sleeve section.

KIMONO TYPE

Kimono sleeves are cut in one with the bodice, and therefore lose the original curve of the lower armscye.

Problem 5

THE DRAFT FOR BASIC KIMONO SLEEVE I WITHOUT A GUSSET

To Draft this Sleeve Use the Master Pattern Sleeve with an Elbow Dart

1. Figure 75 illustrates the method of establishing a new center line on the sleeve block. Line *AB* is the center of the normal sleeve only from the top of the cap to the elbow, since the sleeve curves forward at this point. Because the shoulder line usually continues into a seam down the top of a kimono sleeve, the line *AB* should be replaced by a new vertical division line which falls down the center top of the arm all the way to the wrist. The procedure for establishing this line is as follows:

(a) Mark the center of the wrist line, point *C*.

(b) Measure $5/8$ inch from *C* toward the back seam line and mark *D*.

(c) Rule a line from *A* to *D* to establish the placement of the top seam line of the kimono sleeve.

Note. For a fitted kimono sleeve without a top seam, or for a straight loose sleeve with a top seam but without a horizontal elbow dart (see the dotted lines in Figure 75), use the original center line *AB* rather than *AD* in drafting.

DRESS DESIGN

corner *M*. Extend the sleeve line *ML* up to meet the side seam at *O*. Line *MO* should be 1½ inches.

6. Trace around the blouse front and remove the pattern.

Note. The 1½ inches between the side seam of the blouse and the girth corner of the sleeve provide the minimum extra length required on the underarm seam to raise the arm comfortably in a long fitted sleeve without a gusset.

7. Measure the distance between *N* and *O* on the side front of the blouse and an equal amount on the side seam of the back from *I* to *H*.

8. Extend the back seam line of the sleeve (*KJ*) up to a point 1½ inches above the girth corner *J*, and mark point *H* on the side seam of the blouse back. This balances the back and front in relation to the sleeve.

9. Pivot the shoulder corner *D* until it touches the top of the sleeve cap. The measurement between the back shoulder point at *D* and the sleeve center line *YZ* need not equal the corresponding space on the front. Individual blocks vary.

10. Trace around the blouse back and remove the pattern.

11. Mark point *P* on the side seam of the blouse front 6 inches above the waistline. Square out ¾ inch from *P*, and mark *P*¹.

12. Rule lines from *Q* to *P*¹ and *P*¹ to *L* at the elbow. Square in ¼ inch at a point halfway between *Q* and *P*¹, and at a point halfway between *P*¹ and *L*. Make the final underarm line slightly concave by curving in at these halfway points. Use the **original ruled** seam line (not a curved line) when setting in a gusset (pages 165-166).

13. Repeat the procedure in steps 11 and 12 for the back underarm line *FG*¹*K*.

14. Measure down 3 inches along the center line of the sleeve from the top of the cap and mark *C*.

15. Draw the shoulder seam line on the blouse front by following the original line from *A* to within 1½ inches of *B*. Then begin to curve upward to a point ⅛ inch out from *B* and round off to *C*.

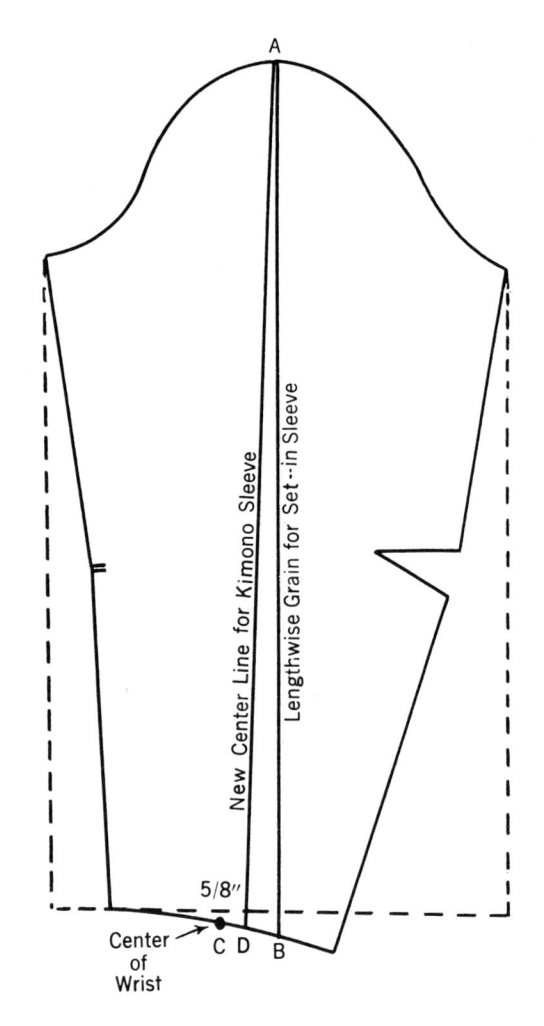

Fig. 75. Establishing top center seam line of kimono sleeve.

2. On pattern paper, rule a line, *YZ*, the length of the sleeve plus 10 to 12 inches (see Figure 76).

3. Place the center line on the sleeve, *AD*, to coincide with line *YZ*.

4. Trace around the master sleeve and remove it. Label the front and back girth corners, *M* and *J*, and the front and back elbow points, *L* and *K*, respectively. The latter points should be 8 inches below the girth points.

5. Place the blouse front with the outer end of the shoulder, *B*, against the top of the sleeve cap, ½ inch from the center line of the sleeve, *YZ*. Pivot the blouse so that the side seam is 1½ inches above the girth

160

SLEEVES

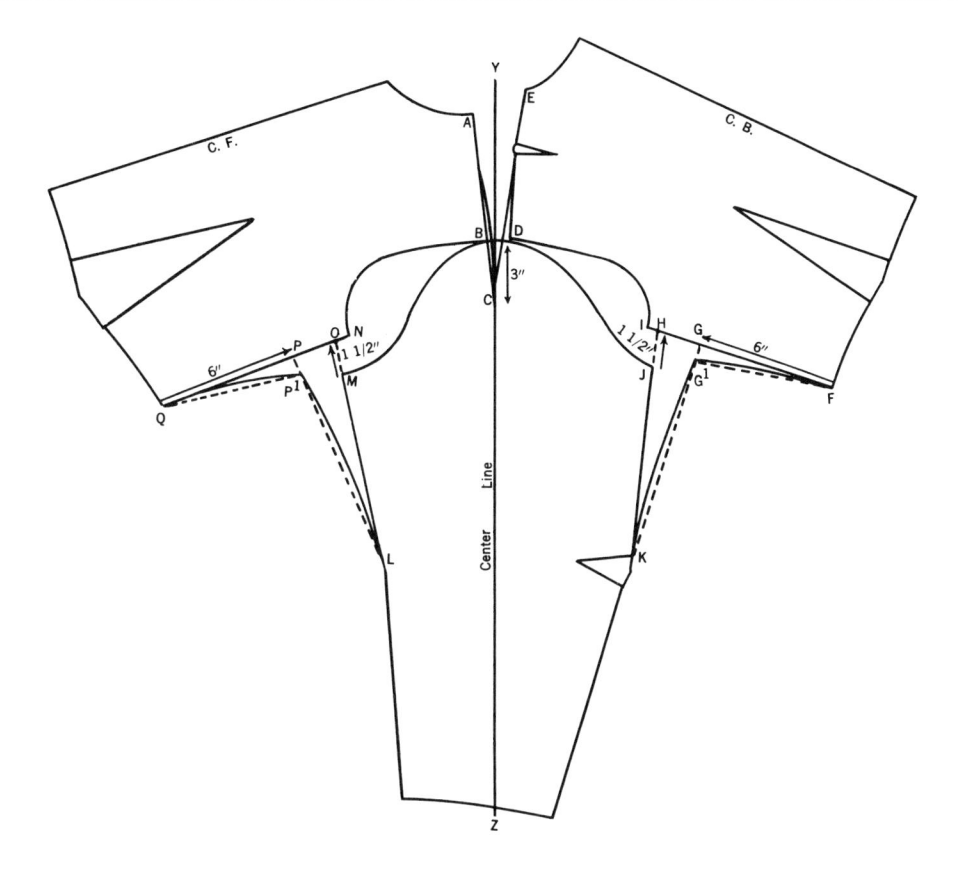

Fig. 76. Draft for basic kimono sleeve Number 1 without a gusset.

16. Repeat for the back shoulder seam line, but curve upward ¼ to ⅜ inch out from *D*. The higher slope on the shoulder seam of the blouse back increases the ease over the back upper arm, and this ease is needed because the arm in a natural position swings forward.

17. The next step will involve either of the two following procedures:

(a) Cut the front and back kimono draft apart on the sleeve center line from *C* to *Z* in order to place the center front and back of the blouse on the straight lengthwise grain.

(b) Or — and this is less frequently done — cut the pattern in one piece, using the shoulder seam line dart *ABCDE*. When this is desired, place the center line of the sleeve on a true bias. This throws a semi-bias at the center front and back.

Variation of Basic Kimono Draft to Provide More Ease Over the Back of the Upper Arm (see Figure 77)

A kimono sleeve sometimes swings forward from the top of the arm to the wrist, drawing tightly over the back of the arm near the girth line. Shoulders which slope forward or a large upper arm may cause this difficulty.

To correct the pattern:

1. Slash the master sleeve on the back vertical quarter division line from the cap to the elbow and spread it 1 inch at the armscye line. This reduces slightly the size of the elbow dart.

2. Follow the basic kimono draft directions. Notice that the distance between the back shoulder point at *D* and line *YZ* is increased. Raise the back shoulder seam above point *D* as much as ¾ inch when drawing the new line *E* to *C*. The other directions remain the same as for the basic kimono draft.

161

DRESS DESIGN

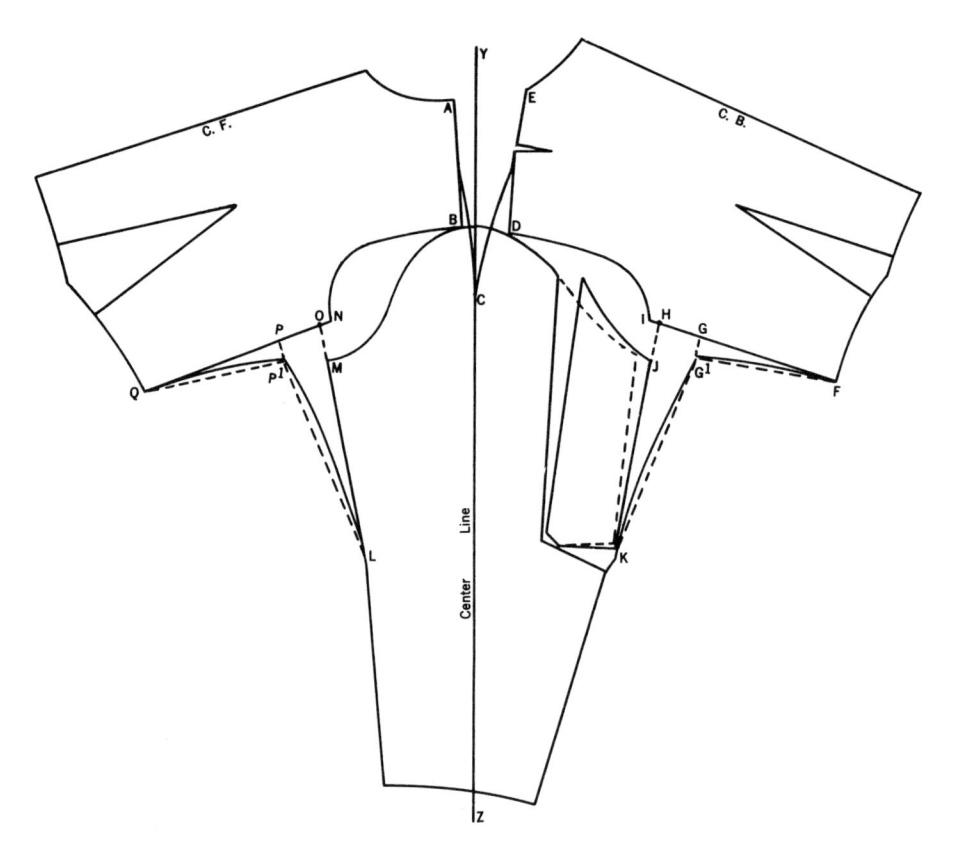

Fig. 77. Variation of basic kimono sleeve to provide more ease over back of upper arm.

Problem 6

DRAFTS FOR BASIC KIMONO SLEEVES WITH GUSSETS (Basic Kimono Sleeves 2, 3, 4)

For smoother fitting kimono sleeves without excessive wrinkling under the arm, place the bodice front and back blocks against the girth corners of the sleeve, or even overlap them to reduce the area between the armscye of the blouse and the armscye of the sleeve. This makes it necessary to set a diamond shaped wedge, called a *gusset*, into the underarm seam to give extra ease and length.

The procedure for drafting basic kimono sleeves 2, 3, and 4 is essentially the same as that for the basic kimono draft without a gusset.

Basic Kimono Sleeve 2 (see Figure 78)

1. Place the blouse front shoulder point B 3/8 inch from the center line of the sleeve YZ. The placing of this point varies, however, with the fullness desired in the cap of the sleeve. You can even move the front shoulder seam at point B as much as 1 inch from the center line YZ, thereby increasing the sleeve width across the top by making the dart BCD larger.

2. Place the blouse side seam NQ so that it touches the sleeve girth corner M, and mark point O where they touch.

3. Measure NO on the side seam of the blouse front. This is a distance of 1½ inches on the diagram, but it may vary with individual blocks. Mark H the same distance down from I on the side seam of the back.

4. Place H against the girth corner J of the sleeve.

5. Pivot D at the shoulder point to touch the sleeve.

6. Measure up from the front waistline point Q the length desired for the side seam and mark P. The side seam can be any length extending between Q and

162

SLEEVES

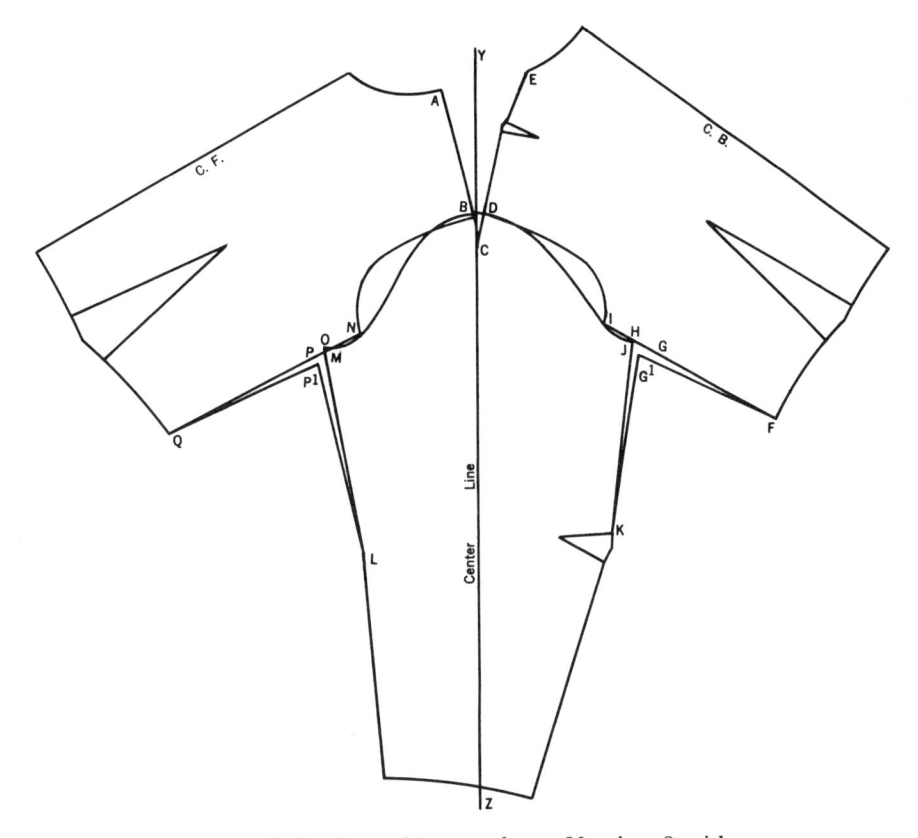

Fig. 78. Draft for basic kimono sleeve Number 2 with a gusset.

O. In the pattern shown in Figure 78, Q to P measures 6½ inches, which allows ¼ inch extension on the underarm line of the blouse and ¼ inch on the sleeve girth so that these two lines will meet at P¹. To widen the sleeve further, decrease the length of the side seam on the blouse or increase the space between the shoulder point B and the sleeve center line YZ.

Draw lines Q to P¹ and P¹ to L. *Do not curve the line when adding a gusset.*

7. Repeat this process for the back underarm seam FG¹K.

8. Draw the completed shoulder line to point C. Figure 78 shows point C moved to within 1 inch of the top of the sleeve to square the shoulder silhouette. This point may be moved up or down from the top of the sleeve to vary the curve of the top center seam line. Raise the shoulder line from B ⅛ inch and from D ¼ inch. (Compare the spaces between A and E on Sleeves 1 and 2.) As the underarm seam length decreases, the shoulder dart widens.

Basic Kimono Sleeve 3 (see Figure 79)

In this draft the girth corner of the bodice and the sleeve overlap to reduce the excess between the armscye of the blouse and sleeve still further, as shown by the smaller open space between BN and BM in the front, and DI and DJ in the back.

Follow the same procedure for this draft as for the previous one, with the possible variations in space between the bodice shoulder seams and the center line of the sleeve. Balance the back and front of the bodice evenly so that the front underarm seam from Q to P equals the back from F to G, and so that MO on the front of the sleeve equals JH on the back. **In Figure 79, QP is 6½ inches and MO is 1¾ inches.**

Basic Kimono Sleeve 4 (see Figure 80)

This draft practically eliminates the excess between the sleeve and blouse armscyes and will fit almost as smoothly as a set-in sleeve, but will require a larger underarm gusset to free the arm. In Figure 80, the underarm seam QP is 5¾ inches, and MO is 2½.

DRESS DESIGN

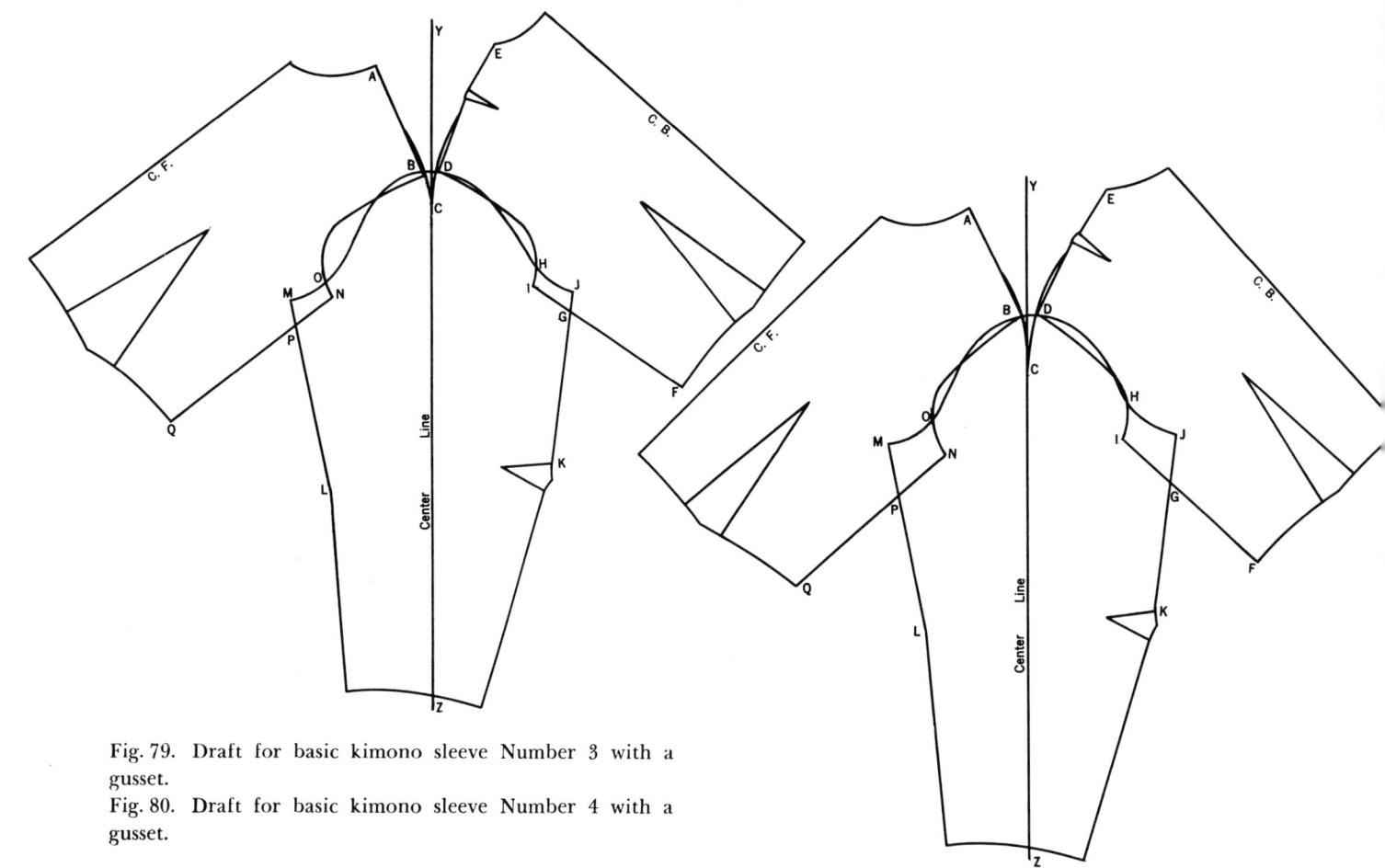

Fig. 79. Draft for basic kimono sleeve Number 3 with a gusset.

Fig. 80. Draft for basic kimono sleeve Number 4 with a gusset.

Comparison of Kimono Drafts (see Figure 81)

The kimono sleeve drafts illustrate a progressive decrease in the length of the underarm seam of the sleeve and a sharpening of the angle between the underarm seam of the blouse and the sleeve. Whenever this angle is sharper than a right angle, it will be necessary to set in some form of gusset so that the arm can be raised comfortably without pulling up the waistline. As the angle sharpens, the underarm length of the sleeve shortens, whereas the overarm length remains constant. Therefore, when seen on the figure, the overarm length appears longer in comparison to the underarm, and with each succeeding draft more nearly resembles the comparative arm measurements when the arm hangs at the side. The diagonal wrinkles falling from the top of the arm toward the underarm seam which characterize the typical kimono are almost eliminated in sleeves 3 and 4. The Japanese, or unshaped, kimono fits the arm smoothly when it is held at a right angle to the body. The set-in sleeve, the opposite extreme, fits smoothly when the arm is down at the side. Thus wrinkles appear on the top, or in the overarm length, of a set-in sleeve when the arm is held out, whereas wrinkles appear at the underarm of a kimono sleeve when the arm hangs down.

Because of this shortness of the overarm measurement as compared to the underarm, the long fitted kimono sleeve tends to pull the blouse away from the side of the neck when the arm is lowered. To offset this, the center top line of the sleeve can be cut on the bias to let the fabric give with the lengthening of the top of the arm as it drops to the side. The greater the slope on the top of the sleeve (as shown to a marked degree in Sleeve 4), the less the sleeve tends to pull down from the shoulder line and away from the side of the neck.

SLEEVES

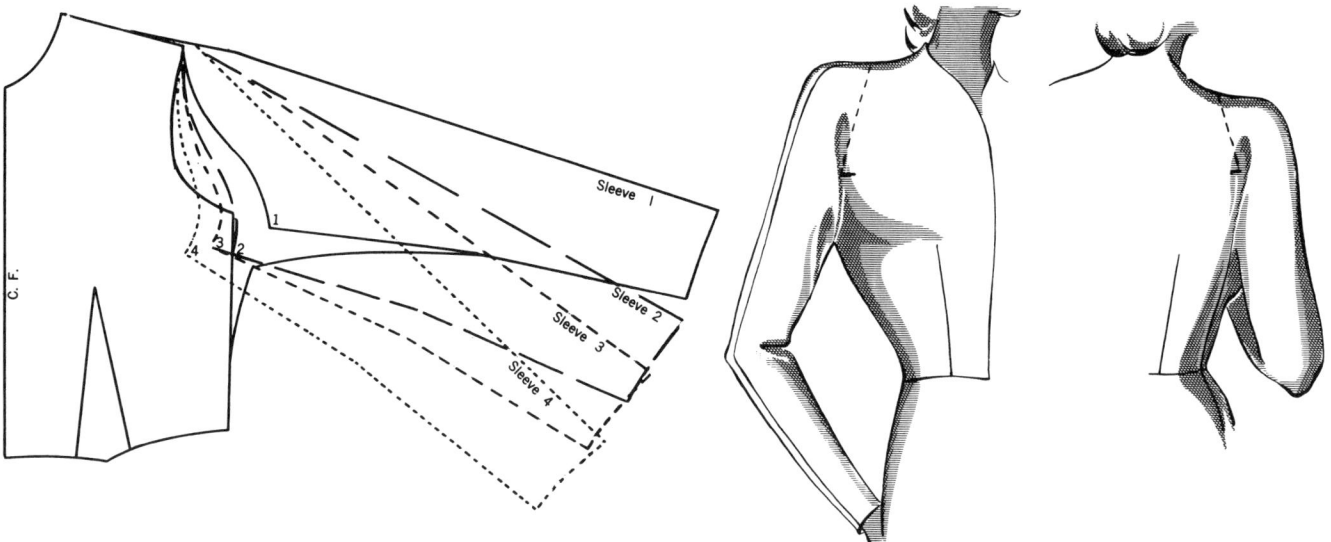

Fig. 81. Comparison of basic kimono sleeve drafts (Sleeves 1, 2, 3, and 4).

Fig. 82. Marking front gusset line when dress is on — Method A.

Fig. 83. Marking back gusset line.

Problem 7

GUSSETS

Using Sleeve 3, follow the directions below for cutting and setting in a gusset. The same procedure applies to all patterns requiring gussets.

1. There are two ways of determining the slash line for the gusset (see Figure 82). Method A should be used in designing a garment for an individual, and Method B should be used in working with standard sized pattern blocks.

Method A

(a) Try on the muslin proof with your arm hanging at your side.

(b) Mark a pin line from the underarm seam up along the inner edge of the natural fold which forms at the front and back of the sleeve along the normal armscye of the body (see Figures 82 and 83).

(c) Slash from the underarm at the juncture of the sleeve and the side seam along the line marked in step *b* for approximately 3 to 4 inches, the length depending on the tightness when the arm is raised. The gusset when set into the garment will fall with the lines of the fold and be inconspicuous when the arm is down.

(d) With slashes made, determine the exact length needed in the gusset so that the arm may be raised above the head without pulling up the waistline.

Figures 84 and 85 show a gusset set in. AD and DC represent the sides of the front slash line. The distance from A to C is the spread needed to raise the arm.

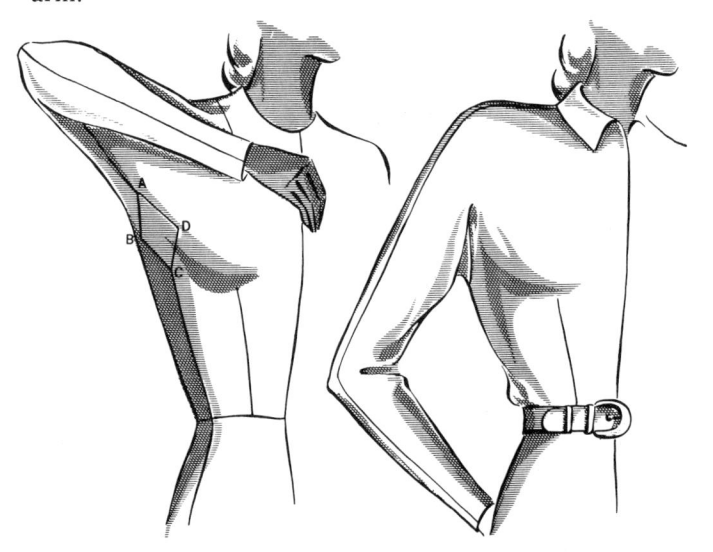

Fig. 84. Gusset set in. AD and DC represent edges of front slash.

Fig. 85. Gusset concealed by front and back fold lines when arm is down.

165

DRESS DESIGN

Fig. 86. Marking gusset line on a pattern.

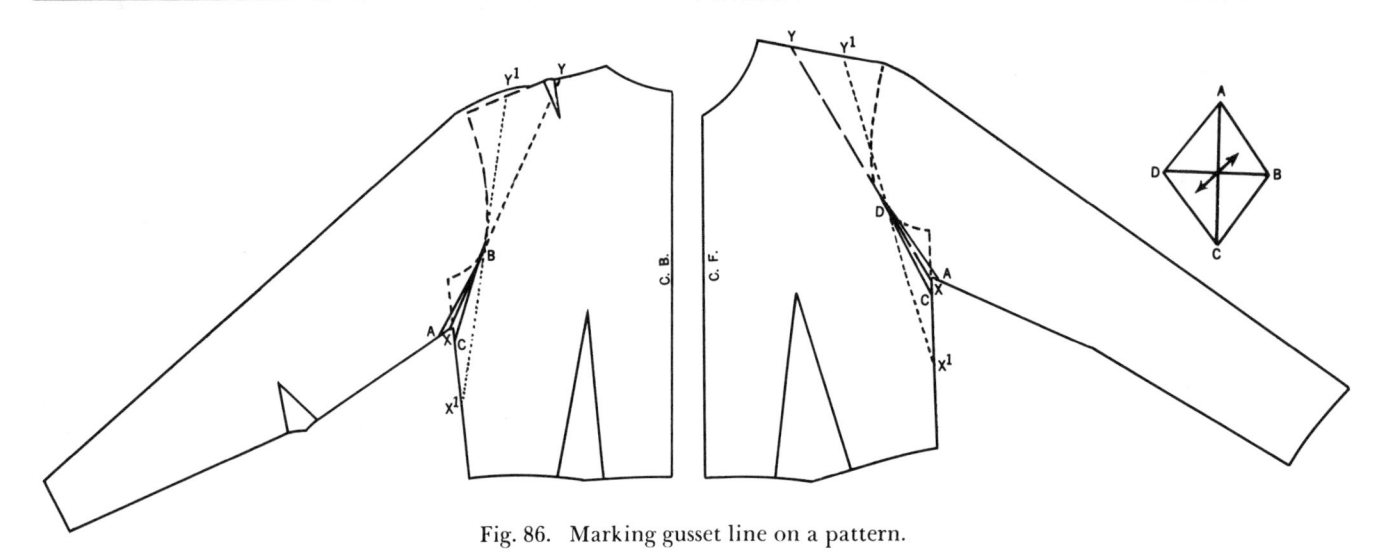

Method B (see Figure 86)

(a) Measure over from the basic neck point along the shoulder seam 1½ inches on the blouse front and 2 inches on blouse back to determine point Y. This gives the correct slope to the slash line XY for a gusset inset, if the underarm depth is approximately 2 inches below the normal scye line (see pages 162-3). As you lower the underarm depth, the slash line will be moved farther toward the armscye end of the shoulder seam as illustrated by dotted line X¹Y¹.

(b) Rule slash lines XB and XD which are directed *toward the point where the normal armscye begins to curve under the arm.*

2. Mark the seam line on either side of the slash for a seam allowance of at least ¼ inch tapering to nothing at points D and B.

3. To draw the gusset pattern, rule a vertical line the length required from A to C, and rule a horizontal line BD through the center of AC and perpendicular to it. Place a ruler on point C and extend it toward the horizontal line, touching it at a point that will make DC equal to the seam line marked along the slash XD. Then rule C to B in the same way. Join points A to D and A to B.

4. Place the gusset on the lengthwise grain of the fabric as indicated, so that the length AC and width DB will be on the true bias. Cut with a ⅜ inch seam allowance.

Note. When making the actual garment, machine stitch the seam lines marked for the gusset before slashing from the underarm to points D and B. This stays the narrow seam allowance and the still weaker corners. Stitch before joining the underarm seams in order to handle the blouse flat. Next slash the gusset line halfway between the two stitching lines and join the underarm seam of sleeve and blouse. Turn under the seam allowance along the slashed lines so that the stitching is concealed, and lap the garment edge over the gusset. Pin and baste on the clearly marked seam lines. Slip-baste if you are using a plain seam. If you are top-stitching, stitch exactly on the edge.

Bodice Insets as Substitutes for Gussets (see Figures 87 and 88)

Variously shaped bodice insets ingeniously lengthen the kimono blouse under the arm. The two types of insets here presented explain the general principles involved. The inset may either be shaped to harmonize with the design of the garment, or it may merely be an inconspicuous strip under the arm.

KIMONO BLOUSE WITH STRAIGHT UNDERARM INSET (see Figures 87a, b, and c)

The straight underarm inset may vary somewhat in width, but will be less conspicuous if it enters the bodice armscye not more than 1½ to 2 inches from

SLEEVES

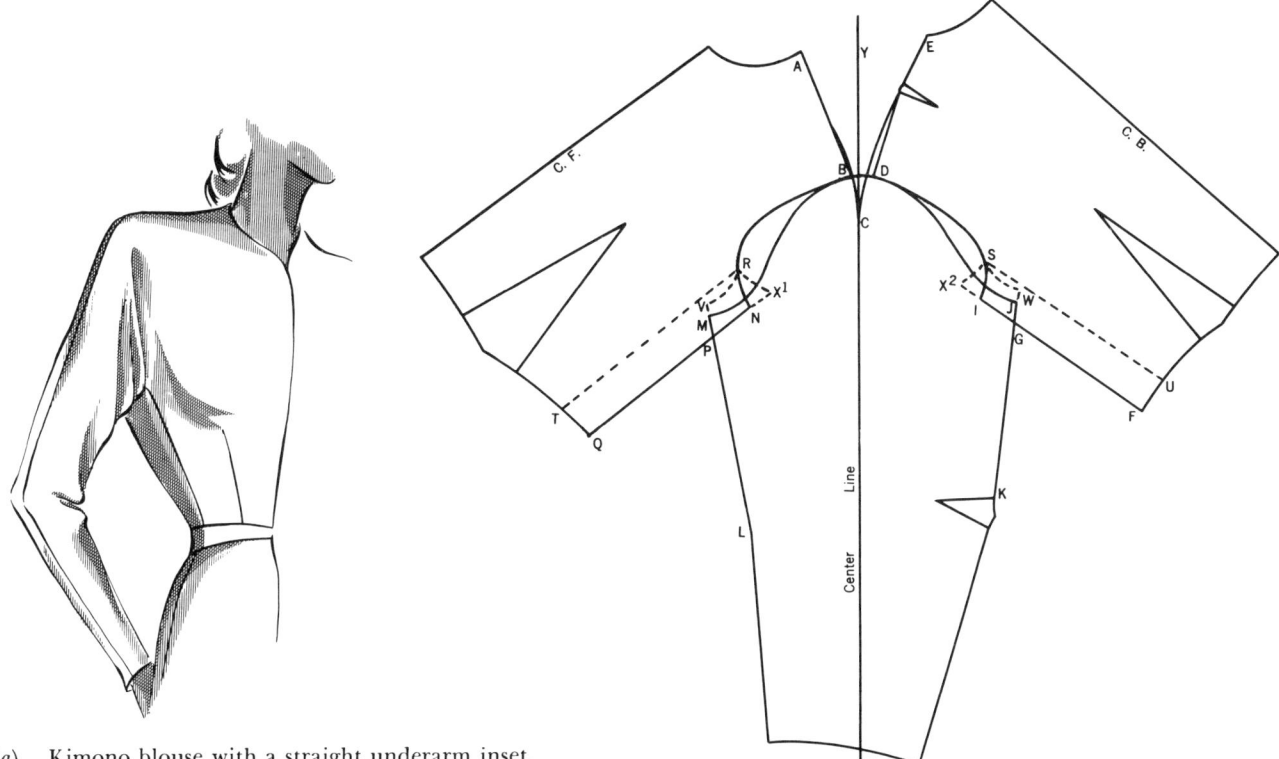

Fig. 87 (a). Kimono blouse with a straight underarm inset.

Fig. 87 (b). Draft for kimono blouse with straight underarm inset.

the original underarm seam line. However, if narrower than this, it fails to serve its purpose.

Figure 87b shows draft 3 of the basic kimono sleeve. It is better, however, to use draft 2 when more ease is desired around the armscye.

1. Establish lines RT and SU for the edges of the underarm inset by measuring in from the side seam lines NQ and IF 1½ inches.

2. Draw the front sleeve armscye line from R to V and the back from S to W. The curve from R to V should equal the length of the front blouse armscye line RN, and that from S to W should equal the length of the back blouse armscye line SI. To provide seam allowances on both edges, the curve must fall at least ⅜ inch within the inset seam lines drawn from R in front and S in back. Figure 87b shows an increase of ½ inch on the length of the sleeve underarm seam above the front and back girth corners M and J.

3. Extend both the front and the back underarm seam lines NQ and IF 1 inch for additional underarm length. RX^1 should equal RN and SX^2 should equal SI.

4. Trace $ACZLPVRTA$. There should be at least ⅜ inch between VR and RT for seam allowances.

5. Trace the back, $ECZKGWSUE$, checking to see that there is at least ⅜ inch between SW and SU as in front.

6. Trace the insert from the front $RTQX^1R$ and back $SUFX^2S$. Join the original front and back underarm seam lines QX^1 and FX^2, cutting the insert in one piece (see Figure 87c).

Note. Before slashing the actual garment between lines VR and RT or WS and SU, machine-stitch from V to R and down on RT for 3 inches. Repeat on the back. This reinforces a ³⁄₁₆ inch seam line.

RV joined to RX^1 and SW joined to SX^2 form the gusset-like extension on the underarm line. Either a wider inset or the use of sleeve draft 2 would allow more extension on the sleeve armscye above M and J, and would make it unnecessary to add to the length of the underarm inset above N and I (see Figure 87b).

167

DRESS DESIGN

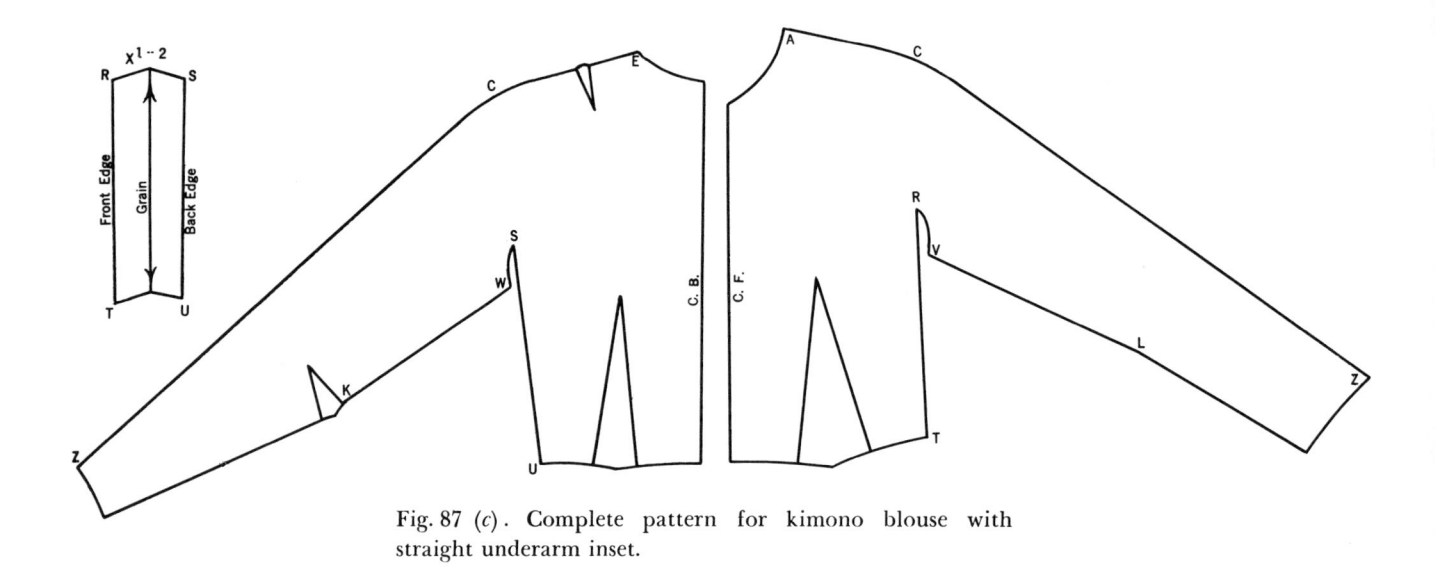

Fig. 87 (c). Complete pattern for kimono blouse with straight underarm inset.

KIMONO BLOUSE WITH SHAPED UNDERARM SIDE SECTION AND DEEP ARMSCYE (see Figures 88a, b, c)

Figure 88b shows the same draft layout as that for the blouse with straight underarm inset, but the side inset begins 1½ inches above the intersection of sleeve and bodice armscyes. Greater length above the front and back girth corners M and J of the sleeve makes it possible to increase the length of the sleeve underarm seam almost 2 inches. The sleeve seam needs greater length as the bodice armscye is lowered.

1. Measure down 1 inch from N and I on the front and back bodice underarm seam to points X^1 and X^2, and draw new curved lines for bodice armscyes RX' and SX^2.

2. Extend horizontal lines through the front and back girth corners M and J. Draw new curved lines for the sleeve armscye from points R and S equal to RX^1 and SX^2, touching the horizontal lines at points V and W.

3. Draw vertical lines from the front and back armscyes at R and S to intersect the horizontal lines through the sleeve girth.

4. Trace the center front section of the bodice, $ACZLPVRTA$, and the side front section, QT^1RX^1Q.

5. Trace the bodice center back section, $ECZKGW$-SUE, and the side back section, FU^1SX^2F.

6. Slash the horizontal line from V up to R and from W up to S. Swing up the girth corners V and W to within ⅜ inch of lines RT and SU to increase the length of the sleeve underarm seam (see Figure 88c).

7. Redraw the sleeve underarm seam lines from V and W.

Fig. 88 (a). Kimono blouse with shaped underarm side section and deep armscye.

168

SLEEVES

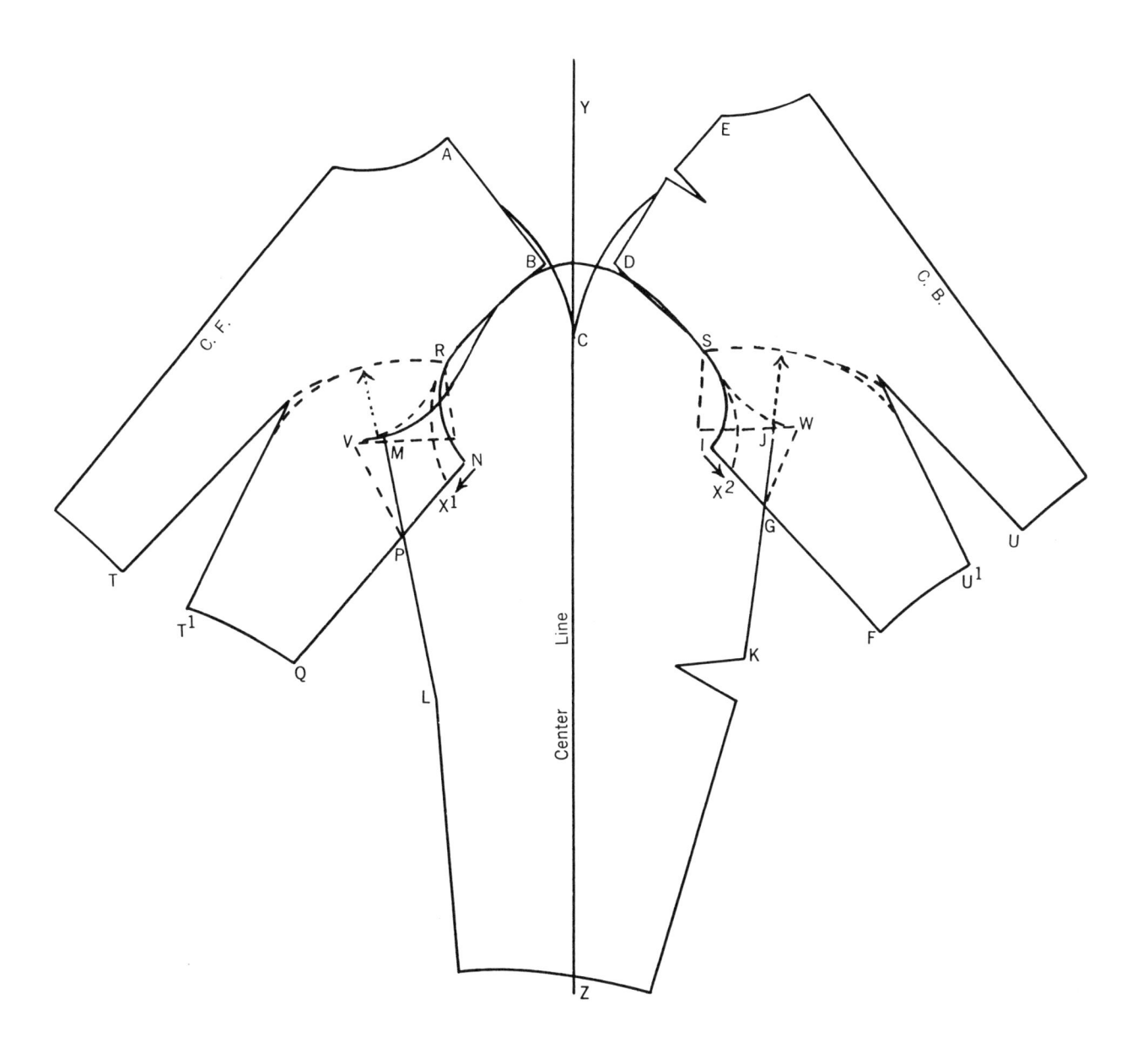

Fig. 88 (b). Draft for kimono blouse with shaped underarm side section and deep armscye.

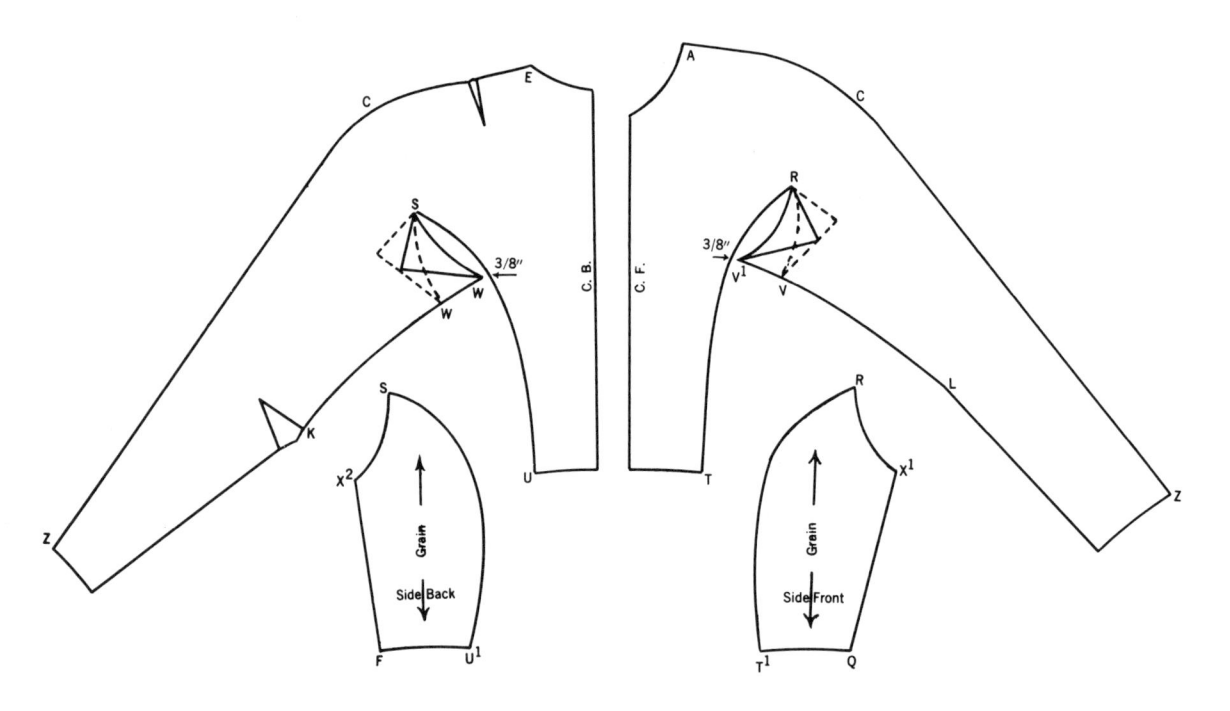

Fig. 88 (c). Draft cut apart and sleeve underarm seam lengthened.

Problem 8

DRAFT FOR KIMONO BLOUSE WITH BELL OR BISHOP SLEEVE

Use the bishop or bell sleeve block (see Problem 3, Set-In Sleeves, pages 120-122).

Study Figure 89 and follow the general procedures for the basic kimono. This draft produces a sleeve very roomy over the upper arm because *the blouse shoulder points B and D are placed approximately 1 inch from the center line YZ.*

1. Place the side seams of the front and back of the bodice 1 inch from girth corners M and J in order to give additional underarm length to the sleeve.

2. Place the back of the bodice so that IH on the side seam of the back equals NO on the side seam of the front.

3. Measure up 6 inches from the waistline on the front underarm seam to point P.

4. Square out ¾ inch to P^1 and join Q to P^1.

5. Measure 8 inches down the sleeve from the girth point M and mark L.

6. Rule the line P^1 to L.

7. Curve underarm line of blouse and sleeve as in Problem 1.

For a sleeve gathered at the wrist, increase the length for blousing above the cuff band. Add at least 1½ to 2 inches below points R, T, and U, and 1 inch below S and Z. Since the underarm and the line over the elbow of the sleeve slip up farther when the arm is raised or bent than the top center of the sleeve, add more length at these points.

SLEEVES

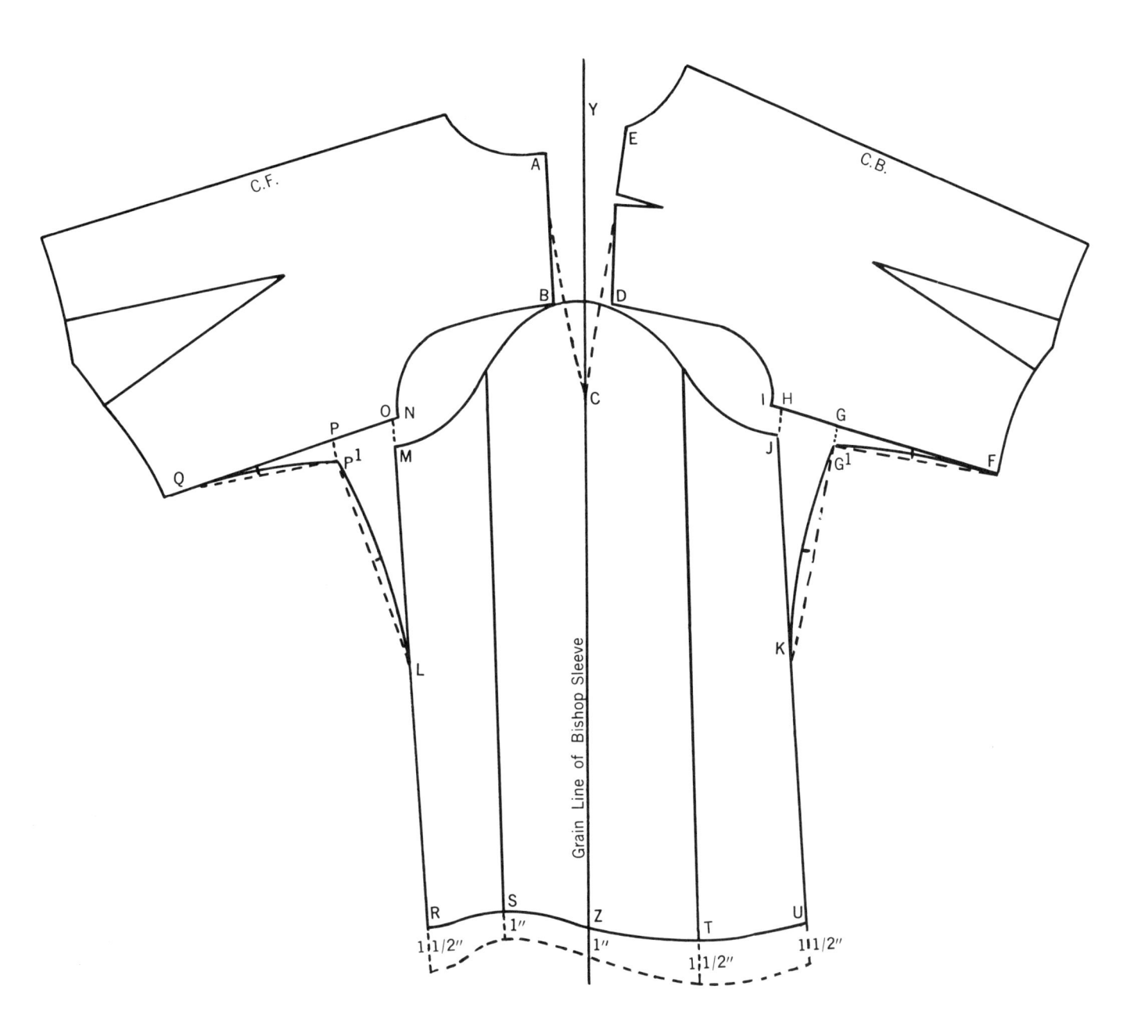

Fig. 89. Draft for kimono blouse with bell or bishop sleeve.

Problem 9

DRAFT FOR THE KIMONO BLOUSE WITH A YOKE
(see Figure 90a, b, and c)

Combining a yoke with a kimono cut offers the advantage of a smooth hanging sleeve with one definite fold at the front and one at the back of the armscye and a clean-cut close-fitting shoulder line, because the needed length at the underarm seam can radiate from a point at the lower yoke edge rather than from the line of the shoulder seam. It also offers the opportunity to increase the overarm sleeve length by lowering the grain slightly at the top center line of the arm. This, however, increases the difficulty of raising the arm unless the sleeve is quite wide at the top.

Follow the general procedure for the kimono layout (see Figure 90b).

1. Place the front corner of the bodice shoulder at point *B*, 1 inch from the center line of the sleeve *YZ*, and the girth corner of the bodice against the sleeve. Trace the blouse front.

2. Repeat for the back, making *IH* on the side seam line of the back equal to *NO* on that of the front.

3. Draw the style-line of the yoke, *R* to *C* and *S* to *C*. Figure 90b shows a yoke extending down on the center line of the sleeve 3½ inches to point *C*.

4. Draw the shoulder seam lines *ABC* and *EDC*, following the original seam lines. *Do not increase the height at B and D.* Draw convex curves ending at point *C*.

5. Measure up from the waist on the front side seam 6½ inches and mark *P*. Measure down on the sleeve 8 inches from *M* and mark *L*. Join *Q* to *P* and *P* to *L*.

6. Repeat for the sleeve line of the back to join *F*, *G*, and *K*.

7. To place the slash lines that are to be spread at the underarm in order to increase its length, measure 1½ inches over from the neck on the shoulder seam and mark *V* on the front and *W* on the back. Then rule lines from *P* and *G* to these points. Mark points *T* and *U* where these lines cross the yoke. (See marking slash lines for gussets, Problem 7, Figure 86, page 166.)

8. Crossmark the yoke and the lower section.

Fig. 90 (*a*). Kimono blouse with a yoke.

9. Trace the front and back of the yoke, *ABCTRA* and *EDCUSE*. Trace the lower front and back of the blouse, *RTCZLPQR* and *SUCZKGFS*.

10. Slash the line from *P* to point *T* and spread 1¾ inches at *P* (see Figure 90c).

11. Repeat for the back.

Note. You will notice that a sharper arc has been produced at *T* in front and *U* in back. This inward curve when attached to the yoke lines *RC* and *SC* causes a definite fold to radiate from points *T* and *U* and to fall along the normal armscye line.

12. Heighten the cap of the sleeve slightly at point *C* if you wish to increase the overarm length. This will reduce the diagonal wrinkling from the top center of the sleeve and deepen the fold hanging at the front and back of the armscye.

Note. Figure 90a shows a very conservative amount of drapery from the one slash line at the front and back. For afternoon or evening gowns of jersey or soft crepe (see Figure 91), slash the basic pattern once about 1½ inches lower on the side seam and again 1½ inches from the sleeve underarm seam, and direct both slashes to points on the yoke edge from which folds should fall. If you wish to obtain gathers or folds in the lower blouse section, spread the slashes along the edge joining the yoke as well as at the underarm. See Figures 92a and b for still another variation of a kimono sleeve with fullness held by a simulated yoke line at the upper armscye.

SLEEVES

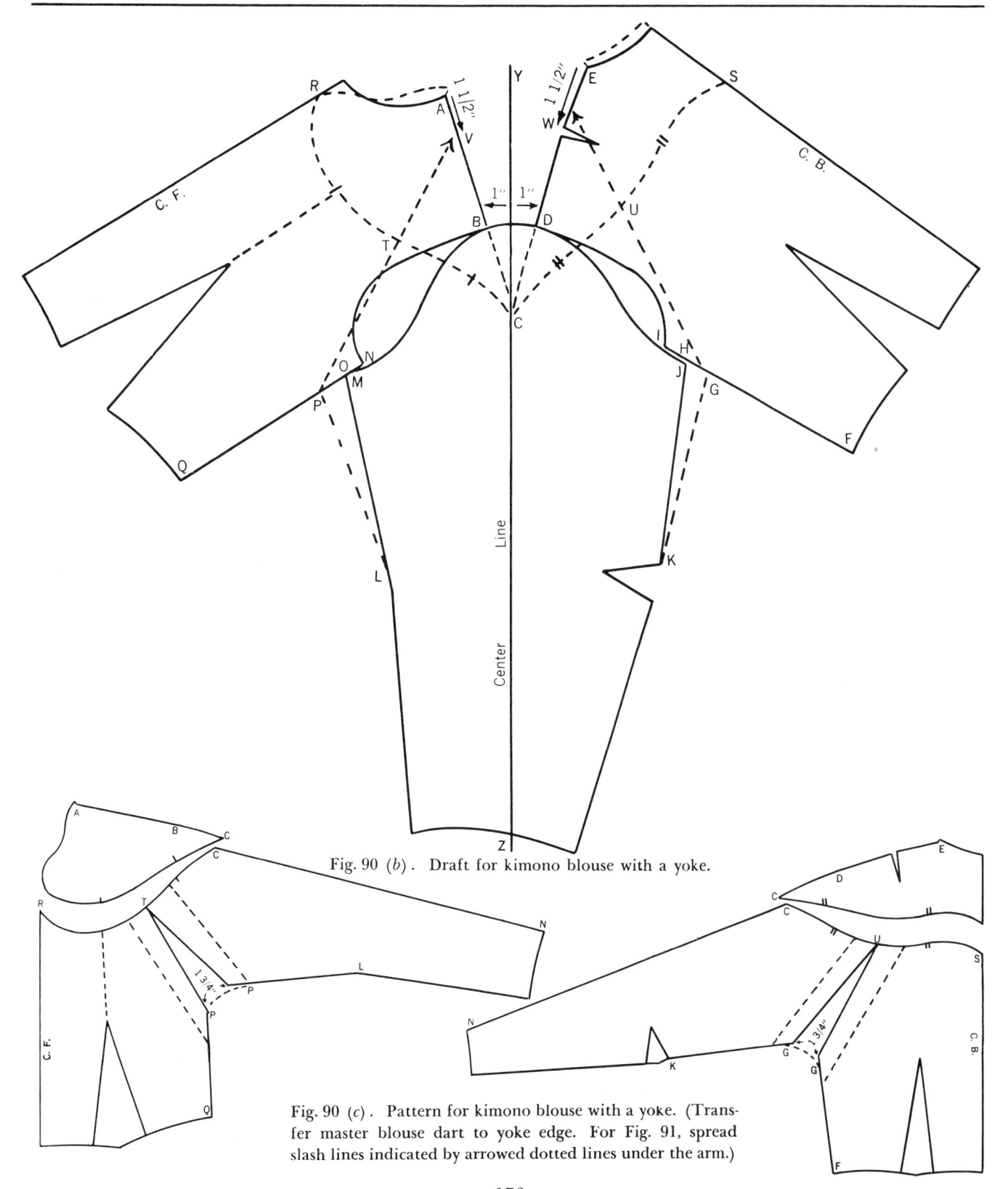

Fig. 90 (b). Draft for kimono blouse with a yoke.

Fig. 90 (c). Pattern for kimono blouse with a yoke. (Transfer master blouse dart to yoke edge. For Fig. 91, spread slash lines indicated by arrowed dotted lines under the arm.)

173

DRESS DESIGN

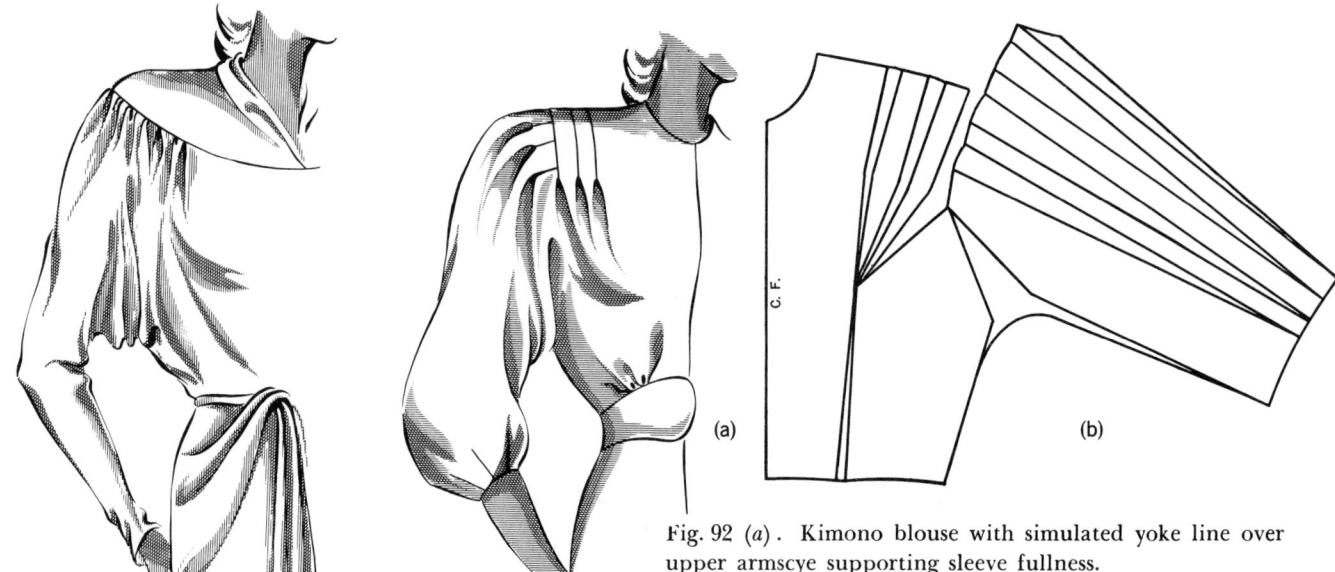

Fig. 91. Kimono blouse with soft drapery falling from yoke line.

Fig. 92 (a). Kimono blouse with simulated yoke line over upper armscye supporting sleeve fullness.

Fig. 92 (b). Pattern for kimono blouse illustrated in Fig. 92 (a). Waistline dart transferred to shoulder and slash made along upper armscye to separate blouse and sleeve. Sleeve slashed for fullness.

Problem 10

DRAFTS FOR SHORT KIMONO SLEEVES

The short kimono sleeve can be made by following several simple steps. First, redraw the shoulder line on the original basic master pattern by ruling a line from the neck end through a point ¾ to 1 inch above the armscye end of the shoulder seam. Lower the armscye at least 1½ to 2 inches at the underarm seam line and increase the blouse width at the top point of the underarm seam at least ¾ inch. The sleeve line may or may not be curved to give it a short underarm seam. Figure 93 shows the blouse front with the possible sleeve lines, *EDC, EDF,* and *EDGF.* In drafting the back, use the same measurements for shoulder line, underarm line, and sleeve.

A more accurate foundation block for developing original short sleeve designs can be made from any one of the basic kimono drafts given in Problems 5 and 6, pages 159-164. When you use this method, choose a draft that allows enough ease to raise the arm in the particular sleeve being designed. For a sleeve extremely short, for one left open on the top of the arm, or for one that is very loose at the lower edge, choose a draft with the minimum underarm length.

The short sleeves shown in Figures 94a, 95a, and 96a indicate a few of the possibilities for blocking original designs from the kimono draft.

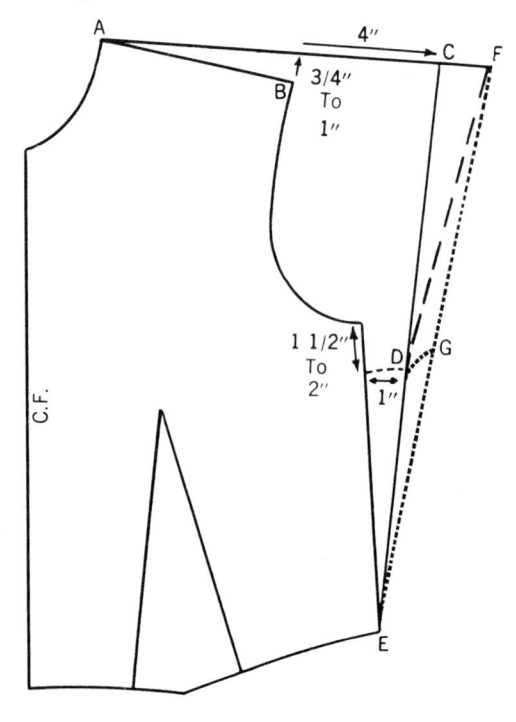

Fig. 93. Draft for short kimono sleeve.

174

SLEEVES

Short Sleeved Kimono Blouse with Simulated Yoke

For this design, use the draft for Basic Kimono Sleeve 2, page 163. Extra underarm length is not necessary in this sleeve because it is either flared or allowed to hang open at the top.

Short Kimono Sleeve with Fullness at the Yoke Edge (see Figures 94a and b)

1. Place the front and back shoulder seams of the blouse so that when they are extended they will meet at C, ½ inch below the top point of the sleeve.

2. Draw a line for the simulated yoke RCS.

3. Draw lines for the lower edge of the short sleeve, UT and TV.

4. Draw lines from the yoke to the lower edge of the sleeve for folds.

5. Cut out the blouse front and back.

6. Slash along the front and back yoke lines from R through C to S, and continue to slash from R and S to the point of the waistline darts in order to transfer most of their fullness to the yoke edge. Note the line drawn above R^1 and S^1 to join to yoke (see Figure 94c).

7. Slash the blouse front from edge R^1C^1 to the lower edge of the sleeve UT, and spread each slash twice the depth of each fold. Repeat for the back.

8. Round off the underarm corners at P and G.

9. Follow the dotted lines indicated from R^1 to X, if a tighter lower sleeve edge produces a more effective drape.

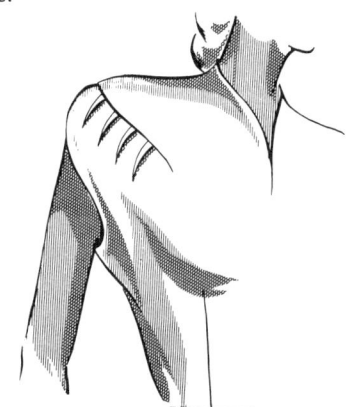

Fig. 94 (a). Short kimono sleeve with fullness at simulated yoke edge.

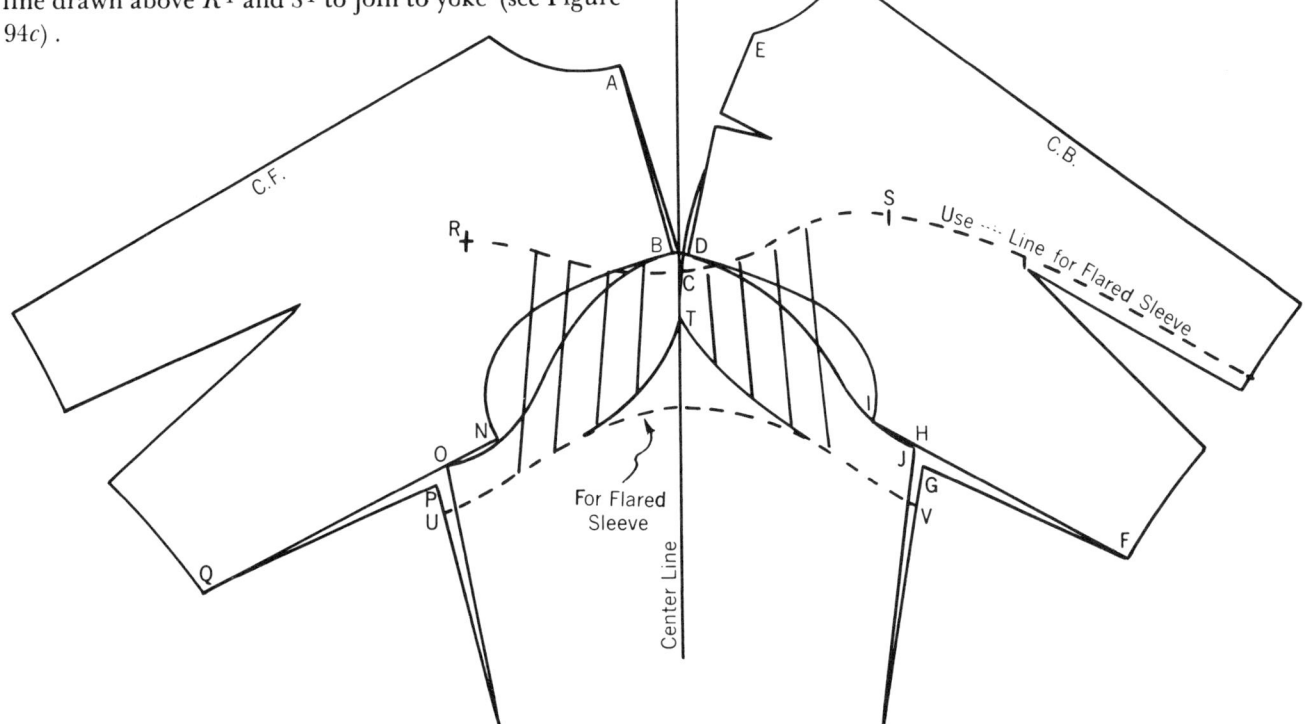

Fig. 94 (b). Slash lines drawn on kimono sleeve Draft 2 for short sleeve blouse with simulated yoke.

DRESS DESIGN

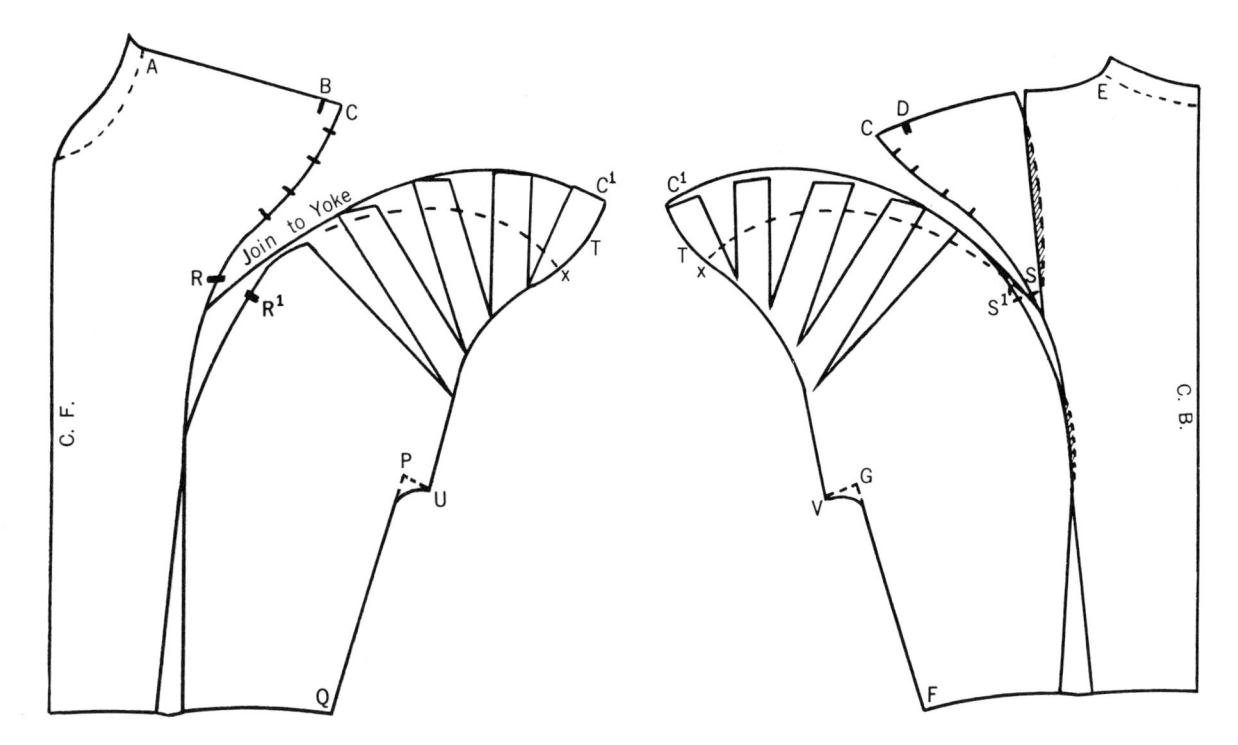

Fig. 94 (c). Pattern slashed and spread for fullness at yoke line.

Short Kimono Sleeve with Flared Lower Edge (see Figure 95a)

Use the draft for Basic Kimono Sleeve 2. Continue the yoke line in back to produce a separate section, not a simulated yoke. Figure 95b shows the yoke and center back cut together and the sleeve and side back cut together. The yoke could also have been separated from the lower blouse. The transfer of the waistline dart to a large shoulder dart in front makes it possible to block a flared sleeve line in one piece with the blouse, but since there is no large shoulder dart in back, the section with the flared sleeve must be cut apart from the yoke. Cut the front bodice in one piece. The space between the center front and side front sections merely indicates extra ease over the bust in addition to that provided by the master pattern dart. Crossmark the yoke edge at each slash line.

1. Slash from the lower edge of the sleeve to the edge joining the yoke. Figure 95b shows a 1½ inch spread between slashes. The width of the dart transferred to the shoulder limits the amount of spread for flare as shown where point C^1 curves back almost to the yoke line RC.

Fig. 95 (a). Short kimono sleeve with flares at lower edge radiating from simulated yoke line.

176

SLEEVES

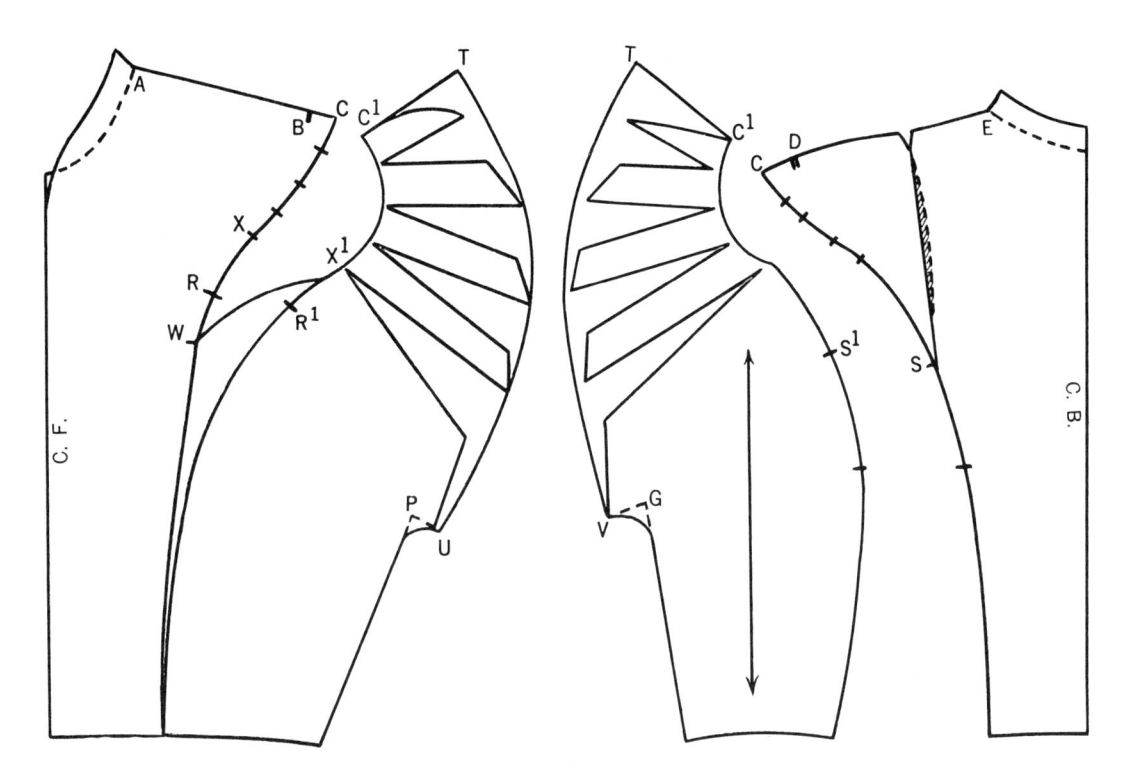

Fig. 95 (b). Pattern slashed and spread for flare at lower edge of short sleeve.

2. Just below point R, taper the width between dart lines RC and R^1C^1 to nothing. Measure down from point C on line RC approximately 4 inches and mark X. Mark a point X^1 the same distance down from C^1 on C^1R^1. Draw a convex curve from X^1 to W, 1½ inches below R. The space between X^1W and X^1R^1 not taken up in the dart will give the blouse front slightly more ease. Since the new line X^1W is longer than XW, ease the convex curve X^1W between points W and X when pinning the dart.

3. Draw a smooth convex curve for the lower edge of the sleeve from U to T and from V to T, and round the underarm corners at P and G.

4. Add a ⅜ inch seam allowance on lines CXR and C^1X^1W when cutting the pattern in fabric. Mark accurately on the fabric the inward curved lines such as C^1X^1 which control the flares, and clip the seam allowance so that the flares will fall in definite clean lines from the yoke edge.

Short Kimono Sleeve with Fullness Draped from Both the Under and Overarm into the Yoke Edge (see Figure 96a)

Use the draft for basic kimono sleeve 2, page 163, and follow Figure 96b.

1. Draw lines for the simulated yoke, RC and CS.

2. Draw lines for the lower edge of the sleeve, UT and TV.

3. Rule lines from the yoke to the side seam at the underarm and to the sleeve underarm for the folds.

4. Crossmark the yoke edge at each slash line, and also draw horizontal lines WW^1 and XX^1 across the front and back group of slash lines.

5. Cut out the blouse front and back.

6. Slash along the yoke line CR and CS. Extend each yoke line slash to the point of the waistline dart in order to transfer most of the dart to the yoke edge.

DRESS DESIGN

7. Slash the lines drawn from the yoke to the underarm and spread them to introduce fullness on both edges, but more at the yoke edge than at the underarm. Use the horizontal markings from W to W^1 and X to X^1 to keep the vertical slashes in line.

8. Draw a new rounded underarm line.

9. Taper off the width between the dart lines at R and R^1 on the bodice front as shown in the directions for the preceding sleeve, step 2.

10. Note that the points halfway between the slashed lines match the crossmarkings on the yoke edge.

Kimono Blouse with Short Puff Sleeves (see Figures 97a and b)

Use the draft for basic kimono sleeve 2, page 163, and follow Figure 97b.

1. Draw a new neckline.

2. Draw a line for the lower edge of the sleeve.

Fig. 96 (*a*). Short kimono sleeve with fullness draped from both under- and overarm.

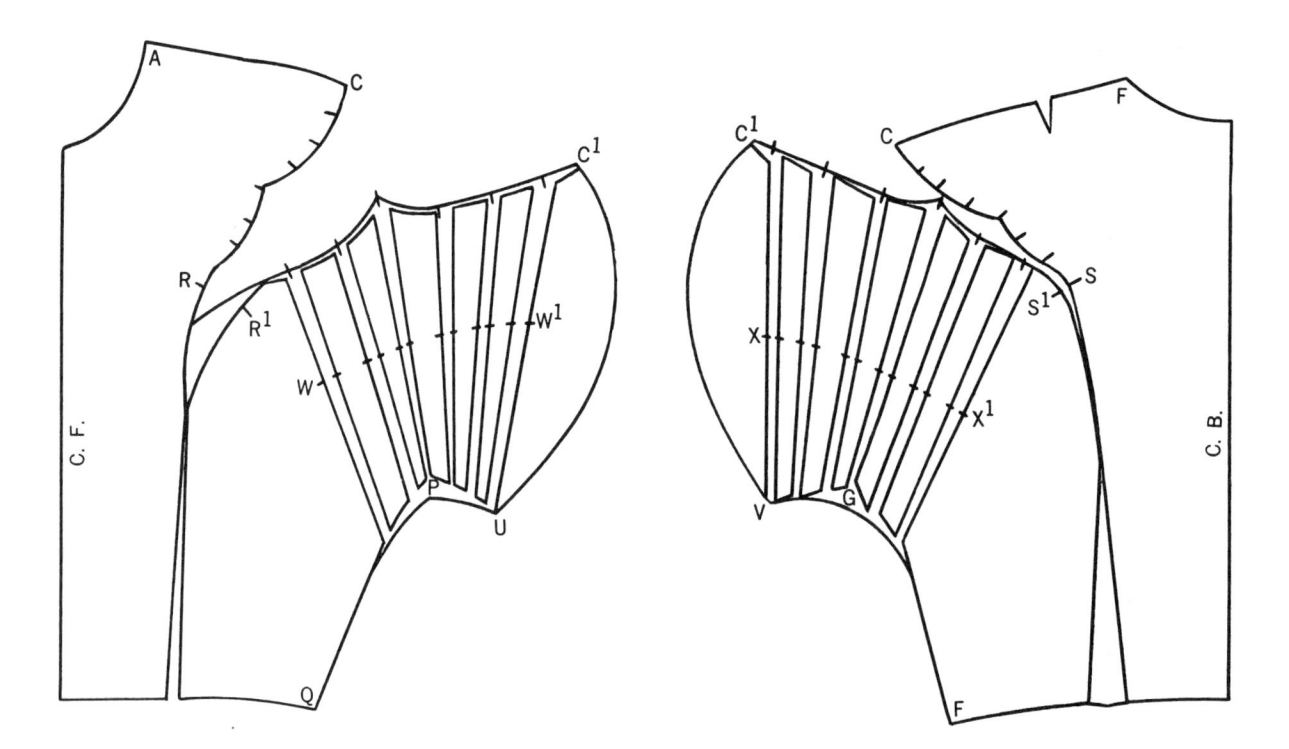

Fig. 96 (*b*). Pattern slashed and spread for drapery at both under- and overarm.

178

SLEEVES

Fig. 97 (a). Kimono blouse with short puff sleeve.

3. Rule slash lines from the neckline to the lower edge of the sleeve.

4. Rule lines on both back and front from the underarm at the point where the sleeve and the side seam intersect to a point 1 inch from the center front and back at the base of the neck, intersecting the new low neckline, front and back at *W* and *X*. Slash and spread these lines to introduce extra length on the underarm for freedom to raise the arm comfortably in a short sleeve which is tight at the lower edge.

5. Rule a horizontal line across the sleeve at right angles to the center line *YZ* to keep the sleeve slashes in line when they are spread.

6. Rule lines from the front neckline to the point of the waistline dart.

7. Trace the blouse front and back. Cut the pattern apart along the top center line of the sleeve to place the center front and back of the blouse on the straight lengthwise grain.

8. Slash through the vertical lines on the sleeve pattern to spread for the puff.

9. Rule a vertical and a horizontal line on a second sheet of paper to serve as guide lines in placing the vertical slashes.

10. Slash line *PW* in front and *GX* in back to the neckline. Spread these slashes 3 inches at the underarm.

11. Slash the three lines drawn from the front neckline through the point of the waistline dart, and spread the dart ¾ to 1 inch at the point for extra fullness along the bust line. Spreading the neckline slashes closes the dart at the waistline.

12. Draw new underarm curves at *P* and *G*, and draw slightly convex lines for the neck and lower edge of the puff sleeve.

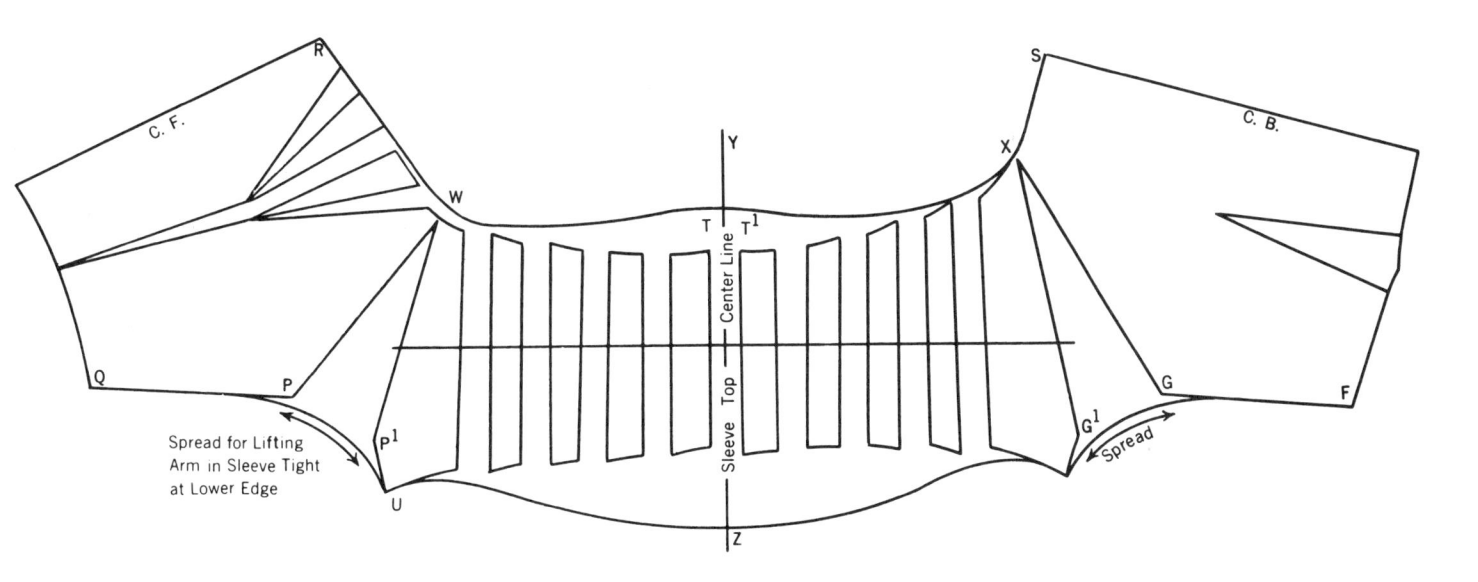

Fig. 97 (b). Draft for kimono blouse with short puff sleeve.

179

DRESS DESIGN

Kimono Blouses with Cowl Sleeves — Short Cowl Sleeve with Folds Produced by Slashing and Spreading the Basic Kimono Pattern (see Figures 98a, b, and c)

Use the draft for basic kimono sleeve 3, pages 163-164 and follow Figure 98b.

1. Draw the line for the lower edge of the sleeve, UC and CV.

2. Draw the cowl lines, RT on the bodice front and ST^1 on the back. The illustration shows the cowl line entering the side seam at R and S $3\frac{1}{2}$ inches above the waistline, and entering the shoulder seam at T and T^1 $1\frac{1}{2}$ inches from the armscye end.

Fig. 98 (a). Short cowl sleeve designed from kimono sleeve block.

3. Draw a second cowl line following the normal armscye in the draft layout, that is from P through B to Y and from G through D to Y. The line passes about halfway between the armscye of the blouse and the armscye of the sleeve.

4. Cut out the blouse front and back (see Figure 98c).

5. Slash the cowl lines to the shoulder line at points T and T^1 and at Y above points B and D (see Figure 98b).

6. Spread twice the depth of the folds between RT and R^1T and PY and P^1Y. Figure 98c shows a four-inch spread. Repeat exactly for the back, since the back and front seam lines when joined must drape as one piece of fabric.

7. Measure 1 inch from R to point W on the front side seam and from S to point X on the side back seam.

8. Draw a convex curve from W to U in front, and from X to V in back. The curve should remove very little at points R^1 and U, S^1 and V.

A convex curve is essential to allow cowl folds to fall into position, since the line TR^1 will fall on TW, and YP^1 will fall on YP. On each cowl line, the edge of the fold must be longer than the line that falls inside the fold.

Short Cowl Sleeve on a True Bias Fold

This sleeve shows another way of producing cowl drapery which also applies to cowls in other parts of the costume. The cowl may begin as low as the waistline or up part way on the side seams, as shown in Figure 99a.

Figure 99b illustrates the pattern layout for a cowl sleeve with the underarm on the true bias.

1. Rule a vertical line YZ on a sheet of paper.

2. Measure up from the waistline on the front and back side seams ($2\frac{1}{2}$ inches in the sleeve illustrated) and mark K.

3. Place the front and back side seams on the vertical line YZ so that they will intersect at K.

4. Pivot outward the corners H and C on the side seams of the front and back equally from line YZ. The amount of pivoting determines the depth of the cowl drapery. In Figure 99b, H and C are each $3\frac{1}{2}$ inches from line YZ.

5. Draw around the blouse back and front.

From here on you may copy the pattern illustrated, drawing in the cowl lines as indicated. But in order to experiment a little, cut the pattern in muslin, leaving 2 inches above the line drawn between the ends of the front and back shoulder seams at B and G. Place YZ on a true bias line ruled on the muslin.

180

SLEEVES

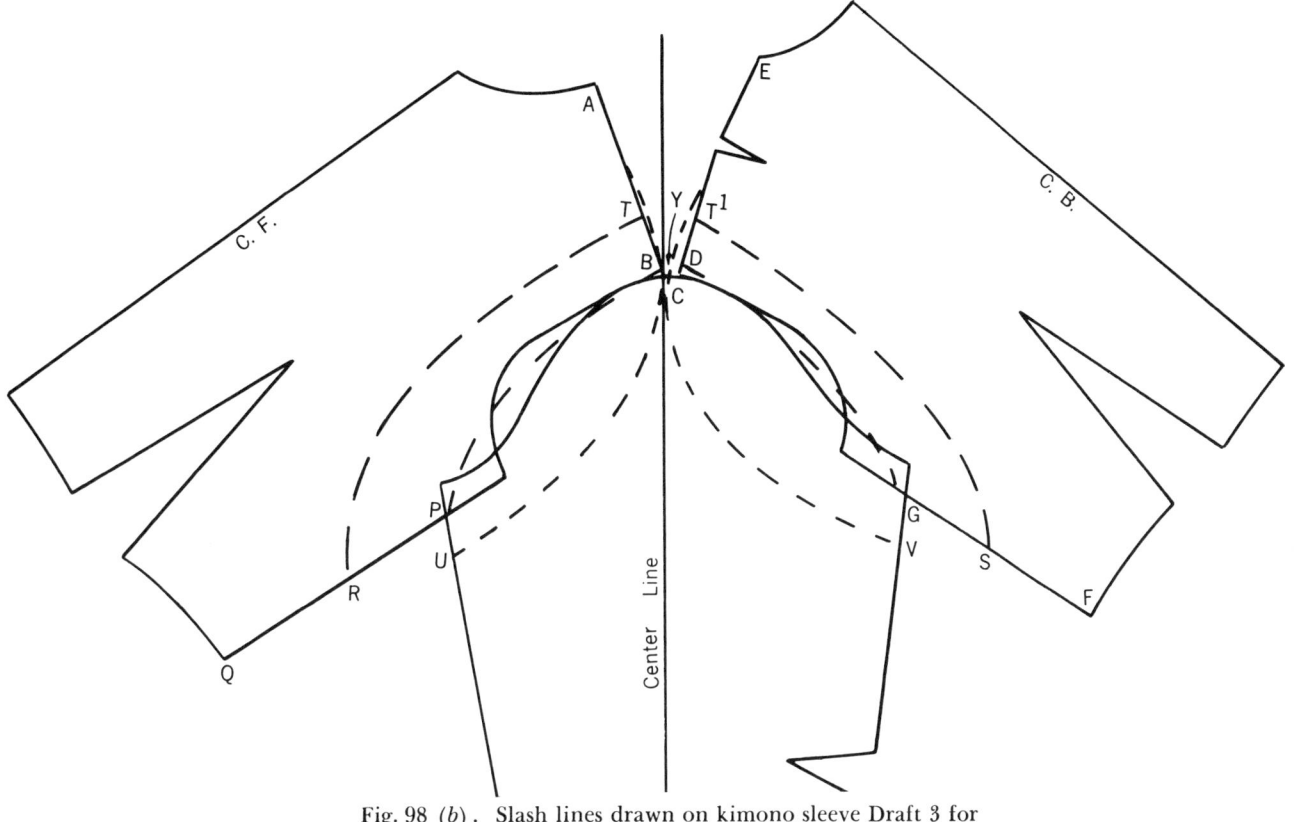

Fig. 98 (b). Slash lines drawn on kimono sleeve Draft 3 for short cowl sleeve.

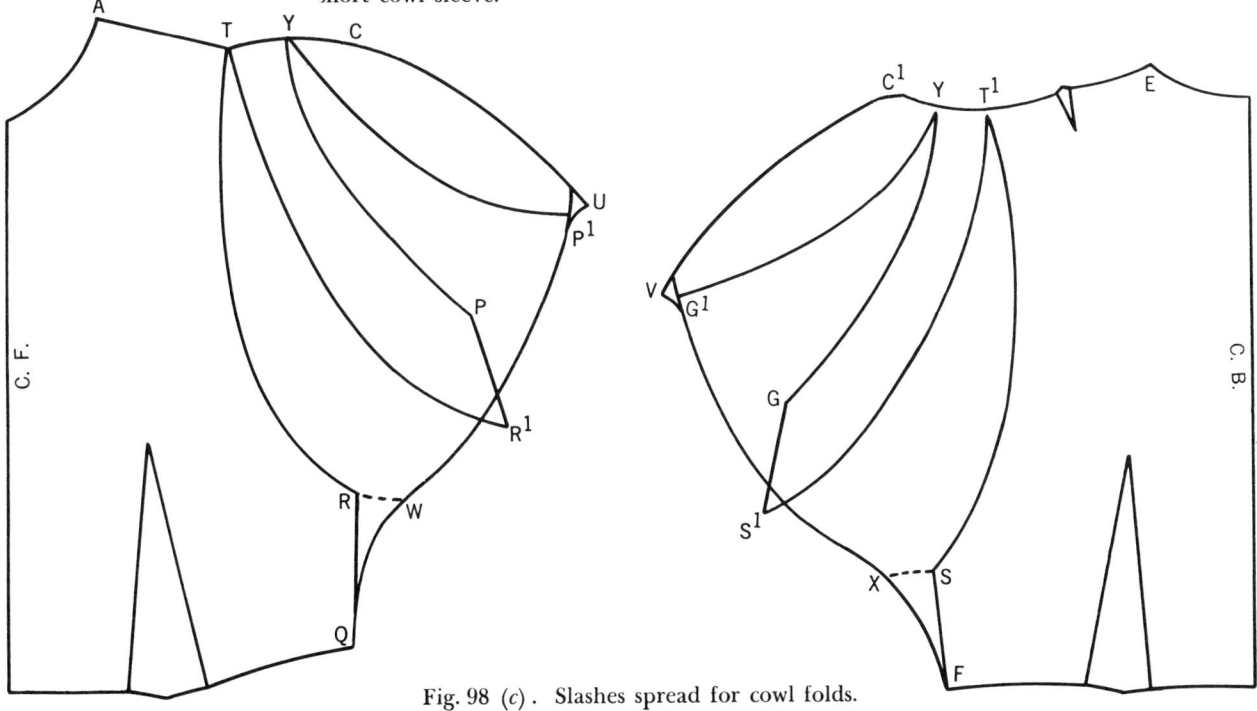

Fig. 98 (c). Slashes spread for cowl folds.

DRESS DESIGN

Experimental draping with the approximate pattern brings out many possibilities for handling the blouse and sleeve cowl. After blocking this particular blouse, the designer did not carry the cowl line in front up to the shoulder point as she had planned, but ended it at the corner *N* by making a neckline slash from the center front. She then raised the section above the slash to form an open neckline. As this section swung upward, the inner edge of the cowl line, *B* to *N*, fell into a deeper fold. The back cowl line from *C* to *B* continued up to the shoulder as planned. She also revised the center front line and front waistline dart by draping to repeat the curve of the neckline. She added an inset to the waistline area below edge *MK* and *KP* since the cowl began above the waistline.

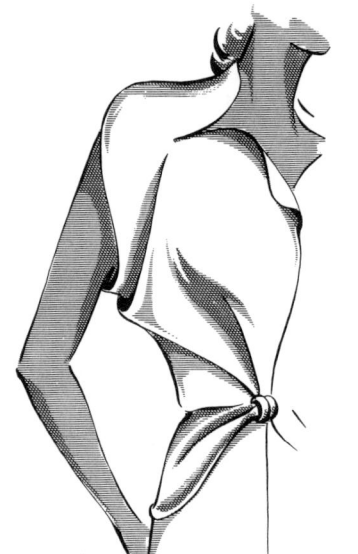

Fig. 99 (*a*). Kimono blouse with short cowl sleeve on true bias fold.

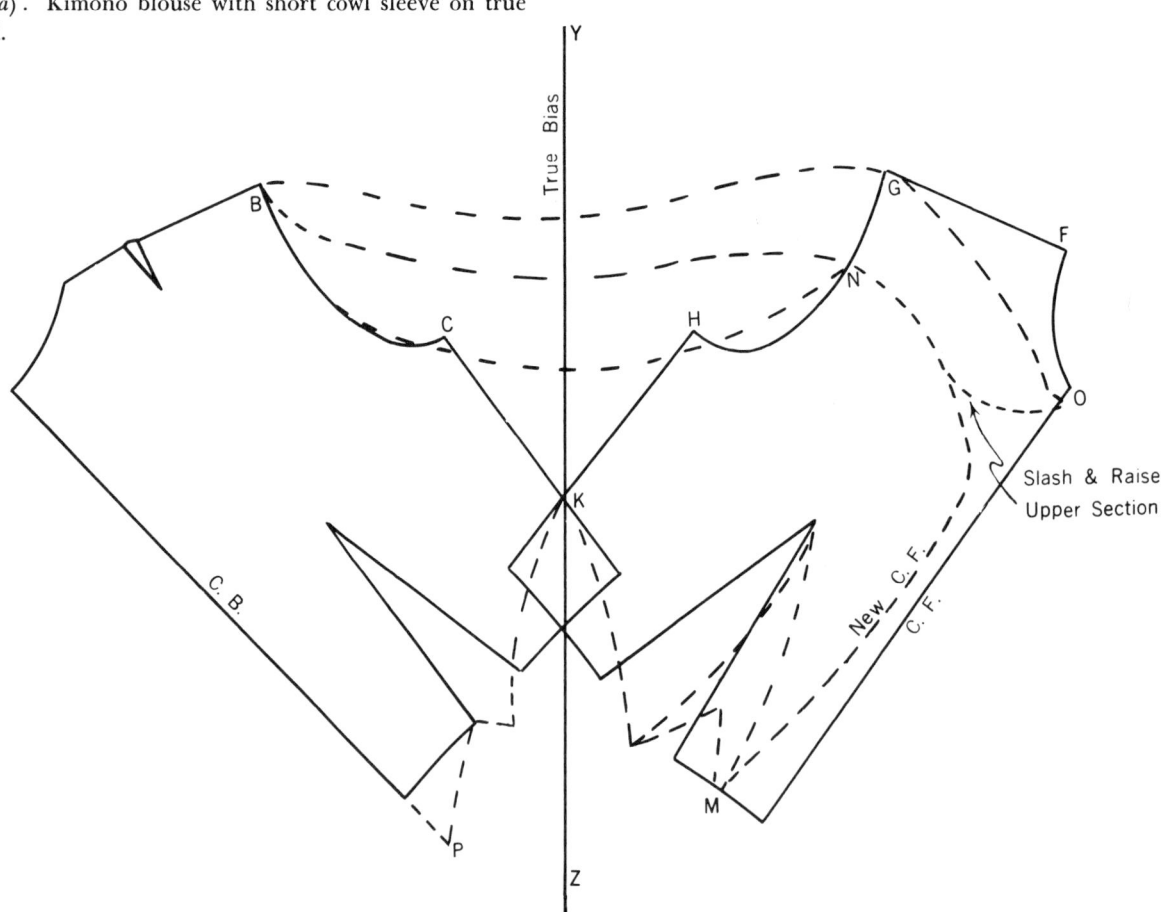

Fig. 99 (*b*). Pattern layout for cowl sleeve with underarm on true bias.

Problem 11

DOLMAN SLEEVE DRAFTS

The dolman, a sleeve with a deep armhole and a wing-like silhouette, belongs to the kimono group because it retains none of the under armscye curve of the normal set-in sleeve. But unlike the true kimono, the dolman sleeve and blouse are cut in two separate units. You will see from the following illustrations that this makes it possible to lengthen the underarm seam of the sleeve section without altering the fit of the main part of the blouse. Also, the overarm length of the dolman sleeve can be made longer than that of the true kimono.

Dolman Sleeve Cut in One with a Yoke Front and with a Deep Armscye Line in Back (see Figure 100a)

Use the draft for basic kimono sleeve 2, page 163, but place the shoulder points B and D 1 inch from the center line of the sleeve YZ. Place C, 2½ inches below Y, the top center point of the sleeve (see Figure 100b).

1. Draw the dolman style-line from R to P on the bodice front.

2. Draw the back armscye line from D to G to correspond to the depth of the front armscye. Figure 100b shows a dolman underarm line 6 inches above the waistline.

3. Rule down from P and G, the girth points at the front and back of the sleeve, to the sleeve points L and K. Draw a new girth line from P to G.

4. Find the halfway point between R and P on the dolman style-line on the blouse front and mark S. The extra length needed for the underarm will radiate from this point.

5. Draw an inward curve from S to P for the sleeve armscye, keeping it the same length as the line S to P on the blouse section. The inward curve on the sleeve will attach to the bodice without bulk along this edge, and will direct the fullness of the sleeve upward from the seam line.

6. Draw a new back armscye line on the sleeve from D to G, adding ⅜ inch or about one-third of the space between the original armscye line of the blouse and the sleeve. Raise the sharp inward curve

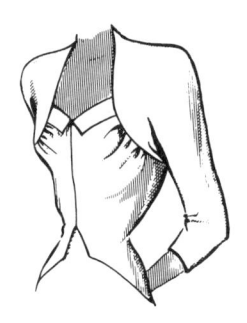

Fig. 100 (a). Dolman sleeve cut in one with yoke front.

of the normal sleeve armscye above point J to prevent it from pulling out when set into the deep armhole. The new line from D to G should be the same length on the edge of both the sleeve and the blouse.

7. Establish vertical slash lines to the sleeve girth PG from S, T, U on the front, and from V, W, J¹, X on the back. These lines will be slashed and spread to raise the lower armscye curve when you lengthen the front and back underarm sleeve seams.

8. Trace the blouse front, RSPQR, and the back, EDGFE.

9. Slash from the line PG up to points U, T, and S on the front. Slash from line PG up to points V, W, J¹, and X on the back (see Figure 100c).

10. Spread the slashes to lengthen the underarm sleeve seam between P and P¹ the same amount that the armhole was lowered on the blouse. Figure 100b shows the armhole line lowered 2⅞ inches. Repeat to spread the back slashes.

11. Draw lines from P¹ and G¹ to the elbow. These lines should be the same length on the front and back, although the angles on P¹L and G¹K are different.

12. Measure toward the back 2 inches from D at the top center dart on the sleeve back, and slash to point C, the end of the dart. Spread the slash ¼ inch to convert part of the dart width into ease over the upper back armscye of the sleeve.

13. Complete by tracing around the slashed and spread pattern.

Note. The blouse front will be softer and prettier if you slash from S and from points 1 inch above and below S to the point of the waistline dart and spread line SP, partially closing the waistline dart. This introduces fullness along the edge of the yoke.

DRESS DESIGN

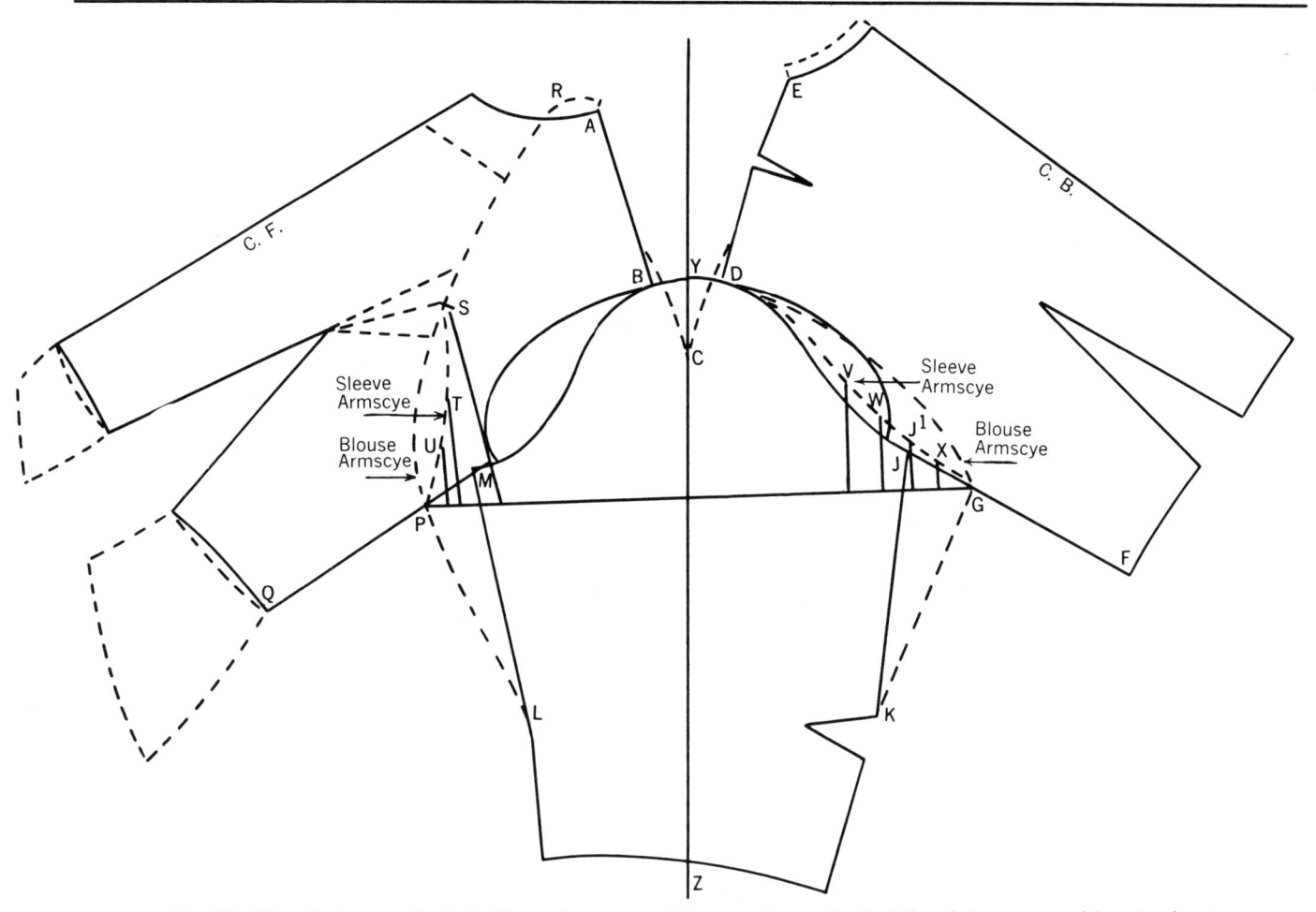

Fig. 100 (b). Design and slash lines drawn on kimono sleeve Draft 2 for dolman cut with yoke front.

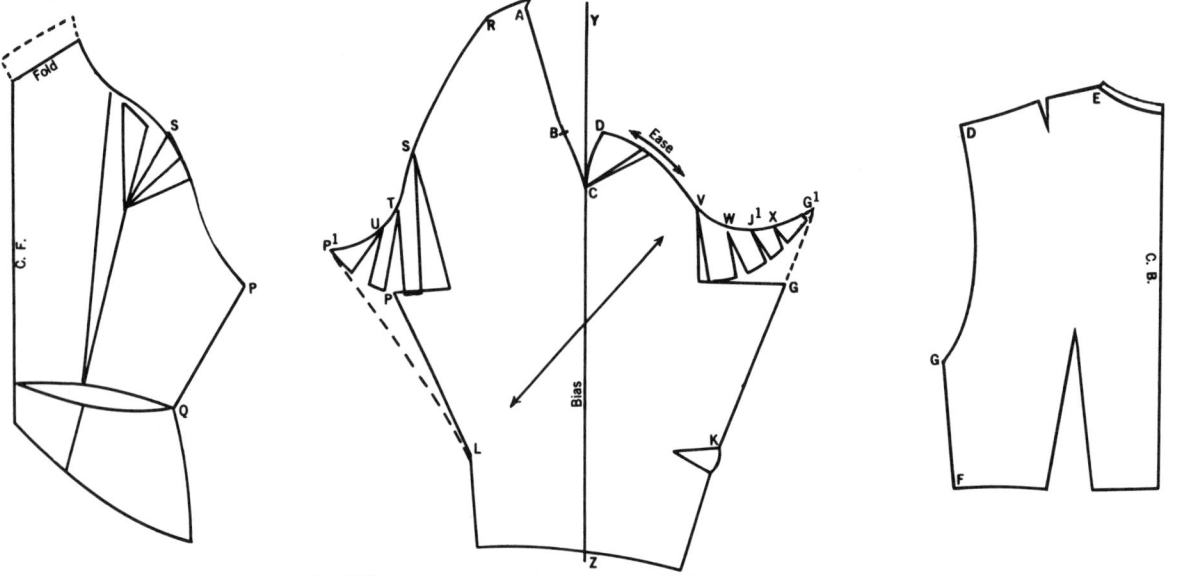

Fig. 100 (c). Pattern parts cut and slash lines spread.

184

Dolman Sleeve with Deep Square Armhole (see Figure 101a)

Figure 101b illustrates the method for designing this sleeve, basing it on kimono sleeve draft 2.

1. Draw style lines *BRP* and *DSG* for the dolman sleeve on the front and back of the bodice. Figure 101b shows the dolman line entering the side seam at *P* and *G*, 4½ inches above the waistline.

2. Measure down 8 inches from the sleeve girth and mark points *L* and *K*. Draw a curve for the underarm from *P* to *L* on the front and from *G* to *K* on the back.

3. Draw slash lines to introduce extra length on the underarm seam. Mark points *T* and *Y* at the halfway points between *R* and *B* on the front and *S* and *D* on the back. Rule lines from *T* and *Y* to the underarm points *V* and *W*, halfway between the original sleeve seam and the blouse side seam.

4. Trace the bodice front, *ABTRPQA*; the back, *EDYSGFE*; and the dolman sleeve, *BTRPVLZKWGSYDCB*. Crossmark the dolman style-line as indicated.

The procedures outlined in the following steps are illustrated in Figure 101c.

5. Slash the sleeve on line *VT* and *WY* (see Figure 101b), and spread the sleeve underarm seam 2 inches at *V* and *W*.

6. Add ⅞ inch to the center top of the sleeve at *B* and *D* and mark *U*. Gradually curve down to points *T* and *Y* to avoid sharp corners. The ⅞ inch increase on the overarm length deepens the fold at *VT* and *WY* and reduces the tendency toward wrinkling from the top of the sleeve cap.

7. Either use the dart at the center top of the sleeve as it is, or convert it to ease along the cap edge by slashing to the point of the dart 2 inches down from *B* and *D*. (See directions for this under previous dolman sleeve variation.)

Note. The single slashes in the front and back (*V* to *T* and *W* to *Y*) give a clean-cut fold at the front and back of the arm. For additional folds, slash from points on either side of *V* and *W* to points above and below *T* and *Y*.

Fig. 101 (*a*). Dolman sleeve with deep square armhole.

DRESS DESIGN

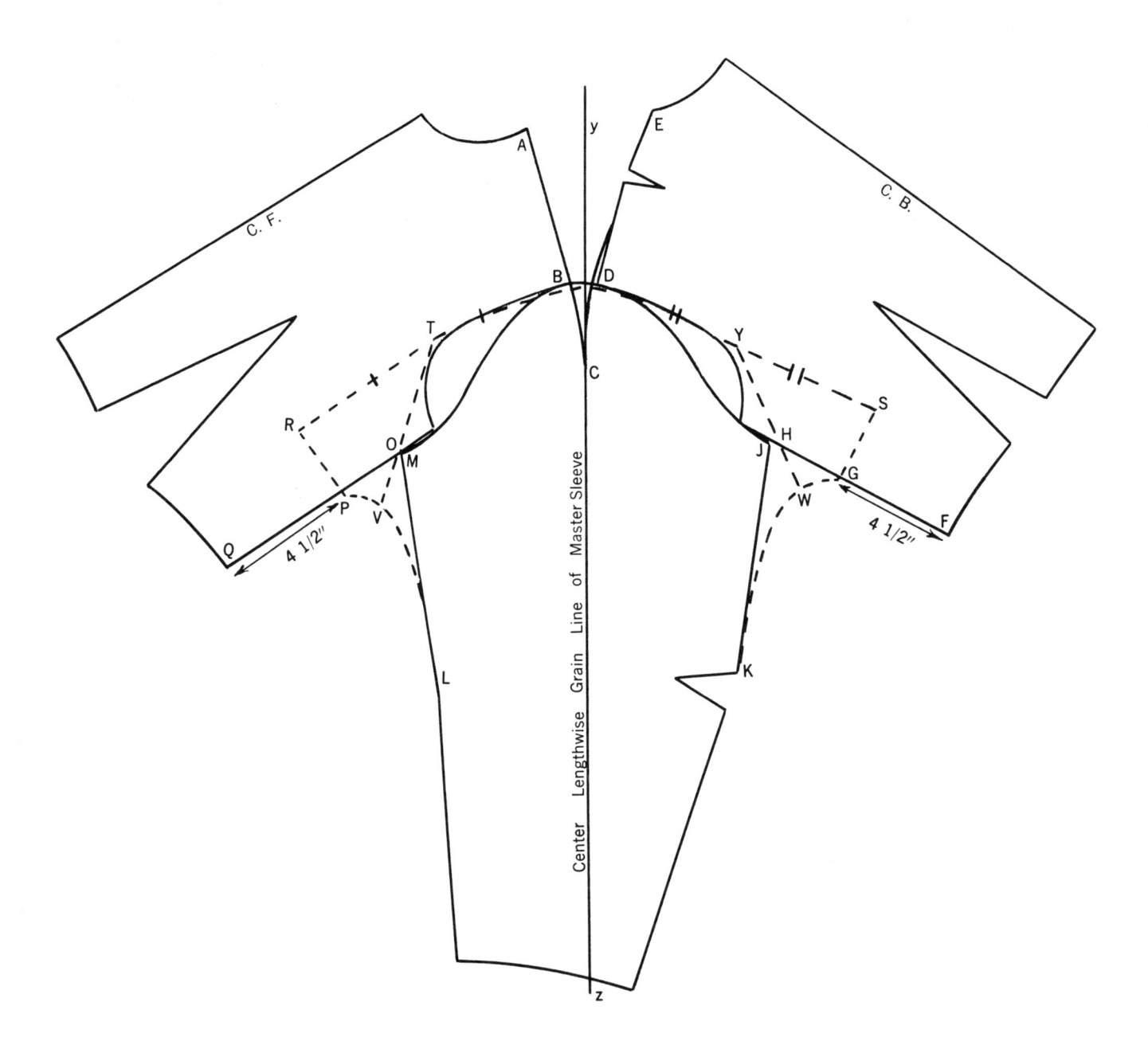

Fig. 101 (b). Design lines drawn on kimono Draft 2 for dolman sleeve with deep square armhole.

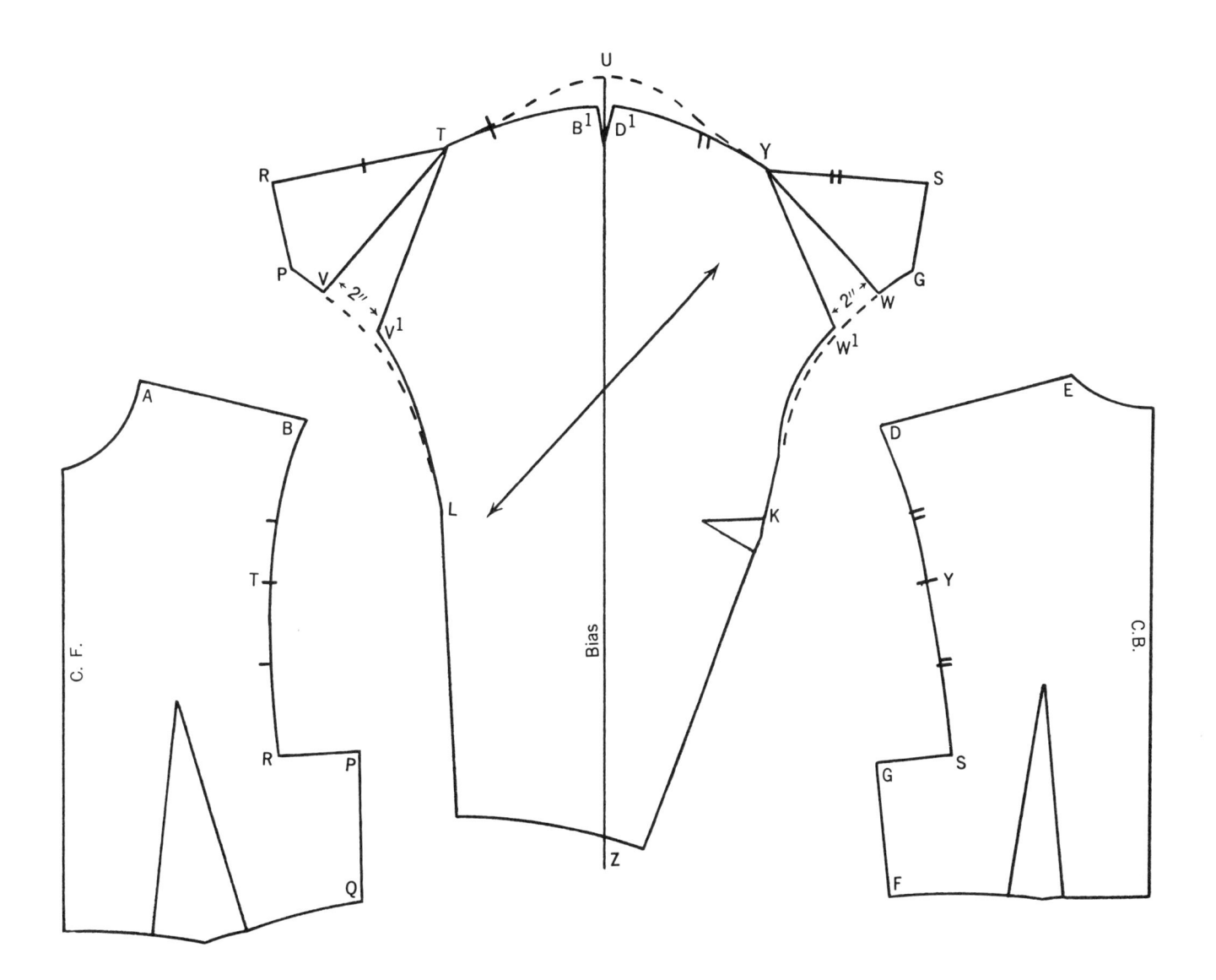

Fig. 101 (c). Pattern cut apart and slash lines spread.

Dolman Sleeve with Style-Line Near the Normal Armscye
(see Figure 102a)

Use the draft for Basic Kimono Sleeve 2, page 163, and follow Figures 102b, c. d, and e in carrying out the following directions.

Fig. 102 (a). Dolman sleeve with style line near normal armscye.

1. Draw the style line for the armscye on the front of the blouse, *BRP,* and on the back, *DSG.* Figure 102b shows the armscye depth lowered $1\frac{7}{8}$ inches below the normal scye line at *N* and *I.*

2. Establish the sleeve armscye line (see Figure 102c). On a second sheet of paper under the draft, trace the section *BRPB,* the front, and *DSGD,* the back (see Figure 102b). Cut out these traced sections. Slash from the *BP* edge to the *BRP* edge of the front, and from the *DG* to the *DSG* edge of the back. Superimpose the slashed sections on the corresponding sections of the draft and spread the *BP* and *DG* edges in order to revise the bulging convex armscye line of the blouse between *BRP* and *DSG* to a slightly concave line for the lower part of the sleeve armscye. Place P^1 in the front and G^1 in the back so that they touch the horizontal lines extending from the girth corners at the front and back of the sleeve.

Shift the position of the entire slashed section BRP^1 and DSG^1 so that the armscye line of the sleeve is slightly separated from the armhole line of the blouse. This will get rid of a part of the excess between the armhole of the blouse and the armscye of the sleeve. Avoid a deep, sharp curve on the lower part of the sleeve armscye, especially on the back, as it would pull when the sleeve is set into the deepened armhole of the blouse.

Pencil carefully around the new armscye line of the sleeve.

3. Rule lines from P^1 and G^1 to the elbow at *L* and *K.*

4. Trace the bodice front, *ABRPQA;* the bodice back, *EDSGFE;* and the sleeve, $BR^1P^1LZKG^1S^1DC.$

5. Rule the sleeve girth, P^1G^1 (see Figure 102d). Erect perpendiculars from the line P^1G^1 to points *U* and *T* on the front armscye of the sleeve, and to *V* and *W* on the back. Slash and spread to increase the underarm sleeve length (see Figure 102e).

6. Raise P^1 in front and G^1 in back at least as much from the girth line as the blouse armhole has been deepened. Figure 102e shows these points raised $2\frac{1}{4}$ inches for easier arm movement and for increased drapery at the underarm.

Note. In order to eliminate diagonal wrinkling from the top of the sleeve, add $\frac{5}{8}$ inch to the overarm length if necessary.

7. Trace around the slashed sleeve to complete the pattern.

8. Place *YZ* on the true bias.

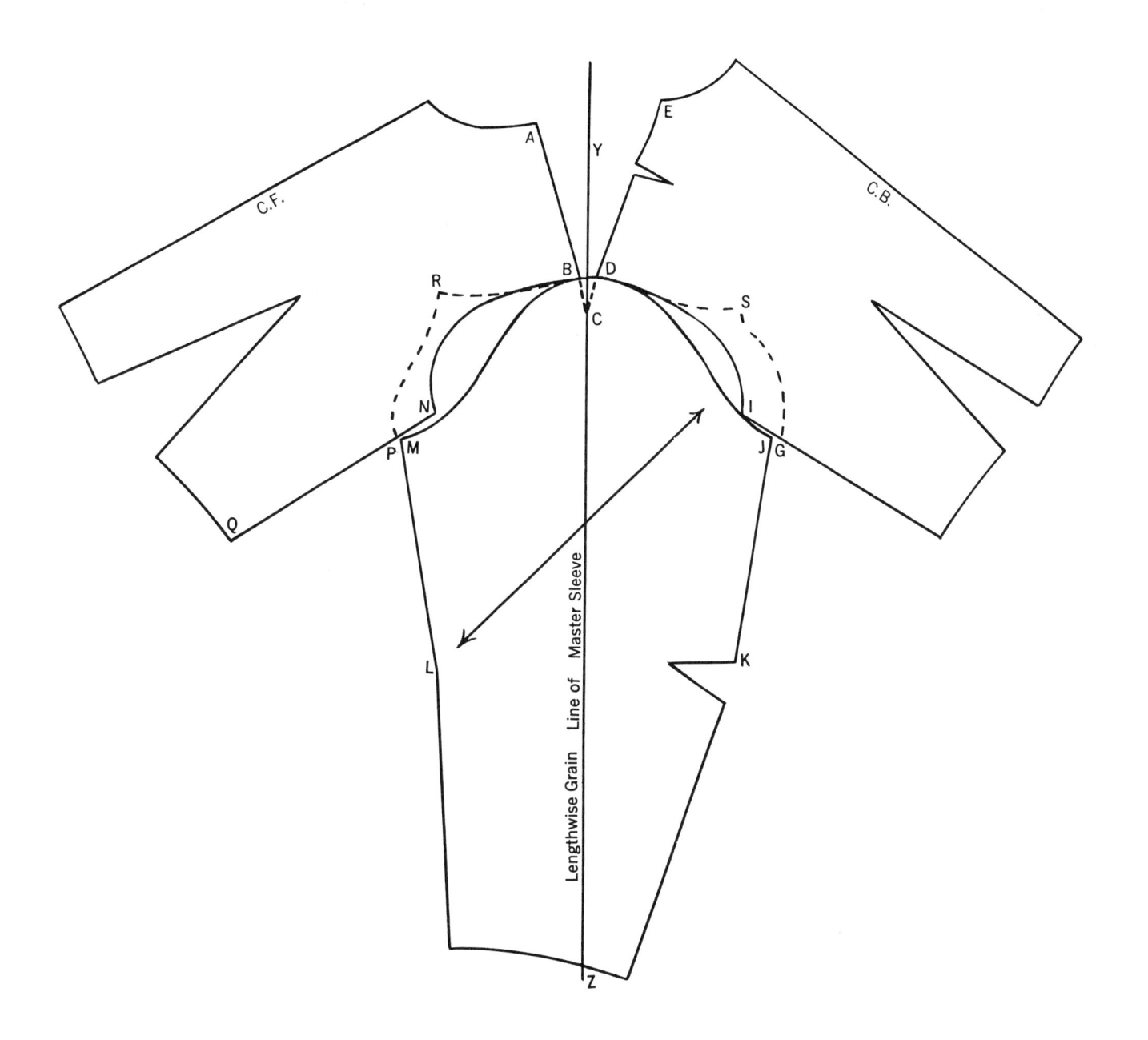

Fig. 102 (b). Design lines drawn on kimono sleeve Draft 2 for dolman with style line near normal armscye.

DRESS DESIGN

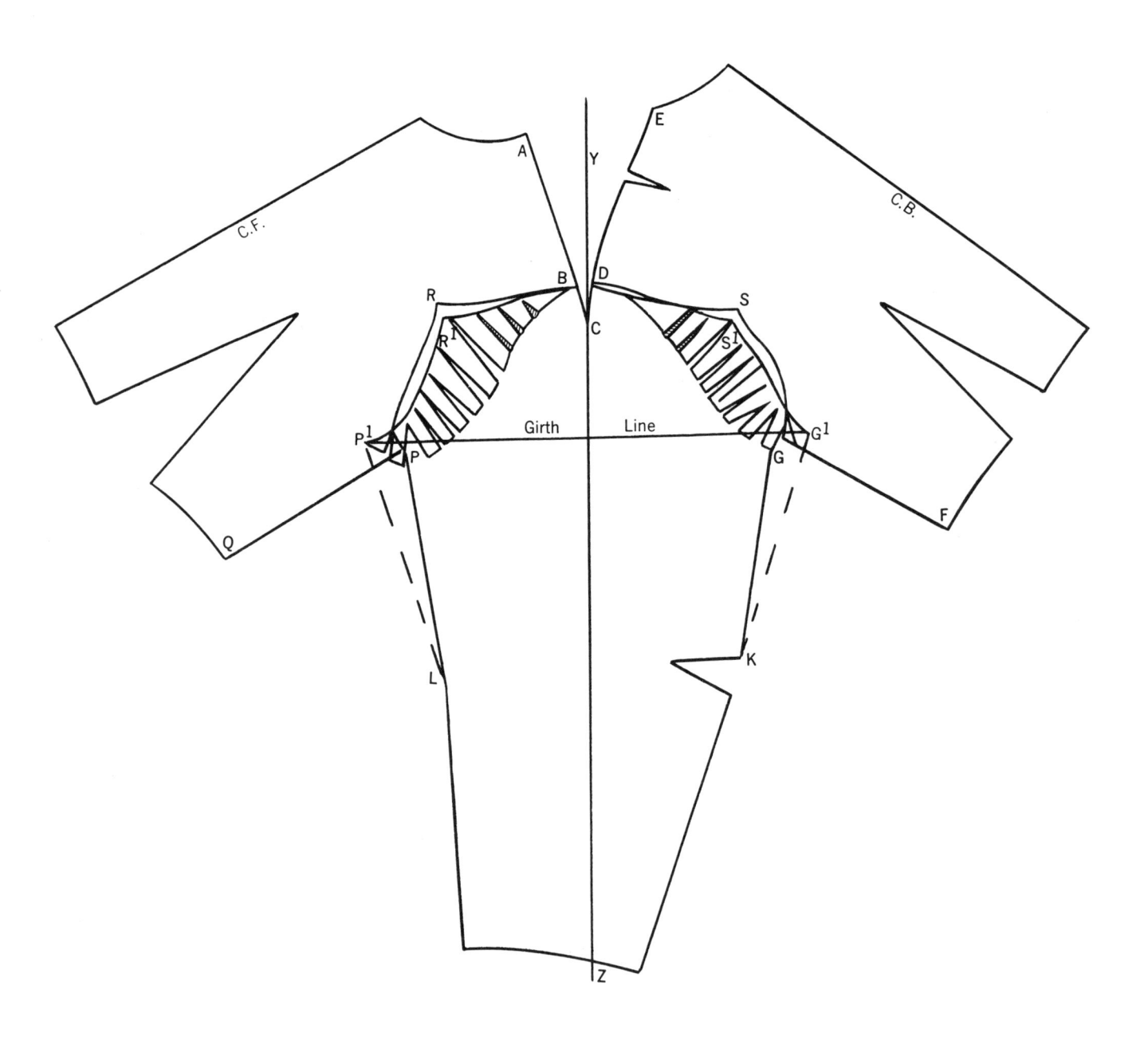

Fig. 102 (c). Sections BRPB and DSGD cut out, slashed, and spread to establish sleeve armscye.

190

SLEEVES

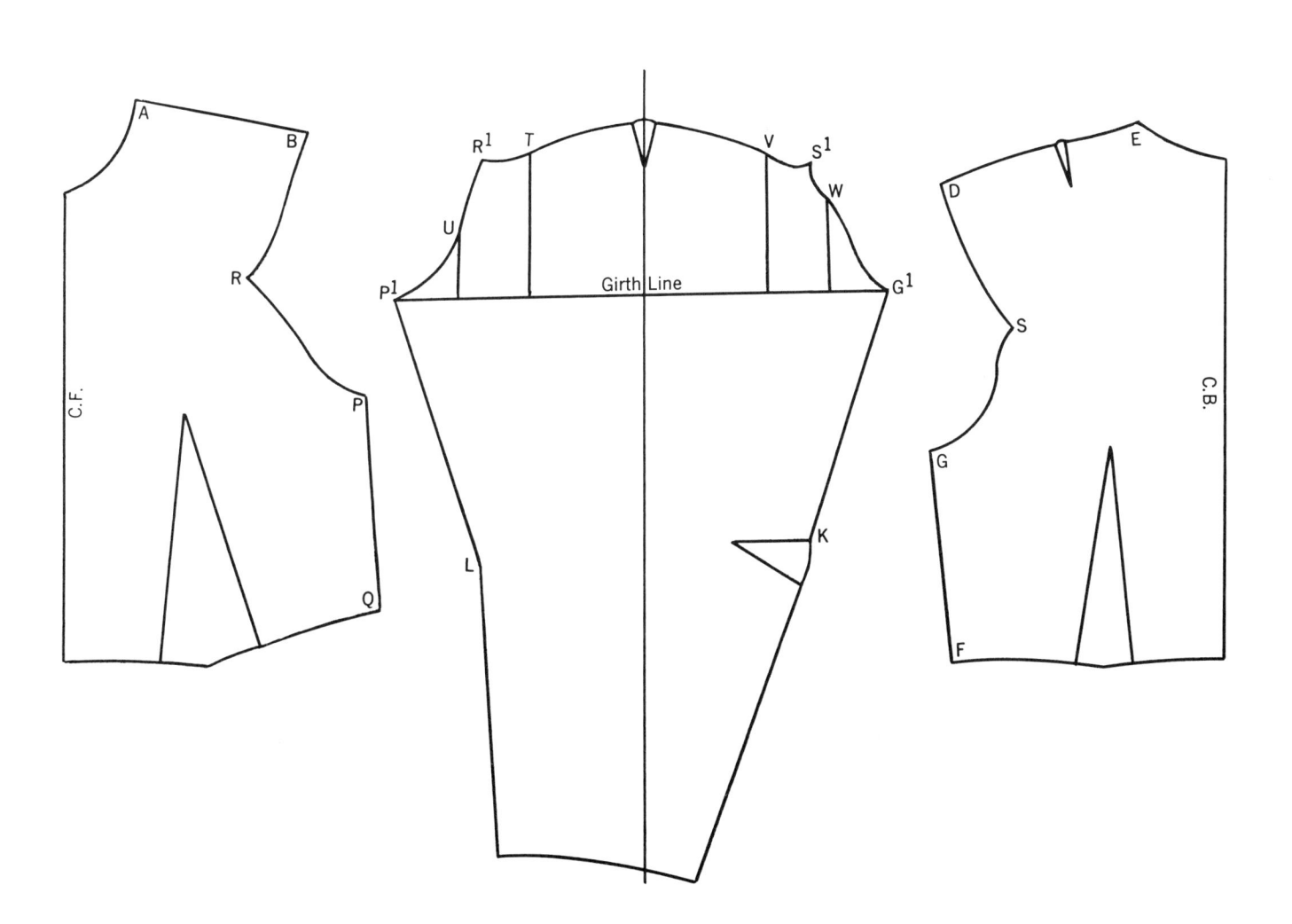

Fig. 102 (d). Pattern parts cut and slash lines drawn.

DRESS DESIGN

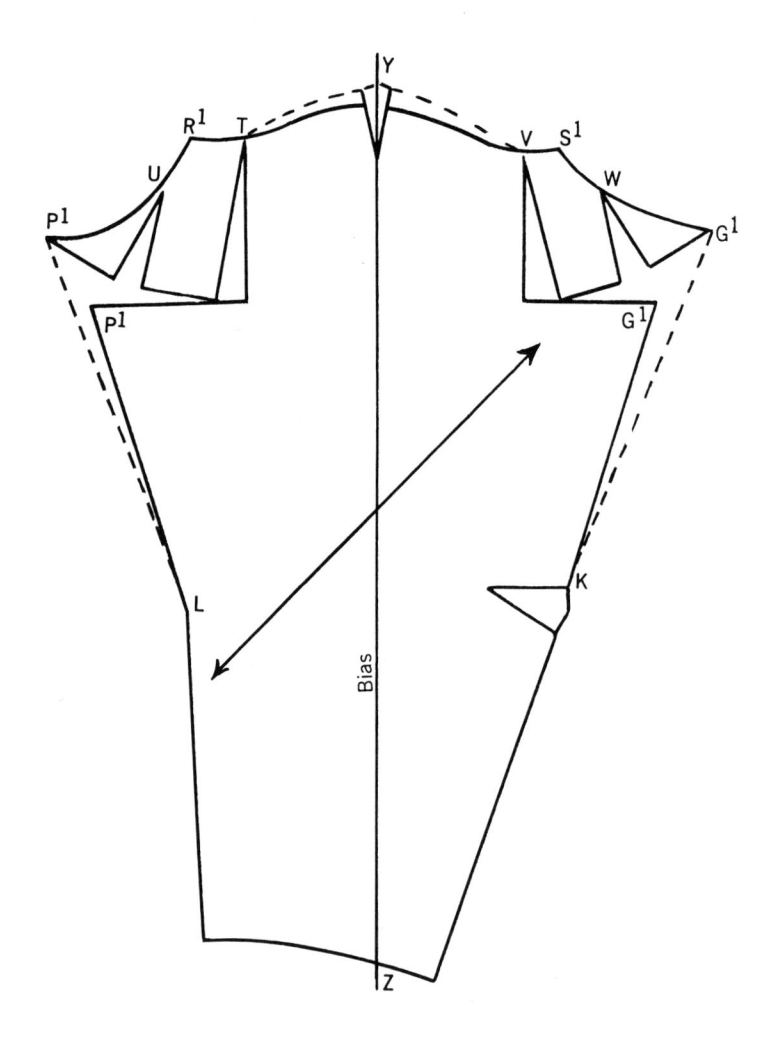

Fig. 102 (*e*). Dolman sleeve slashed and spread to increase length of underarm seam.

5. Fitting

PART I

GENERAL PRINCIPLES OF FITTING

In this chapter the general principles of fitting are discussed; and although the master pattern is the garment to which all the references are made, the solution given for each problem is equally applicable to any type of garment, whether it is in the process of being made or is a ready-made garment that requires alteration.

The careful fitting of the master pattern serves several purposes. The chief one, of course, is to provide a master block on which to develop other designs by the flat pattern blocking method. Every correction, however small, which perfects this pattern is important, because any flaw in the master pattern enters into every design blocked from it.

The fitting of the master pattern is of value even if it is never used for a master block, because its fit may show up inaccuracies in the padding of the form or errors in draping. To determine the cause of an error, try the master pattern back on the form after it has been fitted and corrected. If, after this alteration, the dress fits the form correctly, then draping technique was to blame. But if it does not fit, then the padding should be changed to duplicate the figure more exactly. Fitting the master pattern serves another purpose as well. It provides an excellent way to learn the principles of fitting dresses that are to be worn, without the confusion of intricate details of design. Although you have already learned how to fit a form cover (Chapter 1), the methods used for that in no way apply to the fitting of a garment that is to be worn or a master pattern from which to block designs. The lines of a dress must hang freely and easily both when one is active and inactive, whereas the form cover must fit skin-tight. Fitting a garment to be worn requires far keener judgment to determine what alterations to make, and it requires greater skill to make them. Adequate ease must be provided without producing wrinkles or bulkiness in any part of the garment. Each figure, because of its particular proportions and posture, presents a different problem to the fitter. Perfection of fit goes far beyond mere comfort and wearability. For a good fitter will flatter the figure by skillfully bridging across the too narrow or too flat area into the too broad or rounded one, thus making both less noticeable. She will inject style and smartness as well as comfort into a design.

A basic pattern carefully draped on a personal dress form usually fits with little or no alteration. However, women whose posture varies from that of the standard dress form may not be able to duplicate their variations by padding. And some may find it more convenient to buy master patterns made by a commercial pattern company than to pad forms and drape their own. Therefore, it seems worthwhile to analyze the causes and corrections of fitting faults.

Knowing where to place the lengthwise and crosswise grain on the body eliminates much of the guesswork from fitting. The center front and back are, of course, the vertical balance lines and must hang perpendicular to the floor. Less well known are the horizontal balance lines of the blouse and skirt. The scye line, the balance line of the blouse, is a level line $\frac{1}{2}$

DRESS DESIGN

inch below the armpit when the arm is down at the side and is the lowest point of the armhole. It crosses just above the largest circumference of the bust and over the shoulder blades. In draping the basic pattern (Figure 1), you will remember that the same crosswise thread [1] was kept on the scye line. This was done by taking up the excess above the bust and shoulder blades in shoulder darts and the excess below this line in waist or underarm darts. In order to maintain this balance when irregularities in body proportions or posture cause variations in length from shoulder to scye line, make adjustments above this line, at the armscye, the shoulder, or along the neck edges; or through darts from these edges.

Fig. 1. Fitting the master pattern.

---

[1] Placing the same crosswise thread on the entire scye line gives excellent balance to the fabric grain of the master pattern when the dart ease is distributed between shoulder and waistline. But the same crosswise thread cannot follow through the entire scye line when the dart ease is not thus distributed above and below the bust. The significant point to remember in correct fitting is that you should have that level of the garment which was intended for the scye line fall on the true scye line of the person being fitted.

In the skirt the balance line is at the hip level. All alterations should be made above it to keep the crosswise grain equally balanced in the lower part of the skirt on the left and right sides of the center line and at the back and front of the side seam. Figures 2a, b, c, d, e, and f show various postures to illustrate how the same body measurements may present quite different balance problems. On the first figure, with correct posture, the waistline and hip level appear parallel to the floor, and a vertical line through the center of the side hip also passes through the center of the side of the waistline, the center of the knee, the ankle bone, and up from the waistline through the center of the shoulder and ear. On each of these figures the shoulder and arm have been thrust back to show the side of the waist and hip and are therefore not in a natural position. The third figure leans back at the waistline; thus the center back of the waistline is lowered and the center front is lifted. The fourth leans back from the hips in a position which lengthens the center front and shortens the center back. The fifth figure leans back from the knees, stretching out the length along the front of the leg up to the center front of the waist, and shortening the length of the leg in back. On each of these three figures (2c, d, and e), the center front is longer than the center back from the waist to the hip level, and a skirt made for a figure with correct posture will swing forward at the center front and cup under the hips in back. To correct the hang of such a skirt on one of these figures, you must start at the hip level and first restore the lengthwise lines to the perpendicular from there down, and then adjust the skirt to the individual variations from hip to waist by working from the hip level up to the waistline. For the postures shown in Figures 2c, d, and e, extra length should be provided from the center front of the hip level to the center front of the waistline, and some length should be removed at the center back between the hip level and the waist.

Figure 2f tilts forward from the hip to the waist and back from the waist to the shoulder. This lifts the back hips and consequently shortens the space between the waist and the hips at the back. This, combined with a backward tilt from waist to shoulders, produces a very exaggerated sway back. Swinging the hips up in the back lifts the hip level of the skirt at the back and causes the center back line of the skirt

FITTING

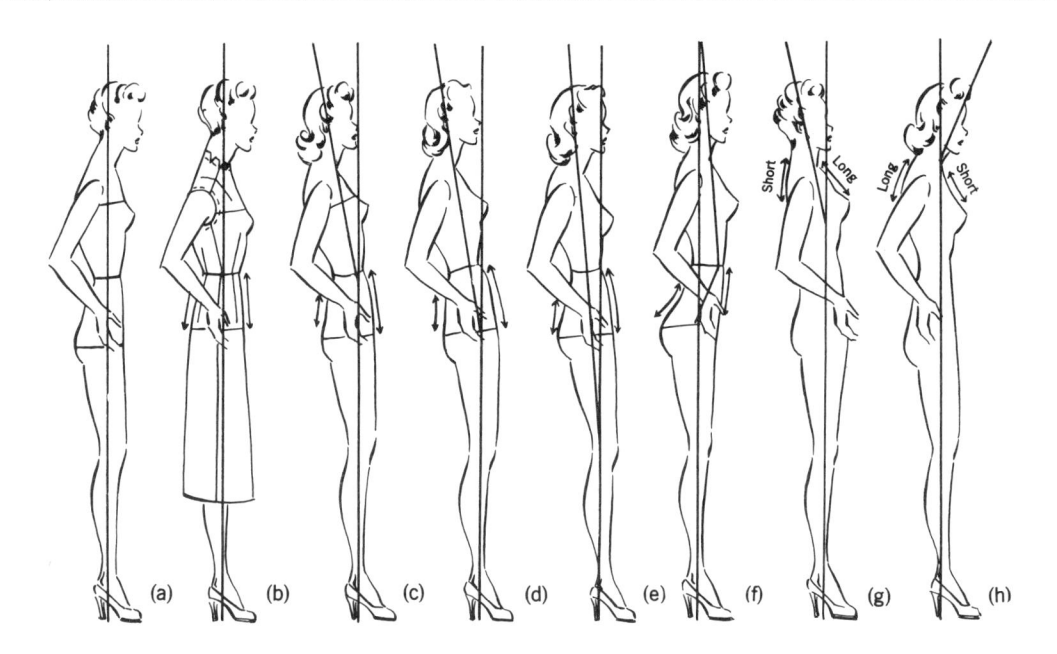

Fig. 2. (*a*) and (*b*) Correct posture; (*c*) Figure leans back from the waist; (*d*) Figure leans back from the hips; (*e*) Figure leans back from the knees; (*f*) The sway-backed figure; (*g*) Overly erect posture; (*h*) Head tilts forward.

to project out from the body. The adjustment for this fault must also be made from the hip level to the waistline.

More detailed discussion is given under *Fitting Problems of the Skirt,* pages 219-229, but this example shows that skirt fitting proceeds from a hip balance line up to the waistline and from the hip level to the lower edge. It also shows that a posture which causes any variation from the usual length from the hip level to the waistline will make fitting alterations necessary.

Figures 2*g* and *h* illustrate postures which produce fitting problems in the blouse. On the over-erect figure, (Figure 2*g*), the length from the center back of the neck to the scye line is shortened. Also, the length from the center back of the neck to the bust line is increased, a variation which will be especially noticeable in trying on a jacket with a high collar, as this posture makes the jacket hike up in the front and spring out at the lower front edge. The stoop-shouldered and flat-chested figure with the forward head, (Figure 2*h*), has the opposite fitting problem. On this figure, necklines push up in front and pull down in back, and proper balance in the blouse can be restored only by adjusting the length from the scye line to the shoulder in back and front. This may require changes in the front and back armscye length, shoulder seams, and neckline. All variations in the length of the blouse which occur below the scye line should be adjusted at the waistline.

A balanced garment sets comfortably and does not shift out of position when one moves. Even a jacket worn unbuttoned, if it is correctly balanced, tilts neither forward nor back, but retains the proper position at the shoulder and neckline. More detailed alteration instructions for Figures 2*g* and *h* are given under *Fitting Problems of the Blouse,* pages 198-218.

When you begin a fitting, study the entire garment from front, back, and side views and make a careful analysis of any possible flaws before ripping a single seam. To learn to fit successfully, one must observe the figure keenly and study the relationships among its contours just as a sculptor would do. One must become conscious of grain in order to know where and when to adjust it. And one must learn to trace wrinkles and unwanted bulges to their origin in order to know whether they are caused by figure irregularity, mistake in pattern shape, or posture.

DRESS DESIGN

Fitting which requires the readjustment and repinning of several seam lines on the figure is, in fact, draping of the most difficult type. Since the body is never entirely motionless and there is little chance to anchor the fabric in position, it takes skill and deft handling to pin accurately and without pricking the model. In addition to basic skill needed in handling, fitting also demands an understanding of pattern shapes. Curves in a pattern edge do not necessarily indicate that a *curved* seam line will appear in the garment but may denote a flare or simply ease over a rounded part of the body. To fit without an understanding of this relationship between pattern shape and body contour, and to work simply on the pattern edges, is to assume that the body is a flat board. The amateur, in her zeal to remove one bulge or wrinkle, may unwittingly create another that is even more serious. It would take years of practice in fitting by trial and error to gain an understanding of pattern shapes equal to that acquired by a short study of draping and pattern blocking. It is this understanding of pattern shapes and grain that gives one mastery of the principles of fitting.

There are two possible fitting procedures, and both have their advantages. The first one is to open the seam lines and "redrape" the section requiring alteration. This method is useful when some experimenting is necessary in order to determine what changes will improve the fit and even the design of the garment. It is also a good procedure for an alteration involving only a short seam line. But for a complicated alteration, it requires not only skill in draping on the part of the fitter but also tiresome standing for the person being fitted. The second method requires less of both persons involved. For alterations can simply be indicated during the fitting by pinning up darts and tucks where there is excess; marking lines for slashing and spreading where more ease or flare is desired; and marking in new lines with pins where a seam or a dart line is poorly placed but the fit is correct. This is really fitting through "blocking," and has the double advantage of requiring less of the fitter's time and of being easier for the amateur to do. There is also less chance of losing the lines that are already correct — an advantage of no small value. The changes are transferred to a paper pattern which is then altered and used in remarking the correct lines on the dress.

Both methods are shown in the diagrams that accompany the discussion of fitting problems in the blouse, skirt, and sleeve. To avoid repeating directions, the general procedure for changing a pattern through blocking is given on page 197.

During all fittings the model should stand before a mirror so that the fitter may see her results without having to move away from the model. Watching the progress of the fitting also encourages the model to keep her head up and face forward. The too-curious person who insists on twisting around to see what is happening is the fitter's bane. The fitter should stand or sit as she works, whichever position brings the part requiring adjustment to her eye level. All fitting should be done with the garment right side out, and it should be done on only one side. All changes should be transferred to the other half of the garment after the fitting.

PART II

PREPARATION OF THE MASTER PATTERN FOR FITTING

I. Mark the following with clear pencil lines:

Blouse and Skirt

1. All seams, darts, and crossmarkings.
2. Neckline, armscye, neck placket line at center back, and placket line in left side of skirt and blouse.
3. Center front and back.
4. Hemline.

Sleeve (prepare only one)

1. Underarm seam.
2. Armscye line.
3. Center lengthwise grain.

FITTING

4. Girth (should be a right angle to lengthwise grain).
5. Elbow line and dart.
6. Wrist and placket line.

II. Stitch (machine-baste):

1. Darts in blouse, skirt, and sleeve.
2. Underarm seams of blouse, skirt, and sleeve. But leave a 6 inch placket at the left side of the skirt; a 4 inch placket at the left side of the blouse; and a 2 inch placket at the wrist of the sleeve.
3. Shoulder seams.
4. The center back of the blouse. But leave a 10 inch placket at the neckline.
5. The waistline (hand-baste). Turn under the skirt waistline seam, top-baste it, and lap it over the waistline of the blouse, matching center front and back, side seams, and darts. *Caution.* Since the skirt appears similar in back and front, be careful not to reverse it. Match the center front of the skirt carefully to the center front of the blouse.
6. The skirt hemline (use long hand-basting stitches). Turn on the hemline and edge-baste; baste the upper edge of the hem.
7. The wrist edge of the sleeve. Turn and edge-baste by hand.

III. Press

Press the muslin pattern well in order to check the fit more accurately and to observe the silhouette lines more carefully. Never use moisture in pressing muslin patterns.

IV. Foundation garments

Fit over a foundation garment and wear a slip.

V. Adjust the master pattern on the person

1. Pin the neck and side plackets closely, being careful not to catch pins into the slip.
2. Pin the shoulder pads into place if they are in vogue and are to be a part of the dress.
3. Adjust the garment on the figure with the center front and back lines at the exact center of the figure and perpendicular to the floor. Also smooth the shoulder seam lines, the waistline, and the neckline into correct position.
4. Clip the neckline if it is too high; and clip the front and back of the armscye if it binds because of a large seam allowance.

Note. If you are fitting your own master pattern, you may prefer to place the opening down the center front of the blouse rather than at the center back.

PROCEDURE FOR ALTERING A PATTERN BY THE BLOCKING METHOD AFTER MARKING CHANGES

1. Separate the part to be altered from the rest of the garment.

2. Mark with a pencil: (*a*) a wrinkle or bulge pinned in as a dart or a tuck; (*b*) the position of slashes for spreading or lapping the pattern; (*c*) the revised line of a seam or a dart.

3. Place over paper and trace a copy of the pattern, including all inner lines as well as the outer contour lines. (Do not include seam allowances.)

4. Make the alterations on the paper pattern.

5. Place the altered paper pattern back over the original and match the grain lines. Trace the revised lines on the muslin pattern.

Note. The same procedure applies to fitting an actual dress that is to be worn, except that tailor's chalk, pins, or thread lines should be used instead of pencil markings.

The remainder of this chapter is intended primarily as reference material which you can consult when fitting problems arise. Consequently you will best understand the following pages if you use them when you are making some direct application of the procedures they discuss to a specific problem. Do not by any means limit the use of this chapter to the fitting of the master pattern, which has merely served conveniently as a garment simple enough to be readily analyzed. It will also be valuable to you in fitting actual garments to be worn and should be used for this purpose.

DRESS DESIGN

PART III
FITTING PROBLEMS OF THE BLOUSE

Some of the commonest fitting problems in the blouse, and some of those which require greatest care, come in the neckline area. Others come at the armscye, the shoulder, the underarm seam, the bust line, the shoulder blades, and the waistline. In the following pages, problems arising in connection with each of these areas will be taken up in turn.

FAULTS IN THE NECKLINE AREA

Problem 1

LOOSENESS IN FRONT NECKLINE

Sometimes the fabric buckles out or appears loose at or near the center front of the neckline. This fault indicates too much width across the neckline from shoulder seam to shoulder seam. Either the dress form was too heavily padded across the collar bone, or the fabric was not pushed away from the center front enough when it was pinned around the neckline.

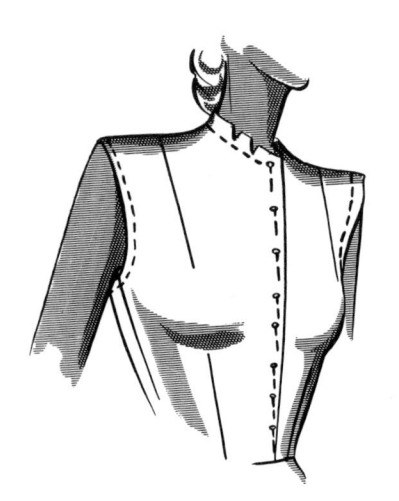

Variation A. Figure 3a shows noticeable looseness at the center front extending from the neckline down to the waistline, where it tapers off to nothing.

To correct this fault by blocking, follow the directions given below (see Figure 3b).

1. Pin the excess into a long dart from the neck to the waistline (see Figure 3a).

2. Use this dart line as a new center front line, and trace a paper pattern from the muslin front following the general procedure for altering a pattern by the blocking method (see page 197). Figure 3b shows that the simple procedure of bringing the center dart line of the paper pattern to the original center front line of the muslin pattern revises every edge and inside line in a single operation. It is simple to reblock the pattern, but to redrape it on the model would be tedious and might be inaccurate.

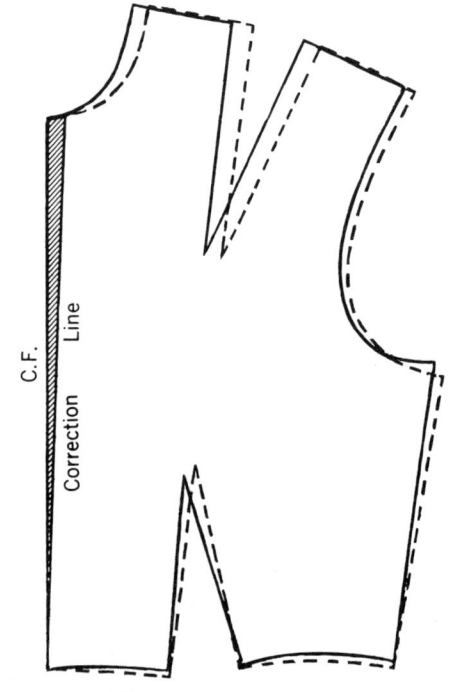

Fig. 3. (a) Fabric is loose at center front of neckline; excess tapers off at waistline; (b) Correction line pivoted to center front to remove excess. Dotted lines indicate pattern before alteration.

FITTING

Variation B. Figure 4a shows looseness near the center front of the neckline which points toward the bust but does not extend below it.

Fig. 4 (a). Fabric is loose at center front neckline; excess tapers off at end of shoulder dart.

To correct by blocking (see Figure 4b) follow the directions below.

1. Pin the excess into a diagonal dart tapering from the neck to a point near the end of the shoulder dart as shown in Figure 4a, and then pinch up an equal amount on the opposite side to retain the balance across the chest and to guard against over-fitting.

2. Take off the blouse and trace the front on paper, including the correction dart from neck to bust.

3. Slash through the center of the original shoulder dart to the point of the bust.

4. Slash the inner edge of the new neck dart to the point of the shoulder dart or to the bust, and lap out the correction dart by bringing the two lines of the dart together, thereby increasing the size of the shoulder dart.

5. Retrace the paper pattern on the muslin master blouse pattern.

Since this change involves only the neckline, the shoulder dart, and the shoulder seam from neck to shoulder dart, the alteration can also be made on the person by the following draping procedure (see Figure 4c).

1. Open the shoulder seam from the neck to the shoulder dart. (Opening only part of the seam in this manner causes less danger of losing the correct fit over the shoulders.)

2. Smooth the excess from the neckline along the shoulder seam line into the shoulder dart, keeping the crosswise grain level at the scye line in front and back.

3. Re-mark the shoulder seam, crossmarkings, and front neckline.

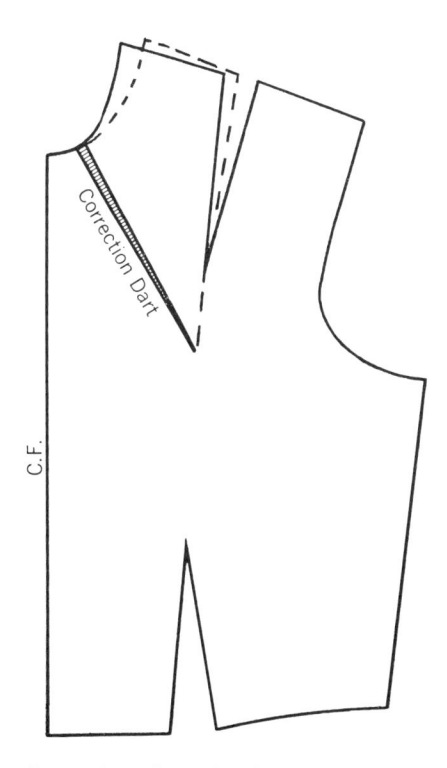

Fig. 4 (b). Correction dart closed at neckline and transferred to shoulder dart. Dotted line shows pattern before alteration.

Fig. 4 (c). Excess at neckline transferred into shoulder dart.

199

DRESS DESIGN

Problem 2

DIAGONAL WRINKLE FROM NECKLINE

A diagonal wrinkle radiates from the side of a too-tight neckline toward the lower point of the shoulder dart or toward the waistline dart. This fault, the exact opposite of that in the preceding problem, is caused by letting the crosswise threads drop from the center

Fig. 5 (a). A wrinkle radiating from neckline to the end of the shoulder dart.

front to the armscye during the draping. The curve of the blouse neckline then becomes sharper than the curve of the neck, and this forces ease to radiate from the neckline when it is stretched around the neck. This same fault appears when a person's neck is larger around the base than is the neckline of the pattern. If the difference is only slight, correct the fault by clipping the neckline, or retain a high neckline by letting out the neckline end of the shoulder seam. (Do not confuse this problem with the one in which wrinkles radiate from the intersection of the neckline and shoulder seam, a fault usually caused by sloping shoulders, or by too little shoulder padding in the costume, if the pattern allowed for padding.)

Variation A. Figure 5a shows a wrinkle radiating from the neckline to the end of the shoulder dart. The crosswise grain drops from the center front of the neckline toward the shoulder dart but is level at the scye line.

To correct by blocking (see Figure 5b), proceed as follows.

1. Pin the excess into a dart tapering from the end of the shoulder dart to neckline as shown in Figure 5a.

2. Mark and crossmark both sides of the new dart and trace a paper pattern from the blouse front.

3. Slash through the center of the shoulder dart to the point of the bust.

4. Slash one side of the correction dart and lap out the excess, thereby reducing the size of the shoulder dart (see Figure 5b).

5. Re-mark the muslin from the altered pattern.

It is also possible to correct this fault by draping. This is done simply by reversing the procedure illustrated in Figure 4c.

1. Open the shoulder seam as far as the shoulder dart.

2. Open the shoulder dart and readjust it so that the crosswise grain is level from the center front to the shoulder dart. This lifts the side of the dart nearer the center. Reduce the depth of the shoulder dart until the diagonal wrinkle from the neckline disappears. Then repin the dart.

3. Push the excess along the shoulder seam toward the neckline. The front edge of the shoulder seam at the neckline is now higher than the back edge.

4. Re-pin the shoulder seam and crossmark it.

5. Re-mark the front neckline.

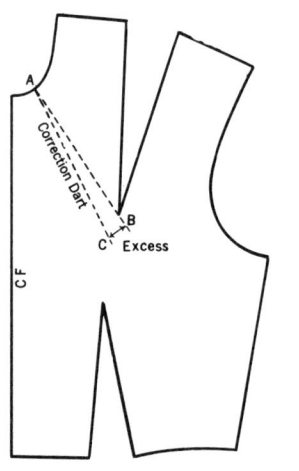

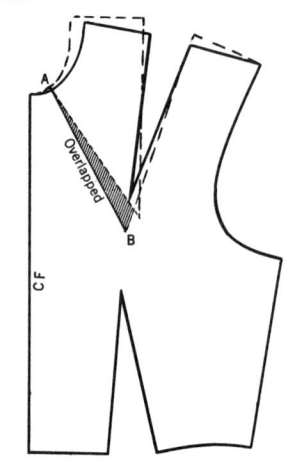

Fig. 5 (b). Correction dart closed to remove excess below shoulder dart. Step 1 — Mark correction dart to show excess. Step 2 — Bring AB to AC. Dotted line shows blouse before alteration.

Variation B. Figure 6a shows a similar but larger wrinkle which runs to a point below the bust. The crosswise grain shows a noticeable drop from the center front to the side below the scye line.

To correct by blocking (see Figure 6b), proceed as follows.

1. Pin the excess into a dart beginning at the point of the waistline dart and tapering to nothing at the neck as shown in Figure 6a.

2. Follow the procedure illustrated in Figure 5a. (See Figure 6b). It would be impractical to correct this fault by redraping the pattern on the model.

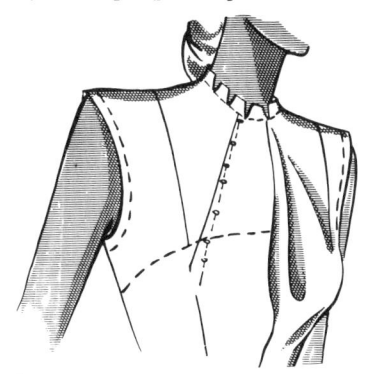

Fig. 6 (a). Large wrinkle radiating from neckline to a point below the bust.

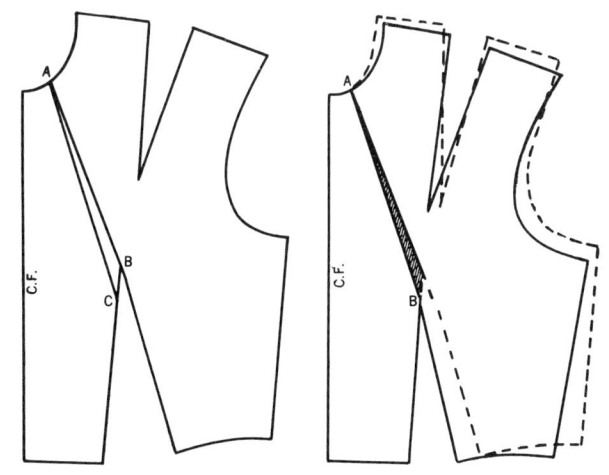

Fig. 6 (b). Correction dart closed to remove excess below bust line.

Problem 3

BLOUSE FRONT WITH HORIZONTAL WRINKLES ACROSS BASE OF NECK (see Figure 7a)

Horizontal wrinkles in the blouse front, sometimes with a crosswise fold near the bust line if the neckline is loose, occur most frequently on a round-shouldered, flat-chested person, because her chest is concave between the shoulders and the scye line in the front, and her back contour is convex. This makes the blouse too long in front above the scye level. By leveling the crosswise grain at the scye line, you can push up the excess length in the blouse front between the scye line and the base of the neck. The horizontal wrinkles due to excess length may run through the armhole or may taper off to nothing there. To get rid of them, pin a horizontal tuck dart across the upper part of the chest (see Figure 7b), and correct by blocking. Figure 7c shows how to change the pattern.

To fit out the excess length on the figure, rip the shoulder seam and raise the front edge until the crosswise grain at the scye line is level and the blouse fits smoothly from the scye line up to the shoulder. Pin the new shoulder seam and mark a new front neckline.

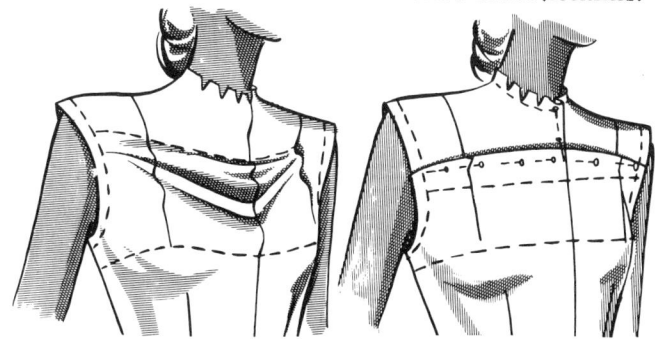

Fig. 7 (a). Blouse wrinkles horizontally below the base of the neck on a flat chested figure.

Fig. 7 (b). Excess between shoulder and scye line pinned out in a horizontal tuck.

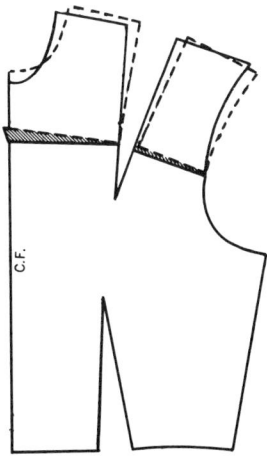

Fig. 7 (c). Correction tuck lapped out to shorten center front above scye line. This also tightens neckline slightly.

DRESS DESIGN

Problem 4

BLOUSE BACK WITH HORIZONTAL WRINKLES ACROSS BASE OF NECK (see Figure 8a)

The over-erect figure with shoulders and head carried far back will have a shorter-than-normal back scye depth, and the excess blouse length in back will push up into a neckline which is too high or into horizontal wrinkles just below the neckline. Or if it does not push above the scye line, it may sag into wrinkles across the lower back with the crosswise grain dropping noticeably at the center back.

When these irregularities occur, fit the garment in exactly the same way as in the preceding problem (see Figures 8b and c).

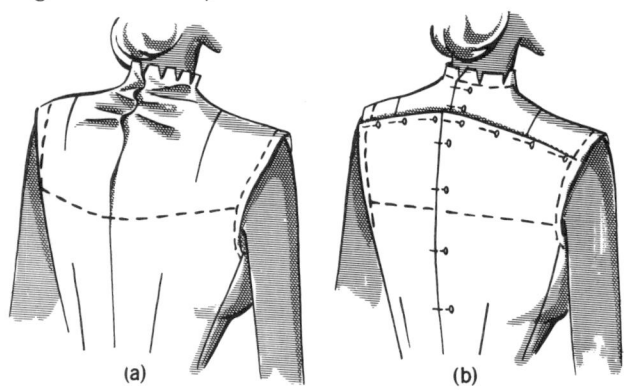

Fig. 8 (a). Blouse back wrinkles horizontally across the base of the neck on an over-erect figure.

Fig. 8 (b). Excess pinned out into a horizontal tuck or dart in order to make the scye line level.

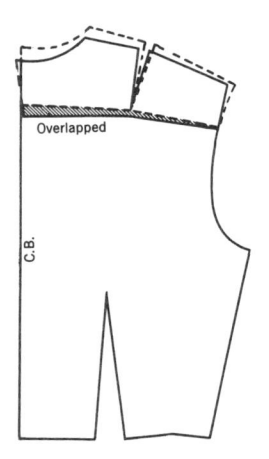

Fig. 8 (c). Pattern corrected. Dotted line shows shape of blouse before alteration.

Problem 5

NECKLINE PULLED DOWN AT CENTER BACK AND TOO HIGH AT CENTER FRONT (see Figures 9a and b)

This fault is related to the one illustrated in Figure 7a, which shows horizontal wrinkles across the front neckline. The round- or stoop-shouldered posture lengthens the back scye depth so that either the center back of the neckline pulls down or the center back of the waistline pulls up. The more forward the head, the longer the back scye depth needs to be. Otherwise the shoulder seams pull toward the back. Also, the back of the blouse will be too narrow between the armscye lines, since the rounded back brings the arms forward and increases the width needed between the back armscye lines.

To correct this fault by blocking, follow these steps:

1. Pull down the crosswise grain at the center back until the blouse scye line is level. Then measure the amount needed to raise the neckline to its proper height.

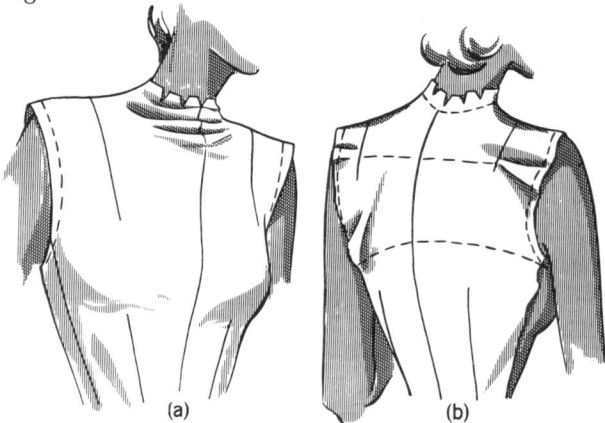

Fig. 9 (a) and (b). Round shoulders and forward-tilting head cause wrinkling at the front of the neck and pulling down at the back of the neck.

2. Mark a line across the blouse where the shoulders show the most prominent bulge. Or if you are using a muslin pattern, slash and spread it along this line (see Figure 9c).

3. Trace a paper copy of the blouse back.

4. Figures 9d and e illustrate the method of marking the paper pattern and of slashing and spreading.

FITTING

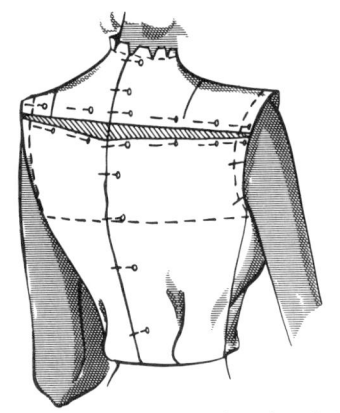

Fig. 9 (*c*). Shows correction by slashing.

5. Re-mark the blouse lines from the spread pattern.

To correct the same fault by draping, proceed as follows:

1. Open the shoulder seams and level the crosswise grain at the scye line, thereby reducing the back shoulder seam allowance.

2. Pin in a small dart at the neckline and increase the ease or the size of the shoulder dart.

3. Re-pin the shoulder seam.

4. Mark a new line at the armscye to add width as far down as necessary.

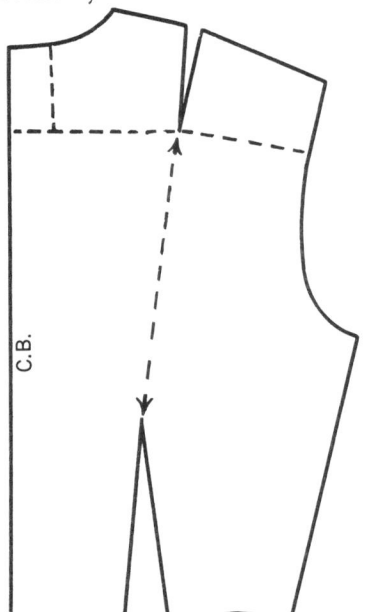

Fig. 9 (*d*). Lines marked for slashing and spreading a blouse back for round shoulders.

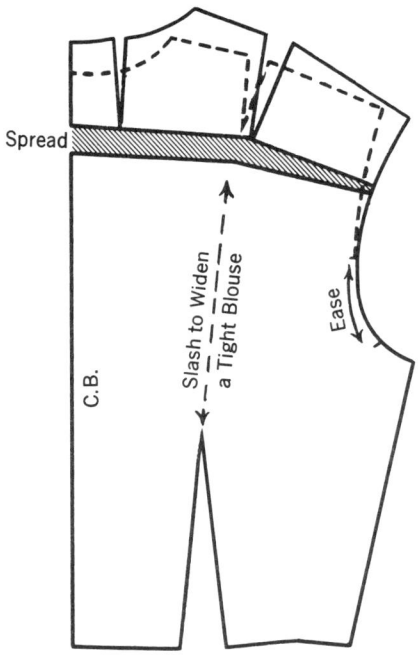

Fig. 9 (*e*). Pattern spread to increase length of the scye and width of the upper blouse.

To make round or stooped shoulders less obvious, fit the entire back of the blouse with plenty of room. To counteract the round-shouldered look, there must be ease on all sides of the shoulder blades — above, through a neck dart and shoulder ease; beside, through ease along the armscye held up by shoulder pads or shrunk out at the lower armscye curve; and below, by blousing above the waistline instead of using a long figure-fitting waistline dart.

If the entire back is somewhat tight, slash the pattern lengthwise through the shoulder and waistline darts and spread to introduce width as well as to increase scye length (see Figure 9*e*).

FAULTS IN THE SHOULDER AREA

Since faults in fitting between the bust line and the shoulders, front or back, require corrections involving the shoulder seam, any changes in the shoulder seam line itself should be made only after carefully checking the grain, ease, and smoothness of fit through the bust, chest, and armscye. If the fit proves satisfactory in all these details, any faults observed near the shoulder seam must be due to a lack of adjustment between the shoulder seam line of the garment and the shoulder line of the body.

DRESS DESIGN

Problem 6
SHOULDER SEAM LINE SLOPES TOO SHARPLY

A person with very square shoulders will very often find that there is too much shoulder slope in ready-made clothes and in commercial patterns. This fault may also appear in a master blouse draped on a personal dress form if the shoulder pads used at the fitting are thicker than the shoulder padding on the dress form. When shoulders are very square and the blouse shoulder seam slopes too much for them, fitting problems of two different kinds arise. A distinction must be made between the two types of faults. One kind occurs when the back or front of a blouse fits correctly from the scye line up to the armscye end of the shoulder seam but is too long from the scye line to the neckline end of the seam (see Figure 10a). The second, and the more serious kind of fault arises when the blouse is too short from the scye line to the armscye end of the shoulder seam, thereby pulling the entire blouse from waist to shoulder out of line (see Figure 10b). Patterns in Figures 11a and 11b show the difference in these two fitting problems.

To correct the blouse shown in Figure 10a, decrease the slope of the garment shoulder *by fitting looseness out of the neckline end of the shoulder seam* as shown by the pinned seam on the right side of the figure. Do not make the mistake of letting out the armscye end

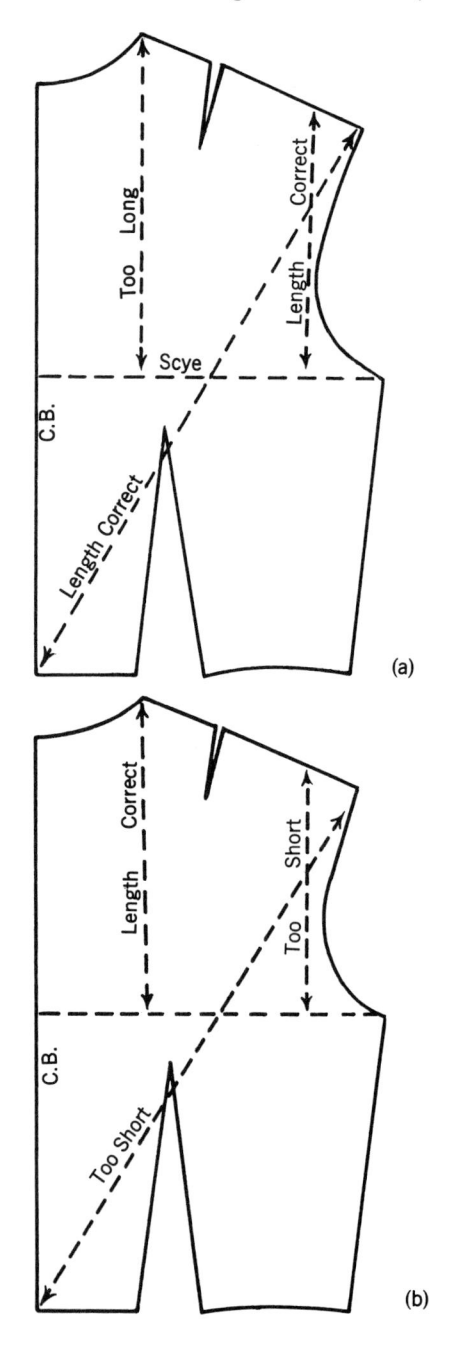

Fig. 10 (a). Blouse is too long from scye line to neck end of shoulder seam. (See Figure 11 (a)).
Fig. 10 (b). Blouse is too short from scye line to armscye end of shoulder seam. (See Figure 11 (b)).

Fig. 11 (a) and (b). Shoulder slope wrong.

FITTING

of the shoulder seam with the idea that the neck would then settle down to fit the body. This would merely allow the whole top half of the garment to droop by making it too long from the shoulder to the scye line. To make this alteration on a ready-made garment which has a collar, pin the excess length into a tuck from center back or center front to a point on the shoulder seam line where it fits correctly. In this way, ripping and changes in pattern shapes can come after the fitting.

To correct the blouse illustrated in Figure 10b, which is too short from the scye line to the top of the armhole, decrease the slope *by letting out the armscye end of the shoulder seam* until the crosswise grain drops enough to be level at the scye line. See the corrected right half of the blouse in Figure 10b. It would be wrong in this case to straighten the shoulder by taking in the neckline end of the shoulder seam, because that would raise the scye line of the entire blouse above the position for which it was intended. Since the results of this error in fitting can not always be traced immediately to their source, let us look again at the left half of the blouse in Figure 10b. This section draws downward at the armhole end of the shoulder seam. The crosswise grain pulls upward from the center back waistline (or center front as the case may be) toward the armhole end of the shoulder seam, and noticeable diagonal wrinkles form in this direction. The waistline pulls up at the side, and the ease from the end of the waistline dart strains toward the end of the shoulder seam away from the shoulder blade, where it was intended to be. Figure 11b analyzes a blouse back pattern which has this fault in fitting. The alteration is simple enough in a muslin pattern, but is complicated in a ready-made garment by the necessity of refitting the sleeve.

Pinning the Shoulder Seam

You may mistakenly believe that the alteration of a shoulder seam is an easy matter, but if you rip it entirely apart, it is actually one of the most difficult seams for an amateur to re-pin accurately. It is important to balance this seam correctly in order to balance the back and front scye length, and yet when the shoulder seam is completely ripped, the whole blouse slips out of place. Not only must the center front and back be kept centered on the body, but the crosswise grain at the scye line front and back must be held level as well. It helps to have the person being fitted hold the center front in position near the chest and neckline area while the fitter smooths the fabric up from the scye line and establishes one shoulder seam edge at a time. Pin the front seam edge first, turning under the raw edge and pinning it as in draping. Then smooth the back up from the scye line, slip the back seam under the front, and pin the two together.

Problem 7

SHOULDER SEAM LINE LOOSE AT THE OUTER END, DIAGONAL WRINKLES FROM NECK TO ARMSCYE

Figure 12 shows a shoulder seam loose at the armscye end, with diagonal wrinkles falling from the neckline end of the seam into the hollow in front of the arm. Similar wrinkles fall toward the back. This is because the shoulders slope more than the shoulder seam of the garment. Sometimes similar wrinkles occur when the shoulders are narrow and the unsupported length beyond the end of the shoulder bone drops into diagonal lines along the armscye. When a square broad-shouldered silhouette is in fashion, correct these drooping lines by adding thickness to the outer edge of the shoulder pads. To fit the slope of the shoulder, reverse the procedure outlined in Problem 6 (see Figure 10b). That is, take up the armscye end of the shoulder seam until the crosswise grain at the scye line is level (see the corrected right shoulder seam in Figure 12).

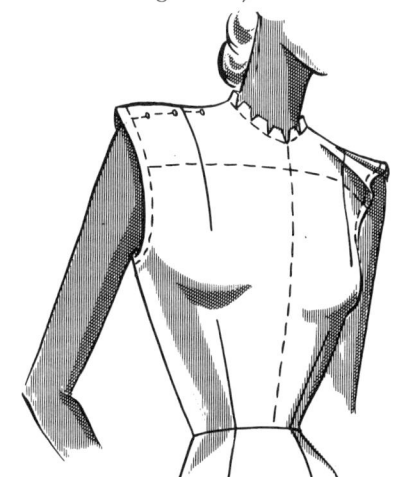

Fig. 12. A figure with sloping shoulders has excess length at armscye end of shoulder seam.

205

DRESS DESIGN

Problem 8

SHOULDER SEAM STANDING ABOVE HOLLOW AT CENTER OF SHOULDER

Figure 13a shows a shoulder seam which fits at both ends but fails to settle down into the hollow at the center of the shoulder. Thick shoulder pads exaggerate this fault. If the shoulder position and fit are otherwise correct, simply pin a small tuck across the hollow along the seam line without ripping the seam. If the fabric appears looser in front than in back, pin more of the tuck out of the blouse front. It is also possible that the shoulder seam is properly curved but has a wide unclipped seam allowance that keeps it from stretching out to its full length. In other words, the raw edge of the seam may be tighter than the seam line. To correct this, clip the seam allowance (see Figure 13b).

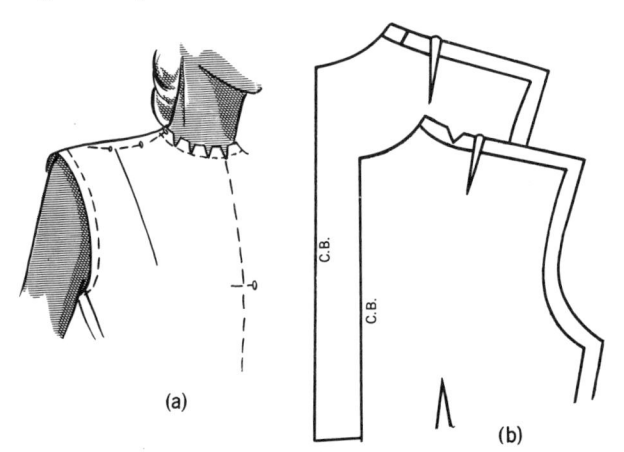

Fig. 13 (a). Pinning along curve in shoulder seam.
Fig. 13 (b). Tight seam edges must be clipped above a curve.

Problem 9

SHOULDER SEAM IN UNBECOMING POSITION

When a shoulder seam line fits smoothly but needs to be moved forward or back for the proper appearance of the garment, it is unnecessary to rip the seam. Simply mark the new line with pins (see Figure 14a). Figure 14b shows how to transfer this new line to the under layer of fabric by tracing, then folding so that the new edges will come along this line. Turn the seam allowance toward the front if the line is to be moved forward and trace along the new pinned line with the wrong side of the blouse next to the carbon paper or chalk board. Then turn the seam allowance out of the way to transfer the line to the wrong side of the blouse front.

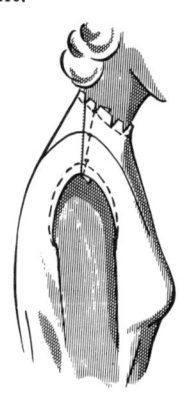

Fig. 14 (a). Shoulder seam line is in an unbecoming position.

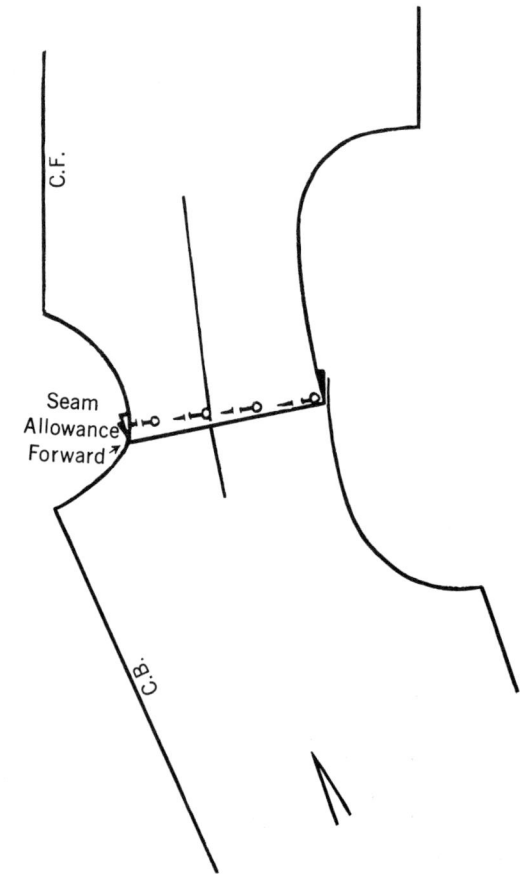

Fig. 14 (b). Shoulder seam moved forward, but same fit retained, by tracing along pin line.

206

FITTING

Problem 10

DRAWING AT NECKLINE END OF SHOULDER SEAM

When this occurs, the neckline end of the shoulder seam generally fails to fit smoothly because the base of the neck is unusually broad and slopes up the side from the center of the shoulder (see Figure 15a). A neck with a broad base requires a definite upward curve at the neckline end of the shoulder seam. Clip the shoulder seam along the curve before fitting the blouse as explained in Problem 8.

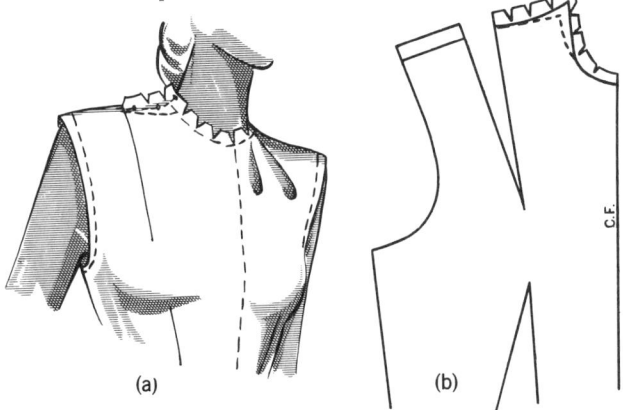

Fig. 15. (a) Broad neck base — the pattern draws at the end of the shoulder seam. (b) Neckline end of shoulder seam and side of neck seam let out for broad neck base.

Clipping the neckline seam to relieve the tightness is decidedly not the answer to this problem, because the side of the neckline should come above the broadest neck measurement to make the base of the neck seem smaller and to minimize the difference between it and the upper part of the neck. Another reason for keeping the line high is that roll collars attached to a broad low neckline will buckle away from the slender upper part of the neck.

To refit the neckline for a looser yet higher line, rip the neckline end of the shoulder seam for at least 1½ inches. Hold the center front line in place and smooth the neckline toward the front from the shoulder, letting out some of the front shoulder seam allowance. Mark a new curved line which follows the side of the neck, and clip from the raw edge to this new line in one or two places. Repeat this procedure for the back. Then re-pin the seam and mark a new side neckline. Figure 15b shows the pattern change.

Problem 11

SHOULDERS OF GARMENT TOO NARROW FOR BROAD-SHOULDERED, ANGULAR FIGURE

The angular figure with large bones should have roomy garments that give the illusion of rounded contours. If the shoulders are broad but the chest and bust line are rather flat and narrow, the blouse should have a definite vertical fold of fabric beginning at the upper half of the armscye and tapering to nothing at the waist (see Figure 16a). This will act as a transitional line between the broad shoulder and the narrow chest. Do not fit this figure closely at the underarm. Broad shoulders support so much extra width that the shoulder dart in front and the waistline dart in back can be somewhat reduced, letting part of the excess go into looseness at the sides of the figure. (See Figures 16b and c for altering the pattern.)

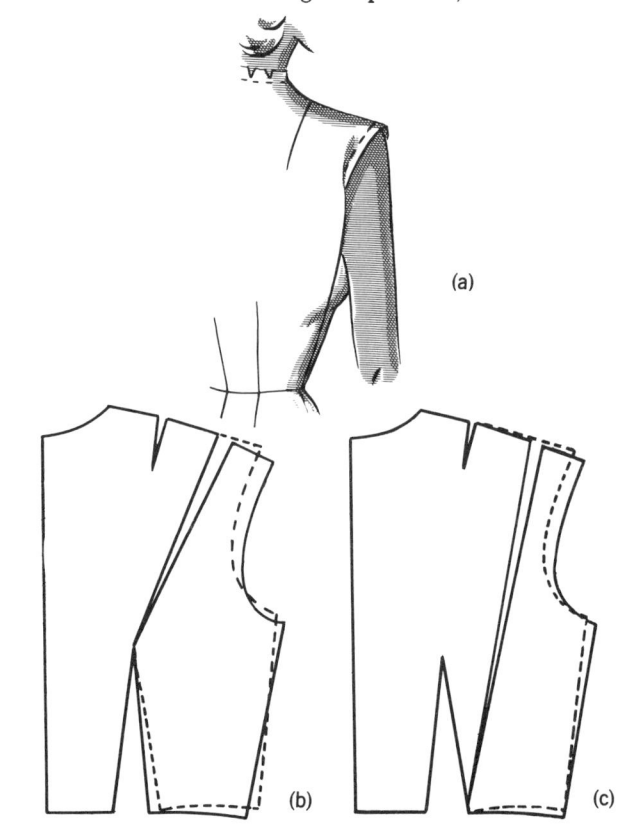

Fig. 16. (a) Vertical fold at armscye softens line between broad shoulders and narrow chest. (b) Shoulder line widened and waistline dart reduced. (c) Shoulder line widened; waistline dart not reduced.

DRESS DESIGN

Problem 12

SHOULDER SEAM LINE TOO BROAD FOR NARROW-SHOULDERED FIGURE WITH LARGE BUST

This problem again is one of equalizing body proportions. If the shoulders can be made to appear broader through the use of shoulder pads, the bust line will appear less heavy and the ease needed by the large bust will be more becomingly supported above the hollow usually present in front of the arm. Instead of cutting off the extra shoulder width, use it to increase the depth of the dart. In garments other than a master pattern, this width is often placed in a front and back dart on the armscye line (see Figure 17).

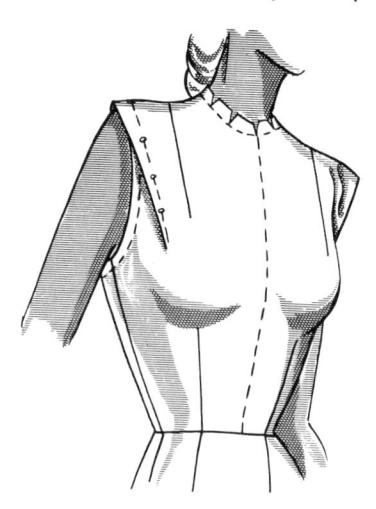

Fig. 17. Dart along armscye bridges between narrow shoulders and large bust.

FAULTS IN THE ARMSCYE AREA

Because any fitting changes near the bust or shoulder blades probably involve the armhole, observe the ease around the scye and bust line before fitting armscye faults. The armscye line should fit with enough ease to allow the arm to move freely without binding, but also without gapping at the front or back armscye edges. You can usually trace a gapping armscye to inadequate darting for the shoulder blades in the back or for the bust in the front. The armscye may gap, however, even when the darting is adequate. Corrections for this fault will be discussed in the following problems.

Problem 13

ARMSCYE GAP CAUSED BY INADEQUATE DARTING

Variation A. Figure 18a shows looseness at the lower curve of the back armscye tapering toward the upper end of the waistline dart. The crosswise grain is level at the upper back line but rises noticeably toward each side seam from the waistline up to the armscye, where it gaps. The pouch at the armscye was produced by an attempt to fit the waistline by pushing the excess over toward the underarm seam instead of taking up a large enough waistline dart. This also raised the crosswise grain toward the side seams. To eliminate the excess at the armhole and to provide more ease at the lower point of the shoulder blade, pin the excess into a dart running from the armscye to the point of the waistline dart. Remove the blouse and alter the pattern by the standard procedure. Transfer the excess at the armscye into a larger waistline dart (see Figure 18b for the pattern change).

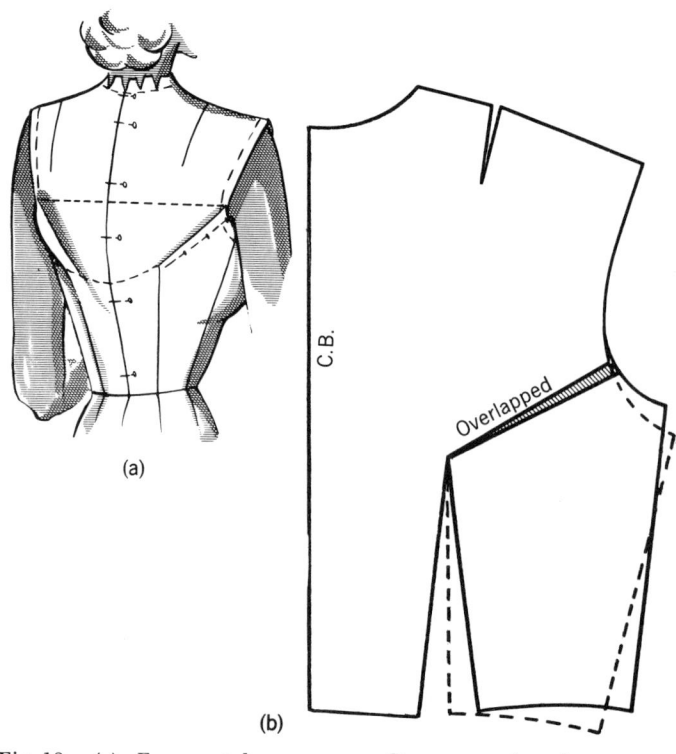

Fig. 18. (a) Excess at lower curve of armscye pinned out into correction dart. (b) Excess at lower armscye transferred into waistline dart. Dotted line shows pattern before alteration.

FITTING

Variation B. Figure 19a shows looseness at the upper part of the back armscye with the crosswise grain near the neckline dropping from the center back to the armhole line. To correct this difficulty, take up the superfluous length by using thicker shoulder pads, or transfer it to a larger dart on the back shoulder seam and a dart at the neckline. At the upper armscye, pin the pouch into a dart pointing to the top of the shoulder blades (see the right side of Figure 19a).

The excess should be transferred to darts at the neckline and shoulder as shown in Figure 19b and described below.

1. Draw a short vertical line for the neck dart intersecting a horizontal line drawn from the end of the pouch.

2. Draw a line through the center of the shoulder dart to meet the horizontal correction dart.

3. Slash the horizontal line from the end of the pouch to the end of the neck dart.

4. Slash the neck and shoulder darts and spread to close the correction dart. In order to spread the neck dart, also spread slightly along the horizontal line. Redraw the neckline from the dart to the center back.

Variation C. Figure 20a shows a pouch at the center of the front armhole radiating from the point of the bust. Pinch up the excess at the armscye into a dart tapering to nothing at the bust. Figures 20b and c show how to transfer this excess equally to the shoulder and waistline darts or entirely to the waistline dart. Choose the method that keeps the crosswise grain more nearly level at the scye line. A third method is to transfer the excess at the armscye into a horizontal dart at the underarm seam approximately 1 to 1½ inches below the armscye (see Figure 20d).

If you correct the faults described in Variations *A, B,* and *C* by fitting the garment directly on the person, determine which seam lines to open and revise from the diagrams showing the pattern changes.

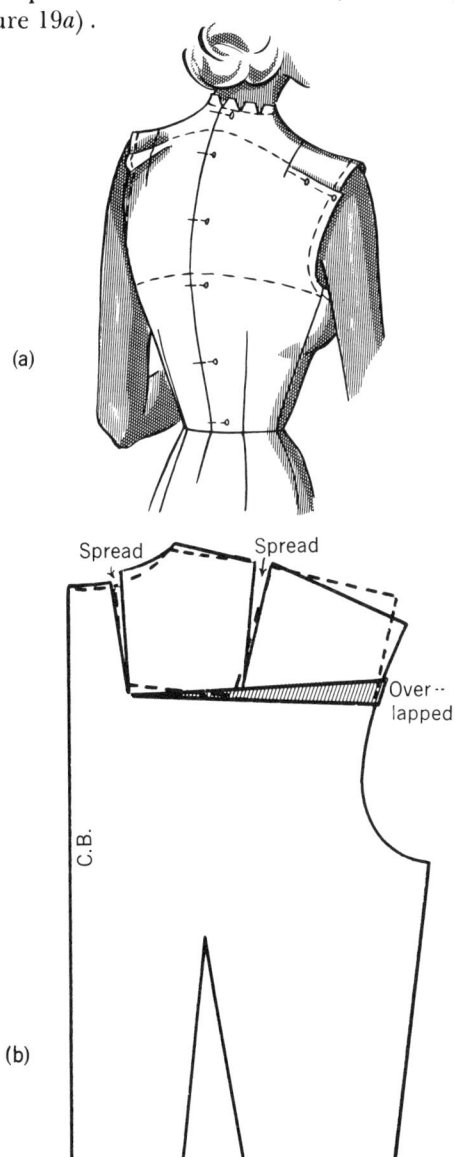

Fig. 19. (a) Excess at upper armscye pinned out into correction dart. (b) Excess at upper armscye transferred into neck and shoulder darts.

Fig. 20 (a). Excess at front armscye pinned out into correction dart.

DRESS DESIGN

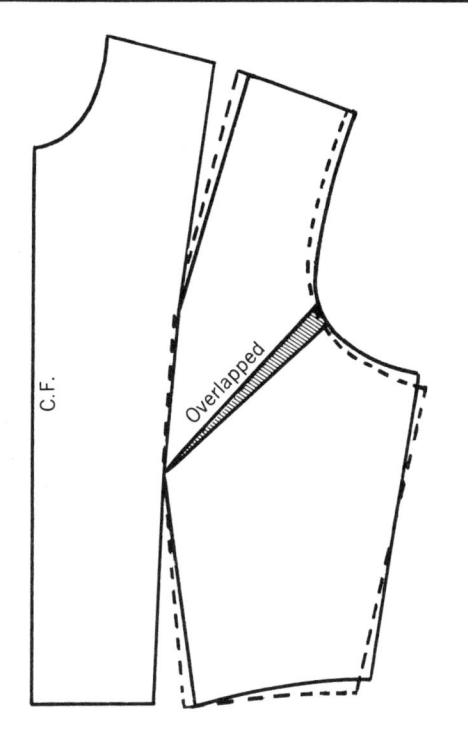

Fig. 20 (b). Correction dart at armscye transferred into larger shoulder and waistline darts.

Problem 14

ARMSCYE GAP CAUSED BY EXCESS LENGTH FROM SCYE LINE TO SHOULDERS

The round-shouldered and flat-chested figure may have too much length from the scye line to the shoulders in the front of the blouse. If so, correct this defect according to the directions given in fitting problems in the Neckline Area, Problem 3, page 201. The over-erect figure may have excess length from the scye line to the shoulders in the back of the blouse and this should be handled as explained in fitting problems in the Neckline Area, Problem 4, page 202. The very slope-shouldered figure may have excess length from the scye line to the shoulders in the back or front and the difficulty may be corrected according to the directions given in fitting problems in the Shoulder Area, Problem 7, page 205.

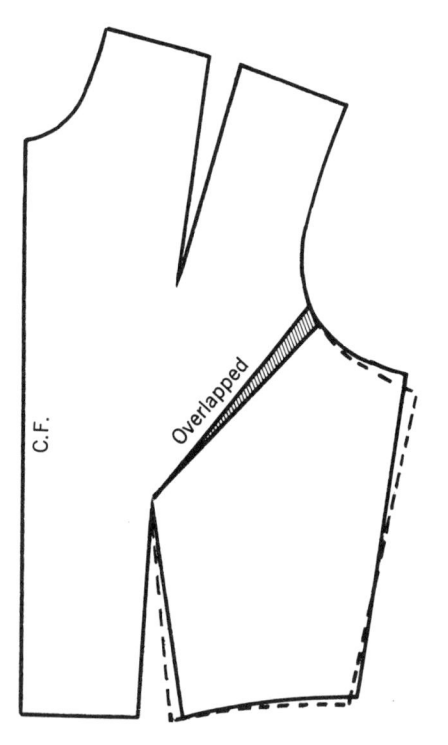

Fig. 20 (c). Excess transferred into waistline dart.

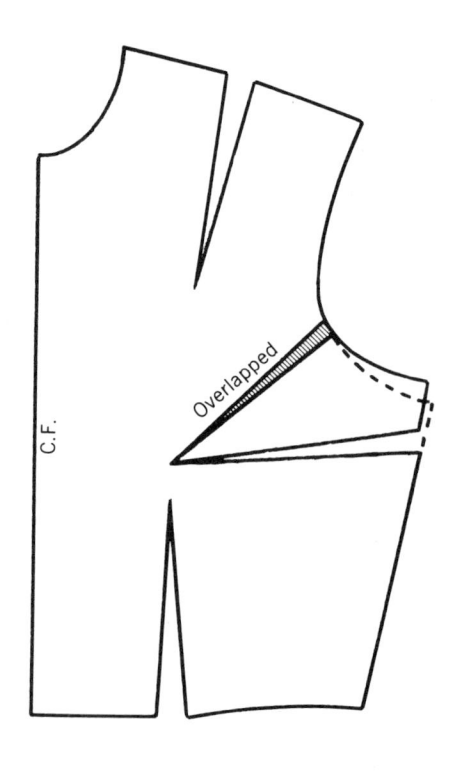

Fig. 20 (d). Excess transferred into underarm dart.

FITTING

Problem 15

ARMSCYE GAP CAUSED BY EXCESS WIDTH AT UNDERARM

Variation A. Figure 21a shows a long triangular pouch at the lower armscye tapering to a point near the waistline end of the dart. The crosswise grain rises noticeably from the dart to the side seam. To correct this, pin the excess into a long dart tapering from the armscye to nothing at the waistline as shown in Figure 21b, and change the pattern as indicated in Figure 21c.

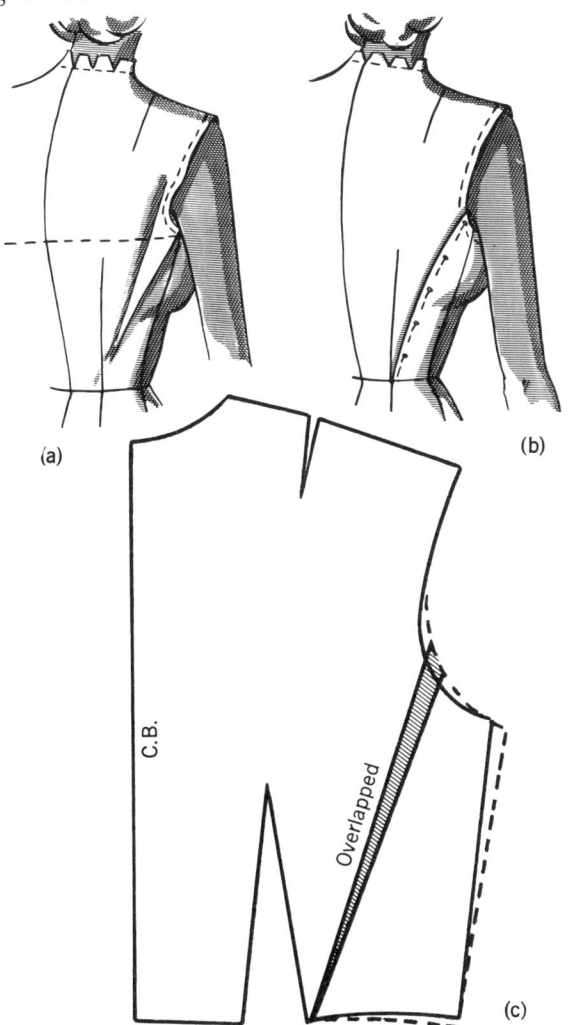

Fig. 21 (*a*). Excess width at underarm causes looseness at lower curve of armscye. (*b*). Excess pinned out. (*c*). Correction dart overlapped to reduce width of blouse at under arm.

Variation B. Figure 22a shows an almost vertical fold starting with excess at the armscye and tapering to nothing at the waistline near the side seam. The direction of the fold in this case is more nearly vertical than in the previous one since the crosswise grain rises less toward the side seam. Either change the pattern by overlapping the correction dart (see Figure 22b), or rip the underarm seam, lap the front over the back to take in the back seam, and lower the back armscye curve.

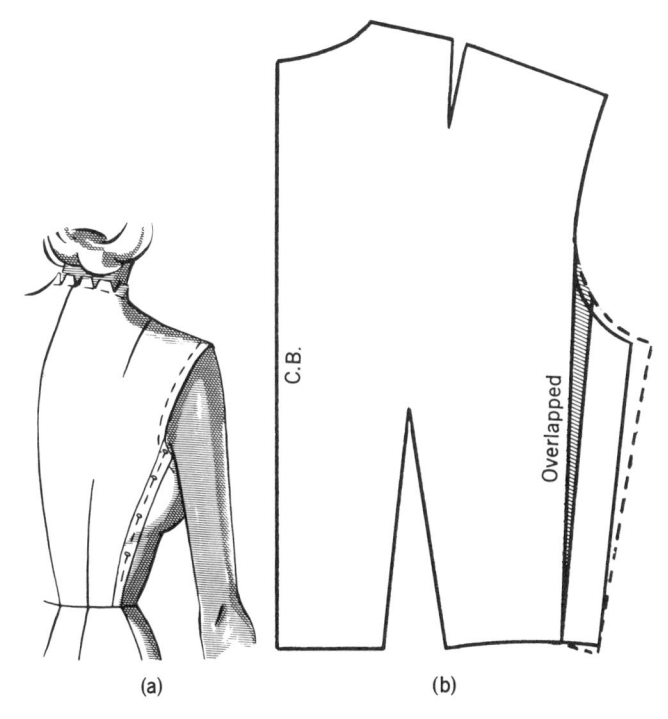

Fig. 22. (*a*) Excess width in blouse back near underarm seam pinned out in correction dart; (*b*) Correction dart overlapped.

Problem 16

ARMSCYE GAP CAUSED BY INCORRECT BALANCE OF BACK AND FRONT UNDERARM SEAMS

See fitting problems of the underarm seam, pages 212-215 for instructions to be followed in correcting this difficulty.

DRESS DESIGN

Problem 17

UNCOMFORTABLE BINDING AT ARMHOLE

Tightness in the armhole does not necessarily indicate that the armhole should be lowered at the underarm seam. In fact, lowering it may even add to the discomfort of the blouse. The armhole size depends on several things: first, the length from the scye line to the armhole end of the shoulder seam as determined by the slope from the neck to the armhole end of the shoulder seam; and second, the amount of width under the arm which can be taken in or let out by the underarm seam (see Figure 23).

The armhole line may be uncomfortable for any one of a half dozen different reasons.

1. The shoulder seams may be too sloping. See fitting problems of shoulder seams, page 204.

2. There may be inadequate width in the side of the garment from the point of the bust to the side seam and from the shoulder blades to the side seam. See fitting problems of the underarm seam, pages 213-214, for changing the underarm width.

3. The lowest point of the armhole may be marked above the true scye line, which should be 1½ inches below the armpit when the arm is raised.

4. The seam allowance on a sharply curved armhole may not have been clipped enough to let it spread the length of the seam line. Remember that the intensity of the armhole curve increases as the amount of darting increases (see Figure 24).

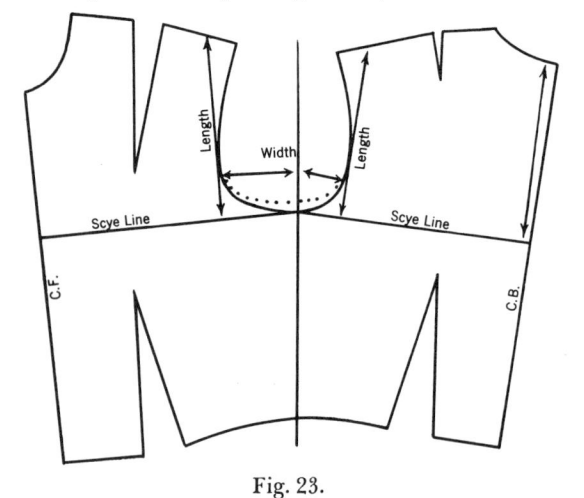

Fig. 23.

5. Even if the armhole circumference is adequate, its lower curve may push up at the armpit because the slope of the underarm seam from the armscye to the waistline has been increased. See fitting problems of the underarm seam, pages 213 214.

6. There may be overdarting in the blouse. An excessively large waistline dart will exert a downward pull on the lowest point of the armhole, and the shoulder dart, if too large, will exert an upward pull on the armscye line.

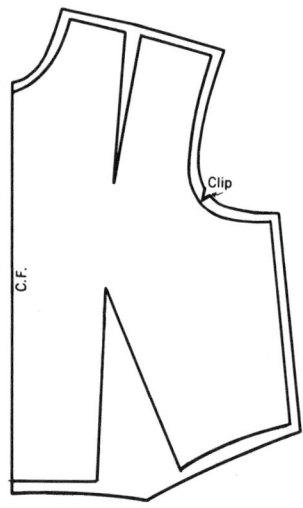

Fig. 24. Seam edge is shorter than seam line on sharply curved armhole.

FITTING PROBLEMS OF THE UNDERARM SEAM

Figures 25a through f show how changing the slope of the underarm seam by taking in the waistline at the side automatically alters the line and fit at both the armscye and the waistline. Figure 25a shows the back and front seam lines balanced correctly. Here the crosswise grain at the scye line is level and the lowest point of the armscye curve is approximately 1½ inches below the center of the armpit when the arm is raised.

Problem 18

ARMSCYE AND WAISTLINE PUSH UPWARD UNDER THE ARM AFTER WAISTLINE HAS BEEN FITTED IN AT SIDE SEAMS (see Figure 25b)

The line which formerly fell at the normal armhole depth now rises above it at the armpit, and the waist-

212

FITTING

line marked on the garment rises above the true waistline at the underarm seam. The armscye circumference does not change, but the length which previously hung down under the armpit now hangs away from the body at the lower curve of the armhole.

To correct this on the figure, mark in a new lower armscye to give the normal armhole depth and let out the front and back waistline at the side seam to lower the waistline on the side of the blouse. Sharpening the slant on the side seam, of course, causes the lower armscye curve to hang away from the body, and if this is undesirably exaggerated, revise the lines of the blouse to fit the smaller waistline by taking up larger darts.

To correct the size of the waistline by the blocking method, pin the excess at the side of the waistline into a vertical dart tapering to nothing at the point where the armscye begins to curve under the arm (see Figure 26a). Then lap out the dart width in the pattern (see Figure 26b). This method will retain the original armscye depth and waistline. The crosswise grain will follow the scye line of the body to the point where the excess is darted out, but will rise from there toward the side seam.

Problem 19

GAP ON FRONT OR BACK ARMSCYE BECAUSE FRONT AND BACK SEAMS TAKEN IN UNEQUALLY

Figure 25c shows what happens when the front seam is taken in at the waistline and the same crossmarkings are still matched. The greater slope on the front edge of the seam causes the front armscye and waistline to rise, and pushes a pouch out on the back armscye.

Figure 25d shows what happens when the back seam is taken in at the waistline and the original crossmarkings are still matched. The greater slope on the back seam edges forces the back armscye and the waistline to rise and pushes a pouch into the front armscye.

Figures 25e and f show that if the more sloping side is lifted above the original crossmarking, it then is the side that gaps at the armscye.

The faults are exaggerated in the illustrations to point out that even the smallest shifting of the crosswise grain or sloping of the underarm seams has an important influence on the balance of the blouse.

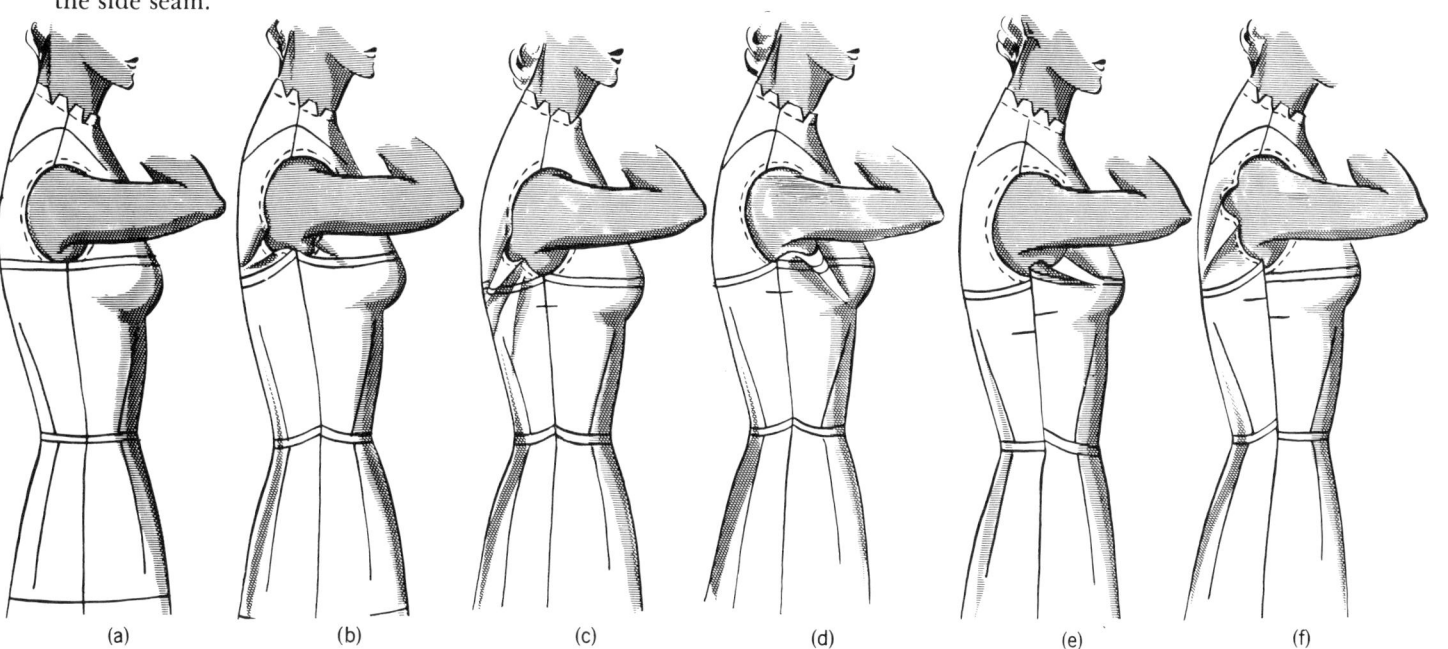

Fig. 25 (a). Front and back underarm seam correctly balanced. (b). Waistline fitted in at the side seam. (c). Front underarm seam taken in at waistline — crossmarking matched. (d). Back underarm seam taken in at waistline — crossmarking matched. (e). Front underarm seam taken in at waistline and crosswise grain lifted. (f). Back underarm seam taken in at waistline and crosswise grain lifted.

DRESS DESIGN

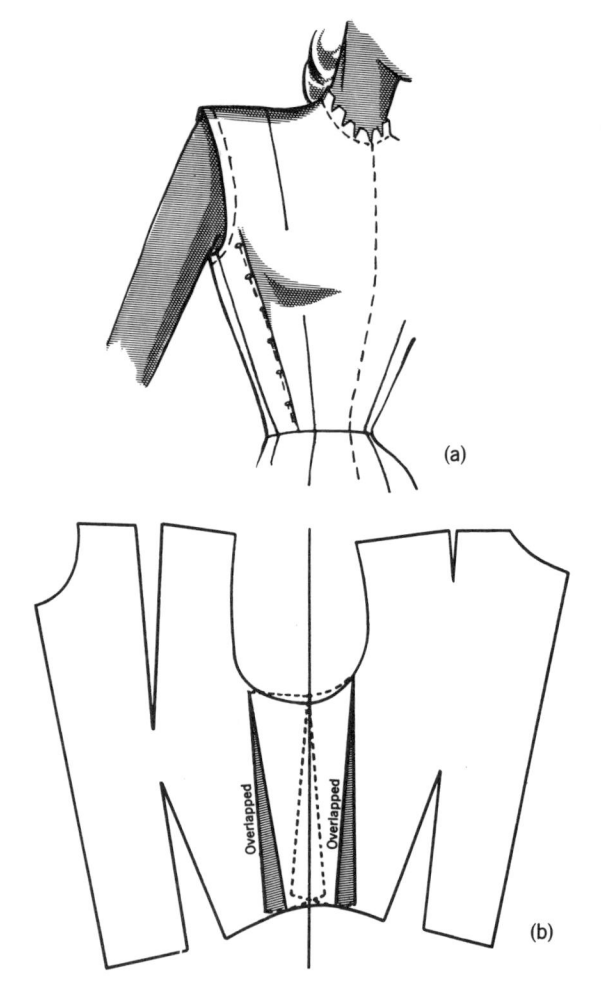

Fig. 26 (a). Excess at waistline pinned into a vertical dart tapering off at armscye.

Fig. 26 (b). Proper method of altering the underarm width of the blouse, by overlapping the side front and side back. Dotted line shows why altering the side seam causes the armscye and waistline to push upward.

ALTERATION OF THE UNDERARM SEAM

Since the underarm seam, like the shoulder seam, controls the balance of the front and back scye lines, the fitter must be able to see the "set" of the front and back of the armhole as she pins the seam lines. She will usually find it more convenient to sit rather than to stand to do this. The armhole, both in back and in front, should hang free and slightly away from the body but not enough to produce pouching. When the dress is viewed from the side, there must be consistency in the amount of looseness on the front and back armscye — that is, in the shape of the armhole as it hangs away from the body. If the side seam is to balance correctly, the person being fitted should raise her arm no more than necessary for the fitter to see the armscye end of the seam. The model must hold her arm at a right angle to the side of her body (that is, pointing neither back nor front, but straight out) in order to avoid uneven strain on the back and front scye lines. The fitter should determine the front line first, and should not attempt to establish both back and front lines at the same time. The model should hold the center front line of the blouse in position at the waistline. If it is necessary to correct this seam, smooth the fabric along the waist over to the side seam line and pin to the foundation garment to anchor the position of the cloth after lifting or lowering the crosswise grain at the waistline enough to keep the scye line of the blouse level. Observe the fit around the armhole. Then establish a straight seam line from the lower point of the armscye to the point pinned at the waist, and turn under the raw edge, pinning at a right angle to the edge as in draping. Repeat this procedure to establish the back seam line. Lap the front over the back, pinning at the armscye and the waistline. Check the balance at the scye line, and check the shape of the armhole in back and front. Then pin between these two points from armscye to waist.

Problem 20

SAGGING OF THE UNDERARM SEAM

Figures 27a and b show an underarm seam that sags into wrinkles below the armscye. When the seam sags in this manner, the blouse is probably too loose under the arm and there is almost certainly too little darting for the bust in front or for the shoulder blades in back. The pouch due to insufficient darting normally shows up in the armhole but may drop down below the armpit into diagonal wrinkles if the blouse is loose under the arm. Although the fault is purposely exaggerated in Figures 27a and b, it may frequently be overlooked unless the fitter checks the underarm seam from the side view with the model's arm slightly lifted. Study the crosswise grain at the scye line to determine whether the excess should be

214

FITTING

pushed up into the shoulder dart or down into the waistline dart and also to see whether both back and front have too little darting or whether the fault exists only in the blouse back or in the blouse front.

To correct the error, push the excess into the armscye and then transfer it to the shoulder or waistline dart according to the procedures given under fitting problems in the Armscye Area, Problems 13, 14, and 15, pages 208-211. If the sagging occurs on the front only, before making the above corrections, raise the crosswise grain of the front seam above that on the back. If the sagging occurs on the back, reverse the procedure.

FITTING PROBLEMS AT THE BUST LINE AND SHOULDER BLADES

Problem 21

BULGE IN BLOUSE FRONT BETWEEN SHOULDER AND WAISTLINE DARTS CAUSED BY OVER-DARTING

Figure 28a shows darts too large to fit the small bust smoothly. with the result that there is puffiness between the points of the shoulder dart and the waistline dart. The center front of the blouse also puffs out, because it is too long between the base of the neck and the waistline. (Overdarting sometimes shows up simply in excessive center front length.)

To subtract the excess length and width which bulges out from the bust line, make the darts smaller. To do this, follow the procedure outlined below.

1. Pin the excess width into a tuck from the point of the shoulder dart to the point of the waistline dart.

2. Pin the excess length into a horizontal tuck from the center front to the bust point, meeting the vertical tuck between the two darts (see Figure 28a).

3. After removing the blouse, pencil along each side of the pinned tucks and crossmark them.

4. Following Figure 28b, trace the blouse pattern on paper and draw lines from both sides of the horizontal tuck at the bust point to a point along the armscye where it begins to curve under the arm.

5. Slash the pattern along the inner edge of the shoulder dart.

Fig. 27 (a) and (b). Insufficient darting causes sagging at the underarm seam if the blouse fits loosely.

DRESS DESIGN

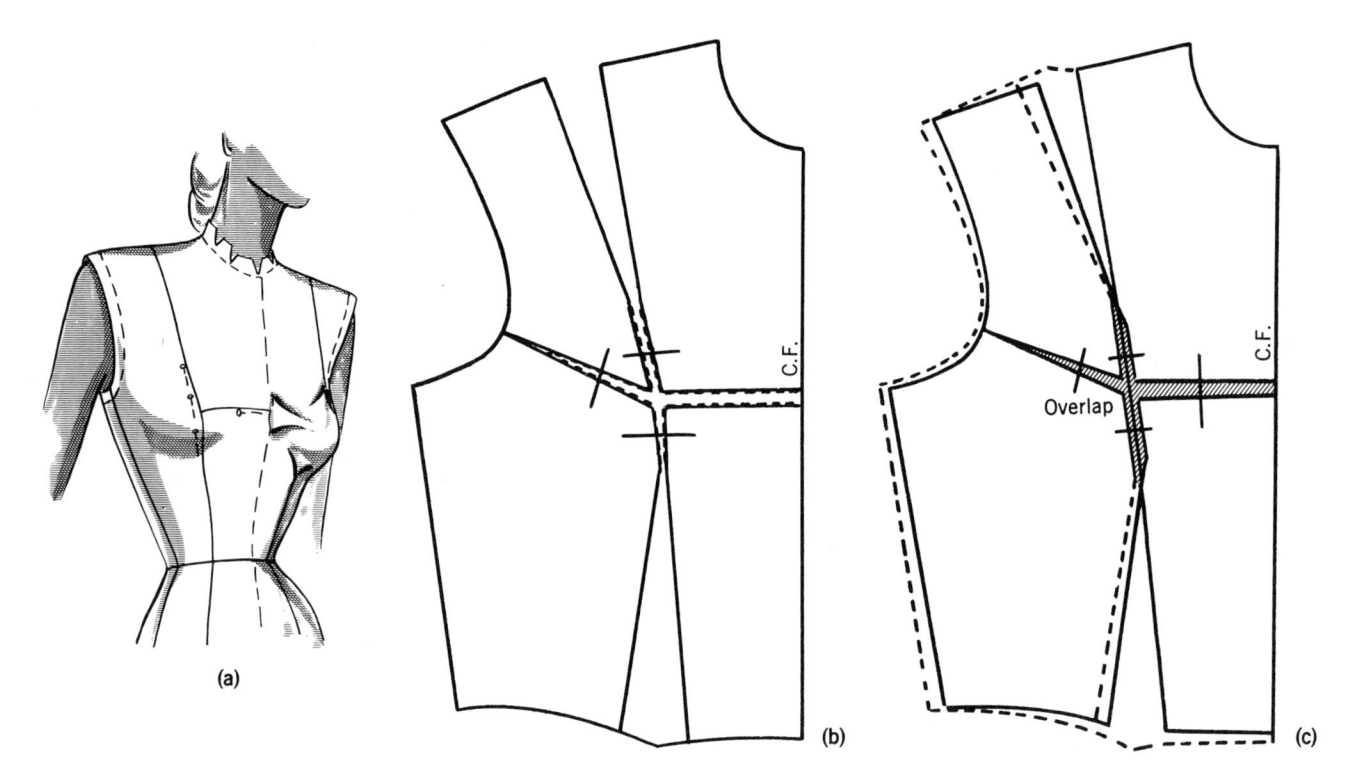

Fig. 28 (a). Overdarting produces a bulge between shoulder and waistline darts — Excess should be pinned into vertical and horizontal tucks. (b). Correction tuck lines marked to indicate excess in length and width. (c). Overlapping of the correction lines eliminates bulge by reducing the size of the shoulder and waistline darts. Dotted line shows pattern before revision.

6. Slash along the upper edge of the horizontal tuck from the bust point to the armscye and to the center front.

7. Lap the two sections to shorten the pattern.

8. Lap out the excess width and match the cross-markings (see Figure 28c).

9. Close the dart from the bust point to the armscye. With the partial closing of the shoulder and waistline darts, the curve of the armscye is now also less intense.

Problem 22

BULGE IN BLOUSE BACK AT END OF WAISTLINE DART CAUSED BY OVERDARTING

The left side of Figure 29a indicates the effect of overdarting at the waistline and thus giving more ease over the shoulder blades than is needed. The center back of the blouse is also too long between the neck and the waistline. The right side of the figure shows the bulge pinned out on a line tapering from the end of the waistline dart to the armscye. Figure 29b shows how to mark the excess on the pattern and lap it out to reduce the waistline dart to the correct size. When the dart is made smaller, the bulge at the shoulder blade drops down into excess length at the waistline. Re-mark the waistline from the center back to the inner edge of the waistline dart so that it corresponds to the length lapped out of the outer edge of the dart.

Figure 29c shows how to lap out a bulge along a line pointing to the juncture of the neck and shoulder seam lines. This bulge occurs whenever the crosswise grain begins to drop from a point as high as the neckline end of the shoulder seam. Follow the same procedure for correcting this as for correcting a bulge pointing toward the armscye.

216

FITTING

Fig. 29 (a). Bulge at shoulder blades caused by making waistline darts too large — Excess at armscye should be pinned into a dart.

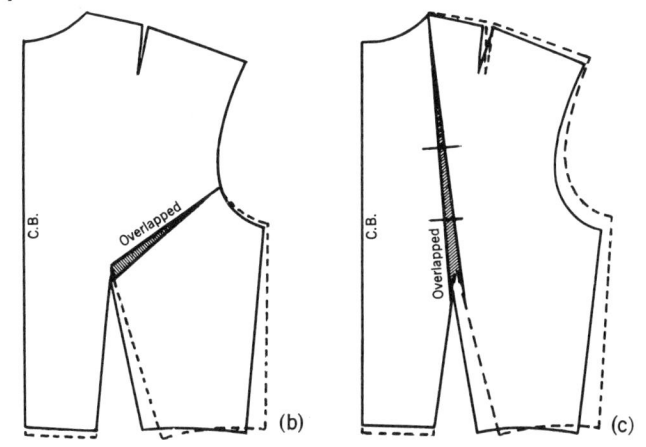

Fig. 29 (b) and (c). Excess overlapped in blouse back pattern to eliminate bulging above dart and too much length at the center back.

Problem 23

TIGHTNESS OVER BUST AND SHOULDER BLADES BECAUSE OF TOO LITTLE DARTING

To correct the fit of a blouse which pulls too tightly over the bust and shoulder blades, increase the size of the darts in order to retain the ease at the front and back where it is needed. Letting out the side seams simply increases the width of the blouse under the arm, since it does not revise the pattern shape in such a way as to direct the ease to the curve of the bust and shoulder. Darts pointing toward a body curve hold both extra width and length over that part of the figure.

To increase the size of the darts follow the directions

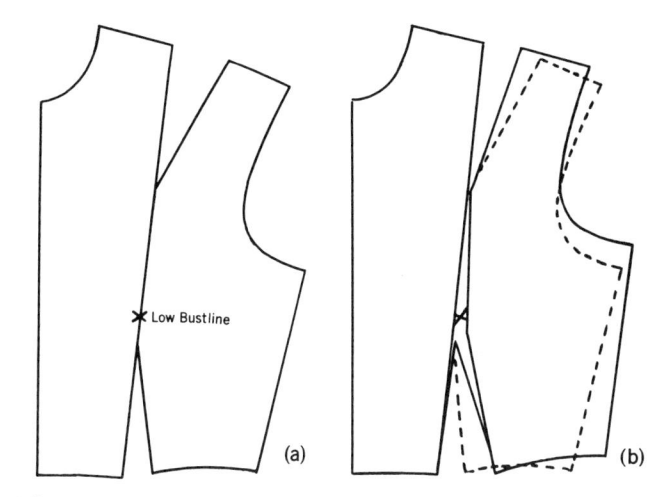

Fig. 30. Altering blouse front to fit a lower bust line. (a) Bust point marked; (b) Blouse front slashed and spread from waistline to point of shoulder dart.

given in Problems 21 and 22, pages 215-217 and refer to Figures 28a and b and 29a and b. But the pattern should be spread to introduce ease rather than lapped to take it out. On the back of the blouse, you may wish to extend the slash to the neckline in order to establish a neckline dart, and through the center of the shoulder in order to increase the shoulder ease.

Problem 24

BUST LINE OF GARMENT PLACED TOO HIGH

When this fault appears in fitting a commercial pattern, it may be due to an unusually low bust line in the model. If it shows up in a pattern draped on a personal dress form, the bust padding may have been placed too high, or the model may have worn a different style of brassiere when the dress form cover was fitted from that worn while fitting the master pattern. See Figures 30a and b for lowering the bust line.

1. Mark on the blouse the point of the bust and determine how much more width is needed for comfortable ease along the actual bust line.

2. Make a paper copy of the blouse front and slash it from the waistline dart to the point of the shoulder dart (see Figure 30b).

3. Open the waistline dart to spread it at the point of the bust. This will partially close the shoulder dart. Re-mark the darts.

217

DRESS DESIGN

Problem 25

BUST LINE OF GARMENT PLACED TOO LOW

Study Figures 31a and b, and follow the procedure given in Problem 24.

Use this same method to correct curves placed too high or too low for shoulder blades.

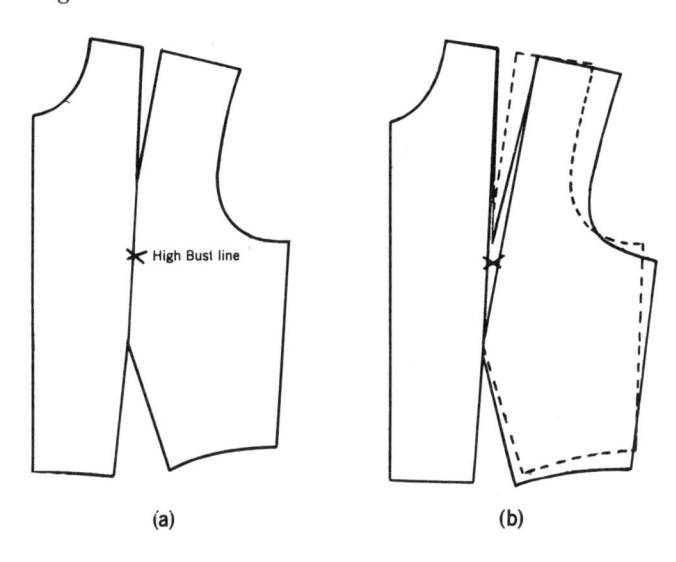

Fig. 31. Altering blouse front to fit a higher bust line. (a) Bust point marked; (b) Blouse front slashed and spread from shoulder seam to point of waistline dart.

The Importance of Marking the Point of Bust and Shoulder Blade on the Master Pattern

It is necessary to know the exact point of the body curve in order to keep the pattern constant in width across the broadest part of the bust or the most rounded part of the shoulder blades when darts are transferred from one position to another. Figures 32a and 33a show two patterns of the same size, but on one the waistline dart is marked for a high bust point, and on the other, for a low bust point. Notice the difference in pattern shape when the waistline dart is transferred to a shoulder dart. (See Figures 32b and 33b.) Had the point of the bust been marked too high for the low bust line, the width at the low bust line would then be inadequate when the darting was transferred to the shoulder. It is not accurate simply to assume that the top point of a stitched dart is the true point of the body curve as the stitching may not have been continued all the way to the point. But when darts are to be transferred from one position to another, the width of the pattern must remain constant across the broadest part of the body curve, and therefore, the dart for this purpose should be continued up to the point of the curve so that the pattern is pivoted from that point.

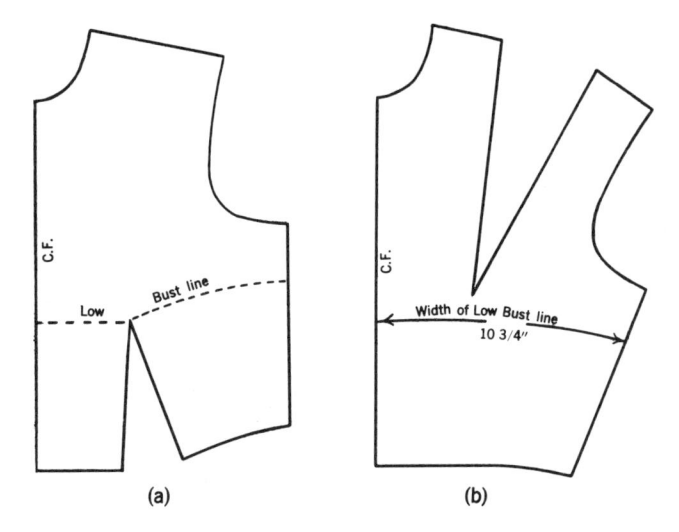

Fig. 32 (a) and (b). Dart for a low bust point transferred to shoulder.

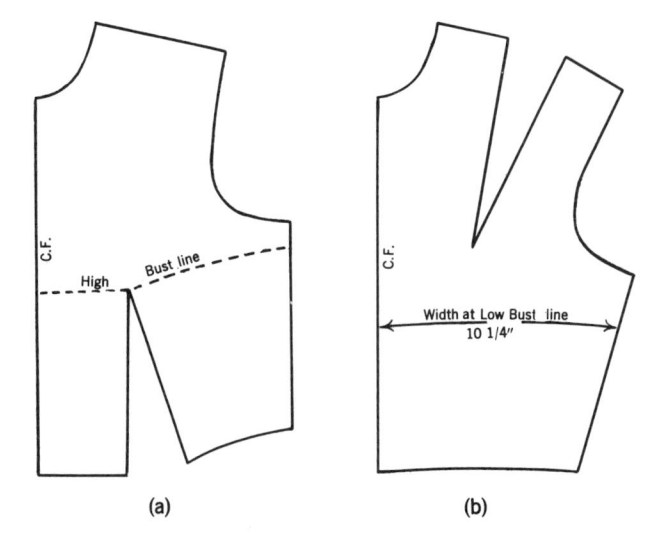

Fig. 33 (a) and (b). Dart for a high bust point transferred to shoulder.

218

FITTING

PART IV
FITTING PROBLEMS OF THE SKIRT

The fitting problems of skirts are generally less complicated than those of blouses. But because the skirt has fewer supported edges, since the entire area below the hips swings free, the slightest fault in the balance of grain is at once made obvious by the way the skirt hangs. Postures which differ from a normal position frequently require alteration of the skirt pattern (see pages 194-195 and Figures 2c, d, e, and f). Bony structure and weight distribution must also be considered as factors in fitting, since they too can change the "hang" of a skirt. Keep in mind that the outward curves of the body lift the crosswise grain, and therefore a skirt tends to jut out below these curves unless there are darts or ease to hold in enough length and width to fit satisfactorily at these points.

The key to the fitting of skirts is found in observing the grain of the fabric and in knowing when the crosswise grain should be lifted and when dropped. This explains why learning to drape skirts also prepares you to fit skirts. Review the discussion of the hip level as the balance line for skirt fitting (pages 194-195).

Problem 1

SKIRT STANDS OUT AT CENTER FRONT

This may occur for either of several reasons. The figure may lean back from hips to shoulders, or the abdomen may be large and protuberant.

(a) Reason: The figure leans back from hips to shoulders.

Figure 34a shows a skirt which stands out at center front and clings against the calf of the leg in back because the figure leans back from the hips to the shoulders. At the hip level, the crosswise grain drops at the center back and rises at the side seams. The waistline rises at the center front and drops at the center back, and this pitches the side seams forward from waist to hem. The skirt is large enough, but appears to be tight across the back of the hips, and it cups in below this point. The *hang* of the skirt, not its *size*, needs adjustment.

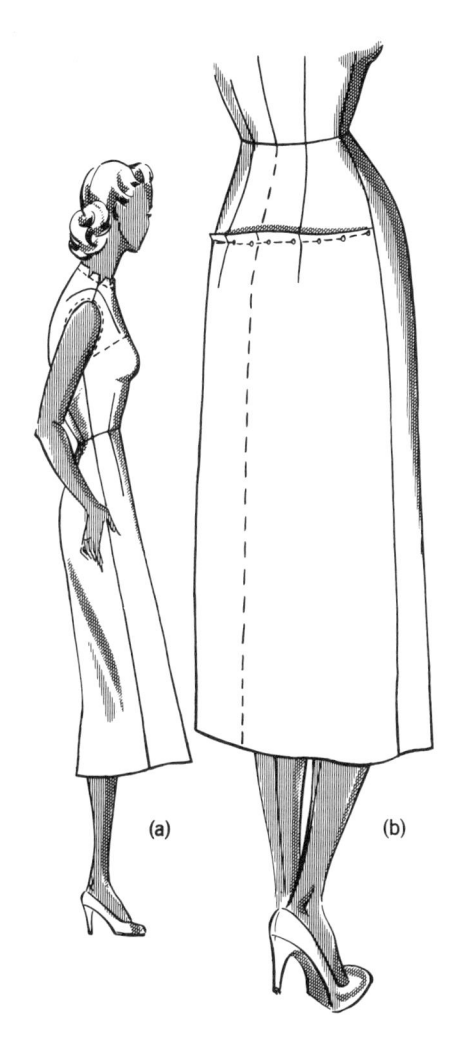

Fig. 34 (a) and (b). Skirt alteration for figure which leans back from hips to shoulders.

Raise the center back by pinning a tuck just below the waistline, tapering it from the center back to the side seam (see Figure 34b). If lifting the center back fails to correct the side seam, lower the center front a little at the waistline. Then remove the skirt, pencil each side of the correction dart, and trace a paper copy of the corrected part. Lap out the horizontal dart and lay the pattern again on the muslin skirt to

219

DRESS DESIGN

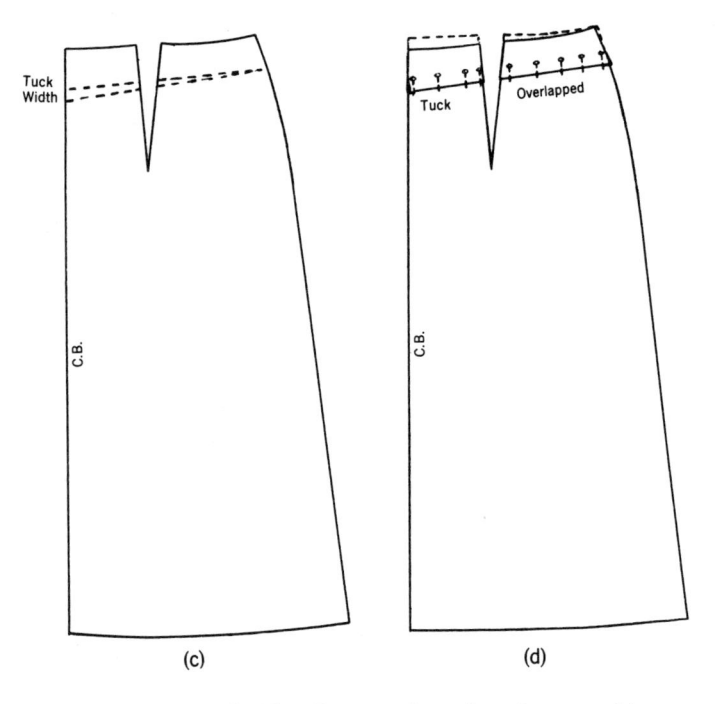

Fig. 34 (c) and (d). Pattern alteration shortens skirt at center back between hip level and waistline.

re-mark the waistline and the upper part of the side seam line. To make the adjustment on the person, raise the waistline across the back and readjust it at the side seam. (See Figures 34c and d for change in pattern shape.)

(b) Reason: A large abdomen.

Figure 35a shows a skirt which stands out at the center front because of a prominent abdomen, which lifts the crosswise grain at the center front on the hip level, thereby shortening and swinging out the entire center front line of the skirt from hip to hem. The large abdomen requires extra length from the center front of the hip level up to the center front of the waist, together with additional width across the largest part of the curve so that the skirt front from hip level to hem can hang in a plumb line.

Figure 35b shows a slash through the center of the waistline dart to the hemline, and another along the hip level from the center front to the side seam. These slashes increase the width around the abdomen and the length at the center front.

To alter this skirt on a person, redrape as follows:

1. Rip the side seam. If the skirt is tight, the wrinkles held above the curve of the abdomen will drop down at the center front.

2. Adjust the crosswise grain from the center front to the side seam at or slightly above the hip level, so that the center front of the skirt hangs perpendicularly.

3. Anchor the skirt securely to a foundation garment at the hip level and re-pin the side seam from hip to hem.

4. Then pin it from hip to waist, pushing any excess length along the front seam up to the waistline and over from the side seam into the front dart.

Note. Maternity skirts to be worn with long loose jackets are cut out over the rounded abdomen to avoid pulling the center front lines of the skirt so far forward and to allow them to hang perpendicularly.

Fig. 35 (a). Large abdomen lifts crosswise grain at center front.
Fig. 35 (b). Pattern alteration widens and lengthens skirt between hip level and waistline.

FITTING

Problem 2

CUPPING UNDER THE HIPS IN BACK
(see Figure 36a)

(a) *Reason:* The crosswise grain has not been lowered enough from the dart at the side back toward the side seam.

In the two-gore master pattern skirt, the crosswise grain at the back hip level should drop toward the side seam slightly in order to provide some flare at the hem. If the crosswise threads along the hip level are not dropped as they approach the side seam, the lengthwise threads at the center back, which should hang perpendicularly to the floor, will cling against the legs. Correct the hang of the skirt by slashing from the lower point of the dart through the hem and transferring part of the dart to width at the hem. This overcomes the cupping if the skirt is not too narrow at the hip level (see Figure 36b). The hip level line remains constant and the spread begins below it.

(b) *Reason:* The skirt is tight across hips which are prominent in back rather than wide from side to side.

If the hips curve out more at the back than at the side, introduce width at the back rather than at the side seam line. This may be done by either of two methods: (1) Slash from the hem to a point on the waistline just outside the dart, and spread the skirt from waistline to hem. Or, (2) slash through the waistline dart and continue through the hem in order to spread the center and side sections apart as much as is needed at the hip level (see Figures 36c and d).

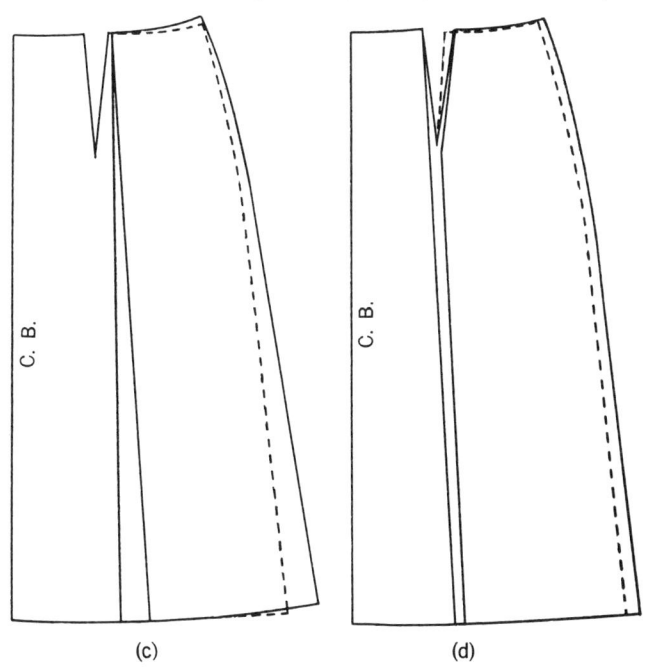

Fig. 36 (c). Skirt slashed and spread from hem to waist for hips prominent in back.
Fig. 36 (d). Skirt slashed and spread from hem through dart for hips prominent in back.

Both methods introduce ease at the back where it is needed. Also see Figure 35b for still another treatment, which introduces length and width over the body curve by combining a vertical slash with a horizontal one at the hip level.

Since the dart at the waistline may be made deeper in two ways producing quite different results, let us examine both methods. First, to *retain the same size at the hip level,* pivot the dart from its lower point and

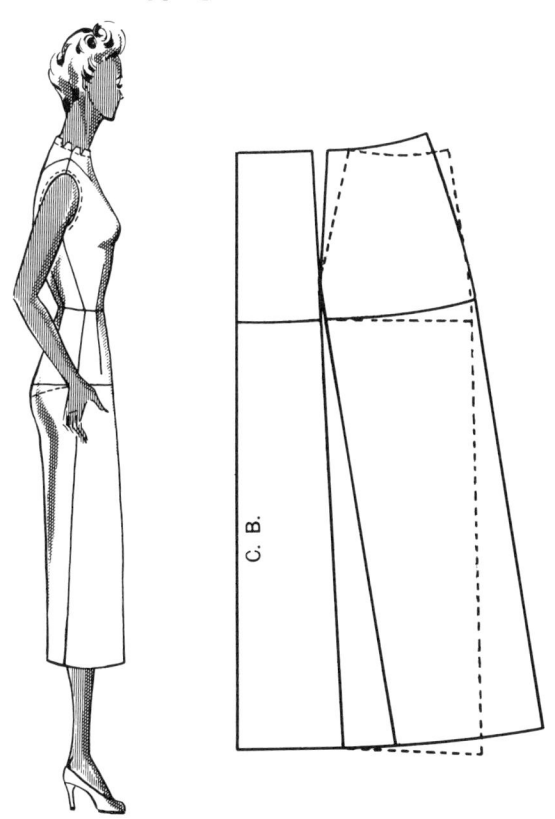

Fig. 36 (a). Skirt cups under hips in back.
Fig. 36 (b). Part of waistline dart transferred to skirt width below hip level.

DRESS DESIGN

lap out the flare at the hem line, transferring it to a larger dart at the waist. The dotted lines in Figure 36*b* show the relationship between the size of the dart and the width of the lower edge of the skirt. Second, to *increase the size at the hip level* when the added width is needed at the end of the dart (rather than at the side), slash the skirt apart from the waistline end of the dart to or through the hem and spread the dart at both ends (see Figure 36*d*).

(*c*) *Reason:* The skirt is tight across the hips, which are broad and have a definite curve on the side between waistline and hip line.

To alter for this figure, add the necessary width to the side seam itself (see Figure 36*e*). It should be remembered, however, that the two-gore is unflattering to this figure, since it does not flare from back to front at all and such flare is needed to counterbalance the flatness from front to back and the width from side to side. This type of skirt should therefore be avoided by persons with figures of this sort.

Note. A slight cupping under at the back may be corrected by raising the waistline at the center back as shown in Problem 1, but not if the skirt is noticeably tight across the hips.

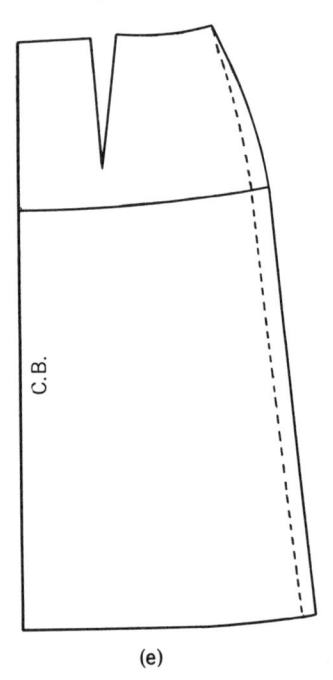

Fig. 36 (*e*). Width added to skirt at side seams for hips wide from side to side.

Problem 3

SKIRT WHICH STANDS OUT AT CENTER BACK WITH SIDE SEAMS SWINGING TO THE BACK FROM WAISTLINE TO HEM (see Figure 37a)

On a sway-backed figure the hips rise at the back, and this raises the center back of the skirt so that it juts out and pulls the side seams toward the back from waist to hem. The length from the waistline to the hip level at the center back is shorter than normal, so that a skirt which fits snugly from the waist to the hips often wrinkles horizontally just below the waistline, since the hip level of the skirt cannot slip below the hip level of the figure. The horizontal wrinkles

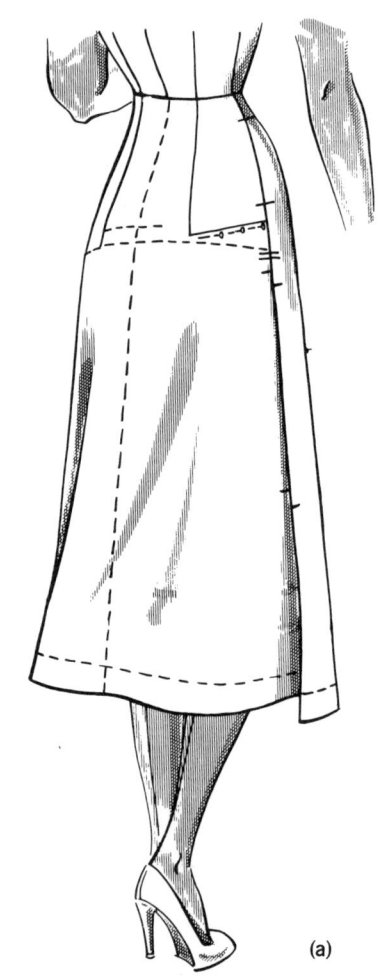

Fig. 37 (*a*). Sway-backed figure causes skirt to swing out at center back.

FITTING

between the hipline and the waistline can be removed by hollowing out the waistline at the center back or by letting out the side seam between waist and hip until the skirt is loose enough to drop lower on the figure. If the sway-back is pronounced however, the center back and the side seam lines will still not hang perpendicularly, and it will be necessary to raise the crosswise grain along the hip level from the center back to the sides.

To make this correction on the person, follow the procedure outlined below.

(a) For a skirt with the correct hip level size:

1. Open the side seam and raise the back edge above the front until the center back falls perpendicularly.

2. Re-pin the back to the front at the hip level in order to retain the corrected balance between back and front, and anchor the skirt securely to the foundation garment.

3. Pin the side seam from hip to hem.

4. Pin the seam from hip to waist, letting out the seam allowance on the back as you smooth the excess upwards.

5. Rip the back waistline seam as far as the dart in order to take up the amount which has been let out on the side seam into a deeper dart.

To reduce the fitting time, open the side seam from the hem up to the hip level. Lift the grain on the back edge of the side seam and take up the excess length into a horizontal dart that tapers to the end of the basic waistline dart. Re-mark the back hemline. Remove the skirt and make a paper pattern copy from hip to waist, tracing in the lines of the pinned horizontal dart. Lap out the horizontal dart which spreads the waistline dart and thereby revises the side section of the waistline seam, the waist dart, and the upper part of the side seam (see Figure 37b).

(b) For a skirt too narrow across the hip level:

Add more width to the hip level by letting out the back edge of the side seam as well as by raising the crosswise grain from the center back to the side seams. Follow the other directions as given for (a), and see Figure 37c for the pattern change.

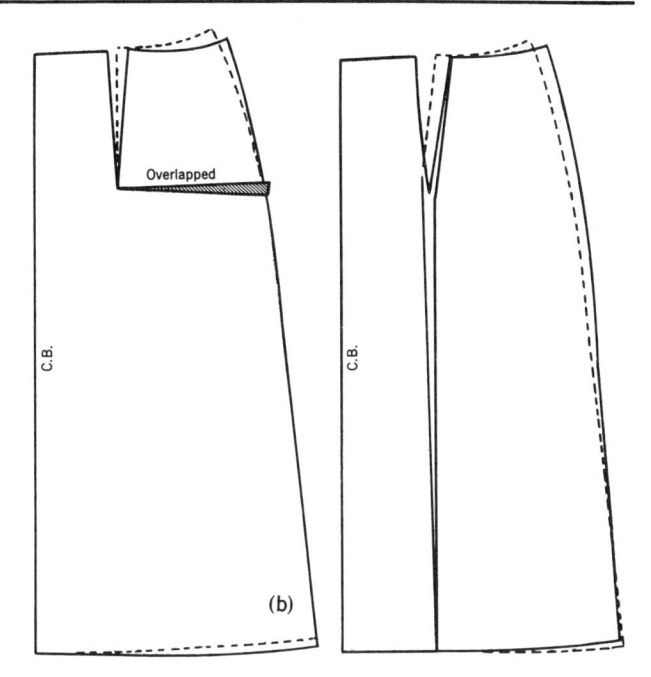

Fig. 37 (b). Alteration for skirt that swings out at back hem line, with side seams that swing to the back.

Fig. 37 (c). Alteration to widen hipline and to correct backward swing of skirt.

Problem 4

SKIRT WHICH CUPS UNDER THE ABDOMEN
(see Figure 38a)

(a) *Reason:* The crosswise grain has not been lowered enough at the hip level from the center front to the side seam. (This corresponds to the fault in the skirt back discussed in Problem 2a, page 221.)

Because the crosswise grain is not lowered enough at the front side seam, the lower skirt width is transferred up above the hip level, where it is taken up into too large a waistline dart. The skirt has the appearance of being smaller below the hips than above them. To refit this on the person, rip the side seam, the waistline from the side seam to the dart, and the waistline dart. Drop the crosswise grain at the front side seam until the center front hangs perpendicular to the floor. Anchor the front and back at the hip level. Pin the side seam from hip to hem, letting out the front seam allowance to give ease below the hip level. Make a new smaller dart at the waistline. Re-pin the side seam from hip to waist, taking in a larger front seam allowance. Re-mark the waistline from the dart to the side seam.

DRESS DESIGN

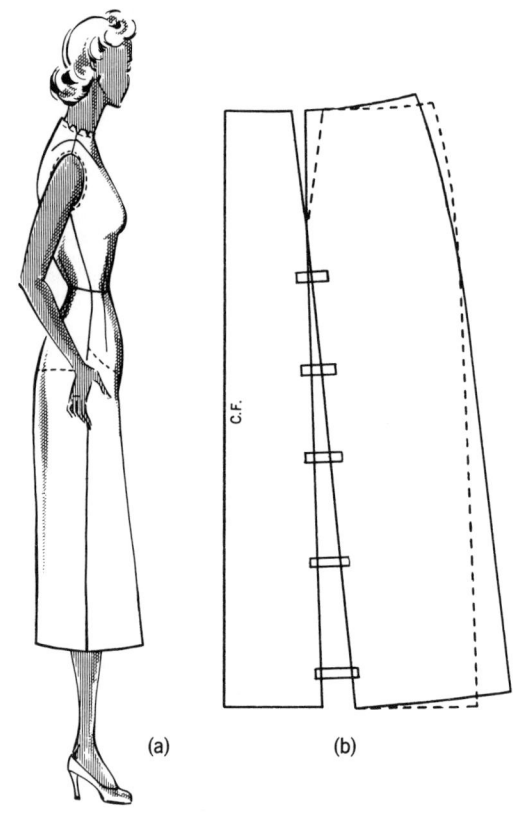

Fig. 38 (a). Skirt cups under abdomen.
Fig. 38 (b). Part of dart transferred into wider skirt from hip to hem.

To make this correction more simply, slash from the hem to the lower point of the dart while the skirt is on the person, and spread the lower section until the center front hangs perpendicular to the floor. Control the amount of the spread by inserting muslin strips or gummed tape. When the pattern for the skirt front is laid flat, the spread lower section partially closes the waistline dart (see Figure 38b).

(b) *Reason:* Hips prominent at the back.

This corresponds to the cause given for the fitting fault in the skirt back discussed in Problem 3. The ease and flare which should fall below the hip level at the front is drawn to the back, and the backward swing of the side seams indicates to what extent this has happened. The skirt front is the correct size, but the drawing back of the side seams pulls the fabric tight under the abdomen and over the thighs (see Figures 37b and c).

To correct this fault, lift the crosswise grain at the center front on the hip level until the center front and the side seams are perpendicular to the floor. Then slip the excess up out of the center front by deepening the curve at the waistline.

Note. This simple alteration corrects the fault if it is not too exaggerated; otherwise it must be corrected according to the procedures given in Problem 3.

Problem 5

SKIRT FLAT IN FRONT AND BACK WITH TOO MUCH OUTWARD SWING AT SIDES
(see Figures 39a and b)

(a) *Reason:* The side seams slant out too much from hip to hem.

If the side seam slants out too much, the skirt swings out at the sides. Alter the pattern for a straight silhouette by reducing the slope from hip to hem until the side seam forms a line perpendicular to the floor. After making this alteration, increase the hem circumference if necessary by slashing from the hem to the darts at the front and back and transferring some of the dart to the hem width. For an example of this alteration, see Figure 38b.

(b) *Reason:* The waistline of the skirt is too loose.

When the waistline does not fit, it drops lower at the center front and back than at the sides, where it is supported by the hip bones. The crosswise grain at the hip level drops toward the center and rises toward the side seams, swinging the flare away from the center out toward the sides. This fault may be corrected by taking up deeper darts or by taking in the side seams at the waistline in order to tighten it.

(c) *Reason:* A figure with a pronounced, high curve on the side of the hip.

Figures 39a and b show a decided curve on the side of the hip, beginning just below the waistline, and lifting the side seam so that the crosswise grain does not drop enough from the center to the side. This throws the flare from the center of the skirt to the side of the figure. To correct this broad silhouette, lower the crosswise grain at the side seam to allow the flare to fall at the side front instead of directly on the side. If the outward swing is equal on both the back and front edges of the side seams, rip the waistline seam from the side front to the side back and let it out until the side seam drops perpendicular to the floor. If the skirt fits too snugly, let out the side seam from

224

FITTING

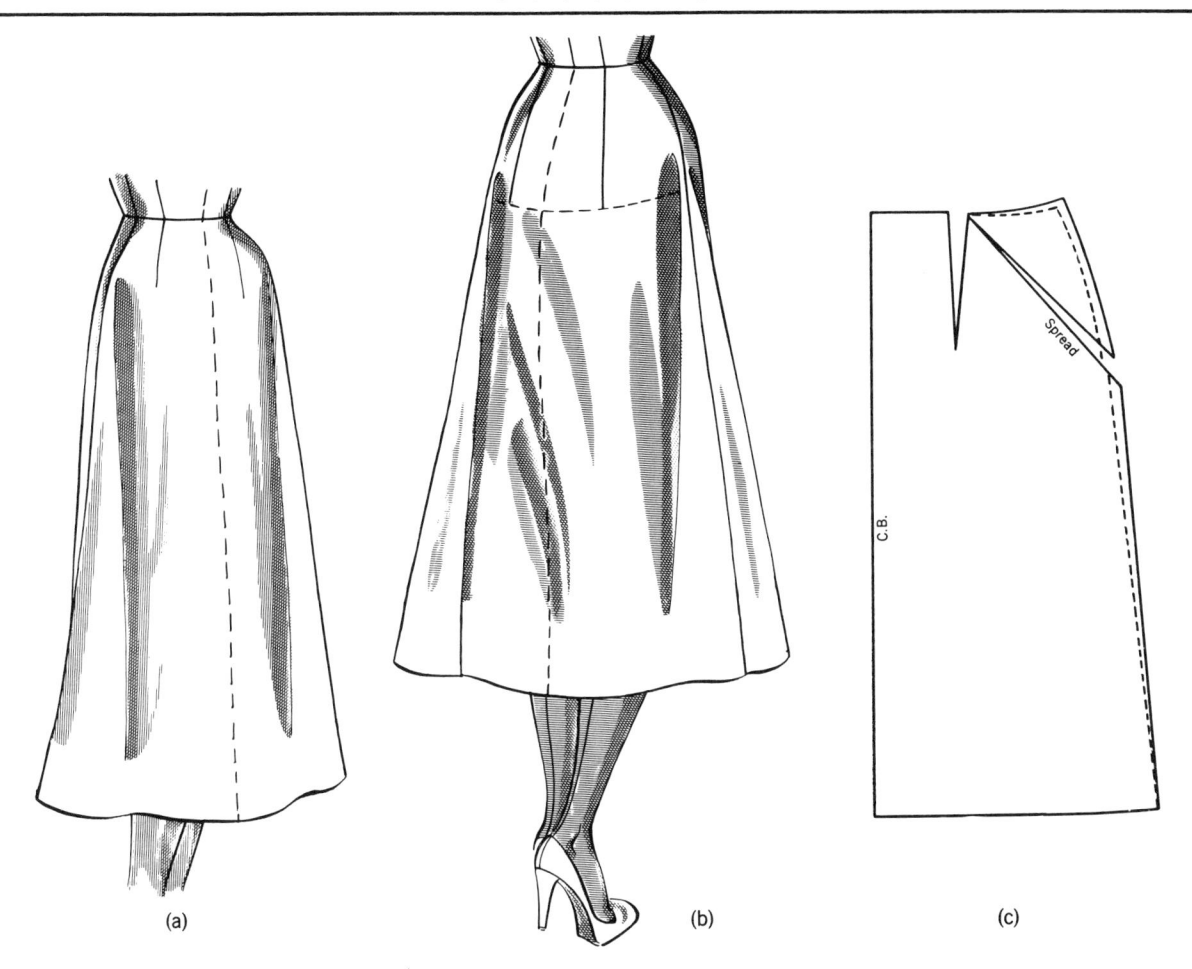

Fig. 39 (*a*) and (*b*). Skirt hangs flat at center front and back and swings out too much at the sides.

Fig. 39 (*c*). Side seams lengthened for a very curved side hip.

just below the hip level up to the waistline. If the waistline seam allowance is too narrow at the sides to let it out, adjust the crosswise grain by raising the waistline at the center front and back.

See Figure 39*c* for the alteration to lengthen the side seam line over a high curve on the side of the hip. Slash from a point on the side seam where the hip curve is most pronounced up to a point on the waistline approximately halfway between the center front and the side seam. Spread the slash at the side seam an amount to equal the extra length required over the curved hip.

(*d*) *Reason:* A figure with unusually prominent front hip bones.

A prominent front hip bone lifts the crosswise grain and lets it drop at the center front. The flare falls below the hip bone rather than on the side seam as in Figure 39*a*, but the silhouette still appears flat at the center front and wide from side to side. To narrow the silhouette, allow ease above or beside the hip bone, or both above and beside it, and place most or all of the front dart above the bone rather than in the usual position close to the center front. To increase the length along the side of the front hip bone, rip the side seam from the waist to the hip level and ease the front seam on to the back seam. See Figure 40 for the pattern alteration. For additional width, let out the front edge of the side seam, tapering it from the waistline to the hem. Pin in the ease at the waistline directly above the hip bone. Re-pin the side seam. On the master pattern, carefully re-crossmark from the front side seam to the back between the hip level and the waist, and mark the exact amount of ease to go into the waistline. When working with wool, shrink in the ease.

225

DRESS DESIGN

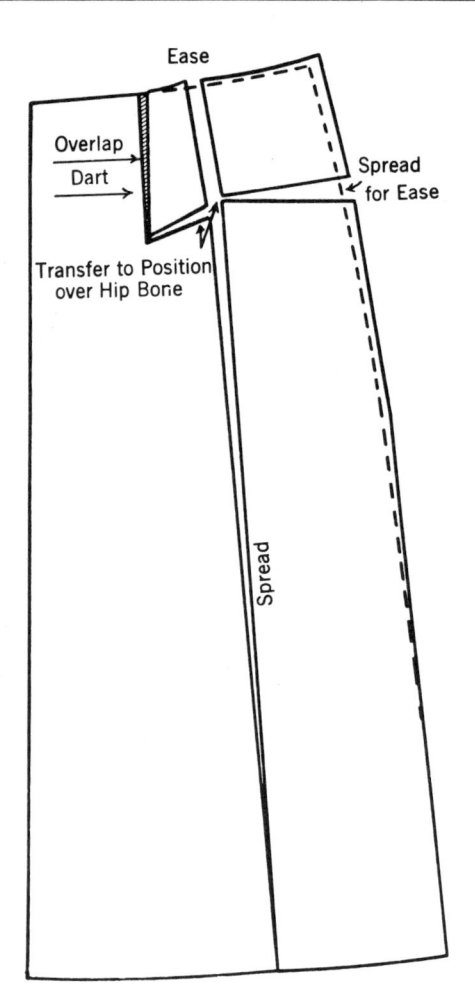

Fig. 40. Pattern alteration to provide increased length and width over hip bone.

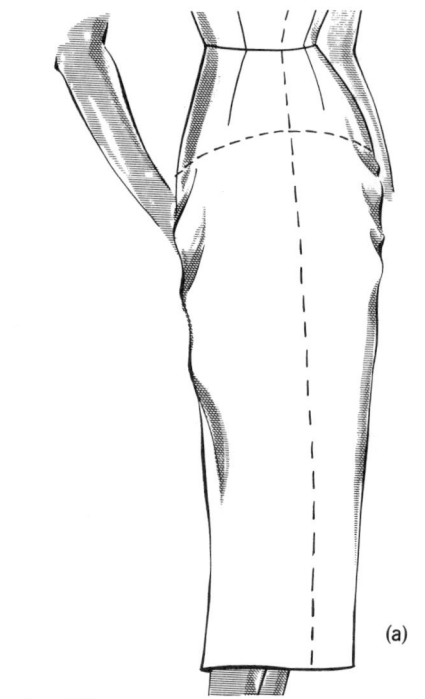

Fig. 41 (*a*). Side seams cup in below the hips, producing diagonal wrinkles.

Problem 6

SKIRT CUPPING BELOW THE HIPS ON THE SIDE SEAM (see Figure 41a)

(a) *Reason:* The side seam of the skirt bows out between the hip and the hem.

Bowing out between the hip and hem on the side seam of a skirt pattern where it should be ruler straight makes the seam line longer than the area directly in front and in back of the seam, and the extra length sags, forming diagonal wrinkles. Figure 41*b* illustrates how the side seam should be ruled straight from hip to hem if the skirt is too loose, and Figure 41*c* illustrates how it should be ruled from a low hipline if the skirt is too tight.

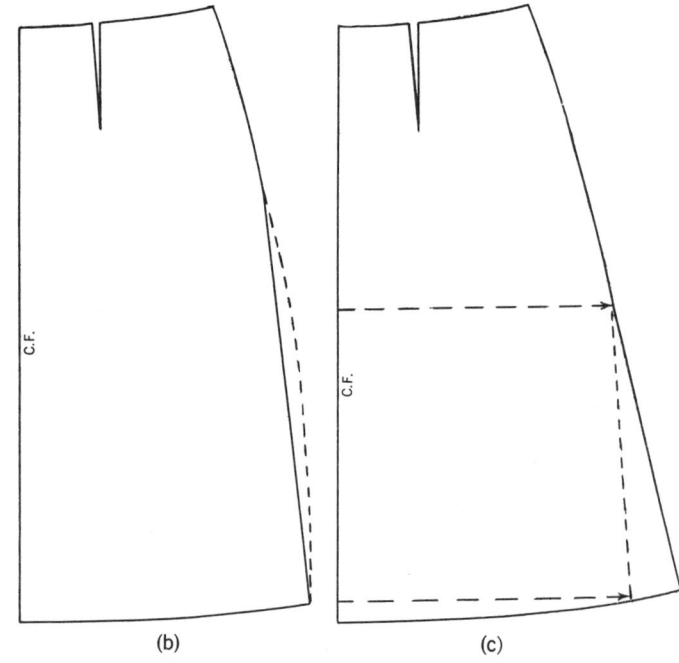

Fig. 41 (*b*). Curved side seam ruled straight from hip to hem, if skirt is too loose.

Fig. 41 (*c*). Curved side seam ruled straight from a low hipline, if skirt is tight over thighs.

226

FITTING

(b) *Reason:* The side seam is too sharply curved from the waist to the hip.

Too much length from waist to hip drops below the hip level into a sagging seam. This happens if a side seam is too sharply curved over the hips to fit the figure. Since the extra length is not held up by a rounded hip line, it drops down below the hip level. A similar difficulty arises if the curved seam from hip to waist is stretched in handling. For this reason, pinning, stitching, and pressing of the curved part of the seam should be done with the utmost care. (See Figures 63 and 64 in Chapter 3 for the method of transferring excess length between hip and waist into the waistline dart.)

Problem 7

FRONT EDGE OF SIDE SEAM CURVED TOWARD THE FRONT AND SAGS INTO DIAGONAL WRINKLES (see Figure 42a)

This occurs when the hip level crossmarking on the front edge of the side seam is dropped below the corresponding marking on the back edge. This happens more often on the front than on the back because the front is usually eased to the back from hip to waistline (see Figure 42b), and if the crossmarking at the hip level is lost or ignored, the extra length which should be retained above the hip level drops below the hips, producing the curved seam line shown in Figure 42a. To correct the direction of the seam line, rip the seam from the hip level to the hem and raise the front crosswise grain from the center front to the side at the hip level until the side seam hangs perpendicularly. Put the excess on the front edge above the hip level into ease, or transfer it to the waistline dart as shown in Figures 63 and 64, Chapter 3.

Problem 8

FRONT SIDE SEAM CURLED TOWARD THE BACK NEAR THE HEMLINE

This occurs when the front edge of the side seam has been eased onto the back. In Figure 43 the front seam was eased to the back near the lower edge of the skirt so that the fabric just in front of the seam is longer than the seam itself, and therefore sags, causing the seam line to curl toward the back. Mark the point where the seam begins to curl. Rip and re-pin this portion of the seam on the person, since the error

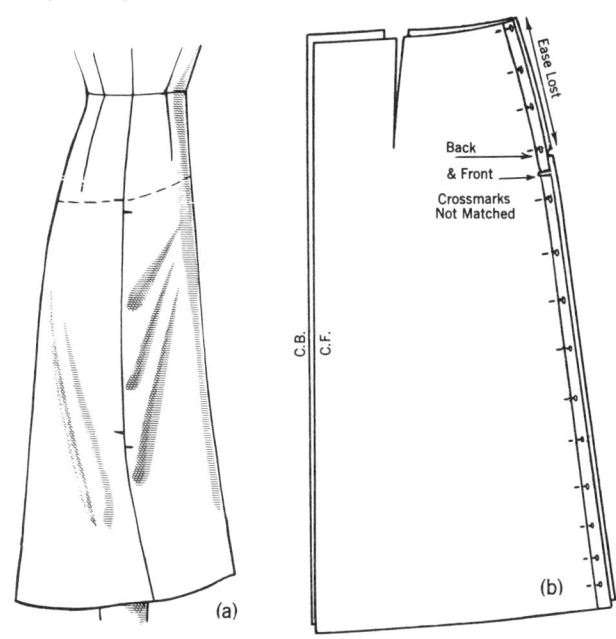

Fig. 42 (*a*) and (*b*). Crossmarkings not matched at hip level — side seam swings forward.

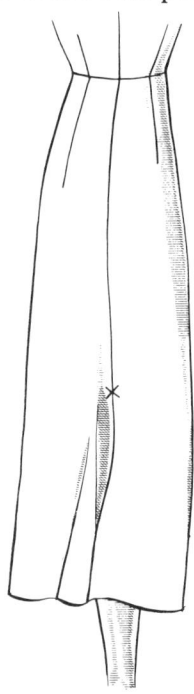

Fig. 43. Front side seams eased to back near lower edge. Seam curls.

227

DRESS DESIGN

is easier to see this way than when the skirt is lying flat on the table. In working with a slippery crepe, however, if the ease starts higher, it will be more accurate simply to indicate the position of the ease and correct by re-pinning and basting with the skirt on the table where seam-line markings on the wrong side can be watched.

Problem 9

THE CENTER FRONT LINE TILTED SIDEWISE
(see Figure 44a)

If the skirt was cut off-grain, or if the model has one hip higher than the other, the skirt is likely to tilt sidewise in this manner. Figure 44b shows that when the crosswise threads fail to match in both the upper and under layers of fabric, the crossgrain tilts diagonally across the figure, causing the center front line of the skirt to swing toward one side. The skirt cannot hang correctly until it is recut with the grain balanced.

To balance the two sides of the skirt for a figure with one hip higher than the other, let out the waistline seam allowance on the side of the higher hip until the crosswise grain at the hip level drops equally on the left and right sides of the skirt center line.

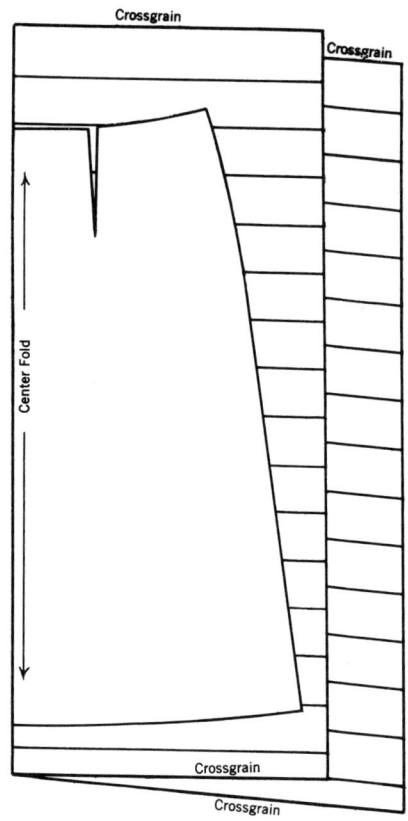

Fig. 44 (b). Crosswise threads must exactly match on left and right sides of center to produce balanced skirt lines.

Problem 10

SKIRT PULLS TIGHT OVER HEAVY THIGHS

A narrow skirt cannot be adapted to a figure with heavy thighs, since the extra width needed on this lower level exceeds the amount needed along the hip line. And when a person sits, the thighs round up on the front of the leg, and take up much more ease than when she stands. If width is merely let into the side seam, the skirt will still be tight over the front of the leg. Instead, a flare must be introduced in front of the side seam. See Figure 45b for the pattern alteration. Slash the skirt front from the hem to the waistline between the waist dart and the side seam so that the added flare will fall over the fullest part of the thigh. When altering during the fitting, drop the crosswise grain at the waistline from the dart to the side seam, and then re-pin the side seam. This not only increases the width but throws flare over the thighs (see Figure 45a).

Fig. 44 (a). Crosswise grain is not balanced on left and right sides of center front. Skirt tilts sidewise.

FITTING

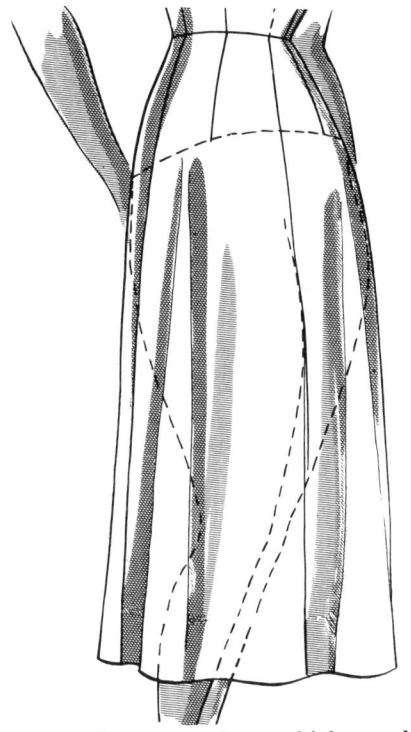

Fig. 45 (*a*). Skirt for figure with heavy thighs needs some flare below hip level.

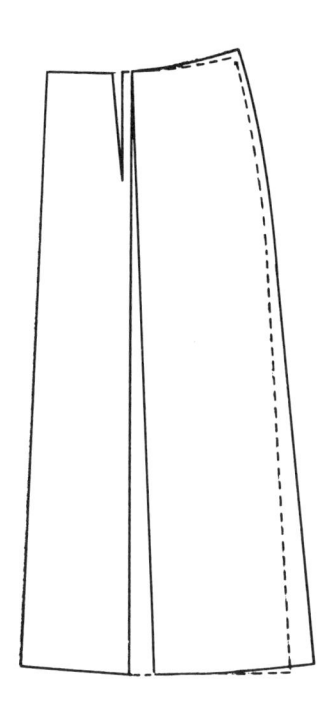

Fig. 45 (*b*). Pattern alteration for a skirt too tight over large thighs.

PART V

FITTING PROBLEMS OF THE SLEEVE

After fitting the master pattern blouse and skirt, pin in the sleeve. If errors previously overlooked show up at this time, postpone pinning in the sleeve until they have all been corrected.

Blouse Armscye Line

Before slipping the arm into the sleeve, re-check the armhole line marked on the blouse. Determine the top point of the armscye at the shoulder seam. By using shoulder pads, it is possible to carry the line of the shoulder seam out beyond the normal shoulder tip to a point which would be intersected by a vertical line carried up from the outside of the upper arm. A very wide shoulder smooths the hollow in front of the arm and above the bust line into a flatter plane. It also conceals the bulge of a fleshy upper arm, gives the effect of flattening wing-like shoulder blades, and makes less noticeable a large bust line. Fashions vary the standard for shoulder width, however, and the lines on the master pattern must be consistent with the prevailing silhouette. The depth of the armscye for a normal set-in sleeve is approximately $1\frac{1}{2}$ inches below the center of the armpit when the arm is extended, which is the same as $\frac{1}{2}$ inch below the armpit when the arm is down. Viewed from above, the armscye line should appear to be a straight continuous line over the top of the shoulder, and viewed from the center front and center back it should look like a straight line almost parallel to the center of the figure as far down as the chest line, where it gradually curves toward the underarm seam. The line from a broad

DRESS DESIGN

shoulder seam to the chest actually slopes in slightly in order to fall at the point where the body and arm meet. The armhole must not fit so closely under the arm, or the seam allowance be so wide at the side where the arm rises, that horizontal wrinkles form when the arm is down. If, in spite of plenty of ease through the scye and bust line, wrinkles form when the arm is down, the armscye seam allowance should be clipped at the point where the underarm curve begins. At the front and back of the armhole there should be a fold of fabric from the chest line down (see page 27), which continues the upper half of the armscye line and hides the underarm curve.

For difficulties involving the blouse armscye, see fitting problems of the Armscye Area, pages 208-212.

Pinning the Sleeve into the Master Pattern

Prepare the sleeve according to the directions under Preparation of the Master Pattern for Fitting, pages 196-197. Check the measurements of a personal sleeve draft or of a commercial pattern before fitting it into the blouse. (See sleeve measurements, Chapter 4, pages 113-114.) The armscye line of the sleeve should be 1 to 2 inches longer than the armhole of the blouse in order to fit smoothly over the outward curve of the upper arm. Clip the sleeve armscye seam allowance at the back and front where the outward curve over the top meets the inward curve under the arm.

When having a sleeve pinned into a dress, stand in front of a mirror so that the fitter can see how it hangs in front or back even when she is working at the side. Relax your arm so that she can move it up, forward, or back without moving the rest of your body, because a sleeve must fit in many different positions. Slip the arm into the sleeve after checking it carefully to see that it is the correct one for the arm.

PINNING IN THE SLEEVE

1. Pin the sleeve to the dress at the shoulder seam line

Ordinarily the center of the sleeve meets the shoulder seam or is 1/4 to 3/8 inch in front of it. To determine the exact position, adjust the sleeve until the lengthwise grain line from the shoulder to the elbow hangs perpendicular to the floor (see Figure 46).

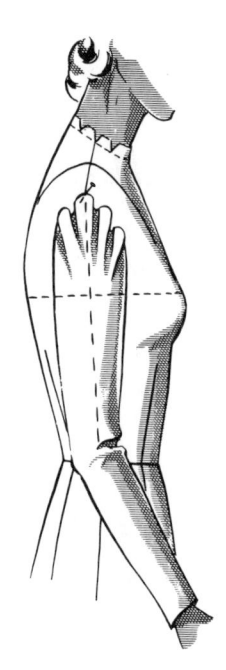

Fig. 46. Step 1 — Pin sleeve at shoulder seam.

2. Pin the sleeve at the underarm seam

With the arm of the model held straight out at the side, the fitter should pin the underarm seam of the sleeve to the underarm seam of the blouse. The two match if the blouse underarm seam divides the front and back equally at the scye line (see Figure 47).

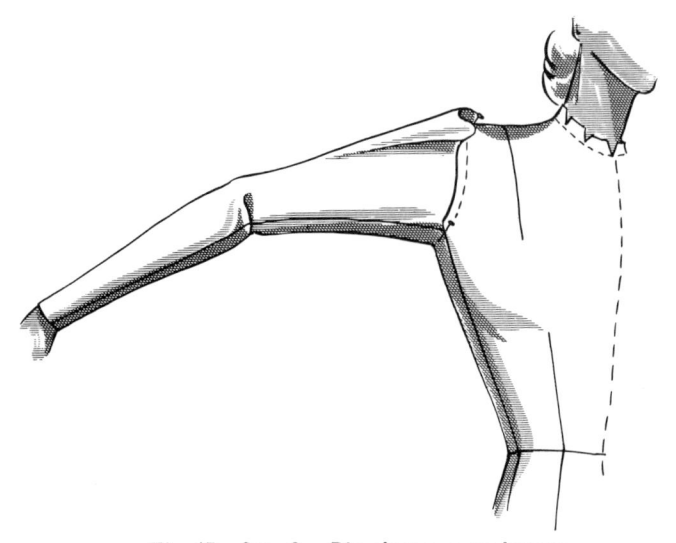

Fig. 47. Step 2 — Pin sleeve at underarm.

FITTING

3. Pin the sleeve to the dress at the chest line

Pick up the sides of the sleeve armscye and lift the back and front equally so that the crosswise grain at the girth of the sleeve is level, with the sleeve hanging in a rounded column, and pin it in this position. These two points, in back and front, should be approximately halfway between the shoulder seam at the top and the underarm seam at the bottom (see Figure 48).

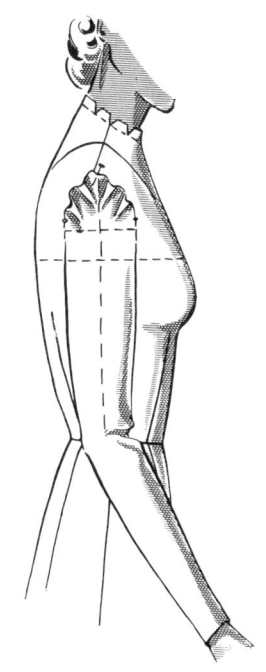

Fig. 48. Step 3 — Pin sleeve at front and back chest line.

4. Pin the sleeve along the front underarm

With the four main points established, begin a continuous line of pinning at the front underarm seam. With the arm of the model hanging slightly away from the side of the body, turn under the sleeve seam allowance, and lapping it over the armhole seam, pin it parallel to the edge. From the underarm seam around the lower armscye curve, stretch the sleeve slightly to the dress, but at a point approximately halfway up the armscye, reverse this procedure and ease the sleeve to the dress. The fitter should test the pinned line for ease by lifting the arm up and to the side. When the arm is down the sleeve should hang in a rounded vertical fold in front of the lower armscye curve (see Figure 49).

Fig. 49. Step 4 — Pin sleeve along front underarm

5. Pin the sleeve along the back underarm as in step 4
(see Figure 50)

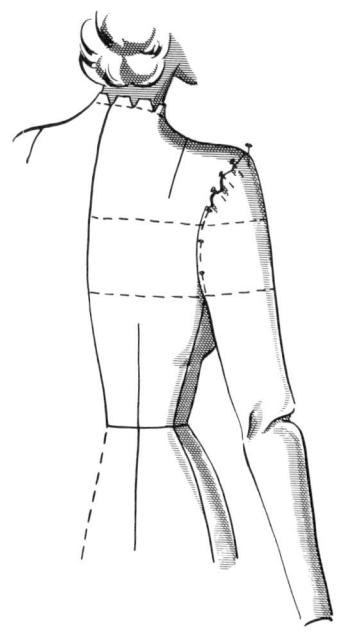

Fig. 50. Step 5 — Pin sleeve along back underarm. (Pinning along top is also indicated.)

DRESS DESIGN

6. Pin the sleeve over the top

After you have pinned the underarm of the sleeve, the points established at the side front and side back of the armhole may need a slight adjustment up or down to keep the crosswise grain level. Before pinning the top half, re-check the shoulder seam point to see that the lengthwise grain is perpendicular to the floor, that the crosswise grain is level at the girth, and that there is an equal amount of ease left in the sleeve for distribution at the front and back of the shoulder tip. Do not attempt to ease the top curve for at least 1 to 1½ inches on each side of the shoulder seam because the grain is straight across the top, but work ease along the more bias sections of the curve at the side front and back (see Figures 50 and 51).

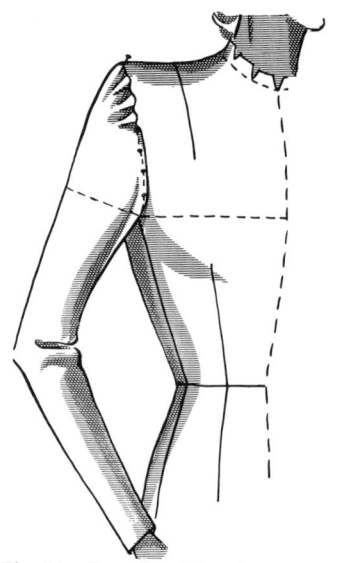

Fig. 51. Step 6 — Pin sleeve over the top.

7. Pin the wrist placket

When pinning the sleeve armscye into the dress, keep in mind that lifting or lowering the crosswise grain controls the hang of the sleeve. If you remember that a sleeve well set in hangs in a smooth rounded column, you will find it easier to decide whether to adjust the crosswise grain up or down. If there are diagonal wrinkles pointing from the girth of the sleeve to the top of the cap, the cap is too short and the sleeve should be pulled down at the top until the diagonal wrinkles disappear.

A poor fit is often considered the fault of the sleeve when the real source of the trouble is inadequate darting for the bust or shoulder blades so that the front or back armscye of the blouse gaps and of course makes the sleeve set badly.

Checking the Sleeve for Freedom of Arm Movement

After pinning the sleeve into the blouse and checking it for appearance when the arms hangs at the side, test it also for comfort in all positions. There must be enough width across the back of the blouse and at the back of the sleeve cap so that it is possible to swing the arms forward and place the hands on opposite shoulders or elbows without straining the back of the dress. It should be possible to reach above the head with no restriction at the arm girth. There should be enough length and width to bend the arm without tightness at the elbow or strain from the back of the armscye to the elbow point.

After completely checking the sleeve, mark any variations in the armscye line on both the blouse and the sleeve. Crossmark the blouse and sleeve armholes at the shoulder seam, the underarm seam, the back and front of the chest line, and at a point halfway between the chest line and the shoulder seam on both back and front. If the underarm seam lines of the blouse and sleeve do not match, re-mark the one which seems to be off center at the underarm seam and then trace a new line without changing the fit. (See directions for moving the shoulder seam position, page 206.)

The sleeve girth is used to check the balance or "set" of the sleeve just as the scye line is used in the blouse and the hip level line in the skirt.

Problem 1

CROSSWISE GRAIN AT GIRTH PULLED UP AT CENTER

In Figure 52a the sleeve has diagonal wrinkles pointing from the shoulder seam toward the back and front of the armhole line. The crosswise grain over the top of the arm should be level in a normal set-in sleeve. When it rises at the center, this indicates that the sleeve cap is too short. To correct this fault, let out the seam allowance over the top half of the sleeve armscye until the crosswise grain at the center of the

FITTING

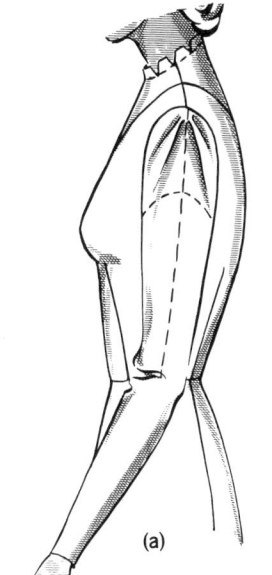

Fig. 52 (a). Sleeve cap is too short.

for increasing cap height.) For a large alteration of this type, change the pattern according to the procedure shown in Chapter 4, Figures 27a and b.

Note. If you attempt to tighten the sleeve at the elbow, even though you do not take in any width at the girth, this change will shorten the height of the cap and cause diagonal wrinkles. To tighten a sleeve at the elbow make the alteration on the vertical quarter divisions (see Chapter 4, pages 123-125).

Problem 2

CROSSWISE GRAIN AT GIRTH PULLED UPWARD AT FRONT OF ARMSCYE

The sleeve shown in Figure 53a has the lengthwise grain line tilted forward from the shoulder to the elbow for one of the following reasons.

(a) A prominent shoulder ball needs more height on the front of the sleeve cap than at any other point. In the normal draft, the highest point is at the center of the sleeve, and some sleeve patterns round up higher along the back armscye curve than along the front. To increase the height the required amount, let out the sleeve armscye seam allowance in front of the shoulder seam until the cap fits over the prominent bone and the grain settles down to a level line at the girth (see Figure 53b).

girth is level. If the seam allowance at the top of the sleeve is too narrow to let out, rip the armhole seam from under the arm to a point about 2 inches below the shoulder seam, and lower the underarm curve of the sleeve armscye to increase the height of the cap. Altering the fault in this second way, however, makes the base of the cap narrower. (See Figures 52b and c

Fig. 52 (b) and (c). Cap height increased. Seam let out at top of cap. Deeper seam taken in at underarm.

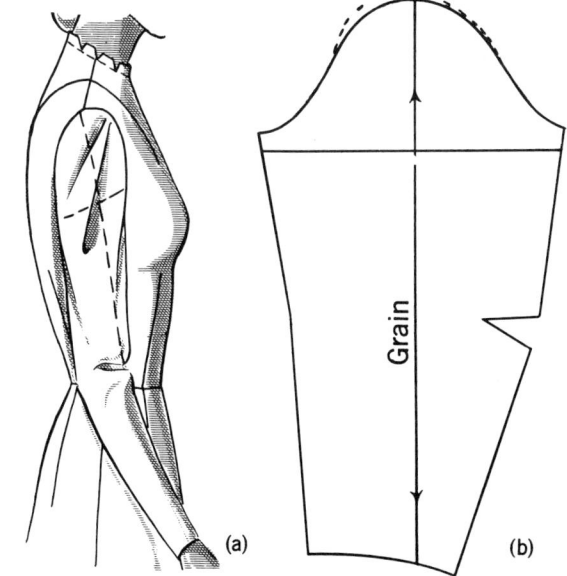

Fig. 53 (a). Front of sleeve cap is short; (b) Addition made to cap height in front of center line of sleeve for a prominent shoulder ball.

DRESS DESIGN

(b) The center lengthwise line of the sleeve may have been placed too far back at the top of the dress armhole. This frequently happens if it is matched to a shoulder seam line placed unusually far back. Restore the center line to the vertical position by moving the sleeve forward until the crosswise grain is level.

(c) An over-erect figure with shoulders thrown back requires a longer armhole in the front of the blouse than in the back. To set the sleeve so that the lengthwise grain is perpendicular to the floor, move the center line forward, in front of the shoulder seam. The cap height *behind* the center line of the sleeve may need to be increased.

(d) The sleeve may have been carelessly cut so that the girth line does not follow the crosswise grain. The only possible correction is to re-cut it.

Problem 3

CROSSWISE GRAIN AT GIRTH PULLED UP AT BACK OF ARMSCYE

The sleeve shown in Figure 54a has the lengthwise grain line tilted back from shoulder to elbow for one of the following reasons.

(a) If the sleeve cap is too short at the top back for square, erect shoulders, it pulls in the opposite way from the one described in Problem 2. Let out the seam allowance on the cap behind the center line of the sleeve until the grain is level at the girth (see Figure 54b).

(b) If the center lengthwise line of the sleeve is too far forward at the top of the armhole, move it back until the girth line is level.

(c) Round shoulders and flat chest require a longer armhole at the back of the blouse than at the front. To set the sleeve so that the lengthwise grain is perpendicular to the floor, move the center line of the sleeve behind the shoulder seam. The height of the cap in front of the center line may then need to be increased.

(d) The girth line of the sleeve may have been cut off the grain, with the result that it will slant in the opposite way from the sleeve described in Problem 2. If so, re-cut the sleeve.

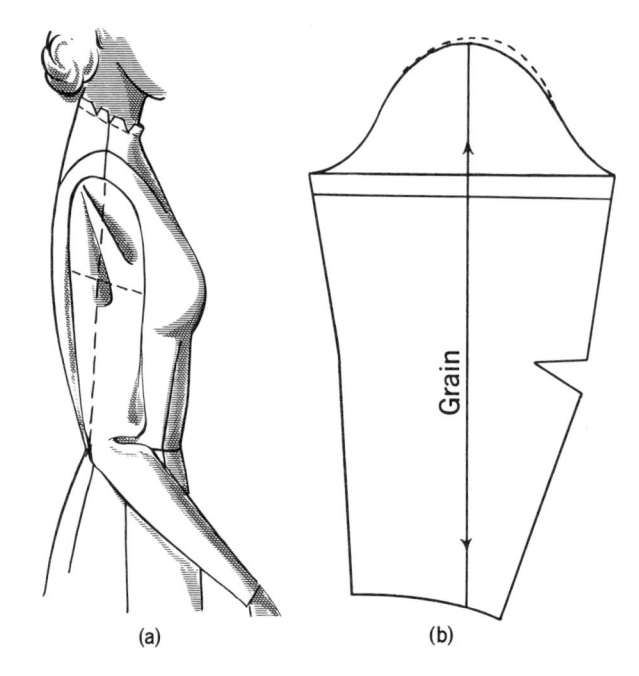

Fig. 54 (*a*). Back of sleeve cap is short; (*b*) Addition made to cap height in back of center line of sleeve for square erect shoulders.

Problem 4

SLEEVE DRAWS ACROSS UPPER ARM WHEN ARM IS RAISED (see Figure 55a)

(a) If the armscye of the blouse is too low, set the armscye line of the sleeve higher at the underarm of the blouse.

(b) If the sleeve cap is too long the cap width rather than the sleeve girth will bind across the arm when it is lifted. For this reason sports dresses and shirts have short sleeve caps. (See the Sleeve with Lower-Than-Normal Cap Height, Chapter 4, pages 125-127.) To correct this fault, increase the width of the cap by letting out the armscye seam allowance at the sides of the cap, and decrease the height by lessening the depth of the sleeve underarm curve, thus decreasing the seam allowance under the arm (see Figure 55b).

(c) If the girth of the sleeve is ¼ to ½ inch too small, let out the underarm seams from girth to elbow. But for a large increase, redraft the pattern with a new girth measurement.

FITTING

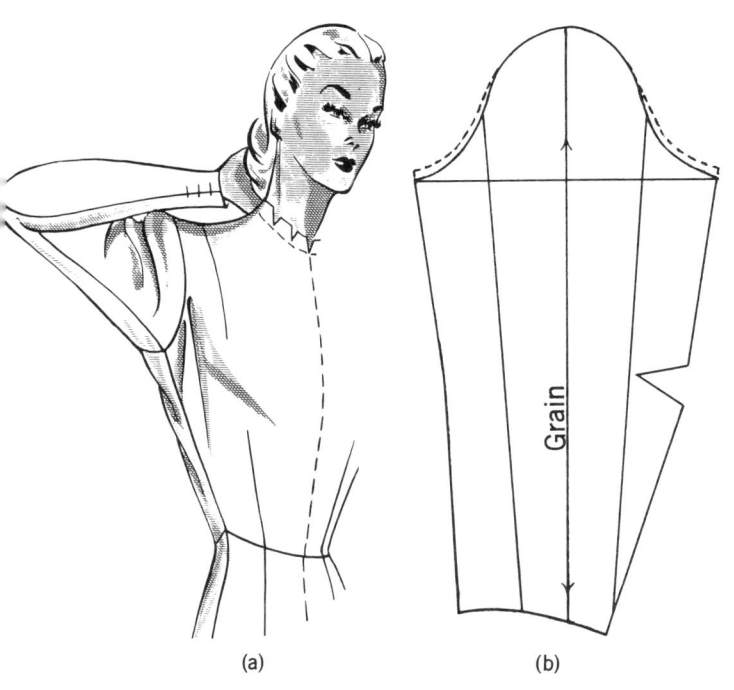

Fig. 55 (*a*). Sleeve draws across upper arm when arm is raised; (*b*) Dotted lines show armscye seam let out to increase cap width and to decrease cap height.

Problem 5

SLEEVE PULLS WHEN ARM IS BROUGHT FORWARD

(a) If the back lower armscye of the sleeve and that of the dress are hollowed out too deeply, rip the seam along the back of the armscye. Have the model bring her arm forward and re-pin the sleeve, letting out the seam allowance on both the blouse and the sleeve.

(b) If the blouse armscye is too low, set the sleeve higher at the underarm.

(c) If the sleeve girth is too narrow, remedy this fault by following the directions in (*c*) of Problem 4 above.

(d) If wrinkles show only in the armscye of the blouse back, not of the sleeve, the armscye of the sleeve is too small for the back armhole of the dress. Increase the size of the sleeve armscye by letting out the back edge of the sleeve underarm seam. The let-out must be an even amount from girth to elbow. For another method of making this alteration, increasing the width by slashing and spreading, see pages 123-125.

Problem 6

SLEEVE PULLS AT BACK OF ARMSCYE WHEN ELBOW IS BENT (see Figure 56a)

(a) The sleeve armscye may be too deeply hollowed out at the back, thus shortening the length from the back armscye to the elbow point. If so, let out the seam allowance on the back armscye to add necessary length (see Figure 56*b*).

(b) The elbow dart may be either too high or too low to provide ease exactly at the point where the elbow bends. If so, change the position of the dart.

(c) The elbow dart may be too small to provide enough length for the bent elbow. If so, slash from the elbow dart to the front edge of the sleeve, and spread to increase the size of the dart (see Figure 56*c*).

(d) If the elbow circumference is too small to allow for flexing the arm, increase it a little by letting out the underarm seam allowance.

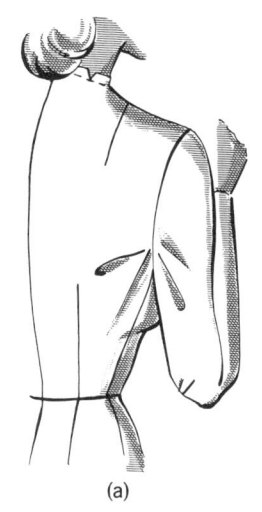

Fig. 56 (*a*). Sleeve pulls at the back of the armscye when the elbow is bent.

Problem 7

ELBOW OF SLEEVE DRAWS WHEN ARM IS BENT AND SLEEVE PULLS UP FROM WRIST

Problem 6 (*b*), (*c*), (*d*) deals with this fitting difficulty.

DRESS DESIGN

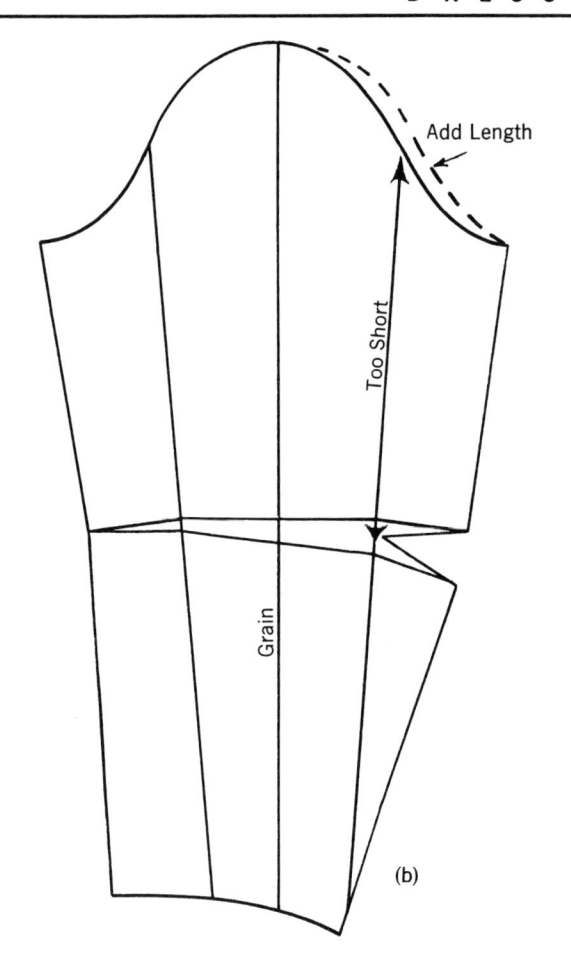

Fig. 56 (b). A back armscye that is too deeply curved shortens the sleeve from the armscye to the elbow.

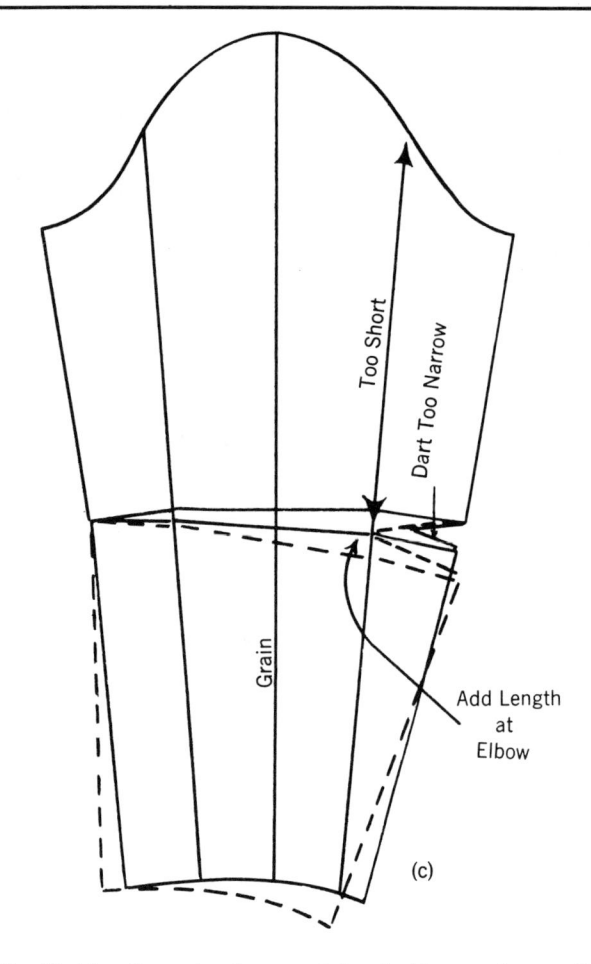

Fig. 56 (c). Dart size increased by slashing and spreading from the elbow dart to the front edge.

Problem 8

SLEEVE SEAM FROM ELBOW TO WRIST TWISTS TOWARD THUMB WHEN ARM IS BENT (see Figure 57)

The front seam line, as it would appear on the flat pattern, probably slopes in too much toward the center of the sleeve from the elbow to the wrist. The front seam line in a normal sleeve pattern with an elbow dart should be almost on the straight grain, and the normal position of the seam when the sleeve is being worn is on a line with the center of the palm. Correct the seam direction by straightening the front seam edge of the pattern and making the back seam edge more bias.

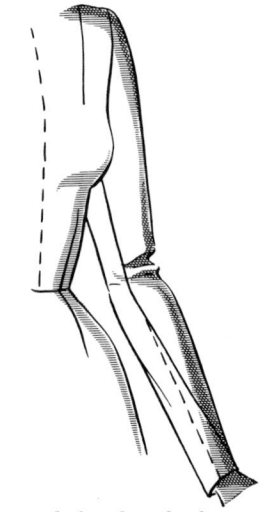

Fig. 57. Seam twists toward the thumb; front edge of seam is too bias.

236

FITTING

Problem 9

SLEEVE SEAM FROM ELBOW TO WRIST TWISTS TOWARD THE LITTLE FINGER WHEN ARM IS BENT
(see Figure 58)

(a) When this happens either the elbow dart is too small or the back seam edge is too sharply biased, since the size of the dart and the degree of the bias on the back edge of the seam must correspond if the seam line is to be held at the center of the palm. (See Analysis of Master One-Piece Sleeve, pages 118-119.)

(b) If the dart does not point to the elbow, make it do so in order to have the back part of the sleeve from elbow to wrist equal the length of that part of the arm when bent.

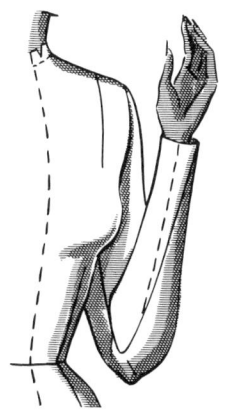

Fig. 58. Seam twists toward the little finger; elbow dart is too small to bring back seam edge in to the center of the palm.

Problem 10

SLEEVE DRAWS OVER MUSCLE AT BACK OF ARM NEAR GIRTH LINE

(a) A large upper arm often requires extra width and length over the back girth muscle but no extra length on the back armscye line. Figure 59 shows a sleeve slashed and spread to increase girth width without altering cap width. Slash the sleeve along the center lengthwise grain line from girth to top of cap and from girth to wrist. Slash along the girth line and lap out horizontally at the center to allow the sleeve to widen at the girth line without changing size at wrist or top of cap. Redraw the top of the

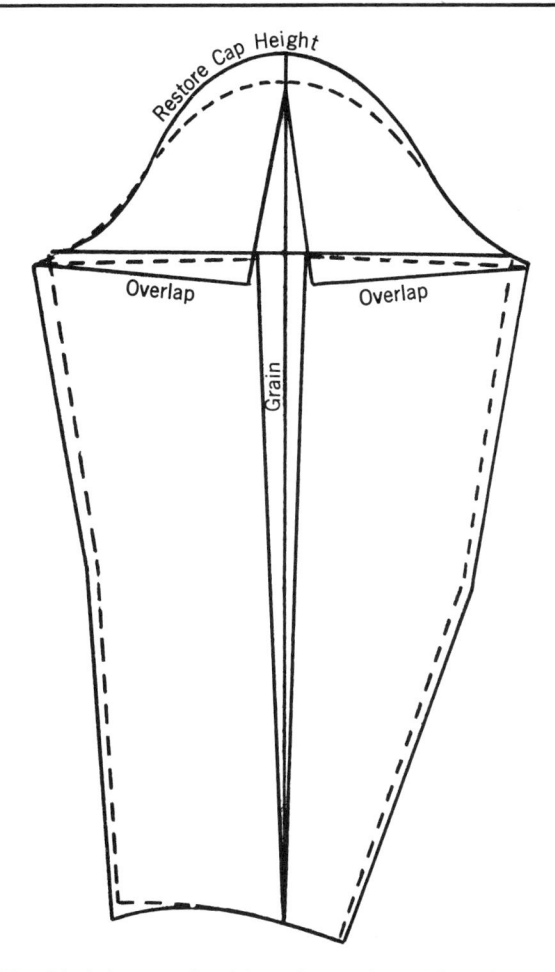

Fig. 59. Girth increased, without increasing width of cap.

armscye to equal the original cap height. Figures 60a and b show a sleeve slashed on the back quarter division and through the elbow dart. The elbow dart is then spread in order to allow the back part of the sleeve to widen and lengthen.

(b) If the lower part of the sleeve armscye line is too straight, the sleeve falls tight over the large muscle at the back of the arm. Figure 61a shows that an inward arc swings fullness into the area below it when the arc is joined to a straighter line. When this sleeve is set into the armhole of the dress, the area falling below the armscye seam between the points X and X will actually be fuller than the seam line. Figure 61b shows that a straight line forces no fullness to fall below it. This sleeve will be approximately as tight in the area falling below the points X and X as the seam line.

DRESS DESIGN

(c) A large upper arm with rolls of flesh at the underarm requires more room just below the armhole of the sleeve on the underside of the arm but no increase in the armhole size of the blouse. See Figure 62 for increasing the size of the back underarm section of the sleeve by slashing and spreading along the back quarter line above the elbow. Take up the excess length on the armscye into a short dart under the arm where it is concealed and yet provides the extra room in the sleeve where the arm is heavy.

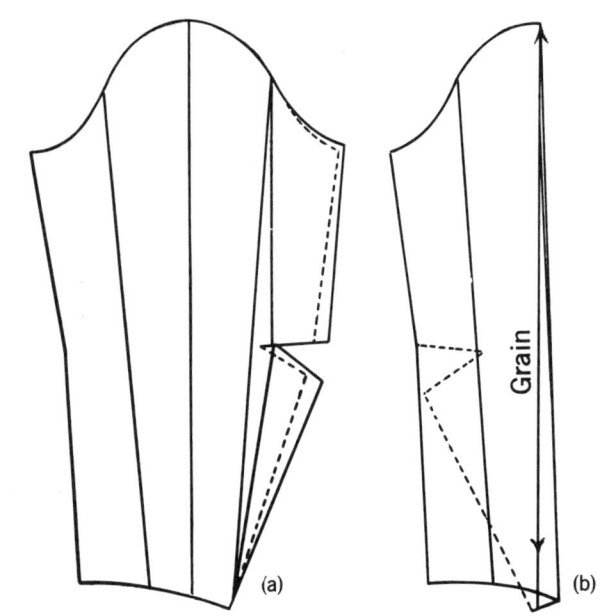

Fig. 60 (a). Width increased for the elbow and back upper arm; length of armscye remains unchanged.

Fig. 60 (b). Sleeve folded. The fold will not fall on the lengthwise thread.

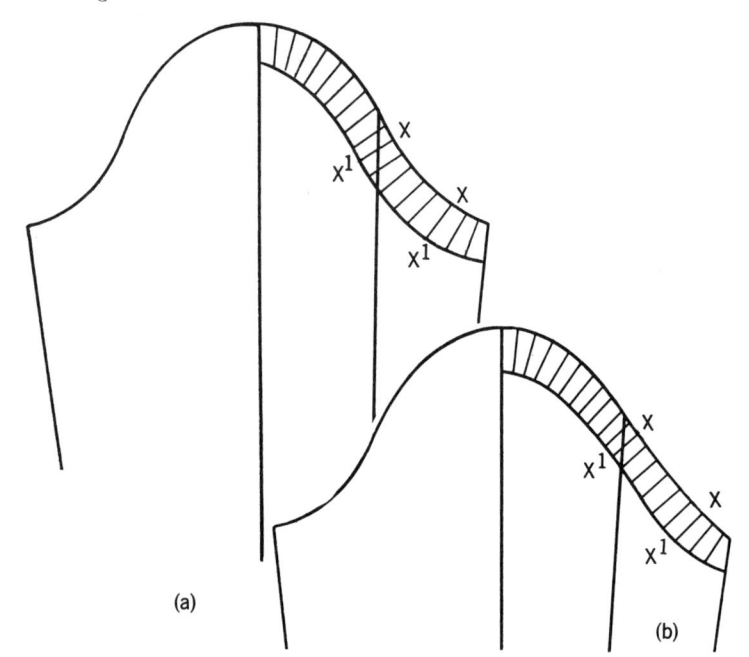

Fig. 61 (a) and (b). Effect of armscye curve on sleeve fullness below armscye.

Fig. 61 (a). An inward curve (x–x) when stretched out forces fullness into the area below it (x^1–x^1).

Fig. 61 (b). An almost straight line (x–x) forces no fullness to hang below it (x^1–x^1).

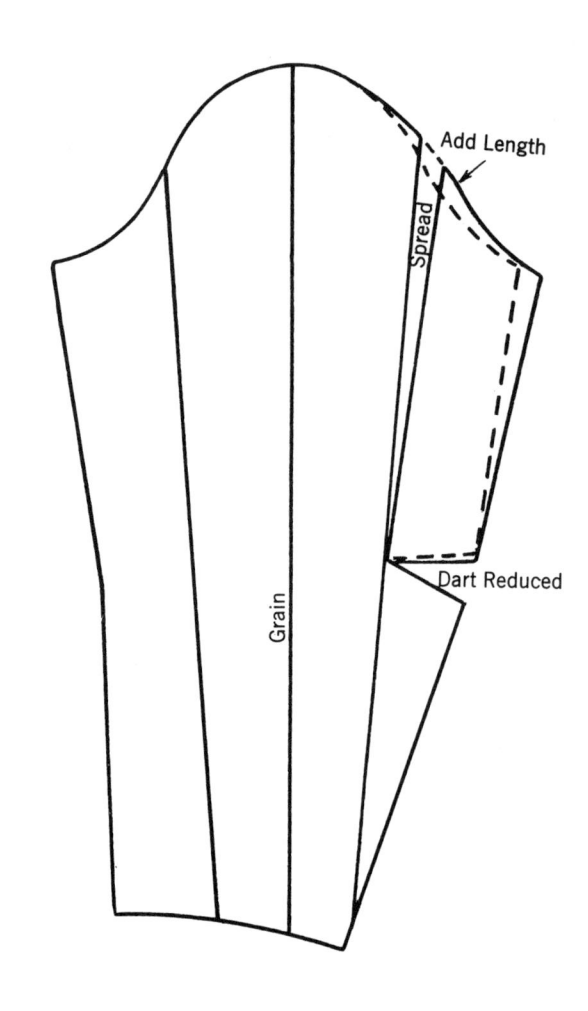

Fig. 62. Alteration for arm with large girth but small elbow.

FITTING

Problem 11

SLEEVE FALLS IN LOOSE FOLDS AT FRONT OF ELBOW

If an arm is large around the girth but small around the elbow, a sleeve may fit the girth correctly but be too loose to fit trimly from the elbow to the wrist. Figure 63 shows the method for reducing the width of the front quarter of the sleeve. Slash vertically on the front quarter division from the wrist to the armscye and again on this division horizontally on the elbow line to the front seam edge. Spread the elbow slash at the quarter division line in order to lap out vertically the excess width in the front half of the sleeve above and below the elbow line. Correct the lower edge as indicated. Notice that any change in the slope of the underarm seam of the sleeve must be accompanied by an alteration of the armscye curve.

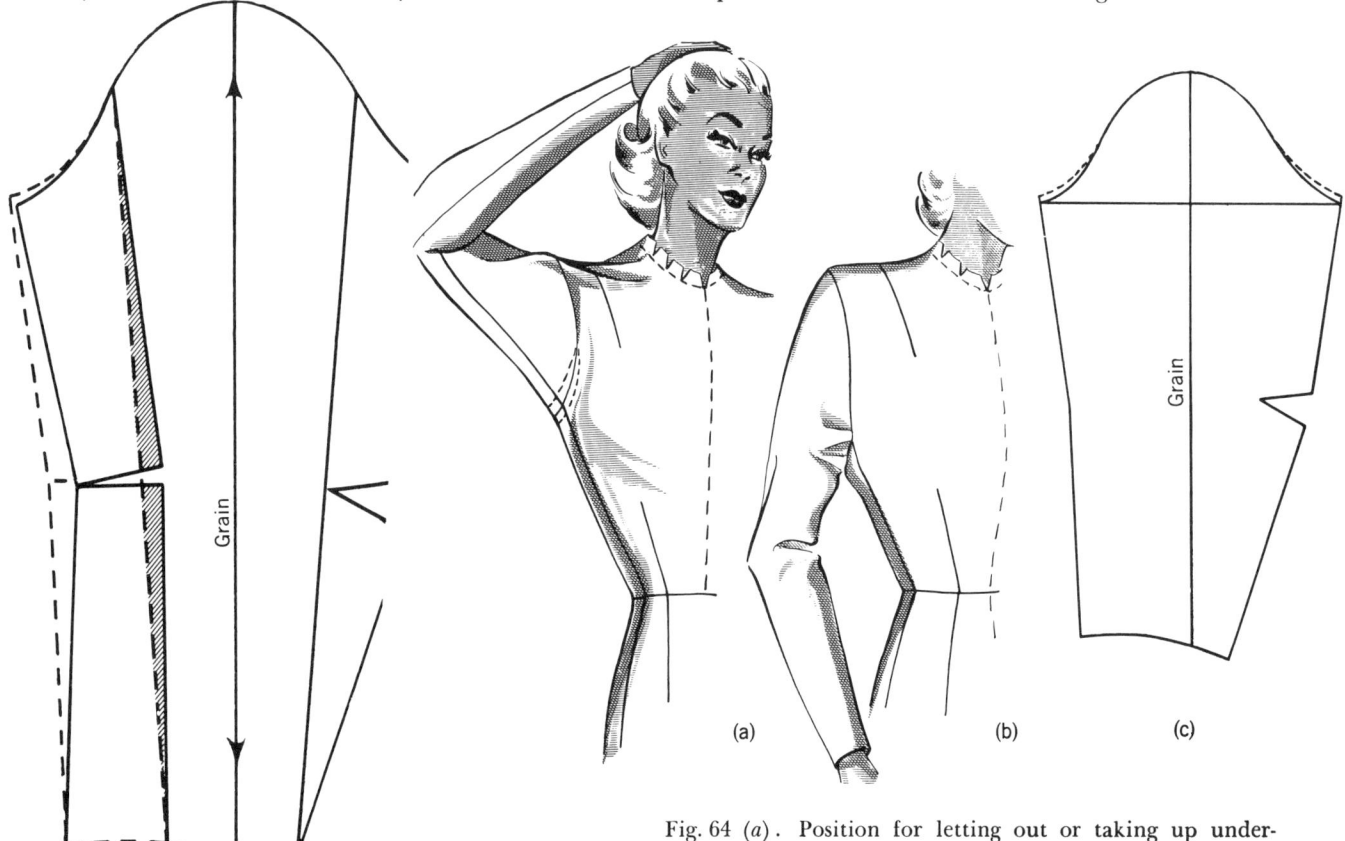

Fig. 63. Alteration to eliminate excess width at front of elbow.

Problem 12

SLEEVE FALLS IN HORIZONTAL WRINKLES UNDER THE ARM JUST BELOW ARMSCYE LINE WHEN THE ARM IS DOWN (see Figures 64a and b)

If the sleeve cap is shorter than the armhole of the blouse from the chest to the underarm seam, the excess length on the underarm seam of the sleeve produces blousing at the underarm. Some extra length on the sleeve underarm is needed for raising the arm, especially in tightly fitted blouses. But if the blousing is excessive, it shows as horizontal wrinkles at the front and back just below the armpit. To correct this difficulty, reduce the underarm seam length, but not enough to make it uncomfortable to raise the arm.

Note. See Figure 64c for correcting the reverse of this problem, too little underarm length.

Fig. 64 (*a*). Position for letting out or taking up underarm length on sleeve and blouse.
Fig. 64 (*b*). Sleeve with too much underarm length for the normal set-in sleeve.
Fig. 64 (*c*) Alteration of underarm length.

DRESS DESIGN

Problem 13

DIAGONAL WRINKLES ACROSS SLEEVE FROM BELOW ARMPIT TO ELBOW (see Figure 65)

If the slope on the front is not the same as on the back, the front and back girth corners will not match when the sleeve is folded unless the corners are forced together, and this causes the sleeve to twist. Figure 66a shows a sleeve with greater slope on the back than on the front and Figures 66b and c show what happens when this sleeve is folded. Compare Figure 66d, which illustrates a folded sleeve with the same slope on back and front underarm seam edges. Remove a sleeve which twists and check it for accuracy of cut according to the directions on pages 118-119.

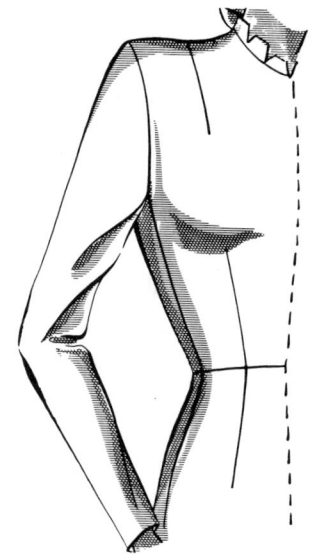

Fig. 65. Sleeve twists from armpit to elbow.

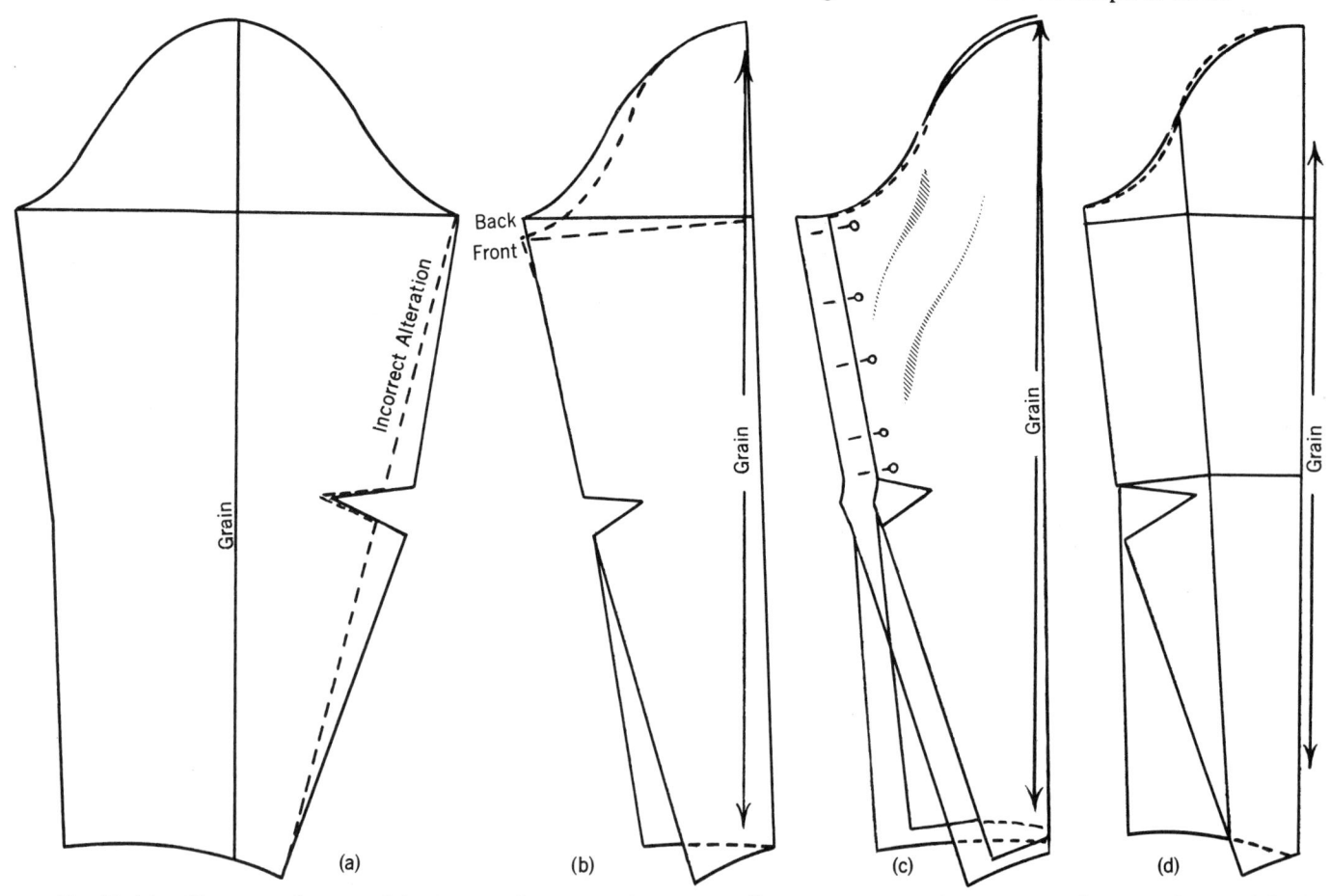

Fig. 66 (a). Slopes on front and back seam lines are mismatched. (b). Girth corners fail to meet, because slopes of back and front seam lines do not match. (c). Sleeve twists when back and front girth corners are forced to match. (d). Folded sleeve with correct slope.

240

FITTING

Problem 14

ARMSCYE OF SLEEVE UNCOMFORTABLY HIGH

If the binding is due to the blouse armhole size, see fitting the Armscye Area of the blouse, pages 208-212.

To enlarge the sleeve armscye:

1. Let out the seam allowance over the top curve to add to the width and height of the cap.

2. Let out the underarm sleeve seam to increase the armscye length along the underarm curve, but do this only if the underarm curve of the sleeve is too short for the underarm curve of the blouse.

3. Either redraft the sleeve with wider girth and higher cap, or slash and spread the pattern.

Problem 15

SLEEVE ARMSCYE EXCEEDING LENGTH OF BLOUSE ARMHOLE BEYOND THE USUAL 1 TO 2 INCHES

1. **Enlarge the blouse armscye** (see fitting of armscye area, pages 208-212).

2. Reduce the sleeve armscye by:

(a) Deepening the seam allowance along the sides of the upper edge of the sleeve cap.

(b) Deepening the seam allowance of the underarm seam if the sleeve girth is too large.

(c) Redrafting the sleeve with a narrower girth and therefore a narrower cap.

Note. If the girth measurement exceeds the elbow measurement by more than the usual 2 inches, the sleeve draft will have a very wide cap and too large an armscye.

Problem 16

SLEEVE TOO LARGE AT WRIST

To reduce the wrist size, pin out the excess on the back edge of the seam only. Remove the sleeve and fold the back line against the front from elbow to wrist. Slanting the back edge more intensely makes it slide above the front at the wrist line, so that a new wrist line must be marked. Increase the elbow dart to take up the extra length on the back edge.

To enlarge the wrist measurement, reverse this procedure. See Figure 67 for both changes.

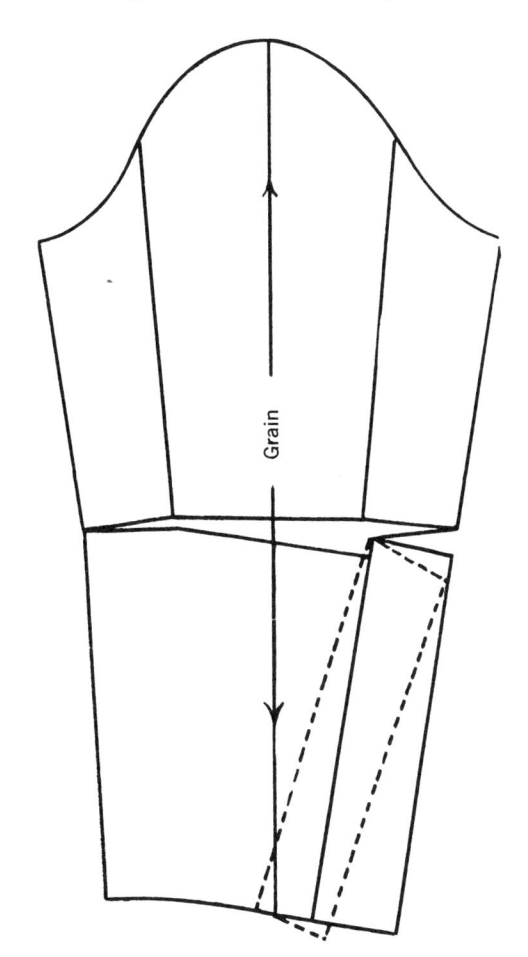

Fig. 67. Dotted section is pivoted back to reduce dart and widen wrist, forward to increase dart and narrow wrist.

DRESS DESIGN

PART VI
COMPLETING THE MASTER PATTERN AFTER THE FITTING

Marking the Balance Lines (see Figure 68)

After fitting the master pattern, mark the balance lines — the scye line in the blouse and the hip level line in the skirt, as well as any other lines which will be helpful in designing patterns on the master block. Place a tape measure around the body under the arms so that its upper edge just touches the armhole at the side seams. Adjust it at the center back, center front, and sides so that it is level. Pencil the muslin blouse around the top edge of the tape, and mark the most prominent point of the shoulder blades. Place a second tape across the bust line in the front, but raise it to the scye line at the back. Pencil the upper edge of the tape across the front only and mark the point of the bust. Measure down 3 inches from the base of the neck on the center front line, and place a level tapeline from this point to the armscye. Pencil this line. Measure down 4 inches from the base of neck on the center back (or farther if necessary to match the chest line in the front) and mark a level line. This line, when carried across the sleeve to match the line in front, should be level all around the chest.

Pin a tape around the largest hip measurement, 7 to 9 inches below the waist, and adjust it at the center front, center back, and sides until it is level. (See marking the hip level, Chapter 1 page 8.) Pencil the upper edge of the tape. If special darting is required for prominent hip bones, mark these points.

All marking of balance lines must be postponed until a second fitting if important alterations involving a change of grain are made at the first fitting.

Making Alterations in the Master Pattern and Re-checking the Dress Form

Take off the master pattern and mark all alterations indicated at the fitting. If there are many important changes, duplicate them on the opposite half and prepare the garment for a second fitting. This is usually not necessary when it has been carefully draped on a well padded personal form.

If the master pattern did not fit well, re-check the dress form by placing the altered master pattern on the form again, readjusting the padding, or re-marking the basic lines to conform to the fitted pattern. If the fitted master pattern fits the dress form, a review of the changes that were made during the fitting will help explain to the beginner her mistakes in draping or her posture variations from the standard dress form.

See Chapters 2, 3 and 4 for suggestions in checking the accuracy of the flat pattern pieces of the blouse, skirt, and sleeve.

Mark and measure the basic lines on the pattern pieces as shown on the following charts.

FITTING

Fig. 68. The marking of balance lines.

DRESS DESIGN

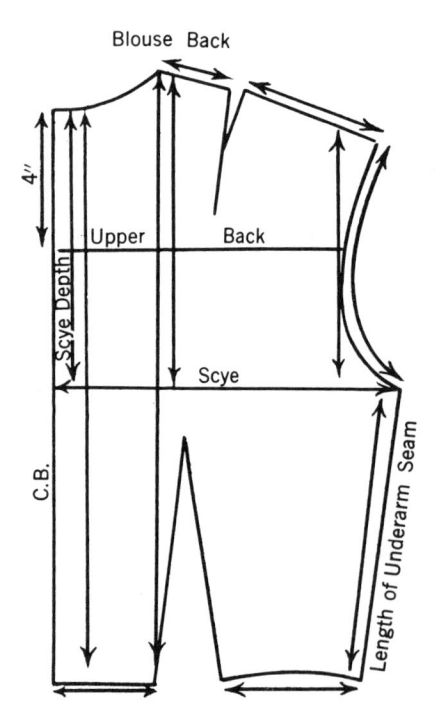

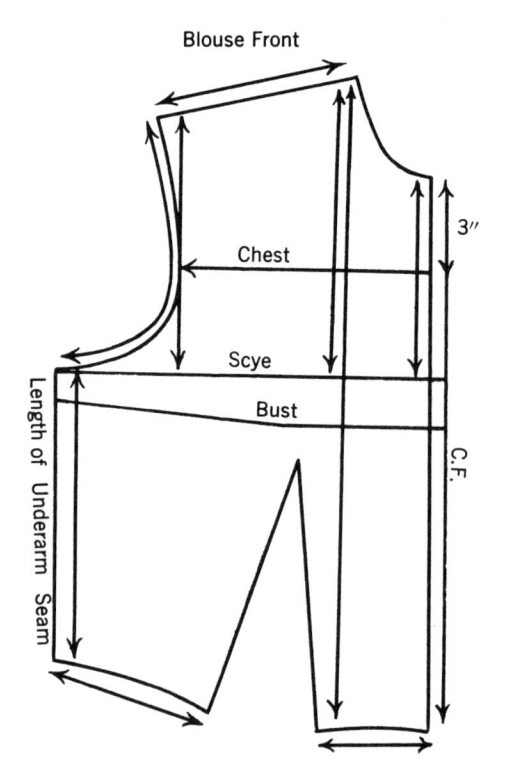

MASTER PATTERN MEASUREMENTS

BLOUSE

WIDTHS
1. Shoulder seam (front) . . . .
   Ease on back . . . .
2. Basic neckline . . . . (total)
   C.B. to shoulder . . . .
   C.F. to shoulder . . . .
3. Chest (3" down on C.F.) . . . .
4. Upper back (4" down C.B.) . . . . . .
5. Scye circumference . . . . (total)
   C.B. to side seam . . . .
   C.F. to side seam . . . .
6. Bust circumference . . . . (total)
   C.F. to side seam . . . .
7. Waist circumference . . . . (total)
   C.F. to side seam . . . .
   C.B. to side seam . . . .

LENGTHS
1. Center — base of neck to waist
   Center back . . . .
   Center front . . . .
2. Shoulder seam (at neck) to waist
   Front . . . .
   Back . . . .
3. Underarm seam . . . .
4. Scye line to upper edge of blouse
   Back — C. Back—neck to scye . . . . . .
            Shoulder at neck to scye . . . .
            Shoulder at armscye to scye . . . .
   Front — C. F. neck to scye . . . . . .
            Shoulder at neck to scye . . . .
            Shoulder at armscye to scye . . . .
5. Armscye length . . . . (total)
   Back . . . .
   Front . . . .

244

FITTING

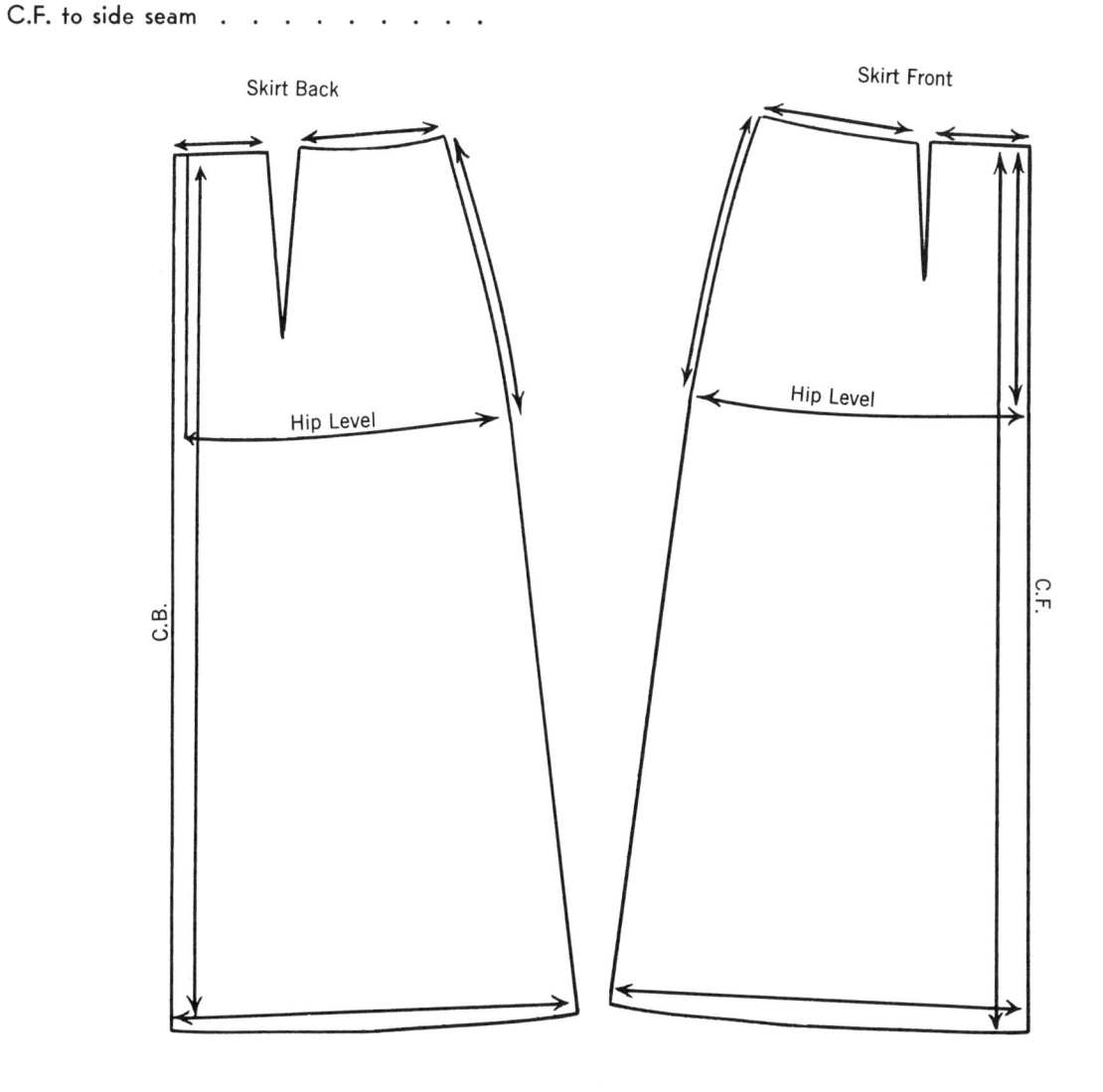

MASTER PATTERN MEASUREMENTS

SKIRT

WIDTHS
1. Waistline circumference . . . . (total)
    C.B. to side seam . . . .
    C.F. to side seam . . . .
2. Hip level circumference (taken over largest part of hip line) . . . . (total)
    C.B. to side seam . . . .
    C.F. to side seam . . . .
3. Hem sweep . . . . (total)
    C.B. to side seam . . . .
    C.F. to side seam . . . .

LENGTHS
1. Waist to hem
    Center back . . . .
    Center front . . . .
    Side seam . . . .
2. Waist to hip level
    Center back . . . .
    Center front . . . .
    Side seam . . . .

Skirt Back

Hip Level

C.B.

Skirt Front

Hip Level

C.F.

DRESS DESIGN

MASTER PATTERN MEASUREMENTS

SLEEVE

WIDTHS

1. Girth . . . .
2. Elbow . . . .
3. Wrist . . . .
4. Cap (at chest line of blouse) . . . . . .
5. Dart depth . . . .

LENGTHS

1. Overarm . . . .
2. Underarm . . . .
3. Cap height . . . .
4. Armscye . . . . (total)
   Back . . . .
   Front . . . .
5. Armscye ease (difference between measurement of dress and sleeve armhole). . . . .

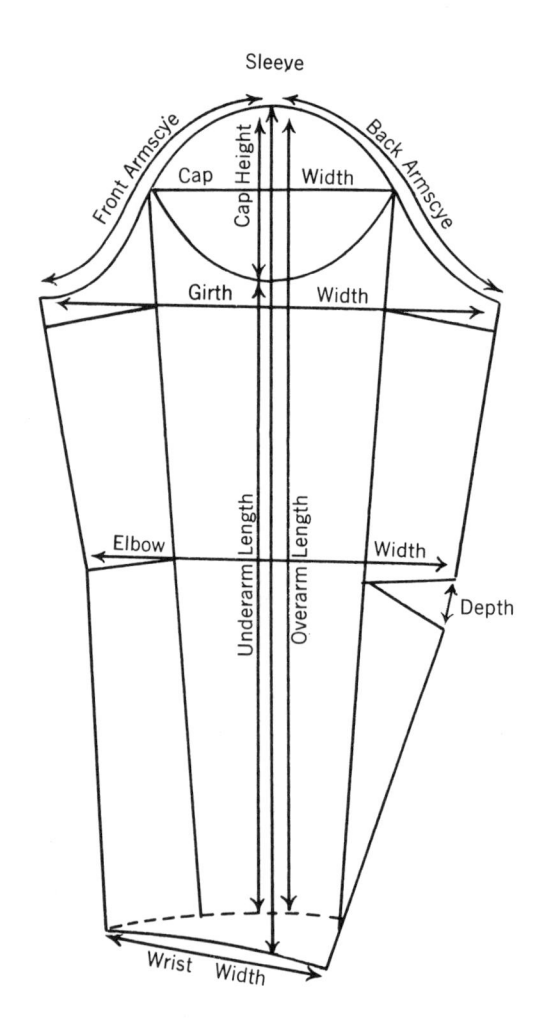

6. Collars and Necklines

Although this chapter, on the designing of collars and necklines, is the last to deal with basic cuts, it has not been placed last because its importance is least; but rather because of the difficulty of the subject. The neckline or collar acts as a background for the face, and should therefore be considered the most important area of the entire costume. It should be given careful thought both from the point of view of fashion and of individual becomingness, and should always be an integral part of the costume.

In this chapter, patterns for the basic types of necklines and collars are developed both through draping and through the flat pattern blocking method. In a few cases, where accuracy is of primary importance, draft directions are given. Of the three methods, draping offers the most opportunity for creating original effects, but because no part of the dress requires more precision of fit than the neckline, it is essential that the dress form neckline be padded and shaped to duplicate your own precisely.

COLLARS

Some explanation here of the terminology commonly employed in discussions of collars will save repetition in the following problems. The following are the principal terms used:

Style-line denotes the free outside edge of the collar as opposed to the neckline edge sewed to the garment.

Stand refers to the height of the collar roll, usually the amount the collar rises above the basic neckline to which it is attached. It is that part of the collar which extends from the neckline to the roll-line.

Roll or *fold* is the turning line of the collar along the top of the stand.

Break is the point where the lapel begins to fold back from the edge of the garment, and *break-line* refers to the fold-line of the lapel and the tailored collar.

Collars are classified according to their various characteristics — width, shape of outside edge, neckline shape, and roll. The most important of these characteristics is the way the collar rolls from the neckline edge, and this is largely determined by the relationship of the neckline edge of the collar to the neckline of the garment. For instance, if the collar neckline has the same curve as the garment neckline, it lies flat; if the collar neckline is less curved (or even convex) it rolls; and if the collar neckline is more inwardly curved (or more concave) it ripples. It is essential, then, to think of the collar roll as resulting from the relationship of the two shaped lines which are joined — the neckline of the garment and that of the collar.

If a collar is not entirely flat, its width also influences the height of the roll. That is, the stand increases as the collar widens. A collar flattens out until it finds its own circumference on the body. For example, if its circumference 2 inches from the basic neckline is only as great as the body circumference 1 inch from the basic neckline, there is that extra inch of collar width to go into a soft roll around the neckline, giving the collar a ½ inch stand. A straight strip sewed to the basic neckline produces a stand one-half its width, since its circumference at the outside edge is the same as that of the basic neckline. A concave collar neckline provides a greater circumference on the outside edge of the collar, and stands less than one-half its width, since the outside edge of the collar slides out on the shoulders farther from the basic neckline. As the collar neckline takes on a more in-

DRESS DESIGN

ward curve, the circumference on the outside edge increases, and therefore the *proportion of its width* that goes into the stand decreases.

The looseness or tightness of the collar along the roll-line is another important factor in determining the collar style. Since the upper part of the neck is smaller than the base, a close fitting roll-line must be the same length as the basic neckline or even shorter, and this can be achieved only by a straight line or a convex curve on the neckline. Figure 68, page 272, showing a diagram of a wide tailored collar with a reverse curve, gives a graphic explanation of the relationship between the shape of the neckline and the length of the fold-line. A collar with an inward curve along the neckline, such as the pattern shown in Figure 14, page 253, has a fold-line greater in length than the circumference of the neck, and thus a rather soft easy roll that stands away from the neck. See also the rolled Peter Pan Collar, Figure 13, page 253.

By learning to use the three types of lines, straight, concave, and convex, for collar necklines, you can design an infinite variety of collars adjusting curves to the right degree or combining line directions until you produce the exact effect you wish. In all collar designing, check the fit on the model by using the entire collar, not one half. The pull across the back of the neck by the opposite side is essential in determining the fold-line of the collar.

PART I
DRAFTING AND FLAT PATTERN DESIGN

In this chapter, we shall consider the drafting and flat pattern designing of collars and necklines before we discuss the relevant draping procedures. This is done because the subtle modifications achieved by draping logically follow, rather than precede, the drafting process.

Problem 1

THE BUILT-UP NECKLINE (see Figure 1)

Before building up the neckline of a master pattern blouse, you must revise the basic neckline. As it is, the basic blouse has lengthwise threads very slightly stretched away from the center front to make the arc or curve of the neckline somewhat sharper than the curve of the neck itself. The circumference of the blouse area which could be extended 1 inch above the basic neckline would therefore be too small to fit the upper part of the neck. For this reason, the size of the basic neckline must be slightly increased, and also the grain must be shifted, so that the lengthwise threads are perpendicular to the neckline rather than slightly stretched away from it. (See Draping Procedure for the Built-up Neckline, Figures 18-21.)

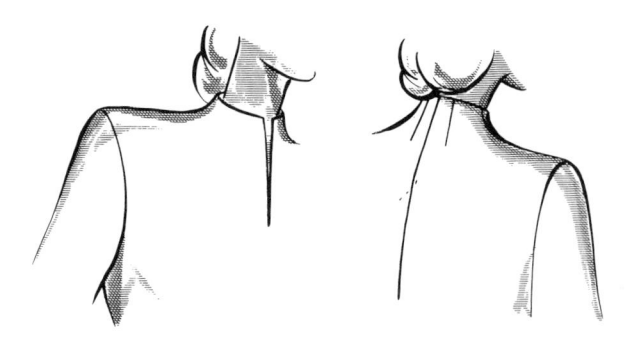

Fig. 1. The built-up neckline.

BLOUSE FRONT

For your convenience, have blocks for the front and back of the blouse with built-up necklines ready to use whenever you design dresses with necklines higher than the basic one. The following directions explain how to make these blocks.

Slash lines (see Figure 2)

1. Cut a copy of the master pattern blouse front, and on it draw a line from the halfway point, J, on the neckline to the end of the basic waist dart, D. Slash from J to D.

COLLARS AND NECKLINES

2. Draw a line from the halfway point, *K*, on the shoulder seam, to the end of the basic waistline dart, *D*. Slash from *D* to *K*.

Pattern guide (see Figure 3)

1. Draw around the master pattern on another sheet of paper, but do not cut it out. Draw a dotted line from the center front of the neckline, *A*, to point *L*, ½ inch out from the center front of the waistline.

2. Measure ½ inch on the shoulder seam from the neck end and mark *M*.

Spreading

Spread the pattern on the slash lines to increase the neckline size and shift the grain (see Figure 4).

1. Place the pattern shown in Figure 2 over the pattern shown in Figure 3, matching the center front, *AB*, to the new sloping dotted line *AL*, in order to shift the grain slightly. Keep the pattern in this position throughout the remaining steps.

2. Draw along the edge of the pattern from *A* to *J*.

3. Spread the slash *JD* to increase the size of the neckline until the shoulder corner *I* touches point *M*. This spreads the slash ⅜ inch at the neck. Draw a curved line from *J* through *I* and follow the pattern edge to *K*.

4. Spread the slash *DK* at *D* until the width at the armscye end of the side seam, *G*, equals the original pattern size.

5. Draw around the pattern section marked by the points $KHGFED^1$. The inner edge of the waistline dart D^1C remains the same. Extend D^1C to C^1 to equal the length of D^1E. Connect C^1 and *B*. The *final center front line remains AB*. The new pattern is $ABC^1D^1EFGHKIJA$.

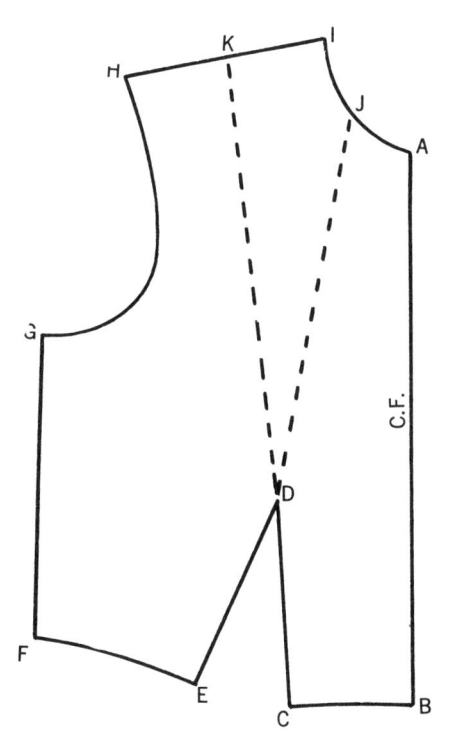

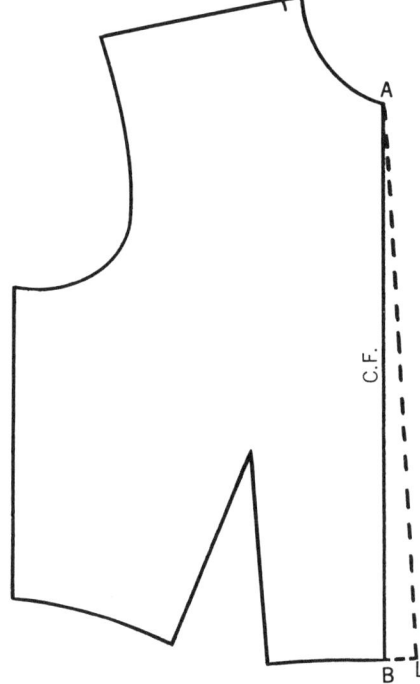

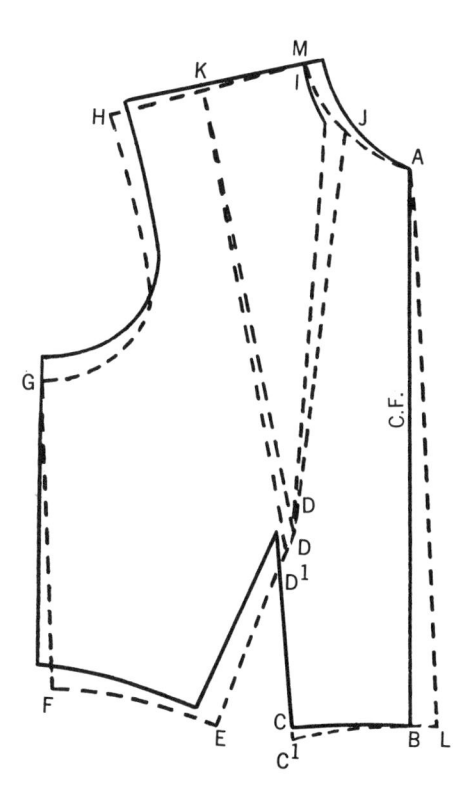

Fig. 2. Slash lines.

Fig. 3. Pattern guide with temporary center front line AL.

Fig. 4. Slash lines spread to shift grain and increase neckline size.

DRESS DESIGN

New neckline

Draw the built-up neckline on the final pattern (see Figure 5).

1. Extend the center front line *AB*. Mark a point 1 inch up from *A*, and label the new point *N*.

2. Extend a line from the shoulder corner, *I*, parallel to the center front, mark on it a point 1 inch up from *I*, and measure in at a right angle ½ inch to establish the neckline end of the shoulder seam. Label this *O*.

3. Draw the upper edge of the neckline, *N* to *O*, parallel to the basic neckline.

BLOUSE BACK

To revise the blouse back for a built-up neckline, transfer some of the waistline dart to a neckline dart which will shift the lengthwise grain slightly and provide a fitting line at the back of neck.

Establishing the neck dart (see Figure 6)

1. On a copy of the master pattern blouse back, place a dot, *J*, on the neckline 1½ inches from the center back.

2. Place a second dot, *K*, 2 inches below the neckline and 1⅝ inches from the center back. Join *J* to *K*. This will be the length of the dart when it is stitched.

3. Draw a line from *K* to the point of the waistline dart, *D*.

4. Slash from *J* to *K* to *D*, and spread ¼ inch at the neckline, tapering off to nothing at *D*.

5. Draw around the new pattern, *ABCDEFGHIJ¹-JA*.

6. Draw the new dart, following line *KJ* for the inner edge and *KJ¹* for the outer edge. Make line *KJ¹* equal *KJ*.

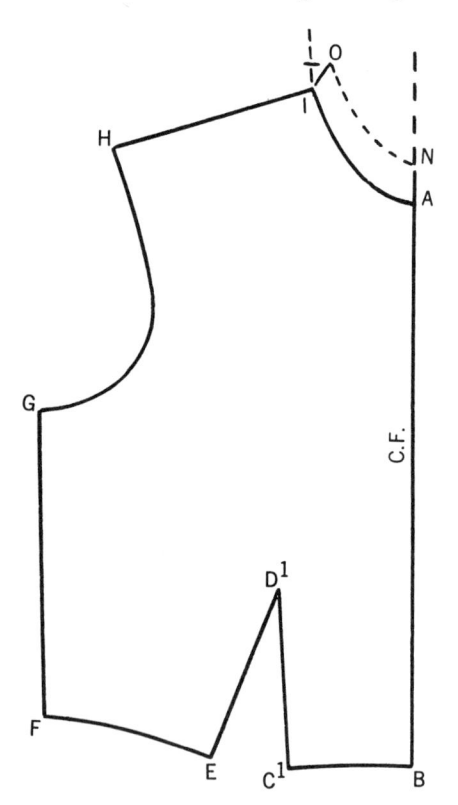

Fig. 5. Built-up neckline drawn.

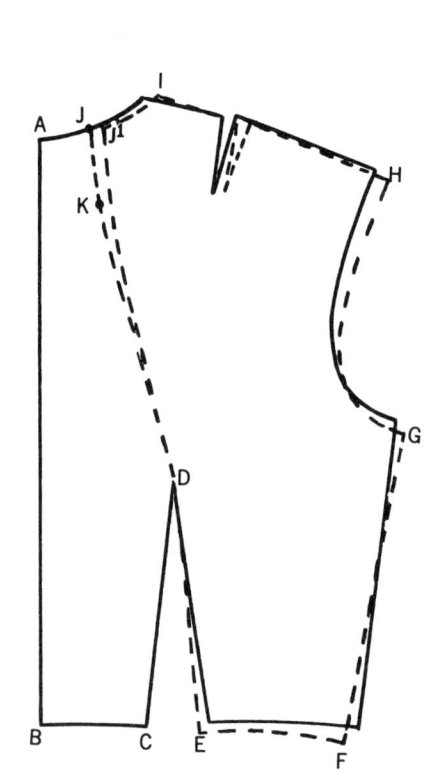

Fig. 6. Part of waistline dart transferred to small neckline dart.

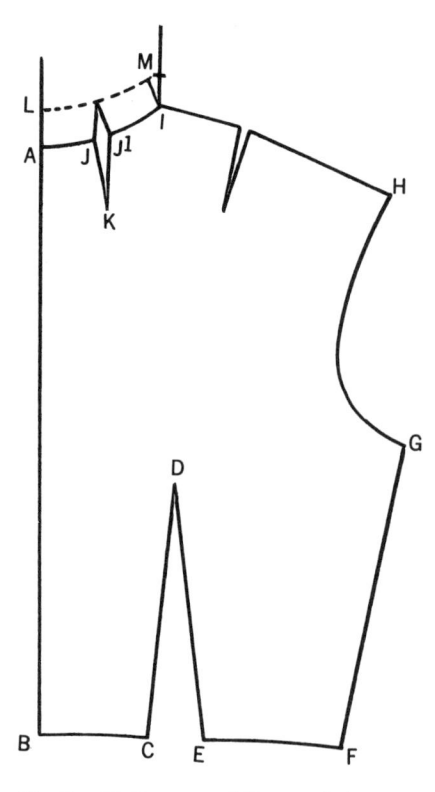

Fig. 7. Built-up neckline and dart drawn.

COLLARS AND NECKLINES

Drawing the built-up neckline on the final pattern (see Figure 7)

1. Extend the center back line up through *A* and mark a point 1 inch above it, *L*.

2. Extend a line from the shoulder corner, *I*, parallel to the center back; mark on it a point 1 inch up from *I*; and measure in at a right angle 3/8 inch to establish the neckline end of the shoulder seam. Label this *M*. Join *I* to *M* to complete the shoulder seam.

3. Draw the upper edge of the neckline *L* to *M* parallel to the basic neckline.

4. To complete the dart, rule a line from *J* to the neckline edge, *LM*, sloping the line very slightly away from the center back. Rule a line from *J¹* to intersect the neck edge at the same point.

Problem 2

FLAT COLLARS DESIGNED FROM THE MASTER PATTERN

Narrow Flat Collar, Not Wider than 3 Inches (see Figure 8)

1. Place the shoulder seams of the master pattern blouse back and front together so that they touch at the neckline and overlap ½ inch at the armhole. The overlapping at the end of the shoulder lessens the sharp neckline curve across the shoulder seam.

2. To remove the sharp curve at the center front of the neckline, place a dot ½ inch below the neckline at the center front, and another on the neckline halfway between the shoulder seam and the center front. Join these two points with a smooth curve. This increases the neckline length about ¼ inch on each half of the pattern.

3. To remove the excess length, draw the final line for the neckline ⅛ inch above the original neckline curve.

4. For a slight roll to cover the seam joining the collar and the dress, subtract ⅛ inch from the center back of the collar and the same amount from the center front. A collar should usually be ¼ inch shorter than the dress neckline from center back to center front. (Even the flattest collar must roll enough to cover the seam.)

5. Measure from the neckline at the center back and at the shoulder seams the width of the collar, and draw in the style-line (the outer line of the collar).

Note. Design a flat collar for a low neckline in the same way, but change the neckline on the blouse front and back before you block the collar.

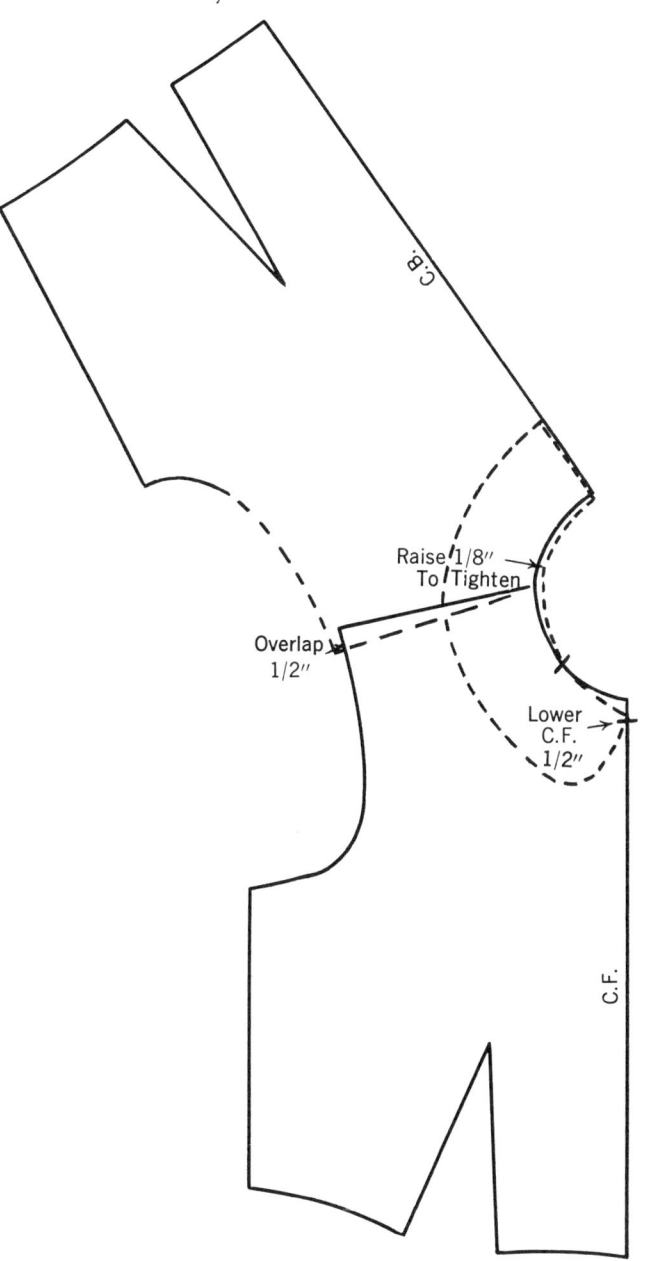

Fig. 8. Flat collar sloper designed from master pattern blouse.

DRESS DESIGN

Wide Flat Collar—"Bertha" (see Figure 9)

1. Place the back and front of the master pattern so that the shoulder seams touch at both the neckline and the armscye but do not overlap.

2. Remove the sharp curve on the center front of the neckline as you did for the narrow flat collar.

3. Remove the length that this adds as you did for the narrow flat collar.

4. To keep the collar flat in the back, increase the circumference of its outer edge by sloping out its center back line 1/8 inch. This tightens the arc at the center back and prevents the neckline from rolling up when a wide flat collar is preferred. The looser outer edge of the collar makes it fall more gracefully over the shoulder blades. For still more ease, or even for a rippling edge, slash from the outer edge of the pattern to the neckline at a point at least 1 inch from the center back.

5. Draw the style-line as you wish.

Note. Wide collars sometimes have shoulder seams so that the width beyond the armscye can curve down over the arm (see Figure 10). Also see the lay-out plan for the sleeve with a dropped shoulder line, Chapter 4, pages 157-158.

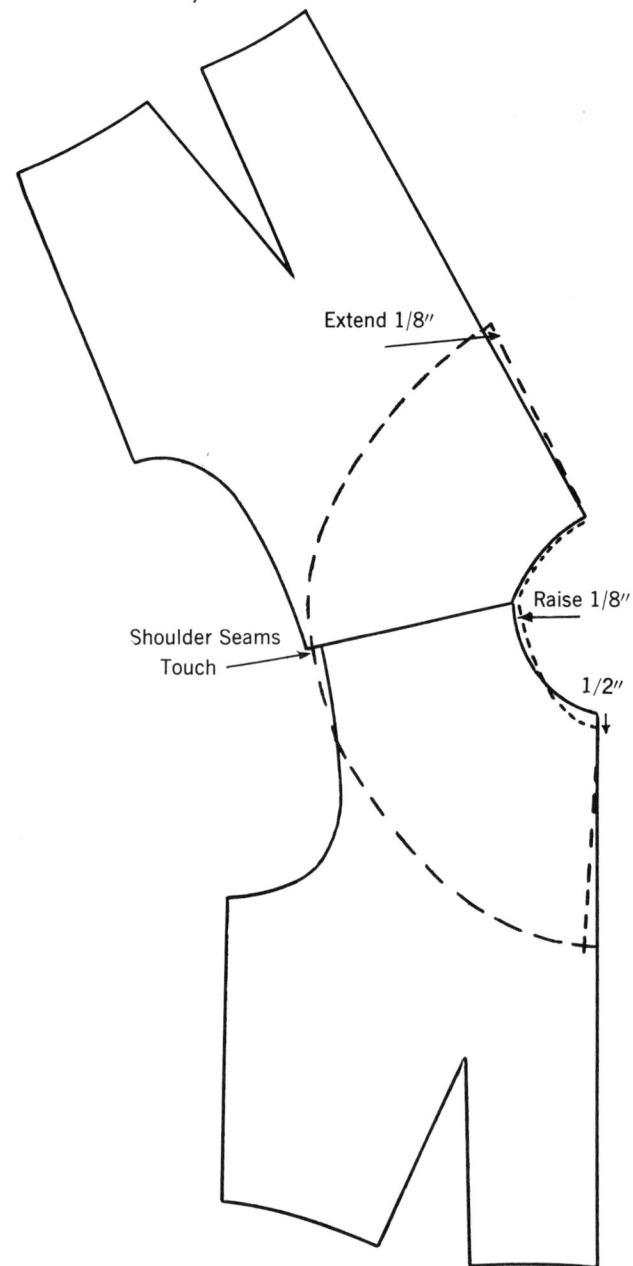

Fig. 9. Wide flat collar designed from master pattern.

Fig. 10. Wide collar. Curved over arms with shoulder seams.

Problem 3

COLLARS DESIGNED FROM THE COLLAR PATTERN SLOPER

Rippled Collar (see Figure 11)

To design rippled collars from the sloper made in Problem 2, first draw lines from the outside edge perpendicular to the neckline where the flares will be most flattering and consistent with the rest of the design. Then slash and spread to produce ripples of the size desired. Figure 12 shows that the placement and spread for the flares must be considered in relation to the number and position of seams in the collar. The one in Figure 12 requires either a shoulder seam or a seam or opening down the center back. To produce a collar that ripples evenly around the entire neckline,

COLLARS AND NECKLINES

many complete circles, each with a small inner circle whose size determines the degree of flare, are cut and sewed together with tiny seams on the lengthwise grain.

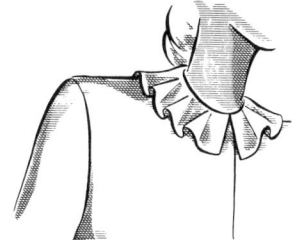

Fig. 11. Rippled collar designed from collar sloper.

Note. See Figure 27 for the pattern shape of a collar which rolls high in the back but lies flat at the center front.

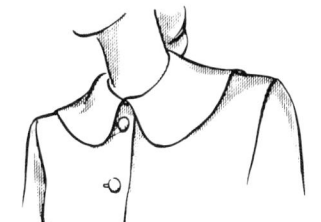

Fig. 13. Rolled Peter Pan collar.

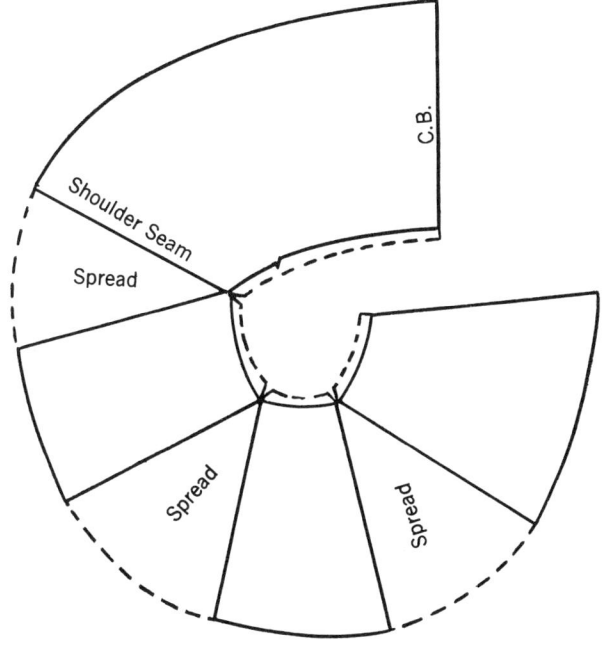

Fig. 12. Flat collar sloper slashed and spread for rippled collar.

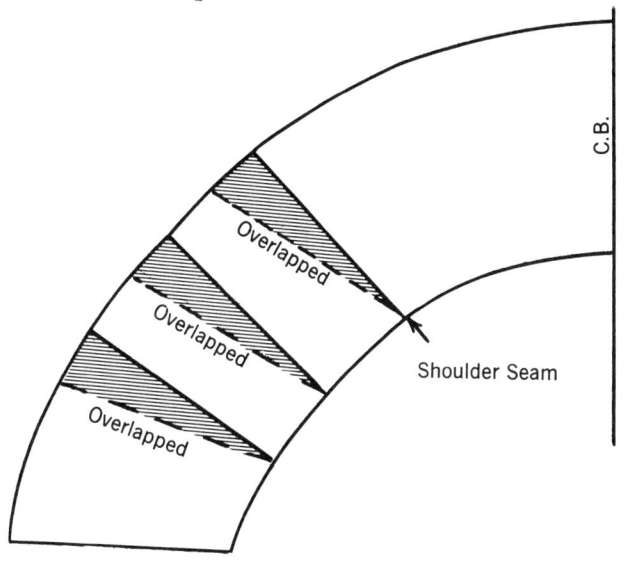

Fig. 14. Flat collar sloper slashed and overlapped for rolled Peter Pan collar.

Rolled Peter Pan Collar (see Figure 13)

This is sometimes referred to as a full-roll collar because it rolls from center back to center front. The Peter Pan collar, although often thought of as similar to the flat collar, actually has a soft roll which falls away from the side of the neck unlike the high-roll collar which clings along the fold-line. To design this collar, slash and overlap a copy of the collar sloper, as shown in Figure 14. Keep the roll soft and low at the center back by placing the first slash at the shoulder position. A straight line across the center back produces a high, close-fitting roll.

Problem 4

DRAFT FOR A HIGH-ROLL COLLAR (see Figure 15)

To appear smartly tailored, a high-roll collar should cling to the neck at the center back and sides. Since the neck is smaller at the fold-line than at the base, a collar cut from a straight strip of material tends to buckle along the fold-line. However a convex curve at the neckline edge of the collar increases the length so that it fits comfortably at the base and yet clings at the fold-line.

Note. Never attempt to make a high-roll collar wide.

This collar can be so easily drafted from the neckline measurements that draping directions will not be given. If you wish to drape it, follow the directions for the narrow standing collar (pages 262-263 and Figures 36 and 37), but introduce less convex curve.

DRESS DESIGN

Fig. 15. High roll collar.

The Draft (see Figure 16a)

1. Draw a line *AB* the length of the basic neckline from center back to center front. For a coat or jacket, measure over a garment.

2. Square out from *A* the collar width — not more than twice the height of the stand.

3. Continue *AC* down ½ inch to *D*.

4. Square out from *D* 2¼ inches. If the curve on the neckline begins closer to the center back than this, it will overtighten the outside edge of the collar.

5. Draw a line from *D* through *E* to *AB*, ending at point *F*. This line will be the length of the neckline from center back to center front minus 1¼ inches.

6. Follow the straight line *AB* for the last 1¼ inches. The original point *B* will be slightly too far out because the line curves from *D*. Move point *B* back toward *F* so that line *DEFB* equals the neckline measurement from center back to center front.

7. Square out from *C*.

8. Square out from *B*, cutting the top line at point *G*.

9. Finish the center front line of the collar.

(a) To shorten the fold-line, indent the center front line *BG* ⅛ inch at *H*, a point ⅜ inch nearer the neckline *B* than the halfway point between *B* and *G*. Join *B* to *H*.

(b) To lengthen the outer or free edge, draw a line from the center front at point *H* to intersect line *CG* at a point ½ inch beyond *G*.

10. Duplicate for the opposite side and cut out the pattern.

Note. Increase the length of the outer edge of a coat collar at the center back to ensure its rolling down enough to cover the neckline seam. This can be done by sloping out the center back seam on the under collar (see Figure 16b), and slashing and spreading the top collar pattern at the lower edge (see Figure 16c).

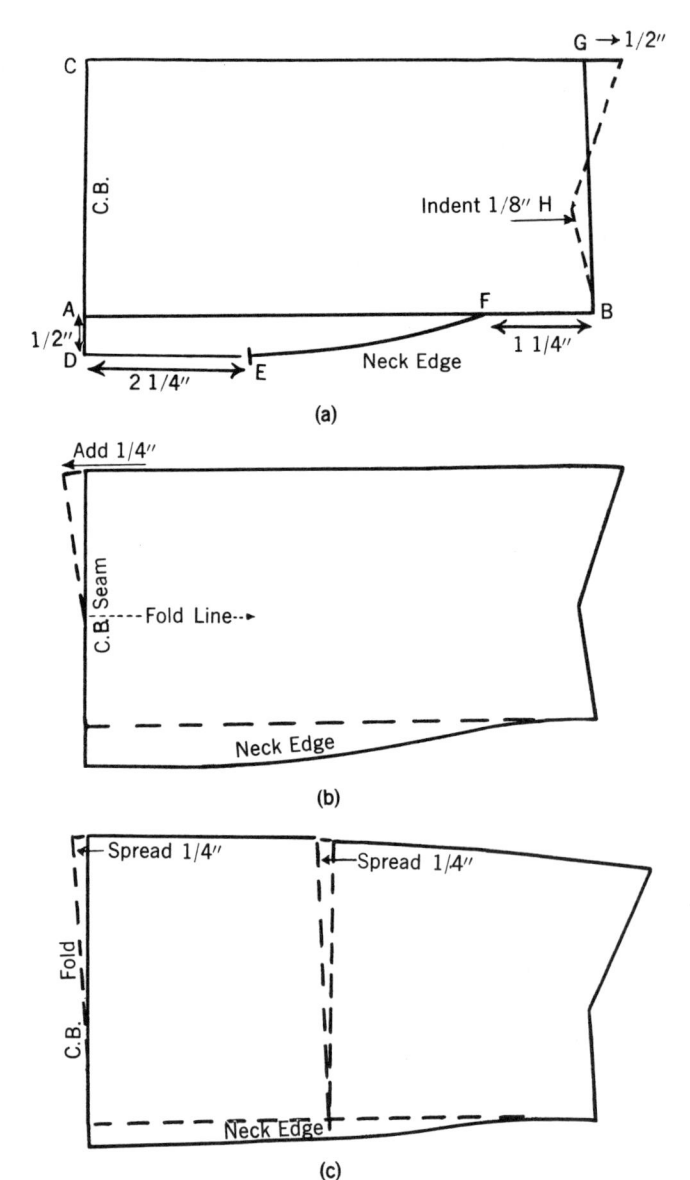

Fig. 16. Draft for high roll collar. (*a*) Draft of pattern for the collar; (*b*) Under-collar of wool coat with CB seam; (*c*) Top collar of wool coat.

254

COLLARS AND NECKLINES

Problem 5

DRAFT FOR A CONVERTIBLE COLLAR (see Figure 17)
(See also the Draping of a Convertible Collar)

Measurements needed for the drafting of this collar are given below:
Center back to center front along the basic neckline.
Center back to shoulder seam.
Center back to break-line.
Height desired for stand.
Collar width from fold-line to outer edge at center back and shoulders.

To construct the neckline of the collar, follow these directions.

1. Draw horizontal line *AB* one-half the length of the neckline, or the length of the measurement from the center back to the center front.

2. At *A*, erect a perpendicular, line *AI*.

3. Measure up from *A* ¾ inch and mark *C*. This establishes the depth of the inward curve at the center back.

4. Draw a smooth curve from point *C* to line *AB*, making it the length of the neckline from the center back to the shoulder seam plus 1 inch. Mark point *E*.

5. Continue on line *AB* the length of the neckline from *E* (the point 1 inch in front of the shoulder seam) to the break-line of the lapel at point *F*.

6. Draw a line ½ inch above and parallel to *AB* in order to establish the approximate rise for the outward or convex curve at the end of the collar.

7. Draw a convex curve from *F* up to the parallel line drawn in step 6 and make the curve from *F* the length of the neckline from the break to the center front. Label the center front neckline point *G*.

Note. This completes the neckline of the collar and gives it a compound curve. It is possible to draw a straight line from the center back to the break-line and then curve upward as shown from *F* to *G*. However a straight neckline produces a collar which pulls tighter on its outside edge than one with a curved line.

To construct the style line of the collar, perform the following steps.

1. Measure up from *C* the height of the stand and mark *H*. In blouses that are to be worn under suits, a satisfactory stand is about ¾ inch, and it can seldom be higher than 1⅛ inches.

2. From *H* measure up twice the height of the stand and mark *I*. Since there is an inward curve on the neckline of ¾ inch at center back, the collar will tend to stand one-third of its width and fall two-thirds of its width. If the neckline is constructed as a straight line across the back, the stand from *C* to *H* and the fall from *H* to *I* must be made equal.

3. Square a line from *I* the length of *AB*.

4. Square out from *AB* at point *E*. Measure up from *E* on this line the length of center back, or from *C* to *I*, and mark point *J*.

5. Follow out from point *I* on *IK* about half the distance from *I* to *J* before curving in to point *J*.

6. Draw a line through *G* parallel to the center back. The collar may end on this line, or it may slope out from *G* and end 1½ inches or more beyond it for a collar both longer and wider at the pointed ends.

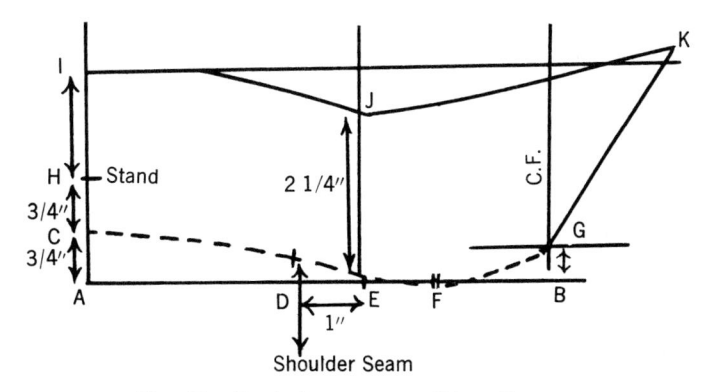

Fig. 17. Draft for a convertible collar.

DRESS DESIGN

PART II
DRAPING

Problem 1

DRAPING PROCEDURE FOR THE BUILT-UP NECKLINE

A neckline that curves up against the side of the neck is usually more becoming than one that stops abruptly at the base of the neck, since it forms a softer transitional line. Moreover, it creates an impression of height in the figure and slenderizes a short heavy neck (see Figure 1).

Front of Garment

1. Placing the center front line marked on the fabric to coincide with the center front of the form, and with the top edge of the cloth 1½ inches above the shoulder line, pin it at the following points (see Figure 18):
    (a) Base of neck.
    (b) 1 inch above base.
    (c) Bust line.
    (d) Waistline.

2. Pin the fabric to the form again 3 to 4 inches from the center base of the neck at the chest level to support the crosswise grain perpendicular to the center front.

3. Pin around the base of the neckline marked on the form from the center front to the shoulder seam, smoothing with the thumb of the left hand ahead of the pins, which should be placed by the right hand. Pencil the basic neckline with short broken lines to guide you later in placing the blouse correctly when you fit it.

4. Pencil the shoulder seam line. Cut it with a ¾ inch seam allowance, cutting from the armscye end of the shoulder toward the neck and stopping at a point 1½ inches from the neckline to slash diagonally to the intersection of the shoulder line and the neckline (see Figure 19).

5. Before marking the shoulder seam line above neck base, pull the lengthwise threads above the base of the neck forward toward the center front from the slash point. This eases the fabric above the base of the neck and avoids a tight upper edge that would draw down and form horizontal wrinkles around the lower part of the neck.

Note. The diagonal slash at the shoulder and neck intersection is not only important but necessary, since it makes it possible to pull forward the lengthwise threads above the basic neckline into a position more nearly perpendicular to the neckline. It is impossible to achieve an absolutely smooth fit over the two planes (the horizontal area around the collar bone and the vertical plane of the neck) with one uncut or undarted piece of material unless the fabric has some flexibility. Soft-textured wool is ideal because the lengthwise threads above the basic neckline can be forced out of their normal position perpendicular to the crosswise threads by stretching and shrinking.

6. Pencil the neck end of the shoulder seam line and cut it with a ⅜ inch seam allowance (see Figure 19). Turn under the seam allowance and pin it perpendicular to the edge.

7. Measure up from the base of the neck the desired neckline height, usually between ½ and 1 inch. Mark and cut it with a ¼ inch seam.

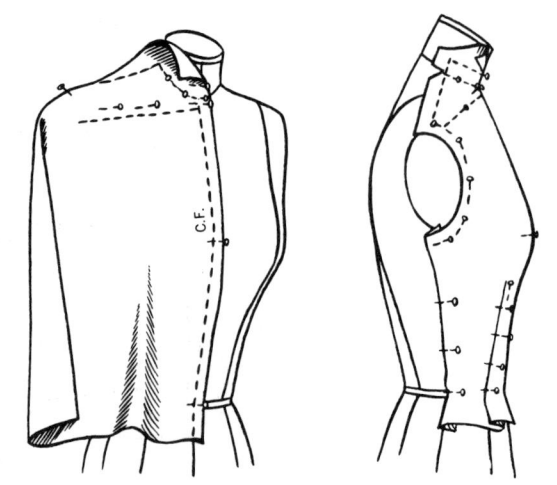

Fig. 18. Draping procedure for built-up neckline. Front of garment, steps 1 to 3.
Fig. 19. Steps 4 to 7.

256

COLLARS AND NECKLINES

Back of Garment

1. Place the fabric with the marked center back line at the center back of the form and with the top edge 1½ inches above the shoulder line; then pin it at the following points (see Figure 20):
   (a) Base of neck.
   (b) 1 inch above base.
   (c) Shoulder blade.
   (d) Waistline.

2. Pin again to the basic neckline 1 inch from the center back. Do not allow the crosswise grain to drop, but keep it perpendicular to the center back.

3. Place a small neckline dart about 1½ inches from the center back. It should be from ⅛ to ¼ inch deep at the base of the neck and should taper off to nothing both near the upper edge of the neckline and 2 inches below the neckline.

4. Continue to pin the fabric to the basic neckline, smoothing ahead of the pins and keeping the crosswise grain level until you reach the shoulder seam.

5. Pencil the shoulder seam line and cut it exactly as you did the front (see Figure 21).

6. Force the lengthwise threads from the point of the slash toward the center back before marking the shoulder seam line above the base of the neck.

7. Finish the shoulder seam line by slipping the back seam allowance forward under the front and pinning it perpendicular to the edge.

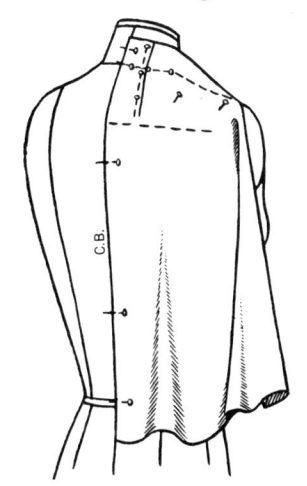

Fig. 20. Back of garment, steps 1 to 4.

8. Measure up from the base of the neck the desired neckline height, and mark and trim the seam to match the front.

Note. If a center back seam is used, it provides another fitting line and can even be substituted for the small neck dart.

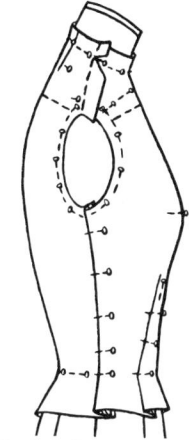

Fig. 21. Back of garment, steps 5 to 8.

Figure 22, illustrating a variation of the built-up neckline, shows that darts or yokes entering the neckline make it possible to fit the built-up neckline even more closely and offer interesting design possibilities as well.

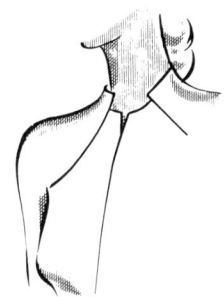

Fig. 22. Built-up neckline with dart variation.

Problem 2

DRAPING PROCEDURE FOR THE FLAT COLLAR
(see Figures 23a, b, and c)

A flat collar is particularly suited to a young child or a young woman with small, delicate features. It is a basic collar form, however, and since it can be interpreted in many different ways, it has great versatility.

DRESS DESIGN

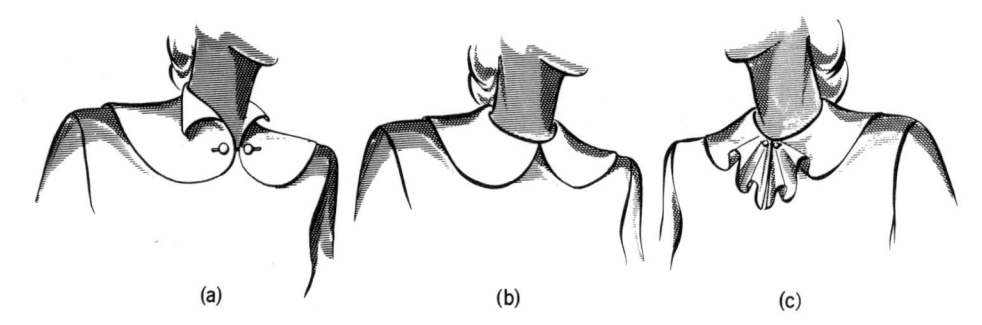

Figs. 23 (a), (b), (c). Flat collar with variations.

1. Find the center back line on the fabric by measuring from the selvage the planned width of the collar from the center back to the outside edge at the shoulder plus 2 inches. Pencil the center back line on the lengthwise grain. The approximate lengthwise measurement is the depth of the collar plus 9 inches.

2. Pin to the form the center back line marked on the muslin, allowing the collar depth at the center back to hang below the basic neckline. Clip on the center back line from the basic neck up 6 inches or more (see Figure 24a).

3. Trace a crosswise thread along the neckline for at least 1 inch from the center back to prevent the grain from dropping. Pin the muslin to the neckline of the dress form 1½ inches from the center back.

4. Beginning at the center back, cut along the neckline 1½ inches, allowing a ⅜ inch seam. Clip to within ⅛ inch of the neckline at this point.

5. Continue to smooth and pin the fabric toward the shoulder seam, clipping the seam allowance at intervals of 1 inch. Keep the crosswise grain from the center back to the shoulder seam almost level. Lowering the grain loosens the lower edge, and lifting the grain tightens the lower edge, causing the collar to roll.

6. Smooth the muslin over the shoulder to the center front so that both the neckline and the lower edge of the muslin lie flat. (See directions for Variation A.) Continue to pin and clip at one-inch intervals, stretching the neckline slightly.

7. Pencil the outside edge of the collar and cut it (see Figure 24b and directions for Variation B).

8. Pencil the basic neckline and crossmark at the shoulder seam.

9. Remove from the form and smooth and true the lines. Mark the final neckline ⅛ inch above the one marked on the form in order to introduce a slight roll that covers the seam line when the collar is attached to the garment.

10. Fold the fabric on the center back line and duplicate the other half of the collar to try on.

Variation A (see Figure 23a)

Since a flat collar is so extremely uncompromising in line that it is usually too harsh and flat for an adult, it is generally wise to take advantage of the many interesting variations that are almost bound to happen accidentally when you are draping. For instance, by clipping to the neckline at a point about ¾ inch in front of the shoulder seam line and flipping the fabric over above the neckline, you will have a lapel on top of the flat collar — a rolling transitional line more flattering to the neck and face than the flat collar. A crisp fabric will interpret this as a half standing lapel. The pattern shape for this variation is illustrated in Figure 25a.

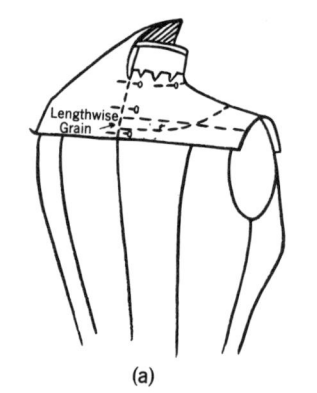

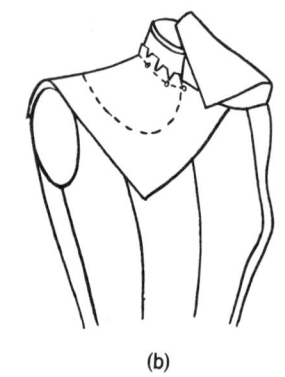

Fig. 24. Draping procedure for flat collar. (a) Steps 1 to 6; (b) Steps 7 and 8.

258

COLLARS AND NECKLINES

Variation B (see Figure 23c)

The fabric within the curve marked for the center front, if it is not cut away, may be interpreted as a small jabot, indicated in the pattern shape shown in Figure 25b.

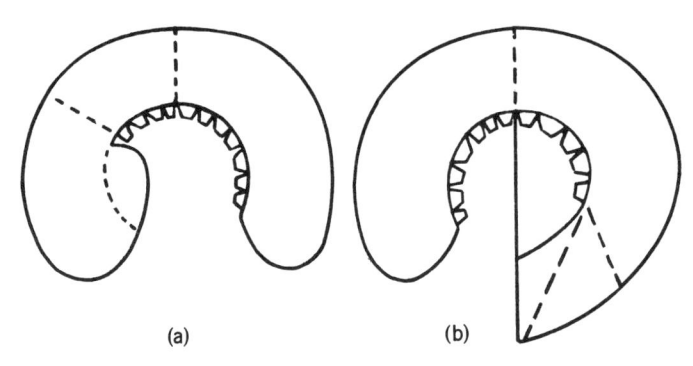

Fig. 25. Flat collar variations. (a) Collar pattern for Fig. 23 (a); (b) Collar pattern for Fig. 23 (c).

Problem 3

DRAPING PROCEDURE FOR A COLLAR WITH A HIGH ROLL IN BACK AND FLAT AT CENTER FRONT (see Figure 26)

Collars that roll up against the neck in back are more becoming and give a more tailored appearance to a costume than those which reveal the base of the neck at the back.

To drape a collar of this kind, proceed as outlined below:

1. Cut off a strip of muslin with the lengthwise grain measured the depth of the collar at the center back plus 4 inches. (For a collar which comes to a low V at the center front, add several more inches.) The crossgrain direction of the strip should equal the measurement of the neckline planned for the garment plus 2 inches for manipulation.

2. Pencil the center back line on the lengthwise grain of the muslin.

3. Measure up from the crossgrain edge 4 inches on the center back line and square out from this point the neckline length from the center back to the shoulder seam. A collar with a high roll in back has a straight, not a curved, back neckline (see the pattern shape, Figure 27).

Fig. 26. Collar rolls high in back, lies flat in front.

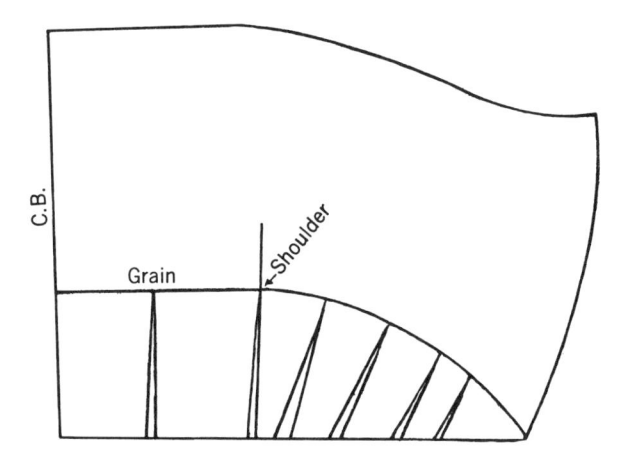

Fig. 27. Pattern shape for collar shown in Fig. 26.

4. Pin the muslin to the form with the 4 inch allowance hanging below the base of the neck and with the center back line on the center back of the form. Pin at the base of the neck and above the base the desired height of the stand (see Figure 28).

5. Pin along the neckline from the center back to the shoulder seam.

6. Clip from the bottom edge up to the base of the neck. (Thus far the collar is turned up against the neck of the form.)

7. Pin the fabric to the form above the basic neck at the shoulder line the desired height of the collar stand.

259

DRESS DESIGN

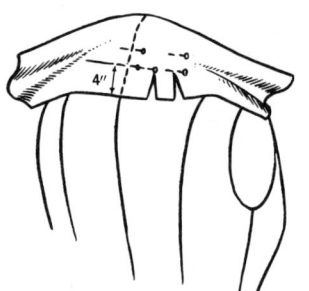

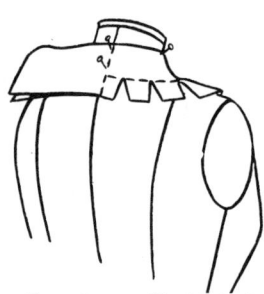

Fig. 28. Draping procedure for collar that rolls high in back, lies flat at center front. Steps 1 to 7.
Fig. 29. Step 8.

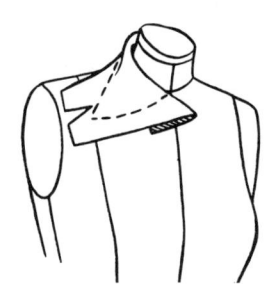

Fig. 30. Step 9, shows marking for both basic and V-necklines.
Fig. 31. Step 9, shows outside edge marking.

8. Fold the muslin over on itself and anchor the outside edge to the form at the center back so that it will not shift (see Figure 29). Pencil the outside collar edge from the center back to the shoulder, and clip from the raw edge to the penciled line.

Caution. Keep the collar anchored at the back so that the center back marking remains perpendicular to the neckline, and pin the fold-line at the side.

9. Finish the collar from shoulder line to center front (see Figure 30).

(a) *For a V-neckline,* fold the fabric back from the shoulder to the lowest point of the center front and mark the outside edge of the collar. Then flip the fold up out of the way to mark the neckline edge of the collar.

(b) *For a basic neckline,* fold the muslin back from the shoulder, but follow the base of the neck. This requires an inward curve at the neckline to prevent the collar from buckling away at the side. Flip the fold up out of the way and mark tentatively the line following the base of the neck on the form. Clip to within ¾ inch of this line, and again check the fit of the collar along the fold-line. When the curve is satisfactory, mark the outside edge (see Figure 31).

10. Remove the pattern from the form after cross-marking the point which matches the shoulder seam. True the pattern lines and duplicate the opposite side.

Note. After the neckline of the collar from the shoulder to the center front is established, any change in the width of the collar at the shoulder seam will also change the stand. For instance, narrowing the collar at this point will lower the stand, and vice versa.

Problem 4

THE USE OF BIAS FOLDS IN COLLAR DESIGNING

Many collars can be made from bias folds. Because it is pliable, cloth cut on the bias curves more subtly and gracefully than a shaped piece of fabric. When attached to a high neckline, a roll collar made from a straight strip cut on the grain rises half its width, whereas one made from a bias fold stretches along its outer edge and thus reduces the height of its stand. Vary the amount of roll by varying the amount you ease or stretch the neck edge of the bias when you attach it to the garment. For example, to force a collar to roll up very close to the neck (see Figure 32a), stretch the neck edge of the bias fold when you attach it to the neckline of the garment. Always handle the double thickness of cloth cut on the bias as if it were one layer. That is, never separate the two when you join the fold to the garment. For a flatter collar (see Figure 32b), stretch the outside or folded edge of the bias and ease the neck edge when you join it to the dress. The success of the flatter collar will depend on the pliability of the fabric. You can steam a bias fold of wool into a curved shape before applying it (see Figure 33).

Bias folds are effective around necklines of low-cut evening bodices, since the fold rolls gracefully over the seam and clings or flares along the free edge according to the way you manipulate it, and according to the inward or outward curve of the neckline to which you apply it (see Figures 32c, and d).

Both wide and narrow shawl collars (see Figure 32e) can often be more successfully made from bias folds than from shaped pieces with seams on the out-

260

COLLARS AND NECKLINES

side edges. To avoid seams at the ends of the collar, curve the neckline edge back to the fold edge (see Figure 34a), and then stretch the fold edge and ease the neckline to straighten the convex curve (see Figure 34b), or even to make it concave (see Figure 34c). The bias shawl collar is especially satisfactory when made of wool because of the excellent shrinking quality of this material.

Tie collars (see Figure 32f), although usually straight bands cut on the lengthwise grain, can also be made of bias folds, either to get a soft roll line around the neck or to play up the diagonal line of a plaid or stripe.

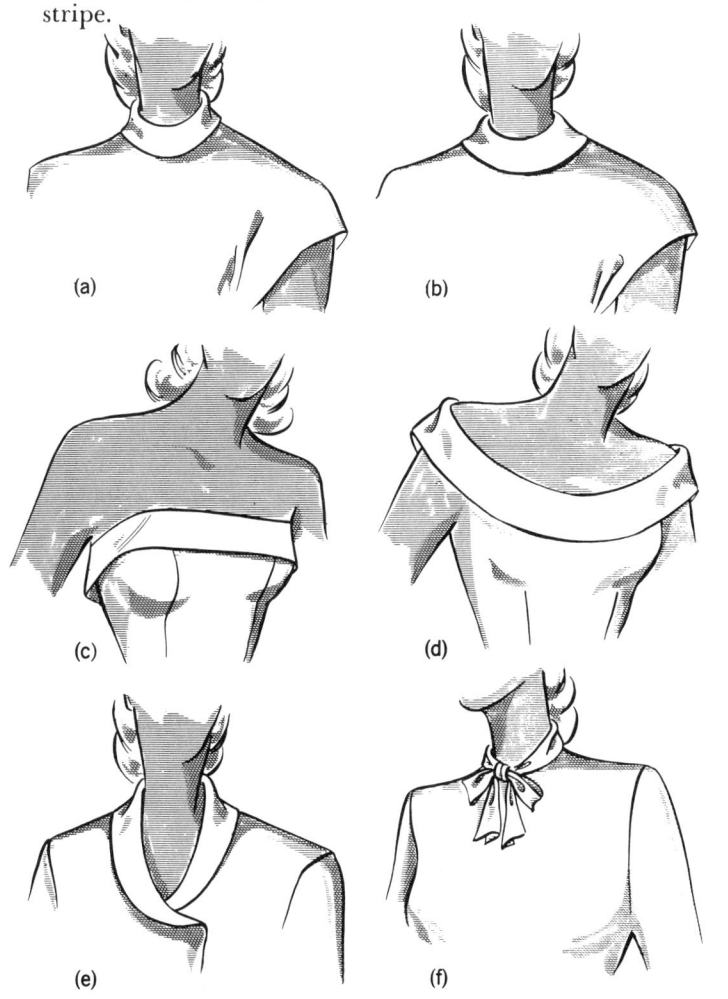

Fig. 32. Bias folds used in collar designing. (a) High bias roll (bias stretched at neckline); (b) Low bias roll (bias eased at neckline); (c) Bias flares when attached to outward curve; (d) Bias clings when attached to inward curve; (e) Bias shaped for a shawl collar; (f) Bias for a high roll collar ending in a tie.

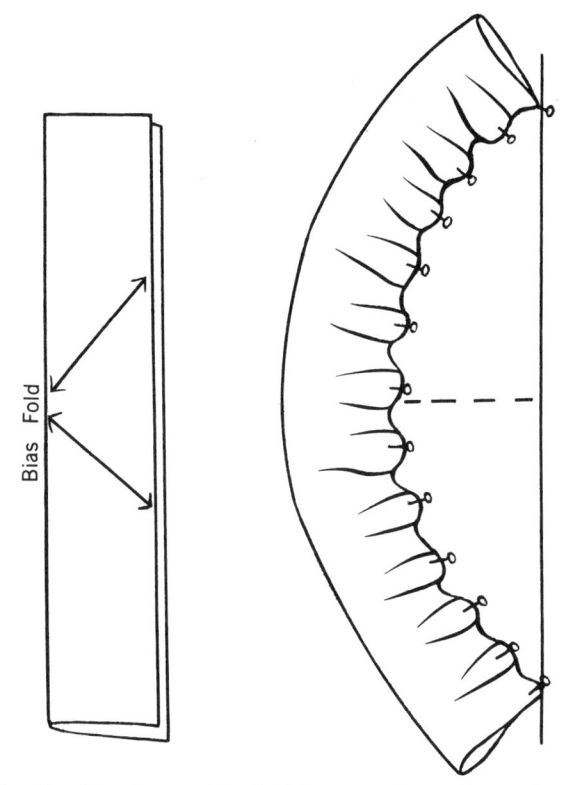

Fig. 33. To shape a bias fold by steaming and pressing.

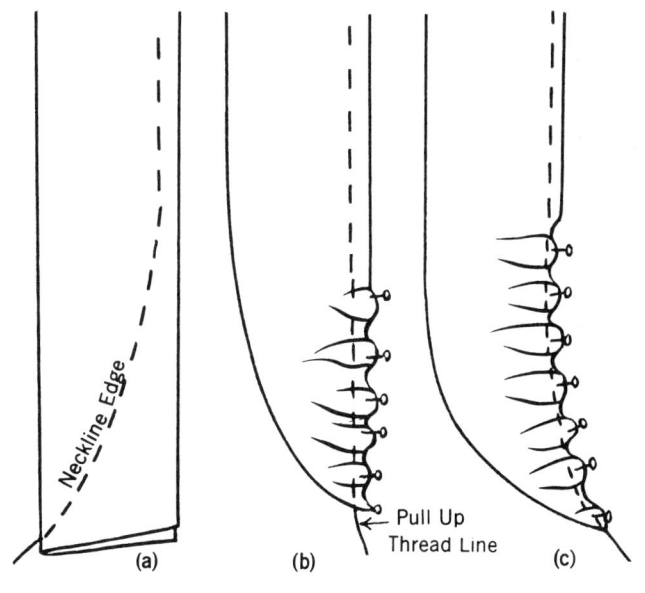

Fig. 34. To shape the end of a bias fold shawl collar. (a) Cut off end of bias collar in a convex curve; (b) Stretch fold edge, shrink neck edge to bring neckline into a straight line; (c) Shrink still further and ease to neckline to produce a concave curve

DRESS DESIGN

Problem 5

DRAPING PROCEDURE FOR A NARROW STANDING COLLAR (see Figure 35)

The narrow standing collar, commonly called the military, Chinese, or Mandarin collar, is particularly becoming when the neck is slender without being either extremely long or short, and when the column of the neck is straight. This type of collar must be made of a fabric firm enough to hold its shape.

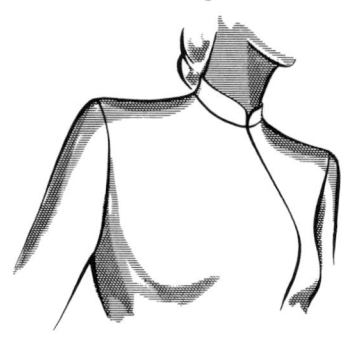

Fig. 35. Narrow standing collar.

The collar must be shaped so that it fits the neck closely along its free edge and at the same time fits comfortably at the base of the neck. Since the measurement around the base of the neck is at least 1¼ inches longer than that 1 inch above the base, a straight strip of fabric would gap at the upper edge. To fit both circumferences, a collar must have a convex curve on the lower edge.

1. Cut a strip of fabric crosswise equal to the basic neckline measurement plus 2 or 3 inches. Make the width of the strip the collar height plus 1¾ inches. Mark the center back line on the lengthwise grain. Pencil the crosswise grain line ⅜ inch above the lower edge for a distance of 1¾ inches from the center back before placing the muslin on the form. Figure 38 shows the pattern shape for this collar.

2. Pin the center back line to the center back of the form, leaving a ⅜ inch seam allowance below the basic neckline (see Figure 36).

3. Pin the strip to the basic neckline from the center back over at least 1¾ inches following the same crosswise thread. From this point drop the grain slightly, so that the collar will cling to the side of the neck. At the point where the collar crosses the shoulder seam, the neckline marking may be ¼ inch above the crosswise thread on which the center back was started.

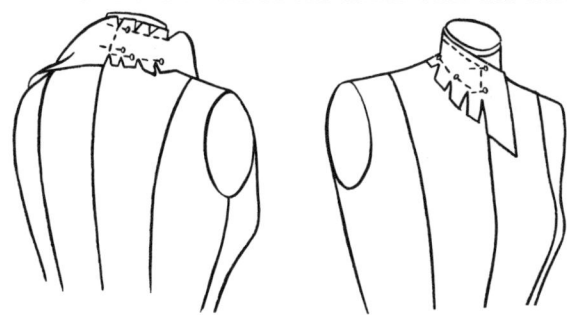

Draping procedure for narrow standing collar. Fig. 36. Steps 1 to 3. Fig. 37. Steps 4 and 5.

4. Clip from the raw edge of the seam allowance in toward the basic neckline, so that the muslin can be smoothed around the neck to fit both circumferences. The closer the upper edge of the collar should fit, the more the crosswise grain should be lowered. The sharpest drop in the grain should begin about 2 inches from the center front. The lower edge of the collar at the center front should be somewhere between ⅝ and 1⅛ inches above the crosswise thread at the center back (see Figure 37).

5. Mark the center front line perpendicular to the neckline edge; mark the upper edge of the collar; and mark the neckline edge. Crossmark at the shoulder seam line.

6. Remove the pattern from the form. True the lines and cut the duplicate half.

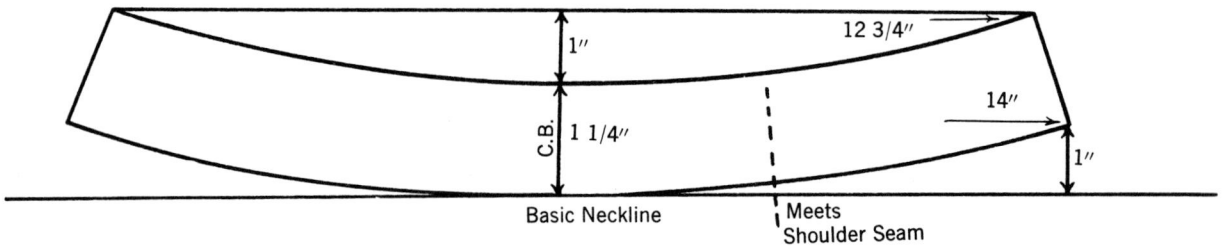

Fig. 38. Pattern for narrow standing collar.

COLLARS AND NECKLINES

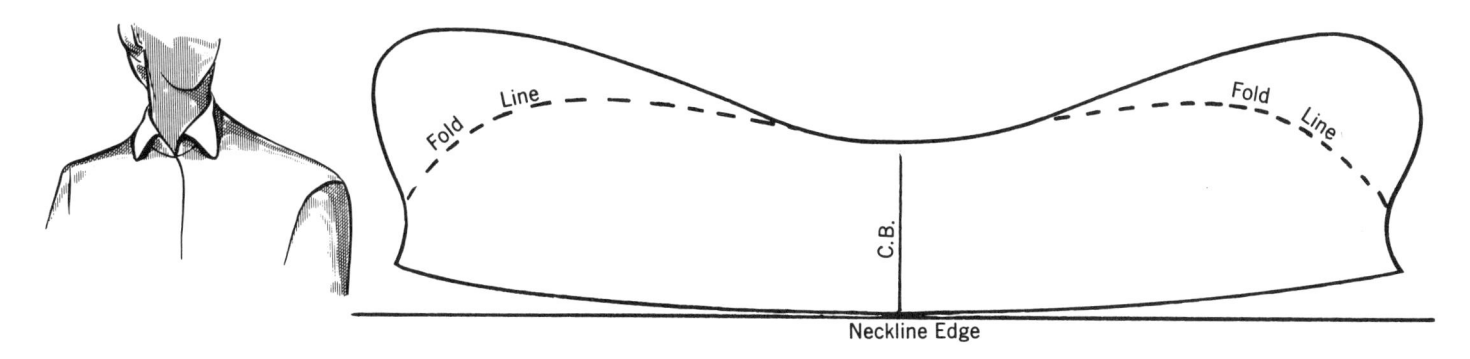

Fig. 39. Wing collar—a variation of the narrow standing collar.

Fig. 40. Pattern shape for collar shown in Fig. 39.

The Wing Collar Variation (see Figure 39)

The wing collar is one which fits snugly around the back and sides of the neck, rolls over slightly along the upper edge at the side front, and turns down at the center front. It is a variation of the narrow standing collar. Follow the same draping procedure, but lower the grain somewhat less from the shoulder to the center front to avoid overtightening the roll along the upper edge. Figure 40 shows the pattern shape for this collar.

Problem 6

DRAPING PROCEDURE FOR THE COLLAR CUT IN ONE WITH THE BODICE FRONT
(see Figures 41-50)

A collar cut as an extension of the bodice front offers the designer many opportunities to vary her collar effects, and because it is cut all in one piece, she avoids the risk of cutting up her design. When this collar is interpreted freely, it leads to invention through the use of excess both above the shoulder and within the neck area as explained in Chapter 7, pages 288-293.

1. Determine how far the fabric must extend beyond the center front to provide the desired width for the lapel or collar which turns back from the center front. Mark the center front line parallel to the selvage for the length of the blouse front plus 5 or 6 inches which will extend above the shoulder line for the back of the collar.

2. Place the muslin on the form with the 5 inch extension above the shoulder seam, and match the center front lines (see Figure 41). Anchor the muslin to the center front at the base of the neck *and also 1 inch above the base.* Pin the cloth to the form at the bust and waist. Pin it to the form at the chest line to keep the crosswise grain level when the pins at the neckline are later removed to turn back the collar or lapel.

3. Pin the fabric to the neckline marked on the form from the center front to the shoulder, smoothing with the thumb of the left hand ahead of the pins, which should be placed by the right hand. It is important to avoid too much looseness, but the neckline cannot fit as snugly as the basic neckline of your master pattern and still allow the collar to roll effectively.

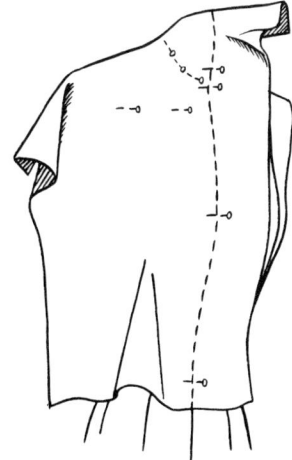

Fig. 41. Draping procedure for collar cut in one with bodice front.

DRESS DESIGN

4. Pencil the shoulder line and cut it with a ¾ inch seam allowance (see Figure 42). Begin to cut at the end of the shoulder and proceed toward the neck. At a point 1½ inches from the neckline, slash diagonally to the intersection of the shoulder line and the neckline.

5. Turn under the shoulder seam allowance and pin it perpendicular to the edge. Pin the muslin to the form at the intersection of the shoulder and neckline. Finish the basic lines of the blouse, marking the armscye, waistline dart, side seam, and so forth. The blouse should be shaped up before the outside edge of the collar is established. This should be done so that you will be able to see the relationship of the collar shape to the background area of the blouse.

6. Check to see that the fabric is still correctly anchored to the form at the upper chest level, and then remove the pins around the neckline.

7. Turn the muslin back on the fold-line desired for the collar or lapel (see Figure 43), determining at this point the width of the center front lap (see Lap Directions, page 41). Determine the lower point of the fold-line by the top button, and begin it at the edge of the lap. The height of the fold-line will increase until it reaches the shoulder seam, and there it should be pinned up against the side of the neck to match the height of the collar stand in back. The stand can vary from ½ to 1 inch, but as the height of the roll increases, the width of the back of the collar should decrease if the collar is to cling to the neck along the fold-line.

8. Pencil the outside edge of the collar front, keeping the roll in the collar pinned against the side of the neck. Cut along the pencil line to the shoulder, allowing a generous seam so that the shape can be altered later on.

9. Carry the extension around to the back of the neck, continuing the fold-line from the front so that the stand at the center back equals the stand at the shoulder seam (see Figure 44). Smooth the under layer of muslin against the neckline, stretching and pinning it to the form.

Notice that the amount of lifting or dropping of the grain along the basic neckline from the shoulder seam to the center back determines the height of the collar roll and the tightness along the edge of the fold. The higher the roll, the more the fabric must be dropped below the basic neckline of the form.

10. Turn the muslin back on the fold-line and establish the center back and lower edge, slashing in from the raw edge to allow the collar to set smoothly (see Figure 45). Lift the upper layer of muslin to pencil the center back line on the under layer.

11. Remove the pattern from the form, smooth the lines, and cut the duplicate half.

Note. This type of collar fits best when the neckline end of the shoulder seam is cut as high as the basic neckline or even ⅛ inch higher, and when the shoulder seam is moved as far forward as possible.

Fig. 42. 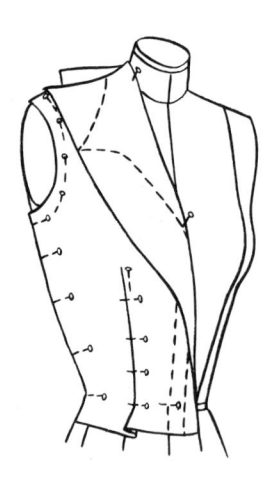　　　Fig. 43. 　　　Fig. 44. 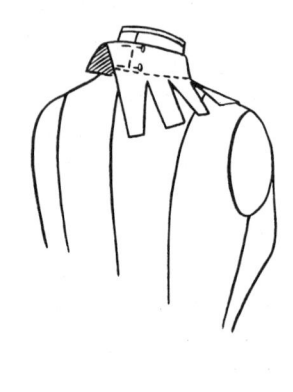　　　Fig. 45.

COLLARS AND NECKLINES

Varying the Roll of the Collar (see Figures 46a, b, and c, and 47)

1. Before establishing the center back and outside edge of the collar across the back, decide whether you want a collar which is flat in front, as in Figure 46a, or a curled one, as in Figure 46b. To produce the curl along the free edge, lengthen the outside edge of the collar. Pull the collar to the front until you get the desired curl, and then smooth the fabric across the back, reducing the height of the fold-line slightly if necessary, and establish the new center back line. The center back line from the outside edge of the collar to the fold-line slants more when the outside edge is lengthened. Clip to the center back seam at the fold-line. See Figure 47 for the collar pattern G A B F with the fold-line BH for the collar shown in Figure 46 a and the collar pattern G A B C with the fold-line BH for the collar shown in Figure 46 b.

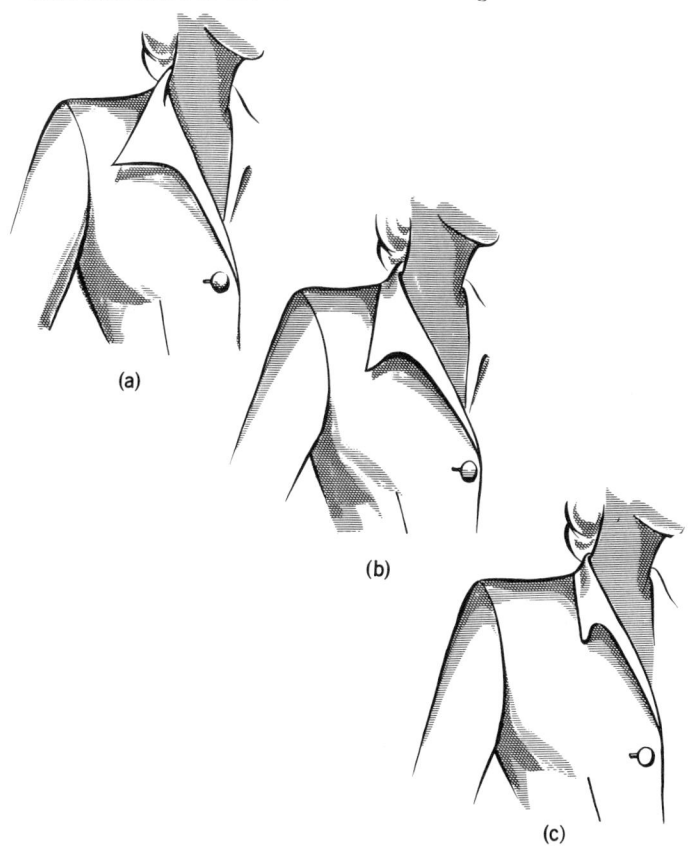

Fig. 46. Varying roll of collar cut in one with bodice front. (a) Collar rolls in back, becomes flat in front; (b) Collar curls in front; (c) Collar rolls high in back and front.

2. Produce the higher roll indicated in Figure 46c by dropping more of the fabric below the basic neckline of the form at the back. (See Figure 47 for the collar pattern G D E F with the fold-line EH).

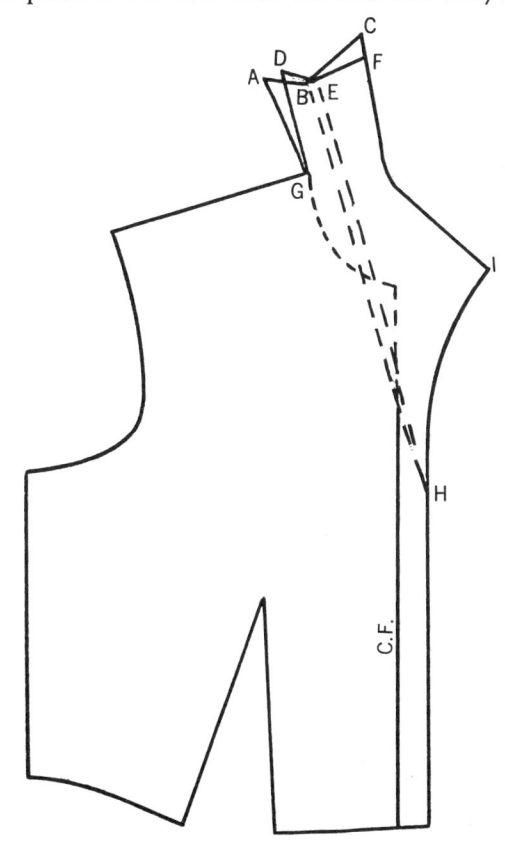

Fig. 47. Pattern for Figs. 46 (a), (b), and (c).

Checking the Fit and Shape of the Collar Pattern

1. *The center back seam* of the collar should not be made a straight line unless it is so marked when on the form. A line sloping in from the neckline seam to the fold-line, and out again to the outside edge, often improves the fit of the collar at the center back and allows the extra length needed on the outside edge of the collar with a rolling effect as in Figures 46b and c.

2. *The neckline seam* may have a slight convex curve near the center back. This produces a close fit along the fold-line and prevents the center back of the collar from standing away from the neck. This precaution is especially necessary for a person with a slightly forward head (see Figure 48).

DRESS DESIGN

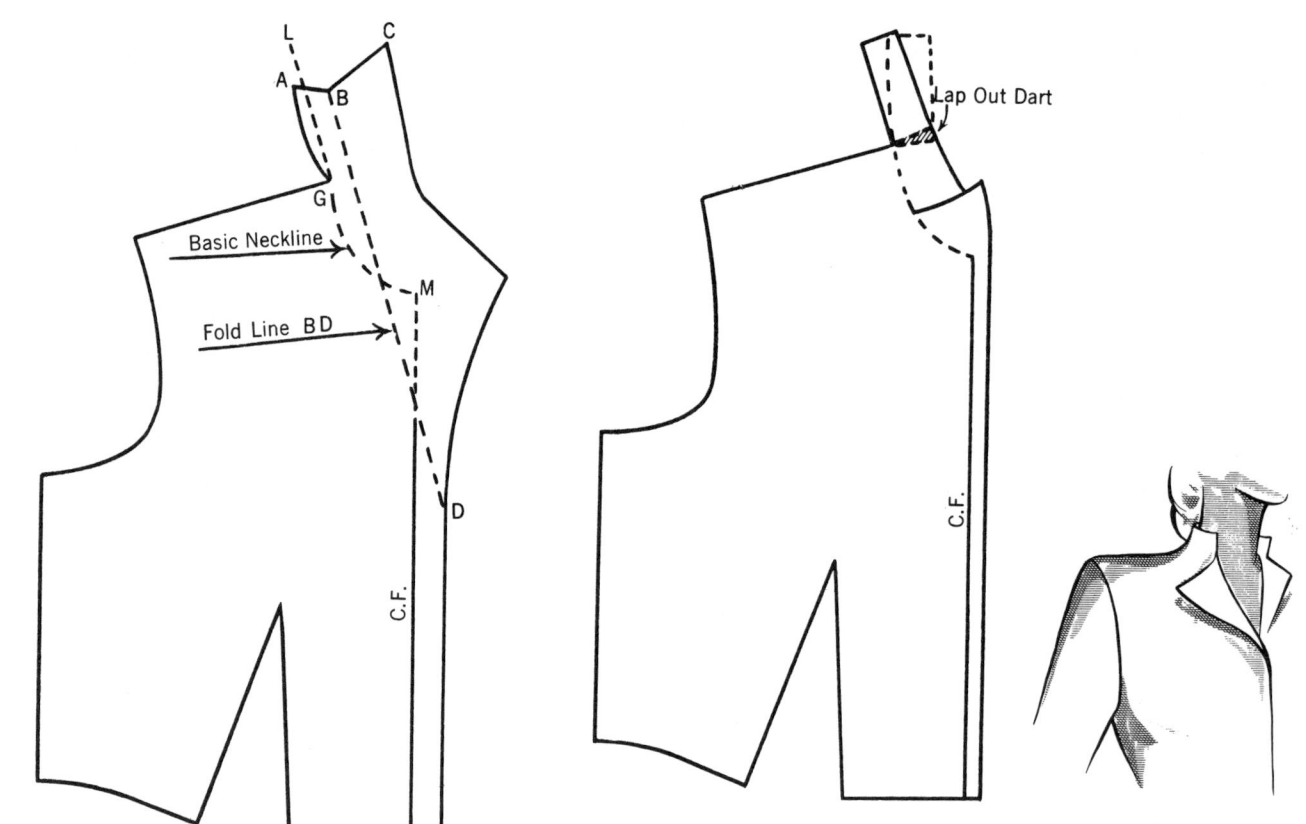

Fig. 48. Use convex curve AG to tighten collar fold-line without tightening neckline.

3. *The angle formed by the shoulder seam and the neckline seam* for a collar with a high roll (about ¾ to 1 inch) should be a right angle. A neckline which meets the shoulder to form less than a 90 degree angle gives a lower stand.

4. *Collar alterations.*

(a) If the collar does not cling to the neck along the fold-line from the side to the center back when the muslin blouse is fitted, pin out excess in a dart which tapers to nothing at the base of the neck. This automatically corrects the pattern shape from the shoulder seam to the center back (see Figure 49, which shows this alteration on the pattern for the collar illustrated in Figure 50). The dotted line shows the altered collar after the dart at the shoulder position has been pinned in.

(b) A dart which follows the basic neckline position beginning near the center front (or sometimes at the center front) and tapering to nothing in front

Fig. 49. Collar alteration to tighten upper edge.
Fig. 50. Variation of collar cut in one with the front of the bodice. See collar pattern, Fig. 49.

of the shoulder seam, takes up the excess at the neckline without destroying the easy roll of the collar. Such a dart is frequently needed to improve the fit of a collar of this type when it fastens high at the center front. The collar or lapel rolls over to conceal the dart line and the facing covers it on the inside.

Problem 7

DRAPING PROCEDURE FOR A CONVERTIBLE COLLAR (see Figures 51a and b)

A convertible collar, as its name implies, can be worn open like a tailored collar or closed as a high-roll collar. However, a collar with enough length along its outer edge to close comfortably cannot possibly have a neckline with as much convex curve as a tailored collar. Neither can it be a straight band, for this would stand away from the side of the neck when open and would buckle at the fold line when

266

COLLARS AND NECKLINES

closed. Therefore, in order to make the collar cling more closely to the side of the neck both when open and closed, some convex curve is needed on the neckline edge of a convertible collar from the point where it meets the break-line of the lapel to the point where it ends at the center front of the garment.

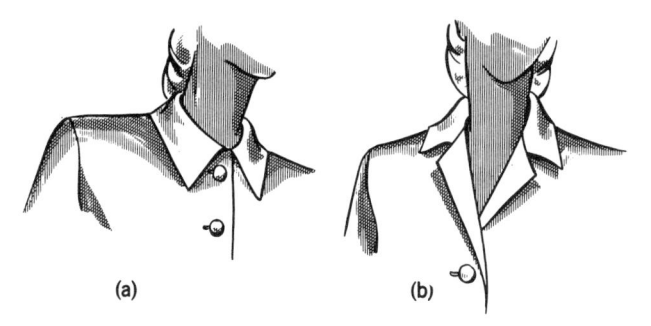

Fig. 51. Convertible collar. (a) closed (b) opened

From the center back to the point where it meets the break-line of the lapel, the collar neckline may be cut straight to produce a collar that stands half its width at the center back and sides when it is worn closed. However, it will be more flexible and will fit better if it is cut with a compound curve — that is, an inward curve from the center back to a point 1 inch in front of the shoulder seam, followed by a straight line to the break-line of the lapel, and then by a convex curve to the center front. Figure 17 shows the pattern shape for a convertible collar.

A convertible collar should be joined to a dress that has a standard basic neckline at the center back and sides. The lap width of the dress (see Chapter 2, page 41) will determine the size of the lapel notch. Start the break-line of the lapel at the top button or fastening. Mark it from the lap edge to a point on the neckline at least 1½ to 2 inches in front of the shoulder seam.

Mark the dress front, showing clearly the center front line, the basic neckline, the lap edge, and the break-line of the lapel (see Figure 52).

1. Fabric measurements for the collar are as follows:

Length — (crosswise grain) neckline length plus 4 to 5 inches for the collar points.

Width — (lengthwise grain) about 5 inches.

2. Fold the length in half and mark the center back.

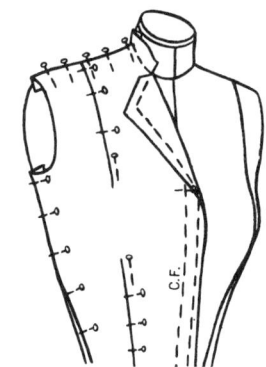

Fig. 52. Figs. 52-56. Procedure for draping convertible collar.

3. Measure up on the center back line 1 inch from the lower edge. Of this, ¾ inch is the allowance for the depth of the inward curve across the back, and ¼ inch is for the seam.

4. Square out 1 inch from the center back at the point measured in step 3, since a curve beginning exactly at the center makes the collar stand away from the center back of the neck.

5. Pin the center back line marked on the muslin to the center back of the form, matching the line drawn in step 4 to the basic neckline (see Figure 53). Clip from the lower edge up to the pin.

6. Pin to the form again ¾ inch above the neckline to hold the muslin level. This pin will come at approximately the height of the stand.

7. Pin along the basic neckline 1 inch over from the center back point. The raw edge of the muslin should be 1 inch below the basic neckline. Clip to the pin.

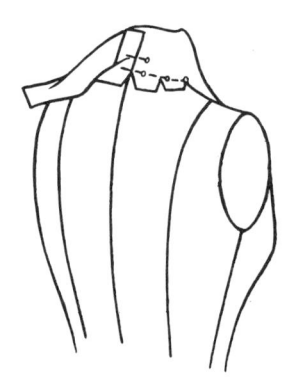

Fig. 53.

267

DRESS DESIGN

8. From the point pinned in step 7, lift the crosswise grain until the raw edge of the muslin is only 3/4 inch below the base of the neck at the shoulder seam. Pin and clip. Do this to produce an inward curve and to increase the ease on the upper edge of the collar.

9. Turn the lapel up against the neckline before pinning the collar from the shoulder seam to the center front (see Figure 54).

10. Proceed to pin the muslin to the neckline, lifting the grain so that at a point 1 inch in front of the shoulder seam, the raw edge is only 1/4 inch below the neckline.

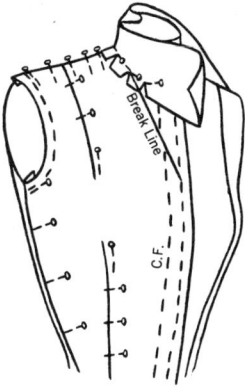

Fig. 54.

11. Continue on the same crosswise thread (1/4 inch above the raw edge) to the break-line of the lapel. Pin and clip.

12. At the break-line, reverse the procedure and begin to drop the crosswise grain to produce an outward curve and to tighten the upper edge of the collar.

13. At the center front, the raw edge of the muslin should be 3/4 inch below the neckline, *i.e.*, the grain should drop 1/2 inch and there should be a 1/4 inch seam allowance.

Note. The above measurements help to guide the beginner, but the looseness or tightness of fit must really determine the amount which the crosswise grain is to be lifted or lowered. If the collar bulges away from the neck at any point, you have raised the crosswise grain too much and created too great an inward curve. The reverse is also true for if the collar pulls tight near the center front, you have dropped the grain too much.

14. Fold the muslin over on itself (see Figure 55). The strip is too wide for the blouse collar at the center back and sides since it stands at least 1 1/4 inches. Clip the outside edge of the collar at the center back and shoulder until the collar settles down to the desired width and stand.

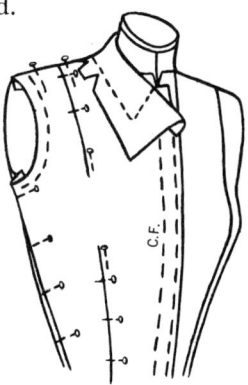

Fig. 55.

15. Turn the lapel and collar back at the center front to see that it sets smoothly in this position, that it clings at the center back and sides and yet does not draw or pull on the outside edge (see Figure 56).

16. With the collar open, mark the outer edge and check it again when you fasten it at the base of the neck.

17. Cut the outside edge with a 1/4 inch seam allowance.

18. Pencil the neckline of the collar and crossmark it at the shoulder seam, at the point meeting the break-line of the lapel, and at the center front.

19. Remove the fabric from the form and duplicate the other half.

Fig. 56.

268

COLLARS AND NECKLINES

Problem 8

DRAPING PROCEDURE FOR A TAILORED COLLAR
(see Figure 57)

Jacket and Lapel

1. Pencil the center front line on muslin 3 to 4 inches back from the lengthwise edge. This distance is determined by width of lapel (see Figure 58).

2. Place the fabric on the form, allowing a 1 inch shoulder seam, and pin the center front at the base of the neck, the bust, and the waistline.

Fig. 57. Narrow tailored collar.

3. In many tailored jackets, the usual shoulder dart is transferred to the neckline, as shown in Figure 58. Keeping the grain level across the bust, swing the excess above the bust line into a neckline dart. The collar and lapel will almost completely hide it.

4. Pin the fabric to the basic neckline of the form, smoothing ahead of the pins.

5. Pin also at the chest line so that the pins at the base of the neck can be removed later without having the muslin shift out of position.

6. Mark the shoulder seam, armscye, waistline dart, and so on, completing the basic lines of the jacket before proceeding with the lapel.

7. Pencil in the lap edge from the beginning of the fold-line to the lower edge of the jacket.

8. Turn the muslin back on the fold, or break-line, to form the lapel (see Figure 59). Pin the fold-line against the form at the shoulder seam line to hold it in position.

9. Study Figure 57 to note the details of a finished tailored collar, and mark as indicated in Figure 59:

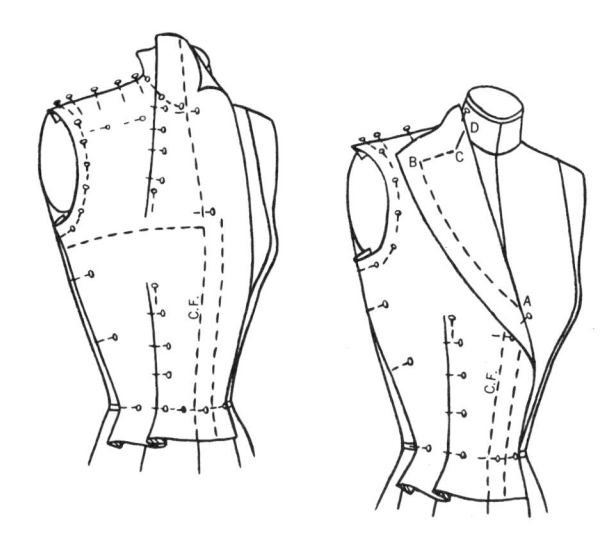

Fig. 58. Procedure for draping a narrow tailored collar. Steps 1 to 7.
Fig. 59. Steps 8 to 11.

(a) The *fold* (or break) line from the lap edge below the top button continuing to the center back of the collar.

(b) *Height* of *roll* (or stand) of collar and lapel. The average stand at the side of the neck is 3/4 to 1 inch.

(c) *The distance from the shoulder seam to the point where the break-line of the collar joins the break-line of the lapel.* This usually measures about 2 inches on the neckline seam.

(d) The *length* and *slant* of the *visible portion of the seam joining the collar* and *the lapel.* Pencil the line *CD*.

(e) The *width* and *shape* of the *lapel notch*. Pencil the upper edge of the lapel, *BC*.

(f) The *size and shape of the lapel* as it continues from the notch to the lap edge. Pencil the line *BA*.

10. Draw the entire line of the lapel from the lap edge to the point where the lapel rests against the neck at *D*. Cut on the seam line along the lap edge and lapel edge up to the point of the notch at *C* (or where the collar joins the lapel).

11. Mark heavily the visible portion of the seam *CD* joining the collar and the lapel. If this line does not show through to the wrong side, place pins through the line and mark on the wrong side as well.

DRESS DESIGN

12. Turn the lapel up against the neck in order to mark the remainder of the neckline (see Figure 60). This must begin as a basic neckline at the shoulder seam and must follow the basic neckline as far as possible in order to swing gradually into the line previously marked for the visible portion of the notch seam. If this line is marked too far above the basic neckline, it tends to come up above the fold-line of the collar. Leave a $\frac{1}{4}$ inch seam allowance on the neckline from the shoulder seam to the point of the notch.

13. Drape the jacket back with a basic neckline.

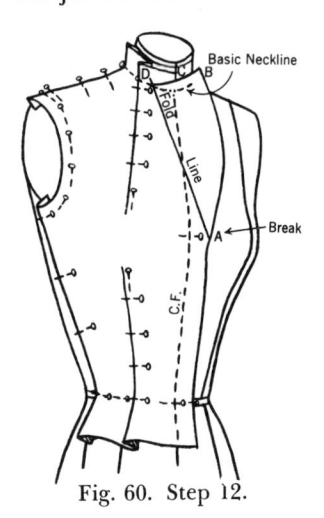

Fig. 60. Step 12.

Narrow Tailored Collar with Convex Curve

1. Begin with a strip about 4 inches wide, with the 4 inch measurement parallel to the lengthwise grain, and twice the length measured on the form from the center back to the notch of the lapel. Pencil the center back line on the lengthwise thread (see Figure 61).

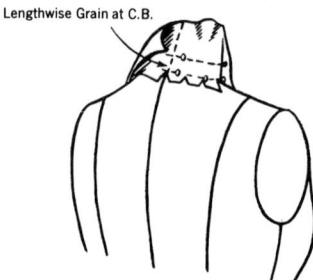

Fig. 61. Tailored collar, Steps 1 to 3.

2. Starting at the center back, pin the muslin at the base of the neckline and 1 inch above the base, leaving a $\frac{1}{4}$ inch seam allowance below the neckline and the bulk of the collar fabric above the neckline.

3. Carry the same crosswise thread along the neckline for approximately 2 inches, or to a point 1 inch back of the shoulder seam. Then begin to drop the grain so that the collar will fit the basic neckline yet cling to the neck at the fold-line. This gives the neckline of the collar a convex curve.

4. To drape and pin the collar to the front of the jacket, keep the lapel turned up flat against the front of the neck rather than rolled over (see Figure 62). Continue to drop the grain on the collar all the way to the point of the notch so that the muslin fits above the basic neckline with neither strain nor excess. A smooth, gradual curve is formed on the collar neckline, swinging from behind the shoulder seam point to the end of the collar.

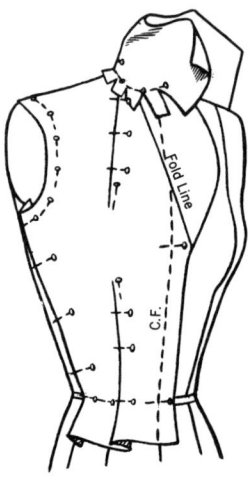

Fig. 62. Step 4.

5. Fold the collar back on itself and mark the outside edge. At the center back, the collar edge should fall at least $\frac{1}{4}$ inch below the basic neckline (see Figure 63).

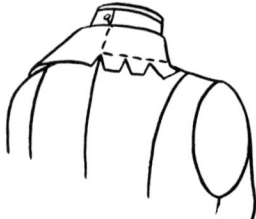

Fig. 63. Step 5.

270

COLLARS AND NECKLINES

6. Pencil the collar neckline and crossmark it at the shoulder seam and also where the break-line of the collar meets the break-line of the lapel (see Figure 64). Pencil the collar fold-line from the center back to the break.

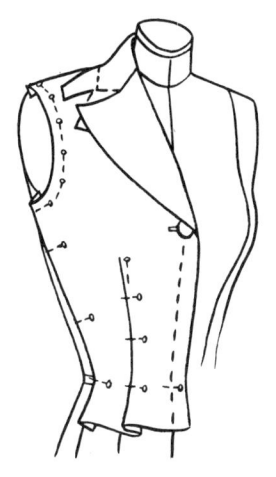

Fig. 64. Step 6.

7. Remove the collar and jacket from the form and true the lines. The shape of the collar pattern is illustrated in Figure 65 and the pattern for the undercollar in Figure 66.

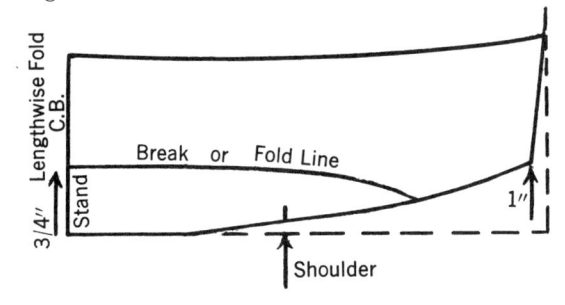

Fig. 65. Pattern for typical tailored suit collar (add ⅛ inch plus seam allowances to all pattern edges except center back when cutting upper collar).

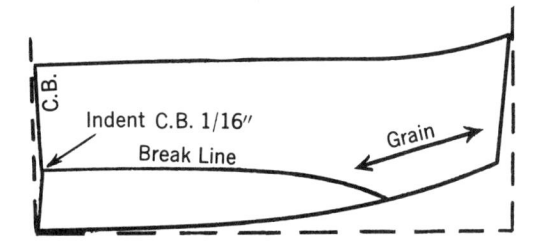

Fig. 66. Pattern for under collar (note grain position).

Wide Tailored Collar with Reverse Curve

The wide tailored collar should be draped in a slightly different way from the narrow one, since on a collar with a straight or convex neckline, the stand or roll rises as the width increases. A stand higher than 1 inch is apt to seem uncomfortably high at the back of the neck in any garment except a heavy winter coat with a collar especially high for warmth. To make the collar wide with less roll (Figure 67), a slight concave curve will be needed across the back of the neckline, reversing into a convex curve from a point back of the break-line. To keep the collar from gapping away from the neck at the side, carry the concave curve only a little beyond the shoulder seam. From that point make the line almost straight until it reverses into a convex curve.

Fig. 67. Wide tailored collar.

1. Begin with a strip of fabric the width of the finished collar plus the seam allowances and about 1 inch for the concave curve. It will be helpful to rule a line on the muslin 1¼ inches from the lower edge on the crosswise grain. Then rule the center back line.

2. Start at the center back and pin the muslin at the base of the neckline and 1 inch above the base. Allow 1¼ inches of width below the neckline.

3. To avoid producing a point at the center back, carry the same crosswise thread along the neckline for 1 inch. Clip from the raw edge up to the basic neckline and begin to lift the crosswise line. The crosswise line drawn on the muslin shows clearly how much the grain is lifted and the resulting amount of inward curve. The amount the grain is lifted will be determined by the width of the collar and the height

271

of the stand. In the collar sketched, the crosswise grain was lifted only ½ inch to give the necessary inward curve before reversing the line into a convex curve. Vary the curve until you obtain the desired roll.

4. The remaining steps are like those given for the narrow tailored collar. Figure 68 illustrates the pattern shape.

Note. By studying the shape of a collar with a reverse curve, one can plainly see that its length at the fold-line is controlled by the character of the inner collar line. Thus in Figure 68, the length between A and B is equal to that between A' and B' because the neckline is straight. But the length between C and D is less than that between C' and D' because the neckline is concave; whereas the length between E and F is greater than that between E' and F' because the curve is convex. A clear understanding of this relationship between the shape of the neckline and the length of the fold-line enables one to produce collars with the exact degree of roll desired.

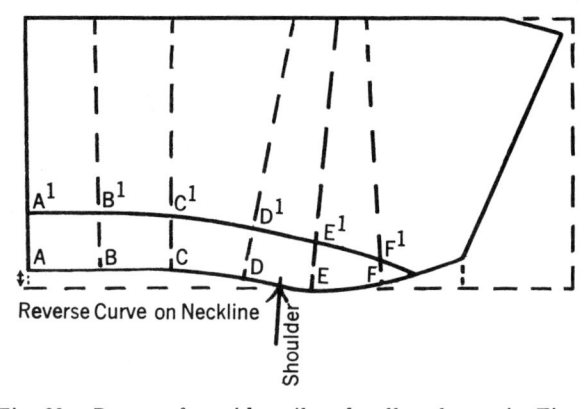

Fig. 68. Pattern for wide tailored collar shown in Fig. 67.

7. Sources of Inspiration in Design

THE BACKGROUND FOR DESIGNING

After mastering the principles and techniques of draping and blocking standard patterns, the student will be able to apply her information to the designing of more unusual and complicated cuts. Although the underlying principles of carrying out intricate designs are exactly the same as for standard patterns, it is of course necessary to practice cutting patterns for many designs of varying degrees of difficulty before one develops the confidence and ability required to design any pattern that she may want.

The imaginative student can hope not only to interpret the designs of others but also to create new ones. Many women have a secret urge to design clothes for themselves whether they design them for anyone else or not, but the urge is often stifled by fear of criticism, lack of confidence, and lack of skill. So much pleasure and satisfaction can be derived from creating original designs that anyone who wants to do it should be given as much help and encouragement as possible. Luckily, there are definite and tangible ways of acquiring the necessary background for designing as well as of developing the ability to use source material creatively.

Ask any student to suggest where she should look for ideas for dress design, and her answer will be immediate and without hesitation — in fashion magazines, shop windows, and the clothes of recognized fashion leaders. It is doubtful, however, whether she has any plan beyond looking for one particular idea which she can copy exactly, or at most, adapt to her own purpose. The same student will probably be much less familiar with the method of using current magazines as a source of background information on fashion trends and details of cut. Every woman, whether a student of dress design or not, will glance through fashion magazines without prompting. But students of dress design need to be taught to recognize the difference between reading for casual enjoyment and a really serious study of fashions.

A would-be designer should scrutinize carefully the best current fashion magazines, not with any thought of copying, but rather with the intention of saturating her mind with general impressions of fashion trends. Too often a novice sees only the cute tricks that happen to appeal to her fancy at the moment, and too often she does not pause to look at a design if some small detail of it is not what she personally likes. The potential designer, however, must look for more than minor details and clothes that suit her own taste. She must consciously cultivate an awareness of current fashion silhouettes and must analyze the subtle fashion changes that influence them. She must observe and analyze the details of each line and cut in order to acquire a fund of fashion and style information. Constant observation of current fashions supplies one basis for recognition of intrinsically good lines, those that are certain to last, and of distinguishing them from the fads and tricks of the moment.

To be sure, this is not by any means the only necessary background for designing. The student should take for granted that she will also need the general training in the fine arts that will enable her to apply the principles of design to every costume, at first consciously, but after long experience, instinctively.

The first steps, then, are to steep one's mind in current fashion information, to develop an understanding of principles of design, and to acquire the technical skill in draping and blocking which makes it possible to carry a design through to completion. Only then can a student feel confident that she has acquired the necessary background for designing really beautiful clothes.

SOURCES OF INSPIRATION

It is impossible to saturate one's mind with fashion information without being stimulated to creative activity. A file of clippings of the best designs of each year furnishes an imaginative mind with endless suggestions. This is obviously the most readily available source material, but there is a danger in relying on it exclusively, for it is so simple and easy to transfer an idea from one costume to another that the source may unwittingly be merely copied rather than used to stimulate the imagination to the invention of a new idea.

Another source of inspiration closely related to current fashions, and only slightly less familiar to the beginner, is historic, peasant, and national costume. Every student of costume design must become thoroughly acquainted with this source and learn to appreciate its value to the designer. But it is almost as easy to interpret too exactly a Grecian or a medieval gown as it is to copy a clipping from a current magazine, since here also it is all too easy merely to transfer a basic idea from one costume to another. And designs taken too literally from such sources will be neither original nor appropriate to a modern setting. Unless costumes from past eras or foreign countries can be used to inspire new designs suitable for the present time and place, they should not be used at all.

Current and historic costumes are both so familiar that they are sure to be used as sources of inspiration without further urging. Moreover, there are so many other prolific sources of inspiration that have scarcely been explored at all, that the suggestions in the following pages are limited to problems of fabric texture and to the many ways of handling fabric through draping and flat pattern blocking. The authors present these less familiar sources with confidence that the careful study of each exercise will not only stimulate the student's imagination, but will also lead her to investigate the possibilities of innumerable other techniques that she will invent for herself.

Suggestion 1

DEVELOPING LINE ARRANGEMENTS BY SKETCHING

Sketching, the most obvious medium for developing an idea, has long been used by designers because it is the quickest way of embodying an intangible idea in tangible form. Some ability to get an inspiration down on paper quickly before it is lost is a great asset to the designer, and the sketch is usually the first step in working out a design already in mind.

You can also use sketching, playing with lines on paper, to create new designs. Starting with a lay figure (see Figure 1), a sheet of transparent tracing paper, a pencil, and an eraser, but with no definite idea for a design in mind, you can work abstractly to create many designs by merely using a certain set of lines in various arrangements. To create the designs illustrated in Figures 2, 3, 4, and 5, the designer simply placed a sheet of tracing paper over the lay figure, drew a costume silhouette, and then placed the lines within the silhouette. In each case she used the same combination of two horizontal and two vertical lines — an excellent basic design because it offers so many possibilities for variation. She let the two verticals represent the French dart line and the lines of the six-gore skirt panels as these structural lines divide the silhouette into pleasing spaces; and she thought of the horizontals as yokes, pockets, Eton jackets, peplums, or merely as abstract space divisions. Try this yourself.

The first step is to draw the verticals and horizontals within the silhouette. Figure 2 shows where not to place them — and incidentally points up the fact that designing does not consist solely of thinking up a new and different idea, but rather involves an understanding of design principles and a feeling for form. Always place lines to produce interesting shapes that not only flatter the lines of the figure but accent and harmonize with the costume silhouette already drawn. Figure 2 shows what happens when lines are placed mechanically, without regard for good space division and without consideration of either the curves of the figure or the silhouette line of the costume. In this sketch, the designer intentionally drew the verticals in one continuous straight line from shoulder to hem line in order to show what happens when the narrowing of the figure at the waistline is ignored. The result

SOURCES OF DESIGN

Fig. 1. Lay Figure on which to design with transparent paper.

Fig. 2. Monotonous spacing.
Fig. 3. The same line combinations as in Fig. 2, but with the spacing improved.

is that the center panel not only looks stiff and blocky, but it fails to slenderize the waistline; and because the panel is perfectly straight, it exaggerates to the point of distortion the curve over the side of the hip.

Now study the horizontals. The upper one cuts across the blouse exactly halfway between the shoulder and the waistline. This is the most monotonous spacing possible, and besides, the horizontal falls exactly at the highest point of the bust, a cross line that should always be avoided in costume design because it overemphasizes the curve of the bust. The lower horizontal cuts the skirt exactly in half — always monotonous spacing.

Next, notice the sleeve. The contour lines should not be parallel, and they will not be if the sleeve is wider at the top than at the lower edge, or the reverse. Look at the sleeve length — exactly to the elbow, an awkward half and half division as well as a length uncomfortable to wear. The entire spacing of this figure shows just how badly a promising set of lines can

275

DRESS DESIGN

turn out when the principles of design have been ignored and no feeling has been shown for the relationship of structural lines to the silhouette itself.

Now study Figure 3. The designer used exactly the same basic combination of lines here as in Figure 2, but with completely different results. This time the verticals emphasize the width of the shoulders and the slenderness of the waist. That is, they repeat the silhouette, and thereby strengthen its effect. Moreover, the skirt paneling divides the width at the hips into three unequal parts and thus avoids the monotony of exact repetition. The paneling is narrower at the waist than at the hip, and it flares out toward the hem to strengthen the lines of the silhouette. Both the blouse and skirt horizontals have been raised to form an interesting relationship between the area of the yoke and the lower section of the waist and between the peplum and the lower section of the skirt. Notice also that both yoke and peplum vary in depth. Next, look at the sleeve, which this time is three-quarter length instead of the awkward elbow length shown in Figure 2. So much for the spacings.

The next step, after placing lines to break up the contour into interesting spaces, is to convert the design from an abstract set of crisscrossed lines to a real dress with style and originality. First of all, there are obviously too many lines crossing one another. Erase some of them, and let your imagination have full play in deciding which ones to rub out. By erasing across various connections you can develop many different designs from the same set of lines. Figures 4 and 5, for instance, show two entirely different conceptions developed from precisely the same combination of lines. The dress shown in Figure 4, geometric and tailored, might be interpreted as a wool dress, whereas the lines of Figure 5 suggest a soft afternoon dress, possibly of rayon crepe.

These examples serve merely to show what can be done by different interpretations of one set of lines. Obviously, they do not begin to exhaust the possibilities. On tracing paper over the lay figure, see how many other designs you can invent from this same set of lines. Then analyze them for beauty of proportion and, of course, for wearability. Even a person who has always considered herself to be unimaginative will find that from this starting point she can create innumerable designs very quickly. She will also discover that it is an excellent way to train her

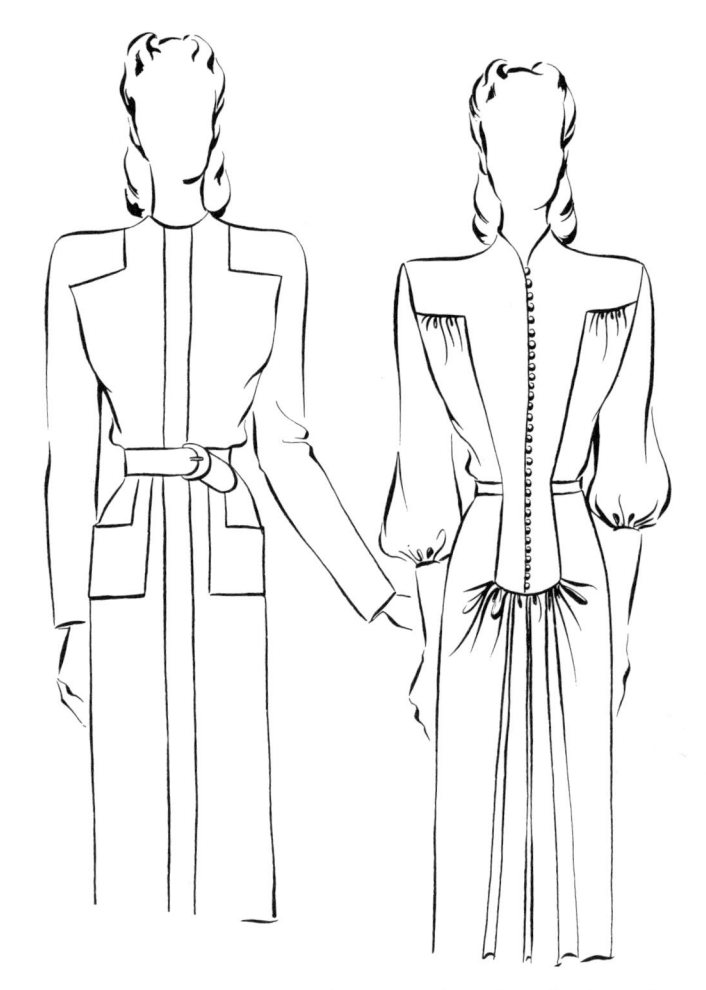

Fig. 4. Geometric, tailored interpretation of two horizontal and two vertical lines.

Fig. 5. Soft, curved interpretation of the same line divisions as in Fig. 4.

eye to an awareness of good proportion, unity, rhythm, and balance.

A beginner may consider it futile to draw lines clear through the design both vertically and horizontally when perfectly well aware that she is going to erase some segments of them. But this is *not* a waste of time. Drawing lines through the entire composition forces you to think of it as a whole instead of as a heterogeneous mass of details. In other words, it helps to keep the design unified. It has the second advantage of lining up darts and seams, for although you may erase a section of a line, the eye picks it up again on the same axis. If you practice this exercise conscientiously these points will become evident.

SOURCES OF DESIGN

After exhausting the possibilities of this combination of lines, try others, always realizing, however, that you must group several lines to form enough spaces to suggest ideas. For example, one vertical center line and one horizontal line at the waist are too meager to stimulate the imagination very effectively; and, aside from the fact that such a design could not possibly have much interest, it would be impossible to fit a garment with so few seams.

After formulating ideas into clear pencil sketches, cut patterns for the designs from the master block to test their practicality.

Suggestion 2
STUDYING THE FABRIC

Texture, Surface Interest, and Body

Give a student with little draping experience a dress length of expensive fabric, tell her to drape and cut it on the form, and she will probably be too terrified to get either a good idea or to apply the principles she has learned — and with good reason. But actually working with the fabric on the form reveals the "feel" or texture of it and its draping quality. It is possible to experiment without cutting into the piece at all and to substitute muslin for dress fabric when draping to cut.

The following qualities of fabric are of utmost importance to consider when designing.

Texture Interest Without Pattern

Matelassés, Bouclés, Ratinés, and all Nubbed Surfaces. For a fabric with definite surface interest, such as a matelassé, a coarse bouclé, or a nub weave, plan the design so that it does not compete for attention with the fabric itself. Compose it of large unbroken areas rather than intricate fine details. Flat crepe, in direct contrast to these pronounced textures, has a surface so lacking in interest that it needs to be given texture appeal by the addition of stitching, embroidery, self-cordings, and so on. But never use such applied design on matelassé or on any other nubby texture which is not suited to surface decoration.

Twilled or Ribbed Fabrics. Twills, reps, herringbones and piqués form a second class of fabrics with definite diagonal, horizontal, or vertical line effects that must be taken into consideration when designing a costume. A diagonal twill weave in particular presents several problems. It has a right and wrong side, and in wool fabric the twill usually runs from left to right, whereas in cotton and rayon it runs from right to left, regardless of which end is used for the top. The only way to change the direction of the twill is to use the material horizontally in some areas. Moreover, any change in the direction of the grain is quite conspicuous, and is likely to cause a mismatched effect at certain seams, such as the French dart line or the center seam of a four-gore skirt.

Twills and ribbed weaves generally suggest straight lines rather than soft curves or draped effects.

Patterned Fabrics

Patterned fabrics, such as checks, plaids, stripes, and floral motifs, present many more problems for the designer than do either of the two preceding groups. The pattern of a fabric may be the chief inspiration for a particular design. Indeed, you must take the cue for structural lines from the pattern of the fabric whenever you select a material with a dominant pattern.

Spaced Floral Prints. Large spaced floral prints suggest softly gathered effects, suitable for dressy afternoon or formal evening wear. It must also be remembered that every cut through a large floral design will be very conspicuous. And because it is not possible to match floral patterns, obvious seams and cuts will utterly destroy the effectiveness of the gown by chopping up the motif. The aim should be to hide as many as possible of the necessary joinings in soft fullness, and to place seams, if at all feasible, under the arm, where they are least evident. In short, the pattern of the fabric, whenever it is an important one, should always take precedence over the cut of the design. Tiny checks, polka dots, and fine florals, on the other hand, should be handled almost like fabrics with no pattern at all.

Figure 6 is a design suitable for a large floral print. It has no center front or center back seam, but if such seams were necessary the design should be changed so that there would be fullness over the joinings to make them less noticeable. The sleeves are lapped on top of the arm to avoid a seam, and the side seam of the skirt is concealed in gathers. Thus the underarm

DRESS DESIGN

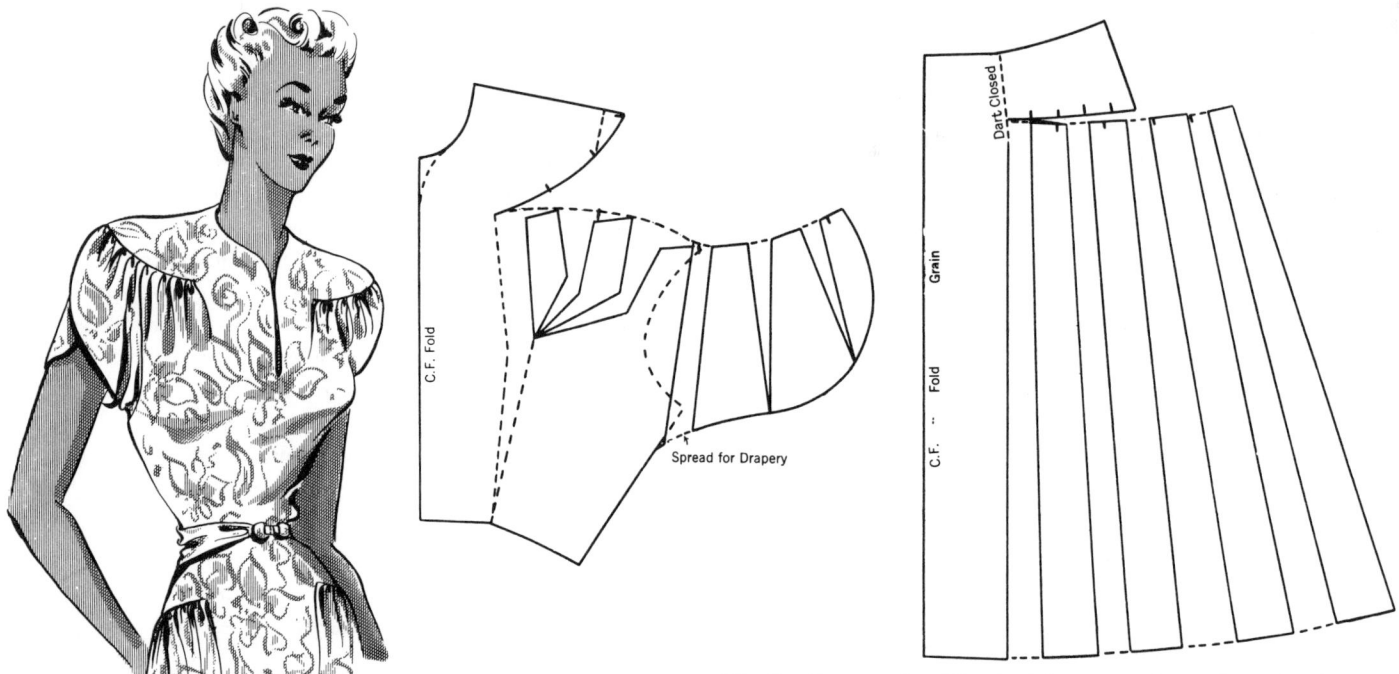

Fig. 6. Design suitable for a large, floral print.

Fig. 7. Pattern for Fig. 6. There are four pieces in the dress.

blouse seam, the only seam that appears mismatched, is fairly well covered by the arm. Figure 7 shows that the pattern for the entire dress has just four pieces.

The larger the motif, the more limited is its use. And very large ones are generally suitable only for floor-length evening gowns, since they require long skirts to provide space for enough repetitions of the pattern. Obviously, too, large patterns are at their best on tall slender women and never appear to advantage on short, stocky, or rotund figures.

Plaids. A plaid is another type of patterned fabric that demands special designing. Here again the pattern of the cloth must be the dominant factor in the choice of the design. But whereas the design for a floral should be soft and flowing, that for a plaid should be brisk and staccato to be in harmony with the geometric lines of the pattern. Pressed pleats should be substituted for gathers where fullness is required, and straight lines should be used in place of curves. Seams should be visible but carefully matched in both directions. Another problem peculiar to plaid is the need of co-ordinating angular lines with the natural curves of the figure. This requires skill and ingenuity. Navajo Indian rug designers change the figures in their patterns to angular shapes without a qualm, since weaving technique requires angularity; but a dress designer cannot eliminate a woman's curves so easily! Her alternative is to adapt the harsh oppositional lines of a plaid to the soft curves of the figure by using the plaid diagonally. In this way she makes a transition between figure curves and an angular pattern. A woven plaid is of course on the bias when used diagonally, and in most fabrics tends to stretch and thus produce soft curves instead of angles.

Figure 8 shows a dress designed especially for plaid. Notice that in the skirt the pressed pleats follow the lines of the plaid, since it is better to lay the pleats straight along a dominant line of the plaid than to gore out at the pleat edge. The left and right halves of the blouse front are each cut in one piece with a deep dart running to the neck. This throws the grain on the bias above the dart and repeats the diagonal line over the hip in the side sections of the skirt. A biased sleeve with a matched seam on top of the arm completes the effect of the bias along the silhouette lines of the figure. A word of caution in regard to cutting any plaid: maintain a sense of order in the costume by carefully matching the plaids at all seams. To do this, flare both edges of a gored seam to the same degree.

278

SOURCES OF DESIGN

Fig. 8. Structural lines that emphasize the character of plaid.

Since the difficulties of handling plaid around the curves of the silhouette are so obvious and also impose limitations on the way in which the cloth can be cut, plaid is often used merely to accent a solid color. For example, a straight pleated skirt of plaid with a jacket of a solid color avoids the problem of shaping plaid over the curve of the bust.

Plaid is notorious for enlarging the apparent size of the figure and because of its strong, straight-line character and its opposition to curves, for overemphasizing a pleasantly rounded figure. Large, angular patterns are at their best on girls with very subtle curves, and seem to be particularly harmonious with the sudden motions and lively manner of adolescents.

Stripes. Stripes as well as plaids need special designing and handling. They are perhaps more widely used than any other kind of patterned fabric and involve the designer in many problems. Unless stripes are very interestingly spaced and very wide, they tend to be monotonous if allowed to run in the same direction throughout a costume; at the same time, they seem confused if allowed to go in too many directions in a single design. Like plaids, stripes usually suggest straight-line costumes; and yet unlike plaids, they are not oppositional or static and are, therefore, more versatile in interpretation. For example, Figure 9 shows a design for a very fine stripe, perhaps in cotton chambray or rayon crepe. The fabric is soft enough to gather well and the stripe runs both horizontally and vertically. Indeed, it would be very insignificant if it did not. A tiny, unimportant stripe benefits from a good deal of interest in cut.

Figure 10 shows a very wide stripe in a hand-woven suiting. The object here is to play down the interest in the cut of the garment in order to set off to advantage the dominant stripe, which is far too important to use in more than one direction — in fact, too important to repeat again in the skirt. Try to adjust wide stripes on the form so that they come at the most becoming positions on the figure; and also try to match the pattern across the sleeve, so that the sleeve and body of the jacket appear as one unbroken unit. This is an advanced problem in designing, for although there must be darts to fit the jacket, they must be invisible. In this example three small darts under the arm, in addition to a horizontal one along the waistline, fit the jacket without being noticeable and lift the grain of the peplum so that the lower stripe does not sag toward the side seam.

Stripes need not be used to emphasize a straight-line effect. In fact, when used diagonally, stripes, like plaids, tend to take on the effect of curves. The striped taffeta evening bodice (see Figure 11) shows such an effect. Not only does the stripe conform to the curves of the figure when it is used diagonally, but it is far more active and dynamic than when used vertically or horizontally. It is perhaps unnecessary to caution the student to match the two sides exactly at the center so that the lines slope down at the same angle from each side.

When draping designs for plaids or stripes, the student should work in muslin, lining it off with pencil to get the effect of the fabric to be used.

DRESS DESIGN

Fig. 9. Fine stripes need variety and interest in the costume design.

Fig. 10. A wide stripe is too dominant to use in more than one direction.

Fig. 11. Diagonally used stripes appear to curve around the figure.

Aside from the general effect of floral patterns, plaids, and stripes, there are still other problems of fabric pattern to consider. Woven or printed plaids, stripes, and floral patterns should be examined to see if they have an up and down direction, a right and left side of the pattern, and a right and wrong side of the fabric. Any one of these characteristics adds to the problems of handling, and a fabric possessing all of them is one for an inexperienced person to avoid.

The Body of the Fabric: Stiffness, Weight and Thickness

Except for purposes of explanation and clarification, it is, of course, impossible to separate the consideration of the various characteristics of a fabric into neat little categories. At the same time that you examine the size and dominance of a fabric pattern, you will also consider the qualities of texture that determine the effect it will produce. A little experimental draping will very quickly answer your questions about the sort of silhouette a fabric will give. If you look again at Figure 11, you will notice that the fabric has the stiffness of a taffeta or it would not produce that perky silhouette. The fine striped material shown in Figure 9 obviously has not only a soft texture but also one that lacks bulkiness.

Rayon jersey and moss crepe are outstanding examples of fabrics that fall so close to the figure as to be fairly liquid, and yet in spite of their weight have no bulkiness or buoyancy at all. This is the quality generally meant when it is said that a fabric possesses "drape." A material may lack this quality because of stiffness, bulkiness, wiriness, or buoyancy. A flat unweighted silk crepe or foulard, even though thin and soft, is too light in weight to

SOURCES OF DESIGN

hang in close folds, and a woolen dress fabric is too bulky or buoyant. It is buoyancy that makes wool, if gathered or draped, fall into less definite folds than rayon crepe, and it is this same quality that makes it necessary to restrain the quantity of fullness used in a wool garment and to handle that fullness so that it falls into vertical lines with the folds definitely controlled. If the design for a woolen material is to be gathered at all, select a soft one entirely without wiriness or bulkiness. Use only the very softest crepes for draped or gathered effects which fall into horizontal lines or folds in the costume. These lines run in opposition to the warp yarns which are more tightly twisted and resist gathering or draping.

The body of the fabric, its stiffness or softness, its bulkiness or clinging quality, will also determine whether to shape the fabric to the curves of the body by darts, tucks, or pleats to give a flat, close-fitting effect; or by gathers or flares to give extension. Obviously, the bulkier the fabric, the more likely you will be to fit out all excess into tailored, pressed darts. And conversely, the softer and more clinging it is, the more apt you will be to gather it. If it is stiff but without heaviness, take advantage of this characteristic by letting it puff out into animated circular flares.

The characteristics of the fabric also determine the kind of finish the edges should be given. For a tailored suit, choose a fabric that is firm without bulkiness; that will press into sharp, clean-cut edges on the lapels, the lower edge of the jacket, the sleeve opening, and the hem line; and that will not only *stand* heavy pressing but also *retain* a press. On the other hand, do not take a rayon moss crepe out of character and transpose it into a design so tailored that you must press the edges to a knifelike sharpness. Its beauty depends on light handling and even pressing that leaves its soft dull surface unmarred.

In all experimentation with fabric on the form to discover its "handle," the point to keep constantly in mind is that the design should be planned to play up the natural characteristics of the fabric, and the cut of the garment should be subordinated to fabric interest whenever the texture or pattern is of sufficient importance to warrant first consideration. It is never wise to work in opposition to the natural character of the fabric or to attempt to make it act in any way for which it was not intended.

Suggestion 3
DRAPING FOR GENERAL EFFECT

Suggestion 2 discussed draping with a dress length of fabric for the purpose of learning its texture and body. Another and very important advantage in draping without cutting is that it teaches one how to work for the entire effect rather than for minute detail. It forces the draper to carry the fabric from neck to hem and from front to back, and also to keep the idea simple and natural so as to give a mere impression of the design. The result is almost bound to be smooth, easy-flowing line rather than overworked detail. To preserve the freshness of the fabric, learn to handle it deftly, and to pin it only where necessary; and in doing this, learn to work with speed and lightness and to leave all details until the design is actually draped and cut in muslin.

The dress form itself can be a challenge to inventiveness. Just as the flat lay figure gives a basis for sketching space divisions in relation to the two-dimensional silhouette, the dress form provides a three-dimensional shape the actual size of the figure on which to experiment with fabric. The form suggests where it will be advantageous to extend or confine the silhouette of the costume, and shows the merits of curved or straight lines and of horizontal or vertical dominance in line direction. Inconsistency in the scale of major space divisions, or in appropriateness of detail to the entire figure, becomes apparent at once. The challenge is to retain the figure's most pleasing attributes and to emphasize them through the lines of the dress and by subtle illusion to modify the less desirable proportions. Since the dress is for the wearer rather than the wearer for the dress, the form as a source of design inspiration is the nearest approach to the figure itself.

Valuable suggestions also come from draping the uncut fabric on yourself. You see your features, the tilt of your head, your characteristic posture in relation to the fabric and the lines into which you drape it; and immediately you can sense the harmony or disharmony between the draped fabric and yourself.

Figures 12 and 13, showing the draping of a dress length on the form, illustrate these points. In Figure 12, the fabric is a soft, heavy, fluid crepe. Starting at the shoulder with one end of the material, the designer formed the neckline, then drew the fabric to-

DRESS DESIGN

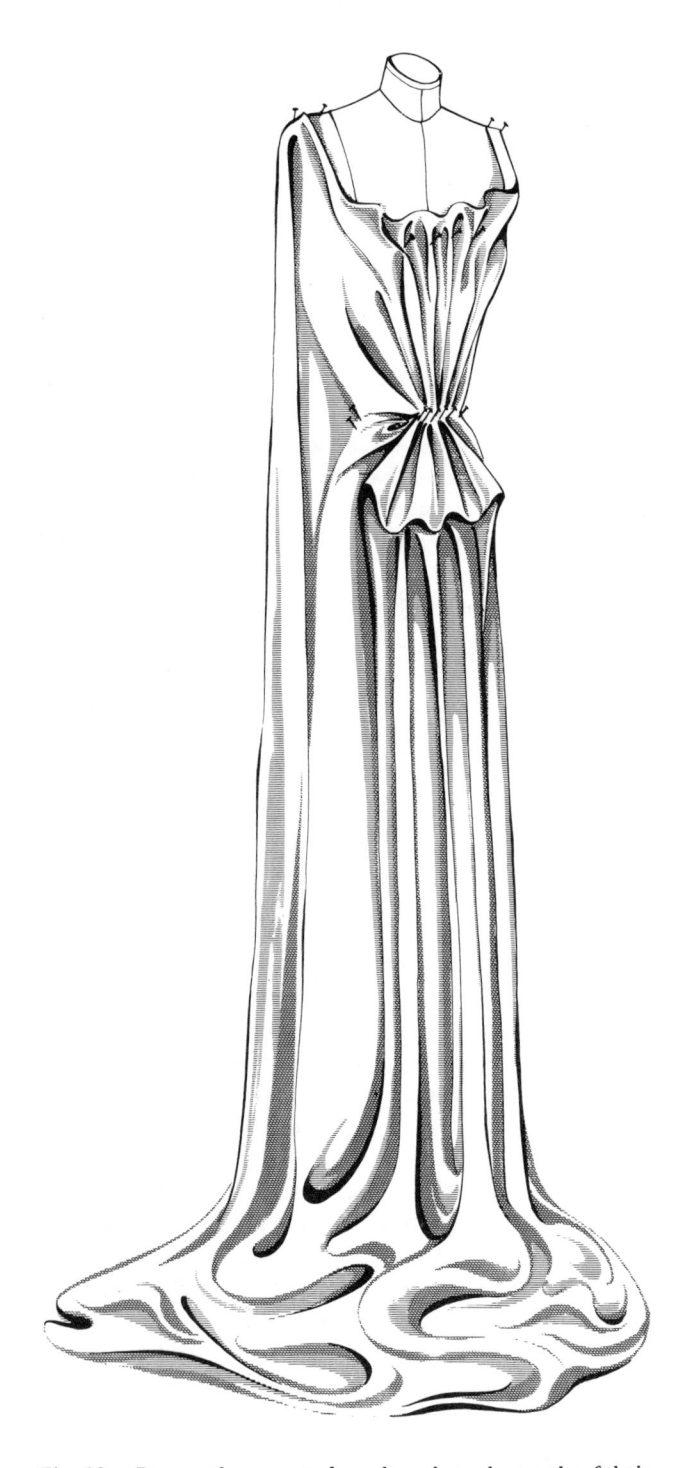

Fig. 12. Drape the uncut dress length to learn the fabric texture and to work for a quick impression of the entire design.

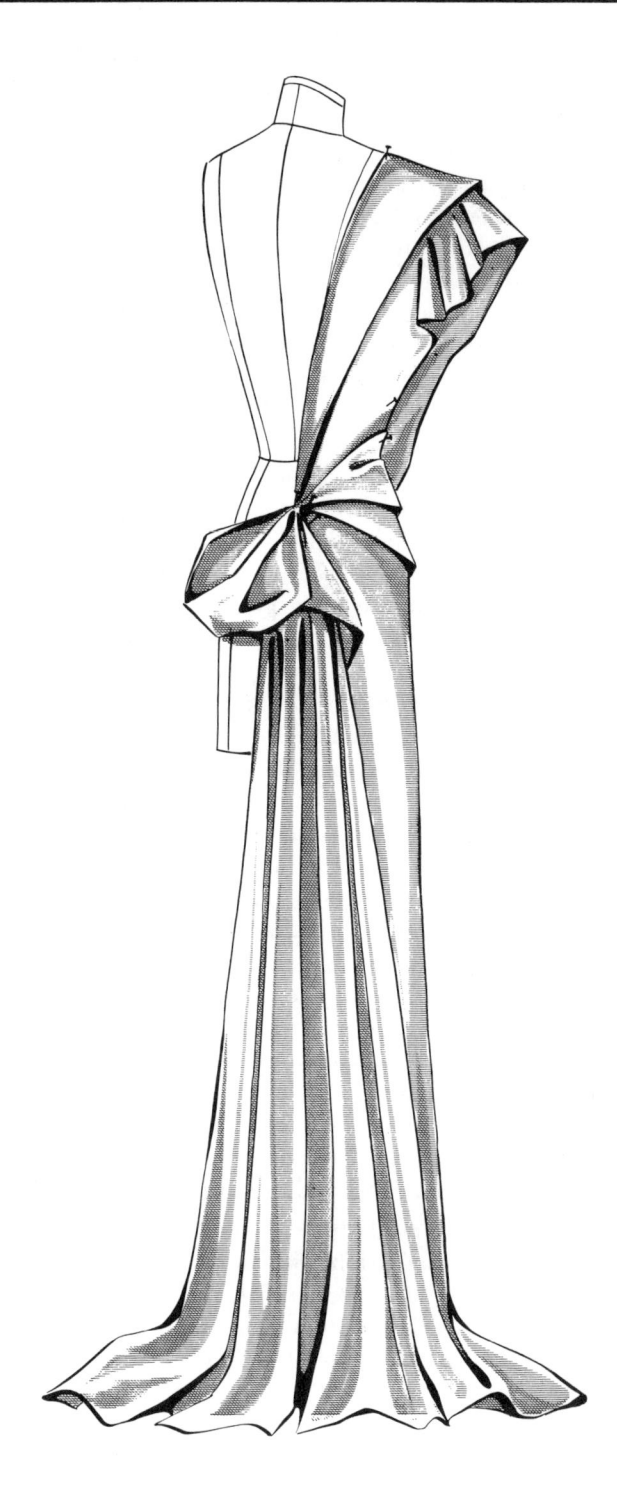

Fig. 13. Drape taffeta lightly for quick effect. To avoid injury to the fabric, pin it with needles and only where necessary.

gether at the waistline, pushed it up under the peplum drapery, and let it hang to the floor — all of this without cutting even a slash. Moreover, she used very few pins, so that the fabric would not be injured. Figure 13 shows a stiff taffeta draped up into a bustle at the center back. Here the designer started the draping by placing one end of the fabric at the center front of the skirt; then she pulled it around to the back, draped it up, and let it fall to the floor into lines natural to the taffeta. She then threw the opposite end of the taffeta over the shoulder from the front and draped the bodice from the waistline up toward the shoulder. Since in handling the taffeta she had to be especially careful to pin and crush it as little as possible, she substituted steel needles for pins and used very few of these.

Suggestion 4

DRAPING WITH MUSLIN FOR DETAILS OF DESIGN

Slashing "Accidentally" to Produce Flares and Ripples

Many ideas develop only after making a slash to release the excess fabric beyond the normal seam position. This type of "accidental" cut will often inspire a person with any imagination at all to recognize possibilities for the development of a good detail or even for the entire theme of a dress. But the experiment can be freely indulged in only when draping with scraps of muslin, for then an error in judgment, a slash in the wrong place, involves nothing more than a fresh start with a second scrap of practice material. Unhampered by fears of cutting too far or in the wrong places, the experimenter can work with speed and let ideas develop as they will.

When a slash is made through the excess beyond the seam to a seam line, the fabric falls over and forms drapery which can be handled in an endless variety of ways. Moreover, it is possible to analyze this "accidental" occurrence and to make it happen at will. Hence by this method those who are in the habit of producing stereotyped effects can learn to inject unusual or even original ideas into their designs.

At which seams or which points can you expect these possibilities for ideas to occur? Principally, they will develop at points of articulation, or structural points on seams suitable for design emphasis. If you slash from above the shoulder to the intersection of shoulder and neck, a cascade of drapery will fall at the neck — a very logical focal point for design interest. If you cut to the intersection of the shoulder seam and the armscye, drapery will fall from the outer end of the shoulder. Again, if you cut horizontally along the waistline from the side seam toward the center front, the fabric will ripple out into a peplum. Or if you slash toward the center back along the waistline, a flare will spring from the end of the slash. At whatever point you slash, from beyond a seam toward an intersection, the fabric will curl away from the point of the shears and fall into a circular cascade or ripple. It is easy to see what a varied source of inspiration this action of cloth can become.

Figure 14 illustrates flare produced by a slash to the intersection of the neck and the shoulder. The effect shown could only have been produced by draping, since after the first slash was made, many other ideas might have resulted. The only known fact with which the draper started was that some sort of detail would develop from the excess fabric above the shoulder. When such a graceful circular ripple fell out of the dart, she carried the effect still farther by dropping the grain at points along the shoulder to repeat the ripples. Figures 15a and b show the draping procedure, and Figure 16 the pattern shape, which produced this effect. In this case it seemed interesting to continue the flares around the arm to the back armscye line. This one detail would be enough to furnish interest for an entire costume. The skirt and sleeve can then serve merely as background for the shoulder frill, or in a subtle way can emphasize it by repetition, so long as the repetitions are kept subordinate. It is never wise to strain for more than one good idea at a time. If a second one occurs to you, keep it for a second costume. The beauty of any design depends on the development of one main theme, and on playing up variations of that theme rather than introducing a competing one.

This one example illustrates that anyone who is groping for an idea ought to cut away excess fabric with the utmost caution and alertness, particularly when approaching those structural locations where original treatment is most likely to develop. One should also experiment with the fabric beyond the normal seam line to see how many details may develop from any piece of excess fabric.

DRESS DESIGN

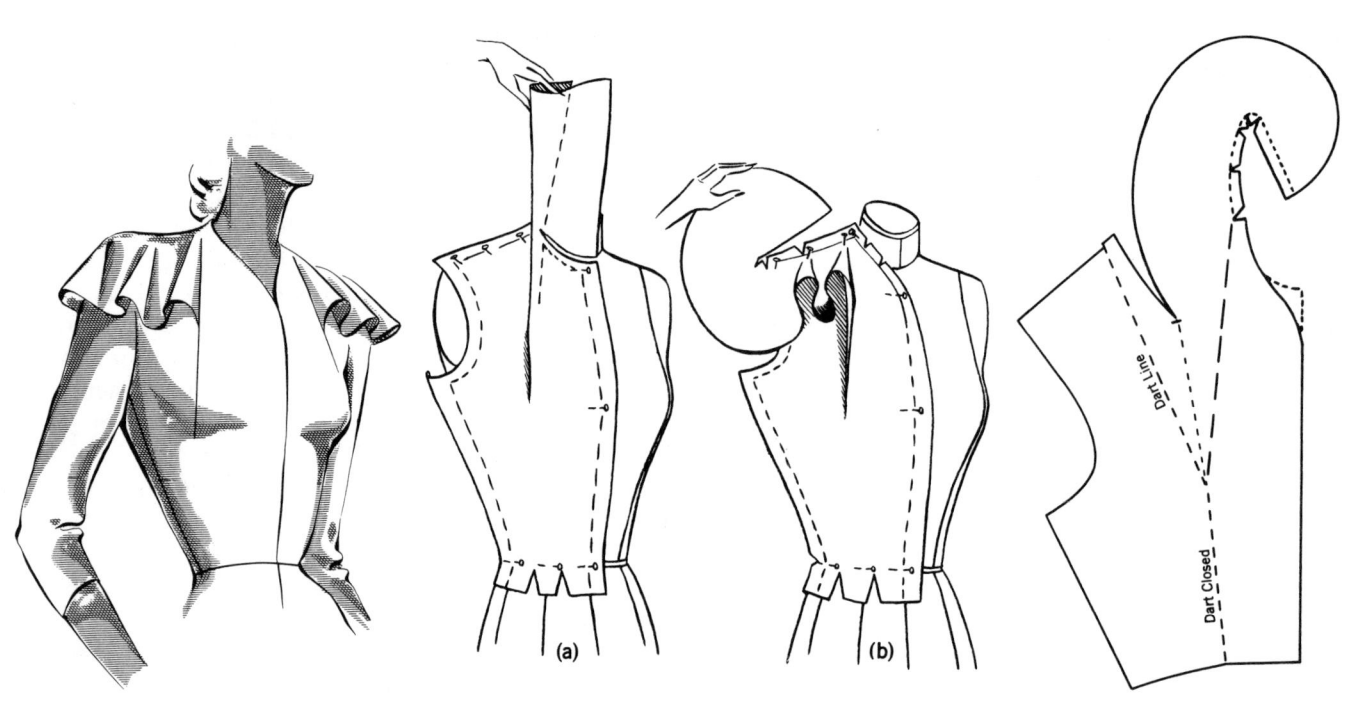

Fig. 14. Ripples produced by slashing to the intersection of neck and shoulder.

Fig. 15.(a),(b). Draping procedure for effect shown in Fig. 14.
Fig. 16. Pattern for Fig. 14.

Figure 17 shows the result of another "accidental" cut — a horizontal slash along the waistline from the side seam toward the center front but stopping short of that point. The fabric fell from the point of the shears into a rippling flare later interpreted as a peplum. The diagonal line from the end of the slash to the side hip repeats the motif of the diagonal dart to the neck and gives it emphasis. Whenever you make such slashes and separate the two edges, you must use an inset to fill in the space. The inset may be frankly a space filler, or it may be so carefully designed that it adds interest to the entire costume. In this case, the inset is really the back of the peplum extended around to the front, as Figure 18 shows. The diagram also shows that there was no separation of the pattern sections along the waistline until the peplum front dropped downward into a flare.

The design illustrated in Figure 19 was achieved by a very similar procedure. To obtain the effect of a perky peplum flare without a waistline seam across the center back, it was necessary to slash along the waistline away from the center back and to separate the two edges of the slash sharply. This left a triangular space across the center back of the waistline

Fig. 17. Rippling peplum from a horizontal slash along the waistline.

284

SOURCES OF DESIGN

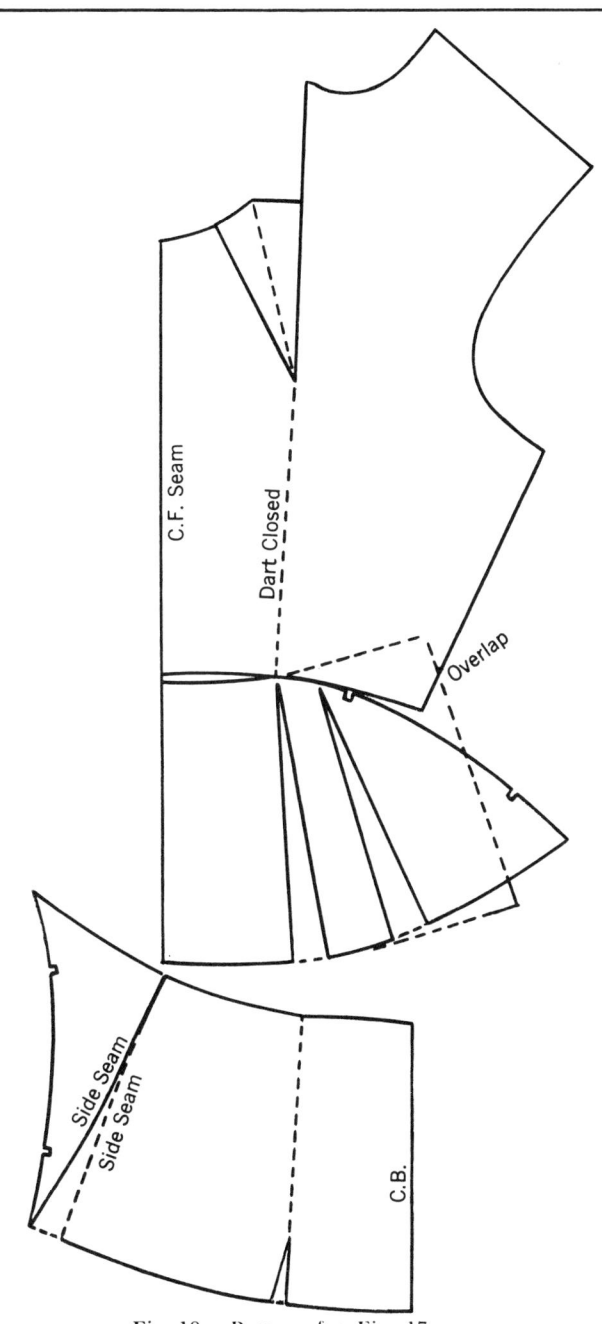

Fig. 18. Pattern for Fig. 17.

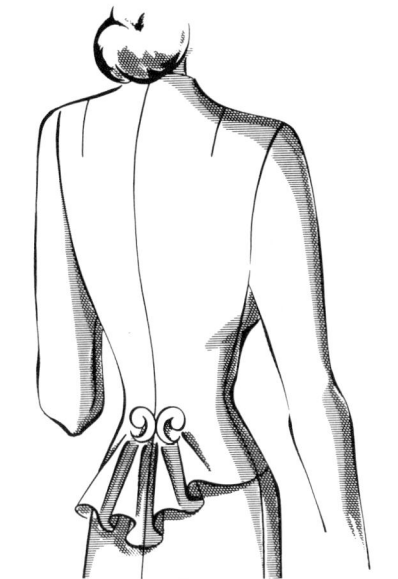

Fig. 19. Rippling flare produced by slashing along waistline at center back.

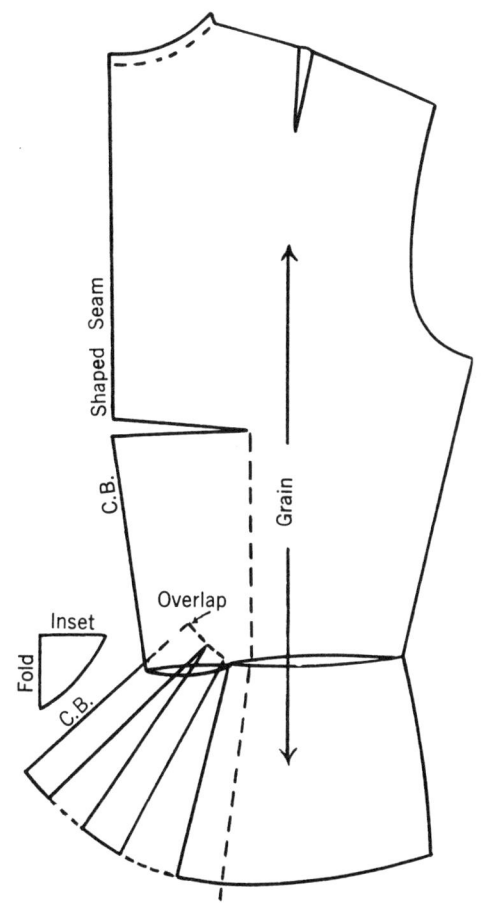

Fig. 20. Pattern diagram for Fig. 19.

that had to be filled in. It would have been possible to set in a plain triangle, but the pair of scrolls shown in Figure 19 serve not only as the necessary inset but become the decorative feature of the costume as well, and when repeated at the front of the neck, give balance and emphasis to the whole design. Figure 20 is the pattern for the design illustrated in Figure 19.

285

DRESS DESIGN

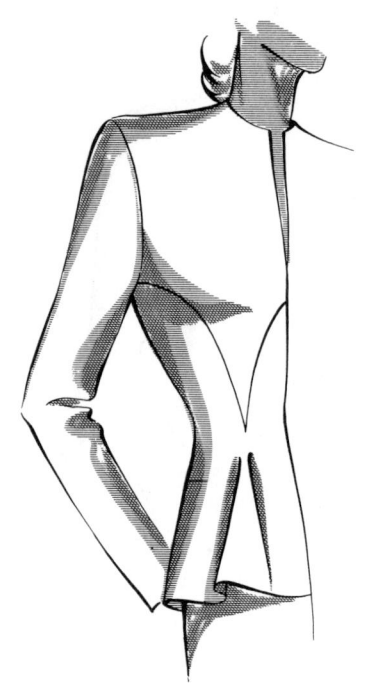

Fig. 21. Peplum rippling from a vertical slash down to the waistline.

Figure 21 shows the results when a vertical slash was made to the point on the waistline where the basic dart normally falls. When the slash was spread apart at its top end, a striking flare rippled into a peplum below the waistline end of the slash. Figure 22 shows the pattern for this design.

Figure 23 illustrates a peplum flared at the center back somewhat similar in character to that shown in Figure 19. The method of producing the ripple is so different, however, that it warrants special mention here. If you compare the two illustrations, you will note that in Figure 19 there is no possible way of creating the sudden flare at the center back without the introduction of an inset into the waistline slash. The back of the jacket shown in Figure 23, on the other hand, is cut completely apart by the long, curved seams from below the shoulders to just below the waist. Cutting off the side back sections makes it possible to drop the grain very suddenly on these sections in that short space from the points on the curves where the lines touch the waistline down to the point where they meet the center back line. This introduces the flaring circular folds across the center back. The problem was to induce the folds to ripple out rather than to

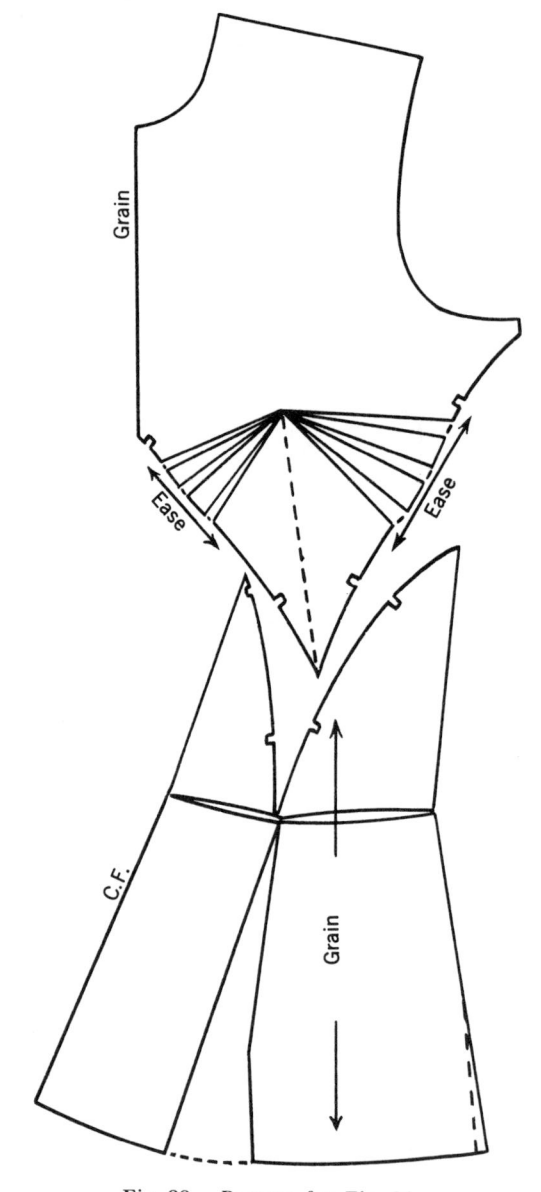

Fig. 22. Pattern for Fig. 21.

fall flat, as they would have done if the grain had not been dropped from the point where the first fold was introduced. There was also the problem of keeping the waistline close-fitting. Dropping the grain only along the downward curve below the waistline into the center accomplished this. Study Figure 24, the finished block pattern, which shows that the unpressed folds spread more at the lower edge than at the top. This is a blocking procedure with results comparable to those of lowering the grain when draping.

SOURCES OF DESIGN

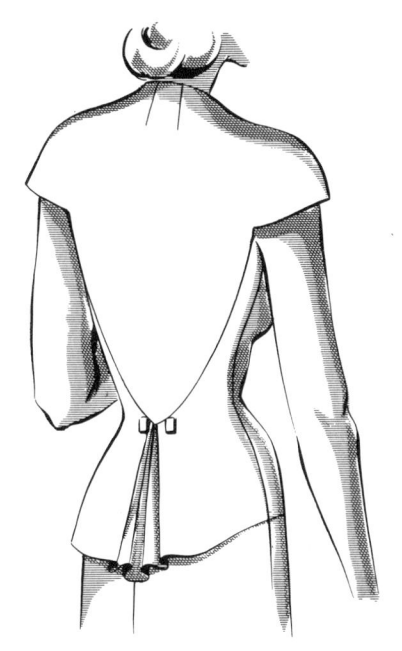

Fig. 23. Flare at center back produced by lowering the grain from the waistline to the center back seam of the peplum.

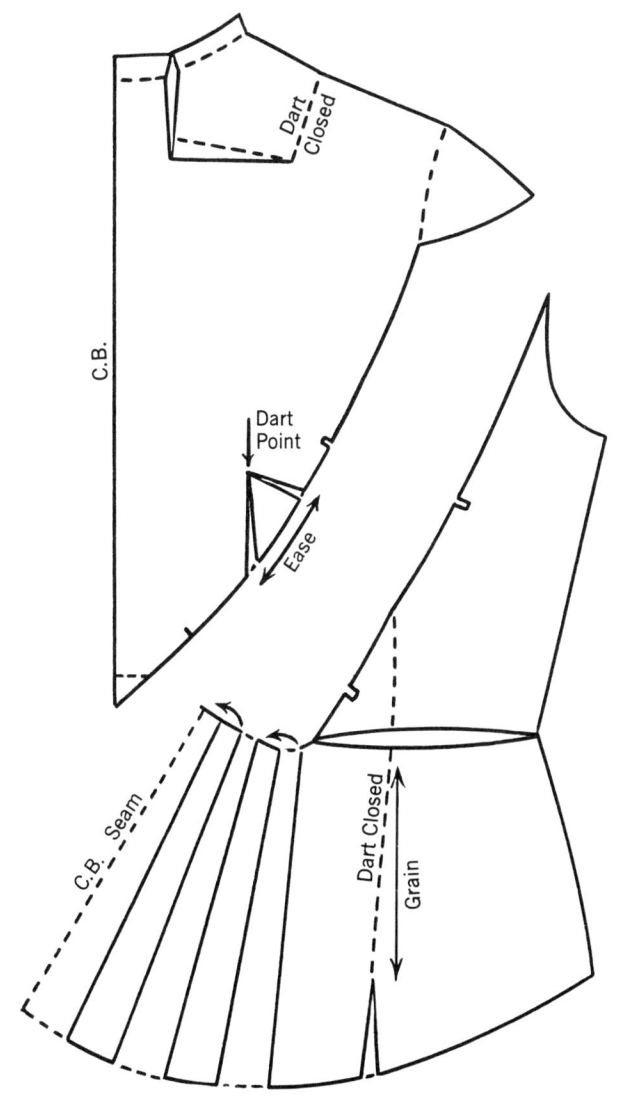

Fig. 24. Pattern for design shown in Fig. 23.

Another point that may be puzzling is the presence of ease along the side edges of the center section, whereas ease is usually found along the edge of the side section. The reason for this reversal is that the center back section is very wide and the cut falls well below and outside the point of the basic waistline dart. The ease helps to curve the fabric around the form and will not be visible if the seam is carefully joined.

You will remember that the blouse shown in Figure 14 illustrated one way of producing ripples at the shoulder. And at first glance, the effect shown in Figure 25 may appear similar, for here too there is a shoulder frill. But there the similarity ends. The costume illustrated in Figure 25 is an asymmetric design combining two opposite ways of handling fabric — drawing it up into draped folds along the first half of the shoulder length, and then reversing the procedure by lowering the grain from there in order to throw flares along the lower edge. The method of developing the pattern is also different, as this one was partially blocked and partially draped. Starting with a carefully blocked pattern of the main body of the blouse, on which the draped folds to the shoulder were marked, the draper added a fairly large piece of extra fabric to see what effect she could get by draping the shoulder area on the form. By slashing through the excess above the shoulder to the shoulder seam, and then by dropping the grain, she finally developed the circular frill. There was some doubt whether to lay the circular folds *through* the shoulder seam edge, or just to it; but the experimental draping quickly decided that issue. Letting the ripple lines run *to*, but not *through*, the shoulder seam created a lighter, more buoyant effect. The diagram of the completed pattern (see Figure 26) shows that the shoulder edge beyond the drapery is a sharp arc from which the flares spring.

DRESS DESIGN

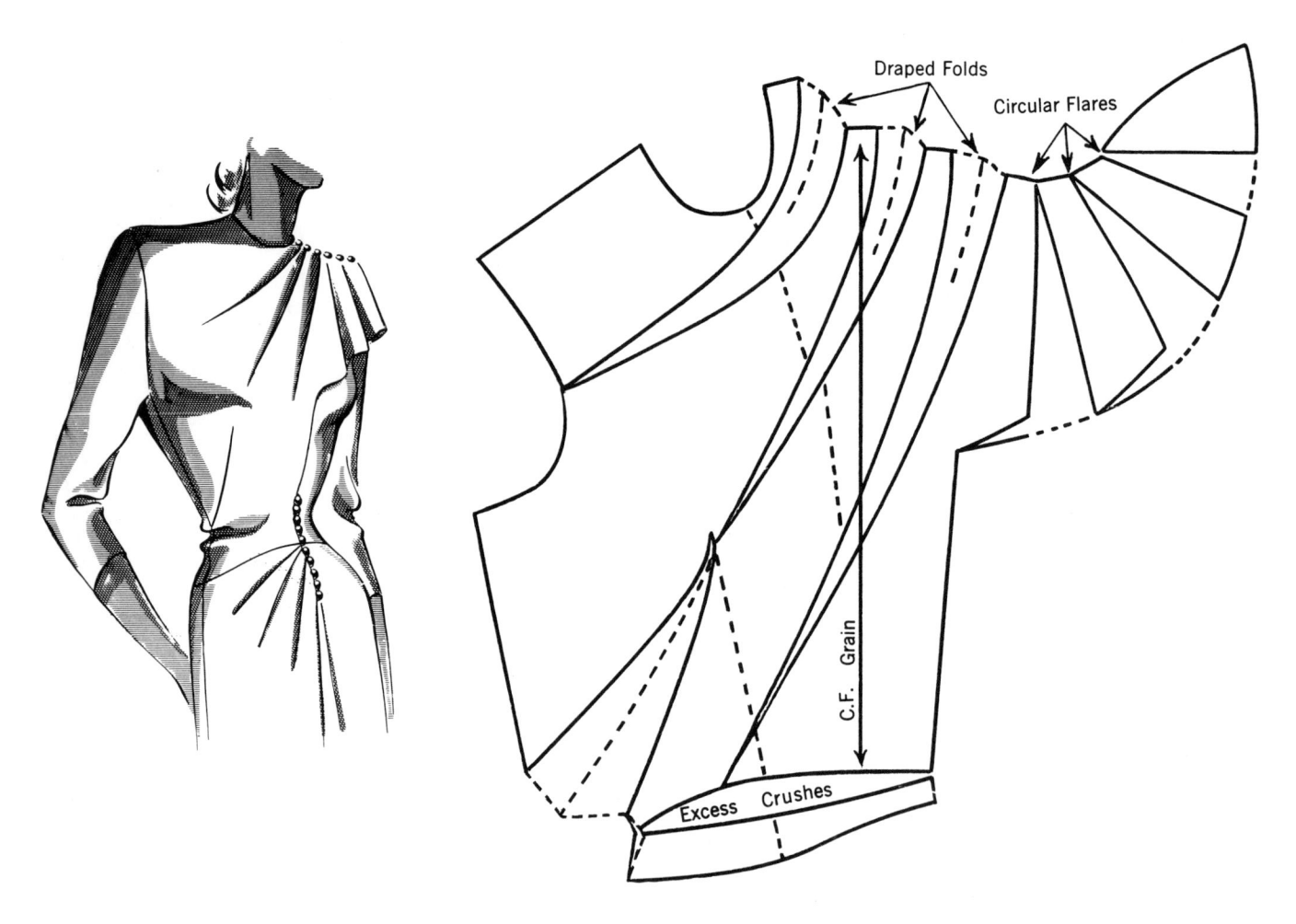

Fig. 25. Draped folds and circular ripples combined at the shoulder.

Fig. 26. Pattern diagram for garment shown in Fig. 25 with draped folds and circular flares.

The diagrams of the patterns for all of these designs show the trued up, blocked patterns. They also show the advantages of combining draping with blocking. After you have developed ideas by experimenting on the form with scraps of practice fabric, the blocking of the accurate pattern becomes a fairly quick process and makes it unnecessary to drape the design to completion.

Distributing Gathers and Folds Along Slash Lines to Produce Drapery

This experiment is somewhat similar to the previous one of slashing to produce flares, but instead of dropping the grain for a ripple, the aim this time is to try gathering the free edge of the slash or draping it into folds.

Figure 27 shows a shoulder dart converted into drapery with an extension carried around to the back. It also illustrates the effect of slashing the dart line and distributing gathers along it. If the fabric is soft and heavy, the lines of the design are as fluid and rhythmical as in the illustration. Although this idea seems complicated, you can readily block it to perfect the pattern shape. The diagram of the flat pattern (see Figures 28a and b) shows that the center front line has become a sharp arc, and the separation of the two sides of the slash shows the location and size of the dart.

SOURCES OF DESIGN

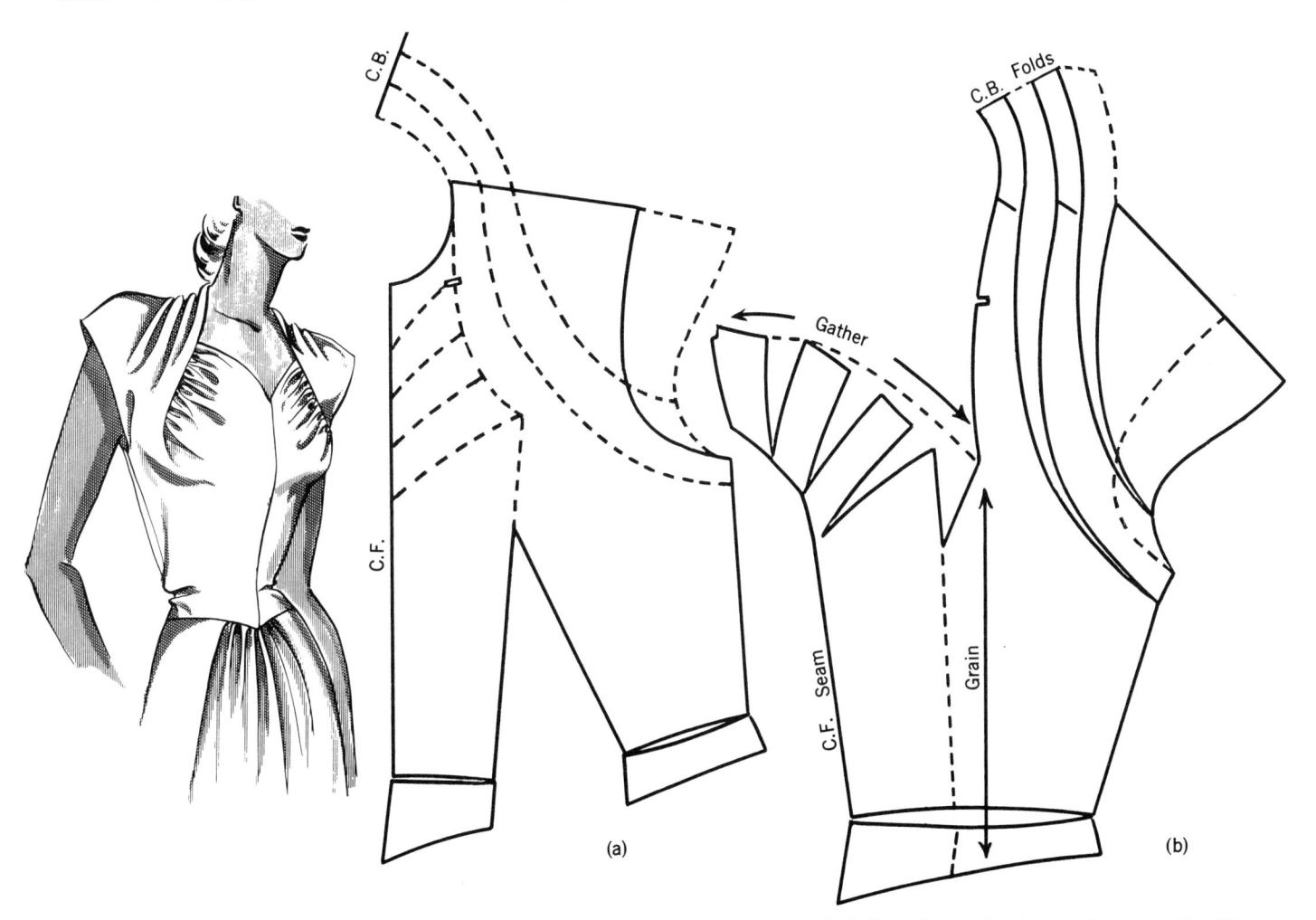

Fig. 27. Shoulder dart converted into drapery and slashed to push in gathers.

Fig. 28. (a) Slash lines drawn for design shown in Fig. 27; (b) Slashes spread for folds and gathers.

Simulated yokes (see Chapter II, pages 000-000) employ this method of slashing to push in gathers or folds along the cut line. A more unusual version of this same basic technique is shown in the asymmetrical bodice design in Figure 29. Two slashes running to the neck at the side front support gathers radiating toward the shoulder on one side and toward the underarm on the other. After the design is developed in a rough form by draping, the pattern should be trued up by exact blocking. For blocking not only establishes the grain line correctly, but also insures a pattern with shoulder, armscye, and underarm seams of exactly the same length even though not of the same shape on both sides. Study Figures 30a and b, which show two steps in producing the flat pattern.

Another method of developing folds, as we have already seen, is to introduce them into a vertical slash. One way of using this technique was illustrated in a skirt (see Chapter 3, page 109), and similar methods were shown in two sleeves, one with a simulated cuff (see page 138), and the other with a vertical slash below the elbow along which gathers were distributed (see page 134-137.)

A graceful skirt design (see Figure 31) shows this same principle of slashing back to push in gathers. The skirt has a yoke with a crossed simulated belt, along the lower edges of which gathers have been worked in. The seam at the center front is concealed in the gathers of the skirt. Figure 32 shows the method of slashing and spreading used to obtain this cut.

DRESS DESIGN

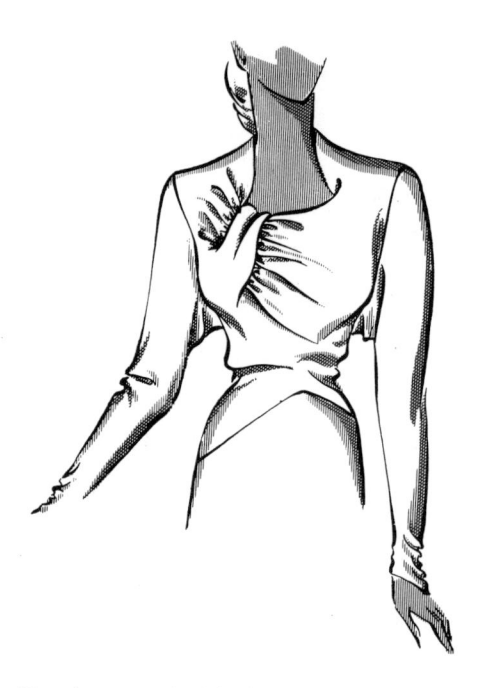

Fig. 29. Asymmetrical bodice slashed at the neck to push in gathers.

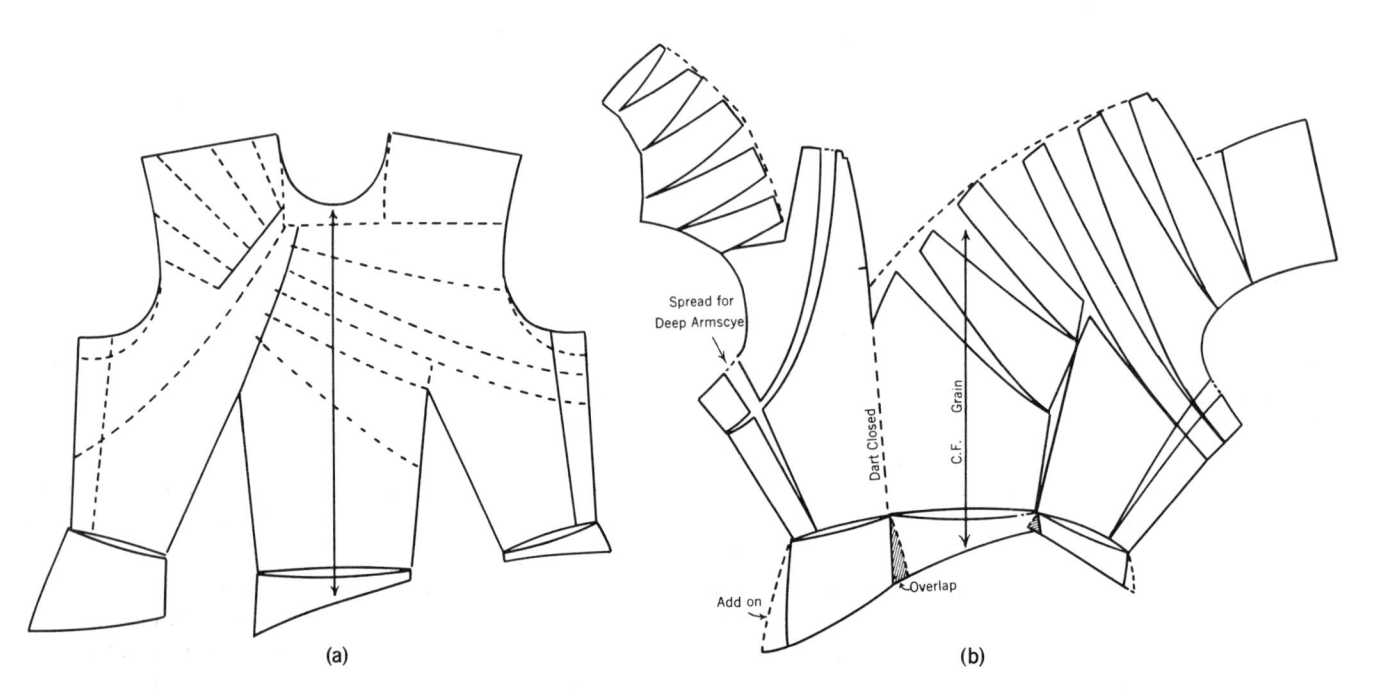

Fig. 30. (a) Slash lines drawn for folds and gathers; (b) Slashes spread. Underarm, armscye, and shoulder seams are equal in length on right and left halves.

290

SOURCES OF DESIGN

Fig. 31. Slashing back along a skirt yoke to push in gathers.

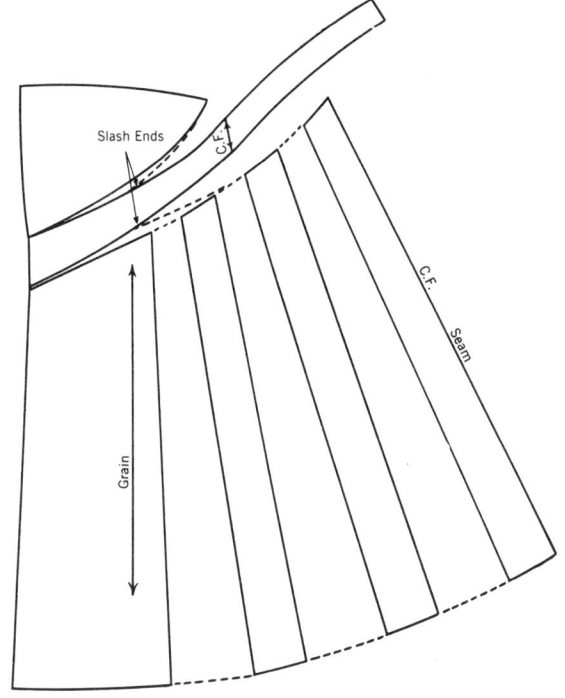

Fig. 32. Pattern for dress shown in Fig. 31.

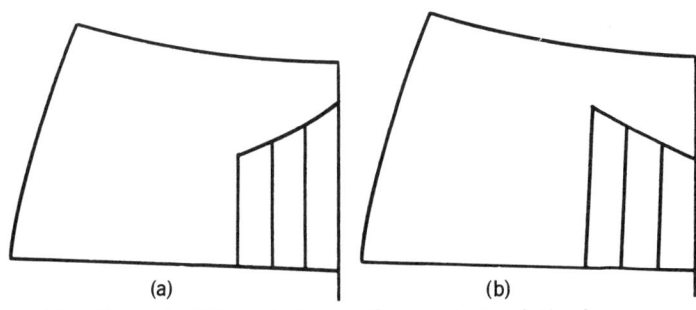

Fig. 33. (a) When slashed and spread, the full edge can be easily gathered into a descending yoke line; (b) When slashed and spread, the full edge will not push back into an ascending yoke line without puffing at the corner.

Slashes should be made to the side seam, but tapered to nothing at the point on the hip where the belt appears to end. If a suggestion of draping toward the side hip is desired, however, the slashes should be tapered to a small dart rather than to a fine point.

Figures 33a and b illustrate an important technical point concerning the shape of simulated skirt yokes. When you make a slash from the seam edge of the pattern (which is at the center front in the skirt under discussion) downward as in Figure 33a, as you spread the pattern you gain more and more length on the gathered edge to fit back into the shorter yoke line. But study the diagrams of the two yoke segments. If you slash in the opposite direction, that is, from the seam edge upward, you will have trouble, because you must push a gathered edge which is shorter at the center front up into an ascending yoke edge. Because you must raise the grain of the gathered edge as you draw up the fullness, the skirt gathers tend to curl and puff from the outer end of the yoke line instead of falling into straight vertical lines. (See also Chapter 2 on simulated yokes for an explanation of the same principle applied to blouses.)

DRESS DESIGN

Folding Extra Fabric Beyond the Normal Cutting Line to Produce Drapery

One should never cut along the base of the neckline without first experimenting to see what interesting neck treatments may be offered by the excess fabric both within the curve of the neck and up beyond the shoulder seam. Figures 34 and 35 show two ways of folding excess to form necklines which are unusual and becoming. If you can accomplish the feat of creating pleasing lines around the face, then you will have made considerable progress in designing. The remaining costume lines may take their cue from the neckline detail, or may be used merely as a foil to the neck design by being kept severely plain. Figure 34 shows a striking neckline set off by the simplicity of the other lines of the costume, whereas Figure 35 shows how the neckline may serve as inspiration for the peplum detail. When the designer draped the jacket illustrated in Figure 35, she turned the excess under below the waistline at the front, draped it up to the waistline at the back, and terminated it in a cascade. This peplum illustrates another way of producing a striking effect by folding off excess.

Fig. 35. The fold of excess at neckline inspired the fold of excess below the waistline.

Again in Figure 36 the waistline detail illustrates what may be achieved by folding back the excess left beyond the center front line. Another possibility is to leave the excess at the lower edge of the peplum and fold it up to form a pocket. In fact, there is no limit to the number of interesting variations that can be developed from the single expedient of folding back the excess beyond the normal pattern edge — and all one needs besides the idea and the will to experiment is a dress form and a few scraps of muslin.

Fig. 34. Folding off excess to form a becoming neckline.

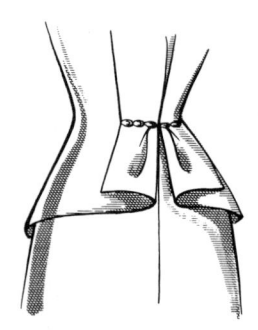

Fig. 36. Folding back excess beyond center front.

292

SOURCES OF DESIGN

Tying Excess into Knots or Bows

In general, the same positions that are advantageous for slashing or for folding excess are also suitable for tying it into knots or bows. Thus it is possible to slash vertically through the excess above the shoulder and to tie it into decorative knots on top of the shoulder. In Chapter 2 it was explained how to tie the excess from a dart at the center front of the neckline into a bow, and also how to plan for knots tied at several points along the center front line. Not only is tying a decorative way of shaping the fabric, but it also serves the purpose of fastening. Moreover, it is one of the simplest and most natural ways to end drapery.

Figure 37 shows how the excess beyond the normal front and back shoulder seam lines can be tied in order to function both as a closing and as a decorative neck treatment. Ties also offer a chance to introduce contrasting color in the facing of the ends, if that detail seems to improve the color harmony.

Figure 38 shows the soft folds from the basic waistline dart and the peplum drawn together at the center front and tied. Incidentally, whenever you use ties to fasten drapery, cut them in one piece with the main body of the pattern in order to avoid a clumsy seam under the knot.

Figure 39 illustrates an extension of fabric wrapped around the waistline to form a softly draped girdle. To make the pattern for this design (see Figure 40), transfer the basic dart to the center front near the waistline, but do not cut it out. Instead, slash the edge of the dart from *A* to *B* and draw the fabric forward to form a sash cut on the bias. The dotted line shows the top of the dart, which is not cut but folded in. Add an extension *CDE* under the drapery to form a support for the skirt at the center front as shown by the dotted line. The ends can be tied at the back or run through a buckle or ring.

Once your eye becomes trained to look for the source of a particular design idea, you will repeatedly see applications of that idea, and will constantly be made aware of more and more possibilities growing out of every possible slash, folding back, or tying of the fabric. And you will soon come to see many other ways in which excess can be manipulated in order to produce original and striking effects.

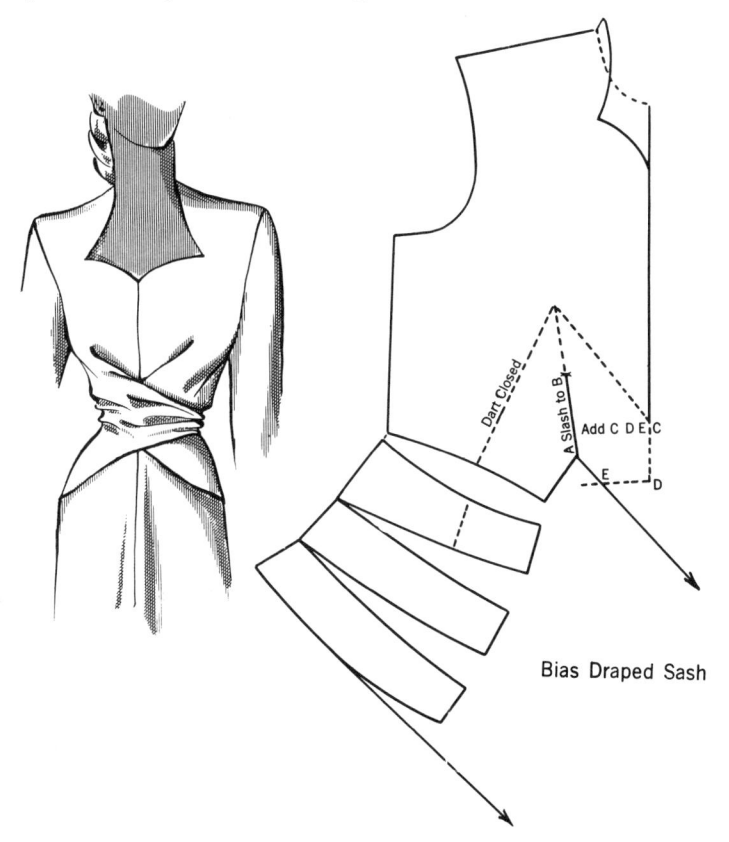

Fig. 37. Excess from shoulder dart and above the shoulder tied to form a becoming neckline.
Fig. 38. Folds from basic waistline dart tied.
Fig. 39. The tying idea interpreted in a wide girdle.
Fig. 40. Pattern for dress shown in Fig. 39.

Suggestion 5
INTERPRETING SILHOUETTES AS COMPLETE DESIGNS

Each year fashion magazines present new trends primarily as silhouettes, for the shape, of course, is the most important characteristic of every costume. Indeed, if you were not interested in cutting a pattern for a garment, the silhouette would show all you would need to know about fashion and style. It shows, for example, the current breadth of shoulder; the shape of sleeves; whether bodices are rib-fitting or bloused; whether waistlines are nipped in or wide; whether skirts are pencil-slim or bell-shaped, short or long, flared at the side, front, or back. It also shows whether there is a vogue for peplums, whether or not they flare, and just where they flare. In short, almost the only important thing the silhouette fails to show is the location of the structural seams and darts required to produce its distinctive outlines.

It is, therefore, a challenge to try to interpret a certain silhouette by placing the seam and dart lines within the contour, not only to produce the desired shape, but also to introduce harmonious seaming detail. There are usually many possible seam and dart positions, and it is good practice to see how many interesting arrangements you can make. All designing is fundamentally interpretation of silhouettes, and only those seams and darts that contribute to the molding of the contour are of vital importance. In carrying out this exercise, you will become increasingly conscious of this fundamental principle and will tend to work more and more for complete effect rather than for minute detail.

The central sketch in Figure 41 illustrates a typical fashion silhouette but shows no seams. Obviously, there must be seams somewhere to produce the rib-fitting bodice and the sharply flared peplum. Surrounding this central silhouetted figure are four possible interpretations of the design, each one with almost the same contour. But the various cuts could not possibly have exactly the same grain location through the flare. Hence the effect of each would vary slightly, though not much. When placing lines within the silhouette, always observe the laws of good space division, and place seams where they will harmonize with the lines of the silhouette. The simplest way to arrive at any of the four interpretations is to draw the structural lines on transparent tracing paper laid over the silhouetted figure, and then to block each interpretation from the master pattern. Figures 42a, b, c, and d show the patterns for each of the four interpretations of the silhouette shown in Figure 41.

This one example of silhouette interpretation should stimulate you to interpret in a variety of ways many others of your own choosing.

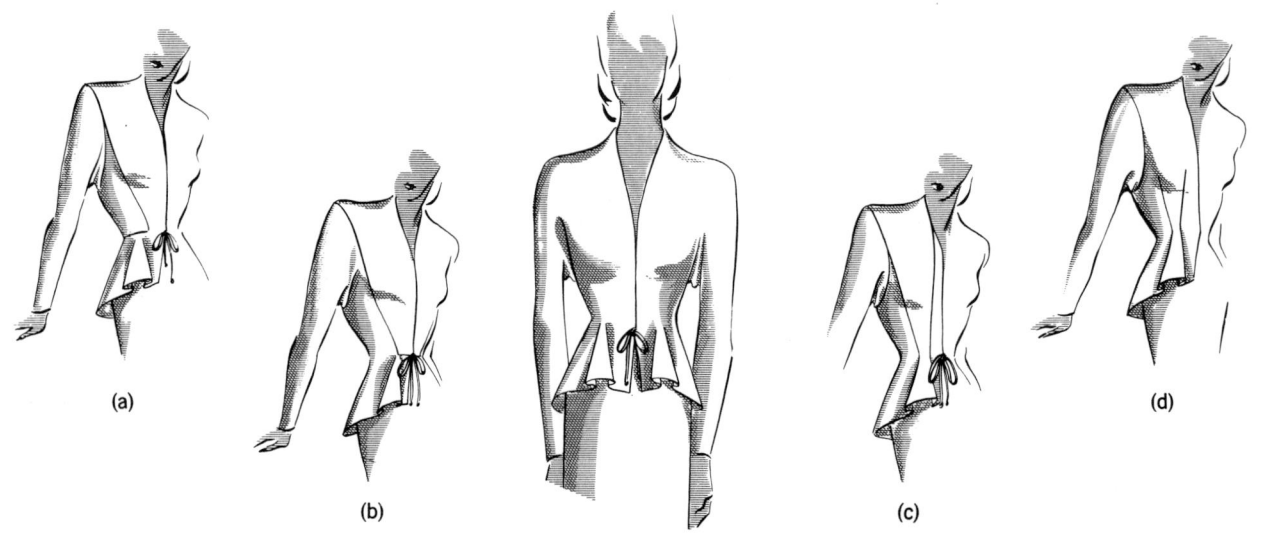

Fig. 41. Sketches (a), (b), (c), (d) show four interpretations of the silhouette shown at the center of the illustration.

294

SOURCES OF DESIGN

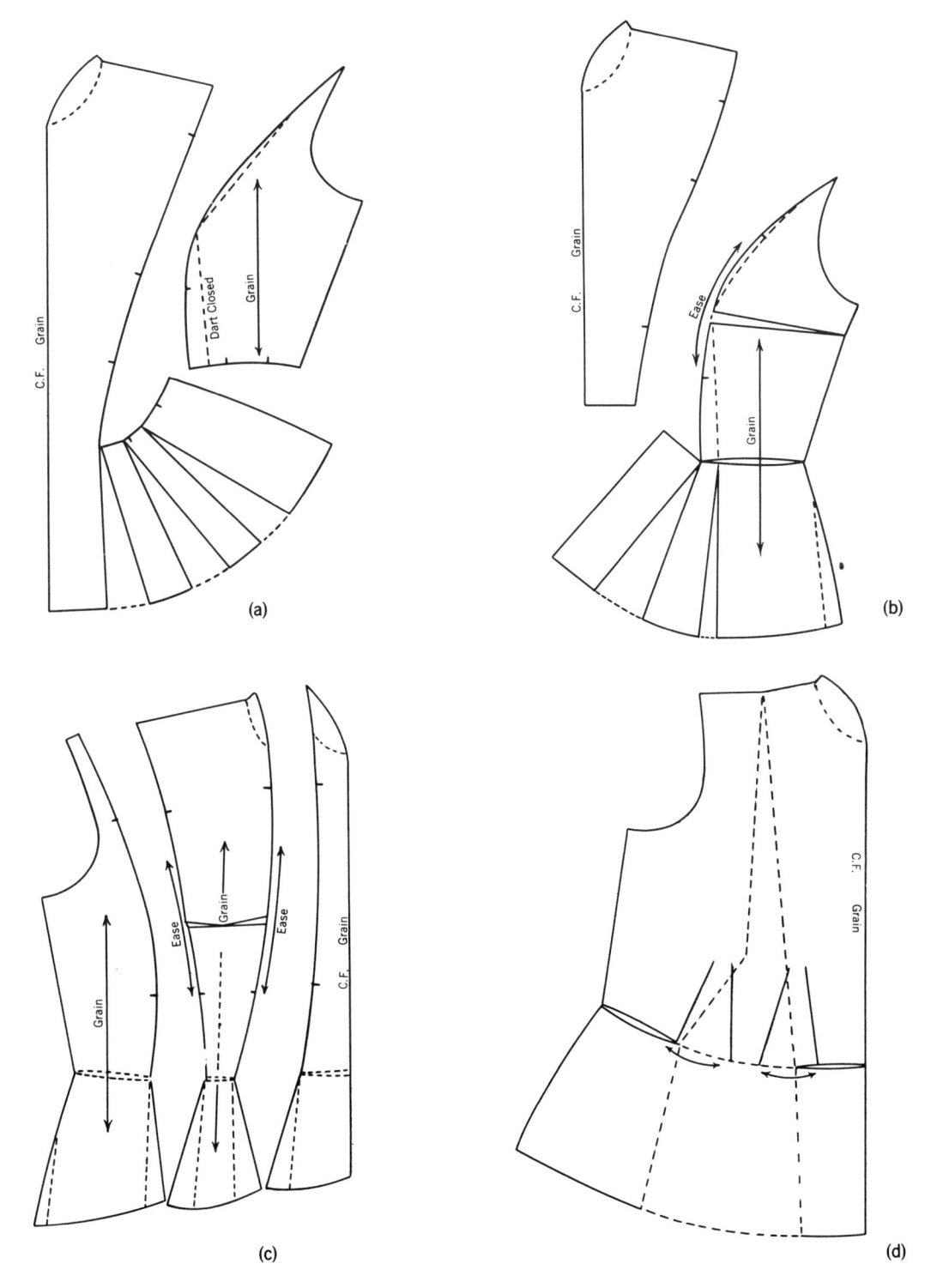

Fig. 42. (a) Pattern for Fig. 41 (a); (b) Pattern for Fig. 41 (b); (c) Pattern for Fig. 41 (c); (d) Pattern for Fig. 41 (d).

295

DRESS DESIGN

Suggestion 6

MOLDING THE FABRIC TO THE FORM BY SEAMS AND BY CONCEALED DARTS

Molding by Seams

The purpose of this experiment is to achieve a smooth, form-fitting costume which takes its inspiration not from a costume silhouette but rather from the contour of the figure itself. To do this, mold the fabric to the form through seams that run from one edge of the pattern to the other, rounding the fabric to the form not only along seam lines but also in the unbroken areas between them. A soft pliable woolen with good shrinking quality is essential for such a design. If you place seams to form the design detail of the costume they will thereby serve the double role of shaping and decoration. The French dart is a familiar example of a line that cuts clear through the pattern, and you have already observed that it molds more effectively than any pair of short darts. If you double or even triple a continuous line, the pattern curves to the contour of the figure as if sculptured.

The three following examples illustrate the same principle but show that the lines can run in different directions. The blouse in Figure 43, a variation of the French dart, repeats the vertical line to strengthen the character of the design and to give a second line along which to shape the fabric. In the design shown in Figure 44, lines radiate outward from the neck over the bust to the underarm. And the costume illustrated in Figure 45 is shaped through horizontal seaming. In the first two of these, the radiation of the lines improves the spacing and avoids the monotony of parallels. As shown in Figure 42, radiation can also focus attention on broad shoulders and a slender waistline, or, as in Figure 44, on the neckline, which is ornamented by a heavy metal chain. In the dress shown in Figure 45, although the lines are parallel, the spaces are graduated in size to give variety.

The pattern diagrams for all three designs (see Figures 46, 47, and 48) illustrate how to distribute the shaping between two seams rather than all at one. To achieve this effect, the seams must be placed so that no one of them falls exactly at the point of the bust.

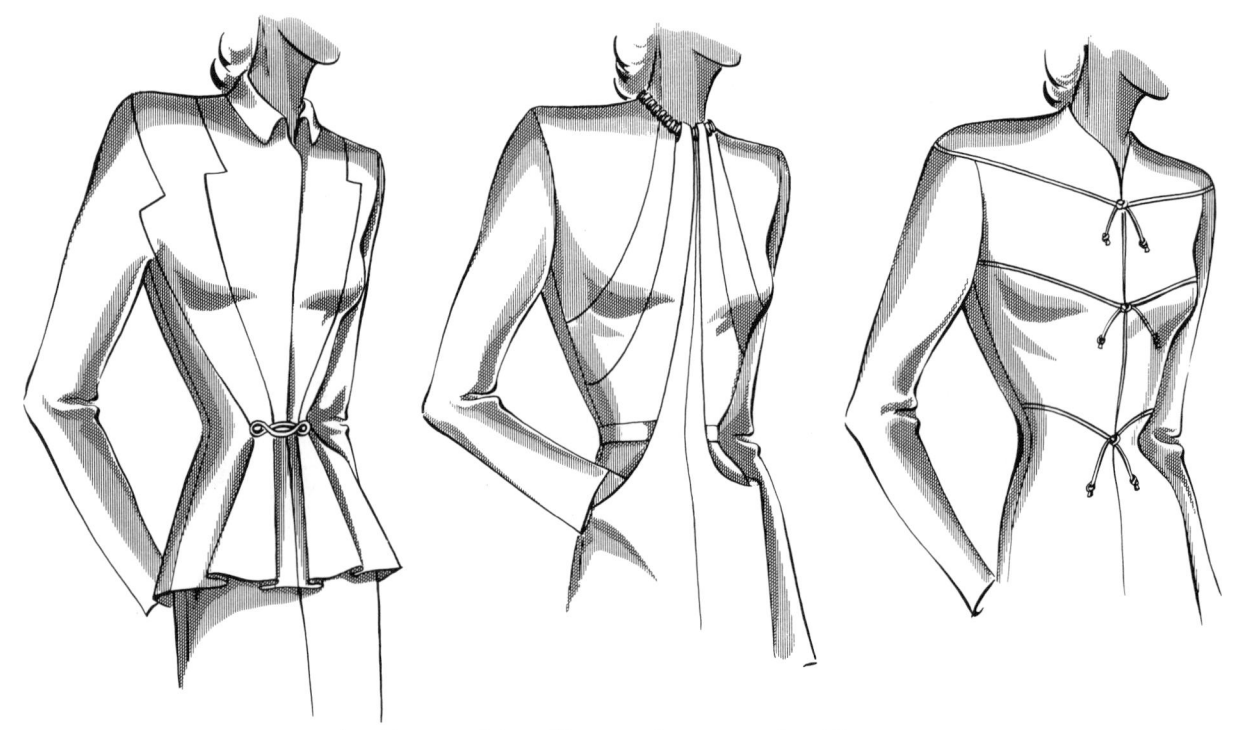

Figs. 43, 44, and 45. Illustrate three ways of molding a garment to the figure through seams that cut entirely across the pattern.

SOURCES OF DESIGN

If you study the patterns, you will notice that in the pattern corresponding to Figure 43, the two design lines fall on either side of the bust point, and the ease is distributed along both edges. In the pattern for Figure 44, the section next to the top falls directly over the bust, and the ease is divided between the upper and the lower edges. The lower section of the blouse shown in Figure 45, which spans a wider space below the bust, has most of the ease along its upper edge. Had a narrower section been used over the bust, ease would have been almost equally divided along the upper and lower edges of that section. In each of the three designs, all of the ease could have been placed on the one edge where it naturally fell when the basic dart was closed and the pattern was slashed on the new lines. However, this would have made it more difficult to ease in the excess invisibly, and would have failed to take advantage of the opportunity to divide the ease and cup or mold the section that falls directly over the curve of the bust. This is the structural advantage of using more than one seam line. Molding, however, is more than a matter of seam lines, and the entire blouse takes on shape because of the intensification of the curves along the edges which distributes the shaping over the whole pattern.

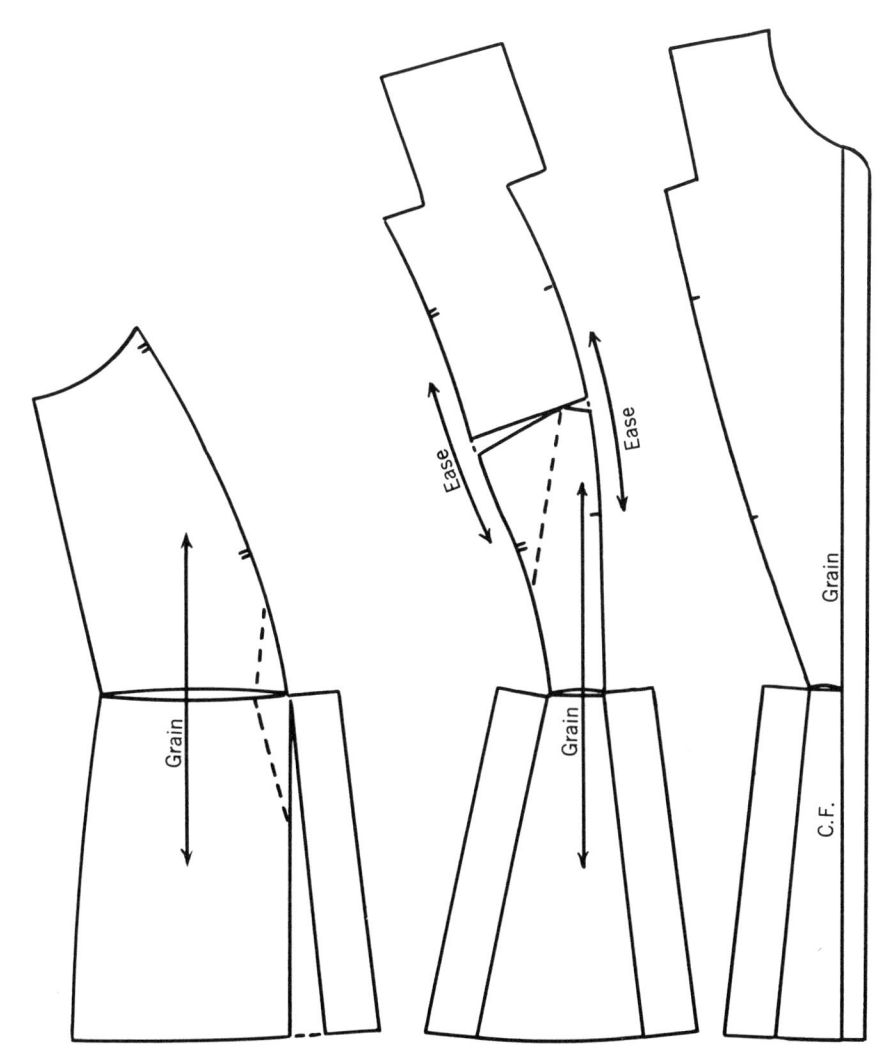

Fig. 46. Pattern diagram for Fig. 43. Ease from the dart transfer is distributed along both edges of the central section.

DRESS DESIGN

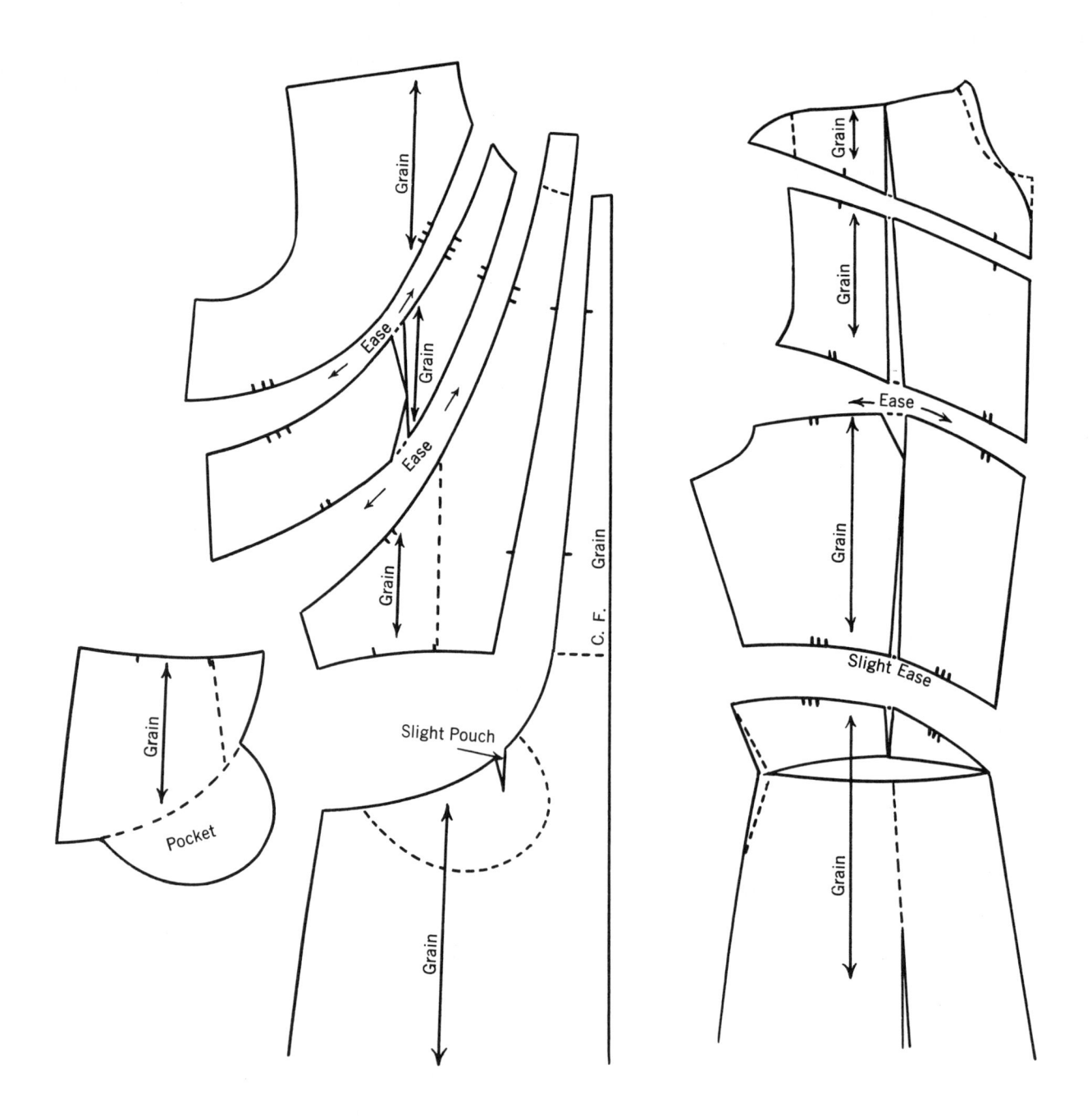

Fig. 47. Pattern diagram for Fig. 44.
Fig. 48. Pattern diagram for Fig. 45. Most of the ease falls at the top of the section directly under the bust. Note the spread along other section edges.

Other additional seaming to emphasize the design, though not necessary to shape the fabric to the contour of the bust, does make it possible to open the lower edge of the top section and the upper edge of the lowest section in order to shape the blouse outward in a smooth convex curve from shoulder to bust and inward from bust to waistline. If the small section falling directly over the bust is cupped excessively on each edge, the bust contour becomes too pronounced. This is especially true if the bust is large. To adjust the shaping to the individual figure, slash and pivot outward the edges attached to the bust section, as shown in Figure 48.

The pattern for the dress shown in Figure 45 (see Figure 48) also clears up another difficult problem — fitting fabric across the waistline when the waistline darts have been closed in both blouse and skirt. When this is done, both waistlines become intense arcs, with the result that there is excess vertical length across the waistline at the side front. Either leave this to break and blouse slightly at the waistline, or stretch the fabric slightly horizontally to reduce the length. Then fit out the excess width by indenting the side seam as shown by the dotted lines across the waistline in Figure 48. Seam tape held slightly tighter than the waistline of the dress, and invisibly tacked on the wrong side, will reduce the width enough to define the waistline. Ease the dress just above the hip bone where greater width is needed below the waist.

Molding the Fabric by Concealed Darts

Figure 49 shows a design with a long S scroll running from the neck to a curve below the waistline. The problem was to figure out how to hide the darting underneath the neck and waistline scrolls so that they would serve the purpose of fitting the fabric to the form. The scrolls are so important that the introduction of obvious darts close to them would not only interfere with their effectiveness, but would give the scroll design the appearance of a useless added detail. Study Figures 50a and b to see how the dart on the right shoulder still serves its purpose although it is curved to follow the scroll. The darts at both sides of the center front below the waistline are also curved to fit the scroll lines. It would have been possible to close the dart on the left shoulder entirely, and to transfer it to the curved dart at the left side of the waistline. But this would have created too much ease to shrink out readily. It also seemed to improve the design to balance the waistline dart on the right side with the small shoulder dart on the left. These two small darts are scarcely visible when carefully pressed. This idea can be developed either by draping or blocking, but eventually the design should be blocked to true up the pattern and to balance the darts.

Fig. 49. Molding the fabric through darts concealed under the design lines.

Figure 51, on the other hand, depicts a design much softer in character than that shown in Figure 49, for it has gathers falling from simulated shoulder yokes and soft fullness repeated in the skirt. Designs with gathers such as this one has are technically deceptive. They seem at first glance to be complicated and difficult to cut, but actually they cause less trouble than designs like the one shown in Figure 49, which must be molded without visible fullness along the design lines. It takes far less skill and ingenuity to put the entire basic dart in one place and distribute it into gathers than it does to get rid of it subtly, as the molded garment requires.

DRESS DESIGN

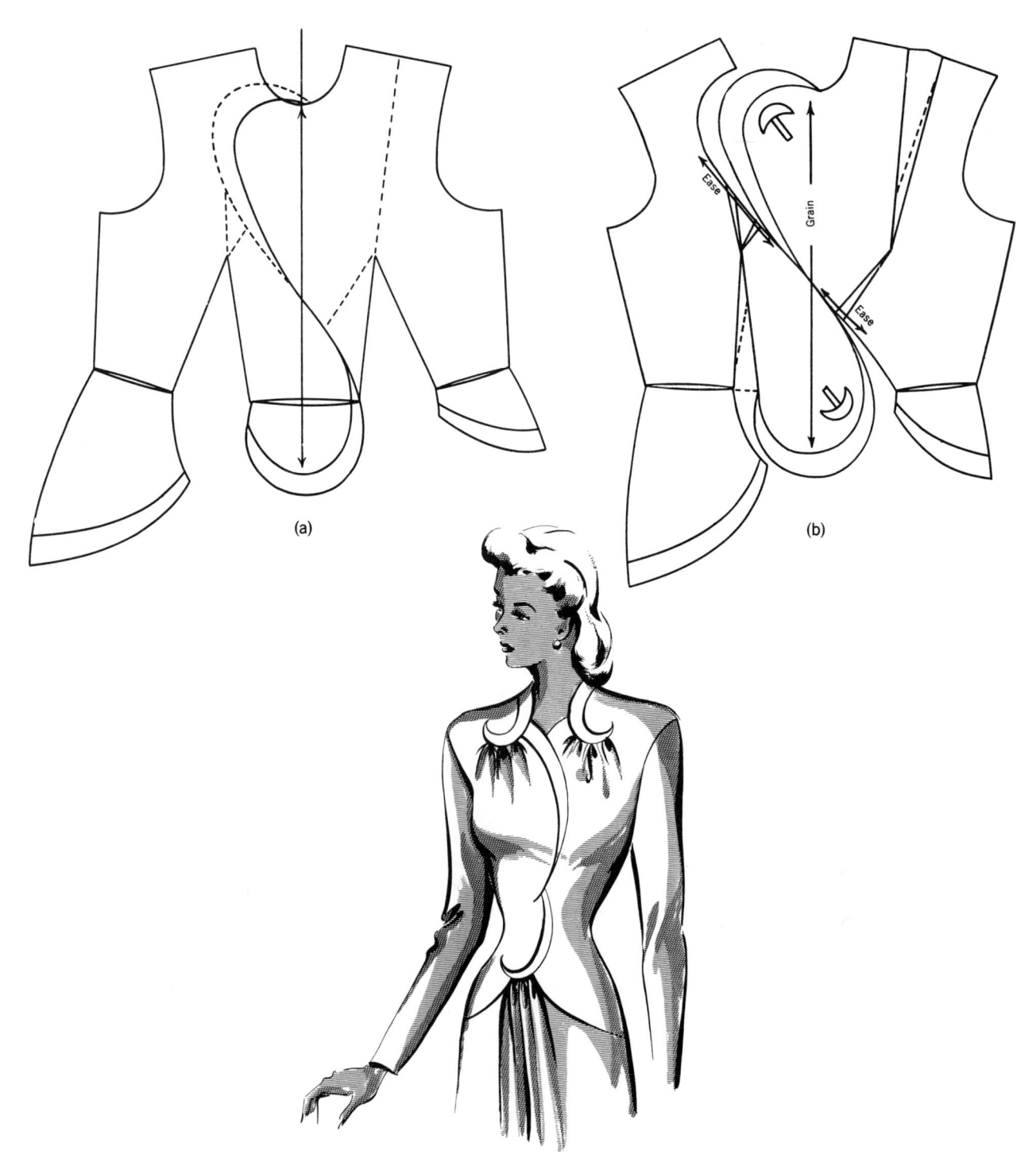

Fig. 50. (a) (above) Pattern for Fig. 49. Dart lines drawn;
(b) Pattern spread to show where darts are concealed.
Fig. 51. (below) Shaping concealed under yoke edge.

300

SOURCES OF DESIGN

Suggestion 7
DEVELOPING THE DESIGN THEME FROM VARIATIONS OF BASIC DARTS

Nothing could be more stereotyped or unimaginative than to use the basic darts — the shoulder, waistline, or French darts — exactly as they are used in a master pattern. But long before you become adept at pattern designing, you will discover that the vertical shoulder and waistline dart positions are two of the best possible locations for darts from the point of view of becomingness. What could be more reasonable, therefore, than to shape the pattern at these standard locations, and at the same time to center the interest there so that the design is both imaginative and becoming? It is not necessary to strain your ingenuity very hard to invent innumerable variations of each basic dart, and in so doing to explore another source of design inspiration.

Variations of the Shoulder Dart

The shoulder is an exceptionally good position for design emphasis. Centering attention high makes the figure appear taller, and also focuses interest around the face, both of which effects are always desirable.

The group of sketches in Figure 52 illustrates a few of the possible interpretations of the shoulder dart. Any of these ideas could have been developed from draping on the form, and any one of them could have been first clarified in a sketch and then blocked. The method used to develop the design makes little difference and varies from one individual to another and from one design to another. All of the designs illustrated furnish good practice problems to be analyzed for design quality and pattern making. In working them, you will gain assurance in designing as well as technical skill.

Variations of the Waistline Dart

A waistline dart, either the standard vertical one or a diagonal one slanting upward from the side seam toward the bust, will be found in most blouses, regardless of other dart locations, in order to fit the waistline more closely and to retain some ease over the lower curve of the bust. If well placed, the vertical waistline dart tapers to define the waistline becomingly. It is good practice to play up this dart position and to make it the center of interest of the costume as well as a standard location for fitting. The group of sketches in Figure 53 shows several possible ways to treat the excess from this dart in order to make a design both unusual and interesting. To gain experience, you should practice blocking the pattern for each of these designs.

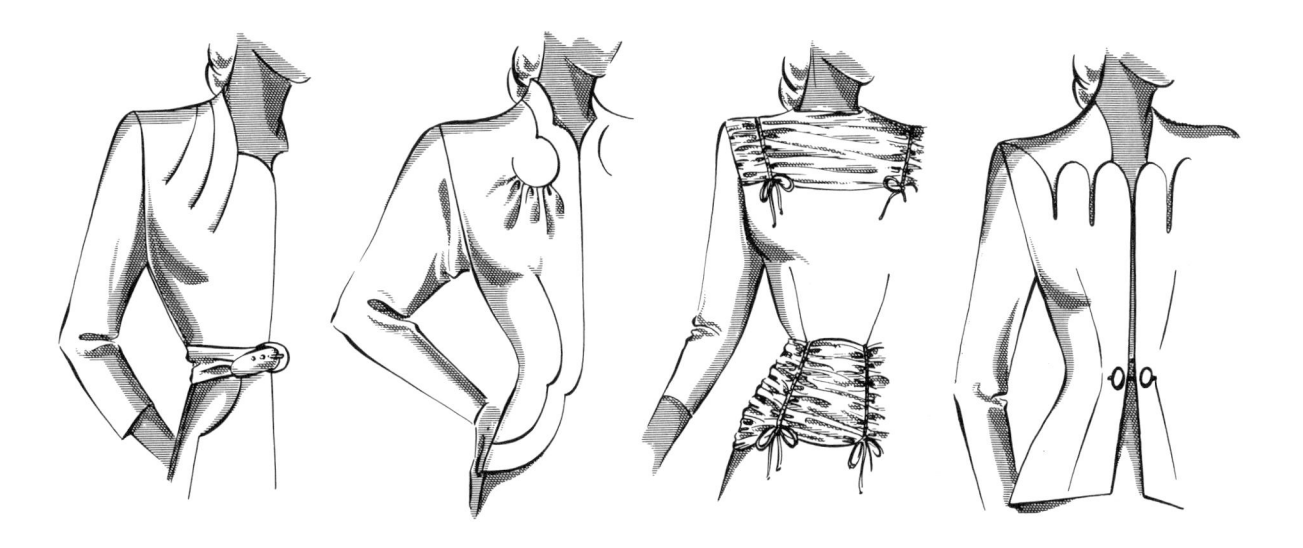

Fig. 52. Four unusual variations of the standard shoulder dart.

DRESS DESIGN

Fig. 53. Six possible variations of the standard waistline dart.

Variations of the French Dart

Several of the illustrations have already pointed up the fact that the French dart line, because it cuts clear through the pattern from one edge to the other, offers a better opportunity for molding the fabric to the figure than any combination of short darts. For this reason it is a favorite in hip length jacket designing where adequate shaping — out over the bust, in at the waistline, and out again at the hipline — requires a continuous seam rather than a series of short darts. Because the inward slanting line from the shoulder to a narrowed waistline is universally becoming, regardless of individual figure faults, the French dart should be fully exploited so that you may see how many unusual variations of the line can be devised.

The group of sketches in Figure 54 shows the use of the French dart in both tailored and soft designs, and one example even shows its effectiveness when used for a close-fitting evening bodice with a contrasting bouffant skirt. For practice, you should see how many variations of this theme you can contrive, and should either block or drape the pattern for each. By experimenting with variations of these three familiar dart locations, you can develop any number of good designs. The prime requisites are the necessary shaping, a clear understanding of generally becoming line locations, and alertness in seeing a possibility for converting a conventional dart into an original theme for a design.

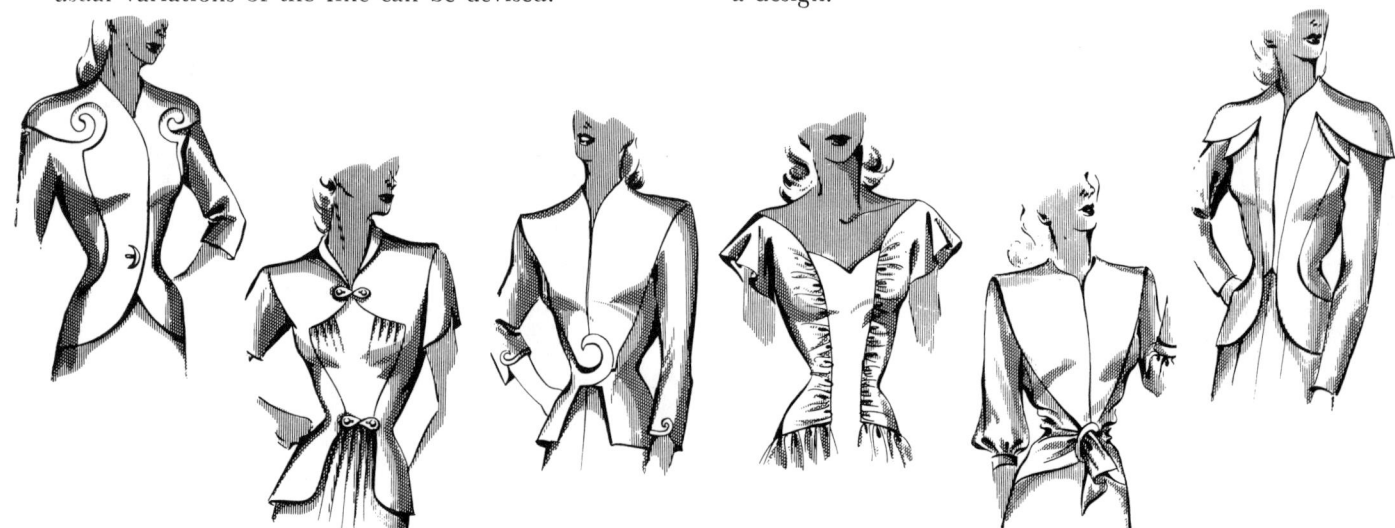

Fig. 54. Six suggestions for converting a standard French dart into the design theme of the costume.

SOURCES OF DESIGN

Other Variations of the Master Dart

Although the shoulder and waistline are generally the most advantageous dart positions from the point of view of becomingness, there are frequent opportunities for play on lines that run from the bust to the center front at the neckline, to the center front seam at the chest, and to the underarm seam near the waistline; or for that matter, to any point on the front half of the blouse pattern. Do not ignore these other locations as possible centers of interest even though they may be less generally becoming to all types of figures.

The dart from the bust to the center front at the neckline should be used sparingly, since its usual effect is to emphasize the size of the bust by slanting outward toward the bust and inward toward the neck. However, when you crush the excess from the dart and add an extension for a tie at the center front of the neckline, many soft, flattering folds are formed which partially counteract the inward pull of these lines. You may fasten the excess with a striking ornament at the neck or even drape it over a necklace to give a more unusual effect. Suit blouses take advantage of the variations of this dart position with great success to focus attention on the center front opening of the jacket.

The dart transferred to the center front line at the chest level offers a chance to vary the theme of horizontal fullness distributed along the vertical center front line. But again this dart position should be used cautiously because of the tendency of horizontal gathers or folds to reduce apparent height and to exaggerate curves. This position, however, like the preceding one, is a particularly good choice for dressy suit blouses, since interest in the jacket opening is usually desirable. The blouse illustrated in Figure 55 shows such a dart, which is obviously appropriate either for a separate blouse or for a dress.

At first glance this seems like a simple transfer of the master dart to the center front, but on analysis it will prove to be a form of cowl neckline with the drapery drawn into horizontal tucks across the bust. Notice that the excess left when the dart is transferred to the neckline at the center front is taken up into tucks and then released at the end of each tuck to fall into soft folds directed toward the shoulder and armscye. This design is easier to drape than to block.

To drape it, pin the straight grain at the center front, and then work from the waistline up and outward toward the shoulder, swinging the entire excess in from the shoulder point toward the center as in the cowl neckline procedure. The bias at the neckline will stretch advantageously to cling to the sides of the neck.

The dart from the bust toward the underarm at the waistline is most commonly used merely as a supplementary fitting dart, but may also serve to a minor extent as the source of an idea. For example, the line may be slashed back and gathers may be pushed in along its upper edge, or it may have a sash extension at the underarm to be carried around the waist to the back, where it can be tied or buckled. To most students, this will undoubtedly be a familiar use of this dart.

Figure 56 shows a more unusual interpretation of the underarm dart. On the front of the blouse, the slash forms a simulated bolero line, which is attached at the underarm seam to a real bolero jacket back. The pattern diagram (see Figure 57) shows how the excess from the dart was left to slide up under the loose edge where it was attached to a support extending to the shoulder. This design is casual, looks effortless, and yet takes careful planning.

Fig. 55.

DRESS DESIGN

Fig. 56.

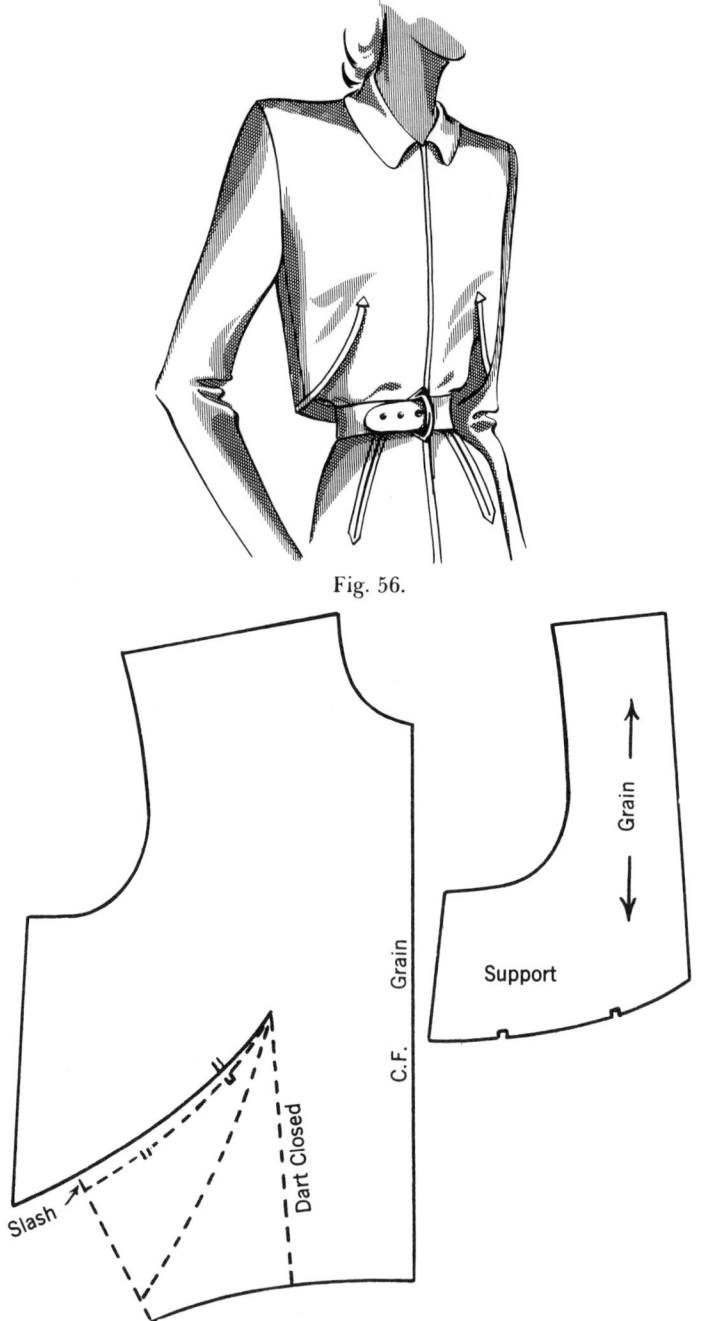

Fig. 57. Pattern diagram for Fig. 56. Arrows show slash line and underarm dart which is left to slide up under the bolero and be attached to the support.

The suggestions here offered for variation of the basic darts in the front of the blouse to produce the theme of the costume are only a few of the many possibilities. The same idea can be applied to the back of the blouse, though to a much more limited extent, since any design that seems to thicken or round out the back over the shoulder blades should be avoided. Because of this, back darts usually serve their purpose better if placed at about the same location as in the master pattern, that is, with the excess divided between the shoulder and the waistline. The plainness of the back may be relieved by button lines, by waistline sashes, or by details which add interest to the silhouette, such as bows, peplums, and draped effects centered at the hollow of the waistline. Therefore, while designing around the basic back darts offers good practice and is often valuable experimentally, waist backs in general can better serve the purpose of carrying to completion the idea started in the front. Never forget that any motif, however interesting, clever, or unusual, must be avoided if it distorts the figure. Intricacy of detail for its own sake does not make good design. It is the beauty of the costume silhouette from all angles — front, back, and sides — that really matters.

Variations of Standard Yokes

Although the conversion of a dart to a yoke is not properly a variation of the basic dart, it is a closely related technique and therefore should be mentioned here. A yoke, as its name indicates, is a segment of a pattern used to support gathers or folds, and is usually placed at the shoulder in the blouse and from the waist to the hips in the skirt. Although yoke cuts are frequently used to shape and mold the fabric to the form without visible fullness beneath the edge, the following example will deal solely with a yoke used conventionally as a means of support for visible fullness.

In Chapter 2 the techniques of both draping and blocking a simple horizontal shoulder yoke were explained. It is possible to vary this standard yoke to produce many other more unusual versions of the idea. Figure 58 shows a design with a crossed shoulder yoke. The fact that the gathers radiate toward the armscye and the underarm from the yoke, but disappear when they reach the seam lines, accounts for their graceful softness and lack of heaviness. Figures 59a and b show the pattern shapes for this blouse and illustrate two important points in yoke designing. The first of these concerns the placing of the yoke. It should be cut to fall across the figure either above the bust, if the curve

SOURCES OF DESIGN

tends to be horizontal, or no closer to the underarm seam than the point of the bust, if the curve is more nearly vertical. Either way, there will be space for the gathers to fall over the bust. If, on the other hand, the yoke line cuts across the figure beside or below the point of the bust, then ease falls on the yoke edge rather than on the edge that should be gathered. The effect is very poor if gathers puff out too close to the underarm, or in the case of a horizontal line, below, rather than above the bust.

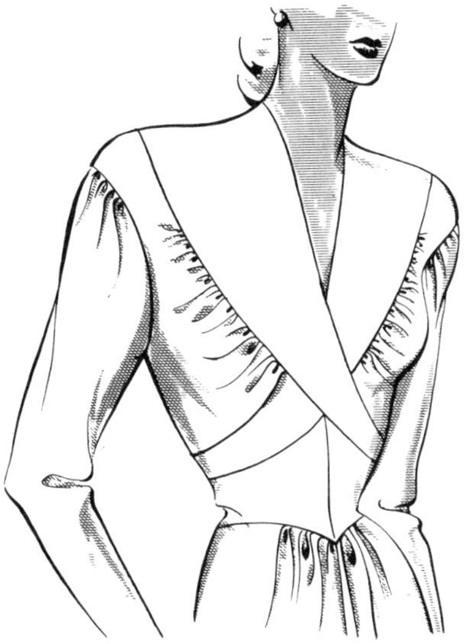

Fig. 58. Crossed shoulder yoke.

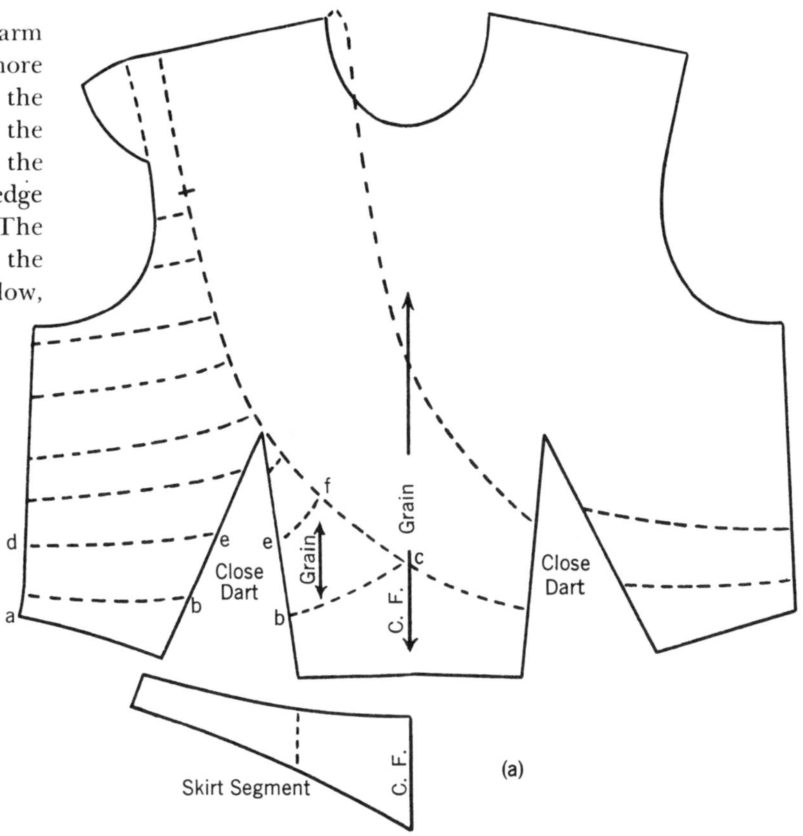

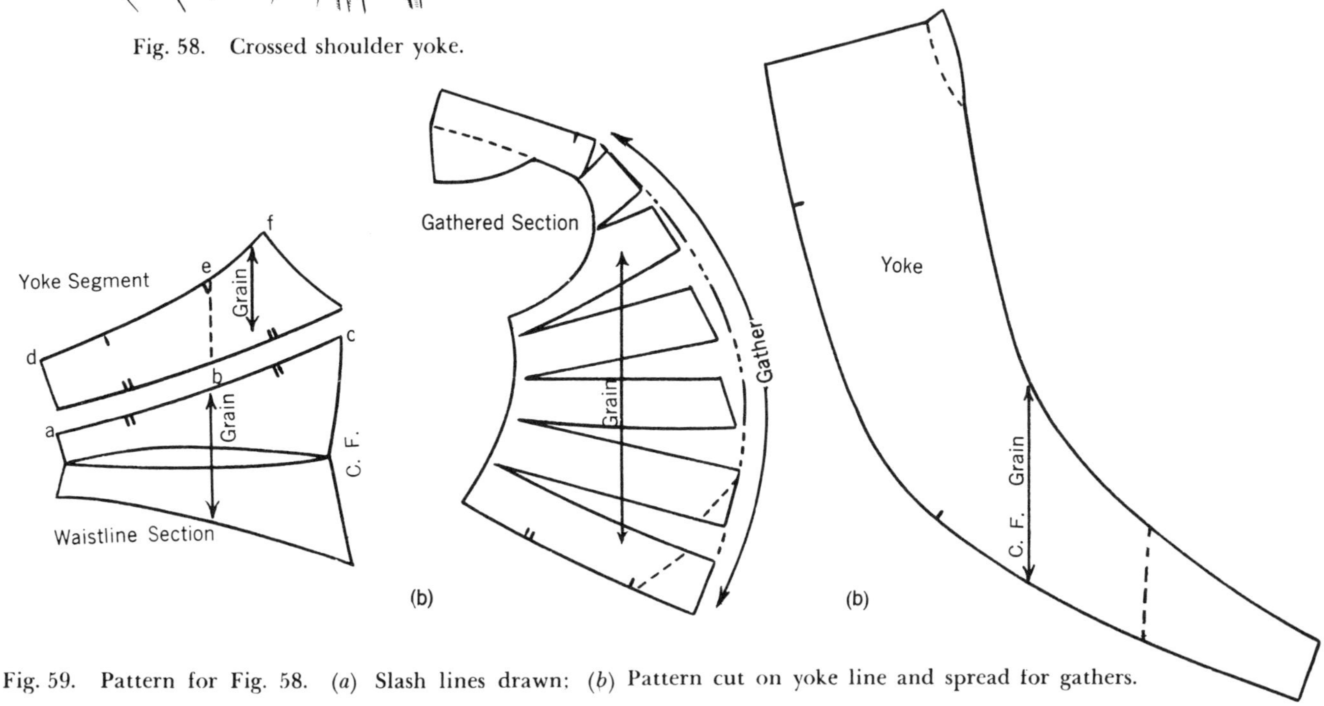

Fig. 59. Pattern for Fig. 58. (a) Slash lines drawn: (b) Pattern cut on yoke line and spread for gathers.

305

DRESS DESIGN

The second point to observe is that the gathers radiate and disappear before reaching the underarm seam. If the slashes for gathers had been cut completely through the underarm seam and if both edges had been spread evenly, then the lines of fullness would have been parallel, horizontal, and altogether lacking the animation of gathers that spring from curved seams like the underarm and armscye seams shown here. This example illustrates the generalization previously made, that gathers and folds are invariably more animated and less inclined to fall into heavy, "clothy," parallel folds when they radiate outward from an arc; that is, when only one edge of the pattern is spread for fullness.

Yokes with suspended fullness are a favorite means of introducing softness to emphasize figure contour and yet of controlling the fullness so that it serves its purpose without billowing out where closeness of fit is essential. Hence various other yoke designs have been illustrated earlier in this book.

Suggestion 8

DEVELOPING UNUSUAL SKIRT CUTS FROM THE BASIC TWO-, FOUR-, AND SIX-GORE PATTERNS

In Chapter 3, the principles of both draping and blocking standard gored, draped, and circular skirts were explained. It should not be difficult now to experiment with the draping and blocking of the more unusual variations of these basic skirt forms.

Figure 60 shows the back view of a two-gore skirt that does not even remotely resemble the standard two-gore cut. Although in its usual form a two-gore skirt is most unsatisfactory for anything except a master pattern, in its many gathered and draped variations it can be very effective. This particular design shows

Fig. 60. The standard two-gore pattern was used to develop this skirt, which is far from standard.

Fig. 61. The basic four-gore skirt pattern was varied to produce this design.

Fig. 62. Pattern for dress shown in Fig. 61.

SOURCES OF DESIGN

fullness drawn up onto a cord at the center back. The sketch of the blouse front shows a repetition of this same motif to form a keyhole neckline. Notice that in the skirt all fullness directed toward the hips disappears before it reaches the side seams. This radiates the gathers and also fits the skirt smoothly at the hip seams.

Figure 61 shows one of the countless variations of a four-gore skirt, and Figure 62 shows the method used to make the pattern for this design.

In order to get the precise effect of the funnel pocket drapery shown in Figure 63, the designer cut the skirt as a variation of the six-gore style. First she cut the belt curve from the master two-gore skirt pattern; then she cut the remainder of the pattern into panels as shown in Figure 64. She next slashed the center front section, spread it for gathers, and added the funnel pocket shape to each edge of the side front seam. Shaping the side front seam does away with puffing below the pockets.

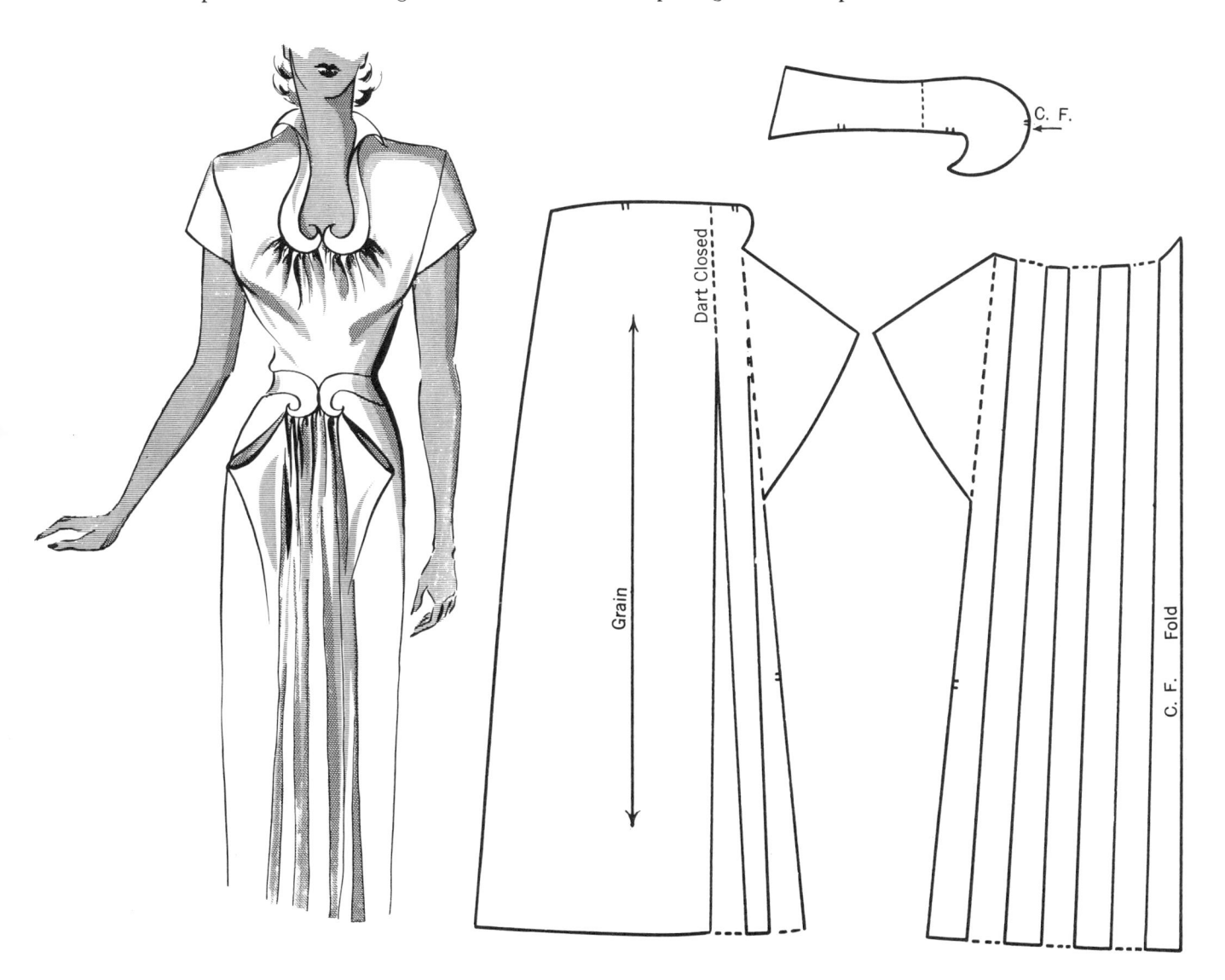

Fig. 63. Funnel pocket skirt derived from the standard six-gore pattern.

Fig. 64. Pattern for dress shown in Fig. 63.

307

DRESS DESIGN

Figure 65 shows another skirt variation, this time with a cowl drapery on the side of the hip. The pattern, illustrated in Figures 66a and b, shows how to place the hip seam on the bias and how to spread the front and back sections of the skirt at the top, thus eliminating the side seam through the drapery. Some of the blousing at the hem on the side seam was taken out by making a diamond-shaped dart. To cut the side seam section above the folds, follow Figure 66a, but extend the side section down to meet the under edge of the top fold. This is an extremely complicated design, and one which will most certainly need some adjustment either on the form or on the model, since cowl folds fall differently in different fabrics.

Figure 67, showing a skirt with a separate piece of fabric set into the seam to form a semblance of cowl drapery, illustrates the point that set-on drapery is usually inferior in design to drapery produced by the cut of the pattern. In this case, the basic skirt is too flat and plain to be suddenly swathed in folds which appear to be stuck on rather than draped into the design. However, the difficulty of draping cowl folds such as those illustrated in Figure 65 explains why draped cowl folds are often added as a bias swathe as in Figure 67, and not produced by the cut of the pattern.

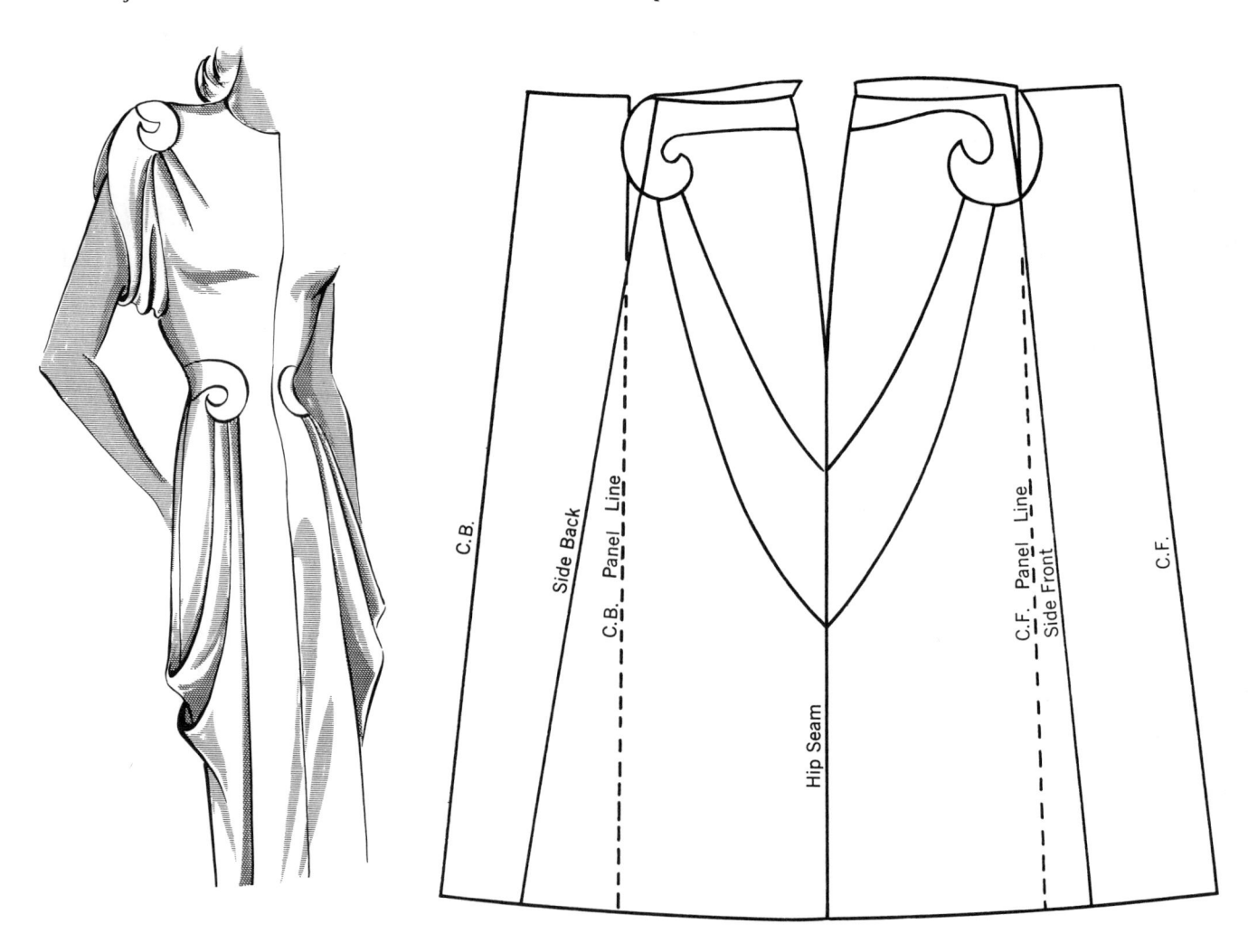

Fig. 65. Deep cowl folds produced by placing the hip seams on the bias.

Fig. 66. (a) Design lines drawn.

308

SOURCES OF DESIGN

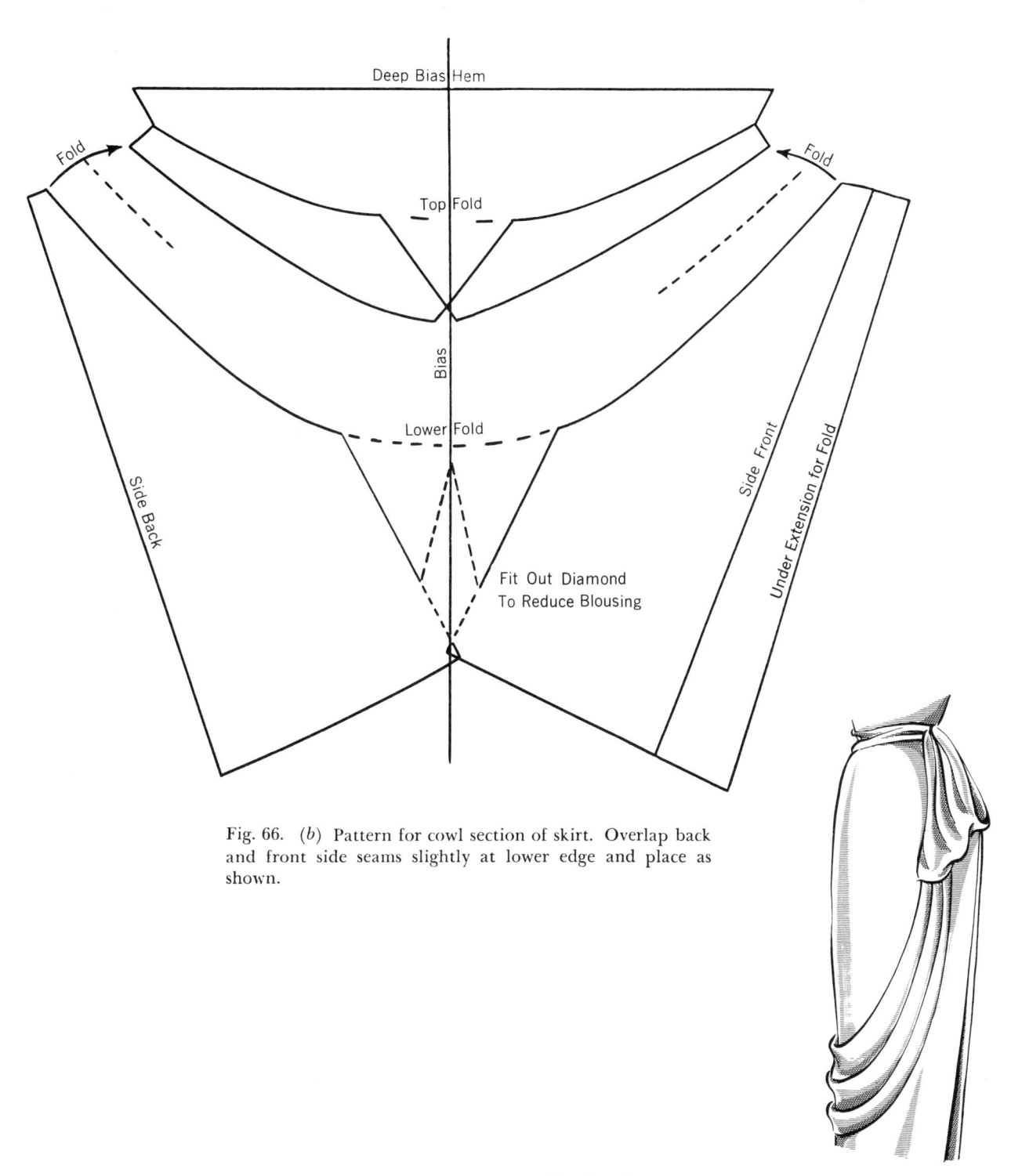

Fig. 66. (b) Pattern for cowl section of skirt. Overlap back and front side seams slightly at lower edge and place as shown.

Fig. 67. Cowl folds added to a basic skirt. The design lacks the rhythm of Fig. 65.

Suggestion 9

CARRYING ONE PIECE OF FABRIC AS FAR AS POSSIBLE WITHOUT CUTTING

This is not by any means a new idea. Under Suggestion 1, Developing Line Arrangements by Sketching, you discovered that erasing crisscrossed lines smoothed up the design and made it continuous instead of cut-up and choppy. This idea has permeated all of the other experiments described in this chapter, because continuity, rhythm, and smooth flow of line are fundamental to good design. The costume shown in Figure 27 (page 289)is an outstanding illustration of this rhythmical quality, especially the folds to the shoulder which are carried across the shoulder seam line around to the center back instead of being ended abruptly at the shoulder. The blouse illustrated in Figure 39 (page 293), with smooth curved lines that merge into a girdle tied around the waist, is another particularly good example of continuity of line.

Figure 68 shows a dress with both the right and left halves of the front cut in a single piece from shoulder to hem. It avoids the usual crosslines at the waistline and yoke and as a result has unbroken rhythm and an effect of uncluttered simplicity of the kind that characterizes the most expensive clothes. It appears to be simple and yet requires the most careful kind of planning to avoid obvious seams while retaining a smooth fit.

This experiment brings out another and more technical point. Regardless of the method used to develop an idea, it frequently happens that in the final blocking of the pattern you will see small pattern pieces that you can attach to larger sections in order to cut them all in one piece and thus to eliminate unnecessary seams. Or you may discover just the reverse to be true. When you spread the pattern out flat, you may find that a hidden seam along the waistline, for example, simplifies the cutting, saves material, and lets you place the grain more advantageously. Exercise your own judgment as to the comparative value of cutting a pattern all in one piece or of concealing seams skillfully. The main point to remember is to work to get the effect of continuity and to hide necessary joinings so well that they will never be noticed.

If you study Figure 69, which shows the pattern for the dress illustrated in Figure 68, you will notice that the skirt folds present no pattern-making difficulties at all. The problem lies in indenting the waistline without a seam and in distributing the excess from the waist dart of the master pattern in order to preserve the smooth, molded effect of the illustration. To accomplish this, the designer distributed the excess around three sides of the bust, easing a very small amount (but not enough to create gathers) along the under edge of the lower horizontal tuck dart, and also easing a very little at the center front to help shape the fabric over the bust and take the flatness out of the pattern. But the biggest part of the dart she transferred to the underarm, and divided it into two smaller darts concealed under the arm.

Molding the fabric across the waistline was possible because the shaped center front line helped to close up the arc between waist and skirt patterns. Notice also that the bias runs vertically across the waistline and that it will therefore mold the fabric to the figure as it hangs. Any excess left at the waistline can be taken out at the fitting by stretching the waistline horizontally. The waistline as well as the center front seam should be taped to stay each the correct **length**. This front pattern plus the three-quarter sleeves shown and a four-gore skirt back for the design can all be cut from two shoulder to hem lengths of fabric, leaving only the blouse back and facings to provide for. The cut is therefore not an extravagant one.

Suggestion 10

DERIVING UNUSUAL EFFECTS FROM ASYMMETRIC CUTS

The design balanced at the side front or side back has always enjoyed the reputation of being more subtle in effect than the one with the two sides absolutely alike. The asymmetric design is less formal and static; but the balance, although not so obvious, must nevertheless be present and must be "felt." The designer must possess much more than skill in pattern making if she is to recognize or "feel" the right location of the lines so that the two unlike sides will seem to have the same weight and importance in spite of their difference in size and shape. To design an asymmetrically balanced costume, especially if it is a complicated one, requires more natural talent — as well as more training and experience in the placing of lines — than to design one exactly balanced at the center.

SOURCES OF DESIGN

Fig. 68. The half front from shoulder to hem cut in one piece.

Fig. 69. Pattern for Fig. 68. Notice the method of shaping the blouse and also of indenting the waistline.

311

DRESS DESIGN

Figures 70 and 71 show two examples of asymmetric balance. In Figure 70, the larger plain area on the right side of the blouse balances the smaller but more detailed left side. The front line swings in continuous movement from the point of the collar to the hip. The straight vertical lines at the side front of the skirt and of the skirt silhouette stabilize the design and furnish relief from the activity of curves and gathers.

The front lines of the costume shown in Figure 71 are almost all curves, the upper one from shoulder to waist forming the loose simulated bolero which is balanced by the reverse curve of the peplum. The straight-hanging sleeves in both Figures 70 and 71 supply necessary relief from drapery, gathers, and curves. In all designing, some plain areas and strong, straight lines should be used as foils to the more detailed or curved sections. In both these dresses, a rhythmical flow of line carries the eye effortlessly through the entire costume from one side to the other and from shoulder to hem.

Two steps in the development of each blouse pattern have been shown because the cuts are so complicated. The pattern corresponding to Figure 70 (see Figures 72a and b) illustrates the point that the shoulder, armscye, and underarm seams must be exactly the same length even though they vary greatly in shape. This point, although mentioned before, cannot be overemphasized, because it is very likely to be forgotten by the beginner, with the disastrous result that the pattern varies in size on opposite sides.

On analysis, the dress shown in Figure 70 proves to be far easier to make than that in Figure 71, because in the former, the gathers at the left side front are attached to the right side at the line of joining. The second costume, on the other hand, shows a loose, free, bolero effect that must have not only a deep facing but also a complete underbody in order to set well (see Figure 73c). This not only complicates the construction but makes the dress expensive because of the large amount of material required. It would spoil the graceful, free-flowing effect, however, to reduce this requirement by sewing down the bolero edge. This is decidedly both an intricate design to make and an expensive one; and it is not for the inexperienced dressmaker.

Fig. 70. Asymmetric design. The smaller gathered space balances the larger plain area.

Fig. 71. Asymmetric balance is achieved through opposing curves and through radiating folds.

SOURCES OF DESIGN

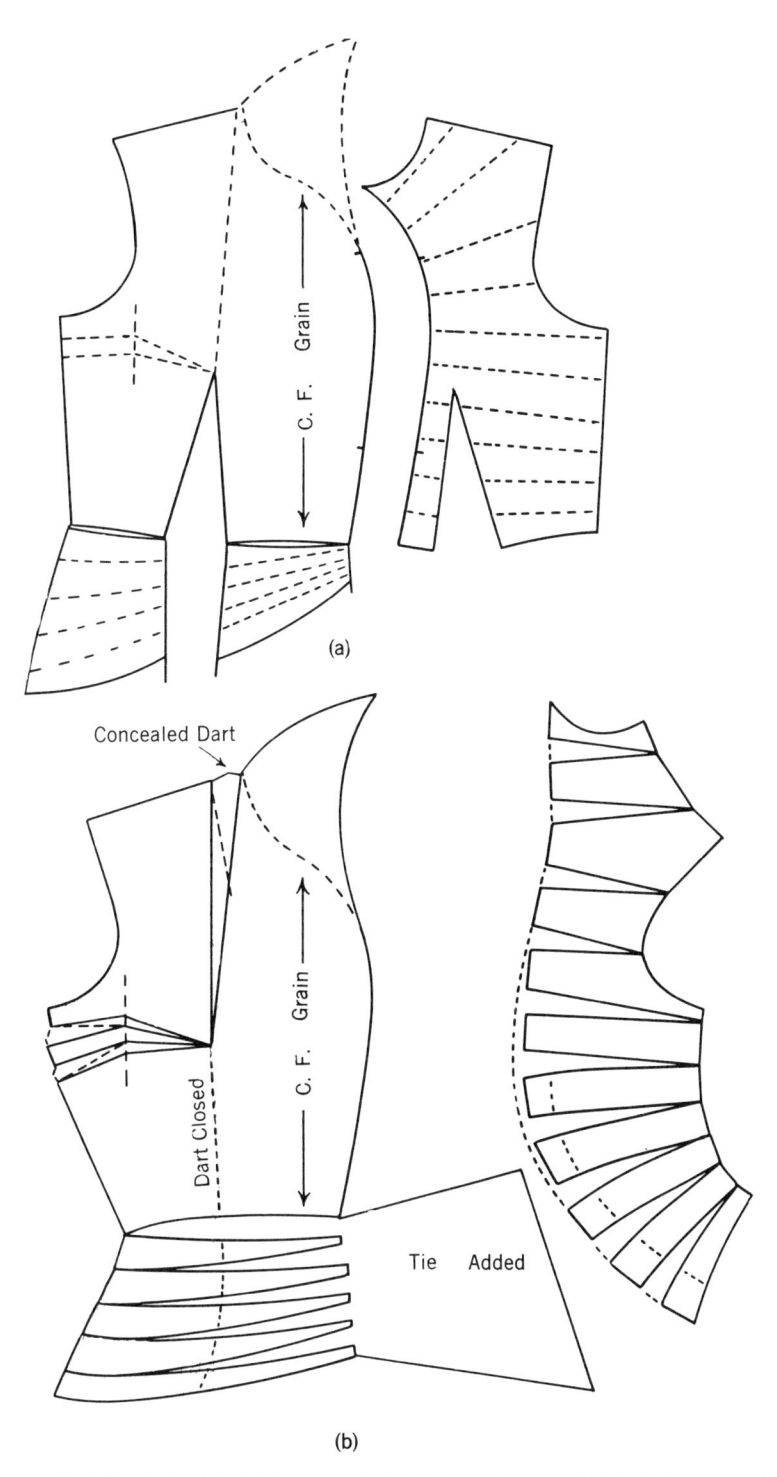

Fig. 72. Pattern for dress shown in Fig. 70. (*a*) Design and slash lines drawn; (*b*) Slashes spread and darts transferred. Note the difference in the shape of the armscyes and the underarm seams.

DRESS DESIGN

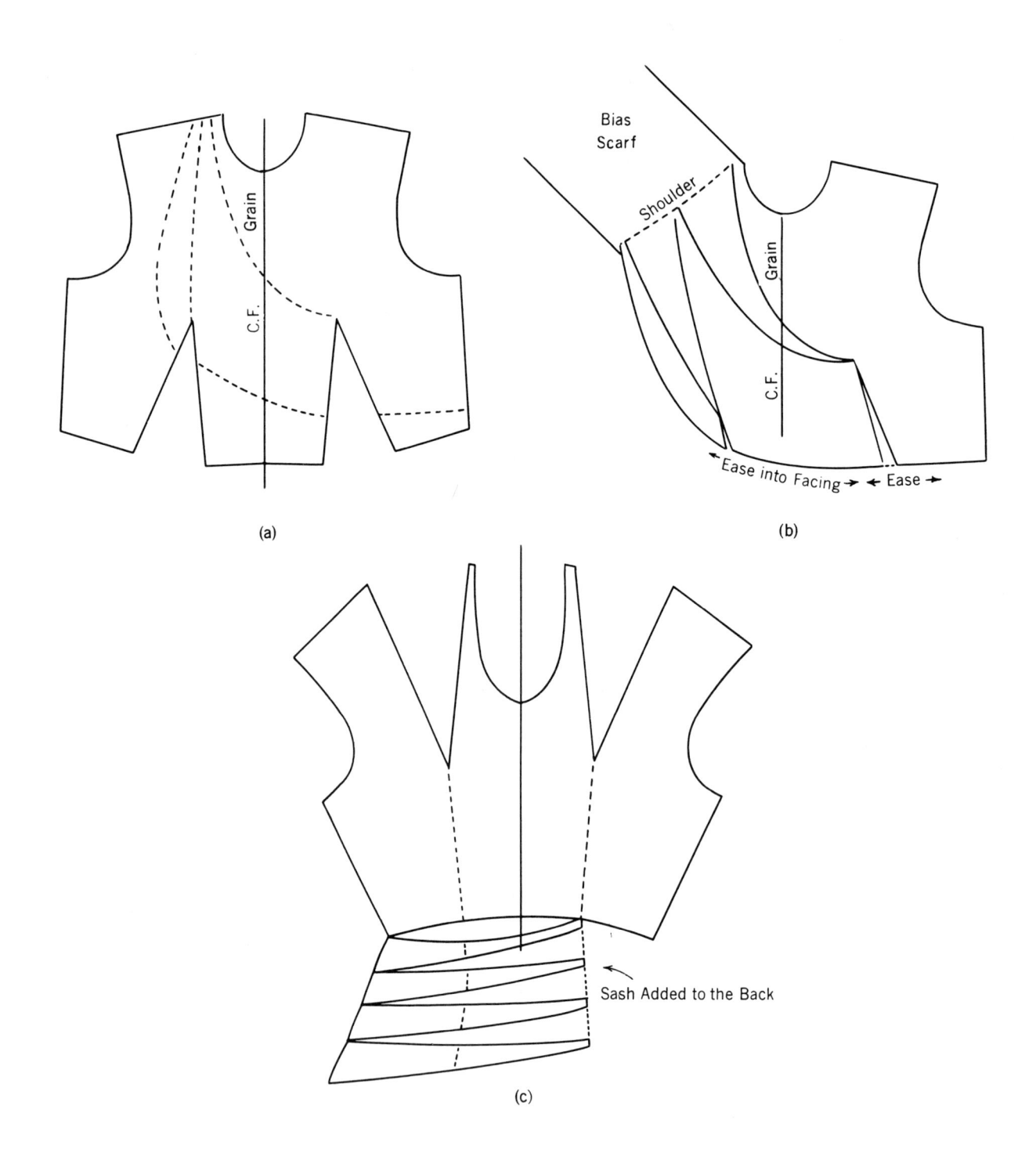

Fig. 73. (a) Bolero Front, Step 1; (b) Bolero Front, Step 2; (c) Underbody and draped peplum section.

SOURCES OF DESIGN

Suggestion 11

DESIGNING FROM A DETAIL

The usual procedure when one plans to design a dress is to make a preliminary examination of fashion magazines or ready-to-wear clothes in order to study details of design as well as silhouettes. You can observe details with two entirely different purposes in mind. You can aim merely to copy them exactly, in which case your designs will show a complete lack of imagination. Or you can plan to use them as a source of inspiration for an original design, which is a very good way to stimulate your imagination. For example, a detail used at the shoulder may suggest a similar idea to be used at the center back of the waistline, or even to be turned upside down. Shoe and handbag designs may have straps, buckles, or even folds that suggest an entire theme for a dress or a suit. There is no limit to the way in which ideas can be adapted in this fashion if you cultivate the habit of seeing possibilities in everything you observe. On the other hand, never forget that silhouette is the fundamental image to keep in mind, and that detail which does not harmonize with the silhouette should never be used, no matter how good it is in itself.

Figure 74 shows how a design might develop from a curve holding fullness along each edge. Notice that the source of the detail in this instance was a very dressy shoe, with a curve supporting fullness along both edges. It occurred to the dress designer that she could use this detail for a simulated belt holding gathers at both its upper and lower edges. She then decided that a sleeve with a simulated cuff would effectively repeat and strengthen the motif. The shoulder yoke further uses the curves and the gathers which run up into it, but there are no gathers at its upper edge since the designer felt that too much emphasis on the basic idea would destroy the effect. The final design could not possibly be called a mere copy of the shoe detail, since the two uses are so different. But if the idea had been taken from another and similar belt, the design could not strictly be considered original. Rather, it would have to be called an adaptation or variation of the original form.

The two steps in diagramming the pattern (see Figures 75a and b) show the all-in-one cut of the peplum, simulated belt, and lower blouse section. Smoothness and continuity of line mark this design and set it apart from more ordinary jackets and sleeves that are cut completely around the waistline and upper edge of the cuff.

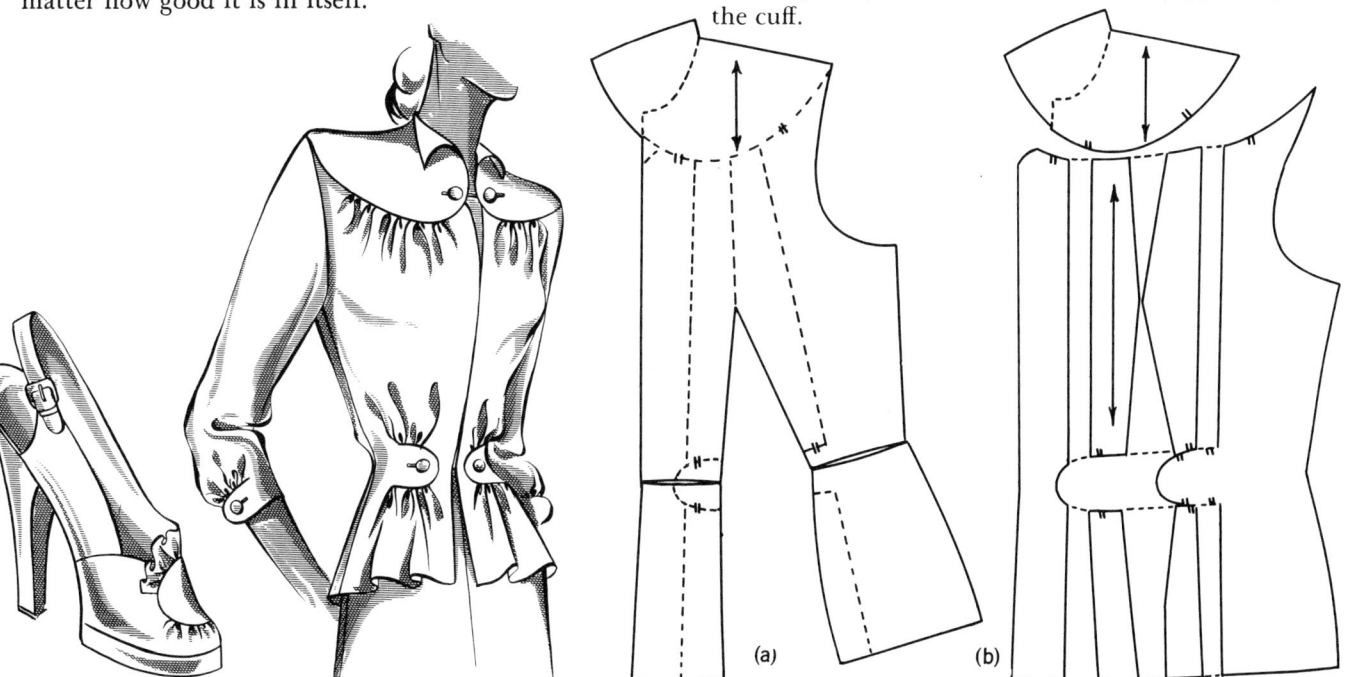

Fig. 74. Design developed from a similar idea used in a shoe design. As used in the dress, the design naturally shows variations.

Fig. 75. Pattern for blouse shown in Fig. 74. (a) Design and slash lines drawn; (b) Pattern cut on design lines and slashes spread for gathers.

DRESS DESIGN

Suggestion 12

INTRODUCING ORIGINAL DETAILS INTO A STANDARD COMMERCIAL PATTERN

Probably a woman's commonest wish in regard to pattern making is for enough skill to change commercial pattern designs to suit her own taste. She may have seen or thought up a design for which she is unable to buy a pattern or she may like to design her own clothes and yet may find it convenient to use a commercial pattern, especially if her figure conforms to standard pattern sizes. The problem in this case is to change the design without altering the size or fit of the pattern, and this is no different in principle from designing on a basic draped master pattern. If the changes are at all intricate, however, the process may be somewhat involved.

Figure 76a shows a standard tailored suit, and Figure 76b shows one converted to a more individual style with softer, less severely tailored lines. A suit was chosen intentionally here to illustrate that it is wiser to leave the carefully drafted collar, lapels, and sleeve unchanged, and to introduce the new design detail on the body of the jacket only.

To design the new pattern, follow the steps below and study the accompanying diagrams (Figures 77a and b).

1. Cut a duplicate of the commercial pattern so that you can keep the original one intact for future use.

2. Pin in the darts and draw the new design lines on the original pattern, with the pattern either pinned up on the dress form or held up on yourself.

3. Remove the pattern from the form and mark the grain in the yoke section before detaching it from the body of the jacket. In the yoke, place the grain parallel to the center front.

Fig. 76. Designing on a commercial pattern. (a) Standard tailored suit; (b) Individual design developed from the standard pattern.

SOURCES OF DESIGN

4. Draw in new dart lines from the point of the bust to the yoke edge and to the two new vertical waistline darts. Divide the large shoulder dart evenly into three tuck darts which can be eased into the yoke edge to form softness rather than visible darting.

5. Draw a waistline seam.

6. Cut the pattern apart along the new design lines and slash it along the new dart lines so that it will lie flat. Cut along the waistline for an inconspicuous seam partially hidden by the pocket flaps.

7. Examine the shapes of the various sections.

There is still too much excess left from the old shoulder dart below the new shoulder yoke to ease it in invisibly. Transfer to the two new waistline darts enough of this to get rid of the superfluous ease at the yoke edge but leave just enough for soft shaping over the bust (see Figure 77b for the method of doing this).

The directions above illustrate a design change which is about as complicated as one would expect to make on a commercial pattern. Frequently a change from a standard pattern involves nothing more difficult than, for instance, leaving a block of extra fabric

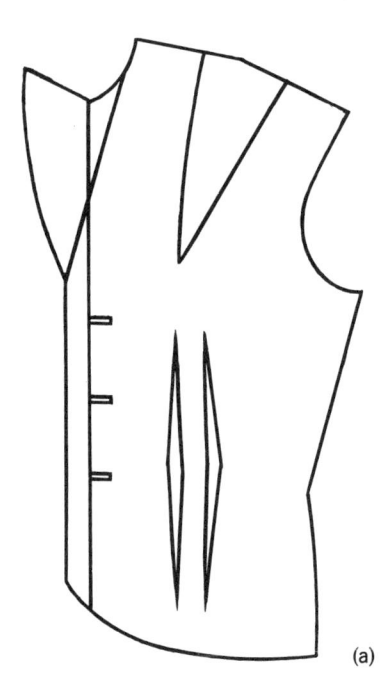

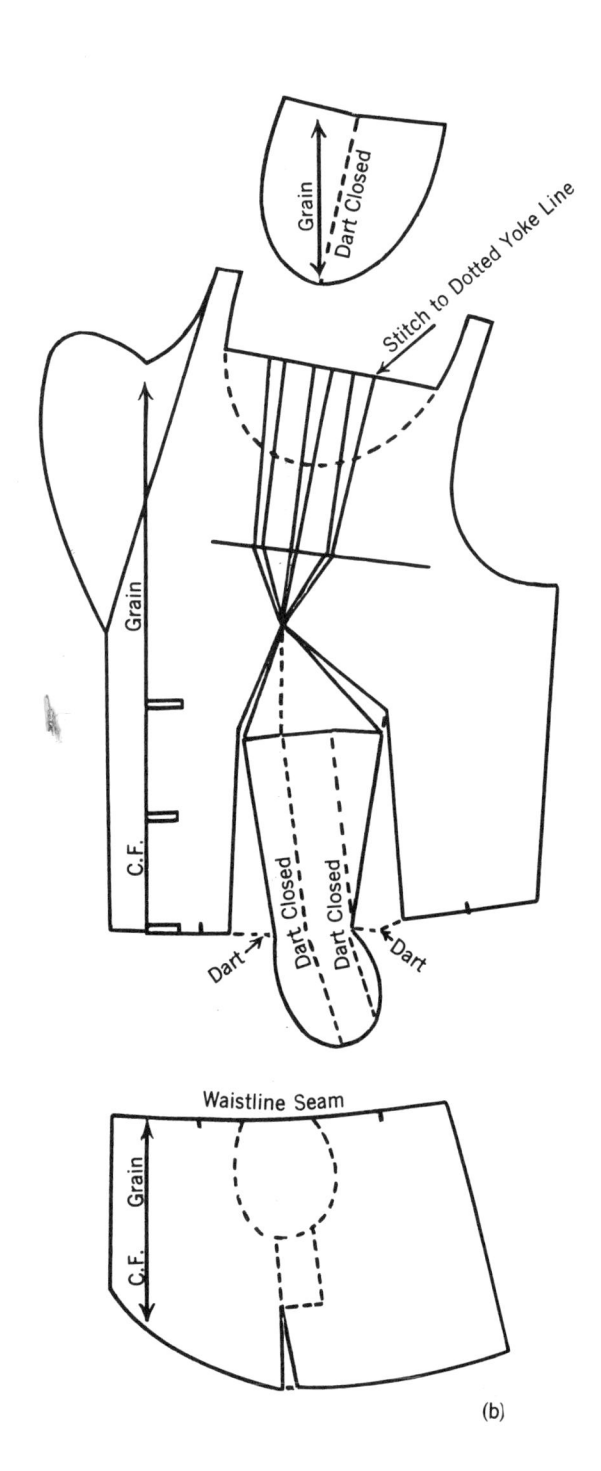

Fig. 77. (a) Tailored suit pattern before the changes were made; (b) Design changes made on pattern of suit shown in Fig. 76 (a).

317

DRESS DESIGN

at the neck when you cut out the dress so that you can later drape this material on the form into whatever new neck treatment you may want. Be careful, if you do this, to drape the new design lines in harmony with the other lines of the costume. (See Figure 78b for a suggested change from Figure 78a, and for one that is very much easier to drape than to block.)

Another change that it is often necessary to make in a commercial pattern is to add fullness at a yoke edge where no fullness previously existed, or to increase the fullness where the amount allowed by the pattern might seem skimpy for a particular fabric texture or figure. To make this change, refer to the directions for transferring the basic dart to a yoke edge, Chapter 2, pages 54-57. The principle is exactly the same.

If you have tried faithfully to carry out each of the suggestions in this chapter, you should have developed your creative ingenuity and your skill in pattern making to the point where you can not only be independent of others for suggestions of design sources, but also self-reliant in figuring out how to cut each pattern. From this point on, how well you do depends entirely on how well you apply what you have learned to your own individual needs and problems.

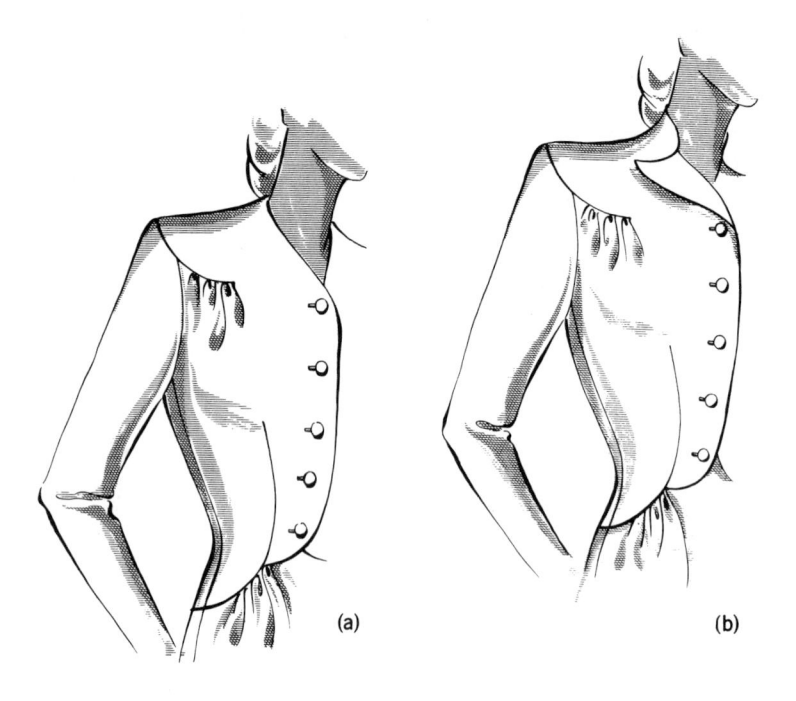

Fig. 78. (a), (b). Suggested change to adapt the neckline to individual features.

BIBLIOGRAPHY

Erwin, Mabel. *Practical Dress Design.* New York, The Macmillan Co. 1940.

Evans, Mary. *Draping and Dress Design.* Ann Arbor, Michigan. Edwards Brothers, Inc. 1935.

Kaplan, Charles and Esther. *Principles and Problems of Pattern Making as Applied to Women's Apparel.* New York, Streimin Studio, 1265 Broadway. 1940. Book I, "Foundation Patterns or Slopers," Revised Edition. Book II, "Style Patterns."

Morton, Grace Margaret. *The Arts of Costume and Personal Appearance.* New York, John Wiley and Sons, Inc. 1943.

Pepin, Harriet. *Modern Pattern Design.* New York, Funk and Wagnalls Company. 1942.

Rohr, M. *Pattern Drafting and Grading.* Revised Edition. New York, M. Rohr, 240 W. 98th St. 1944.

Index

ABDOMEN, fitting skirt for, 220, skirt cups under, 223-224

ALTERATION: *master pattern,* blouses, 198-218; collars, 266; skirts, 219-229; sleeves, 229-241; *methods of,* blocking and draping compared, 196; blocking, general procedure for, 197; *of sleeves,* cap height, 125-127; cap width, 123-125; *see also* Fitting

ANALYSIS, master sleeve pattern, 118-119

ANGLE, of seam intersection, 28

ARCS, hemline and waistline, 106-107

ARMHOLE, 7; *see also* Armscye

ARMSCYE: *of blouse,* deeper than normal, 128-129; dress form cover, 7; fitting of, 208-214; formation of, 7, 21; correction of gapping at, 208-211; side view illustration of, 26, Fig. 31; causes of too tight, 212; *of sleeve,* back, fitting of, 235; deep, in kimono, 168-169; deep, in raglan, 151; deep, square dolman, 185-187; dolman cut in one with yoke front, 183-184; effect on, of fitting girth, 237-238; master pattern, 118-119; modifying length of, 241; raglan, 148-149

ARTICULATION POINTS, emphasis of in design, 283-288

ASYMMETRICAL BALANCE, in blouses alike on opposite sides, 55; in blouses unalike on opposite sides, 311-313; in a draped skirt, 109; equalizing of seam lengths, 290

BACKGROUND, for designing, 273-274

BALANCE, in blouse, 213, Fig. 25, 273-274; in skirt, 228; in sleeve pinned into garment, 231-232

BALANCE LINES, horizontal and vertical, 193; marking of, on master pattern, 242-243; of blouse, 193-194; of skirt, 194; of sleeve, 232

BALANCE POINTS, 27; on skirt seams, 69, Fig. 19; *see also* Crossmarks

BASIC BLOUSES, 16-59

BASIC DARTS, variations of, 301-306

BASIC SET-IN SLEEVES, 113-133

BASIC SKIRTS, 60-111

BELL SLEEVE, blocking of, 123; in kimono blouse, 170-171

BELT, 62

BERTHA COLLAR, blocking of, 252

BIAS: collars and folds at neckline, 260-261; cowl sleeve in kimono blouse, 180; position of, in cowl necklines, 50; position of, in cowl skirts, 308-309; position of, in kimono sleeves, 161

BINDING, of too tight armhole, 212

BISHOP SLEEVE, 120-123: blocking of, from master sloper, 120; blocking of, from "opened" pattern, 122; blousing exaggerated, 122-123; in kimono blouse, 170-171; measurements for, 120; with raglan armscye line, 152; with simulated cuff, 138

BLOCK, MASTER: quarter size blouse to trace, 46; quarter size skirt to trace, 94; quarter size sleeve to trace, 136

BLOCKING: defined, 45; method of pattern alteration, 197; method of designing blouses, 44-59; method of designing collars, 251-253; method of designing sleeves cut in one with bodice, 148-192; method of designing skirts, 92-111; method of designing set-in sleeves, 134-148

BLOUSES, 16-59: blocking of, 44-59; draping of, 16-44; draping of master blouse, 16-27; fitting problems of, 198-218; measurements for master pattern, 244

BODY, of fabric, discussion of, 277

BODY CURVES, provided for by darts: abdomen, 220; back hips, 68; back of shoulder, 24; bust, 16; elbow, 116; hip bone, side front, 70; hip, side, 70; shoulder blades, 26

BOLERO, draped, 312-314

BOWING, of a seam, 81, Fig. 43

BREAK-LINE, of a collar, defined, 247; of a convertible collar, 267; of a lapel, 269; of a tailored collar, 269

BREAK-POINT, of a gored skirt, defined, 72; of a six-gore back, 75; placed high, 96; placed low, 97, 98

BUILT-UP NECKLINE, draft for, 248-251; draping of, 256

BUOYANCY OF FABRIC, effect on handling, 280

BUST, draft provision for, in master pattern, 16; ease around, in master pattern, 48, Fig. 83

INDEX

BUST LINE: dress form cover, 8; fitting of area, 215-218; too high in pattern, 217; too low in pattern, 218

BUST POINT, marking of, in pattern, 218

BUTTONHOLES, placement of, 40

CAP, of sleeve, drawing of curves, 115

CAP HEIGHT, of sleeve: alteration of, 233-235; higher-than-normal, 127; in relation to darted top, 140-144; in relation to sleeve width, 124-125; lower-than-normal, 125-127; normal, 114

CENTER FRONT DART VARIATIONS, 303

CHALK BOARD, 4

CHEST, narrow point of blouse back, 26; narrow point of blouse front, 21

CHINESE COLLAR, draping of, 262

CIRCULAR SKIRTS: *blocking of,* 105-107; the greater-than-normal, less-than-normal, maximum, and normal, 105-107; hem line and waistline arcs of, 106-107; principles of, 111; *draping of,* 81-87; flares, 85; grain placement, 87; the greater-than-normal, less-than-normal, and normal circular, 82-87; principles of, 89; standards for, 86

CLIPPING SEAM ALLOWANCES: for armscye, too tight, 212; for cowl folds, 39; for draped folds, 90; for flare in Franch dart jacket, 36; for low flare in gored skirt, 74; shoulder, 206-207; waistline of blouse, 22; waistline of circular skirt, 85; waistline of draped skirt, 90; waistline of four-gore skirt, 79

COAT SLEEVE, measurements for, 114; two-piece, 130-133

COLLARS: bias, 260-261; blocking of flat, 251-252; blocking of rippled, 252-253; blocking of roll, 253-254; classification of, 247; drafting of built-up neckline, 248-251; drafting of convertible, 255; drafting of high roll, 253-254; drafting of Peter Pan, 253; draping of convertible, 266-268; draping of, cut in one with bodice front, 263-266; draping of, high roll in back, flat in front, 259; draping of narrow standing, 262-263; draping of tailored, 269-272; flat, variations of, 258; patterns for, 251, 255; 259, 261-263, 265-266, 271-272; relationship of neckline to garment neckline, 247; roll or stand, determination of, 247; slopers, narrow flat, 251; slopers, wide flat, 252; terminology for, 247

COMMERCIAL PATTERNS, design changes on, 316-317

CONTROL DART. *See* Dart, basic

CONVERTIBLE COLLAR, draft for, 255; draping of, 266-268

CORRECTION DART, use of, 196, 198-201, 208-211

COUCHING, 8

COWL FOLDS: *blocking of, in* necklines, 50; short sleeved kimono blouse, 180-182; shoulder of long sleeve, 147-148; skirt drapery, 308-309; yoke, 51; *convex curve,* general principle in designing, 180; *draping of,* necklines, 37-40

CROSSMARKING, at hip level, 69

CROSSMARKS, meaning of, 4; mismatched on skirt side seam, 227

CROSSWISE GRAIN. *See* Grain

CUFFS: bands, 130; cutting of, 130; flared, 130; simulated, 138; wide, 130

CUPPING OF SKIRT, at the back, 221; under abdomen, 223-224

CURVES OF BODY, effect on "hang" of skirt, 219

DART: *basic, fundamental, or master,* 16; concealed under design, 299; division of, 47; general function of, 16; method of making parallel, 31; function of, in sleeves, 112; shift or transfer of, 46; standard positions in blouse front and other possible locations, 16, Fig. 2; use in correction of fitting faults, 199; variations of basic, 301-306; vertical, rule for establishing, 20; *in blouse, back,* neck, 25, 250; shoulder, 24; waistline, 26; *in blouse, front,* shoulder, 19; underarm, 29; waistline, 22; *in skirt,* back, 68, 69; side front, 69, 92, 93; *in sleeves,* epaulet cap, 155-156; horizontal elbow, 117; parallel at top of cap, 140-143

DARTING: armscye gapping, correction of, 208, 209, 210; correction, 196, 198-201, 208-211; dress form cover, fitting of, 5; excessive in blouse back, 216-217; excessive in blouse front, 215-216; inadequate in blouse back and front, 217

DESIGN, principles, as background, 273; sources, 273-318

DESIGNING: avoiding unnecessary seams, 310; background for, 273-274; basic dart variations, 301-306; on commercial patterns, 316-317; detail used as a source, 315; draping changes on a pattern, 318; draping without cutting, 281-283; fabric study, 277; folding back excess fabric, 292; for patterned fabrics, 277-281; interpretation of silhouette, 294-295; set-in sleeves from master one-piece sleeve, 134, 148; shaping darts to fit the design, 299; sketching, 274-277; through structural seaming, 296-299

INDEX

DETAILS, of design introduced on commercial patterns, 316-317; draping of, 283-293; source of design, 315

DIRNDL. *See* Straight Skirts, gathered

DOLMAN SLEEVE, cut in one with yoke front, 183-184; definition of, 183; deep square armhole, 185-187, Fig. 101a; drafts for, 183-192; style line near normal armscye, 188-192

DRAFTING, collars, 248-250, 253-255; definition of, 112; dolman sleeves, 183-192; basic kimono sleeves, 159-164; master one-piece sleeve, 113-119; master two-piece sleeve, 130-133; raglan sleeves, 148-153; short kimono sleeves, 174-182

DRAPE, of fabric, meaning of, 280

DRAPED SKIRTS, asymmetrically balanced, 109; blocking of, 108-111; blocking, summary of principles, 111; draping of, 89-92

DRAPERY, gathers and folds along slash lines, 288-291; in kimono sleeve with yoke, 174, Fig. 91; in short kimono sleeve with simulated yoke, 177-178, Fig. 96a

DRAPING, combined with blocking, 288; details, 283-293; to introduce design change, 318; without cutting, procedure for, 281-282

DRESS FORM: armhole, cover for, 15; collar draft, 15; design inspiration, use as, 281; kinds of, 1; padding of, 13-14; selection of, 13

DRESS FORM COVER, fabric for, 3; making of, 3-8; pattern selection for, 1-8

DROP SHOULDER SLEEVE, 157-158

EASE: around bust, 27; around hips, 67; at back edge of shoulder, 24; division of, between two seams, 297-298; skirt, front hip seam edge, 70; around armscye of set-in sleeve compared with raglan, 149; around elbow, 116; around girth of sleeve, 113; over top of sleeve, 134; when sleeve is pinned into garment, 230-232; upper arm, over back of, in kimono draft, 161; at waistline of blouse, 27

EDGES OF A PATTERN, danger of altering, 125

ELBOW, ease in sleeve over, 116; measurement of, for sleeve draft, 114; pulling of sleeve from, 235-236; width of sleeve, decreasing and increasing of, 238-239

ELBOW DART, increasing size of, 236; introduction in master sleeve, 117; transferred to vertical placket, 134-135; wrong location or size, 235

EPAULET SLEEVE, drafting of, 153-154; with darts, 155-156

EXCESS FABRIC, use of in designing, 283-293

FABRIC: body, meaning of, 280-281; for cowl drapery, 51; for draping master patterns, 17; for making dress form cover, 3; patterned, designing for, 227-281; study of, before designing, 277; use of, as design inspiration, 274

FABRIC ESTIMATE FOR: dress form cover, 3; master blouse back, 23; master blouse front, 17; skirts: four-gore, 79; pleated, all-around, 63; six-gore, 72; straight gathered, 61; two-gore, 65

FACING, fitted, cutting of, 40-42

FASHION, influence on dart lines, 19-20; trends, study of, 273

FIGURE, as design inspiration, 296-299

FILLING THREADS, 18; *see also,* Grain, crosswise

FINISH, in relation to fabric, 281

FITTING, adjustment for faulty posture, 194-195; blocking method of, 197; draping method of, 196; fitter, position of, 196; general principles of, 193-196; preparation of master pattern for, 196-197

FITTING PATTERN: blouses, 198-218; bust line and shoulder blades, 215-218; for abdomen, large, 220; for armscye area, 208-214; hip area, 221-228; neckline area, 198-203; shoulder area, 203-208; skirts, 219-229; sleeve shoulders, 233-234; sleeves, 229-241; underarm seam of blouse, 212-215

FLARE IN: four-gore skirt, low placed, 97; short kimono sleeve, 176; six-gore skirt, low placed, 74; six-gore skirt, minimum at side seam, 73; two-gore skirt, 67

FLARES, circular, draping of, 85; formed by slashing, 283-288

FLAT-CHESTED FIGURE, pattern alteration for, 201

FLAT COLLAR, drafting of, 251-252; draping of, 257-259

FLAT PATTERN BLOCKING, definition of, 44-45; method of designing: blouses, 44-59; collars, 251-253; cuffs, 130; kimono blouses, 170-192; set-in sleeves, 134-148; skirts, 92-111

FLORAL PATTERNS, designing for, 277-278

FOLDING BACK EXCESS, use in designing, 292

FOLD LINE, of tailored collar, 270

FOLDS, draping of, into a slash line, 289-291; in draped skirts, 90; placing of, in draped skirts, 108; radiating, draping of, 287-288

INDEX

FORWARD HEAD, 195, Fig. 2h

FOUNDATION: blouse master pattern, 46; skirt master pattern, 94; sleeve master pattern, 136

FOUR-GORE SKIRT, blocking of, 93-97; draping of, 78-81; seams side front and back, 104-105; variation of, 306-307

FRENCH DART, ease over bust, 33; variations in design, 302

FRENCH DART BODICE, blocking of, 53; draping of, 31-36; panel formation, 32-34

FRENCH DART HIP-LENGTH JACKET, blocking of, 57-58; draping of, 36

FRENCH LINING, definition of, 1; drawing pattern, 8-12; measurement chart, 9

FULLNESS, direction control, 49; folds in draped skirt, 90; as gathers, 61; as pleats, 62; gathers in puff sleeves, 144-145; gathers in raglan sleeves, 152; radiation of, 49

GAPPING, of armscye, 208

GATHERS, along a slash line in blouse and skirt, 288-291; along a slash line in sleeve, 134-137; allowance for in skirt, 61; allowance for in sleeve, 137; appropriate use of, 44; radiation of, 306

GATHERED SKIRT, straight, 60-62

GEOMETRIC FABRIC PATTERNS, designing for, 278-280

GIRTH OF SLEEVE, balance line, 232; drawing at back of, 237-238; measurement for draft, 113; to increase for large upper arm, 237-238

GORED SKIRTS, blocking of four-, six,- multi-gore, 81-105; blocking principles, summary of, 105; comparison with straight, 65; draping of two-, four-, and six-gore, 65-81; draping, general procedure, 68; draping, principles of, 81

GORES, definition of, 65; shape of, 81

GRAIN, adjustment of, at hip level, 67; adjustment of at shoulder blades, 25; crosswise and lengthwise, 3, Fig. 3; cutting in on, in skirt gore, 75, 108; fitting significance of, 219; indicator, 52, 53; *lowering*, for: circular flares, 85; cowl folds, 39-40; flares in gored skirts, 67; *raising*, for "draped" skirts, 90

GRAIN POSITION: at girth of sleeve, 232-234; in a blouse, 194; in circular skirts, various possibilities for, 87; in cowl necklines, 37-40; in cowl sleeves, 148; in cowl sleeves in kimono blouses, 180; in gores with equalized flares, 96; in gores with unequal flares, 81; in gored skirts, rule for, 93, 95, Figs. 68, 69; in gussets for kimono blouses, 166; in a standard sleeve, 230; in straight skirts, 60

GUSSET, definition of, 162; pattern for, 166; size of, for various kimono drafts, 163; slashing of kimono blouse for, 165-166

HANDLE, of a fabric, 280-281

HANDLING, influence of fabric on, 280-281

HEM, on sleeve lower edge, 129; sweep or width, 80; comparison of sweep in circular and gored skirts, 81-82

HIP LEVEL, adjustment at, in straight skirts, 60; importance of, in fitting, 194; in two-gore skirts, 67; marking of, on dress form cover, 8; marking of, on master pattern, 245

HIPS, fitting problems: when bones are prominent, 225-226; when broad or prominent in back, 221-222; when curve on side is high, 224, 225; when uneven, 228

HISTORIC COSTUME, as source of design, 274

INSET, 165-166; at waistline center back, 284-285; shaped underarm, 168-170; straight underarm, 166-168; *see also* Gusset

INSPIRATION, for designing, 273-318

JACKET, master hip-length pattern, 57

KIMONO BLOUSE, with bell or bishop sleeve, 170-171; with shaped underarm side section and deep armscye, 168-170; with short puff sleeve, 179; with short sleeves and simulated yoke, 175-178; with straight underarm inset, 166-168; with yoke, 172-174

KIMONO SLEEVE, definition of, 148-159; dolman variation, 183-192; drafts, comparison of, 164, 165; drafts with gussets, 162-164; draft without a gusset, 159-162; draft for short kimono, 174-182

LANTERN SLEEVE, blocking of, 139

LAP, allowance for buttons and buttonholes, 41, Fig. 69; allowance for buttons and loops, 42, Fig. 70; allowance for, in side front skirt, 99; direction of seams, when draping skirts, 76; vertical seam direction, 37

LAPEL, of convertible collar, 267; of tailored collar, 269

LAPPED SLEEVE, blocking of, 147

LAY FIGURE, 275, Fig. 1

INDEX

LEG O' MUTTON SLEEVE, blocking of, 146

LESS-THAN-NORMAL CIRCULAR SKIRT, blocking of, 106-107; draping of, 84-85

LINE ARRANGEMENTS, 274-277

LINE, continuity of, 276

LOOPS, 41, Fig. 70

L-SQUARE, 14, 50; *see also* Tailor's square

MACHINE BASTING, 4

MANDARIN COLLAR, 262

MARKING: balance lines, 242; measurements on master pattern, 244; seams, 28, 29; with carbon paper, 6; with chalk board, 4

MASTER BLOCK PATTERN: balance lines, marking of, 242; blouse, draping of, 16-29; completion of, 242-246, fitting, preparation for, 196-197; quarter size blouse, 46; quarter size skirt, 94; quarter size sleeve, 136; reasons for fitting, 193; skirt, draping of, 65-71; sleeve, analysis of, 118-119; sleeve, one-piece, cap height varied, 125-127; sleeve, one-piece, draft for, 113-119; sleeve, modification of armscye depth, 128-129

MATERNITY SKIRTS, 220

MEASUREMENTS: chart of, for dress form cover, 9; of arm, for bishop sleeve, 120; of arm, for master one-piece sleeve, 113-114; of body with tailor's squares, 14; of body with tape line, 9; of cowl neckline depth, 38; of master pattern skirt, 245; marked on master pattern, 244

MILITARY COLLAR, 262

MOLDING FABRIC, through seaming, 296-299

MULTI-GORE SKIRTS, blocking of, 100

MUSLIN PROOF, 45

NECK BASE, broad, pattern alteration for, 207; back of, 23, 24; front of, 18

NECKLINE, built-up, design variation of, 257, Fig. 22; built-up, draft for, 248-251; built-up, draping of, 256-257; curve, on collars and garments, 247; designing of, 292; fitting of, 198-203

NOTCH, of convertible collar, 267; of tailored collar, 269

NOTCHES, 4; *see also* Crossmarks

ONE-PIECE SLEEVE, quarter size pattern to trace, 136; *see also* Sleeves

OVERARM LENGTH, compared with underarm, 164-165; in dolman sleeve, 183; measurement for sleeve draft, 113

OVER-ERECT POSTURE, alteration of blouse for, 195, Fig. 2, 202

OVERLAP, definition of, 40-42; on wrap-around skirt, 64

PANELING, of blouse, 22, 32, 34; of six-gore skirt, 72; of skirt back, 69, Fig. 20; of skirt front, 70, Fig. 21; sketched in designing, 274-277

PATTERNED FABRIC, designing for, 277-281; florals, 277-278; geometrics — plaids and stripes, 100, 278-280

PATTERNS, alteration of, by blocking, 197; basic, foundation, or master, 17; for collars, 251-255, 259, 261-263, 265-266, 271-272; in relation to body contour, 196; *see also* Master block pattern, blouse, skirt, sleeve

PEG-TOP SKIRT, 89; blocking of, 108, 111

PEPLUMS, blocking of, 108; "draped," blocking of, 110-111; draping of, 87-89; girdle draped all-around, 111

PERPENDICULAR TO FLOOR, skirt seam position, 70

PETER PAN COLLAR, blocking of, 253

PINNING: method when draping, 19; of seams, general method, 4, Fig. 4; of sleeve into armscye when fitting, 230-232; of taffeta, 282-283, Fig. 13

PIVOTING, of pattern at point of dart, 96; of pattern pieces, 99; of pattern to introduce elbow dart, 116-117

PLACKET, in skirt side front, 109; vertical, in one-piece sleeve, 134-135

PLAIDS, designing for, 278-279

PLEATED ALL-AROUND STRAIGHT SKIRT, 62

PLEATS, allowance for in gored skirt, 77; allowance for in straight skirt, 63, Fig. 5; inverted box, 78, Fig. 38; side pleat in a gore, 76, Fig. 34b; tapering of into waistline, 63

PLUMB LINE, position of skirt seams, 70

POSTURE, adjustment for, 194-195; correct and incorrect, 195, Fig. 2; effect on balance lines, 194; forward head, over-erect, round shoulders, sway back, 195

PRINCESS, line, 58; pattern, 2, Fig. 1

PROOF, muslin, 45

INDEX

PUFF SLEEVES, character of, 145; in kimono blouse, 178-179; set-in, 144-145

RADIATION, of folds in "draped" skirts, 90

RAGLAN SLEEVES, 148-153; characteristics of, 148; general classification, 148

RIPPLES, circular, 283-288; equalized and unequalized in gores, 75; in six-gore skirt, 74; *see also* Flares

ROHR, M., general method for drafting master one-piece sleeve, 113; method for drafting bishop sleeve, 120

ROLL LINE, of collar, definition of, 247; of collar cut in one with bodice, variations of, 265

ROUND SHOULDERS, alteration of blouse for, 202-203; alteration of sleeve for, 234

SAMPLE MODELS, of dress form covers, 2

SCROLLS, 285, Fig. 19

SCYE LINE, definition of, 193-194; importance of, in fitting, 194; marking of, on master pattern, 244

SEAM ALLOWANCE, on master blouse, 29; on master skirt, 67

SEAMING, decorative, in sleeves, 139; to mold fabric to body, 296-299

SELVAGE, 17, Fig. 4

SET-IN SLEEVES, designed from master block, 134-148

SHAPING, bias folds for collars, 261

SHAWL COLLAR, 260-261

SHORT CAP IN SLEEVE, uses of, 126

SHOULDER BLADE, fitting over, 216-217; marking of, in pattern, 218

SHOULDER DART, variations of, 301

SHOULDER PADS, influence on cap height, 127

SHOULDER SEAM, alteration of, 206; dart in raglan sleeve, 150; length, 21; pinning method, when fitting, 205; placement of, 20, Figs. 15, 16, 17

SHOULDERS, fitting of, 203-208; broad, 207; narrow, 208; sloping, 205; square, 204; squared by sleeve cut, 143

SHRINKING, bias folds for collars, 261

SIDE SEAM OF SKIRT, alteration of, 226-227; position of, 66; seam that curls, 227

SILHOUETTE: *interpretation of,* 294-295; and relationship to lines within it, 274-277; *of skirts,* circular, 82, 87, Fig. 55; dirndl, 61; draped, 89; four-gore, 78; narrow four-gore, 95; six-gore, 72; two-gore, 65; wrap-around, 64; *of sleeves,* 139; barrel, 152-153; dolman, 183; puff, 145; square shouldered, 143-144, Fig. 57

SIMULATED: belt and cuff, 138, 315; cuffs, 138-139; yoke in blouse, 50; yoke, ascending line compared with descending, 291

SIX-GORE SKIRT, blocking of, 97-99; draping of, 72-78; variations of design, 307

SKETCHING, source of design, 274-277

SKIRTS, 60-111; classification of, 60. *Fitting of,* 219-229; when cut off grain, 228; when cups under hips, 221-222; when cups in on sides, 226; when stands out at center front, 219-220; when stands out at center back, 222-223; when stands out at sides, 224-225; when thighs are large, 229. Measurements for master pattern, 245; variations of basic cuts, 306-309

SLANT, inward compared with outward, 75; *see also* Slope

SLASHING, to but not through an edge, explained, 287; use of, in designing, 283-288

SLEEVE, fitting problems of, 229-241; armscye too high, 241; cap height alteration, 133-135; pinning of sleeve into blouse on wearer, 230-232; underarm seam edges mismatched, 240; underarm seam twists elbow to wrist, 236-237

SLEEVE, master pattern; analysis of, 118-119; cap height, 124-125, higher and lower than normal, 125-127, measurement for draft, 113; cutting off above and below elbow, 129; decreasing or increasing width, 123, 125; drafting of, 113-119; drafting standard size 16, 114-117; hem, cutting of, 129; measurements, marked on, 246; methods of making compared, 112; quarter size for tracing, 136; with vertical placket dart, 134-135

SLEEVES: classification of, 113. *Cut-in-one-with-bodice,* 112, Fig. 2, 148-188: kimono type, 159-192; block for drafting, 160; cowl in kimono blouse, 180-182; dolman cut with yoke, 183-184; dolman with deep square armhole, 185-187; dolman with style line near armscye, 188-192; *see also* Kimono blouse *and* Kimono sleeve; *raglan type,* 148-153, cut in one with yoke, 156-157; drop shoulder, 157-158; epaulet, 153-154; raglan with barrel silhouette, 152-153. *Set-in,* 112, Fig. 1, coat pattern measurements, 114: *derived from master one-piece block,* 134-148; bell, 123; bishop, 120-123; cowl folds at shoulder, 147-148;

324

INDEX

LEG O' MUTTON SLEEVE, blocking of, 146

LESS-THAN-NORMAL CIRCULAR SKIRT, blocking of, 106-107; draping of, 84-85

LINE ARRANGEMENTS, 274-277

LINE, continuity of, 276

LOOPS, 41, Fig. 70

L-SQUARE, 14, 50; *see also* Tailor's square

MACHINE BASTING, 4

MANDARIN COLLAR, 262

MARKING: balance lines, 242; measurements on master pattern, 244; seams, 28, 29; with carbon paper, 6; with chalk board, 4

MASTER BLOCK PATTERN: balance lines, marking of, 242; blouse, draping of, 16-29; completion of, 242-246, fitting, preparation for, 196-197; quarter size blouse, 46; quarter size skirt, 94; quarter size sleeve, 136; reasons for fitting, 193; skirt, draping of, 65-71; sleeve, analysis of, 118-119; sleeve, one-piece, cap height varied, 125-127; sleeve, one-piece, draft for, 113-119; sleeve, modification of armscye depth, 128-129

MATERNITY SKIRTS, 220

MEASUREMENTS: chart of, for dress form cover, 9; of arm, for bishop sleeve, 120; of arm, for master one-piece sleeve, 113-114; of body with tailor's squares, 14; of body with tape line, 9; of cowl neckline depth, 38; of master pattern skirt, 245; marked on master pattern, 244

MILITARY COLLAR, 262

MOLDING FABRIC, through seaming, 296-299

MULTI-GORE SKIRTS, blocking of, 100

MUSLIN PROOF, 45

NECK BASE, broad, pattern alteration for, 207; back of, 23, 24; front of, 18

NECKLINE, built-up, design variation of, 257, Fig. 22; built-up, draft for, 248-251; built-up, draping of, 256-257; curve, on collars and garments, 247; designing of, 292; fitting of, 198-203

NOTCH, of convertible collar, 267; of tailored collar, 269

NOTCHES, 4; *see also* Crossmarks

ONE-PIECE SLEEVE, quarter size pattern to trace, 136; *see also* Sleeves

OVERARM LENGTH, compared with underarm, 164-165; in dolman sleeve, 183; measurement for sleeve draft, 113

OVER-ERECT POSTURE, alteration of blouse for, 195, Fig. 2, 202

OVERLAP, definition of, 40-42; on wrap-around skirt, 64

PANELING, of blouse, 22, 32, 34; of six-gore skirt, 72; of skirt back, 69, Fig. 20; of skirt front, 70, Fig. 21; sketched in designing, 274-277

PATTERNED FABRIC, designing for, 277-281; florals, 277-278; geometrics — plaids and stripes, 100, 278-280

PATTERNS, alteration of, by blocking, 197; basic, foundation, or master, 17; for collars, 251-255, 259, 261-263, 265-266, 271-272; in relation to body contour, 196; *see also* Master block pattern, blouse, skirt, sleeve

PEG-TOP SKIRT, 89; blocking of, 108, 111

PEPLUMS, blocking of, 108; "draped," blocking of, 110-111; draping of, 87-89; girdle draped all-around, 111

PERPENDICULAR TO FLOOR, skirt seam position, 70

PETER PAN COLLAR, blocking of, 253

PINNING: method when draping, 19; of seams, general method, 4, Fig. 4; of sleeve into armscye when fitting, 230-232; of taffeta, 282-283, Fig. 13

PIVOTING, of pattern at point of dart, 96; of pattern pieces, 99; of pattern to introduce elbow dart, 116-117

PLACKET, in skirt side front, 109; vertical, in one-piece sleeve, 134-135

PLAIDS, designing for, 278-279

PLEATED ALL-AROUND STRAIGHT SKIRT, 62

PLEATS, allowance for in gored skirt, 77; allowance for in straight skirt, 63, Fig. 5; inverted box, 78, Fig. 38; side pleat in a gore, 76, Fig. 34b; tapering of into waistline, 63

PLUMB LINE, position of skirt seams, 70

POSTURE, adjustment for, 194-195; correct and incorrect, 195, Fig. 2; effect on balance lines, 194; forward head, over-erect, round shoulders, sway back, 195

PRINCESS, line, 58; pattern, 2, Fig. 1

PROOF, muslin, 45

323

INDEX

PUFF SLEEVES, character of, 145; in kimono blouse, 178-179; set-in, 144-145

RADIATION, of folds in "draped" skirts, 90

RAGLAN SLEEVES, 148-153; characteristics of, 148; general classification, 148

RIPPLES, circular, 283-288; equalized and unequalized in gores, 75; in six-gore skirt, 74; see also Flares

ROHR, M., general method for drafting master one-piece sleeve, 113; method for drafting bishop sleeve, 120

ROLL LINE, of collar, definition of, 247; of collar cut in one with bodice, variations of, 265

ROUND SHOULDERS, alteration of blouse for, 202-203; alteration of sleeve for, 234

SAMPLE MODELS, of dress form covers, 2

SCROLLS, 285, Fig. 19

SCYE LINE, definition of, 193-194; importance of, in fitting, 194; marking of, on master pattern, 244

SEAM ALLOWANCE, on master blouse, 29; on master skirt, 67

SEAMING, decorative, in sleeves, 139; to mold fabric to body, 296-299

SELVAGE, 17, Fig. 4

SET-IN SLEEVES, designed from master block, 134-148

SHAPING, bias folds for collars, 261

SHAWL COLLAR, 260-261

SHORT CAP IN SLEEVE, uses of, 126

SHOULDER BLADE, fitting over, 216-217; marking of, in pattern, 218

SHOULDER DART, variations of, 301

SHOULDER PADS, influence on cap height, 127

SHOULDER SEAM, alteration of, 206; dart in raglan sleeve, 150; length, 21; pinning method, when fitting, 205; placement of, 20, Figs. 15, 16, 17

SHOULDERS, fitting of, 203-208; broad, 207; narrow, 208; sloping, 205; square, 204; squared by sleeve cut, 143

SHRINKING, bias folds for collars, 261

SIDE SEAM OF SKIRT, alteration of, 226-227; position of, 66; seam that curls, 227

SILHOUETTE: *interpretation of,* 294-295; and relationship to lines within it, 274-277; *of skirts,* circular, 82, 87, Fig. 55; dirndl, 61; draped, 89; four-gore, 78; narrow four-gore, 95; six-gore, 72; two-gore, 65; wrap-around, 64; *of sleeves,* 139; barrel, 152-153; dolman, 183; puff, 145; square shouldered, 143-144, Fig. 57

SIMULATED: belt and cuff, 138, 315; cuffs, 138-139; yoke in blouse, 50; yoke, ascending line compared with descending, 291

SIX-GORE SKIRT, blocking of, 97-99; draping of, 72-78; variations of design, 307

SKETCHING, source of design, 274-277

SKIRTS, 60-111; classification of, 60. *Fitting of,* 219-229; when cut off grain, 228; when cups under hips, 221-222; when cups in on sides, 226; when stands out at center front, 219-220; when stands out at center back, 222-223; when stands out at sides, 224-225; when thighs are large, 229. Measurements for master pattern, 245; variations of basic cuts, 306-309

SLANT, inward compared with outward, 75; see also Slope

SLASHING, to but not through an edge, explained, 287; use of, in designing, 283-288

SLEEVE, fitting problems of, 229-241; armscye too high, 241; cap height alteration, 133-135; pinning of sleeve into blouse on wearer, 230-232; underarm seam edges mismatched, 240; underarm seam twists elbow to wrist, 236-237

SLEEVE, master pattern; analysis of, 118-119; cap height, 124-125, higher and lower than normal, 125-127, measurement for draft, 113; cutting off above and below elbow, 129; decreasing or increasing width, 123, 125; drafting of, 113-119; drafting standard size 16, 114-117; hem, cutting of, 129; measurements, marked on, 246; methods of making compared, 112; quarter size for tracing, 136; with vertical placket dart, 134-135

SLEEVES: classification of, 113. *Cut-in-one-with-bodice,* 112, Fig. 2, 148-188: *kimono type,* 159-192; block for drafting, 160; cowl in kimono blouse, 180-182; dolman cut with yoke, 183-184; dolman with deep square armhole, 185-187; dolman with style line near armscye, 188-192; *see also* Kimono blouse *and* Kimono sleeve; *raglan type,* 148-153, cut in one with yoke, 156-157; drop shoulder, 157-158; epaulet, 153-154; raglan with barrel silhouette, 152-153. *Set-in,* 112, Fig. 1, coat pattern measurements, 114: *derived from master one-piece block,* 134-148; bell, 123; bishop, 120-123; cowl folds at shoulder, 147-148;

324

INDEX

deep armhole, 128-129; horizontal gathers below elbow, 134-137; lantern silhouette, 139; lapped across top, 147; leg o' mutton, 146; master block for sleeves loose at lower edge, 119-120; parallel darts at top, 140-143; puff, 144-145; simulated cuff, 138; square shouldered, 143; *two-piece draft,* 130-133

SLOPE, of shoulder seam, 204; of gored skirt, 67, 68; *see also* Slant

SLOPER, of master blouse, quarter size, 46; of master skirt, quarter size, 94; of master sleeve, quarter size, 136; of master collar, narrow flat, 251; of master collar, wide flat, 252

SOURCES OF IDEAS, discussion of, 273-274

SPACING, monotonous, 275, Fig. 2; of skirt panels, 72; of yokes, 42; study of, 274-276

SPORTSWEAR, sleeves for, 125-126

SQUARE ERECT SHOULDERS, fitting sleeves for, 234

SQUARE SHOULDERED SLEEVE, 143

STAYING, of a seam, 299, 310

STAND, of collars, definition of, 247; of tailored collar, 269

STIFFNESS, of fabric, effect on handling, 280

STITCHING, of hip to waist curve, 103

STRAIGHT SKIRTS, 60-65; all-around pleated, 62; gathered, 60; wrap-around, 64

STRAP SLEEVE, 153-154; *see also* Epaulet

STRING COLLARS, from bias folds, 261

STRIPES, designing for, 279-280

STYLE LINE, of a collar, 247

SUMMARY OF: blocking circular skirts, 111; blocking draped skirts, 111; blocking gored skirts, 105; draping circular skirts, 89; draping gored skirts, 81

SWATHE, bias, used as cowl substitute, 308-309

SWAY BACK, alteration of skirt for, 222-223

SWEEP OF HEM, 80-82, 96

TAGBOARD, 45; cutting of, for master blouse, 58

TAILORED COLLAR, narrow, 269-271; wide, 271-272

TAILOR'S SQUARE, 14. *See also* L-square

TAPERING, pleats into waistline, 63; skirt panels, 72

TAPING, of a seam, 299, 310

TEN-GORE SKIRT, blocking of, 100

TEXTURE, importance of in designing, 277, 282, Figs. 12, 13

THIGHS, large, alteration of skirt for, 228-229

TRACING WHEEL, 4

TRANSFER, of darts in blouses, 54, 56; of darts in skirts, 95; of dart in sleeve, 134-135; of pattern markings, 29, 71

TRENDS, study of, 273

TRUEING OF A PATTERN, for blouse, 28; for skirt, 71

TURTLE NECK, bias, 261

TWILLS, designing for, 277

TWO-GORE SKIRT, draping of, 65-71; variations of, 306-307

TWO-PIECE SLEEVE, draft of, 130-133

TYING, use in designing, 293

UNDERARM, measurement for sleeve draft, 113

UNDERARM DART, variations of, 303-304

UNDERARM INSET, in kimono blouse, 166-168; shaped as side section, 168-170

UNDERARM SEAMS: *of blouse,* fitting of, 212-215, for excess width, 211, for sagging of, 214-215; pinning method, 214; taking in of, 213, Fig. 25; *of sleeves,* length, comparison of in kimonos and in dolman, 163-165, 183; lengthening of, for deep armscye, 128; lengthening in dolman, 187, Fig. 101c; lengthening or shortening in blouse and sleeve, effect of, 239

UNDER COLLAR, of high roll type, 254; of tailored type, 271

UNDERCREASE OF A PLEAT, 76

UNDERLAP, definition of, 40; for buttons and buttonholes and buttons and loops, 41-42

UPPERARM, large, sleeve alteration for, 237-238

WAISTBAND, 62

WAISTLINE, dart in blouse back, 26; dart in blouse front, 22; dart variations in design, 301-302; position on dress form, 7; shape of in gored skirts, 66

WAX CARBON PAPER, 6

WEIGHT, of fabric in relation to draping, 280

INDEX

WING COLLAR, variation of standing, 263

WRAP-AROUND SKIRT, draping of, 64-65

WRINKLES: *in blouse,* diagonal from neckline, 200; diagonal from neck to armscye, 205; general causes of, 195; horizontal across neck base, 201, 202; underarm, 215; *in skirt,* diagonal toward the side seam, 227; *in sleeves,* at back of armscye, 235; diagonal from below armpit to elbow, 240; horizontal at underarm, 239

WRIST, correction of size on draft, 116; dart in leg o' mutton sleeve, 146; measurement for sleeve draft, 114; to increase or decrease size of, 241

YOKES, blocking of, in blouses, 54, 56; blocking of in skirts, 103-104; cowl, 40; cut in one with dolman sleeve, 183-184; cut in one with kimono sleeve, 172-174; cut in one with raglan type sleeve, 156-157; designing of, 305; distributing gathers under, 43; draping of and spacing, 42, 43; simulated: in blouses, 50; in kimono blouse, 175-178; use of in designing, 289-291; variation from standard, 304